CANADIAN BUSINESS

A CONTEMPORARY PERSPECTIVE

CANADIAN BUSINESS

A CONTEMPORARY PERSPECTIVE

Steven H. Appelbaum

Concordia University

M. Dale Beckman

University of Victoria

DRYDEN

Harcourt Brace & Company, Canada

Toronto   Montreal   Fort Worth   New York   Orlando
Philadelphia   San Diego   London   Sydney   Tokyo

Canadian Cataloguing in Publication Data

Appelbaum, Steven H., 1941–
    Canadian business : a contemporary perspective

Includes bibliographical references.
ISBN 0-03-923199-2

1. Business. 2. Business enterprises – Canada.
I. Beckman, M. Dale, 1934–   . II. Title.

HF531.A6 1994   658   C94-931988-0

Publisher: Scott Duncan
Editor and Marketing Manager: Donna Muirhead
Projects Manager: Liz Radojkovic
Projects Co-ordinator: Cheryl Teelucksingh/May Ku
Director of Publishing Services: Jean Davies
Editorial Manager: Marcel Chiera
Production Editor: Louisa Schulz
Producton Manager: Sue-Ann Becker
Reprints/Special Orders Co-ordinator: Denise Wake
Production Supervisor: Carol Tong
Substantive Editing: Elizabeth Reid
Copy Editor: Beverley Endersby
Cover Design: Brett Miller
Interior Design: Steve Eby
Typesetting and Assembly: Pixel Graphics Inc.
Printing and Binding: Edwards Brothers Incorporated

Cover Art Illustrator: Anson Liaw

This book was printed in the United States of America

    3   4   5   98   97   96

To

Barbara,
Wendy,
Jill and Glen,
Geoffrey,
Eric and Jessica

and to

Bobbi, a key contributor

PREFACE

The year 2000 is fast approaching. It will be an exciting time for the world of business. *Canadian Business: A Contemporary Perspective* opens the door to understanding many business challenges and opportunities. Never before have organizations — from the smallest business to the largest corporation — placed greater emphasis on business knowledge.

The authors Steven H. Appelbaum and M. Dale Beckman are respected and well-known in the introductory business market. Each brings to this text extensive knowledge and years of experience. Dr. Appelbaum, a professor of management for twenty years, presently teaches at the Faculty of Commerce and Administration, Concordia University. He served as the faculty Dean from 1983-1990 and has received such prestigious awards as the Distinguished Teaching Award in 1994 and the First Graduating Class Award for outstanding new contributions to university life. He has published numerous articles in professional journals and is an editorial board member of the *Journal of Management Development*. He is the author and co-author of successful textbooks including *Principles of Modern Management: A Canadian Perspective* (three editions) and *Contemporary Canadian Business* (three editions).

Dr. Beckman, co-author of *Contemporary Canadian Business*, is Professor and Head of the International Business Program at the University of Victoria. He established and directed the Center for International Business Studies at the University of Manitoba (where he served as Head of the Department of Marketing) and was previously Chair of the M.B.A. program. Dr. Beckman's business experience includes advertising and marketing management and sales administration for a pharmaceutical company, as well as consulting for various firms and associations. He has authored and co-authored several marketing books including *Foundations of Marketing* (five editions), which has been used by more than 140,000 students.

For the past ten years, *Contemporary Canadian Business* has introduced students to business. It won recognition as the Top Canadian Book published by Harcourt Brace & Company, Canada in 1990. It became the standard against which all other introductory business texts are measured. The reasons?

1. It was written with an entirely Canadian perspective, reflecting the Canadian business setting with readily identifiable cases and real-world examples to illustrate the application of fundamental business concepts discussed in the text.
2. Written in a rigorous and lively style, it satisfied the dual course objectives of providing a solid foundation for more advanced business courses, while communicating the challenges and opportunities of a career in business.

3. It was written for both the instructor *and* student unlike other traditional texts that are written for the instructor.

This new text, *Canadian Business: A Contemporary Perspective,* incorporates all these elements *and* takes a further revolutionary step to better accommodate the needs of instructors and students. Each chapter is designed as a separate, self-contained module to meet the needs of the *specific* course. This innovative modular format offers you, the instructor, the opportunity to customize your book for your course. You can select only the modules you want, and by including your own materials, you can create a text that is uniquely suited to your course. Because the modular format allows for flexibility, it also enables key portions, especially statistics, to be updated on a more frequent basis, and new modules to be added regularly. The text can thus remain contemporary and relevant.

This new text also contains an excellent pedagogical system that will motivate student learning in the dynamic field of business. It is designed to meet the needs of instructors and students in several special ways:

Each module begins with **The Focus of this Module** and **Key Terms** to give students an overview of the contents that follow. These can be used as a quick reference and studying tool for students.

An **Opening Vignette** follows. It contains a Canadian business story that is directly relevant to the materials in the module.

To facilitate learning, a **Running Glossary** appears in the margin area to explain key terms and concepts where they occur.

To make the content a "hands-on" experience for students, **Developing Your Business Skills** boxes highlight important skills needed to be successful in business. Thought-provoking questions are included to allow student participation.

Issues in Business boxes present current (sometimes controversial) issues. These are followed by questions which encourage attention to and learning of the module content.

Business Review questions are included at the end of each major section to promote revision and learning as the student progresses through the materials.

Instead of the traditional end-of-chapter questions section, each module concludes with **Interactive Summary and Discussion Questions** followed by two **Case** studies. Each case includes questions to encourage student interaction.

All these features, plus a lively writing style, work together to make the text a teaching and learning tool that is absorbing and interesting to read.

ANCILLARIES

Complementing the text is an extensive set of materials for instructors and students that further assist teaching and learning. They are:

Instructor's Manual. Written by Cliff Bilyea (Wilfrid Laurier University), it is an excellent resource tool for the instructor. It includes: lecture outlines, transparency masters, and illustration files; suggested answers to review, interactive summaries, and case questions; supplementary lecture material, assignments, and cases; experiential exercises; and suggestions for guest speakers and term papers.

Study Guide. Also prepared by Cliff Bilyea, it helps students to comprehend business principles and applications. Each chapter follows the organization of the text and develops students' skills with numerous types of real-world problems and exercises.

Test Bank and Examaster Computerized Test Bank. A computerized test bank enables instructors to edit, revise, or add to a test bank containing about 35-40 multiple choice questions for each module. The *Test Bank* has been prepared by Brian Hawker.

Transparency Acetates. These additional four-colour acetates supplement the *Instructor's Manual.*

Business Disks. These contain complete interactive programs for the computer cases supplement. They are designed to be duplicated so that each student has his or her own disks.

Computer Cases Supplement. This manual is designed to increase the student's level of analytical thinking in the basic business course and integrate the use of microcomputers in the business curriculum. The manual contains a special set of materials describing the use of a technique or business concept that can be adapted to the microcomputer.

Chopsticks Computer Simulation (IBM). This innovation places students in the role of manager, requiring them to make decisions in all key areas of business.

Stock Market Game. It is an 8-10 week game that gives students hands-on experience investing money wisely as they track four stocks on a weekly basis and create a profitable portfolio.

Videos. Twenty-three videos on 13 cassettes come packaged together. Videos include: Plimoth Plantation, Lincoln Electric, Bolivia's Debt, Brew Ha-Ha, Sea World, and Global Marketing.

Video Instructor's Manual. The video includes titles, outline, teaching objectives, warm-up, recap, experiential activities and handouts, and multiple choice questions and answers.

Quality Module. The materials in the module cover everything from the definition of quality to total quality management (TQM) to TQM's effects in businesses and industries. They also include discussion and review questions, and application exercises.

Career Design Software by Eric Sandburg. This is a comprehensive, computer-based career development package that helps students decide on a major, identify their best skills, discover a career direction, evaluate entrepreneurship, determine workplace preferences, network, create custom resumes, succeed in interviews, locate desirable employers, and develop communication skills.

Dryden Applied Business Series. This series emphasizes real-world application through the discussion of current events and issues in the business world.

ACKNOWLEDGEMENTS

As always, many dedicated individuals, in addition to the authors, have been involved in producing this project. We would like to thank Louis E. Boone and David L. Kurtz for their inspiration over the three editions of *Contemporary Canadian Business*. Special thanks to Brian Hawker who, in addition to preparing the test bank, was also instrumental in the review and development of the manuscript. Cliff Bilyea greatly assisted in the development of this text with his review, comments, and ideas. To him, we also owe our thanks for writing the *Instructor's Manual* and *Study Guide*.

A text can only be enriched by the invaluable suggestions and ideas of colleagues and reviewers. Reviewers from across Canada have added considerably to the strength of this text. They are

Tony Atkinson (Mount Allison University)
John Chyzyk (Brandon University)
Dorothy Derksen, John Redston, and colleagues (Red River
    Community College)
Johan DeRooy (University of British Columbia)
Al Ersser (Mohawk College)
William Grier and Shripad Pendse (Saint Mary's University)
Peter Kelly (Wilfrid Laurier University)
John Lille (Centennial Community College)
Carole Lusby and Joy Vertes (Ryerson Polytechnic University)
Don Mask (Dawson College)
Lloyd McConell (University of Calgary)
John Miteff, Fran Smyth, William Ward, and colleagues (Seneca
    College of Applied Arts and Technology)
Paul Tom (Acadia University)

Professor Appelbaum wishes to extend his thanks to Barbara Shapiro — his other co-author, full-time partner and wife — for her help in discussing and developing the modules on management, human resources, behavioural sciences and life itself. Thanks also to Laurie St. John for her professionalism and flexibility.

Professor Beckman would like to extend special thanks to Paul Levy and Ian Stuart for their respective contributions to the development of the accounting and operations management modules. He is also grateful for the assistance of Glenn Martin and Jane Collins of the University of Victoria.

Many professionals at the College Division of Harcourt Brace & Company, Canada deserve special kudos for their dedication in helping to make this a text of which we can all be proud. Thanks to Scott Duncan for his encouragement and input and Donna Muirhead for her advice and firm belief in the authors and the text. We wish to express our deep gratitude to Cheryl Teelucksingh for her dedication, hard work, and guidance. Many thanks go to Liz Radojkovic who, amidst other projects, still gave her utmost and diligently followed the manuscript through to its final stages. We would also like to extend our appreciation to May Ku for securing the permissions in this text, researching the photos, and helping to put all the bits and pieces in their places. This text has been further enriched by Elizabeth Reid who fine-tuned and helped to rewrite important portions of the manuscript. Our thanks to Beverley Endersby for her effort and care in copy-editing.

What good is a manuscript without a dedicated production team? We owe our deep appreciation and thanks to the staff members in the Harcourt Brace Publishing Services Department whose combined skills and efforts helped to bring this project to life. They initiated an effective editorial and production plan that met all deadlines and made possible the modular format. Unfailing in their support and unlimited in their enthusiasm and determination to help bring life to this innovative modular format, they deserve special praise. The dedicated team members who were instrumental in creating this revolutionary text include Jean Davies, Sue-Ann Becker, Marcel Chiera, Carol Tong, Louisa Schulz, Denise Wake, Brett Miller, and Debbie Fleming. Thank you all for a job well done!

A Note from the Publisher

Thank you for selecting *Canadian Business: A Contemporary Perspective* by Steven H. Appelbaum and M. Dale Beckman. The authors and publisher have devoted considerable time and care to the development of this text in a modular format. We appreciate your recognition of this effort and accomplishment.

We want to hear what you think about *Canadian Business: A Contemporary Perspective*. Please take a few minutes to fill in the stamped reply card at the back of the book. Your comments and suggestions will be valuable to us as we prepare new editions and other books of this format.

BRIEF CONTENTS

Number	Abbreviation	Title
1	BUS	Business and the Canadian Economic System
2	OWN	Forms of Business Ownership
3	ENT	Entrepreneurship in Small Business
4	LEG	Legal Concerns for Business
5	SOC	The Social Responsibility of Business
6	MGT	The Management Process
7	ORG	Organizational Structure
8	PEO	Why People Work
9	HRM	Human Resource Management
10	LR	Labour Relations
11	GLO	Business in a Global Environment
12	INF	Information in the Electronic Age
13	OP	Operations Management
14	MKT	Marketing: Bridging the Gap Between Producer and Consumer
15	PRI	Product Management and Pricing Strategy
16	DIS	Distribution
17	COM	Marketing Communications
18	ACC	Accounting
19	FIN	Managing the Firm's Finances
20	SEC	Investors and the Securities Market
21	BAN	Money and Banking
22	FUT	The Future of Canadian Business
23	IND	Index

CONTENTS

BUS **BUSINESS AND THE CANADIAN ECONOMIC SYSTEM** BUS1

What Is Business? BUS4
Economic Systems Around the World BUS4
    Capitalism BUS6
    Socialism BUS6
    Communism BUS7
    Enterprise and Government BUS9
    Mixed Economies BUS9
Development of the Canadian Economy BUS10
    Business and Enterprise to 1759 BUS10
    British Colonial Rule (1759 to 1867) BUS11
    The Era of National Policy (1867 to 1900) BUS11
    From Growth to Decline (1900 to 1930) BUS11
    Depression and War (1930 to 1950) BUS12
    Postwar Prosperity (1950 to 1980) BUS12
    Recession, Recovery, and Recession (1980 to the Present) BUS12
The Canadian Economy Today BUS15
The Challenge of the Future BUS16
    Competition BUS16
The Entrepreneur in Private Enterprise BUS17
Ground Rules of the Private Enterprise System BUS17
    Private Property BUS17
    Profit BUS18
    Freedom of Choice BUS18
    Freedom to Compete BUS18
Factors of Production BUS18
    Natural Resources BUS19
    Labour BUS19
    Capital BUS19
    Entrepreneurship BUS19
The Measure of National Output BUS20
Productivity and Competitiveness BUS20
The Structure of the Marketplace BUS22
    Perfect Competition BUS23
    Monopolistic Competition BUS24
    Oligopoly BUS24
    Monopoly BUS24
The Business Process BUS25

OWN **FORMS OF BUSINESS OWNERSHIP** OWN1

Ownership: From Proprietorship to the Corporation OWN2
    Sole Proprietorship OWN2
    Partnership OWN3
    Incorporation OWN7

The Structure of a Corporation OWN12
    Shareholders OWN12
    The Board of Directors OWN13
    Top Management OWN16
How Should the Corporation Grow? OWN17
The Government in Business: Crown Corporation OWN17
    Privatization OWN20
    Private Enterprise in Public Affairs OWN20
Co-operatives OWN21

ENT   **ENTREPRENEURSHIP IN SMALL BUSINESS** ENT1

Defining Small Business ENT4
The Entrepreneur ENT4
The Scope of Small Business ENT6
    Retailing ENT6
    Service Firms ENT6
    High-Tech Firms ENT7
Characteristics of Small Business ENT10
    Organization ENT10
    Staff and Managerial Style ENT10
    Innovation ENT11
    Niche Marketing ENT11
    Management Expertise ENT11
    Financial Capability ENT13
    Paperwork ENT15
    Compensation ENT17
Franchising ENT17
Special Cases in Small Business Ownership ENT24
    Family-Owned Business ENT24
    Women as Entrepreneurs ENT24
Conclusion ENT26

LEG   **LEGAL CONCERNS FOR BUSINESS** LEG1

Where Do Laws Come From? LEG4
What Is Business Law? LEG5
How Is Property Exchanged? LEG7
    Real Estate Law LEG7
    The Sale of Goods LEG8
    Intellectual and Industrial Property Law LEG9
What Makes a Contract Legal? LEG13
Is It a Tort or a Crime? LEG15
What Is An Agent? LEG16
How Are Financial Transactions Handled? LEG16
What Happens When One Can't Pay? LEG17
Why Does the Government Regulate Business? LEG18
    Competition LEG19
    Administrative Agencies LEG20

Who Decides Questions of Law? LEG20
    Provincial Courts LEG21
    Federal Courts LEG22
    The Supreme Court of Canada LEG22

SOC   **THE SOCIAL RESPONSIBILITY OF BUSINESS** SOC1

Regulating Business Behaviour SOC5
What Are the Social Issues Facing Business? SOC7
    How Business Treats People SOC7
    Responsibility to Employees SOC7
    Responsibility to Business Associates SOC13
    Responsibility to Investors SOC14
    Responsibility to Customers SOC14
    Responsibility to the Community SOC17
How Business Treats the Environment SOC18
    Keeping the World Clean SOC19
    Reducing Waste SOC20
    Using Energy Wisely SOC23
    Government and the Environment SOC23
How Business Practice Relates to Economic Issues SOC24
    Inflation: An Issue Still With Us SOC24
    Unemployment SOC25
The Scorecard on Social Responsibility in Business SOC27

MGT   **THE MANAGEMENT PROCESS** MGT1

Management and Managers MGT3
    Levels of Management MGT4
    Managerial Skills MGT6
    Managerial Roles MGT10
Mission, Goals, and Objectives MGT11
    Objectives as Standards MGT12
    Goals and Profits MGT12
Managerial Functions MGT13
    Planning MGT13
    Organizing MGT14
    Leading MGT17
    Controlling MGT19
Making Decisions MGT21

ORG   **ORGANIZATIONAL STRUCTURE** ORG1

Influences on the Organization's Structure ORG4
    A Hierarchy of Goals ORG5
    Grouping People to Achieve Goals ORG5
    Delegation ORG7
    Span of Control ORG7
    Degree of Centralization ORG8

How Much Growth Is Necessary ORG11
Designing the Organization's Structure ORG12
Line Structure ORG13
Functional Structure ORG14
Line-and-Staff Structure ORG15
Matrix Structure ORG16
Committee Structure ORG18
The Horizontal Organization ORG18
Organizational Charts and Organizations ORG21
The Informal Organization ORG24

PEO   **WHY PEOPLE WORK** PEO1

The Hawthorne Studies PEO3
Content Theories of Motivation PEO4
A Hierarchy of Needs PEO5
Dissatisfiers and Motivators PEO7
Existence, Relatedness, and Growth PEO7
Acquired Needs PEO7
Process Theories of Motivation PEO10
Meeting Expectations PEO10
Setting Goals PEO11
Is It Fair? PEO11
Theory X and Theory Y PEO12
Morale PEO13
Improving Motivation in Today's Workplace PEO15
Management by Objectives PEO16
Job Enrichment PEO18
Flextime and Alternative Work Schedules PEO20
Compressed Workweek PEO22
Job Sharing PEO22
Styles of Management and Motivation PEO22
Why People Work: Continuing Studies PEO23

HRM   **HUMAN RESOURCE MANAGEMENT** HRM1

What Is Human Resource Management? HRM3
Human Resource Planning HRM5
The Right Worker for the Job HRM7
What Is the Job? HRM7
Avoiding Discrimination in Job Specifications HRM8
Looking for Candidates HRM9
Creating the Short List HRM9
Aptitude and Attitudinal Testing HRM10
The Job Interview HRM10
The Company Medical HRM11
Welcome on Board HRM11
Employment and Human Rights HRM12

Pay Equity HRM12
Employment Equity HRM12
Harassment HRM17
Developing Employees' Skills HRM19
On-the-Job Training HRM20
Classroom Training HRM20
Management Development Programs HRM21
Assessment Centres HRM22
Performance Appraisal HRM22
Employee Counselling HRM23
Employees on the Move HRM23
Employee Compensation HRM25
What Is Each Job Worth? HRM25
Approaches to Compensation HRM25
Employee Benefits HRM28
Occupational Safety HRM28
Human Resources in the Future HRM29

LR   **LABOUR RELATIONS** LR1

What Is a Labour Union? LR3
Labour Unions: A History LR3
Strength in Numbers LR4
Development of Labour Unions in Canada LR4
Labour Legislation LR7
Legal Designation of the Workplace LR7
Dues Checkoff LR8
Joining the Union LR9
Reaching a Collective Agreement LR9
Negotiating Units LR10
The Bargaining Zone LR11
Conciliation LR14
Mediation LR14
Arbitration LR14
Tools of Power LR15
When a Contract is in Place LR18
Wildcat Strikes LR18
Work to Rule LR18
Grievance Procedures LR18
Concerns for Organized Labour LR21
Technological Change LR22
A Changing Work Force LR23
Labour and Management: Future Relations LR24

GLO   **BUSINESS IN A GLOBAL ENVIRONMENT** GLO1

The Global Challenge GLO4
Entering the World Market GLO4
Modes of International Activity GLO6

Indirect Exporting and Importing GLO6
Direct Exporting and Importing GLO6
Licensing GLO6
Joint Venture GLO7
Foreign Production and Marketing GLO7
Multinational Enterprise GLO7
Starting International Operations GLO7
Management Commitment GLO7
Adequate Resources GLO7
Viable Product GLO8
Strategic Planning for Export GLO8
The Market GLO8
The Price GLO9
Distribution GLO9
Marketing Communications GLO9
The Intricacies of International Business GLO10
Social and Cultural Factors GLO10
Economic and Political Barriers to Trade GLO12
Tariffs GLO12
Non-Tariff Barriers GLO14
National and International Law GLO15
International Agreements and Economic Alliances GLO15
General Agreement on Tariffs and Trade GLO15
Regional Economic Alliances GLO17
Macroeconomic Factors GLO19
International Trade Terminology GLO19
The Balance of Trade GLO19
The Balance of Payments GLO19
The Exchange Rate GLO20
Countertrade GLO21
Why International Business? GLO22
The Argument for Self-Sufficiency GLO22
The Argument for Specialization GLO22
Canada's Trade Picture GLO23
Canadian Business or Global Competition GLO28

INF   **INFORMATION IN THE ELECTRONIC AGE** INF1

Computers in Management INF2
The Transition in Information Processing INF2
Survival in the Third Wave INF3
Business Applications of Computers INF4
Accounting INF4
Data Analysis INF4
Word Processing INF5
Production INF5
Retailing INF5
Transfer of Information INF6

Types of Information and Information Systems INF7
Marketing Research INF8
Secondary Data INF9
  Government Sources INF9
  Private Sources INF10
Primary Data INF11
  Survey Method INF12
  Experimental Design INF13
  Observation Method INF13
Sampling the Market Research INF14
Comparing Secondary and Primary Data INF16

OP   OPERATIONS MANAGEMENT OP1

What Is Operations Management? OP2
Operations Management and Productivity OP3
  Productivity and Competitiveness OP4
Approaches to the Production Process OP4
  The Job Shop OP4
  The Batch Operation OP7
  Assembly Line and Continuous Operations OP8
Priorities and Process OP11
Planning Production OP12
  Assessing Materials and Timing Needs OP12
  Developing a Schedule OP13
Managing Inventories OP15
  Uses of Inventory OP15
  Types of Inventory OP16
  Just-in-Time Production OP16
The Service Planning Environment OP18
Managing Inputs OP19
  Equipment Maintenance OP19
  Labour Management OP20
  Purchasing Management OP22
Managing the Outputs OP25
  Warehouse Policies and Distribution Costs OP25
Quality Control and Quality Management OP27
  Defining Quality OP27
  Quality in the Production Process OP28
  Quality and Productivity OP29
Managing Change OP29

MKT **MARKETING: BRIDGING THE GAP BETWEEN PRODUCER AND CONSUMER** MKT1

    Bringing Producer and Customer Together MKT3
        Perspective MKT3
        Time MKT3
        Space MKT4
        Needs or Wants MKT4
        Possession MKT5
    The Tools of Marketing MKT5
        Marketing Research MKT5
        Transportation MKT6
        Wholesaling MKT6
        Retailing MKT6
        Buying MKT6
        Advertising MKT6
        Selling MKT7
        Financing MKT7
    Marketing Defined MKT7
    Orientation of Marketing Efforts MKT8
        Product Orientation MKT8
        Sales Orientation MKT8
        Market Orientation MKT9
    Understanding the Customer MKT9
        Market Segmentation MKT9
    Analyzing Consumer Behaviour MKT10
        Information Input MKT11
        Information Processing MKT11
        Decision Process Stages MKT11
        Variables Influencing the Decision Process MKT11
    Marketing Strategy MKT12
    The Marketing Plan MKT12
    The Marketing Mix MKT12

PRI **PRODUCT MANAGEMENT AND PRICING STRATEGY** PRI1

    Goods, Services, and Products PRI2
    Product Classification PRI3
        Consumer Products PRI3
        Industrial Products PRI5
    The Birth and Death of Products PRI5
    Brand Identification PRI9
        Brand Name or Generic Term? PRI9
        Private Brands PRI10
    Product Management PRI11
        Modifying Existing Products PRI11
        Eliminating Products PRI11
    Packaging PRI12
    Pricing PRI12

Setting Prices PRI13
    The Law of Supply and Demand PRI13
    Practical Price Setting PRI14
    Breakeven Analysis PRI15
    Price Lining PRI16
Prices and Corporate Goals PRI17
    Profitability Objectives PRI17
    Volume Objectives PRI18
    Other Objectives PRI18
Prices and Consumers PRI19
    Price-Quality Relationship PRI19
    Psychological Pricing PRI19
    Prices and Inflation PRI19
Pricing New Products PRI21
    The Skimming Price Strategy PRI21
    The Penetration Price Strategy PRI22
What Product? What Price? PRI22

DIS   **DISTRIBUTION** DIS1

The Marketing Channel DIS3
    Using Multiple Channels DIS4
    Conventional and Vertical Systems DIS5
Retailing DIS6
    Evolution in Retailing DIS6
    Marketing Planning for Retailing DIS9
    Types of Retailers DIS10
Density of Distribution DIS13
Physical Distribution DIS14
    Transportation DIS14
    Warehousing DIS16
    Inventory Control DIS16
    Order Processing DIS16

COM   **MARKETING COMMUNICATIONS** COM1

Elements of Marketing Communication Strategy COM3
    Pushing versus Pulling Strategies COM3
Objectives of Marketing Communications COM4
    Providing Information COM4
    Product Positioning COM4
    Increasing Sales COM4
    Stabilizing Sales COM5
Advertising COM5
    Classifying Advertising COM6
    Advertising and the Product Life Cycle COM8
    Advertising Media COM11
Sales Promotion COM13

Point-of-Purchase Sales Promotions COM13
Specialty Advertising COM13
Trade Shows COM13
Samples, Coupons, Premiums, and Trading Stamps COM14
Packaging COM14
Personal Selling COM15
Selling Activities Categorized COM16
Sales Management COM17
Waste or Masterpiece? COM18

ACC ACCOUNTING ACC1

Who Uses Accounting Information? ACC3
Accounting Standards and the Accounting Profession ACC4
Accounting versus Bookkeeping ACC5
The Accounting Equation ACC7
Financial Statements ACC7
The Balance Sheet ACC7
The Income Statement ACC10
Statement of Changes in Financial Position ACC10
Double-Entry Bookkeeping ACC12
Ratio Analysis ACC15
Ability to Pay Current Liabilities ACC15
Ability to Repay Long-Term Liabilities ACC16
Operating Ratios ACC17
Profitability Ratios ACC19
Accounting and Budgeting ACC21
Accounting in Management ACC22

FIN MANAGING THE FIRM'S FINANCES FIN1

Financial Planning FIN2
Cash Management FIN5
The Uses of Credit FIN5
Managing Inventory FIN5
Financing Land, Plant, and Equipment FIN6
Debt and Equity Funds FIN7
Operating Revenues FIN8
Short-Term Sources of Funds FIN9
Trade Credit FIN9
Unsecured Bank Loans FIN10
Secured Short-Term Loans FIN12
Factoring: The Sale of Accounts Receivable FIN12
Long-Term Sources of Funds FIN12
Long-Term Loans FIN13
Bonds FIN13
Equity Financing FIN13

Raising Venture Capital FIN15
Leverage: Borrowing Magnifies the Rate of Return FIN15
The Use of Excess Funds FIN18
Marketable Securities as Substitutes for Cash FIN18

SEC   INVESTORS AND THE SECURITIES MARKET SEC1

Funding a Business SEC4
Common or Preferred Shares? SEC4
Common Shares SEC4
Preferred Shares SEC6
Bonds SEC7
Secured Bonds SEC7
Debentures SEC7
Convertible Bonds SEC8
Retiring Bonds SEC8
The Trade in Bonds SEC9
The Securities Exchanges SEC10
The Toronto Stock Exchange (TSE) SEC10
Other Canadian Stock Exchanges SEC10
Foreign Stock Exchanges SEC10
The Over-the-Counter (OTC) Market SEC11
The Futures Market SEC11
Buying and Selling Securities SEC12
The Cost of Trading SEC13
Bulls and Bears SEC13
Regulating Securities Transactions SEC14
Brokers and Promoters SEC14
Following the Stock Market SEC15
Stock Quotations SEC15
Stock Indexes SEC17
Investors and Their Goals SEC17
Speculation SEC19
Investment SEC19
Mutual Funds: Another Approach to Investing SEC22

BAN   MONEY AND BANKING BAN1

Money: What Is It? BAN2
Separating Buying from Selling BAN3
Practical Money BAN3
Divisibility BAN3
Portability BAN4
Durability BAN4
Stability BAN5
Security Against Counterfeiting BAN5
The Functions of Money BAN6
The Money Supply BAN7

Plastic Money: A Substitute for Cash BAN7
The Canadian Chartered Banking System BAN9
Services Provided by Chartered Banks BAN11
The Banks' Competitors BAN12
The Need for a Central Banking Authority BAN13
The Bank of Canada BAN13
Reserve Requirements BAN14
Open-Market Operations BAN15
The Bank Rate BAN15
Setting the Bank Rate BAN16
Insurance for Depositors: The CDIC BAN16
The Canadian Payments System BAN17
Electronics and Banking BAN18

FUT   **THE FUTURE OF CANADIAN BUSINESS** FUT1
Changes in the Way We Live and Work FUT2
Economic Trends FUT3
The Global Marketplace FUT3
The Job Market FUT7
The Economic Base FUT10
Social Trends FUT12
Population Changes FUT12
Attitudes and Lifestyle FUT13
Balancing Work and Family FUT15
Technological Trends FUT17
International Competition and Co-operation FUT21
Technology and You FUT22
The Changing Biosphere FUT23
Business Strategy Changes FUT24
Balancing the Positive and Negative Aspects of Change FUT29
Tomorrow's Challenges FUT29

IND   **INDEX** IND1

MODULE

◆ BUS ◆

BUSINESS AND THE CANADIAN ECONOMIC SYSTEM

THE FOCUS OF THIS MODULE

1. To define what business is and the role of business skills in the economic system
2. To describe briefly economic systems in place around the world
3. To consider the roles of government and private enterprise in Canada's mixed economy
4. To show how government and private enterprise contributed to the historical development of the Canadian economy, and the challenge global economic trends pose for the future
5. To examine aspects of the private enterprise system, especially the importance of competition and entrepreneurship
6. To explain the concepts of gross national product, productivity, and competitiveness and how they affect business and individuals
7. To describe various competitive market structures
8. To show how business operates to serve the needs of society
9. To define the following terms:

KEY TERMS

business	factors of production
profit	natural resources
non-profit or not-for-profit organizations	labour
	capital
capitalism	gross national product (GNP)
socialism	productivity
communism	competitiveness
private enterprise system	law of supply and demand
mixed economy	perfect competition
National Policy	monopolistic competition
entrepreneur	oligopoly
private property	monopoly

The Montreal Expos baseball team is part of the fabric of the city of Montreal. The team also represents big business to those who own it. After twenty years of ownership, in 1992 Charles Bronfman sold the team to a Montreal business syndicate. As one of only two Canadian clubs, the Expos continue to draw fans to see both the still-impressive Olympic Stadium and a major-league baseball team in a major-league city.

"IT'S NOTHING BUT big business now."

If you read the sports pages, you'll recognize that sorrowful comment. It's a special favourite of professional athletes, though it's also heard from others struck by cost restraint and restructuring in their own industries.

The players complain that their bosses are increasingly hardheaded in the pursuit of profits. It ain't like the old days. (Nor is it, of course, for their wages, which have escalated amazingly.)

The result is a great deal of change and the possibility of much more. That worries the owners. Many fear their costs—some locked in for years ahead—may outstrip their ability to pull in more revenue.

They try to reduce the risk by doing things their employees and fans find disturbing. More players switch teams, voluntarily or otherwise, to reflect the more intrusive forces of supply and demand.

There's nostalgia for a gentler era, for a time of more family feeling and loyalty, less upheaval from year to year and less concern for maximizing profits and franchise values.

That vanished for a reason common to all larger businesses. The more money you have at stake, the more you'll work to protect and enhance it.

This attitude is held by employees too, especially in pro sports. Even rather marginal baseballers can make a million a year instead of $100,000. That calls for businesslike management, toughminded agents, and special advice on how to handle careers and incomes.

In the language of analysts, major-league pro sports is being "industrialized." It becomes more like operating a supermarket chain than a game.

Welcome to the world of Big Business. But it should be said that sports has merely graduated from small to medium-sized.

Financial World's estimate of the combined value of 26 major league baseball franchises (recent expansion teams are omitted) dropped 6 percent last year. The total is $2.8 billion.

Other industries are far larger. Look at stock market valuations of the common shares of single companies. BCE's is more than three times the total for baseball and hockey. Imperial Oil's is more than twice as large.

The largest valuations in baseball—the Toronto Blue Jays, New York Yanks, and Mets—are around $150 million each. Detroit tops hockey at $87 million. The National Football League averages the most, at $129 million per club.

It's still a lot of money. Financial considerations become more dominant, sentiment and hobby-ownership less so.

In all sports, some franchises are vulnerable. Profits seem low or non-existent for many though the figures reported are not trusted.

Financial World puts the combined profits of the 26 baseball teams at less than $100 million in 1992. That's poor on a valuation of almost $3 billion.

It estimates that the 21 National Hockey League teams made about $80 million, a much better return. But their wages still shoot up and attempts to broaden interest in the United States may not succeed.

The frequency of sports ownership by large companies in other industries—the media, beer, and other consumer products—is a mixed blessing. They have deep pockets but are also profit-oriented.

Labatt and CIBC, owners of the Blue Jays, are obliged to do their best for themselves and their shareholders.

The point is that the motives are businesslike—another sign of the changing times in sports.

Source: Excerpts from Jack McArtner, "Sports and Big Business now Closely Meshed,' *The Toronto Star*, May 31, 1993, p CZ Reprinted with permission the Toronto Star Syndicate.

W HAT DRAWS PEOPLE who have succeeded at business to want to own a professional sports team? The sums of money required, not just to buy the team but to pay sky-rocketing players' salaries, are enormous and the risks seem equally so. It seems quite out of character for astute business people to behave like this. Yet we know sports is business—big business. Like all business, it involves the desire and ability to control the enterprise, to know and serve loyal customers, to appreciate the nature of the risks involved and yet to take them, to make goodwill gestures with no thought of return, and to enjoy the whole exercise.

Professional players play one game in stadiums and arenas. Sports club owners play another in money markets and back rooms. Both must know the rules of the game they are playing. To succeed at business, people must know the rules of the economic system.

WHAT IS BUSINESS?

Business is generally defined in terms of private enterprise: the commercial activity that provides goods and services consumers want so that the provider can make a profit. **Profit** is the difference between revenues (the money a company takes in) and expenses (the money the company must spend in order to produce and market its product).

"Business" comprises large mining corporations with employees in countries all over the world; manufacturers that have most of their work force in one place, relying on others to sell their products at home and abroad; farmers who may work alone or employ workers only when the crop is ready for harvesting; construction firms; trucking lines; cable television operators; large department store chains; the corner store; and the kid who negotiates a contract to mow the neighbours' lawn all summer.

But business skills are needed by people in many organizations where the prime interest is not necessarily to make a profit—indeed, these are often called **non-profit** or **not-for-profit organizations**. Few hospitals, public schools, museums, charities, or municipal governments in this country could operate without sound business managers at the helm. So the world of business is actually far broader than the private system.

ECONOMIC SYSTEMS AROUND THE WORLD

Business operates according to the rules and assumptions of the economic system in which it functions. These rules and assumptions can vary widely from the ones we are accustomed to in Canada. To take a historical example, under the feudal system all land was considered to belong to the monarch, who demanded military service from nobles in return for protection and the rights to certain lands. The noble extended his (occasionally her) protection to serfs, who worked the land in return for their labour. Serfs were tied to the land; they could not be forced from their fields if the noble wanted to use the land for something else, but neither had they the right to leave to pursue some other occupation. The rules and assumptions under which people lived and exchanged goods and services were very different from

business
The commercial activity that provides goods and services consumers need so that the provider can make a profit

profit
The difference between revenues and expenses

non-profit or not-for-profit organizations
Organizations whose primary interest is not necessarily making a profit

Orchestre Symphonique de Montréal

1 9 9 3   SAISON   1 9 9 4

CHARLES DUTOIT, DIRECTEUR ARTISTIQUE

For the Montreal Symphony Orchestra, marketing, promotions, and pricing strategies are important elements in their business plan. To promote its upcoming season, the MSO offers price discounts for series subscribers. Concerts that are sponsored by Canadian corporations may also provide the subscriber with additional benefits and gifts.

those we operate under today. Yet vestiges of the feudal system existed in some parts of Europe and Asia until as late as the early twentieth century.

Present-day economic systems evolved—sometimes violently or painfully—from those of the past. From a theoretical perspective, the world economic order can be viewed as a spectrum that ranges from capitalism, also called free or private enterprise, to socialism, or its most extreme form, communism.

Capitalism

capitalism
The understanding that private capital, or money, is used to produce goods and services for a profit, the profit belonging to the owner or owners of the original capital

In *The Wealth of Nations,* published in 1776, Adam Smith theorized that the economy works best in a "system of perfect liberty." **Capitalism** operated on the understanding that private capital, or money, was used to produce goods and services for a profit, the profit belonging to the owner or owners of the original capital. With little or no government control, the economy was ruled to the benefit of all people by the invisible hand of competition. The "invisible hand" ensured that consumers would receive the best possible goods at the best possible prices, because if one producer's prices were higher than a competitor's, or the quality of goods lower, customers would buy from the competitor, forcing the first producer to lower prices or improve quality. Smith believed that the "invisible hand" also applied to labour. An employer who offered poor wages or working conditions would find it more difficult to find workers than would a more generous one.

Smith's thesis was that the free use of capital could only cause the economy to grow. He used the example of a pin factory in which ten employees working at specialized tasks could produce thousands more pins than each worker working individually could produce. Only the initial investment of capital to build and equip the factory and to pay the workers made this possible. And the entire society benefited from having a larger supply of goods.

A pure capitalist system does not exist. The economic system in the United States is probably the closest to it, and certainly Americans are proud of the opportunities their private enterprise system gives them, but, even there, legislation at both the federal and the local level affects the way business operates, and businesses such as public utilities are often state-owned.

Socialism

socialism
A term that embraces a number of approaches to government, business, and society that emphasize some form of common ownership of the means of production and greater economic equality for all people

Though the invisible hand of competition may work well in the provision of goods and services, the labour-saving devices and technology of the Industrial Revolution erased the competitive edge Smith expected workers to have in the setting of wages and working conditions. Mine and factory owners gained almost total power over their workers, often paying them as little as possible to work for long hours in unsafe conditions, while raking in huge profits for themselves. In the early nineteenth century, people like Henri de Saint-Simon and Robert Owen, who were concerned about social conditions, suggested that an economy based on co-operation and sharing rather than competition would curb the excesses of capitalism. **Socialism** is a term used to embrace a number of approaches to government, business, and society that emphasize common ownership of "the means of production" and greater economic equality for all.

Sweden and, to a lesser extent, several European countries are often cited as examples of socialist economies because some of their major industries are owned by the state, which also provides generous social service programs.

Communism

To some who were shocked and angry at the oppression of working people, the "utopian" socialist thought of Saint-Simon and Owen seemed vague and impractical. Karl Marx developed a theory of "scientific" socialism, or communism. With Friedrich Engels in *The Communist Manifesto* and *Das Kapital,* Marx described history as a process of strife and social conflict. He predicted that the class struggle of nineteenth-century workers against their capitalistic bosses would end in revolution, with the workers taking over the means of production in a "dictatorship of the proletariat." The new government would supervise and administer the economy for the good of all. Once the new social and economic order of **communism** was properly established, people would work according to their abilities for the common good and be paid according to their needs; the struggle would be over, and the state, which had supervised the transition period, would "wither away."

Until recently, a large part of the world was dominated by so-called communist regimes. However, establishing the ideal communist state proved far more difficult than Marx had expected. Communist states have never progressed beyond what Marx described as the transition period of state control. In fact, once in power, communist leaders such as Lenin, Stalin, and Mao claimed that central planning by the government to direct economic and political affairs would be needed for a long time to come.

In the late 1980s, the peoples of eastern Europe rejected the communist system, with those of the Soviet Union soon following their example. China, the largest remaining communist state, has actually been opening its doors to free enterprise for even longer, though the same political leadership remains in control. The following Developing Your Business Skills box discusses some of the changes in attitude and approach to business that Russians have found are necessary in a new economic system.

A purer form of communism may be said to exist in small communities such as those of the Mennonites in Manitoba and southwestern Ontario, or the kibbutzim of Israel. These groups own all property in common and work co-operatively for the good of their own community, but operate within the private enterprise system of the countries in which they live.

communism
An economic system under which all property is owned by the community as a whole and people work for the common good according to their abilities and are paid according to their needs

DEVELOPING YOUR BUSINESS SKILLS

SERVING THE CUSTOMER

Almost lost on Nikolskaya Street, two blocks up from Red Square and the Kremlin, the Slavyansky Bazaar makes no claim to Western chic. As restaurants go, it is a sprawling cathedral of a place, with white plaster statues, fading paint, and an arched ceiling as high as a five-storey house.

It is a blissful escape from the harsh realities of the street, with its array of Russian appetizers known as *zakousky*, black bread, butter, caviar, and vodka. The waiters wear white peasant shirts, and the menu is in Russian only. True, the musicians wear white track suits and their instruments are electric, but the music they play is Russian, and even at lunch the fat lady who sings wears a black evening dress.

A Russian visitor is enchanted: "Here there is the illusion of the same thing as in the past. You don't get that feeling in the shops. Even when the things are Soviet-made, it's different now."

Indeed, it is an illusion. Everything is different now. Boris Yeltsin has promised to bring the prosperity of the West to the land of the czars and the commissars. And both Russia and Mr. Yeltsin are counting the cost.

Though it may not have Western chic, the Slavyansky Bazaar does have a place in history. When it opened 123 years ago, its patrons were the great artists and writers and musicians of the day, beginning with Peter Tchaikovsky. More recent history was not quite so illustrious. For 30 years, up to 1966, it served as the canteen of the Central Committee of the Communist Party. The waitresses will tell you that the *apparatchiks* made off with everything of value that wasn't bolted down.

But as she chatters about the *zakousky*, Tatyana, who has worked at the Slavyansky Bazaar for 25 years, says things have changed. Everybody used to eat here before; there was a sewing factory across the street, and the workers could come in for lunch. Now it's only rich people.

Grigory Veshikov, a maître d' straight from Central Casting, talks gravely of preserving the Russian character of the restaurant, and regrets that "we don't have many Soviets." Three-quarters of the diners are tourists or diplomats or foreign businessmen.

Tatyana shrugs. The novelty of only the rich is engulfed in her announcement that she and the other employees are now shareholders. That too has meant changes. She smiles: "Now our job is to please the customers."

For anyone who has ever been in a Russian restaurant, that is a revolutionary perception. It is a small revolution, perhaps, and it certainly hasn't swept the entire country. But it is one more small revolution in a land that is numb from change.

For seven decades, if there was any change it happened with glacial deliberation. There was not much to buy, but what there was you could afford. Stability was comforting.

In that other, now distant world, foreigners were suspect. Foreign goods and foreign ways were for the special pleasure of those with power and privilege. Foreign cars are still a cause for some awe in towns no more than 50 kilometres from Moscow.

Then it started. Mikhail Gorbachev and *glasnost* and *perestroika*. Traditional values were torn out by the roots. Good were the market economy, Westerners, democracy, business, and dollars. Bad were the command economy, stability, communism, and rubles. The Soviet Union died, and a Russia ignored since the time of the czars was reborn....

For a lot of Russians, it is the sudden wealth of other Russians that seems the hardest change to digest. Not too long ago, those who were *beezinessman* were social outcasts. Now, they don't go to jail; they drive Mercedeses.

(continued)

New business where there was no business before, no business culture, and no business laws has led to a spectacular level of corruption. Foreign and Russian business people alike say there is never a deal without a bribe.

One of the benefits of the old days was that the forces of law and order had things pretty much under control. These days, you buy your own Russian-made bulletproof vests for 60,000 rubles, a little over $100.

Mr. Yuri Levada is one of Russia's most respected pollsters.... His conclusion is that this society that has been shaken by change like few others in recent times is ready to be shaken again. "The common man is much more ready for changes, much more ready for economic reform, even in spite of all the difficulties of the last years. There is some grain of hope, hope for a better future, hope that a return to the past is impossible."

Mr. Levada may be right. But, if there is a grain of hope, it is a grim hope. On the streets of the new Russia there is no joy.

Source: Excerpts from John Gray, "Moscow Streetscape," *The Globe and Mail*, March 20, 1993, pp. D1 and D3.

Question for Discussion

What new business skills are Russian business people finding they need as the economic system changes?

Enterprise and Government

Perhaps the greatest difference between capitalism, or the private enterprise system, on the one hand, and socialism and communism, on the other, is where the impetus for economic activity comes from. The "private" in **private enterprise system** implies that business is not controlled by government. Rather, success or failure depends on how well a business understands and meets the needs of the market in competition with others trying to meet the same needs. Competition, the rivalry among businesses to satisfy customer demand and maintain sales and profit, is the essence of free enterprise. Because the market determines the direction the economy takes, free enterprise is often called a "market economy." In a communist system, the central government assesses economic needs according to an all-inclusive plan and, to fulfil this plan, decides what will be produced, how much, and when. This approach is often called a "command economy." Socialist governments may set broad general goals for economic activity and encourage private firms to operate within these guidelines.

private enterprise system
An economic system in which business is not controlled by government; rather, a firm's success or failure depends on how well it understands and meets the needs of the market in competition with others trying to meet the same needs

Mixed Economies

Today most countries of the world are **mixed economies** in which governments exercise some level of control over business through legislation about such matters as minimum wages, safe working practices, product safety standards, and fair trading practices. They also include both private enterprise and public ownership of industries regarded as too vital for the general good to be operated solely on the basis of profit. For example, most municipalities operate their own

mixed economy
One that includes a mix of private enterprise and government ownership of industries regarded as too vital for the national good to be operated solely on the basis of profit, all within a framework of legislation

water and sewage facilities and urban transit systems. Governments may also offer grants of money or other assistance to private businesses to operate in areas of high unemployment or to develop industries that might otherwise be too expensive or too risky to attract investors.

The "mix" in a mixed economy can vary a great deal from one country to another. There has been a recent trend toward "privatization," or the selling of certain publicly owned businesses to private interests, so it may be said that many countries are moving toward the private-enterprise end of the mix.

Canada's mixed economy leans heavily toward the private enterprise system, and business in Canada operates according to its ground rules and assumptions. Our mixed economic system has proved highly effective. It has provided a high degree of economic freedom, a high standard of living, and a valuable social safety net. Private enterprise provides incentive for business people, variety for consumers, and opportunities for both to improve the quality of their lives. Regulation and other kinds of central government control provide benefits and security through appropriate distribution of everyone's taxes. Government does influence our freedom of choice, ways of doing business, and property rights in the attempt to balance the disadvantages of pure capitalism. We still have an incentive to produce, but the gap between rich and poor is narrowed under this philosophy. Canada's standard of living, economic opportunities, and social services remain the envy of people all over the world.

DEVELOPMENT OF THE CANADIAN ECONOMY

Canada has a unique business history. Business has significantly influenced customs, politics, and even family living. Economic development and industrial growth in Canada followed a very different path from development and growth in the United States, where private incentive with very little government interference was the main source of business activity. In Canada, business was forced from the beginning to depend upon government intervention, finances, and policy. This reliance on government continues to affect the way business operates today.

Business and Enterprise to 1759

The various Native groups in the lands that became Canada traded with their neighbours for a variety of items such as furs, silver, and copper. But, when the first European colonies were established, the immigrants expected that commercial activity would be controlled from Europe. Fishing off the east coast was a seasonal operation run by businesses in Portugal, Spain, and England's west country, and settlement was actively discouraged in Newfoundland. The colony of New France was expected to provide furs for the profit of the French court; trapping and trading operations were to be strictly licensed.

However, some fishing families soon decided it was more efficient to "winter over" near the fishing grounds. In New France, the entrepreneurial spirit of the *habitants* could not be limited by government order, and *coureurs de bois* like Pierre Radisson and Médard Chouart des Groseillers soon began to trade for furs on their own behalf. By the 1750s, the French had trading posts as far west as the Saskatchewan River.

British Colonial Rule (1759 to 1867)

After Quebec became a British colony, a consortium of French-Canadian and Scottish businessmen formed the North West Company from the network of trading posts and canoe routes that stretched west from Montreal. The North West Company soon found itself competing for both furs and territory with the Hudson's Bay Company (founded by English merchants at the suggestion of Pierre Radisson in 1670, after a particularly painful experience with French bureaucracy). In 1821, the two groups merged.

Thus, in the West, fur trading was the major business activity. The Atlantic zone of Nova Scotia and Newfoundland concentrated on fishing. In the early 1800s, demand for lumber saw business increase in Quebec and New Brunswick. After the American Revolution, new settlers from the United States and Britain demanded manufactured products from Europe. The desire for trade led the government to support the expansion of the St. Lawrence water system through the building of canals. However, great hopes for this waterway never came to fruition, and by 1867 it was severely underutilized. Thus, at Confederation, the new country was already shouldering a large national debt.

The Era of National Policy (1867 to 1900)

Canada had great resources—timber in British Columbia; wheat in the Prairie provinces; oil and timber in Ontario; timber and a commercial and manufacturing base in Quebec; and fish, iron, coal, and timber in the Atlantic provinces. Shortly after Confederation, the government instituted the **National Policy**, which was intended to bring settlers to the western prairies and to increase the manufacturing of goods within the country by imposing high tariffs in order to discourage the importation of goods, particularly from the United States. The government also agreed to provide financial subsidies to a business group led by Donald Smith to build a railway to transport both goods and people across Canada rather than through the United States.

National Policy
Post-Confederation economic policy of increased immigration, protective tariffs, and improved transportation

From Growth to Decline (1900 to 1930)

Wheat and mining exports at the turn of the century helped to stimulate the Canadian economy. Manufacturing still played only a small part; only 15 percent of the Canadian labour force worked in manufacturing in 1911 whereas agriculture occupied 35 percent of workers. But the amount of capital available for investment in manufacturing and the production capacity for consumer goods were growing all the time. By the close of the 1920s, every second Canadian household owned an automobile. New roads were being built. Mass production in all other areas followed the automobile boom. The refrigerator, washing machine, and radio became part of family life. Government continued to step in, as it had when it financed the Canadian Pacific Railway in the 1870s, to assist enterprises it considered vital to the economy: Ontario set up Ontario Hydro as a crown corporation; the western provinces built their own telephone networks; the federal government formed Canadian National Railways from a number of failing companies in order to ensure an adequate transportation system.

Depression and War (1930 to 1950)

The Depression following the stock market crash of 1929 led to lower demand for goods as consumers and businesses cut back. Farmers in the West suffered the double blow of lack of markets and severe drought. Government intervention was seen as a necessary antidote to the vicious cycle of lower demand and production. Following the example of U.S. president Franklin Roosevelt, Prime Minister R.B. Bennett offered unemployment insurance, higher old age pensions, and regulation of working conditions in the attempt to regenerate the economy. Many of the policies of the "social safety net" Canadians know today had their origins in the 1930s.

The Second World War led to new levels of employment and productivity in new industries such as shipbuilding and aircraft manufacturing. After the war, exploration led to the development of vast resource industries, such as the first significant exploitation of Alberta's oil fields. This much-needed stimulation led to a new problem at the close of the 1940s. Almost one-half of all Canadian manufacturing assets and many natural resources were owned or controlled by foreign investors, many of them from the United States.

Postwar Prosperity (1950 to 1980)

The postwar era brought unprecedented gains in productivity, new resource development, a vast increase in Canadian manufacturing, and the growth of service industries, from fast-food restaurants to management consulting. Consumer goods became readily available, either made in Canada or, increasingly, imported from other countries. Electronic computers revolutionized ways of doing business. The "baby boom" and immigration from all over the world provided an enlarged work force—and new consumers. The new prosperity allowed Canada to expand the social safety net, in particular to include medicare. Though many people at the time opposed what they saw as "socialized medicine," the removal of the profit motive from the provision of medical services, today few Canadians wish to return to a private health care system.

Despite occasional setbacks during economic downturns (business cycles with peaks and troughs occur on a fairly regular basis), the standard of living rose from decade to decade. People began to expect it would do so forever.

Recession, Recovery, and Recession (1980 to the Present)

The 1980s began with an economic downturn caused, in part, when governments around the world tried to battle inflation with high interest rates. As the crisis slackened and industrial investment, employment levels, and consumer demand picked up again, many people felt things had returned to normal. During the mid-1980s, the Canadian economy experienced faster and more productive growth than those of all other industrialized countries except Japan and the United States. The governments of Canada and the United States negotiated a free-trade agreement to improve access for Canadian and U.S. businesses to each other's markets; the North American Free Trade Agreement, ratified in Canada in 1993, is designed to bring Mexico into a similar pact. But the early 1990s brought another global recession as governments, facing a growing burden of national debt, tried to decrease spending. In Canada, the situation was worsened when manufacturing industries began to transfer many of their operations out of the country, particularly out of Ontario, to parts of North America where labour costs were cheaper or distances to their major markets were smaller.

As Canadians pull out of the latest setback, they are examining some of their basic assumptions about the way the Canadian economy has worked in the past and will work in the future.

ISSUES IN BUSINESS 1.1

THE SUNRISE ECONOMY

AT THE BEGINNING of the 1990s, corporate Canada passed an important but unheralded milestone that can only jolt some traditional preconceptions about the country's economy. The top company in the *Canadian Business* Corporate 500 neither fells trees, smelts ore, pumps oil, extracts minerals, nor assembles a product as its primary way to earn money. It sells a service—telecommunications. Equally remarkable may be the fact that Canada's biggest company is no longer a subsidiary of a U.S. multinational. It is owned by Canadians, and a lot of us at that.

BCE Inc., the most widely held company in Canada, with 270,000 shareholders, finally supplanted General Motors of Canada Inc. as top honcho in *Canadian Business*'s annual ranking of industrials. The race had actually been going on for some years. GM's sales have been in a state of decline, having peaked in 1989. BCE's grew steadily every year, regardless of boom or bust.

BCE exemplifies much of the recent transformation of Canadian industry, especially in the upper reaches of the top 500 companies. To grow, the company has struck a balance between providing a sophisticated service—telecommunications—and making sophisticated products—communications equipment. It strikes a similar balance with customers. As one of Canada's truly global companies, BCE has by far the largest share of the domestic telecommunications market, and its subsidiary Northern Telecom Ltd. is the third-largest communications equipment manufacturer in the world.

If the 1980s and early 1990s felt like a roller-coaster ride, that's because they were. The era began in the pit of the worst recession since the 1930s and ended in the second worst. Yet, sandwiched in was one of the wildest decades in memory: a boom that both propelled winners to dizzying heights and pummelled losers into exhaustion.

(continued)

Companies weather such change only by changing profoundly themselves, and you only have to visit some of them to realize this. Walk into Maple Leaf Foods Inc. and the first thing you notice is a head office that in two years shrank from 225 employees to 28. If you visit IBM Canada Ltd., you may notice something funny about the secretaries—they scarcely exist. Many executives use voice mail while their former secretaries hold down new jobs, usually somewhere on the front lines, dealing directly with customers.

On a larger scale, it's time to dispel myths, such as the one that says we have an economy only so long as there are trees to chop down and oil to pump. Try these numbers on for size: our corporate top twenty in 1982 consisted of no fewer than six energy companies (oil and gas and pipelines), accounting for 25 percent of the revenue of this group. In 1992, there were three energy companies in this tier, with about 8 percent of the revenue and less than half the sales in 1982.

When we rank the 500 a decade from now, we expect to see many of these trends continue as Canadian industry strengthens its hold on "the sunrise economy." You see this with Imasco Ltd. when it branched out from tobacco products to drugstores (Shoppers Drug Mart) and with Power Corp. when it bought entry into financial services (Investors Group Inc. and Great-West Lifeco Inc.).

EXHIBIT 1.1 • A DECADE OF CHANGE FOR *CB*'S TOP TWENTY COMPANIES

Forget the "hollowing out" of the Canadian economy. Over the course of the 1980s, revenues of the top twenty companies came more from manufacturing and less from resources.

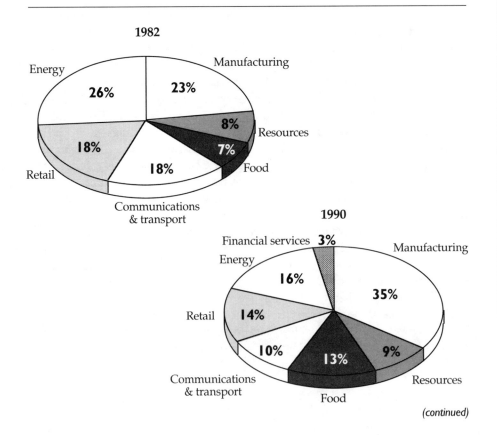

(continued)

Where this may ultimately take us is still anyone's guess. But the guess of that venerable management theorist Peter Drucker (he's now in his 80s) is that we are heading toward a deep structural shift in the world economy where economic growth can no longer be based on consumer demand. He says the new markets will be neither consumer nor producer, but for varying types of infrastructure and facilities that serve both consumers and producers.

As it happens, the growth areas Drucker points to for the next decade bode well for a Canadian industrial structure that is often stronger in capital equipment areas than in consumer goods. For example, the antiquated phone systems of the former Soviet Bloc would be familiar to Alexander Graham Bell himself. This isn't an investment any of these countries can postpone, but the precursor to economic development itself—business must communicate. A safe bet is that demand for these goods and services will keep BCE where it is now—at the top of the heap—over the next decade.

Source: Adapted from Randall Litchfield, "The Sunrise Economy," *Canadian Business*, June 1992, pp. 85–86. Reprinted with permission from Randall Litchfield.

Questions for Discussion

1. What does Randall Litchfield mean by the term "the sunrise economy"?
2. What sort of changes can be expected in the management structures of business?

THE CANADIAN ECONOMY TODAY

Some people feel government has come to play too large a role in our economy in recent years. In addition, some Canadian industries are all but controlled by a few large and complex corporations. While this situation has sometimes led to reduced competition, large corporations have used their increased productivity to generate higher profits, employment, and wages. And yet, in the face of the apparent domination of the business world by government and the giant firms, more and more Canadians are going into business for themselves, founding small companies that reflect the personality of the owners. Companies offering services rather than manufactured products form a growing sector of the Canadian economy.

Consumer concerns, occupational health and safety, the environment, and higher fuel costs have affected Canadian business. Financial scandals, infrequent but spectacular, have led to greater government regulation as legislators try to protect consumers, workers, and businesses themselves from a loss of confidence in the system.

As a result of challenges like these, business has become more socially responsible; the impact on society of a business decision is now weighed in most management decision-making. Business has become more conscious of its operating costs, particularly energy costs. Management continues to struggle with the problems of predicting and then reacting to new government regulations and requirements. Business has found new markets abroad but has encountered increasing competition from foreign producers at home. Writers may some day describe the current era as one of the most challenging for Canadian business.

THE CHALLENGE OF THE FUTURE

Canadians are confused about the state of business and the economy. After the recession of the 1980s, the economy bounced back, and employment soon surpassed [its] earlier levels. In the mid-1990s, though employment levels have risen marginally from those at the worst of the slump, experts say that the same jobs will not come back—that Canada has priced itself out of many of its traditional industries—and that the country must focus on its skills in technology, information, and service to meet the competitive challenge of the world marketplace.

BUSINESS REVIEW 1.1

1. Discuss how the collapse of communism around the world is affecting the Canadian economy today. What opportunities do you see for Canadian business in the future?

2. How do you think Canadian business must change to meet the challenges of the end of the twentieth century?

Competition

Competition on a global scale works much as it does in a smaller environment. Companies must be constantly aware of changes—not only in their customers' desires and needs but also in the costs of raw materials, efficiencies in production, and technology that may improve their product, or make it obsolete. Success or failure depends on how well their products stand up against those of their competitors with regard to price, quality, and service. To remain competitive, companies must develop long-term strategies and revise them regularly.

Companies that satisfy customers succeed. Those who do not, fail. Consider these examples: Ford, once the dominant automaker in North America, slipped behind General Motors; both are now challenged by sales of Japanese, Korean, and German cars, which they once regarded as interesting curiosities but no threat to their own market. Eaton's was for many years the leader in catalogue sales; Sears surpassed it, and Eaton's closed its catalogue operation; more recently, in-home customers seem to prefer to shop through specialty catalogues such as Lee Valley for tools or Marci Lipman for "art to wear" clothing, or through television shopping channels. The last recession brought changes to many fine restaurants; in the affluent 1980s, chefs produced extensive menus at lavish prices to serve formally in exquisitely decorated rooms, but people became more cautious with their money, and restaurants that survived reduced the numbers and types of menu items, streamlined their kitchens to decrease waste, turned to less exotic ingredients, lowered prices, and found less expensive ways to create a friendly and pleasant atmosphere; restaurants that continued in their old extravagant ways folded. The post office once had a virtual monopoly on the delivery of letters and small parcels; then couriers such as Purolator began to offer businesses faster, more efficient service, and Canada Post decided to try to serve this market by buying into Purolator; today both mail and courier services are facing new challenges from fax machines and electronic banking.

Competition guarantees that the private enterprise system will continue to provide the goods and services that make for high living standards and sophisticated lifestyles. Few organizations that offer a product or service can escape the influence of competition. Even non-profit organizations must compete: the Canadian Cancer Society competes for contributions with the Canadian Heart Foundation, your local university or art gallery, and other non-profit enterprises. The armed forces compete in the labour market with private employers.

THE ENTREPRENEUR IN PRIVATE ENTERPRISE

An **entrepreneur** is a person who plans and organizes a business endeavour, taking the risk in hopes of making a profit. We tend to associate the imagination, expertise, and risk taking of entrepreneurship with small and new companies, but entrepreneurs may also see possibilities in existing companies and reorganize or redirect them to create more profitable ventures. The investment and the risk Dave Nichol of Loblaws took in setting up President's Choice, a whole line of interesting and innovative food products, was enormous.

entrepreneur
A person who plans and organizes a business endeavour, taking the risk in hopes of making a profit

The words *enterprise* and *entrepreneur* have the same root. Without entrepreneurs who take risks there would be no private enterprise system; customers would have no new products to choose from, and life would be a lot less interesting.

GROUND RULES OF THE PRIVATE ENTERPRISE SYSTEM

Those who have grown up in an economy dominated by private enterprise may assume that its ground rules are logical, almost axiomatic. A glance at other economic systems has demonstrated that they are not universal, yet they are fundamental to our system. What exactly are these ground rules and why are they important?

Private Property

People in Canada believe they have the right to own **private property** and to do what they wish with it—to buy, use, sell, or leave it to their children. Property may be *tangible*, such as land, buildings, and material goods, or *intangible*, such as inventions, music, or literature. The latter, *intellectual property*, is protected through patent and copyright law. Not all property in Canada is private; some, such as national parks, the Parliament Buildings, public museums and their holdings, and the desks and equipment bought by government departments, is owned by the Crown (the government) for the benefit of all Canadians.

private property
Property, tangible or intangible, that may be bought, used, and disposed of at the will of the owner

Without the security of private property rights, people would have less incentive to buy goods, and demand for the products of the economy would suffer.

Profit

The entrepreneur who takes risks has the right to any profit made after the costs of the undertaking and the payment of taxes that maintain the services provided by the government. Risk, of course, entails the possibility that there may be loss rather than profit.

Many regard the "profit motive" to be the engine of the private enterprise system.

Freedom of Choice

The private enterprise system relies on people to choose what goods and services they will buy. It also requires them to choose what jobs they will accept for what salary and under what working conditions. It allows them to choose whether they will take risks by going into business for themselves instead of working for a regular salary, or investing their savings in a business they believe will succeed rather than leaving them to collect interest in the bank.

Individuals make these choices for their own benefit. But competition would be meaningless if people were not free to choose.

Freedom to Compete

Under the private enterprise system, individuals or companies may enter and compete in any industry they wish. They will, of course, succeed or fail according to their ability to serve and please their customers. But, just as in sport, people expect a level playing field for competition in business. The public, through the government, expects to set rules for the operation of business that are fair to all interests while limiting competition and enterprise as little as possible. Such rules prohibit deceptive advertising and packaging, pricing practices designed to eliminate competition, and fraudulent dealings in financial markets.

Such laws stem from an even more fundamental ethical standpoint that is concerned with how people treat each other and the world around them. Whether the law covers a particular issue or not, we expect business to respect individuals and their rights to privacy and quiet enjoyment, and to operate in a manner that will avoid damaging the natural world that we all share.

Government involvement and business ethics reduce the impact of problems that might occur in a pure capitalist system. They protect consumers, workers, and the privately owned firm itself. Though some may question how much a company should listen to the concerns of outside interests or the amount of power the government has and the way it exercises it, the public's overview helps keep business, labour, consumers, and government in an equitable balance.

FACTORS OF PRODUCTION

factors of production
The basic inputs of the production process: natural resources, labour, capital, and entrepreneurship

The object of a business is to produce some form of output. To do this, the business must have certain inputs. Economists have categorized inputs into four **factors of production**: natural resources, labour, capital, and entrepreneurship. Let us see how the factors of production would apply to a small computer software firm that has decided to put out a new product: a computer game devised by a team of enthusiasts on the staff.

Natural Resources

Natural resources are the raw materials businesses use in their work: land, air, water, forests, mineral deposits. Our software firm will use few of these directly, apart from the land on which the business sits, but other companies who sell various supplies to the firm will use forest products to make desks, paper, and packaging materials, and oil and minerals to make the plastics and metals used in the computer and diskettes. The firm will also use electricity (generated from water, coal, oil, or uranium) for light and power and oil or natural gas for heating.

Theoretically, all these natural resources will still exist in some form after the firm has used them: the building site, the paper, the electricity and oil (in the form of energy). Originally, economists called this first factor of production *land*, because that was ultimately where the resources came from and would return. The firm must pay its suppliers for the materials it uses just as purchasers of its product must pay the firm. Because of the permanent nature of materials, in whatever form, and their relationship to land, the payment for this factor of production is called *rent*.

natural resources
The land and materials from the land that businesses use in the course of their work

Labour

Labour refers to to the people necessary to do the physical and mental work of the business. In order to produce the computer game, our company has a manager, an accountant, a graphic artist, several programmers, packagers, shippers, and sales personnel.

The payment for labour is in the form of *wages*.

labour
The people who do the physical and mental work required by the enterprise

Capital

A business needs **capital** to finance its activities, whether in the form of investments, loans, or profits ploughed back into the company. The entrepreneur who started our software firm approached friends to invest by buying shares in the company. This offering did not provide enough capital to equip the office, buy computers, and hire workers, so the company also sought a loan from the bank. The company is also planning to reinvest some of the profit made from sales of the computer game in more sophisticated equipment to use in future projects.

The factor payment for capital is called *interest*.

capital
The funds from investments, loans, or profits ploughed back into the company that finance its activities

Entrepreneurship

Without entrepreneurship, our software firm would not exist. The entrepreneur has taken risks in forming the company in the first place and is now taking more risks in deciding to develop and market the game idea of some of the company's workers. If the game is a flop, the entrepreneur will sustain a loss. But the game may be a great success.

As a good business person, our entrepreneur will have reduced the risk by assessing the probable demand for the product, likely by hiring a market research consultant (more labour). But it is not the market research consultant who made the decision to devote resources, labour, and capital to the project. After all these other factors of production have been paid, the factor payment that remains is *profit*.

THE MEASURE OF NATIONAL OUTPUT

Why should we care whether our software company fails or succeeds with its new venture? If it fails, the factors of production put into creating the computer game will have been wasted. If it succeeds, and people enjoy the game, they will support not only the company and its workers but also companies from which the software firm buys its supplies; the trucking firms that transport the supplies and the final product; and the retail stores that sell the product, as well as all the employees of these concerns, who will be able to spend more on goods and services provided by still other businesses and other individuals. In the long run, everybody benefits. How well people live—their *standard of living*—depends on an entire economy's level of output.

gross national product (GNP)
The measure of a country's output based on the value of all the goods and services produced in the economy over the course of a year

The **gross national product (GNP)** is the measure of a country's output based on the value of all the goods and services produced in the economy over the course of a year. Comparing the gross national product from one year with that of the next gives economists a crude measure of the state of health of the economy. Dividing the GNP by the number of people in the country to find the GNP per capita determines the standard of living.

Of course, things are not really that simple. For example, the prices of goods and services change continually—usually upward. Inflation, what we call the gradual (or sometimes rapid) rise in prices, has to be taken into consideration. So year-to-year comparisons of GNP include the inflation factor to provide what is called the real gross national product. The arithmetic of the standard of living may not always indicate the *quality of life* for the majority of people in a country. This depends on other factors as well as the GNP, such as how much of the country's wealth is devoted to military spending rather than to consumer goods or health care, or how the wealth is distributed through the population—if a tiny minority holds most of the wealth, the quality of life for the rest of the population will be much lower.

PRODUCTIVITY AND COMPETITIVENESS

productivity
A measure of the output of goods and services in relation to the inputs of natural resources, labour, and capital, most often thought of in terms of output per worker

Are Canadians getting the most out of the factors of production at their disposal? **Productivity** is a measure of the output of goods and services in relation to the inputs of natural resources, labour, and capital, or to any one of these. For example, by careful cutting, a shirt manufacturer may be able to increase the number of shirts it can produce from the same bolt of fabric; by efficient working practices, it may be able to produce more shirts per worker; and an expenditure on new sewing machines may eventually yield a better return on the funds invested in the company. Productivity is most often thought of in terms of output per worker.

Gains in productivity are what allow people to receive higher real wages—wages that rise faster than the cost of living. Productivity increases must exceed wage increases if workers are to receive higher real wages. In contrast, if wages go up 5 percent and productivity only

2 percent in real terms, prices will have to go up 3 percent. The standard of living in a country can rise only when there is an overall increase in productivity.

A country's competitiveness in the global marketplace can also be measured in terms of increases in productivity. In Canada, productivity gains have been shrinking in recent years in comparison with those in such countries as Italy, Japan, and France. Recent assessments of productivity indicate that increased levels of productivity depend on five factors: technology, labour, education, government policies, and management. This five-pointed star for increased productivity is shown in Figure 1.1.

Various reasons have been given for the low rate of productivity growth in Canada. These include: high inflation, a decline in the work ethic or basic desire to work, failure to invest in new plants and equipment, the difficulty of increasing productivity in service-oriented industries, excessive government regulation, inadequate research and development of new products, the high cost of energy, the limited availability of capital, and high interest rates caused by uncertainty about the country's economic future. But perhaps the most damaging factor of all is that many Canadians do not realize that Canada is lagging behind in this crucial area. If Canada is to remain competitive, it is clear that productivity must be seen as a major responsibility of the total management system.

Competitiveness is "a fuzzy concept," Alan Toulin points out:

It means one thing to labor and another to industry and still another to government. Yet any set of workable policies will have to find support among these groups and with a larger public which is only hazily aware of the subject.

But, people don't seek competitiveness for its own sake. In economic terms, being competitive means increasing our real income and, along the way, improving the quality and quantity of the jobs available in the economy. The ultimate public policy objective is an improving level of security and well-being for all citizens.[1]

competitiveness
A measure of the productivity of one company or country against others

FIGURE 1.1 • FIVE-POINTED STAR FOR INCREASED PRODUCTIVITY

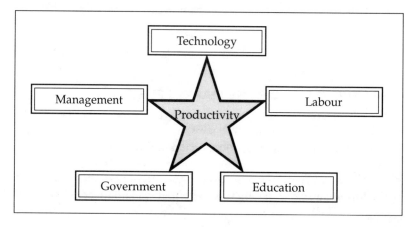

ISSUES IN BUSINESS 1.2

COMPETITIVENESS

IN THE 1990s, the key issue will be excellence in business practice at all levels of the enterprise, not just on the production floor. Countries which have emphasized and achieved a large measure of strength in the implementation of production techniques—notably Japan, Germany, and Switzerland—will have to go beyond that to imaginative emphasis on the techniques of quality throughout the marketing and service organizations. In developing the Miata, for example, Mazda designed the car in California close to its major target market to get the best information on what its target client wanted. Mazda tested more than 100 different combinations of exhaust sounds in order to produce a sports car with the right "sound."

Competitive companies require that there be a broad knowledge at every level of the business enterprise. To be competitive in the future, companies will require people who have the inclination, desire, and ability to understand the rationale of the business throughout the many facets of the enterprise.

This is very important as each employee will have not only to perform his or her duties, but to be able to make suggestions on how the process may be more efficiently or effectively performed.

This is highlighted by contrasting the typical Canadian and U.S. company with those in Japan. In North America, knowledge is too often concentrated at the top of the hierarchical management structure, whereas it is more spread out in Japan.

Quality is the name of the game in the 1990s. Indeed, every facet of the organization today—management, production, marketing, accounting, globalization, localization, values, etc.—feels the impact of the emphasis on efficiency and quality which is moving from the factory to every other area of the firm.

Countries and companies must operate in an open environment which will allow them to react quickly and efficiently if they want to be competitive with the rest of the world. This means providing the opportunity for new ways of looking at problems and, in some areas, drastically changing work methods.

Source: Excerpts from Richard Fogler, "Competitiveness Is More Than Strategy," *The Financial Post*, August 29, 1991, p. 11. Reprinted with permission from Richard Fogler.

Questions for Discussion

1. Name several areas of the business process where competitiveness is becoming an issue. Give an example of the sort of change required in at least one area.

2. Who does Richard Fogler believe should be the experts in a company—the people managers should listen to?

THE STRUCTURE OF THE MARKETPLACE

In the private, or free, enterprise system, we hear a lot about competitiveness and competition. But sometimes it seems to the casual observer that there is no real competition and that prices are mysteriously set in stone.

Ideally, in a free market economy, prices are determined according to the **law of supply and demand**. When sellers have a large supply of

law of supply and demand
An economic law that says market price is determined by the intersection of the supply and demand curve in a free market economy

a product that they wish to sell and few people want to buy, the price will fall; conversely, when buyers want more of a good than is available for sale, the price will rise. When the demand of the buyers is satisfied by the supply the sellers have to offer, the actual price is established (see Figure 1.2). In the real world, of course, things are not quite that simple. The type of product, the number of sellers, the relative ease or difficulty of entering the market, and the power of individual sellers or buyers influence the way prices are set. Market structures are usually divided into four types: perfect competition, monopolistic competition, oligopoly, and monopoly.

Perfect Competition

The law of supply and demand is most fully effective in what is called **perfect competition**. In perfect competition, a common product is sold by many sellers in a market where there are many buyers. All the sellers and buyers are aware of each other, and each individually is too small to influence the final price unduly. If sellers see good opportunities in the market, it is easy to enter; if they do not find it profitable, it is easy to withdraw.

The most commonly cited example of this type of market is the agricultural industry, where potatoes, carrots, or apples are grown by a large number of farmers and are similar from farm to farm. The price of each commodity is set by what the market will bear. A visit to a local farmers' market will reveal similar prices from one stall to the next. At the end of the day, when sellers are eager to dispose of their remaining merchandise and few buyers remain, prices will drop.

(Agricultural products that fall under the control of marketing boards are *not* examples of perfect competition. Marketing boards usually limit supply in order to keep prices high enough to cover the costs of production. Doing so ensures that the producers will be able to stay in business and guarantees consumers a reliable source of supply.)

perfect competition
A market easy to enter or withdraw from, governed by supply and demand, where many sellers sell a common product to many buyers and each individually is too small to influence the final price unduly

FIGURE 1.2 • SUPPLY AND DEMAND DETERMINE PRICE

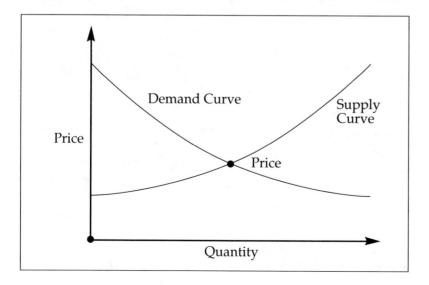

Monopolistic Competition

monopolistic competition
A market with many sellers and buyers that is relatively easy to enter or withdraw from, and where sellers can differentiate their products from those of competitors that may be essentially similar

While one potato may be very like another, some people will tell you that one over-the-counter cough remedy or one pair of jeans is definitely not like another; others regard all cough remedies and all jeans as essentially similar. **Monopolistic competition** exists in a market when the sellers can make their product appear different (in quality, convenience, or image, for example) from the products of competitors. The "monopoly" aspect lies in the differentiation—each seller has a monopoly on its particular style—and the "competition" aspect in the fact that there are many sellers and buyers and it is relatively easy for sellers to enter or withdraw from the market.

Oligopoly

oligopoly
A market in which a few sellers dominate and have significant influence over the product's price

Oligopoly is a market in which a few sellers dominate because of the large investments required to enter it. The product may be the same, as in perfect competition—for example, steel or cement—or similar, as in monopolistic competition—for example, automobiles. Because of the limited number of sellers, each can have a significant influence over the product's price. Prices seldom vary much, because any unjustified jump in price would eliminate the seller from the market, and a substantial price cut would immediately have to be matched by other producers, thus reducing the profit margin for all. Laws such as the Combines Investigation Act of 1985 prevent sellers in oligopolistic industries from actually getting together to fix prices.

Monopoly

monopoly
A market in which there is only one seller, usually regulated by government

In a **monopoly**, there is only one seller. If a monopoly were not controlled in some way, it would be completely free to supply its product at a price that would yield the most profit. The Combines Investigation

Via Rail Canada is a crown corporation with the mandate to provide passenger rail service from one end of Canada to the other. Because it offers extensive services across Canada, Via Rail continues to be a non-threatened monopoly. Via Rail Canada separated from Canadian National Railways (CNR) in 1978. Today, Via owns its own trains; however, it must lease the railway-track access from CNR.

Act prohibits attempts to monopolize markets except under conditions in which having a single supplier is the only practical way to deliver the product. Electricity and natural gas are examples of such products. In the public interest, firms selling these products are regulated by the provincial and federal governments (some are actually owned by the government), but because of the huge investment required to enter the market at all, the firms are also protected from competition.

If a firm has a monopoly, it may have little incentive to improve service. New technology may change people's and governments' views of which industries require monopolies. Telephone service used to be seen as an area that required a monopoly, but the government has recently licensed a number of firms to compete in the provision of long-distance services. Cable television companies have a monopoly on providing service within a designated area, but are finding they may be challenged by new satellite technology.

The four types of market structure can be illustrated by various stages in the wine and beer industries. Table grapes are an undifferentiated product whose price is determined by the law of supply and demand in perfect competition. Wine produced from special "varietal" grapes, by contrast, is a highly differentiated product sold by small producers under many labels in a monopolistically competitive market. Cottage breweries occupy the same sort of market, but they hold only a small portion of the entire beer market, which is dominated by a few giant beer companies operating in an oligopoly. In many provinces, the retail sale of alcoholic beverages is a government-owned or government-controlled monopoly. Characteristics of the four types of market structure are summarized in Table 1.1.

BUSINESS REVIEW 1.2

1. What factors of production does a business use as inputs in order to produce an output? How are these inputs paid for?

2. Explain the relationship of gross national product, standard of living, and quality of life.

3. Describe how effectively the law of supply and demand operates in each of the four marketplace structures.

THE BUSINESS PROCESS

A business's objective is to make a profit by serving the needs of a market or markets through the use of the factors of production—natural resources, labour, capital, and entrepreneurship. The business manager's job is to control these variables in the most efficient way possible to produce goods and services that will satisfy these markets.

What are these markets? Ultimately, the consumer is the market for all business, but not all businesses serve the consumer directly. Many supply the needs of other businesses that, in turn, serve the consumer,

TABLE 1.1 • MAJOR CHARACTERISTICS OF MARKET STRUCTURE

Type of market	Characteristics			
	Number of firms	Product	Control over pricing	Ease of entry
Perfect competition	Many	Similar	None	Easy
Monopolistic competition	Many	Different	Some	Relatively easy
Oligopoly	Few	Similar or different	Substantial	Difficult
Monopoly	One	No readily available substitute	Usually regulated by government	Virtually impossible

perhaps still indirectly. For some businesses, an important market is government, which uses the products of business in providing the services legislated by the voters' elected representatives. A fourth major market is the export market; sales to foreign countries provide the funds that allow the consumer to buy products from abroad. Some businesses serve several of these major market sectors; others concentrate on one.

Figure 1.3 is a diagram of the business process as it affects everyone who is part of the Canadian economic system.

FIGURE 1.3 • A DIAGRAM OF BUSINESS AND SOCIETY

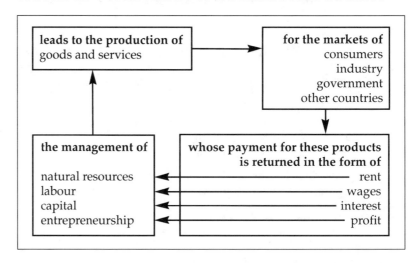

INTERACTIVE SUMMARY AND DISCUSSION QUESTIONS

1. What do Charles Bronfman, Wayne Gretzky, Harry Ornest, and Norm Green (all Canadians who own major league sports teams) have in common when we consider the decisions that need to be taken during the buying or selling of professional teams? What is unique about the decision-making styles they employ in dealing with these businesses?

2. Excellence! Quality! Competitiveness! What must the contemporary Canadian organization know about these terms to survive and prosper throughout the second half of the 1990s?

3. Why are entrepreneurs so important in the Canadian mixed-economy system?

4. Productivity is a measure of how efficient production is and is related to the amount of goods and services produced by people within a specific time period. Today, *productivity* is a major buzzword. Why is it so crucial? Explain.

5. You know that the basic systems of competition are perfect competition, monopolistic competition, oligopoly, and monopoly. Match each of these systems with the following businesses:
   (a) Hydro-Québec
   (b) Ford of Canada
   (c) Emile Roberts Turkey Farm
   (d) Kmart

6. Describe and give an example of the economic systems discussed in this chapter: private enterprise, communism, socialism, and mixed economy.

7. How does Canada rate in terms of overall competitiveness in relation to such countries as Sweden, Japan, the United States, and Germany? What must be done to increase Canada's ability to compete?

8. The study of business is interesting and important to students for different reasons. Some feel it can help in the selection of careers. Are there other reasons to study the field of business as a university/college topic, or even as a blueprint for the future?

CASE 1.1

MOGULOMANIA

FASCINATING MOVIES could be made about Kenneth C. Irving (1899–1992) and Jack Kent Cooke (1912–). Both Canadian by birth, they got their start as hustling salesmen in the 1920s. Both became fabulously wealthy and then left their native land, Irving for an offshore haven, Cooke to make more millions in the United States. Both were fanatically hard workers who never stopped trying to expand their empires. Their lives have been classic capitalist success sagas, the truth on which fiction gets based.

Yet, how very different the Irving and Cooke movies would be, almost as different as Canada and the United States. K.C. Irving made money in one region of Canada, kept it there, becomes a tremendously powerful but obsessively private person, passes his empire to sons who also live quietly and without ostentation, and gradually fades away. J.K. Cooke is always on the move, changes his name and his citizenship, lives in and perhaps for the limelight, and in his old age becomes a kind of pathetic tabloid star. His biographer calls him "The Last Mogul," which is absurd. He will soon vanish and be forgotten. The Irvings, on the other hand, who are characterized in their biography as Canada's wealthiest family, seem to have built an enduring dynasty.

Irving and Cooke made their fortunes in two of this century's greatest growth industries, the automobile and broadcasting. K.C. Irving started out selling Model-T Fords in Kent County, N.B.; went into gasoline and spare parts, car dealerships, and bus lines; and never slowed down. In the

(continued)

1940s, he expanded into forest industries, newspapers, and shipping, but the Irving Oil Company Ltd., with its tankers, refineries, and 3,000 service stations, is still the chief pillar of the empire. In a strategy designed to minimize taxes and, perhaps, liability to anticombines persecutions, Irving moved suddenly in 1971 to the Bahamas, then Bermuda.

His three sons, J.K., Arthur, and Jack, have inherited the family enterprises, and are starting to bring along the next generation. The Irvings may or may not be Canada's richest family; certainly they are the butt of jokes about being the only family that owns a province. ("How would the Irvings downsize?" the Royal Canadian Air Farce asks. "By selling Moncton.")

They are now expanding their oil and gas business in Maine and other eastern states. As well, through their Cavendish Farms Ltd. operations, the Irvings have entered the frozen-food wars against New Brunswick's upstart French-fry barons, the McCain family.

Young J.K. Cooke first got a name in Toronto newspapers as leader of a dance band: Oley Kent and His Bourgeois Canadians. In the 1930s, he peddled soap and encyclopedias, then hooked up with another go-getter from Toronto, Roy Thomson, who gave him a Stratford, Ontario, radio station to manage. Jack "Kent" Cooke's big breakthrough came after 1944 when he took over a little 1,000-watt radio station in Toronto; renamed it CKEY; upped its power, the pace of its programming, and the frequency of its commercials; and began coining money. Dubbed a "wonder boy" in the Toronto media, Cooke bought and sold magazines (*Liberty*, *Saturday Night*), tried to buy newspapers (*The Globe and Mail*), and dabbled as a sportsman by owning the old Toronto Maple Leaf baseball team in the International League.

In 1960, Cooke decided that Toronto and Canada were too confining—government regulators, who did not like his freewheeling style, seemed to be frustrating him at almost every turn—so he upped and became a U.S. citizen and went off to California. He went into pop radio and newspaper ownership there, struck it really rich in cable television, and indulged his jock-sniffing inclination by ownership forays into three professional sports—NBA basketball (Los Angeles Lakers), NFL football (Washington Redskins), and NHL hockey (Los Angeles Kings). The millions poured in. Cooke gradually sold out and moved east, where he still has a major winner in the Washington Redskins. He lives with what seems to be his fifth or sixth wife (the actual count is four) on his estate in Middleburg, Virginia, a long way from high school dances in 1920s Toronto.

The Irvings like to run their personal lives quietly and simply. There was a little wild oats and one divorce in the second generation, but nothing like the Cooke mess. We have here the two great variations on the rags-to-riches epic. With Cooke, it's capitalist acquisition and sordid dissipation leading to dissolution; with the Irvings, it's acquisition, retention, transmission, and then more acquisition. As befitting the Scots and Christian people of Atlantic Canada, the Irvings hold fast to the fundamentals long after the Toronto-bred city folk have surrendered to the glitz and glamour of the American way.

Source: Adapted from Michael Bliss, "Mogulomania," *Report on Business Magazine*, April 1992, pp. 27–28. Reprinted with permission from Michael Bliss.

Questions for Discussion

1. While Jack Kent Cooke and K.C. Irving are very different individuals, as business personalities they both appear to have certain characteristics that led to their success. Describe these.

2. If both Cooke and Irving were beginning their careers in 1995, what would they find different about the Canadian economic climate from when they entered business nearly three-quarters of a century ago?

CASE 1.2

THE SEARCH FOR QUALITY AND THE COMPETITIVE EDGE

LAST YEAR, chartered accountants Arthur Anderson & Co. set out on a search for the best-managed private companies in Canada. By December, after countless hours of sifting through financial data and interviewing CEOs, the search team had narrowed its universe to a list of 50 firms. These finalists were as diverse a group as one could imagine: with locations scattered from Halifax to Vancouver, their annual sales range from as little as $2.2 million to as much as $162.2 million, and they are involved in everything from producing radioactive isotopes for medical use to providing investment counselling, to making industrial equipment.

Still, their philosophies are remarkably similar. Asked what gave them a competitive edge, top executives of the 50 companies mentioned customer service more often than any other factor, and employee morale almost as frequently—the twin pillars of success in the post-industrial era, as proclaimed by the most influential contemporary management theorists.

Employee and customer satisfaction are linked concepts: workers who feel their contributions are properly rewarded and recognized are attentive to the quality of their service or product. Customers respond with their own show of loyalty, which, in turn, bolsters employees' sense of achievement. That is the positive link, says Robert Glegg, president of Glegg Water Conditioning Inc. (GWC) of Guelph, Ontario. But there's a downside too: in order to satisfy customers, management may ask employees to work harder, longer hours than the norm, as well as make other personal sacrifices. So GWC management makes constant trade-offs. "If we tried to satisfy every customer need, we'd upset our staff—and vice versa," says Glegg.

The after-sale relationship with the customer is as important for other manufacturers of big-ticket machinery as it is for GWC. After all, machine downtime is disastrous for manufacturers that must pay overhead expenses whether or not their plants are operational. So Glegg Water Conditioning Inc. has eight service engineers ready to jet anywhere in North America within 24 hours, 365 days a year, to service the demineralizers it sells to paper mills, power plants, semi-conductor-makers, and other manufacturers that require impeccably pure water.

"We might get by with fewer engineers," confesses president Robert Glegg. "But we decided to have more than necessary to guarantee prompt service. If a customer calls from California and says, 'I need an engineer here in the morning,' he doesn't want to hear why we can't do it. We send someone on the next plane." It costs GWC in the low six figures annually to maintain the additional mobile trouble-shooters. Still, Glegg figures it is worth it, because it is customer service that wins repeat business and references.

GWC's service orientation can demand superhuman efforts from its 100-plus employees—one service engineer worked 72 hours round the clock to get a system up and running for a Texas-based customer. So Glegg constantly bolsters worker morale. Competitive compensation is just the beginning. "Paying someone a lot is never a positive on its own," Glegg says. "It merely removes a possible negative."

At monthly executive meetings, GWC managers are expected to report on staff satisfaction along with financial issues. And Glegg himself tests the esprit de corps by lunching regularly with small groups of employees. "These are two-way conversations on where we are going, new projects, people, problems," says Glegg. When he hears about a problem, he acts on it. A few years ago, when the firm was building additional office space, it decided on an open concept. Lunching

(continued)

with project engineers, however, Glegg learned they didn't want to give up private offices. The plans for the extension were immediately changed.

Source: Adapted from Ian Allaby, "The Search for Quality," *Canadian Business*, May 1990, pp. 31, 37. Reprinted with permission from Ian Allaby.

Questions for Discussion

1. What makes Glegg Water Conditioning Inc. an outstanding company? Why was it cited as one of the best-managed private companies in Canada?
2. Describe the success of GWC by referring to Figure 1.3.

NOTES

1. Alan Toulin, "Canada Needs Goals for Competitiveness," *The Financial Post*, August 21, 1991, p. 11

PHOTO CREDITS

BUS 2   Montreal Expos

BUS 5   Courtesy of the Orchestre symphonique de Montréal

BUS 24   Via Rail Canada Inc.

MODULE
◆ OWN ◆

FORMS OF BUSINESS OWNERSHIP

THE FOCUS OF THIS MODULE

1. To describe the three types of private business ownership

2. To discuss the advantages and disadvantages of running a business as a sole proprietorship

3. To discuss the advantages and disadvantages of running a business as a partnership

4. To discuss the advantages and disadvantages of running a business as a corporation

5. To describe how a corporation is owned by its shareholders and controlled by its board of directors

6. To discuss government enterprise and crown corporations

7. To describe the features of the collective ownership of co-operatives

8. To define the following terms:

KEY TERMS

sole proprietorship	dividends
partnership	preferred shares
general partner	proxy
limited partner	board of directors
joint venture	outside director
corporation	chief executive officer
shareholders	merger
private or closely held corporation	subsidiary
	parent company
public or publicly held corporation	crown corporation
	privatization
common shares	co-operative

WHEN JOSEPH OF NAZARETH set up business as a carpenter, he was what we would now call a sole proprietor. He owned his own tools, ran his own workshop, kept all the profits from his business, and was responsible for any losses. Sole proprietorship is still the most common *form* of business ownership in Canada today. But for various reasons, as we shall see, most business *activity* is conducted by incorporated companies, owned either by private individuals through the acquisition of shares of stock or by all citizens through the government.

BUSINESS CORPORATIONS come in many sizes, from the one-person music-copying outfit to Canadian Pacific or General Motors of Canada. Their shares may be owned by a single person or family or by tens of thousands of people across the country or elsewhere in the world. They may be crown corporations, owned by the government. Non-profit organizations, too, usually find that incorporation is the most practical way of conducting their affairs.

OWNERSHIP: FROM PROPRIETORSHIP TO THE CORPORATION

The businesses that are still run as sole proprietorships are usually very small. Entering into a partnership agreement may enlarge the scope of the business. Sometimes individual business people find it convenient to operate some part of their business or to provide mutually desired services in co-operatives.

Sole Proprietorship

sole proprietorship
The ownership, and often the operation, of a business by a single individual

Sole proprietorship is the oldest and simplest form of business ownership: the ownership, and often the operation, of a business by a single individual. In law, there is no distinction between the sole proprietor as a private citizen and as the owner of the business. The proprietor owns all the assets of the business, keeps all the profits, and is responsible for all its debts. Many large businesses start out as small, independent sole proprietorships, but today this business structure is most often used for temporary businesses or to provide free-lance services of various types.

Advantages of Sole Proprietorship. All profits of a sole proprietorship belong to the owner (once personal income taxes are paid). Being completely in charge gives the owner a real incentive to be as efficient as possible.

A minimum of legal requirements makes it easy to go into business as a sole proprietor. Most provinces require that the name of the business be registered to prevent two or more companies operating under the same name. Some types of businesses, such as restaurants, retail

stores, motels, hairdressing salons, and repair shops, require municipal licences and must comply with zoning regulations. For example,
Bill Wong cannot set up a car restoration business in his backyard in a
residential area.

Closing down the business is also uncomplicated. The proprietor
simply ceases operation. A local sports fan can organize an exhibition
game in the local arena, arrange advertising, print tickets, hire ushers,
contract with concessionaires, and wind down the business as soon as
all outstanding debts are paid.

Many sole proprietors enjoy the flexibility and freedom "being
one's own boss" brings them. The owner need not consult anyone
about management decisions, so there are no long, seemingly unproductive meetings required to discuss plans, introduce new ideas, or
convince the boss of the value of a particular strategy. Decisions can be
translated into instant action.

Accounting procedures for sole proprietorships are much simpler
than for other forms of business. As far as the law is concerned, sole
proprietors are private individuals and are taxed as such.

Disadvantages of Sole Proprietorship. Anyone planning to go into
business alone must consider the lack of security of doing without a
regular paycheque and fringe benefits that come with employment.
As well, the fact that all profits of a sole proprietorship belong to the
owner has a flip side: if the business loses money, the owner is personally responsible for all losses. This unlimited financial liability can
mean the loss of personal possessions as well as the assets of the
business.

The ease of going in and out of business also means there may be
lack of continuity. When a sole proprietor dies, retires, goes bankrupt,
or simply changes interests, the business is terminated. Legally,
another person cannot "take over" a sole proprietorship; a new business must be set up. This can be a major annoyance for clients, who
have to begin new relationships, learning how another individual
operates.

Most sole proprietors are not management people first and fore-
most. They are designers, plumbers, or music teachers. "Being one's
own boss" means all decisions are made by the owner, and if they are
poor ones, no one is there to give advice. This may also make it difficult for sole proprietors to raise money to expand the business, as
lending institutions may not trust a business plan drawn up by one
individual.

While accounting procedures are simpler, tax rates may be higher.
All the income of a sole proprietorship is taxed as personal income,
and once a business reaches a certain size, it may be advantageous to
incorporate.

The advantages of operating as a sole proprietor can also be seen as
its disadvantages.

Partnership

Under provincial partnerships acts, a **partnership** is a voluntary legal
agreement among two or more people who decide to operate a business

partnership
A voluntary legal agreement of two or
more people to operate a business,
sharing the risks and the profits

TABLE 2.1 • ADVANTAGES AND DISADVANTAGES OF SOLE PROPRIETORSHIP

Advantages	Disadvantages
retention of all profits	unlimited financial responsibility
ease of entry and exit	lack of continuity
flexibility and freedom	lack of management expertise
simple accounting procedures	tax disadvantages

---

together, sharing the risks of financing and managing the business and its profits. Partnership arrangements are common among doctors, lawyers, and accountants, whose professional role does not allow them to limit their liability through incorporation. Partnerships are often set up between individuals who wish to run a small business together.

Like sole proprietors, **general partners** operate as private citizens, their profits are treated as personal income, and they are liable for the partnership's debts. But general partners may also bring limited partners into the association. As long as they take no active role in management, the liability of **limited partners** is restricted to the amount of capital they invest in the enterprise. If Marie and Ivanka decide to go into partnership as home renovators, they might ask Ivanka's father to invest in the partnership as a limited partner by providing the capital to buy a truck. Should Marie and Ivanka run up debts and fail in their endeavour, Ivanka's father will lose the money invested in the truck but will otherwise be secure. Marie and Ivanka, however, will be liable for the entire amount owing to creditors.

Most provinces allow for two or three other kinds of partners: *secret* or *dormant partners*, whose investment in and connection to the firm are not disclosed to the public, and *ostensible partners*, who have no financial investment in the firm, but who allow their names and reputation to be used in advertising. In most circumstances, these types of partners have unlimited liability.

It is useful for partners to clarify the arrangement in a written agreement so that all partners have the same understanding of what resources each partner brings to the partnership, the purpose of the partnership, and how to achieve it.

A **joint venture** is a business partnership between individuals or companies for a specific undertaking. For example, a group of people might come together to import a single vintage of a choice wine, or a group of oil companies in partnership with government might come together to investigate and develop new technology to extract oil from tar sands.

Advantages of Partnership. A partnership allows partners to combine personal resources. After expenses are paid, all profits of a partnership are shared among the partners according to the terms set out in the partnership agreement. For example, partnerships are often set up by professionals who wish to share the cost of support staff, facilities,

general partner
A partner responsible for the management of a partnership and liable for its debts

limited partner
A partner who has no responsibility for the management of a partnership and whose liability is restricted to the amount of capital invested in the enterprise

joint venture
A business partnership between individuals or companies for a specific undertaking

and technology. The partners may decide to devote a percentage of their individual fees or to have each partner pay a set amount toward these costs. Marie, Ivanka, and her father may decide the general partners should each draw a regular sum and then share 90 percent of the remaining profits equally, with 10 percent going to the limited partner.

Registering a partnership is a little more complicated than registering a sole proprietorship. The name under which the partnership intends to do business must be registered, along with the names and addresses of the partners, and any necessary licences must be applied for.

Working in a partnership allows the partners to provide complementary technical and managerial expertise. Marie may have the imaginative flair to design a renovation; Ivanka may be better at the detailed finishing carpentry work; Marie may know how to obtain the best supplies at the lowest cost; Ivanka may be better at bookkeeping. As the business expands, Marie and Ivanka may hire Paul to help them paint walls and lay flooring; If Paul impresses them with his work, they might offer to make him a partner in the business.

Banks and other lending institutions consider it less risky to lend money to partnerships than to sole proprietors.

Disadvantages of Partnership. As with sole proprietorships, all the profits of a partnership are taxed as personal income, which may result in higher taxes.

Unlimited personal liability is an even greater concern in a partnership than in a sole proprietorship. If the business venture fails, all partners are liable for the payment of any debts out of their personal wealth. But if some partners are unable to pay, the remaining partners are liable not only for their own share of the loss, but for everything that is owed. Partners are also liable for any actions made by their partners in the name of the partnership.

Working as partners may be a good way to lose friends. Even when a thorough written agreement has been drawn up, misunderstandings about the direction of the company will inevitably arise. Settling disputes among partners may be difficult, and, although setting up a partnership may be simple, dissolving it is more complicated. If one partner wishes to leave, other partners may not wish to buy the leaving partner's interest, and it may be difficult to find another person to buy into the partnership who is acceptable to the other partners. If the partners decide to liquidate the partnership, it may be some time before assets can be fairly divided.

Any time a partner dies or leaves and a new partner is added or buys an existing partner's interest, the partnership is considered to have been dissolved and a new partnership formed. This new partnership must be reregistered. Because some partners remain with the firm, this lack of continuity is less of a problem for clients than it is in the case of a sole proprietorship.

Frisco Bay Industries of Canada Ltd. in Issues in Business 2.1 is a corporation that has been run very much like a partnership.

TABLE 2.2 · ADVANTAGES AND DISADVANTAGES OF PARTNERSHIP

Advantages	Disadvantages
ease of formation	unlimited financial responsibility
complementary expertise	interpersonal conflict
improved access to financing	complications at liquidation
retention of profits	tax disadvantages

ISSUES IN BUSINESS 2.1

WHEN PARTNERS COLLIDE

WHEN BUSINESS partners feud, their company often suffers. But when the partners are also boyhood friends, it can become a gut-wrenching ordeal that affects everyone even remotely associated with the company.

Since starting Montreal-based Frisco Bay Industries of Canada Ltd. in 1970, Barry Katsof and Joel Matlin built a nation-wide clientele for their customized security systems used by banks and large corporations. By 1988, Frisco Bay registered sales of $13 million and employed 200.

Sensing the company's imminent transition to big-league player, Frisco Bay chairman and chief executive Katsof, and Matlin, then president, began to discuss future strategy. But the partners, who had known each other since high school, soon butted heads. Discussions escalated into arguments, and eventually the two stopped talking to each other. The chill between the CEO and the president had fearful employees, wary suppliers, and nervous customers speculating about the firm's fate.

"We had a difference in philosophy as to how to run the company," says Katsof. "Some concepts he was talking about just weren't realistic." Matlin wanted to diversify, while Katsof argued for augmenting existing product lines. The two also differed on management style. "After a company gets to a certain size, there's not enough hours in a day to run it yourself," says Katsof. "If you're going to grow, you have to delegate authority. I perceived Joel had trouble with that process." For his part, Matlin says he wanted to build a full-service security company, but that Katsof and a third partner, Ron Waxman, decided the five-year plan Matlin had prepared "was contrary to their plans."

As Matlin and Katsof's silence continued, operations all but ground to a halt. "When you spend more time fighting than anything else, you're not running the company," says Katsof. "Arguing behind closed doors is one thing, but employees get nervous and managers don't know who to report to when they know the two of you aren't talking."

By August 1988, the board of directors—which included representatives from such demanding institutional investors as Quebec's Caisse de dépôt et placement—decided to end the cold war; Matlin was fired. Frisco Bay obtained an injunction prohibiting Toronto-based Matlin from entering Frisco Bay premises to conduct business. Matlin sued, claiming $450,000 for wrongful dismissal, and market value for his shares.

Anxiety ran high. One day in November, Katsof looked out of his office window to see a car from the Montreal *Gazette,* and his estranged partner posing for pictures. "I don't know what he was trying to do" by going to the press, says Katsof. "I guess it was to show that he was right and we were wrong." When the reporter phoned, Katsof tried to downplay the situation, saying "this

(continued)

sort of thing goes on every day." Nonetheless, the *Gazette* ran the story on the front page of its business section, with a large picture and caption: "Joel Matlin stands outside office of Frisco Bay. He has been locked out."

Matlin says the story was part of his strategy. "I went to the *Gazette* to turn [Katsof and Waxman] into buyers," says Matlin. "What I was saying with the article was, 'You don't have the guts to buy me out.' I got him [Katsof] to think that 'if Joel wants it so bad, I'm going to get it [instead].'"

Meanwhile, Katsof worried about the impact of this now-public spat. Because service contracts form such a critical element for security-sensitive industries, stability is fundamental. Competing against such heavyweights as Honeywell Ltd. and Chubb Corp., Frisco Bay could hardly afford to look insecure. Katsof says he soon received reports from several customers that Matlin had been drawing their attention to the *Gazette* story. Losing any one of its major accounts, such as the Royal Canadian Mint, the Royal Bank of Canada, or Northern Telecom Ltd., would be a monstrous blow.

To help with damage control, Frisco Bay hired management consultant John Fleming of William M. Mercer Ltd. On his advice, Katsof and Waxman, another high-school chum who had joined in 1977 and was now president, sent letters to clients and suppliers, reassuring them they could stabilize the situation. Katsof compiled arguments and figures attesting to Frisco Bay's continuing health and paid personal visits to bread-and-butter clients in Quebec, Ontario, and B.C.

Meanwhile, Matlin had invoked the "shotgun clause" in the partnership agreement, offering to sell his shares for $1.95 each, totalling $3.2 million. Katsof and Waxman had 30 days either to accept his offer or to sell their shares to Matlin for the same price.

Katsof scrambled for financial support for the December 12 deadline. "It was a very, very stressful time," he says. "I wasn't sleeping well at night." He once booked a hotel room for a two-hour nap between meetings with potential backers.

In the end, Katsof and Waxman bought out Matlin. All lawsuits ceased, and Matlin signed a two-year non-competition agreement. Everyone at Frisco Bay heaved a sigh of relief, says Katsof. "We were friends for more than eighteen years. But I had to do what I had to do. When Joel left the company, we could concentrate 100 percent on growing the company again."

Source: Reprinted from Jennifer Low, "When Partners Collide," *Profit*, October 1991, pp. 25–26. Reprinted with permission from Jennifer Low.

Questions for Discussion

1. What led to the dissolution of the partnership at Frisco Bay Industries Ltd.? Cite specific incidents and issues in your response.

2. Would you adopt the strategy Joel Martin used to attempt to force former partners Ron Waxman and Barry Katsof to buy him out? Support your response in reference to what will happen to the new or future firm.

Incorporation

Once a commercial enterprise is established, most owners find it advantageous to incorporate the business. A **corporation** is regarded as a separate legal entity from the individual owners, and their liability for its debts is limited to their investment in it. In law, the corporation is an intangible entity, a "corporate citizen," that can conduct business and enter into contracts and is subject to the law and its penalties just like an individual human being.

corporation
A legal entity with rights and responsibilities that has a separate existence from its individual owners and whose liability for its debts is limited to the owners' investment in it

The Hudson's Bay Company is a Canadian corporation with both a long and a famous history. Although originally important as a fur-trading company, The Bay is now a modern retailing organization with hundreds of stores across Canada.

Probably the first business corporation to have a major influence in the lands that were to become Canada was the Hudson's Bay Company, with a charter granted by Charles II of England. Today, corporate charters are granted under both federal and provincial jurisdiction. A company that intends to do business across the country will apply for a federal charter; one that expects to do most of its business in Red Deer, Alberta, will apply for an Alberta charter. The federal government and the provinces require similar information on a corporate charter, for example, the corporate name, the purposes of the corporation, the registered office and the name of the agent to whom questions regarding the operation of the company should be addressed, the name of the incorporator, and the authorized capital stock.

The capital that investors place in the company is known as its stock, and the investors receive *shares* of this stock that entitle them to a portion of the profits of the company. Shares can be bought and sold; the shares of many corporations, large and small, are traded on the open market at stock exchanges such as those at Montreal, Toronto, and Vancouver.

TABLE 2.3 · ADVANTAGES AND DISADVANTAGES OF INCORPORATION

Advantages	Disadvantages
limited liability	complex to set up
expanded financial capacity	many legal requirements
specialization	lack of secrecy in operations
tax advantages	impersonality and alienation of employees

Advantages of Incorporation. Limited liability is the most significant advantage of corporate ownership over other forms of ownership. Because corporations are considered legal entities separate from their owners, the shareholders (owners) have limited financial liability. If the firm fails, they can lose only the amount of their investments. Personal funds of owners cannot be touched by creditors of the corporation. The limited liability of corporate ownership is clearly designated in the names used by firms throughout the world. Corporate enterprises in Canada and the United Kingdom usually use "Limited" or "Ltd." at the end of their names (Limitée or Ltée in French). In Australia, limited liability is shown by "Proprietary Limited" or "Pty. Ltd." Companies in the United States use "Incorporated" or "Inc.," and many Canadian corporations, especially those with U.S. interests, have adopted this term.

Incorporation allows a company to grow. People with both large and small resources can buy shares in a corporation, thus providing a larger capital base than a sole proprietorship or even a partnership can command. Size and stability also make it easier for large corporations to borrow additional funds—and often at a lower rate of interest than is available to smaller businesses, incorporated or not.

In fact, many of the other advantages of incorporation are a matter of the size of the business rather than the fact of incorporation. For example, the managerial skills of sole proprietorships and partnerships are usually confined to the abilities of the owners, and this remains true for a small limited company. Larger corporations can easily obtain specialized managerial, professional, or trade skills because they offer long-term career opportunities for qualified people. Thus employees can specialize in the work activities they perform best. Many projects can be internally financed by transferring money from one part of the corporation to another. Longer manufacturing runs usually mean more efficient production and lower prices, thus attracting more customers. Some corporations have grown exceedingly large. The largest industrial corporations are listed in Table 2.4.

Many business people see tax advantages in incorporation. As separate legal entities, corporations are subject to federal and provincial income taxes. Corporate earnings are taxed, and any dividends—payments from earnings—to shareholders are also taxed on an individual basis. From the viewpoints of shareholders who receive dividends, this is effectively double taxation of corporate earnings. By contrast, the earnings of sole proprietorships and partnerships are taxed only once, because they are treated as personal income. As corporations can deduct numerous expense items that are not available to individuals, however, and as the rate of taxation on retained earnings above a certain amount is lower than it would be if those earnings were taxed as personal income, it may be worthwhile to incorporate even a small business enterprise.

Disadvantages of Incorporation. Corporations are the most difficult and costly ownership form to establish. Each province has different incorporation laws, some of which are quite technical and complex. Establishing a corporation can require the services of a lawyer. While it may be possible to incorporate the business oneself, most people hire a lawyer so they can be assured that all necessary requirements are met. This, of course, means legal fees. Provinces also charge incorporation fees that add to the cost of setting up this type of business.

Corporate ownership may involve a multitude of legal requirements. A corporation is restricted to the type of business described in its corporate charter. Corporations must also file various reports about their operations. For example, publicly owned corporations are legally required to supply shareholders with financial statements, so it is difficult to keep this information out of the hands of competitors, suppliers, or customers.

The limited liability offered by incorporation is not complete. When a business fails during the first five years after incorporation, it appears that the business was incorporated only to avoid personal liability or has been managed incompetently. Some courts are also beginning to hold directors or managers of corporations responsible for environmental damage caused by the companies. Company owners and directors must also understand the difference between their own interests and those of the company.

As a company gets larger, impersonality may become a problem, especially when workers feel that management is not interested in either their personal concerns or the problems they encounter on the job. Specialization may lead to the feeling that one's own particular job is more important than the welfare of the entire firm. Conversely, managers may not notice that an individual has abilities beyond those required by the job for which the person was hired. Managers themselves may lack the initiative and desire for achievement that propel sole proprietors and partners to make their businesses a success. Poor human relations can quickly damage the productivity and profitability of the business.

TABLE 2.4 • THE 50 LARGEST CANADIAN PUBLICLY HELD CORPORATIONS RANKED BY PROFITS, 1992

Profit rank	Company	Industry group	Profit $000	Revenue $000	Number of employees
1	BCE Inc.	telephone utilities	1,390,000	21,270,000	124,000
2	Bell Canada	telephone utilities	1,006,100	7,904,500	52,897
3	Bank of Nova Scotia	banks	676,224	8,420,179	29,888
4	Northern Telecom	technology	548,300	8,521,100	57,955
5	Bank of Montreal	banks	640,000	8,847,000	32,126
6	Seagram Co. Ltd.	management companies	474,000	5,206,000	14,000
7	Toronto-Dominion Bank	banks	408,000	6,138,000	25,353
8	Imasco Ltd.	management companies	380,400	7,989,800	86,863
9	TransCanada PipeLines	pipelines	328,700	4,007,600	1,791
10	TransAlta Utilities	gas & electric utilities	233,100	1,305,200	2,500
11	Thomson Corp.	publishing & printing	182,000	6,033,000	45,700
12	American Barrick Resources	precious metals	174,940	553,767	1,845
13	British Columbia Telephone	telephone utilities	205,700	2,063,400	14,524
14	Imperial Oil	integrated oils	195,000	9,026,000	10,152
15	CT Financial Services	trust companies	193,227	4,094,468	17,019

(continued)

Profit rank	Company	Industry group	Profit $000	Revenue $000	Number of employees
16	Power Financial	financial services	184,884	6,066,074	7,600
17	TransAlta Corp.	gas & electric utilities	182,500	1,318,200	0
18	Telus Corp.	telephone utilities	177,768	1,241,151	9,753
19	Canadian Utilities	gas & electric utilities	175,077	1,256,636	4,440
20	PanCanadian Petroleum	oil & gas field services	170,600	951,100	1,330
21	Nova Corp. of Alberta	pipelines	164,000	3,085,000	6,300
22	Laidlaw Inc.	management companies	138,492	1,978,927	35,500
23	Canada Trustco Mortgage	trust companies	155,437	3,548,425	15,486
24	Power Corp.	other services	152,258	6,379,209	9,600
25	Placer Dome Inc.	precious metals	111,000	1,090,000	4,700
26	Bombardier Inc.	industrial products	132,800	4,448,000	34,316
27	Molson Cos.	beverages	126,223	2,577,840	16,000
28	London Insurance Group	life insurance	126,000	3,769,000	7,499
29	Anglo-Canadian Telephone	telephone utilities	119,926	2,302,456	17,000
30	Central Capital	other services	117,374	208,951	12
31	Great-West Life Assurance	life insurance	116,850	5,354,592	6,540
32	Hudson's Bay Co.	retailers	116,723	5,164,482	52,000
33	Trilon Financial	other services	109,000	5,760,000	26,708
34	Consumers' Gas Co.	gas & electric utilities	107,501	1,801,349	3,553
35	Royal Bank of Canada	banks	107,000	12,199,000	49,628
36	John Labatt Ltd.	management companies	101,000	3,867,000	12,100
37	Magna International	automotive	98,000	2,358,000	14,500
38	Great Lakes Power	management companies	93,900	226,400	135
39	Great-West Lifeco	life insurance	89,822	5,356,045	6,540
40	Quebecor Inc.	publishing & printing	87,339	2,612,196	16,400
41	Du Pont Canada	chemicals	81,779	1,453,019	4,052
42	Maclean Hunter	publishing & printing	81,200	1,645,400	12,430
43	Shell Canada	integrated oils	80,000	4,657,000	5,593
44	Loblaw Cos.	food distribution	79,800	9,266,100	46,000
45	Noranda Inc.	management companies	79,000	8,666,000	35,000
46	Interprov. Pipe Line System	pipelines	75,500	436,300	1,100
47	Alberta Mortgage and Housing	developers	73,986	501,707	420
48	Hollinger Inc.	publishing & printing	73,971	922,560	4,822
49	Maple Leaf Foods	food products	72,493	2,772,112	10,000
50	Canadian Tire Corp.	retailers	72,293	3,232,836	27,000

Figures are reported in U.S. dollars.
Source: Adapted from *Report on Business Magazine 1000*, July 1993, pp. 58–61.

BUSINESS REVIEW 2.1

1. What does limited financial liability mean?
2. Susan is a sculptor with a background in math and science; Ravi is a painter and video artist who also writes occasionally for the local newspaper; Bob wants to run an art store where he will sell the work of his friends Susan and Ravi along with that of other artists. They are thinking of setting up a business together instead of operating as sole proprietors. Is this a good idea? Should they consider partnership or incorporation? What advice would you give to each of these individuals?

THE STRUCTURE OF A CORPORATION

Many of us think of a corporation in terms of those who work in it for wages—labourers, who work for supervisors, who report to managers; accountants and bookkeepers, who keep track of expenses and profits; salespersons, who bring in those profits. But without the ownership and control structure set up by the corporate charter, there would be no corporation.

Shareholders

shareholders
The people who own shares of stock in a corporation; also known as stockholders

private or **closely held corporation**
A corporation with no more than 50 shareholders that does not offer its shares to the general public and whose financial statements are private documents available only to the shareholders

public or **publicly held corporation**
A corporation whose shares are traded on the stock exchange and whose financial statements must be made public

common shares
Shares whose owners have voting rights and a residual claim to the firm's assets after all creditors and preferred shareholders have been paid

dividends
Payments from the firm's earnings

Shareholders, sometimes called stockholders, are the people who own the shares of stock in a corporation. Most small and medium-sized corporations, such as family businesses, are **private** or **closely held corporations**; in most provinces, a private corporation may have no more than 50 shareholders. In these firms, the shareholders genuinely control and manage the corporation's activities. The general public is not invited to buy shares, and the financial statements are private documents to which only the shareholders have access. Some extremely large firms, such as the T. Eaton Company, are private corporations.

A corporation that wishes to expand may decide to raise capital by "going public" and issuing shares that can be traded on the stock exchange. In a company such as Bell Canada Enterprises, with hundreds of thousands of shareholders, the individual shareholder has very little influence over the conduct of the company. However, information about the company is readily available because the annual report and financial statements of a **public** or **publicly held corporation** must be open for scrutiny by shareholders and potential shareholders alike, who may use them in the decision to sell (or buy) shares.

All corporations must issue **common shares**, which may or may not pay **dividends**—payments from the firm's earnings—depending on the profitability of the corporation. Ownership of common shares allows the shareholder to vote for certain members of the corporation's board of directors and to select an accountant independent of the corporation's management to audit its accounts to guarantee objectivity. In a family-run private corporation, a few family members may hold all the shares.

When a private corporation decides to expand, it may decide to raise capital by "going public"—offering shares for sale to the general public. But if the family wishes to retain control of the corporation, it may choose to issue **preferred shares**, which guarantee the shareholder a fixed dividend in any year the corporation makes a profit but little voice in the running of the company. If the company is liquidated, preferred shareholders will be paid up to their initial investment in the firm after all debts and other claims have been settled. Anything that remains will be distributed among the common shareholders. Preferred shareholders usually do not vote, and their shares are often called *non-voting shares*.

preferred shares
Shares whose owners receive a fixed dividend and have first claim to the firm's assets after all creditors have been paid

It is easy to see that common shareholders are taking a greater risk than are preferred shareholders. The dividends from preferred shares are almost like interest—only if the company does not make a profit is the dividend cancelled. For this reason, the dividends on preferred shares tend to be fixed fairly low. In a good year, a common shareholder will make many times the amount earned by a preferred shareholder.

All shareholders may attend a corporation's annual meeting and ask questions about the previous year's activities as described in the annual report. Because they assume greater risks, only common shareholders have the right to vote. The number of votes a shareholder has is based on the number of shares owned—a shareholder with 200 shares has more influence than one with only 10 shares. Shareholders who cannot attend the meeting may authorize a **proxy** to vote their shares. Because proxies are often held by members of the board of directors, voting usually turns out to be in favour of management policies and the board's own nominees as directors.

proxy
The authority granted to an agent to vote for a shareholder

A variation of the one-share, one-vote system has been devised to allow small shareholders more influence. Cumulative voting is often used to elect directors to the board. The shareholder multiplies the number of shares held by the number of directorships to be voted on. For example, if one owns ten shares and five positions are open, one has a total of 50 votes. One may then choose to cast all 50 for one nominee, 40 for one and 10 for another, 10 for each of five, or any other distribution desired. Thus, if a number of small shareholders vote for the same candidate, they may be able to elect one director who will represent a minority viewpoint, perhaps on some ethical or environmental consideration.

The Board of Directors

At the annual meeting, shareholders elect a **board of directors** to be the governing authority of the corporation. Directors are usually chosen to represent a broad spectrum of experience in business or legal expertise and need not be shareholders in the corporation. Most provinces require that a publicly held company have at least three directors and that the board meet at least once a year. In practice, most large companies have fifteen to twenty directors who meet quarterly

board of directors
The governing authority of the corporation, elected by shareholders

or more often. In the past, directors have been exempt from liability for actions of the firm. Today, both the law and shareholders are demanding more accountability.

The prime function of the board of directors is to represent the shareholders' interests—and today those interests may be ethical or environmental as well as financial. The board must set overall corporate policy and authorize major transactions, such as whether to put more shares on the market (issuing new shares lessens the proportion of the company owned by existing shareholders) or to negotiate a loan to pay for installing new machinery to update a plant, whether to declare a dividend or retain earnings to finance future expansion, whether or not to acquire or sell corporate holdings, whether or not to introduce a new product or enter a new market. How much influence the board has on the day-to-day management of the company depends a lot on the size of the corporation. In small private corporations, the directors may be closely involved; in larger ones, they act more as a review panel for major decisions.

Perhaps the board's most important function is to hire the people who will actually manage the firm. All employees, from the president down, are officially the employees of the board. In practice, the board usually leaves the hiring of most workers to upper management.

To keep the board in touch with the actual working of the corporation, it is customary for at least some board members to be management employees of the firm. The corporation president is sometimes also the chair of the board of directors. But to foster an unbiased review of the company's actions, most members are usually **outside directors**, that is, persons not employed by the company. People who have considerable knowledge and expertise of sound business practice are much sought after as directors and may sit on the boards of several corporations. Issues in Business 2.2 discusses the importance a good board of directors has for a firm. In a letter to *The Globe and Mail* after the collapse of Royal Trustco in 1993, J. Richard Finlay, corporate governance expert, discusses the role of the board of directors and the special responsibilities of outside directors. He asks:

How frequently did the board meet? When the problems became apparent, did it increase the number of meetings? Was a special committee of the board formed to address the mounting concerns? Did the board take steps to secure information and expertise independent of what management was providing?

The board was dominated by two insiders—a CEO and an executive chairman—which may have made it too much a captive of management thinking. Sound governance practices have long prescribed that, in such circumstances, the board should nominate a lead outside director to help ensure that the independent mandate of the board is being fulfilled. Did it take this important step or did it leave all leadership responsibilities to management?

The most important question of all, however, is what lessons have the directors of Royal Trustco, and other directors of Canadian corporations, learned that can be applied in a remedial and preventive way

outside director
A member of the board of directors who is not an employee of the corporation

to other companies? Shareholders will no doubt be asking a similar question regarding the other organizations in the Edgar/Bronfman empire. Clearly the catalogue of corporate casualties in the 1990s has already provided compelling evidence that good governance is a key to corporate survival. But, as the lessons from Royal Trustco attest, good governance depends on good directors with the vision and ability at least to sense that the store is on fire before they see the fire trucks at the door.[1]

ISSUES IN BUSINESS 2.2

MEMBER OF THE BOARD? IN THE HOT SPOT!

TODAY'S FAST-CHANGING, global business environment means senior management and their boards face formidable responsibilities and mounting pressures.

Board members now play a key role in a company's economic vitality, says Sidney Humphreys, president of executive search firm Korn/Ferry International (Canada) in Toronto. "The days of the old-boy network, where company executives appointed buddies to the board to rubber stamp their ideas, no longer exist," he says. "Firms now take board appointments very seriously."

Directors are now selected on a strategic basis, depending on the individual's background and the way he or she complements the rest of the board. They also play a bigger role in the decision-making process, says Patrick O'Callaghan, president and managing partner of executive recruiters Caldwell Partners International Inc. in Vancouver. "In the past, many companies didn't use their boards as effective sounding boards," O'Callaghan says. "Now they genuinely look for real input, direction and ideas. Firms want [members] who can represent shareholders effectively and bring different perspectives to the board."

Korn/Ferry's fourth annual board of directors study shows 89 percent of Canadian chief executives believe that having a strong board gives their company a strategic advantage. "Appointments used to be based on who you know," Humphreys points out. "Now members are handpicked for their background and expertise." When the chief executive officers of Canadian companies were asked to rank the critical issues facing their corporate boards, Korn/Ferry says, the top five were financial results, cited by 95 percent of the CEOs; maximizing shareholder value, 89 percent; strategic planning, 87 percent; management succession, 85 percent; and long-term corporate survival, 83 percent.

The threat of liability from disgruntled shareholders has forced directors to take board responsibilities more seriously. "With all the liability that accrues to board members these days, people no longer view a board appointment as a means to pick up some extra money," O'Callaghan says. Ninety-five percent of CEOs in the Korn/Ferry survey said if a board member isn't doing his or her job, they should be able to ask for the director's resignation. The top causes justifying resignation include insufficient interest and commitment; poor attendance at board meetings; inadequate contributions at board meetings; and a change in an individual's business position during his or her tenure on the board.

Chief executives and chief operating officers comprise the single most-used source of outside directors for Canadian boards. The CEOs responding to Korn/Ferry's survey said they serve on an average of three boards each; 70 percent said they would accept an additional board

(continued)

position. The reasons for accepting board appointments vary, but Humphreys says "the prestige thing" is the biggest factor. "It's another star on the résumé. People also like to share their knowledge with others." O'Callaghan says boards provide CEOs with an opportunity to look at their own business differently. "It's a tremendous opportunity to generate thought-provoking concepts that may or may not apply to their own companies. Boards also provide busy executives with the chance to network or work with other members of the business community."

Still, board appointments are time-consuming. The Korn/Ferry survey shows Canadian boards meet about five times a year, and members spend 60 hours annually on board matters, including preparation time, meeting attendance, and travel.... Directors are compensated for their efforts, most often with an annual payment, plus per-meeting fees. Korn/Ferry says total compensation averages $13,206 in Canada. The survey also found that companies are finding it increasingly difficult to recruit qualified directors. Two-thirds of CEOs said they found it a problem, with 20 percent saying it had become worse during the past year. "The people in most demand are very busy and on several other boards," Humphreys says. "It's a simple case of demand exceeding supply." O'Callaghan agrees there is a shortage of qualified directors. "People just don't have the time." But he adds that many executives take on boards in the later stages of their careers to prepare themselves for retirement.

More companies are likely to appoint directors with international experience in the near future, Humphreys says. Currently, about 15 percent of Canadian boards surveyed by Korn/Ferry reported having international executives as members. Among those firms that placed importance on directors with international experience, 43 percent of Canadian companies considered a director with experience in the United States to be of key importance. Only 14 percent of U.S. firms place the same value on a director with Canadian experience.

Source: Reprinted from Gayle MacDonald, "Board Seat a Hotter Place to Sit," *The Financial Post*, November 19, 1990, p. 36. Reprinted with permission from Gayle MacDonald.

Questions for Discussion

1. What do contemporary Canadian corporations look for when selecting board members?
2. Why do business people accept positions as members of boards of directors?

Top Management

The people in top management, the president and most vice-presidents, are appointed by the board of directors. They are responsible for the actual operation of the corporation, subject to the approval of the board. They make most of the major corporate decisions and delegate tasks to subordinate managers. Even though they are responsible to the board, they often sit on the board themselves.

Corporate law usually specifies that the corporation has a president; a secretary, who is in charge of legal documents; and a treasurer, who is responsible for the finances of the corporation. The most important appointment made by the board is that of **chief executive officer**, who is usually the president but may also be the chair of the board.

chief executive officer
The most important appointment made by the board of directors. This individual is usually the president, but may also be the chair of the board

HOW SHOULD THE CORPORATION GROW?

Traditionally, successful corporations have expanded through effective business management practices, gaining markets by producing a better product than that of their competitors. In some cases, they have grown by joining with or acquiring other firms. When two firms combine their assets, liabilities, and operations, a **merger** occurs. Usually a new company is formed, with the shareholders in both original firms receiving shares on a proportional basis in the new corporation. Recent examples are Montreal Trust and the Bank of Montreal.

A corporation may also decide that it is in its interests to own or control another organization. For example, Harlequin Enterprises Limited, publishers of paperback romance novels, is owned by Torstar Corporation, which also publishes *The Toronto Star*. When all or a substantial part of a corporation's shares of stock are owned by another corporation, it is a **subsidiary** of that corporation. The owner is usually called the **parent company**. Typically, the management of the subsidiary is appointed by the chief executive of the parent company, subject to the approval of the parent's board. Many well-known corporations are actually subsidiaries of other corporations. Among the companies listed in Table 2.4, Northern Telecom is a subsidiary of Bell Canada, and Loblaws of George Weston.

Corporate growth has become a major economic, political, and social issue in recent years. Historically, growth has been seen as desirable, provided it does not restrain competition. But today, some people are questioning the need for such growth. Typically, these critics argue that further enlargement does not significantly improve the firm's productivity, and it may reduce competition in the marketplace. Corporate executives usually reply that significant economies are still available if the firm expands. No consensus has emerged on this question, and it is likely to remain a critical public issue in the decade ahead. Certainly, several Canadian companies that expanded rapidly during the 1980s, including Robert Campeau Corporation, Bramalea, Olympia and York, and Northern Telecom, ran into trouble in the early 1990s. Peoples Jewellers was driven to the verge of bankruptcy by its purchase of Zale's, an American jewellery retailer ten times its size. Developing Your Business Skills points out some of the problems that can occur when corporations enter into mergers and acquisitions hastily without management having thought through all the implications.

THE GOVERNMENT IN BUSINESS: CROWN CORPORATIONS

Not all corporations are owned by private individuals. Corporations can also be owned by the federal or a provincial government. Because Canada is a monarchy, such government-owned businesses are known as **crown corporations**. Most crown corporations operate under government control in order to ensure the provision of a service to large numbers of people. For example, Canada Post is responsible for the exchange of mail across the country and with other countries.

Why have crown corporations? The traditional reasoning has been that certain activities are so important to public welfare that they should not be entrusted to private ownership and control. Most

merger
Two firms combining their assets, liabilities, and operations, usually to form a new company with the shareholders in both original firms receiving shares in the new corporation

subsidiary
A corporation with all or a substantial part of its shares owned by another corporation (the parent company) and controlled by the parent company

parent company
A corporation that owns all or part of the shares of another corporation (the subsidiary)

crown corporation
A corporation owned by the federal or a provincial government

DEVELOPING YOUR BUSINESS SKILLS

EVEN A SMALL M&A REQUIRES CAUTION

Why are some mergers and acquisitions successful while others wind up in the doghouse? According to Carol Beatty, a Canadian business professor, it could have something to do with an acquisition's size.

From analysis of 86 mergers and acquisitions done by 49 Canadian corporate acquisitors, Beatty found that when acquisitors had bought companies with revenues less than 10 percent of their own, the deals later were deemed successful by the purchasers' own reckoning in fewer than 30 percent of the cases. But, when revenues of the acquired companies were more than 10 percent of those of the acquisitors, the success rate was 72 percent.

"It would have been expected that, rather than size, it would have made more of a difference if you went into a different business and a different market," says Beatty. But, following additional research into the failed small acquisitions, she is now beginning to suspect that the deals may have been unsuccessful because of the acquisitor's excessive haste and nonchalance. While there is little reason to believe that small acquisitions should be any less successful than large ones, continues Beatty, "most companies that made unsuccessful acquisitions probably didn't really pay as much attention as they should have."

These findings, which also cover such indices of mergers and acquisitions success as managerial action to set a common corporate vision (see list of variables, below), should send a warning to novices bent on hurried deals, says Michael Cohen, partner in Toronto merger and acquisitions specialists Cohen & Ferguson Translink. But he warns against expecting that size will influence success, since this study merely rationalizes past decisions.

In any case, says Cohen, the market is so slow these days that buyers can take the time they need to think mergers and acquisitions through: "In 1987, if you weren't there with your letter of intent within a month, or even a week, you could lose a deal. Right now, you can take a longer time to make your decision."

The Signs of a Good Merger

From a study of 86 mergers and acquisitions, here are the variables most closely associated with the success of a merger, in order of predictive power:
1. Size of the acquisition
2. Managerial action
3. Lack of terminations and salary cuts
4. Lower price
5. Lack of haste in negotiations
6. Type of acquisition (same business and market)
7. Lack of negative employee reactions

Source: Reprinted from Christian Allard, "Even a Small M&A Requires Caution," *Canadian Business*, August 1991, p. 13.

Question for Discussion
1. What management skills need to be stressed in a merger of companies of widely differing sizes?

The CBC's *Prime Time News* with Peter Mansbridge and Pamela Wallin has changed recently to a new time slot of 9:00 p.m. in order to capture audience share of viewers who prefer to watch the news earlier than 10:00 or 11:00 p.m. The CBC is a crown corporation originally created in 1936 to ensure that Canadian news and culture were promoted throughout the country.

Canadians would be surprised at the idea that the roads they travel on might be owned and maintained for profit by private enterprise. Broadcasting, water purification and delivery, and electricity are other examples of such services that Canada has preferred to entrust to crown or municipally owned corporations. Some nations, including Canada, have used public ownership to foster competition by operating public companies as competitive business enterprises. The CBC competes with CTV for audience share and advertising revenues. Canadian National Railways (publicly owned) competes with Canadian Pacific Railway (privately owned) in a wide range of travel activities. In Australia, Trans-Australia Airlines (publicly owned) competes with Ansett Airlines of Australia (privately owned). Sometimes public ownership replaces privately owned organizations that fail. The CNR was created from a number of companies in financial trouble. At other times, it comes about when private investors are unwilling to make investments because they believe the possibility of failure is too high, or the investment may not provide an adequate return. Petro-Canada Ltd., for example, is a federal crown corporation established in 1975 to search for future oil and gas supplies and assist the federal government in the formulation of a national energy policy. Hibernia is a joint venture on the part of the federal government, the Ontario and Alberta governments, and major private oil companies to produce synthetic crude oil from Alberta's tar sands. In both instances, the capital required for these undertakings was so large and the return on investment so uncertain that few private investors would be willing to participate.

Crown corporations also perform special functions for the public. The Bank of Canada is responsible for regulating credit and currency, while the Central Mortgage and Housing Corporation provides financial capital for private housing.

Crown corporations may also be established in order to assist economic development in particular regions of the country or to take over a private firm that has decided to close its operation, in the event that its closure might harm the region economically. They may exist to undertake basic research, to prevent a Canadian company from being taken over by a foreign firm, to ensure competition, or to provide service that otherwise might not be available.

Since crown corporations are often established for activities too risky for the private investor, they do not always make a profit; indeed, they may not break even. A crown corporation that loses money on its operation relies on the government that owns it to make up the loss. Government assistance often extends to the financing of fixed assets, if the crown corporation cannot raise the money on its own in the private money market.

D. Wayne Taylor examines the prevalence of "public enterprise" in Canada by glancing at the *Financial Post* 500. At the beginning of the 1990s:

---

of the top 50 firms in Canada ranked by revenue, eight were Crown corporations; seven of the top 50 financial institutions were state-owned. Ranked by employees, state enterprises accounted for six out of the top 50; ranked by capital spending, 11 out of the top 50 were Crown corporations.… Even after the latest spate of privatization, there remained in Canada over 400 federal and 200 provincial Crown corporations. These accounted for … 11% of the GNP.[2]

An important type of government activity is carried out by investment management corporations that are set up to manage the large sums of money in public pension and insurance funds. These corporations invest in private firms just as an individual might. The largest is the Caisse de dépôt et placement du Québec, which invests not only to make a profit on the funds under its control but also to support the province's economic development.

Privatization

privatization

Selling a crown corporation to private interests

Today governments are trying to realize their capital investment in many crown corporations through **privatization**—selling them to private interests. For example, the aerospace manufacturer Canadair was sold in 1986 to Bombardier Ltd. for net proceeds of $123 million. Air Canada, once a crown corporation, is now only partially owned by the government. Shares in 45 percent of the airline were offered for sale and are now bought and sold on the open stock market.

Private Enterprise in Public Affairs

Governments are turning to private enterprise as they "contract out" more and more services that used to be automatically seen as government activities. In some cases, a private firm may receive a contract to perform a regular service, such as selling motor vehicle permits or fishing licences. Canada Post is closing many post offices and inviting local entrepreneurs to provide postal services. Even roads may be going private: the Ontario government is considering having private

TABLE 2.5 • LARGE CROWN CORPORATIONS, RANKED BY REVENUE, 1992

Revenue rank	Company	Industry group	Revenue $000	Profit $000	Number of employees
Federal					
1	Canadian National Railways	transportation	4,069,550	-1,005,242	37,255
2	Canada Post Corp.	other services	3,872,759	-127,529	56,000
3	Canada Mortgage and Housing	other services	1,115,352	-369	2,955
4	Canadian Commercial Corp.	other services	761,629	-11,345	80
5	Export Development Corp.	other services	660,314	44,178	525
6	Via Rail Canada	transportation	546,056	141	4,500
7	Farm Credit Corp.	trust companies	423,358	21,566	754
8	Atomic Energy of Canada	industrial products	395,832	1,973	4,503
9	Canadian Broadcasting Corp.	broadcasting	392,440	-83,303	10,131
10	Royal Canadian Mint	metal fabrication	377,971	8,958	763
Provincial					
1	Ontario Hydro	gas & electric utilities	7,900,000	312,000	33,339
2	Hydro-Québec	gas & electric utilities	7,002,000	724,000	18,933
3	Caisse de dépôt et placement	financial services	3,290,000	2,930,000	302
4	B.C. Hydro and Power	gas & electric utilities	2,371,000	220,000	5,498
5	Insurance Corp. of B.C.	property & casualty insurance	2,104,326	-64,186	3,800
6	Alberta Heritage Savings	financial services	1,483,236	1,381,589	0
7	N.B. Power Commission	gas & electric utilities	991,077	25,079	3,158
8	Manitoba Hydro-Electric Board	gas & electric utilities	833,200	17,700	4,321
9	Alberta Treasury Branches	banks	791,043	12,663	3,204
10	Saskatchewan Power Corp.	gas & electric utilities	762,000	107,000	2,392

Source: Adapted from *Report on Business Magazine 1000*, July 1993, p. 111.

companies build a major highway north of Toronto that would bypass the city's traffic and allowing the builders to recover their investment through charging tolls; Prince Edward Island may soon have a "fixed link" to the mainland, a bridge across the Northumberland Strait to be built and operated by a Calgary company.[3]

CO-OPERATIVES

Another alternative to private ownership is collective ownership of production, storage, transportation, and/or marketing activities. **Co-operatives** are organizations whose owners band together to operate all or part of their industries collectively. Instead of working on the basis of one share, one vote, co-operatives work on the basis of one member, one vote. They are often created by large numbers of small producers who want to be more competitive in the marketplace. For example, the Mesta was a Spanish sheep-owners' co-operative formed in the 1200s. By the sixteenth century, it was the biggest economic organization in Spain, herding three million sheep. Its size allowed it

co-operative
An organization whose owners band together to operate all or part of their industry collectively

to exert considerable influence on government policy. Farmers often use co-operatives to market their products or to buy equipment and supplies, as can be seen from the list of the ten largest nonfinancial co-operatives in Table 2.6. United Co-operatives of Ontario runs retail farm equipment stores and sells fuels to both its members and the general public. The co-op now sells gasoline that includes methanol, an agricultural product, to assist its members. In the United States, the co-operative Sunkist Growers uses the well-known Sunkist brand to identify its products.

Credit unions or caisses populaires are financial co-operatives. A credit union is often formed by a union, religious group, or other community organization with common aims to provide deposit and loan facilities for its members. In Canada, this type of co-operative is doing well, especially in Quebec and the West. Assets of credit unions and caisses populaires are so great today that they are capable of competing with the chartered banks across the country. There are also co-operative trust firms and co-operative insurance companies. Most extensive co-operatives are in agriculture (grains, dairy products, and livestock), and perform production and buying activities.

Co-operatives can flourish in many areas of business. In Toronto, the Canadian Booksellers Co-operative, run by smaller, independent bookstores, has been quite successful in competitive bidding situations against the major bookstore chains such as Coles and W.H. Smith. Mountain Equipment Co-op, which started in British Columbia, provides its members with high-quality mountaineering and hiking gear at a discount.

Although many co-operatives began as local small organizations, where members exercised control and accumulated profits as a return on their investment, today co-operatives are big business and must deal with the same challenges and constraints as those with whom they compete. They face problems in raising capital and hiring quality managers, and the membership is currently exercising less control over operations.

BUSINESS REVIEW 2.2

1. What are the differences between a private corporation and a public corporation? Why might a private corporation decide to "go public"?

2. What is a crown corporation? List factors that might lead a government to privatize a crown corporation.

3. Why do individual business people join co-operatives? Are co-operatives a useful form of ownership in Canada today?

as vice-president of finance, while his father had become increasingly averse to risk. Strongco's expansion into manufacturing in the 1970s, meanwhile, had done little to counter the cyclical and seasonal nature of the sagging feed mill industry. So while Sullivan managed to cut pretax losses to $451,000 in 1984, by slashing inventories and instituting work sharing at plants in Winnipeg and Cannington, Ont., he still had the bank breathing down his neck. "The bank was really getting worried," he says, somewhat matter-of-factly. "One more year of losses would have been enough either to put us out of business or radically change what we had." Yet, he also knew that a short-term fix would not be enough. The people who were lending the money wanted to see more corporate culture and less family culture. So Sullivan put together an outside board of directors, a board of "very distinguished businessmen." He's been pitching his ideas to the board ever since.

Apart from letting strangers into the fold, Sullivan also prodded Strongco into strategic planning. "I had tried long and hard to get planning introduced in the company." But it had never worked with his father at the helm. "Family companies just don't spend a lot of time thinking about the future," says Doug Emerson, a "process" consultant at Managerial Design Corp. in Mississauga, Ont., who helped Sullivan draft a strategic plan to realize his vision. "They just blast off and wake up one day realizing that, 'Holy Molly, we're in trouble.'" Now, with plan in hand, Sullivan hit the streets and ultimately landed $2.1 million in venture capital. "I know how to raise money downtown," he says coyly.

But being a good CEO means more to Sullivan than just possessing the requisite hard-nosed market savvy. "Your job as president is to harness your managers' talents somehow," he says. "I believe that there are cultures built up in certain companies that are more militaristic than others, where the word comes down from on high." Not at Strongco, where Sullivan is quick to point out the roundness of the boardroom table, something that he says helps break down some of the hierarchy. A faithful follower of modern management methods, he involves his managers in the company's annual strategic planning process. By letting them participate, "you force them to dream, to blue sky a little bit," he says with conviction. But he also expects superior results.

Sullivan's management approach has allowed him the luxury of keeping both eyes on the big picture, instead of burdening himself with picayunes. "He's a Bay Street kind of guy, making deals, making things happen," says Emerson, his consultant. Even Jordan F. Sullivan Sr., a rugged individualist who has been somewhat softened by his son's modern ways, calls him "a real management type." But the father doesn't see his son much any more, ever since Sullivan moved Strongco's executives to new digs away from the company's main Toronto operations. Though he's still the chairman, Sullivan Sr. stayed behind, close to the physical plant he's known most of his working life. Still, if his control over Strongco's future is now more apparent than real, Sullivan Sr. shows no bitterness. He'll readily admit that only ten years ago he never would have thought Strongco could undergo the metamorphosis it has. Even the outside board of directors, he says, has proven fruitful.

Sullivan is not taking any chances. His strategic plan tries to reflect every contingency, both external and internal to the company. Sullivan figures Strongco will be able to prepare for cutbacks more quickly than during the last recession. Sullivan remains unmoved when he is asked if Strongco will ever go public. It's a business decision for him now. "Within a few years, if the market's good," he says, taking another sip of coffee from the fine bone china. "I don't view this as a family business anymore."

Source: Excerpted from Christian Allard, "Running from the Family," *Canadian Business*, July 1989, p. 13 and 16.

Questions for Discussion

1. Is Jordan Sullivan managing Strongco as a small private family business or as a diversified corporation? Support your response.

2. Describe the corporate culture and strategy of Strongco. Is it working and successful?

CASE 2.2

INCORPORATION A PERMEABLE SHIELD

BUSINESS OWNERS are often tempted to incorporate their enterprises in order to limit personal liability. But they should realize incorporation won't always shield them.

The new company becomes a legal "person" with its own rights and duties. The owners/directors may then find they have duties to the corporation they own.

As directors, they owe a duty of utmost good faith to the new corporation and they must act only in its interest.

In *Aiken* vs. *Regency Homes Inc.*, the Ontario Court of Appeal decided in July 1991 that, when owners/directors of a company used corporate funds to pay personal debts, they committed acts of bad faith.

Israel Katz and Joseph Fishman owned Regency Homes. After the company failed to complete David and Roseanne Aiken's house on time, the Aikens sued Regency and its directors.

The court of appeal agreed with the trial judge that the directors were guilty of inducing the company to breach its contract.

The courts found there had been sufficient funds in Regency to complete the contract. But, because the directors, who were the sole owners of the company, used some corporate money for their own purposes, the company was not able to fulfil its obligations.

The court of appeal said, "In directing the funds of Regency to be used for purposes other than those related to the affairs of Regency, and in particular for purposes other than for the completion of the respondent's home, the appellants Mr. Fishman and Mr. Katz, acted mala fides [in bad faith] and outside the legitimate scope of their authority over the affairs of Regency."

The appeal judges specifically mentioned that Katz's use of company funds led them to the finding of bad faith.

While the result may have been logical and correct in that the courts stopped the directors from hiding behind the company to disclaim responsibility, the decision could have wider implications.

It points up the fact that corporate funds do not belong to the owners of the company. The owners have certain duties and limitations upon their authority. Overstepping these limitations risks a finding of personal liability.... In a 1990 judgement, Justice Roger Conant of the Ontario District Court listed the circumstances under which Canadian courts have been willing to pierce the corporate veil and find directors liable.

This happens if the company is a sham or cloak; is formed for the express purpose of doing a wrongful or unlawful act; is a vehicle for fraud; is an agent for the controlling operator; and in special circumstances where affiliated corporations are used for tax-avoidance schemes.

Of course, the courts won't allow anyone to commit fraud, then hide behind the corporate veil. But, when there is no fraud, the rule is harder to discern.... Recently the courts have often been willing to go farther than Justice Conant's observations.

If there is wrongdoing—and that can mean anything from sharp practice to statutory offences—and the directors benefit from it, they can be found personally liable for the company's offence.

But, if they were acting in the interests of the company and not for their own benefit, they will usually escape personal responsibility.

Source: Reprinted from James Carlisle, "Incorporation a Permeable Shield," *The Financial Post*, October 24, 1991, p. 14. Reprinted with permission from James Carlisle.

Questions for Discussion

1. How does the *Aiken* vs. *Regency Homes Inc.* case illuminate the reality that incorporation will not always shield business owners who have rights and duties?

2. In what kinds of situations can corporate directors be found personally liable for a company's offence?

NOTES

1. J. Richard Finlay, "Board's Role," letter to *The Globe and Mail*, August 5, 1993, p. A24. Reprinted with permission from J. Richard Finlay.
2. Excerpted from D. Wayne Taylor, Business and Government Relations (Toronto: Gage Publishing, 1991), p. 97.

3. Max Ways, "Business Faces Growing Pressure to Behave Better," *Fortune*, May 1974, p. 316.

PHOTO CREDITS

OWN 8   Hudson's Bay Company

OWN 19   CBC *Prime Time News*, with Peter Mansbridge and Pamela Wallin

MODULE
◆ ENT ◆

ENTREPRENEURSHIP IN SMALL BUSINESS

THE FOCUS OF THIS MODULE

1. To describe the role small business plays in the Canadian economy

2. To describe entrepreneurs and the entrepreneurial spirit

3. To show how small businesses thrive in certain sectors of the economy, such as the retail, service, and high-technology sectors

4. To compare the advantages and disadvantages of working as a small business owner-manager with those of working for a large corporation

5. To discuss some of the services government offers to small business

6. To describe the concept of franchising and its advantages and disadvantages for the small business owner

7. To consider the special problems that may arise in family-owned businesses and for women entrepreneurs

8. To define the following terms:

KEY TERMS

small business
entrepreneur
marketing niche
Counselling Assistance to
    Small Enterprise (CASE)
business plan

Federal Business Development
    Bank (FBDB)
venture capitalists
franchise
franchisee
franchisor

ENTERPRISE IS ALIVE and well and living in Canada.

From coast to coast, Canadians continue to risk their money in new businesses.

Take the Toronto ophthalmologist who discovered a new product that did a better job watering his lawn. He told friends and neighbours about the product, and they were interested. He soon had a flourishing sideline importing and selling the watering system.

Or the Moncton developer who restores and revamps older buildings into first-class office space—improving the vitality of the city, as well as creating a booming business.

New entrepreneurs—many of them people who have lost their jobs during the economic downturn—continue to create start-up businesses or take on franchises.

Neither taxation, free trade, nor recession has been able to daunt entrepreneurial spirit.

Becoming a successful entrepreneur is something thousands of Canadians want to do, but few have the nerve to chase their dream.

Many who decide to start businesses, however, say the rewards of being on their own far outweigh the potential pitfalls.

When it comes to the ups and downs that go along with independent business, Brian Miles is one owner-operator who has experienced them all.

Figuratively and literally.

The 41-year-old Montreal native promotes the popular annual Molson's Supercross motorcycle event in Toronto.

More than a decade ago, when Miles was national sales and marketing director with Canadian Kawasaki Motors, a business associate presented him with the chance to promote a fledgling motorcross show. He accepted the challenge, and armed with a good knowledge of marketing, advertising, and motor sports (he's a former motorcycle racer), sold about $300,000 worth of tickets. But the night before the show at Toronto's Exhibition Stadium, disaster struck.

"There was a huge thunderstorm," Miles remembers. "We thought we were finished because we couldn't build the track—everything was so wet and muddy."

Fortunately, a dry wind swept through the area overnight, and by noon the next day, the track was built.

"We would have lost everything, but we were lucky. There was another storm during the event, but nobody left—they loved it."

Supercross became profitable in its third year, says Miles, when, thanks to tireless promotion and "strength in staging the event on time," Molson Cos. Ltd. signed on as the major sponsor. This year, more than 40,000 attended the two-day spectacle at SkyDome—where weather is not a factor. Gross sales topped $1 million, and Miles hopes to sell at least 40,000 tickets next year.

"I'm always striving to make Supercross a better event," Miles says. "And now that we're in the best venue possible, the event has a lot more potential."

Clearly, luck isn't the only thing that has made Miles a successful entrepreneur, and Supercross Productions isn't his only business.

The Miles Advertising Group, an agency spawned from Supercross Productions, specializes in trade-show advertising and promotion. Among other clients, the advertising agency promotes Mosport, the annual Small Business, Spring Boat, and Travel Camping shows, and brings in about $2.1 million in annual revenue. Miles also presents a Toronto area bicycle show each year.

As for the long hours he logs to run several separate businesses simultaneously, Miles takes it all in stride. The most important elements in life, he says, are work and family, and Miles tries to maintain a delicate balance between the two.

"My work is my hobby, and when I'm home, I spend time with my family," Miles says. "Some people are better off working for someone else, but I enjoy working for myself. The key to having your own business is that the harder you work, the more successful you'll be."

Source: Reprinted from Laura Fowlie, "Entrepreneurs Turn Fantasy into Reality," *The Financial Post*, June 25, 1990, p. 33.

B RIAN MILES IS TYPICAL of many small-business people. A successful service provided to other businesses by a small firm is typical of the vital role small business plays in the economy. Canadians increasingly recognize that a strong small business sector is the backbone of the private enterprise system. Small businesses provide much of the competitive zeal that keeps the system effective. And much has been done to encourage the development and continuity of small firms. Anticombines legislation such as the Combines Investigation Act and Restrictive Trade Practices Act is designed to maintain a competitive environment and market structure in which small companies can thrive. Also, Industry, Trade and Commerce Canada, through its regional offices and the Small Business Secretariat, assists smaller firms in many ways. Provincial governments also have programs to encourage the development of small business.

Small business is a vital segment of the Canadian economy. There are more than a million businesses in Canada, and figures from 1988 showed that small firms constituted 97 percent of Canadian companies and employed 42 percent of the country's labour force.[1] They account for about one-third of total sales in Canada. After the recession of the early 1980s, the number of small businesses in Canada increased at a faster rate than those for all other categories of business. Indications are that small business will play a similar role in pulling Canada out of the latest recession.

Small businesses are suited to respond to a wide variety of needs. We tend to think of small businesses as serving individual consumers, but they also fill an important role in helping other businesses operate smoothly. For example, large manufacturers rely on smaller firms as suppliers, and competition among these companies assures them of prompt delivery of the best possible product or service.

Artisans, tradespeople, and shopkeepers have always been vital to the private enterprise system and will continue to strengthen our economy.

DEFINING SMALL BUSINESS

Definitions of small business have been based on various criteria. The difference between "small" and "big" so often depends on the type of business—manufacturing, wholesaling, retailing, service—and on the influence a particular enterprise has within the field. For these reasons, we cannot simply classify a business as one or the other according to sales, the number of employees, or net worth, though these criteria may be useful for certain purposes.

In all likelihood, there is no such thing as a "typical" small business. Probably the most workable concept of such a business is one suggested some years ago. To qualify as a **small business** under this definition, a business must have at least two of the following characteristics:

small business
A business that is independently managed; owned by a small group or single individual, often the manager; operates locally; and/or is not dominant in its field

1. independent management with the managers often owning the firm
2. the capital contribution coming from a limited number of individuals—perhaps only one
3. the firm operating in a local area
4. the firm representing a small part of the overall industry.[2]

Note: Small businesses tend to operate in highly competitive markets, where the business aims to differentiate its product on the basis of price, quality, or service.

THE ENTREPRENEUR

To make a small business work requires a great deal of individual initiative, hard work, and risk taking. Most small businesses are started by a special type of person, the **entrepreneur**. Entrepreneurship begins with the recognition of an opportunity, a need waiting to be satisfied. The entrepreneur is a person who not only sees the opportunity, but is willing to take the risk and make the effort to make it happen.

entrepreneur
A person who plans and organizes a business endeavour, taking the risk in hopes of making a profit

Entrepreneurs share certain psychological traits and are motivated by a similar set of values and needs.[3] Entrepreneurs tend to be independent, self-reliant individuals with a strong desire to achieve. They have a tremendous amount of energy and drive, with a capacity to work long hours. This is important for the success of a small enterprise that generally faces many crises. And while it is obvious that entrepreneurship is at the core of small business, entrepreneurial activity is also important in larger corporations.

Entrepreneurs tend to compete against standards of achievement they set for themselves rather than standards set for them by others. This need for personal achievement tends to be a main motivating force.

They have a high level of self-confidence and believe strongly in themselves and their own abilities to achieve the goals they set. Thus, they are willing to undertake ventures that others might think of as risky. However, psychological testing has shown that they are not reckless gamblers. Entrepreneurs tend to be positive, optimistic types who focus their attention on their chances of success rather than on the chances of failure.

Entrepreneurs are often more driven by the challenge of building a business than the idea of simply getting in and out in a hurry and making a fast buck. They seem to be primarily interested in the creation of an entity. For some, profits are more a means of keeping score than an end in itself.

Entrepreneurs are the product of their family and environment. Parents and family have set high standards of performance, and served as role models in the creation of the entrepreneur.

These special individuals play a key role in the Canadian economy. They are opportunists who are able to recognize the existence of both a need waiting to be satisfied and a way of satisfying that need. They are thus creators of business enterprise. Table 3.1 provides a statistical profile of business owners in Canada.

TABLE 3.1 • STATISTICAL PROFILE OF SMALL BUSINESS OWNERS IN CANADA

New job creation	Percentage	New job creation	Percentage
New jobs created 1978–85 by firms employing fewer than five people	59.6	**How Many People They Employ**	
		Less than five	77.3
New jobs created by firms employing more than 500 people	6.8	5–19	16.6
		20–49	3.8
		50–99	1.2
By Age		100+	1.2
Under 25	4.5		
25–34	23.7	**How They Got into Business**	
35–44	31.4	Founded	68.6
45–54	22.5	Bought	25.3
55–64	13.8	Inherited	5.0
Over 65	4.2		
		Why They Got into Business	
By Gender		Wanted a personal sense of accomplishment	81.4
In 1988:		Wanted to be own boss	73.4
Men	76.3	Wanted variety and adventure	66.0
Women	23.7	Wanted to make better use of training and skills	63.3
In 1981:			
Men	78.7	Wanted freedom to adopt own approach to work	61.8
Women	21.3		
		Wanted to be challenged by the problems and opportunities of starting own business	60.7
By Origin			
Canadian-born	80.0		
Immigrants	20.0	Wanted to be able to develop a product or an idea	57.5
Business founders in 1987 whose fathers were business owners	35.0	Wanted an opportunity to lead rather than be led	56.3
		Wanted to make a direct contribution to the success of a company	55.7
By Education			
Less than secondary school	32.6	It was a time when it made sense	55.5
Secondary school diploma	10.6	Wanted to keep learning	55.5
Post-secondary	56.7		

Reprinted from Daniel Stoffman, "Who Are the Entrepreneurs?" *Report on Business*, 1988, p. 62. Statistical sources: Statistics Canada Department of Regional Industrial Expansion, and the Canadian Federation of Independent Business. Reprinted with permission from Daniel Stoffman.

THE SCOPE OF SMALL BUSINESS

Small businesses operate in almost every industry in Canada. In many cases, they compete not only with each other but also with some of the country's biggest corporations. Small businesses are most often found in the retailing and service sectors. The creativity and innovation associated with new technologies often finds an outlet in a small business set-up.

Retailing

Although there are several big names in retailing, such as The Bay, Sears Canada, Eaton's, and Kmart, the combined sales of small, privately owned retail stores are far larger—and the giant retailers are losing ground. Many common items such as drugs, fast food, clothes, shoes, jewellery, and office supplies are usually sold by small businesses rather than by large ones. In recent years, small businesses have provided the majority of retail sales jobs.

Service Firms

The work of a great many people in Canada involves providing a service rather than a product. Restaurants, funeral homes, banks and trust companies, dry cleaners, theatres, lawyers, dentists, doctors, insurance brokers, chartered accountants, car mechanics, home renovators, and a multitude of other service industries are perfectly suited to the small business structure. Few companies sell services on a national scale. As pointed out earlier, "small" usually means "local."

The small neighbourhood store is an important local business in most communities. These stores are often owned by the proprietor with perhaps some assistance from either his or her family or a small staff. The success of small stores is dependent on both limited competition in the area and a combination of a wide selection, good hours, and a convenient location.

High-Tech Firms

Scientists and inventors may become entrepreneurs almost by accident. A creative notion may give rise to a makeshift prototype put together in a basement or garage, or a stroke of genius may lead to a first-generation software program on a home computer. But it is not easy to interest General Motors or IBM in an unproven, wacky idea. New products usually become commercially available because the faith the innovator has in his or her invention leads to the establishment of a small business to produce and market it.

Of course, one can't just open up shop and start selling. Starting a small business is expensive because of the time that elapses between production, sales, and payment. Companies selling complex technology may require $1 million or more in "seed money." And the business needs to have a clear idea of its market as well as its product, as we can see in Issues in Business 3.1.

ISSUES IN BUSINESS 3.1

LARGER THAN LIFE

W HEN STEVEN SPIELBERG'S $60-million (U.S.) feature film *Jurassic Park* opened across North America in June 1993, Daniel Langlois felt just like one of the hundreds of kids who packed the local theatres. Langlois, the 36-year-old CEO of Montreal-based Softimage Inc., watched in rapt attention as the dinosaurs—in all their monstrous, realistic, roaring, three-dimensional, animated splendour—ran amok in the jungles of Costa Rica indiscriminately devouring plants, animals, and the occasional citizen....

To create most of the dinosaur scenes, California-based Industrial Light & Magic (ILM) used a variety of computer software, including Softimage's unique 3-D computer graphics software, which helped with the animation. "With Softimage, our animators can work twice as fast, even though the jobs we're being asked to do are twice as hard," says Tom Williams, ILM's software manager....

For Langlois, who knows every feature of his company's award-winning program like the back of his hand, the big-screen reptilian fantasy beasts are—in an indirect way—his own creations. "I'm normally involved at the beginning of a major sale, but not when they're using the products," says Langlois. "I'd love to be at ILM now, because I know I could bring a lot of input."

If watching animation created with his programs is about as close to Hollywood as Langlois is likely to get, his consolation prize is guiding the spectacular growth of Softimage, which is very much a corporate creation of his own making.

Softimage is the computer graphics industry's equivalent of a box-office smash. The company's flagship product, Softimage Creative Environment—known simply as Softimage—is the hottest product in the global 3-D marketplace. Last year the company earned a profit of $2.5 million on $14.6 million in sales, and revenues for 1993 are projected to top $22 million....

Softimage is a prime example of a young, smallish high-tech company that's thriving because it's got a perfectly targeted niche product. Softimage's program is an integrated package of modules used by television stations, film and video studios, product designers, and others to create stunningly realistic 3-D animation. Three-dimensional graphics give the added dimension of depth, unlike the "flat" look of 2-D Saturday-morning cartoons.

(continued)

But for all his success, Langlois now faces a challenge that regularly defeats dozens of other promising software companies—making the transition from brilliant start-up to a more mature, mid-size company. The problems begin when young, growth-oriented companies start moving beyond their niches....

Langlois is something of a rarity—a cautious entrepreneur whose remarkable combination of technology smarts and sure-footed business savvy have enabled him to keep Softimage firmly on track since founding the company in November 1986.

A native Québécois, Langlois grew up on a chicken farm near St-Jérôme in the Laurentians. At age 18, he moved to Montreal and received a BA in Design from the Université du Québec, then immediately dived into the heady world of film. He achieved recognition as a special effects and animation specialist, working independently and for the National Film Board on documentaries and short films.

He also unintentionally became a computer programmer. "I had no choice," explains Langlois. "In the early 1980s, there were only a few software programs for creating complex 3-D graphics, and to use them properly, you had to do your own programming."

In 1985, while he was co-directing his best-known computer-animated film, *Tony de Peltrie,* Langlois started thinking about writing a user-friendly animation program. "We won a handful of awards for that film, but doing the animation required a tremendous effort—we worked on it for nearly two years," he remembers.

Langlois took the plunge, and spent most of 1987 and 1988 developing a program that let his fellow animators concentrate on crafting images instead of manipulating computer functions. He also went looking for venture capital, and was lucky enough to be introduced to John Eckert, a former director of Wood Gundy, and Louden Owen, a Toronto lawyer, who had teamed up to look for a hot technology investment. "The product was obviously impressive, but so was Daniel," says Eckert. "He's an unusual blend of artist and natural businessman."

Eckert and Owen put together $350,000 in private financing, enough to let Langlois complete the program and launch it at an international trade show in late 1988. Softimage's product, which runs on powerful desktop workstations from California-based Silicon Graphics Inc., made a sensational splash, and the company was profitable within a year. "They're having a huge impact on the 3-D animation market," says Steve Porter, editor of *Computer Graphics World* magazine of Westford, Mass. "Softimage has a high-quality product that's remarkably easy to use, and they're selling it at a reasonable price. They've edged out their competition in their category and taken about 50 percent of the market."...

The farmer's son who had grown up dreaming of making it big in film suddenly found himself, at the tender age of 35, a wealthy businessman.... It wasn't hard for Langlois to conclude he had a new calling.

Having committed himself to business, Langlois has mapped out an expansion strategy that he hopes will propel Softimage into the software big leagues. Step one is to keep his big customers happy by continually upgrading Softimage's core product, particularly for use in making feature-length films and video games.

Step two is to move beyond the company's 3-D niche by developing high-end 2-D graphic software, which is far more widely used in postproduction film and video editing, and advertising. The third step is to develop less expensive 2-D and 3-D programs for the professional users of multimedia computer programs, which combine text, video, sound, and graphics capabilities. "This is a $2-billion market," declares Langlois. "There are thousands of architectural, design, and advertising firms who employ only a handful of people. They obviously can't afford a $50,000 product, so we're going to go after them with personal computer programs that will sell for under $5,000."

(continued)

But with characteristic prudence, Langlois has already backed off from the rapid introduction of lower-priced products. Within the next several years, the personal computer market will convulse as a new generation of machines operating at up to 25 times faster than current models hits the stores. When the dust settles, Langlois says, "we'll be ready with lower-priced software. But it's not the right time to invest money to bring these products to market."

Such caution is appropriate since Langlois, the wunderkind of the high-end, 3-D animation market, is heading into the unknown. There's no guarantee that Softimage can repeat its success in the 2-D market—though it is a logical extension of its niche—or that the company will learn how to sell to a wider consumer market when it launches its lower-priced products. Servicing a base clientele of 450 well-heeled customers does not a mass-marketer make.

"As niche software companies grow, they've got the double problem of getting into new markets and learning how to operate differently, particularly if they start selling less expensive software," says consultant Michael Darch. "Cheaper software is basically a commodity, and selling commodities is completely different, with different competition, different distribution channels, huge promotion budgets, and rapid increases in administrative costs."...

Langlois, who loves dressing in trendy black, is well aware of the risks his company faces—and he's convinced he's got everything in hand. "These days, analysts have two main questions for us," he says. "They ask if we can deliver the technology we've promised, and they want to know how we'll manage our infrastructure growth. Well, we're ready now with about 75 percent of the technology we need, and we're making the structural changes we need to manage a larger company."...

But for Langlois, the how and why of corporate growth is ultimately a question of personal direction. "When I started Softimage, I thought that I could still do film, but it wasn't possible. The business is too demanding. Now I've reached my first goal—to have a successful company selling high-end computer graphics worldwide. And I don't need money any more—that's solved.

"I'm at the point where I could go back and do film again, but I'm not going to do that," he explains. "The reason, and it's crucial for me, is that Softimage is influencing what people see in film, what they see on television, all over the world. The impact we can have with our software is far greater, far more important than what I could ever achieve by doing film."

If you're Daniel Langlois, and it turns out that your dream differs from your reality, it's only logical not to adjust the set; adjust the dream instead.

Source: Reprinted from Michael Salter, "Larger Than Life" *Report on Business Magazine*, August 1993, pp. 40–47.

Questions for Discussion

1. How did Daniel Langlois develop his product idea?
2. What is his present market? What need he do to protect his share in this market? What precautions should he take before he expands to new markets?

BUSINESS REVIEW 3.1

1. Name three products or services you have purchased from small businesses during the last week.
2. Interview a relative or acquaintance who operates a small business. How well does this person fit the statistical profile of small business owners in Table 3.1?

CHARACTERISTICS OF SMALL BUSINESS

An executive in a large corporation might find it difficult at first to recognize many small businesses as "business." A closer look will reveal that the same activities, constraints, opportunities, and obligations are present in both types of businesses, but they may look very different, and the rewards and penalties may have different effects. These differences are summarized in Table 3.2.

Organization

A large business is usually a public corporation. A small business may be a sole proprietorship or partnership in which the owner or owners are answerable to no one but themselves. But that freedom comes with a price the corporation executive might not be prepared to meet—unlimited liability. If the small business is incorporated, the risk for the owner-manager is still greater. Should the firm go bankrupt, personal savings may be protected, but there is no severance package or unemployment insurance to cushion the blow.

Staff and Managerial Style

Our executive may be used to calling on employees who are experts in their fields—lawyers, accountants, secretaries, and mechanics—whenever necessary. The small business owner-manager will probably have fewer support personnel on staff and will hire outside consultants and technicians only when their services are needed. A permanent employee of the business is likely to help out in many areas that a large corporation would expect to assign to several people with different skills and job descriptions. The owner-manager's family is likely to be involved in the business, and members can be called on

---

TABLE 3.2 • DIFFERENCES BETWEEN SMALL AND LARGE BUSINESSES

Small Businesses	Big Businesses
Greater risk and liability	Greater security and limited liability
Use of ouside experts, flexible roles for employees, keeping overhead low	Experts on staff, more rigid job descriptions, higher overhead
More personal management style	Impersonality
Adaptability, faster innovation	More careful consideration of change
Filling of marketing niches	Larger market segments
Self-taught, perhaps ineffective, management	Trained management
Financing from family, venture capitalists, banks, and government	Financing from working capital, profits, bond issues
Paperwork a burden on owner and staff	Expert staff to handle paperwork
Often inadequate compensation	Adequate salary, benefits package

to pick up the telephone, run messages, make deliveries, and provide extra hands at busy times. This approach to staffing helps keep overhead in a small firm low.

The nature of the staff leads to a different managerial style from the one familiar to our executive. The owner-manager will have much more knowledge of his or her employees, and thus will be aware of the individual capabilities of each and ready to promote from within, instead of assuming that capable workers are best suited only to their present duties. Knowing people means one is more likely to take the constraints of their personal lives into consideration. The result may be occasional chaos when a key employee is at home with a sick child, attending a course, or taking that once-in-a-lifetime opportunity to join a spouse on a trip to Australia, but management flexibility will usually be paid back in dedication when the firm needs it most.

Innovation

New products and services come from all sectors of business, but when a small company recognizes an opportunity, it is often ideally suited to get it on the market quickly. Our executive might look on in amazement, thinking of the many meetings of technical experts, financiers, production workers, and marketers that must go on before a large corporation is ready to launch a new product.

Niche Marketing

A **marketing niche** is a small portion of the entire market with special needs. Big businesses cannot take advantage of every commercial opportunity. Because their overhead costs are so high, any project must be large enough to cover these costs before it will return a profit. For example, many large publishers must turn down what they know are valuable and worthy projects because the books are not likely to generate enough sales to justify not only editorial and production costs but also the expense of the support staff the firm must maintain. This opens up an opportunity for one of Canada's many small presses to produce books to serve a specific marketing niche. For example, Canada's Wings of Eastern Ontario produces books on aviation.

Of course, certain types of goods and services can best be provided by small businesses. In Toronto, Daniel et Daniel specializes in preparing gourmet foods for small social gatherings. Carol Wood sells her own art and items made by fellow potters, woodworkers, and fabric artists at Local Colour, her store in Flesherton, Ontario.

Management Expertise

An executive from a large corporation may look at many aspects of small business with envy, but the lack of management expertise found in many small firms may come as a shock. Few people who start small businesses are truly prepared to function as managers. Thousands of small businesses open every year. About a third fail within a year, and half within the first five years. Though general economic conditions play a large part in business failures (see Figure 3.1), the key factor is almost always the quality of management.

marketing niche
A small portion of the entire market with special needs that an enterprise can serve

FIGURE 3.1 • CUTTING BACK

Problem areas identified by small businesses affected by recession

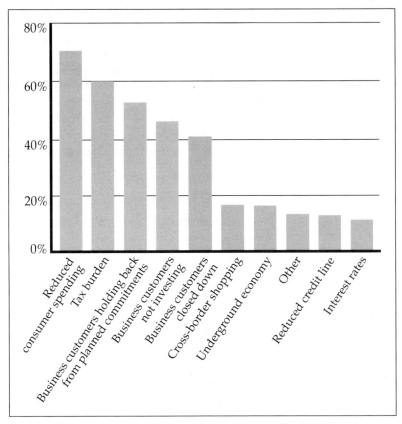

Source: Graph data from the *Canadian Federation of Independent Business*, June 1992.

But statistics tell us that no one is more persistent than small business entrepreneurs. Those that fail often learn from their mistakes and will soon try again—and again, if necessary. Eventually, they may succeed.

Ineffective or poor management can take many forms. There is, of course, no one single approach to *effective* management. But it is clear that good ideas may lead to bankruptcy if the entrepreneur does not fully understand the basic business principles. Learning the ropes does not happen quickly or automatically. Donald Rumball, executive director of the National Entrepreneurship Development Institute in Montreal, observes:

An incredible number of people don't know how to start a business or make it grow. They need help with a business plan and marketing. The biggest difficulty is they often don't know how much they don't know.[4]

Sometimes small businesses fail because their owner-managers get carried away with their eagerness and excitement to sell their new product or service. Kenneth Eaton, head of Associated Business Consultants, puts it this way:

An entrepreneur is an optimist by definition, and over-optimism is what does companies in. When things are going well, the average businessman assumes they will continue to go well. When a problem arises, he assumes it will go away quickly by itself. By the time he wakes up to the fact that he really has a problem, it's often too late to do anything about it.[5]

In other words, the road to entrepreneurial disaster may be paved with false assumptions. Not everyone will jump at an innovative idea or a cheaper product. The chances of selling something new increase with adequate preparation. This includes background research. Is there a market for the new product or service? How strong is the competition? Is the timing right? Research and a little detective work can help the entrepreneur to avoid costly mistakes. Knowing how to find available published reports, conduct surveys and interviews, and analyze consumer behaviour is part of the business education our corporate executive takes for granted. These are a few of the many tools a budding entrepreneur can use to turn up valuable information and insights.

Governments at various levels understand the problems that small business may have with management expertise, and offer assistance of various types, such as management training seminars and various consultation services. **Counselling Assistance to Small Enterprise (CASE)** is part of the service of the Federal Business Development Bank. CASE provides management counselling, using retired business people selected for their management expertise. For example, CASE asked Joe Reid, a retired data processing expert who first worked with electronic computers in 1955, to advise the owner of a small boat engine repair shop on the Trent Canal. The owner was trying to adapt an inventory control software program designed for motorcycle repair work, but Reid's knowledge of the field led him to suggest a program that could be used as it stood.

Counselling Assistance to Small Enterprise (CASE)
Management counselling for small business operators by retired business people; a service of the Federal Business Development Bank

Financial Capability

New entrepreneurs almost always need more money to start their businesses than they expect. Without adequate financing, inexperienced owner-managers will find they run short of capital during slow periods or will be forced to pass up the opportunity to expand when the market grows faster than their ability to produce. The corporate executive, with access to working capital, profits from existing products, the bond market, and a solid reputation at the bank, would be frustrated by the financial strait-jacket that small business people often find themselves in.

Nearly always, the first source of funding is personal savings or family guarantees. Few lending institutions are willing to lend to

business plan
A description of the nature of a business, its prospects, and how the entrepreneur intends to achieve its goals

Federal Business Development Bank (FBDB)
A crown corporation that provides financing, management training, and consulting to small business

entrepreneurs who are not putting any money into the business themselves. Banks are usually careful about lending money to small businesses, especially new ones, because of their high failure rate. They require detailed information in the form of a **business plan** about the nature of the business, its prospects, and how the entrepreneur intends to achieve its goals to justify any loans. Developing Your Business Skills discusses some of the elements of a good business plan.

Small businesses rarely look beyond their banks, but there are other sources to turn to. Because of the importance of the small business sector to the Canadian economy, the **Federal Business Development Bank (FBDB)** may be willing to step in if a business does not have other sources of financing available to it on reasonable terms. The FBDB is a crown corporation with branches across the country that provides not only financing but also management training and consulting to small business. The FBDB may be more willing to support risky but promising new ventures than the somewhat conservative chartered banks, but still expects to see a sound business plan. Under the Small Business Loan Act, the federal government will also guarantee some loans to small business; that is, agree to pay the lender if the borrower goes bankrupt.

Most provinces have similar programs available to small business: for example, through regional development corporations in Ontario; the Enterprise and Development Group in Manitoba; the Industry Development branch in Saskatchewan. Municipal governments may also provide loans or loan guarantees to small businesses opening up in the area.

COIN is a match-making database operated by provincial chambers of commerce. It introduces entrepreneurs to developers and represents the largest pool of capital available in Canada. COIN makes about a hundred matches each month. Investors may be prepared to invest from $50,000 to $1 million, though some loans may be for as little as $5,000.[6]

venture capitalists
Individuals or groups of investors prepared to take a risk in lending money to promising new ventures

Venture capitalists—individuals or groups of investors prepared to take a risk in lending money to promising businesses—also need to be inspired by the potential of the business. Venture capital is a high-risk activity, because loans are usually made to borrowers without a history of proven performance, and venture capitalists expect a high rate of return on their investment—up to 35 or 40 percent. Sometimes a venture capitalist will want some form of ownership in the company as well. Thus venture capital is an option for small business.

DEVELOPING YOUR BUSINESS SKILLS

THE BUSINESS PLAN

An entrepreneur without a business plan is as helpless as a sailor without navigational equipment; without it, it's almost impossible to stay on course, and chances are, each one will sail into trouble.

According to the Canadian Federation of Independent Business, 55 percent of firms with one or more employees don't survive their first five years, even in good economic times. But a proper business plan can help prevent a firm's demise. And what's more, nearly all lenders insist you have one.

(continued)

There are many inexpensive sources to tap when drawing up your plan. Trade and business publications, annual reports of public companies, and industry associations are invaluable. Government sources, such as the Ontario Ministry of Industry, Trade and Technology's self-help centres, and community college entrepreneurship centres are easily accessible.

There's no such thing as a standard business plan because of the diversity of industries and circumstances particular to each, but there are a number of key elements one should contain. They include:

- A description of the company, including its name, when it was formed, what its purpose is, and what the key product or service is.
- A market analysis that justifies the introduction of the product or service. It is essential to demonstrate knowledge of the competition and that the product or service has been test-marketed. There should also be a description of marketing strategy that includes pricing, distribution plans, and promotion.
- An operations overview explaining how the business will be run. This should include capsule biographies of the management team, emphasizing experience and priorities.
- A financial snapshot of the business's cash position and how additional money will be raised.
- A five-year financial plan, including revenue and net-income projections.

Price Waterhouse suggests keeping the business plan to 20–25 pages. It should include a one-page executive summary that explains the business, the product, the industry, and the market. Other ground to be covered includes a management and implementation plan; a discussion of risks and pitfalls of the particular business; financial statements; and a sensitivity analysis to show how the entrepreneur would react if something went wrong.

Entrepreneurs should look at what they can withstand should economic conditions change.

Some of the most common mistakes in business plans can be the most lethal. Too many would-be entrepreneurs treat the competition too lightly; others don't have a marketing strategy.

Business plans being formulated now must make allowances for the tough economy gloom.

Source: Excerpts from Kirsten MacLeod, "You've Got to Have a Plan," *The Financial Post,* April 22, 1991, p. 14.

Paperwork

Bookkeeping, records, correspondence, and, above all, government forms can put a disproportionally heavy burden on small firms. Small business people complain bitterly of excessive government regulation and red tape. The cost of doing the paperwork the government requires is quite significant. The regulation of small companies also accounts for a large portion of the government's own paperwork costs. A survey by the Canadian Federation of Independent Business (CFIB) found that one firm in ten identified regulatory paperwork as its most important problem. This subject ranked fourth among all problems encountered by small firms.[7]

All those forms and regular reports required by various government regulations add up, especially in small businesses with small staffs. In most cases, the owner-manager takes the paperwork home to complete in off-duty hours. In the large corporation, in contrast, support staff skilled in data collection and document preparation are available and better equipped to handle the load.

The Federation of Independent Business believes that politicians and government officials are often mistaken in their impression of small business and underestimate the time it takes to deal with government paperwork.[8] Issues in Business 3.2 presents some views of the vice-president of the CFIB concerning government regulation as it affects Canadian competitiveness.

ISSUES IN BUSINESS 3.2

WE'RE DRIVING OURSELVES OUT OF BUSINESS

A S A FORMER civil servant and banker, and an economist, Catherine Swift may seem an unlikely critic of government, but the Canadian Federation of Independent Business's vice-president has a reputation for shooting from the hip when talking about how government treats business.

"It's my personality, but it's also the CFIB's nature," says Swift, 38, who concedes she can be hard on politicians, but she also explains why: "Public policy has always been a major love of mine."...

Her belief is that while Canadian business and the economy are vastly—and poorly— overregulated, there is an important role for government in society....

Her greatest complaint is that both the federal and the provincial governments tend to regulate business from a big business perspective, with a view toward providing panaceas rather than effectiveness.

"Unfortunately, it's the triumph of politics over logic and common sense, the short term over the long term, and all those sorts of things—our political system fosters it," says Swift, who argues we need a more representative system that doesn't punish dissent.

She also notes that the federal government tends to accept only those studies that reinforce its position. She uses as examples research done by her organization on the goods and services tax and the free-trade agreement. (The CFIB and its membership opposed the GST, but supported the trade deal.)...

"It's a joke. On free trade, we were the buddies, the government couldn't say enough good things about us; how wonderful our research was, but the GST, well, that was quite a different kettle of fish despite [our] having used exactly the same methodology."

John Bulloch, president of the CFIB, says Swift is the best research director in the organization's 20-year history, adding, "She has that fire in her belly you have to have around here. She combines a strong intellectual capacity with very strong communications skills."

As is the case with many policy makers and experts, Swift's greatest preoccupation these days centres on Canada's lack of competitiveness and burdensome tax levels....

"We're driving ourselves out of business. If something doesn't happen, I don't think we can continue to follow the path we're on. Cross-border shopping is merely a symptom of the greater disease—which is lack of competitiveness.

She laughs about the government's attempts to deal with competitiveness.... "Talk about the ultimate oxymoron. They're going to create some new government thing to be more competitive when one of our problems is that we've got too much government. What a joke," she says.

Source: Excerpts from Geoffrey Scotton, "This Government Gadfly Can Deliver a Swift Kick," *The Financial Post,* May 10, 1991, p. 6.

(continued)

> **Questions for Discussion**
> 1. Do you believe Catherine Swift represents small business in this country well as the vice-president of the Canadian Federation of Independent Business? Support your response.
> 2. How does Catherine Swift characterize the federal government's relationship with small businesses?

Compensation

Every two weeks, our executive in the large corporation takes home a paycheque—probably not as big as the executive feels it should be, but it comes regularly and covers most needs. With the cheque is a list of deductions, not only for taxes, but for pension plans and health, drug, and dental benefits. Our owner-manager cannot rely on any of this. Compensation is directly related to how well the business is doing, and any benefits must be negotiated with insurers and paid for out of this fluctuating income.

The Canadian Federation of Independent Business reports that a small number of business owners do very well, but most earn less than the average paid employee—and they spend more hours on the job. Many owners have been employees first, gaining skills and expertise. When they start their own businesses, they usually take a considerable drop in income. "The risks of starting and running a business are high at the best of times, and during hard times the earnings of many business owners plunge. In tough times the money a business owner takes home is usually cut to the bone in the struggle for the survival and long-term viability of the enterprise."[9]

FRANCHISING

Not every small business is started by a visionary with a new and better idea to sell. Not all people who want to go into business for themselves want to begin from the beginning, designing their own premises, setting up their own marketing plan, conducting their own advertising. To the less adventurous, franchising has considerable attraction. Ken Waxman calls franchising "the middle ground between perfect self-employment, where you're creating your own enterprise, and working for a corporation."[10]

A **franchise** is a licence to a dealer to do business in the name of a supplier. The agreement specifies the methods to be used in marketing the supplier's product. The dealer or **franchisee** is usually a small business retailer who has obtained the right from a supplier, the **franchisor**, to sell a specified product or service. The dealer usually pays an initial fee in addition to fixed royalties or commissions for the privilege of using the producer's name, trademarks, and processes in a specified geographical area and for sharing in promotional campaigns. A franchise agreement usually dictates such decisions as building design, location, management techniques, personnel policies, and accounting procedures. The franchisor pays careful attention to promoting a common image across franchises. The franchisees benefit from shared advertising, which they pay for collectively.

franchise
A licence to do business in the name of a supplier specifying the methods to be used in selling the product

franchisee
The purchaser of a franchise operation who receives the right to sell a product and assistance in management of the business in return for various fees and royalties on sales

franchisor
The supplier of a recognized good or service who grants licences to independent businesses to sell the product in accordance with the supplier's business policies and practices

The Second Cup Coffee Company is a successful Canadian franchise that is often found in shopping malls and pedestrian malls. These specialty stores are well known throughout Canada for their wide selection of coffees and coffee supplies. The franchise arrangement provides the businessperson with the opportunity to go into business for themselves as well as the assurance of a business with an established reputation in the marketplace.

Between 1980 and 1990, the number of franchised outlets in Canada more than doubled. Franchises now account for more than a quarter of all retail sales.[11] Franchising has come to dominate certain segments of retailing—fast-food restaurants, car rentals, motels, health spas, and so on. Names like Budget, Holiday Inn, Weight Watchers, and Radio Shack are widely recognized today. The franchises associated with some fast-food chains are truly household words. Some, such as Kentucky Fried Chicken, have been around for a long time. Others are relative newcomers.

Prospective franchises can assess their chances of success by considering the performance records of existing franchise outlets. They should look carefully at the type of support the franchisor is prepared to offer, particularly at the beginning. Does it go beyond supplying the product? Does it teach merchandising techniques to its franchisees? Responsibility for day-to-day management and financing rests not with the franchisor but with the franchisees, who must consider their own business skills and attitudes to risk. The probability of success depends largely on work done before signing the franchise agreement. The advantages and disadvantages of franchising are compared in Table 3.3.

TABLE 3.3 • ADVANTAGES AND DISADVANTAGES OF FRANCHISES

Advantages	Disadvantages
Performance record on which to make comparisons and judgments	High cost of obtaining and operating a franchise
Widely recognized name	Consumer judgment of the business on the basis of other, similar franchises
Shared advertising expenses	Restrictions on business decisions

EXHIBIT 3.1 • FRANCHISE AGREEMENTS

FRANCHISE AGREEMENT
THIS AGREEMENT made this ^C day of ^C 1992

BETWEEN

PIZZA NOVA TAKE OUT LIMITED, a corporation incorporated under the law of the Province of Ontario, (hereinafter called the "Company")

OF THE FIRST PART

– and –

^C
(hereinafter called the "Franchise Owner" or "Owner")

OF THE SECOND PART

WHEREAS the Company has developed and operates a restaurant system (hereinafter called the "Pizza Nova System") which includes all proprietary rights in certain valuable trade names, trade marks and service marks, and other valuable trade marks and service marks designated for use in connection with its restaurant system, including special designs and colour schemes for restaurant buildings and signs, formulae and specifications for certain types of food products and methods of operation; and

WHEREAS the Company grants franchises whereby it licenses the use of said trade names, trade marks and service marks within the Dominion of Canada; and

WHEREAS the Owner recognises the benefits to be derived from being identified with and franchised by the Company and being able to utilize the Pizza Nova System, trade names, trade marks and service marks which the Company makes available to its franchises; and

WHEREAS the Owner desires to be franchised to operate a restaurant pursuant to the provisions hereof and at the location specified herein.

NOW THEREFORE IN CONSIDERATION of the mutual covenants herein contained, the parties agree as follows:

ARTICLE I
GRANT OF FRANCHISE AND TERM

1.01   The Company hereby grants to the Owner for the following term, and subject to the conditions set out in this agreement, the franchise to:

(a)   adopt and use the Pizza Nova System in the restaurant located at ^C (the "Restaurant") and at that location only;
(b)   advertise to the public that the Owner is a franchisee of the Company; and
(c)   adopt and use, but only in connection with the sale of those food and beverage products which have been designated by the Company at the Restaurant, the trade names, trade marks and service marks which the Company shall designate from time to time to be part of the Pizza Nova System.

1.02   The term of this agreement shall be co-terminus with the existing lease during its original term and, at the Owner's option, co-terminus with any renewal of said lease.

1.03   This franchise shall be exclusive within the radius of one (1) kilometre from the Restaurant. The Owner acknowledges that Pizza Nova has established several existing locations and may establish more locations in the future. The Owner acknowledges and agrees that the Company shall have the exclusive right

(continued)

to determine and adjust from time to time all boundaries of the area of this and other franchises established by the Company from time to time and shall be the sole and binding arbitrator in the event of a dispute between or among franchisees.

1.04   The Owner shall operate the Restaurant utilizing the Company's trade names, trade marks and service marks without any accompanying words or symbols of any nature, unless first approved in writing by the Company.

ARTICLE II
FRANCHISE FEE

2.01   In consideration of the grant of franchise, the Owner covenants and agrees to pay upon execution of this agreement a franchise fee in the amount of $^C.00 dollars of lawful money of Canada. No further franchise fee shall be payable during the term thereof. The Owner acknowledges and agrees that the franchise fee has been fully earned by the Company. If the Restaurant is not open for business within six (6) months from the date of this franchise agreement, the Owner shall have the right to terminate his franchise agreement and obtain an immediate refund of the franchise fee upon written request to the Company.

ARTICLE III
ROYALTIES

3.01   In consideration of the services to be rendered by the Company, the Owner covenants and agrees to pay to the Company, in addition to any other payments required to be made under the terms of this agreement, a weekly royalty fee of six percent (6%) of the Gross Sales in any such week.

3.02   The Owner covenants and agrees to pay said royalty fees together with payments for all stock sold to the Owner, all advertising costs due with respect to Gross Sales, and any other charges required under this agreement and made in any week commencing with the opening of business on Monday of each week and ending with the closing of business on the subsequent Sunday night or Monday morning of each week, as the case may be, no later than 8:00 p.m. on the Tuesday of the following week. Said payment or payments shall be made to the head office of the Company and shall be submitted together with inventory listing, daily sales reports and all other reports required by the Company from time to time.

3.03   For the purposes of this agreement, the term "Gross Sales" is defined in Schedule "A" annexed hereto, and the Owner's expenses shall include only those expenses which, in the reasonable opinion of the Company, are incurred by the Owner in the usual and ordinary course of business.

ARTICLE IV
COVENANTS OF THE COMPANY

4.01   In consideration of this agreement and the royalties provided in Article III hereof, the Company covenants and agrees, during the term of this agreement, to use its best efforts to maintain the high reputation of the Pizza Nova System and in connection therewith to provide the following services and assistance pertaining to the restaurant:

(a)   The provision of an efficient system for bookkeeping and stock controls. The Company will bill the Owner for the cost thereof on an hourly basis;
(b)   The provision of a general advertising campaign for the Pizza Nova System;
(c)   General advice and assistance with respect to promotion and management of the Restaurant, including the formulation and installation of general procedures and policies for carrying on the Restaurant business;
(d)   Opening supervision and assistance;
(e)   The Company's confidential standard business policies and operations data and instructions manuals, if any, established from time to time;
(f)   Such special recipe techniques, food preparation instructions, new restaurant services and other operational developments as may, from time to time, be developed by the Company.
(g)   Sale of all materials and supplies at cost to the Company., plus handling charges.

Source: Reprinted with permission from Pizza Nova.

Once having made the decision to own and operate a franchise, the business person has the advantage of using a widely recognized name, which virtually guarantees the availability of customers. Additional benefits include a fine-tuned set of management policies and strategies, a made-to-measure accounting system, predetermined quality control standards, and standardized forms for personnel and other uses.

The careful franchisee will keep in mind that there are disadvantages in this kind of arrangement. The most obvious is the ongoing expense of paying fees and royalties. These costs vary from franchise to franchise, depending on sales, public image, brand name recognition, and management reputation.

Negative publicity as the result of poor performance elsewhere in the franchise system may adversely affect the business. Because franchisees share a common image, customers will tend to judge all outlets according to the mistakes of a few. This is why franchisors stress strict adherence to the same standards in management and production in order to protect the entire system's reputation. Lastly, as noted earlier, the limits and obligations established by the franchisor restrict the decision-making freedom of the franchisee. The prospective small business person must weigh carefully all benefits and drawbacks before determining exactly how much independence he or she wants.

Sometimes franchise agreements turn sour when franchisees feel the franchisor is acting in bad faith. Consider the experience of Dave Michael in Issues in Business 3.3.

ISSUES IN BUSINESS 3.3

FRANCHISE FOLLIES

DAVE MICHAEL, A FORMER advertising salesman and manager of a Consumers Distributing store in Toronto, bought his first Pizza Pizza Ltd. franchise in 1983 for $90,000. "I was a customer," says Michael, a husky, straightforward 35-year-old who grew up in the city's west end, a few blocks from his store. "I was impressed with their service. Having done a bit of selling myself, I knew that if you had confidence in your product, it should be an easy sell."

With his wife's help, working twelve hours a day, seven days a week, Michael paid real estate fees, telephone fees, advertising fees, and cartage fees to Pizza Pizza, plus royalties (6 percent of sales, withdrawn twice a week from a specially arranged bank account) and occasional fines to the company for infractions, such as an employee not wearing a name tag. His hard work paid off. Over eight years, Michael nudged his first store's average sales up to more than $13,000 from $3,000 a week. His reward? Pizza Pizza opened another store in the area, immediately cutting his delivery sales by 50 percent.

Still, Michael liked the system enough to try his luck with another Pizza Pizza outlet in 1991, for $165,000, in Orillia, Ont. "There's a balance," he explains, holding his hands palms up like a set of scales. "I'll put up with this much bullshit if I'm making that much money." Wiser by now, however, he tried to limit his vulnerability to the franchisor in his second contract. "I now pay my rent directly, not into a rental pool," says Michael on a Sunday afternoon at his Etobicoke, Ont., bungalow. "I answer my own phones. My advertising fee is 4 percent, not 6 percent of sales. They couldn't open another store in my area unless I approved it first. The only thing I couldn't include

(continued)

in my contract was the cartage fee, which was 1.5 percent of sales at the time. They said it was being revised. Six months after I bought my second store, they raised my cartage fee by 100%. I was paying more for cartage than I was for rent."

Pizza Pizza says it is now adjusting the way in which it levies fees for such things as cartage, advertising, and rent. "We have a 25-year track record and 245 outlets," says Stan White, vice-president of marketing for Pizza Pizza in Toronto. "We encourage potential franchisees to seek legal, accounting, and banking counsel and to visit some of our franchises before they get involved. Unfortunately, underperformers seem to emerge in bad times."

Michael, however, is now one of 51 Pizza Pizza franchise operators who are suing the company for dealing in bad faith with its franchisees. "There'd be lots more of us," he says, "but some people are scared."

To a hard-working, ambitious Canadian like Michael, it's a rude shock to find yourself battling a franchise system that you had patronized yourself as a customer and then paid thousands of dollars to join. After all, a franchise is supposed to be an idiot-proof alternative to starting a business from scratch, allowing you to enjoy the independence of working for yourself without the risk of losing your shirt if the business falters. In fact, the franchisor will even supply the shirt, along with the pants, the shoes, and the funny hat, for a fee. If you're lucky, the franchisor will also provide the support you'll need to keep your operation afloat, from accounting services to marketing programs. All you have to do is turn the key in the door, switch on the lights, and start making money.

Many of the 500-odd franchise systems operating in Canada do live up to their promoters' sales pitches. Companies such as Midas and McDonald's have been around long enough to establish a track record and refine their systems. They provide franchisees with a comfortable income in return for their efforts. But others don't, despite their well-known names and high profiles. In both the United States and Canada, an increasing number of franchisees are complaining—sometimes in court—of inflated promises, soaring franchise fees, and even outright fraud. And in most of Canada, there is little legislation to protect the unlucky ones.

But there's no shortage of Canadians buying the franchising pitch as an alternative to self-employment or a salaried job....

Even when the economy turned sour potential franchisees were still lining up at the door—especially ex–middle managers armed with hefty severance packages....

Laid off or nudged out of their comfortable mid-level management positions, these refugees from the corporate world wanted to put their business experience to good use without gambling against the enormous odds involved in starting a business from scratch. The odds sound good: Only about one in five franchisees fails outright in its first few years, compared with four out of five independent business startups. But what they don't tell you is how hard you may have to work just to keep your head above water....

"Except in Alberta, there's little protection for a franchisee," observes Toronto franchise lawyer John Sotos. "Franchisees don't benefit from consumer legislation, because they're considered to be sophisticated investors and business people."

Alberta requires franchisors to prepare extensive documentation similar to a prospectus issued by a company selling shares to the public. It describes in detail the financial history of the company, the background of the owners and principals, and the exact fee structure. Franchisors also have to describe any restrictive covenants in the franchise agreement and the conditions under which a franchise can be transferred or terminated. Compliance with Alberta's regulations can cost the franchisor from $5,000 to $20,000, a factor that discourages some franchisors from operating in the province. Other provinces rely on the franchise industry to regulate itself, leaving disgruntled franchisees with no alternative to a court battle to seek a remedy for a franchisor's negligence or fraud....

(continued)

For every successful lawsuit against a franchisor, however, there are others who hang on until the money runs out, then merely walk away from their businesses, whether or not the franchisor was negligent or misrepresented the franchisee's potential sales. "The numbers aren't huge," says Sotos. "Most franchisors are reputable. They try to do the right thing. But there's a subclass of franchisor that causes problems, based on franchisor greed, mismanagement, opportunism, exploitation, and corruption in the system. And the economy exacerbates the problem."

Like the careless driver who causes all of us to pay higher insurance premiums, a relatively few bad franchisors have brought discredit to the entire industry. Other provincial governments, such as British Columbia's, are considering regulations similar to Alberta's, a prospect that concerns the Canadian Franchise Association (CFA) and many franchisors, who do not relish the thought of the additional costs involved in compliance. "If franchisors aren't more prudent in their selection of franchisees, if they don't reduce the number of failures, we could see legislation," says Mike Claener, vice-president of Midas Canada Inc. and a director of the CFA. Like many other reputable franchisors, Midas operates in Alberta and is fully prepared to comply with similar legislation in other provinces. "But if legislation were passed in Ontario, a lot of franchisors [operating in the province] wouldn't make the grade," Claener adds.

In business for more than 30 years, Midas has kept its turnover of franchisees to a minimum. Some franchisees have operated their shops for 20 years. With more than 100 franchisees now operating 206 outlets, the company goes to great lengths to govern its own operations efficiently. Franchise candidates spend a full day in interviews with Midas executives. They also complete a personality profile that identifies their strengths and weaknesses as business people and franchise operators.

"We also make sure they know financially what they're getting into," Claener adds. "While they may have positive cash flow, we tell them they won't make any money in the first three years. In the third year, they may break even. So we don't get people saying we told them they'd make $400,000 in their first year. We keep our franchisees up to date in new technologies, and we make sure they understand who we are."

Midas applies no pressure on applicants to buy a franchise. "We want to open new shops," says Claener, "but we don't want our franchisees failing across the country. If you have to expand to make money, your franchise system is in trouble."

Midas franchisees, who include a former accountant, a department-store manager, a fireman, and an oil-rig worker, need at least $125,000 in unencumbered assets. They should be prepared to make a total investment of $250,000, "and in this climate, even more," says Claener, "because the takeoff is slower." In return they receive exactly what Midas promises—"a focused program with strong advertising and marketing support."

Other franchise systems have equally good track records. Dairy Queen, McDonald's, and Tim Horton, for example, apply similarly thorough procedures to screening and selecting franchisees. "I bought my first Dairy Queen 27 years ago," says Regina's Jack Nicolle, who has bought and sold several franchises since then, including an interest in the Regina Pats junior hockey team. "I was selling cars at the time. I suppose I've felt ticked off at them from time to time over the years, but they've never misrepresented themselves. The things I've wanted to do with my franchise, I've done."

For Nicolle and hundreds of others, franchising has lived up to its potential. But the process of finding a good one is not easy, cautions Sotos. "In addition to checking out the franchisor, you have to do a self-evaluation, identify your own strengths and weaknesses, decide if you can follow the dictates of other people about the way the system should operate. If you're buying a franchise, you should never take anything for granted."

(continued)

Dave Michael, still embroiled in an ugly legal battle with Pizza Pizza, agrees. "If you're thinking of buying a franchise, get advice from an experienced franchise lawyer before you sign anything. And listen to what he tells you."

Source: Excerpts from Bruce McDougall, "Franchise Follies," *Report on Business Magazine*, August 1993, pp. 27–32.

Questions for Discussion

1. Why is Dave Michael suing his franchisor? What has the franchisor done that Dave Michael considers acting in bad faith?

2. What does Midas do to ensure that prospective franchisees properly understand the nature of the franchise contract?

SPECIAL CASES IN SMALL BUSINESS OWNERSHIP

Two business ownership arrangements—one very old, the other relatively new—warrant a quick look.

Family-Owned Business

"From rags to riches to rags in three generations" is a well-known adage. Why do some family businesses fail when the second or third generation enters the scene? Family business consultant Aaron Pervin says that 70 percent of family businesses are liquidated when the founder retires and only 13 percent are passed on to the third generation.[12]

The Canadian Association of Family Enterprise has compiled a list of the most common mistakes made in managing a family business. These include conflicts within the family on how the business should be run; competition between siblings for control; decisions being made in an autocratic manner by the founder; the exclusion or driving away of talented non-family managers due to family politics or incompetence; and the failure of founders who are accustomed to being self-reliant to adequately share information with other managers.[13]

Women as Entrepreneurs

It seems strange in this day and age to regard women in independent business as a special case. Women have been taking the same risks as men in setting up their own businesses with more and more frequency. Many come from families of entrepreneurs, but they have tended to start businesses rather than operating the family's business or buying an existing one.[14]

The main problem women face is the same one that anyone does: inadequate management expertise. Many women entrepreneurs find themselves taking business courses at community colleges and universities to upgrade their skills just as their male counterparts do. There is one area where women do feel they face greater obstacles than men, as is illustrated in Issues in Business 3.4.

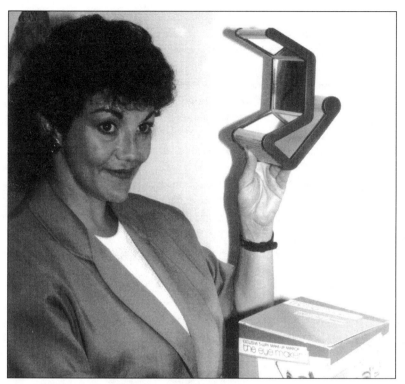

Chips Klein is a successful Canadian inventor and entrepreneur. She invented The Eye Maker, a three-way makeup mirror. Her company, Chipco Canada Inc., has sold over 800,000 Eye Makers worldwide. Chips Klein is also the co-director of the Women Inventors Project, a non-profit organization that assists women inventors and entrepreneurs in Canada.

ISSUES IN BUSINESS 3.4

BARRIERS TO WOMEN STILL THERE

FEMALE ENTREPRENEURS AREN'T making as much headway as is commonly thought, and many think they're unfairly treated by bankers, business professors told a conference recently.

Contrary to popular belief, statistics show that over the past five years, women have not been "making that much headway in terms of numbers of businesses started," Dina Lavoie, a professor at the University of Moncton, told the eighth conference of the Canadian chapter of the International Council for Small Business in Trois-Rivières, Quebec.

In addition, many small businesses started by women stay just that. In Canada, only 5 percent grow into medium-sized businesses, compared with 15 percent in the United States.

A study of Canadian banks and female-owned small business borrowers found that businesses owned by women obtained smaller loans—on average, $44,000 less than those given to men, said Larry Wynant, a professor at the University of Western Ontario in London.

His study, carried out with colleague James Hatch and published earlier this year, was commissioned by the Canadian Bankers' Association.

(continued)

Wynant and Hatch concluded there was little difference between the terms and conditions of loans made to men and women business owners in the sample of bank loan files examined at the six chartered banks.

But Wynant said further research showed there was a strong perception among women that they were unfairly treated by the banks because they were women.

The study also discovered that businesses owned by women were less likely to be incorporated and were smaller, younger, and more likely to be in the retail and service sectors.

Another study found that men and women do receive the same credit terms. What is different is how they feel about the experience.

"Women leave their banker feeling less happy than their male counterparts about the relationship," said Lola Fabowale, a researcher at Carleton University in Ottawa.

Fabowale said there was no smoke without fire and suggested that this more "qualitative aspect of the banking relationship warrants more attention from researchers."

Source: Reprinted from Sonita Horvitch, "Barriers to Women STILL There," *The Financial Post*, November 22, 1991, p. 48.

Questions for Discussion

1. What indicators are there that barriers to women entering small business are still in evidence?

2. What can be done to reduce these barriers to women entrepreneurs? Be specific.

BUSINESS REVIEW 3.2

1. If you had the choice between a job as an executive in a large corporation and working as an independent business person, which would you choose? List the benefits and drawbacks of each option.

2. What advantages does a franchisor gain from a franchise agreement? a franchisee? What safeguards should be built into a franchise agreement?

CONCLUSION

Small business has always had a powerful attraction for people of independent spirit looking for self-fulfilment and self-respect. The monetary rewards may not be great, but self-employed people make a vital contribution to society, creating goods and selling services in market niches often overlooked by big business—and they do it on their own terms.

Small businesses flourish from necessity and creativity. They have long been the fertile ground of the private enterprise system from which great industries have sprung. Life in a small business is seldom boring or routine; it allows those who stagnate in a controlled environment to take charge of their own careers and move ahead as far as their energy and commitment will take them. Where there are individuals with ideas and the will to take them to the public, small business will always thrive.

INTERACTIVE SUMMARY AND DISCUSSION QUESTIONS

1. At the beginning of this module, you read about Brian Miles and his promotion of Supercross motorcycle events. In addition to this special case, what other examples can you draw from to demonstrate that "entrepreneurship is alive and well and living in Canada"?

2. It is widely felt that Canada's industrial future is heavily linked to high-technology organizations. What role would small business play in this crucial future?

3. Comment fully upon this statement: "An entrepreneur without a business plan is as helpless as a sailor without navigational equipment; without it it's almost impossible to stay on course and chances are, each one will sail into trouble."

4. It has been said that "franchising is the middle ground between perfect self-employment, where you're creating your own enterprise, and working for a corporation." Visit several owners of local franchise businesses in your neighbourhood or near your school. Ask these individuals why they chose to purchase a franchise in lieu of starting an independent business. Ask them to describe some problems they experience with their franchisor.

5. In Issues in Business 3.4 you learned that, "contrary to popular belief, statistics show that over the past five years women have not been making that much headway in terms of numbers of businesses started." What is the current status of women in the field of small business?

CASE 3.1

IS IT POSSIBLE TO LEARN ENTREPRENEURIAL SKILLS IN A CLASSROOM?

TWO YEARS AGO, Peter Belle, 42, figured he'd had enough of the corporate rat race and decided to start his own business. So, he did something about it—by going back to school. Last year, Belle enrolled in the University of Toronto's entrepreneurial studies program. Then, last October, fortified by what he'd learned, he began his own Toronto car and truck rental and leasing company.

"I had already been in the MBA program at the U of T," explains Belle, formerly a purchasing manager for several companies. "But I wanted to take some courses that would give me practical advice on how to start a business, not just business theory. Studying entrepreneurship, for example, I learned how to write a business plan, take it to the bank, and get financing—steps I followed to start my own company. I'll still be living hand to mouth for a couple of years before I see big growth, but I'm happy. I think I'll be able to achieve things I wanted in a lot less time than if I was working for someone else."

Since more and more Canadians share that same dream, entrepreneurial studies programs are springing up all over the country. Along with the University of Toronto, York University, the University of Western Ontario, the University of Calgary, Laval University, and the University of Ottawa, scores of community colleges are also offering entrepreneurial courses. "About 30 percent of all Canada's business students are studying entrepreneurship in some form," says Jerry White, professor of entrepreneurial studies at the University of Toronto and a national expert on the phenomenon. "And there are thousands of courses in the subject nationwide, from inexpensive high school adult education classes to whole university programs."

Amidst all the activity, some business people still chuckle at the idea of teaching entrepreneurship—a skill they see as too fraught with intangibles to be communicated in a classroom. But educators like White defend their programs' effectiveness. "We don't really 'teach entrepreneurship,'" he explains, "if you mean that we throw a switch and start producing business people.

(continued)

"What we are providing, however, is a means by which people can evaluate themselves to see if they are entrepreneurial. We do teach some the ropes, like the physical steps involved in starting a business—but mostly, we're helping people bring out of themselves what might be there already. Just by doing that, we're increasing their chances of success."

Rein Peterson, director of administrative studies at York University (also called Enterprise York), agrees. "I don't know that you can really teach entrepreneurship," he reasons. "Many of our students have been preprogrammed to think that they'll fail if they go into business for themselves. We teach skills, how to recognize opportunities, and how to get access to business resources. Although students can do this on their own, we help them shorten the learning curve."

This reasoning is exemplified by 30-year-old Robert Walker, a graduate of the entrepreneurship program at the University of Toronto. Two years ago, in conjunction with earning his MBA at the school, Walker took an additional specialization in entrepreneurship built around courses in marketing and franchising—and one more in which he and some of his fellow students actually ran a business. "Based on our academic qualifications and work experience," he explains, "we were selected to manage a business consulting group. It was a nonprofit enterprise but we still had to negotiate terms with clients to make our expenses." The firm, notes Walker, ended up conducting business for small companies who couldn't otherwise afford a consultant, and big corporations, including Petro-Canada. "We prepared business plans, mini-market studies, new product feasibility studies," he enthuses, "even financial analysis. So, we were both operating as a company and dealing daily with procedures a company needed to know. You can't tell me it's not possible to learn entrepreneurship."

That's the message, say entrepreneurship program academics, that they'd like the business community to hear more clearly. "Not one school in this country offers an MBA in entrepreneurship," says Jerry White, "compared to about 70 in the United States. And there's a tremendous lack of endowed chairs in the subject and qualified academics at any level. What we need to solve all these problems is much greater financial support from the business community."

And the payoff for the business sector? The ripple effect of successful entrepreneurial start-ups, asserts White and others, can be a huge boon to the economy. "Entrepreneurs," White says, "are people who are potentially going to go out and create jobs. And they're not going to rely on others to take care of them; they're going to be willing to determine their own destiny. That's a plus for Canada."

Source: Reprinted from Michael Rozek, "Risky Business," *Canadian*, Vol. 4, No. 5 September 1990, pp. 16 and 18.

Questions for Discussion

1. Argue the pros and cons of the idea of teaching entrepreneurship in a classroom. Support both positions fully.

2. What are some advantages to current students soon to be prospective entrepreneurs as well as to the general Canadian economy of offering business entrepreneurship as a formal university program?

CASE 3.2

THE ADLERS—MAKING DOUGH FROM BAGELS

THE WAY DAVID ADLER tells it, he should be thanking his children for pointing the way to a new business opportunity.

It started on a family vacation to Washington, D.C., in the summer of 1988. The hotel they were staying at offered a complimentary breakfast, but that wasn't good enough for the kids.

"We got up every day to walk across the street and eat in the most beautiful bagel restaurant that was the most stunning enterprise," Adler says.

After living in New York, Adler and his wife, Randi, had developed a taste for ethnic foods, especially those from their own Jewish culture. But their bagel cravings couldn't be sated back home in Nova Scotia, not unless they did something about it themselves.

From the idea planted in Washington, Bagel Works was born last summer.

Their outlet may seem a modest start, but the Adlers are intent on seeing Halifax's first bagel bakery and restaurant fill a niche in the fast-growing specialty foods market.

From their studies of food consumption in the Halifax area, the pair has determined there's a vast market out there for good bagels.

"You really want to know what our market is? It's people who eat bread," Adler says.

But Bagel Works is trying to break into one of the tougher markets in Canada for specialty foods, says Don Shiner, a professor of marketing at Halifax's Mount St. Vincent University.

Although studies have shown that specialty foods are the fastest-growing part of the market, Atlantic Canadians tend to be conservative in their tastes. That makes western or central Canada more fertile territory for a specialty food venture, Shiner says.

The Adlers' confidence springs from their experience in other businesses.

When they moved to Nova Scotia from New York in 1976, David, a carpenter, built a house on property near Lunenburg, southwest of Halifax.

He left his carpentry trade to start up a business importing industrial supplies. By the time they sold out in 1983, David had already begun his new career as a broker in Halifax. Randi also started a new career in sales, then management.

William Ritchie, chairman of Scotia Bond, the Halifax investment firm where Adler worked, was surprised when he learned his broker was opening a bakery and restaurant.

Ritchie says Adler is well-equipped to face the challenges of small business: "The very nature of a successful broker means he has some of the characteristics of the entrepreneur."

The Adlers' new business was indirectly urged on by their extended family. A gathering of 50 relatives in Halifax in the summer of 1989 produced rave reviews of the city, except in one respect: everyone missed a good bagel.

When he mentioned his bakery idea to an old friend in New York who had entered the bagel business, Adler was given a hint of how widespread bagels had become.

"When [my friend] heard there weren't any bagels here, he was prepared to believe that pizza hadn't been discovered here yet," he says.

With that friend's help, the Adlers entered a sort of bagel university, studying the baker's New York business, as well as the rising popularity of bagels in markets from New York to Ottawa to Winnipeg.

Convinced of the demand, the Adlers jumped at the opportunity. Armed with a secret recipe for a New York–style bagel—less sweet than its Montreal cousin—the business was born.

Source: Reprinted from Michael Redmond, "Making Dough from Bagels," *The Financial Post*, November 23, 1990, p. 17. Reprinted with permission from Michael Redmond.

(continued)

Questions for Discussion

1. Explain the Adlers' success in the bagel business. Refer specifically to their product concept.

2. How did the Adlers circumvent some of the problems normally associated with a small business? Explain.

3. If Bagel Works is successful and the Adlers want to franchise it, what factors will they need to consider?

NOTES

1. Dina Lavoie, *Women Entrepreneurs: Building a Stronger Economy,* Background Paper (Ottawa: Canadian Advisory Council on the Status of Women, Feb. 1988), p. 1.

2. These features are suggested in *Meeting the Special Problems of Small Business* (New York: Committee for Economic Development, 1947), p. 14.

3. Based on W. Jennings, *Entrepreneurship: A Primer for Canadians* (Toronto: Canadian Foundation for Economic Education, 1985), pp. 21–23.

4. Scott Haggett, "Self-Employment a Risky Business during Recession," *The Financial Post,* October 5, 1992, p. 20.

5. "Doyle Hoyt Survives Bankruptcy, Succeeds Second Time Around," *The Wall Street Journal,* November 29, 1977.

6. Kara Kuryllowicz, "Where Entrepreneurs Can Go to Bankroll Fledgling Businesses," *The Financial Post,* April 22, 1991, p. 14.

7. "Reporting Burdens and Business Restrictions Survey Results," Canadian Federation of Independent Business, December 4, 1980, p. 1.

8. Eric Beauchesne, "Doesn't Pay to Be Own Boss: Survey," *Montreal Gazette,* January 29, 1991, p. D3.

9. Beauchesne, "Doesn't Pay to Be Own Boss," p. D3.

10. Ken Waxman, "The Franchise Phenomenon," *Independent Business Reporter,* The Royal Bank of Canada, Fall 1990, pp. 5–6.

11. Waxman, "The Franchise Phenomenon," pp. 5–6.

12. Jennifer Low, "Dad, When Are You Going to Let Go?" *Profit,* October 1991, pp. 28, 30.

13. The Canadian Association of Family Enterprise, as reprinted in Deidre McMurdy, "Family Misfortunes," *Maclean's,* May 18, 1992, p. 44.

14. Taxation Statistics, Revenue Canada, Table 12, various years.

PHOTO CREDITS

MODULE
◆ LEG ◆

LEGAL CONCERNS FOR BUSINESS

THE FOCUS OF THIS MODULE

1. To discuss where our laws come from and what "business law" means

2. To define various types of property and discuss laws affecting the exchange or sale of property

3. To describe the significance of patents, trademarks, and copyrights in preserving intellectual and industrial property

4. To define a legal contract

5. To demonstrate the differences between criminal and civil law and between crimes and torts

6. To discuss agency and the responsibilities of principal and agent

7. To describe the exchange of money through negotiable instruments

8. To discuss bankruptcy and proceedings under the Bankruptcy Act

9. To discuss government regulations, especially the role of administrative agencies in the regulation of certain industries

10. To outline the structure of the Canadian court system

11. To define the following terms:

KEY TERMS

law	implied warranty
common law	express warranty
statutory law	patent
Civil Code (*Code civil*)	copyright
property	trademark
real property	contract
tangible personal property	tort
intangible personal	product liability
property	strict product liability

(continued)

negotiable instrument   regulated industry
bankruptcy   administrative agencies
metric system

THE AIR CONDITIONING in Elizabeth Lennon's office has broken down and the temperature in her sunny corner of a renovated Toronto mansion is inelegantly hot. No sweat. Lennon is so cool and collected it's almost unnerving. . . . As cool as she was in 1983 when she joined two other lawyers and set up Cavalluzzo, Hayes & Lennon. The risk paid off: the firm has grown from three to fourteen lawyers. Along the way, Lennon has become well liked and respected in the legal community, says lawyer Chris Paliare, of labour law firm Gowling Henderson.

"There aren't very many women who are partners to begin with, let alone who set up their own business," says Paliare.

Lennon, 41, is co-chair of the national legal committee of LEAF, the feminist Women's Legal, Education & Action Fund. She regularly represents the 31,000-member Federation of Women Teachers' Associations of Ontario. . . .

"As a client, they [the women teachers' federation] are a feminist lawyer's dream come true," Lennon says.

"Their policy initiatives and the kind of things they want to deal with are very congenial to my views; they are very quick to identify sexual equality issues arising under collective agreements."

Lennon has the thoughtful, measured speech of her profession and an air of quiet gravity when talking about cases.

But colleagues praise her warmth and her keen sense of humour. A committed feminist, she breaks into peals of laughter upon learning a prominent magazine recently celebrated 100 years of women in medicine at Dalhousie University by running 10 beauty makeovers of faculty and students.

Becoming a lawyer was not one of her long-time goals. Born in Saskatchewan, she grew up expecting to become an academic and studied medieval literature at Yale. But she didn't find the atmosphere welcoming.

"Women are extremely underrepresented in senior positions in faculties still and they were virtually invisible then," Lennon says.

Disenchanted, she dropped out and returned to Canada. She wound up in law school after a stint as assistant at Dalhousie's medical library. Her interest in labour law was sparked by involvement in the Canadian Union of Public Employees' organizing drive at the library.

Lennon loved the Maritimes and would have stayed, but she found career possibilities were limited.

She landed a job at then-prominent law firm Golden, Levinson, but couldn't shake the lure of the academic world until she'd taken a year off to do graduate work in law at Harvard, with renowned Canadian professor Paul Weiler.

Building a successful practice has not been easy. She had a son, Graeme, while working on the bar administration course and, during the next few years, she and her husband had little money. "Not enough for a nanny, even if I had wanted one." Lennon hasn't forgotten what it was like to trundle her son to day care each day, boarding streetcars with bulging briefcases.

During the 1980s, Lennon's caseload changed. Instead of handling mostly labour matters, two-thirds of her time is now spent on cases dealing with women's issues, especially Charter and Pay Equity Act cases.

"One of my overriding concerns about some of the emerging trends in labour is freedom of association," she says. A series of lower court rulings, human rights decisions, and sexual equality decisions have reflected "a trend toward focusing on rights as inhering in individuals and failing to recognize that equality is a collective goal." . . .

Lennon is "an unsung hero . . . of progressive issues for women," says Leo Gerard, director of the Ontario Steelworkers. This view is echoed by Stephen Krashinsky, a partner at Toronto labour law firm Sack Goldblatt Mitchell. Lennon has a "passionate commitment to social justice . . . and the pragmatism necessary to win individual cases," he says. . . .

Lennon says some of her most satisfying work is not the "big, high-profile Charter cases . . . but arbitration cases in which the issues are just as complex or just as important."

Source: Adapted from Jennifer Lanthier, "Cool Lawyer Likes to Handle Hot Issues," *The Financial Post*, August 30, 1990, p. 13.

L AW IS THE BODY of rules of conduct a society recognizes as binding. Some of these rules are based on long-standing custom; others are enacted by the governing authority. But what the law actually means is open to interpretation. Elizabeth Lennon is involved in areas of law that have gained attention in the last decade as Canadian society has taken a new look at how individuals and groups are treated in everyday life, in the courts, and on the job.

The spur that has goaded us into this flurry of activity is probably the Canadian Charter of Rights and Freedoms. In Canada, our complex body of law arises from our history as a French and a British colony, leading up to the creation of the confederation of Canada. Canada was created by the British North America Act (BNA Act), an act of the British Parliament that came into effect on July 1, 1867. The

law
The body of customary and enacted rules of conduct a society recognizes as binding

BNA Act was patriated to Canada in 1982 as the Constitution Act. In 1984, the Charter of Rights and Freedoms became incorporated into the legal framework of this country.

Many areas of law beyond the labour law that interests Lennon affect business. The Constitution Act divides legislative powers between the federal and provincial governments. Some of the major powers given to the federal government relating to business are the regulation of trade and commerce, the power of taxation, banking, currency, bills of exchange, bankruptcy, interest, patents and copyrights, as well as "general and residual authority in relation to all matters not coming within the classes of subjects assigned exclusively to the Legislatures of the Provinces."

The powers given to the provincial legislatures include all matters relating to property and civil rights in the province, direct taxation within the province in order to raise revenue for provincial purposes, local works and undertakings and "generally all matters of merely local or private nature." In the area of business law, matters such as contract, torts, sale, leasing, partnership, property law, and security arrangements fall within provincial legislative jurisdiction.

WHERE DO LAWS COME FROM?

common law
The body of unwritten law based on court decisions in early England

statutory law
Written laws enacted by legislative bodies

Civil Code (*Code civil*)
System of law used in Quebec, based on the system used in France

The broad body of legislative jurisdiction of the federal government and of all provinces except Quebec is based on the principles of English **common law**. The common law is the body of unwritten law based on court decisions in early England. However, while common law plays an important role in Canada's legal system, more emphasis is placed on **statutory laws**, those written and enacted by legislative bodies. In Quebec, the law falling within provincial jurisdiction is based on its **Civil Code**. This code stems from the same laws that form the *Code civil* of France. The Canadian Charter of Rights and Freedoms has affected both federal and provincial legislation since its incorporation in 1984.

Courts are frequently called on to determine whether or not a particular statute is "constitutional"—that is, whether the enacting legislature has the authority to legislate on this matter in accordance with the Constitution Act. The interpretation of a particular statute can be the central issue in many court cases. Statutes must be worded in a precise, reasonable, and unambiguous manner if they are to be enforceable.

Business must operate within the framework of federal and provincial law and also that of municipal by-laws. Consequently, familiarity with business law is essential for the smooth operation of many enterprises. Executives must have enough broad understanding of the law in order to make responsible decisions—and to know when it is time to bring in a lawyer for legal advice.

Law changes as society changes. No system of law, written or unwritten, is permanent. Laws reflect the beliefs of the people they regulate, and both courts and legislatures are aware of this fact. Laws are constantly being added, repealed, or modified as the requirements of society and government dictate.

WHAT IS BUSINESS LAW?

Generally speaking, all laws apply to business, because any business entity—however it is organized—must obey the same laws as an ordinary citizen. The term business law is used for the aspects of law that relate directly and specifically to business activities.

Some laws apply generally to all forms of business, but some affect only certain types of business. For example, some laws regulate small business and others large corporations; the restaurant industry has one set of legal interests and the oil exploration industry another.

Laws have different applications. Some, such as the Income Tax Act enacted by the federal government, have universal application to businesses and individuals alike. Other federal statutes regulate only one industry, such as oil and gas or television communications. Provincial statutes, such as workers' compensation laws that govern payments to workers for injuries incurred on the job, regulate all business conduct within the province, regardless of the size or nature of the enterprise. Municipal by-laws, backed up by provincial regulations (and often by federal incentive programs) control decisions made by the construction industry on where and what to build.

Decisions in any area of business may have legal consequences. When owners, managers, and employees conduct any form of business transaction, they must, consciously or unconsciously, take the law into account. Some decisions require little more than normal sensitivity to well-known guidelines; others may call for complex legal study. Managers must use their understanding of basic legal principles to decide when they need legal help. For example, most organizations will retain lawyers to handle contracts and to advise on compliance with various regulations.

Smaller firms call on legal expertise from time to time: to set up partnership agreements or to apply for corporate charters; to help negotiate lines of credit at the bank; to check the details of major contracts. Larger firms often call in outside lawyers only in specific complex cases, finding they have enough day-to-day legal work to make it worth having lawyers permanently on staff, as described in Issues in Business 4.1.

ISSUES IN BUSINESS 4.1

KEEPING YOUR COUNSEL

IN 1985, GM OF Canada's vice-president and general counsel Ross McFarlane noticed an uptake in the number of human rights disputes at the company. McFarlane believed the increase was permanent, so rather than continue farming out the work to law firms, he hired an in-house human rights specialist. The move turned out to be a smart one. "If you're having any regularity in the kind of problem you're facing," McFarlane says, "there's no question that going in-house is cheaper."

Oshawa, Ont.–based GM is one of many Canadian companies discovering the benefits of using staff lawyers to handle more of their legal work, particularly recurrent problems in the areas

(continued)

of human rights, product liability, industrial and intellectual property rights, and the environment. Savings on legal fees is the advantage most often cited, but in-house counsel can also educate management and other employees about potential legal problems—thus helping the company avoid disputes. Staff lawyers can't handle every problem that crops up. Still, their importance is such that Canadian law firms view them with a slightly jaundiced eye.

Almost 13 percent of all the practising lawyers in the country now work for corporations, according to Derek Hayes, senior vice-president and general counsel for Canadian Imperial Bank of Commerce and chairman of the Canadian Corporate Counsel Association. "And it's growing very rapidly," he says. CIBC [in 1990 employed] 23 staff lawyers, compared to 6 in 1984.

Spiralling legal fees are fuelling the trend. Big-name private firms charge fees ranging from $100 an hour for a first-year associate's services to more than $300 an hour for a senior partner's. Meanwhile, general counsel—the senior legal officers of Canadian corporations—earn an average $140,000 to $150,000 a year.

For Hayes of the CIBC, there are clear savings in using staff for routine legal chores, such as real estate transactions. CIBC employs a law clerk who does nothing but title searches and registrations. "We can buy or sell a building just as well as having somebody outside do it," Hayes says. "And there are lots of areas like this one that you can bring in-house and do for half the price."

There are other benefits as well as economy. According to Sonja Gundersen, general counsel at Apple Canada Inc. in Toronto, "you end up giving very good practical advice just from the fact that you know how the business works." McFarlane says in-house counsel is becoming indispensable in keeping top management abreast of legal problems as they unfold. "We know how our corporation works, our vulnerabilities," he says.

Corporate counsel can also teach rank-and-file employees about potentially litigious matters. "We're now working with the Canadian Auto Workers to educate our people on the do's and don'ts of human rights situations," says McFarlane. "We understand and resolve problems before they become human rights complaints."

Of course, even the staunchest proponents of in-house counsel acknowledge that some work must go to a law firm. "When it gets down to doing a complicated securities transaction that might involve the U.S., Canada and Japan," says Hayes, "I don't have the people who are trained to do that. It wouldn't be worthwhile because we might do one of those a year for the bank."

It seems to be generally accepted that the toughest and most complicated corporate problems will continue to be handed off to law firms for the foreseeable future. But, says Hayes, in order to keep good people on board, "you've got to be very careful that you don't just have them do the dredge work and leave the sexy stuff to outside firms."

Neither Hayes nor McFarlane nor Gundersen sees the move toward greater in-house work causing serious discord between corporations and law firms. The firms, say Hayes, are reconciled to the fact that the trend will continue and that it's now corporate general counsel who call the shots. He recalls a conference ten years ago when two representatives of large firms "stomped on the table and jumped up and down" because he told them that from then on he expected them to send in detailed bills showing precisely who worked on what file and at what price. That sort of behaviour, he says, is "a thing of the past."

Despite Hayes's advocacy of the use of in-house counsel, he's hoping that its growth will slow—at least at CIBC. "I hope for my sanity we don't get to over 25," he says, when asked whether he'll be adding more lawyers to a staff that's grown nearly fourfold in just six years. The law firms, it would appear, don't have to worry about being shut out of corporate work just yet.

Source: Reprinted from Christian Allard, "Keeping Your Counsel," *Canadian Business*, July 1990, pp. 65, 66, and 68.

(continued)

Questions for Discussion

1. What are the advantages for an organization in relying heavily on in-house counsel? Be specific.

2. List areas of legal practice that may be best handled by in-house counsel. Which areas should probably be handled by an outside firm?

BUSINESS REVIEW 4.1

1. Explain the difference between common law and statute law.

2. Consider two businesses in your area. For each, imagine and describe three occasions on which the firm should seek legal help.

HOW IS PROPERTY EXCHANGED?

Business is often thought of as the exchange of property. The law recognizes several types of property.

The word *property* comes from the Latin *proprius*, which means "one's own." **Property** is defined as anything of value that a person owns and that the owner has the right to use or dispose of. Property is classified as real property, or personal property, which can be tangible or intangible.

Real property, or real estate, is land and any buildings or other structures permanently attached to the land.

Tangible means "able to be touched." **Tangible personal property** is physical items such as furniture, trucks, computers, paper, and any goods a company might own.

Intangible personal property is a right or interest of some kind, usually represented by some kind of document. For example, the money in a bank account is represented by the figures in a bank book, shares in a corporation by a share certificate, the idea for a new invention by a patent. Intangible property in the form of ideas is also known as *intellectual property*.

Property law falls within the jurisdiction of the provinces. In all provinces except Quebec, the law of property is based on common law as modified and formalized by provincial statutes. In Quebec, the laws regarding property are found in the Civil Code.

Real Estate Law

Land is bought and sold by the transferral of a legal document known as a *deed*. A *lease* allows someone to rent the use of real property for a certain time.

The exchange of real property is a thriving business of its own, but all businesses are to some extent concerned with real estate and real

property
Anything of value that a person owns and that the owner has the right to use or dispose of

real property
Land and any buildings or other structures permanently attached to the land; also called real estate

tangible personal property
Physical items such as furniture, trucks, computers, paper, goods in inventory

intangible personal property
A right or interest of some kind, usually represented by a written document

estate law because all businesses need premises in which to conduct their operations. A large retail chain might own its own warehousing space in several places and rent locations in shopping malls and office buildings across the country. Such a firm might have its own real estate experts on staff at head office, but smaller businesses are more likely to use the services of a real estate company. As with most other major decisions, it is always best to have a lawyer look over any real estate documents before signing them to ensure that the company is getting exactly what it expects. For example, when a client wishes to buy a property, a lawyer will search the title to the property to see that there are no *liens* registered against it that give a creditor a claim to a certain part of the property's value. A lien goes with the property and would have to be paid by the buyer even though the debt was incurred by the previous owner. Liens are most commonly registered for payment of back taxes. They have also been registered to cover the costs of cleaning up pollution on the property that was endangering groundwater or nearby properties. Other services that serve the real estate needs of business and individuals are mortgage brokers, architects, real estate developers, and contractors.

The Sale of Goods

Millions of sales transactions regarding tangible property occur each day. The law of sale applies to transactions in which goods or products are exchanged for money or on credit. Although sales may be of real estate and services as well as goods, only tangible personal property is covered by the law of sale.

The law of sale falls within provincial jurisdiction. The common law provinces (all provinces except Quebec) have each enacted a substantially similar sale of goods act, based on the long-standing customs of merchants as expressed in English common law:

1. Both parties must intend to complete the sale; a seller cannot claim payment for an item from an unwilling buyer, nor can a buyer insist that someone sell an item.
2. The sale is concluded by the "express or implied acceptance" by one party of an "express or implied offer" by the other.
3. The sales agreement may be concluded verbally, but if it is for over a certain dollar value, it should be in writing if it is to be enforceable by law. The sales receipt (of which the seller retains a copy) is usually considered to be a written contract.
4. When goods are bought on credit, *title* (the actual ownership) does not pass to the buyer until the final payment is made. So if the buyer fails to make payments as set down in the sales agreement, the seller may *repossess* the goods.
5. When buyers purchase goods for later delivery, they have certain rights to inspect goods before accepting or rejecting them.
6. Other provisions spell out where the risk of loss lies in the event that the goods are lost or damaged during manufacture, shipment or delivery.

In most aspects, laws of sale are similar in Quebec, even though they spring from a different source.

Ambiguities in a sales agreement, or the absence of certain terms (such as a date) will not keep the agreement from being enforceable. Should either party take the matter to court, the court will look to past dealings, commercial customs, and other standards of reasonableness in evaluating the existence of a legal contract. Such variables will also be considered by a court when either the buyer or the seller seeks to enforce his or her rights against the other where the sales contract has not been performed or has been only partially performed, or where performance has been defective or unsatisfactory. A sale of goods act defines the rights of the parties to have the agreement specifically performed, to have it terminated, to reclaim the goods, or to have a lien placed against them. In case of breach of a sales contract, the parties can decide to settle out of court or the injured party can sue the other. Should the case go to court, the remedy usually consists of an order for specific performance (to do as the contract stated) or monetary damages awarded to the injured party.

A warranty is an assurance that a product will perform as described. Sale of goods acts specify that there is an implied warranty with every item sold, even if there is nothing in writing. An **implied warranty** ensures that the item is not stolen and that the dealer has the right to sell it, that it measures up to the description given, and that it is in good condition and suitable for the purpose stated. A dealer cannot sell a refrigerator that will not keep food safely cold when the temperature rises above 25°C. If the fridge does fail, the customer is entitled to be reimbursed. Most of the more expensive products now come with written express warranties. An **express warranty** is a specific promise of performance that states exactly what the manufacturer or dealer will do if the item or certain components of it fail within a given time. However generous their terms seem to be, most express warranties include a phrase such as "This is the only warranty offered." Manufacturers use express warranties because they limit liability and override the wider protection of the implied warranty. Retailers usually honour the spirit of an implied warranty in the interests of customer goodwill, even if the manufacturer has given an express warranty that will not cover reimbursement.

Intellectual and Industrial Property Law

Patents, copyrights, and trademarks protect intellectual and industrial property and lie within federal jurisdiction and intellectual and industrial property is a key business asset, and owners must be alert to maintain their rights to it.

A **patent** grants an individual inventor or group of inventors exclusive rights to an invention for seventeen years. Inventions can be new devices or processes or key improvements to existing devices or processes that have been arrived at through independent investigation and experiment. Patents are obtained through the patent office in Ottawa. An application for a patent must include detailed technical specifications and performance claims, and inventors usually hire patent lawyers to shepherd their inventions through the process. Part of the procedure is a search to discover whether the invention is really new or whether it has been patented by someone else. Les Davis of

implied warranty
A warranty that the dealer can legally sell an item and that it is as described, in good condition, and suitable for the purpose stated

express warranty
A specific promise of performance stating exactly what the manufacturer or dealer will do if the item or certain components fail within a given time

patent
A guarantee to an inventor of exclusive rights to make, use, or sell an invention for seventeen years

Calgary had to give up the idea of patenting the spaghetti fork he invented when a patent search revealed that about twenty similar forks already existed. However, he has high hopes for the Soc-A-Pad, a sock with a built-in shin pad that he devised in 1986 when he was tired of having his shins beaten black and blue during amateur soccer games. The idea didn't seem worth taking further until 1990, when the Canadian Soccer Association instituted a rule that players in soccer games must wear shin pads. Now Davis is devising a machine to make the special socks.[1] The patent search means a long time can elapse between applying for a patent and receiving it. The term "patent pending" is used on articles to warn others that a patent has been applied for.

The owner of a patent has the right to make, use, and sell the invention. Inventors may also transfer the patent or license others to produce or use the invention for a fee. If a large company fears an invention might cut into its market for another product, it may buy a patent in order to withhold the invention from the market.

copyright
The right of artists, musicians, or writers and their heirs to prevent unauthorized copying or reproducing of their works by others

Copyright is the right of artists, musicians, or writers and their heirs to control the use of their material, that is, to prevent unauthorized copying or reproducing of their works by others. In most cases, copyright does not expire until 50 years after the death of the creator. In Canada, copyright is automatic; any books, poetry, plays, motion pictures, songs, recordings, paintings, sculptures, and photographs are copyright from the moment they are created. Creators usually negotiate a *royalty payment*, usually a percentage of the selling price, for each authorized copy of their work.

The proliferation of recording devices, from photocopiers to VCRs, has made it more and more difficult to detect unauthorized copying. The Copyright Act has recently been revised to expand the protection of creators' moral rights, to increase penalties for piracy, and to include such works as computer software programs, databases, and choreography. Because of the complex regulations that these changes require, not all sections of the new act have yet been proclaimed into law.

trademark
The words, logo, symbol, or other designation registered as a mark to distinguish one company's products from others

A **trademark** is defined by the Trademark Act as a registered mark that is used to distinguish wares or services manufactured or sold by a person or business from those manufactured or sold by others. A trademark may be a word, logo, symbol, or other designation used by a business to identify its product. A trademark may be registered for a period of fifteen years, and the registration may be renewed every fifteen years indefinitely. However, if a trademark becomes used as the generic term for an entire class of products, the individual or company originally granted the trademark loses this protection. Nylon, kerosene, linoleum, shredded wheat, and milk of magnesia are some examples of products whose names were once trademarks but are no longer. Because these have been judged to be generic terms, any number of manufacturers can freely use them. Interestingly, Aspirin, which lost its status as a trademark in the United States early in the century, is still a registered trademark in Canada. Other manufacturers of the painkiller refer to their products as acetylsalicylic acid, or ASA. As people tend to ask for "Aspirin" when they enter a drugstore, it can be seen that a trademark can be a very valuable asset. Fabergé reportedly

The WordPerfect Corporation's products are used internationally for both business and home use. The unauthorized copying of diskettes is a major problem with popular software programs, even though all WordPerfect Corporation products are registered with the U.S. Copyright Office and protected under U.S. copyright law. To deal with this issue, some software companies design the software so that the diskettes can be duplicated only once by either the individual or the company that is licensed to use the product.

paid $200,000 to a California cosmetic firm in order to be able to use the trademark Macho for a new men's cologne.[2]

On the whole, Canadian laws, including the new copyright amendments, offer good legislative protection for intellectual property. But as lawyer Linda Wright says, the problem is enforcement: "It's not because the law doesn't protect you but because of the sheer numbers of people out there counterfeiting."[3]

Wright's concerns are illustrated in Issues in Business 4.2.

The award-winning CN trademark was created by the Canadian designer Allan Fleming in 1960. In 1960, CN wanted to put forth a new corporate image. The logo successfully created a new visual identity for CN. Today, the logo is widely displayed throughout the company, including on rail-cars, employee uniforms, tickets, and company stationery. The logo's simplicity and elegance have contributed to its long durability over more than three decades.

ISSUES IN BUSINESS 4.2

CHASING THE PIRATES

CLEVER CROOKS DON'T have to rob banks these days. Instead, they sell imitation designer watches at sidewalk vending tables, copy computer software for their friends, or market cassette tapes recorded illicitly at rock concerts.

They print the faces of popular cartoon characters on T-shirts and sell them from their vehicles at cut-rate prices. They duplicate patented product formulas and undercut the original's price, or simply steal someone else's brilliant idea and present it as their own.

Great ideas are what make money for most companies today. But each clever new product generates hundreds of people wanting to exploit it. That's why companies are taking unprecedented steps to protect their innovations, by applying for copyrights, trademarks, and patents in record numbers.

For patent and copyright lawyers, work has never been better—or more interesting.

"Some of the subject matter is really fun," says Don Cameron, an intellectual-property lawyer with an interest in computer software copyright at the Toronto law firm Sim, Hughes, Dimock, which specializes in patent, trademark, and copyright litigation. "As far as software goes, the law is constantly being challenged."

Amendments to Canada's copyright laws enshrine legal precedents that extend the same kind of copyright protection traditionally given to books, movies, and songs, to computer software. A big question the courts are now being asked to decide concerns software programs.

Apple Computer Inc. launched suits in the United States against Microsoft Inc. and Hewlett-Packard Ltd. for copyright infringement after they introduced software programs that use a graphical interface suggestive of the type popularized by Apple. The cases are now before the courts and are being watched intently by lawyers and computer companies around the world.

"Clearly, you can't pick up someone's program and make a copy of it," Cameron says. "Other areas are grey areas. Can you copy the 'look and feel' of a program without copying the whole thing?"

Many software developers are now obtaining patent protection as well as copyrighting their software programs.

Patents are useful because they don't just protect the text, but also the function and the way it works. It's a more flexible form of protection.

Cameron adds that it "typically takes three to five years to get patented; it takes three to five years for someone to say, 'Hey, that's a good product. I'm going to copy it,' and another three to five years to get to trial."

Source: Excerpts from Laura Ramsay, "Copyright Protection Keeping Lawyers Busy," *The Financial Post*, July 9, 1991, p. F-6.

Questions for Discussion

1. List the infringements on patents, copyrights, and trademarks suggested in this article.

2. Competition experts suggest that the Apple operating system was copied from one under development at Xerox in the late 1970s. If this is so, does Apple have justification in suing Microsoft and Hewlett-Packard?

WHAT MAKES A CONTRACT LEGAL?

Contract law is important to most aspects of business operation. It is the legal foundation on which normal business dealings rest.

A **contract** is an agreement between two or more parties. If certain conditions are met, the contract is enforceable by law.

1. The contract must be made consciously and by mutual consent. A promise given under duress may be declared invalid.
2. The parties must provide equivalent value or benefit—known as consideration—to each other. For example, legal consideration exists if one party agrees to work for pay and the other to pay for work. It does not matter if the payment is made before or after the work is done or whether the agreement is oral or in writing. (An oral contract is just as binding and enforceable in court as a written one—though it may be more difficult to prove.) Similarly, consideration exists if one party works and the other pays, even in the absence of any exchange of promises.
3. The agreement must be for a legal act and intended seriously. Two competitors who agree to fix prices are committing an illegal act, so any agreement to do so would not be enforceable. Agreements made in fun or involving purely social matters will also not be enforced by the courts.
4. The parties must be *competent* to make the agreement. People judged to be mentally incompetent, young children, and sometimes anyone under legal age cannot be held to an agreement.

contract
An agreement, enforceable by law, between two or more competent parties for a specific legal purpose and for valid consideration

The sales agreements discussed earlier are a specific form of contract. Recently, both federal and provincial governments have been imposing conditions to protect consumers against contractual abuses. For example, many provinces insist on a "cooling off" period for sales agreements made in the consumer's home rather than the seller's place of business.

Because contracts are such an important part of modern business practice, many times the parties do not pay due attention to the actual wording. Common examples of legally enforceable contracts include purchase agreements with suppliers, labour contracts with unions, group insurance policies, and franchise agreements. Unnoticed conditions could prove troublesome.

Standard forms are available for many types of contracts. These are useful because they cover many details ahead of time. The parties should be prepared to add or delete clauses to suit their own specific purpose. An example of a standard form contract is shown in Exhibit 4.1.

BUSINESS REVIEW 4.2

1. Look at the written warranty that came with an item purchased recently. Show how this express warranty limits the implied warranty that would otherwise cover the purchase.

2. A asks B to demolish a neighbour's car because the neighbour persists in parking it too close to A's property line. In return, B will receive a new pair of skis and boots valued at $1,000. Is this a valid contract? Explain.

EXHIBIT 4.1 • EXCERPTS FROM A STANDARD COMMERCIAL LEASE CONTRACT

Commercial Lease

This lease is made in duplicate between:

(1) _____ (the "Landlord")
(landlord name)

and

(2) _____ (the "Tenant")
(tenant name)

The Landlord and the Tenant hereby agree as follows:

1.   The Landlord hereby grants the Tenant a lease of the premises outlined in red on the floor plan attached as Schedule A located on the _____floor of
(number)

_____
(address)

_____(the "Premises.")

   The parties agree that the Premises have a rented area of _____square feet, excluding the exterior walls.

2.   The term of this lease commences on _____ and ends on _____.
(date)   *(date)*

If the Tenant continues in occupation of the Premises with the consent of the Landlord after expiry of the term of this lease, the Tenant shall be deemed to be leasing the Premises on a month-to-month basis but otherwise on the same terms as set out in this lease.

3.   The Tenant may use the Premises for _____
(business purpose)

and for no other purpose.

4.   (a) The Tenant shall pay the Landlord a "base rent" of_____dollars ($_____) per year in equal monthly instalments of _____ dollars ($_____) in advance on or before the first of each month commencing on _____with the base rent for any broken
(date)
         portion of a calendar month in which this lease terminates being prorated.
       (b) The following services and expenses are the responsibility of the Landlord, _____% of the total cost of which services and expenses during the term of this lease shall be paid by the Tenant to the Landlord as "additional rent":
       (c) The Landlord shall invoice the Tenant monthly for additional rent incurred during the preceding calendar month. Each invoice is payable in full thirty days after delivery. The Tenant is deemed to have admitted the accuracy of the amount charged in any invoice for additional rent which he or she has not challenged in writing within the same thirty days.

(continued)

15.　　If not in default under this lease, the Tenant has the right to renew this lease for a further term of _____years exercisable by giving written notice of renewal to the Landlord in the six-month period immediately before the expiry of the original fixed term of this lease. The renewed lease is granted on the same terms as set out in this lease except as to base rent and without any further right of renewal. The base rent payable by the Tenant in the renewed term may be agreed between the Landlord and Tenant but, failing such agreement before commencement of the renewed term of the lease, the amount of the base rent shall be referred to and settled by a single arbitrator agreed upon by the parties or, in default of such agreement, to a single arbitrator appointed pursuant to the legislation governing submissions to arbitration in the jurisdiction whose laws govern this agreement. The decision of the arbitrator is final and binding on the parties with no right of appeal.

Executed under seal on _____.
　　　　　　　　　　　　　　　　　(*date*)

Signed, sealed, and delivered　　　　　　　)
in the presence of　　　　　　　　　　　　)
　　　　　　　　　　　　　　　　　　　　)
　　　　　　　　　　　　　　　　　　　　)
_____　　　)　　_____s
for the Landlord　　　　　　　　　　　　　)　　The Landlord
　　　　　　　　　　　　　　　　　　　　)
　　　　　　　　　　　　　　　　　　　　)
_____　　　)　　_____s
for the Tenant　　　　　　　　　　　　　　)　　The Tenant

Source: Excerpts from *Standard Legal and Business Forms for Canadian Business*, Steve Anderson (ed) published by International Self Counsel Press Ltd. Reprinted courtesy of the Publisher.

IS IT A TORT OR A CRIME?

Law is divided into two basic divisions, public, or criminal law, and private, or civil law. *Criminal law* is concerned with acts against the state and the general public, such as theft, assault, tax evasion, or traffic violations. *Civil law* is concerned with private dealings between individual citizens or businesses on such subjects as property, financial transactions, and personal injury. Most of the laws discussed in this module are part of the body of civil law.

Crimes are acts against society and will be prosecuted in court by crown attorneys on behalf of us all. **Torts** (*tort* is French for "wrong") are civil wrongful acts or omissions that injure another private person or damage that person's property. Many torts, of course, are also crimes and will be prosecuted as such in criminal court. But if the injured party wants redress, the case will have to be pursued in a civil action.

Torts may be *intentional torts*, where the injury inflicted is intentional, as in theft, embezzlement, and fraud. Torts may also be the result of *negligence*, where reckless behaviour or the failure to act causes harm.

One particular type of negligence of importance to business is known in tort law as **product liability**. This holds business liable for any negligence in the design, manufacture, and sale of products and in

tort
Wrongful acts or omissions that injure another private person or damage that person's property for which restitution may be sought under civil law

product liability
Liability for damages caused by negligence in the design, manufacture, and sale of products, and in instructions for their use

instructions for their use. Producers take product liability very seriously. In the summer of 1993, Molson Breweries recalled six million bottles of beer from retail stores in Quebec after cleaning fluid inadvertently left in a bottle-filling machine was found in half a dozen bottles of beer. **Strict product liability** carries the principles of tort beyond negligence. It allows an injured party to seek damages if a product is shown to have caused an injury even when no negligence on the part of the manufacturer can be proved.

Meticulous work by employees and careful supervision of all aspects of production are the best defence against tort liability. As awards for damages have risen dramatically in recent years, however, more and more companies are taking out liability insurance.

strict product liability

Liability for damages when a product is shown to have caused an injury, even if no negligence can be proved

WHAT IS AN AGENT?

Agency is a legal relationship in which two parties, the principal and the agent, "agree that one will act as a representative of the other. The *principal* is the person who wishes to accomplish something, and the *agent* is the one employed to act on the principal's behalf to achieve it."[4]

While the agency relationship can be as simple as one family member acting on behalf of another, the legal concept is most closely associated with business relationships. This is true because all types of firms conduct business affairs through a variety of agents—among them partners, directors, corporate officers, and sales personnel.

In Quebec, the law of agency is contained in the Civil Code. Elsewhere, the law of agency is based on common law principles and decisions in specific cases. In other words, agency law is based on tradition rather than on enacted statutes. The importance of agency law lies in the fact that the principal is generally bound by the actions of the agent.

Holding the principal responsible for the performance of the agent is expressed in the Latin maxim *respondeat superior*, meaning "let the master answer." When judging tort cases involving agency, the court must decide the rights and responsibilities of each party. For example, if an agent commits a wrongful act on the authority of the principal, the principal is liable and therefore answerable. At the same time, the agent is responsible to the principal for any harm the agent has caused the principal if the agent exceeded the authority given. When no agency relationship is found, principals have no responsibility for the acts of other persons.

HOW ARE FINANCIAL TRANSACTIONS HANDLED?

Even though cash is still the most widely used method of payment, a company, or even individual, rarely expects all payments to be made in cash. In fact, the burden of using nothing but cash transactions in today's busy world of commerce would be enormous. Financial transactions are generally conducted by means of **negotiable instruments**, or "commercial paper." A negotiable instrument is a written promise to pay that can be transferred among individuals or businesses. The cheque is the most familiar form of negotiable instrument. Bills of

negotiable instrument

A written promise to pay that can be transferred among individuals or businesses

exchange, drafts, promissory notes, and certificates of deposit can also be used to negotiate the transfer of money.

According to the Bills of Exchange Act, a negotiable instrument must conform to the following requirements:
1. It must be in writing and signed by the maker or drawer.
2. It must contain an unconditional promise or order to pay a certain sum in money.
3. It must be payable on demand or at a fixed future time.
4. It must be payable to order or to bearer.

Cheques and any other negotiable instruments can be transferred to others. To do so, the payee, or person to whom the instrument is made out, must sign the back of the document, a procedure referred to as *endorsement*. There are four specific kinds of endorsement:
1. *Blank endorsement* consists only of the signature of the payee. This makes the instrument payable to the bearer, that is, anyone in possession of the paper. Sending a blank endorsed instrument by mail is not advisable.
2. *Special endorsement* specifies to whom the instrument is payable. In this case, the endorsement will read "Pay to the order of . . ." followed by a name. No one else can then negotiate the instrument.
3. *Qualified endorsement* includes wording such as "without recourse before the endorser's signature. This states that the endorser does not guarantee payment. Therefore, the endorser's liability is limited if the instrument is not backed by sufficient funds.
4. *Restrictive endorsement*, similar to a special endorsement, clearly restricts how the instrument can be negotiated. For example, the restrictive endorsement "For deposit only" followed by an account number means that a lost or stolen instrument cannot be cashed because it limits deposit to that one account.

Many banks and other businesses today use electronic methods to transfer funds, and these methods will eat into the use of negotiable instruments just as negotiable instruments have eaten into the use of cash. However, there will still be occasions when the exchange of commercial paper of various types is essential.

WHAT HAPPENS WHEN ONE CAN'T PAY?

Bankruptcy is the condition that exists when a person or a business cannot pay debts that now exist or as they become due. Bankruptcy law in Canada falls within federal jurisdiction and is contained in the Bankruptcy Act. This act provides for the distribution of the assets of a bankrupt person or business proportionately among the creditors.

An insolvent debtor may voluntarily go bankrupt by way of an assignment into bankruptcy, or may be forced into it by a receiving order made by the court following a petition by a creditor who is owed at least $1,000. A receiving order names a trustee to place a business in receivership. The trustee can sell the business and pay off the creditors.

An insolvent debtor may also make a proposal to its creditors, agreeing to pay them back a certain percentage of the money owing them, for example, 50 cents on the dollar, and specifying the time in which it will

bankruptcy
The state of being unable to pay debts, legally resolved by the distribution of assets among creditors

be paid. If the creditors refuse to accept the proposal, the debtor becomes retroactively bankrupt to the date of the filing of the proposal.

In all cases of bankruptcy, the property of the bankrupt is administered by a trustee. In the case of a personal bankruptcy, certain property of the bankrupt is exempt and is not subject to the claims of the creditors, such as some furniture and clothing and some tools necessary for carrying on his or her trade. These exemptions are subject to provincial law and differ from province to province. In the case of a corporation, the trustee administers all assets.

Secured creditors such as mortgage holders will be paid by enforcing their security. The trustee oversees the distribution of all other assets of the bankrupt to the creditors. Certain creditors, known as preferred creditors—such as the trustee (for his or her fees), the government (for unpaid taxes), and a landlord, if there is one—are entitled to be paid off first. The ordinary creditors rank last and, in most cases, there is little left of the bankrupt estate to satisfy their claims. Many small companies have been pushed to bankruptcy themselves when a major customer declared bankruptcy and left them with large uncollectable accounts receivable.

The early 1990s has been a particularly difficult period for many small to medium-sized organizations that had overextended themselves and were devastated by a recession worse than they had expected. The number of bankruptcies rose dramatically. But though external factors ranging from interest rates to free trade were pressuring businesses, bankruptcy lawyer Gordon Marantz says, "A lot of people we see who are going down the drain could have survived had they done something earlier. One of the things they can't do is admit to their failure. It's just like people that stay in a bad marriage. They can't admit they failed and generally they get to us too late."[5] If businesses seek help in time, lawyers and financial counsellors may be able to strike new agreements with creditors, restructuring the debt to reduce interest payments and extend repayment over a longer period.

WHY DOES THE GOVERNMENT REGULATE BUSINESS?

Since earliest times an important function of government has been the regulation of weights and measures. Citizens have always wanted to know that a merchant would give them the expected length of cloth, whether it was measured by the cubit, ell, or metre, or the usual quantity of vegetables, whether weighed by the mina, pound, or kilogram. Because weights and measures are so vital to the business dealings of Canadians both at home and abroad, their regulation is a responsibility of the Canadian government. Like most other nations, Canada uses the International System of Units (or SI for Système Internationale), commonly known as the **metric system**. The government of John A. Macdonald first permitted the use of the metric system in 1871, but it was not until a century later that Canada began to convert completely from the older imperial system of measurement.

In more recent times citizens have demanded that their governments become concerned with a wide variety of issues affecting such matters as health and safety. As a result, businesses that deal in products and services for the general public tend to be fairly heavily

metric system
The common term for the Système Internationale (SI), the system of weights and measures based on multiples of ten

regulated. For example, businesses in Canada are required to comply with the following acts passed by the federal government and administered by Industry and Science Canada (formerly the Department of Consumer and Corporate Affairs):

Hazardous Products Act
Textile Labelling Act
Consumer Packaging and
  Labelling Act
Weights and Measures Act
Canada Agricultural Products
  Standards Act

Precious Metal Marking Act
Food and Drug Act
Fish Inspection Act
Maple Products Industry Act
Canada Dairy Products Act
Motor Vehicle Safety Act

Competition

There is no disagreement that the basis of our economic system is continuous and dynamic competition. Fair and reasonable regulation of business is intended to prevent the accumulation of too much power in a few hands that might lead to monopolies in some basic industries.

The federal Combines Investigation Act lists agreements and conspiracies that lessen competition; mergers and monopolies; price discrimination and price maintenance; misleading advertising; and other unfair selling practices as offences punishable by fine, imprisonment, or both. The act is administered by the Bureau of Competition Policy of Industry and Science Canada.

Other practices may also reduce effective competition. The Restrictive Trade Practices Commission has authority to review certain trade practices such as refusal to deal, consignment selling, exclusive dealing, tied sales and market restrictions, and may order an offender to change its ways of doing business. Failure to obey such an order is an offence punishable by fine, imprisonment, or both.

The other side of the coin is that some industries are **regulated industries**, subject to governmental controls over decision making that may limit or even eliminate free competition. Examples of such industries where market forces do not determine prices are public utilities and other industries normally considered to operate in the "public interest." The usual reason for restricting competition is to avoid waste and duplication and thus to ensure the production of goods and services everyone needs. The argument is that if a company is not assured a virtual monopoly in such areas as cable television or telephone service, it would not be worth the vast investment in infrastructure to set up the service. Other projects requiring large capital investments such as the construction of pipelines or hydro-electric dams and the requirements for safety in the operation of nuclear power plants may make this type of government regulation reasonable. The weakness of a system that relies solely on government regulation rather than the discipline of free market forces is that service and performance can deteriorate or not keep pace with technological change. As a result, some regulated industries are finding that the administrative agencies responsible for them are looking to more competition to improve service. For example, the Canadian Radio-television and Telecommunications Commission (CRTC) has recently opened the long-distance telephone market to competition in many parts of the country.

regulated industry
Industry where, in the public interest, government controls limit or even eliminate competition

Classic Rock CJAY Radio is a popular Calgary radio station. Like all radio and television stations in Canada, it is regulated by the Canadian Radio-television and Telecommunications Corporation (CRTC). The CRTC provides guidelines, from licensing regulations to Canadian-content prescriptions, to all radio stations.

Administrative Agencies

administrative agencies
Government boards and commissions whose powers and responsibilities are laid out in statute law

Almost every level of government includes **administrative agencies**, also called boards or commissions. Some well-known federal agencies are listed in Table 4.1 Examples of provincial administrative agencies are those which oversee public utilities, rental disputes, liquor outlets, securities commissions, and the licensing of various trades and professions. Municipal agencies include zoning boards, planning commissions, and boards of appeal utilized in the resolution of conflicts and legal entanglements.

WHO DECIDES QUESTIONS OF LAW?

Parliament and the provincial legislatures make the laws, but no one knows how these laws will affect individuals or businesses until they have been *interpreted* by the courts. The court system, or judiciary, is the branch of government charged with interpreting the law when individual cases come before it. Issues in Business 4.3 discusses several cases where the courts have had important effects both on the businesses that came before them and on the way that business is conducted in general. On the other hand, going to court is an expensive procedure. Developing Your Business Skills discusses a method of settling differences which is cheaper, faster, and often more effective than the formalities of court proceedings.

Some interpretations of law are made by administrative agencies. Their powers and responsibilities are laid out in accordance with their powers under the law. These often include the obligation to interpret

Table 4.1 • CANADIAN FEDERAL REGULATORY AGENCIES

Anti-dumping Tribunal (1968) Rules on whether a foreign country is selling its goods in Canada at prices well below production costs. Anti-dumping laws allow the government to impose duties on these imports to balance the price between the foreign and domestic goods.

Atomic Energy Control Board (1946) Regulates the nuclear industry in both commercial/domestic and military applications, and markets the Canadian Candu reactor. As concern over nuclear industry increases so will the importance of this board.

Canadian Radio-television and Telecommunications Commission (1976) Licenses all radio and television stations (including cable and pay TV). Charged with the responsibility of developing and maintaining a bilingual Canadian broadcast system in all electronic media, the CRTC regulates Canadian content, as well as setting the rates that can be charged by cable companies, telephone, and telegraph operations. The CRTC also monitors broadcasting in Inuktitut in the Arctic.

Canadian Transport Commission (1970) Regulates and controls the transportation system in Canada. Striving for efficiency in operations and adequate service for all parts of the country, the CTC monitors motor, air, and water transport, railways, and non-oil-and-gas pipeline transportation.

Energy Supplies Allocation Board (1974) Established after the Arab oil embargo of 1973, this board is responsible for the establishment and administration of resource allocation programs during times of scarcity and emergency. This control board ensures, for example, that hospitals will have enough oil, and ambulances enough gasoline to continue functioning during any crisis.

Investment Canada (1985) Encourages investment in Canada and reviews takeovers and the establishment of new businesses in Canada by foreign-controlled corporations, governments, or individuals.

National Energy Board (1959) Mandated to regulate the oil, gas, and electric utilities industries in Canada for the public interest, and to advise the government on the development and use of energy resources. The NEB authorizes oil and gas exploration operations, distribution, and exports and sets domestic and export prices.

National Harbours Board (1936) Finances and operates major ports in Canada (15 ports handling 25 percent of international trade). New legislation (effective January 1, 1983) increased the local autonomy of NHB ports, with the aim of making them more efficient and accessible to the public.

---

their regulations and make decisions in specific cases within their jurisdiction. Agencies conduct "hearings" instead of trials, but because the legal aspects can be quite complex, many businesses prefer to be represented by lawyers at agency hearings. In many cases, the decision of an administrative agency is final and cannot be appealed, though the courts may review any decision that violates the principles of justice.

Provincial Courts

Within each province there are several levels of courts. Although the titles of these courts may differ from province to province, their functions are approximately the same. Unless a case is assigned by law to another court or to an administrative agency, general trial courts hear most cases, both criminal and civil. Courts of appeal within each province hear appeals from the general trial courts. An appeal is usually filed when the losing party believes that the case may have been wrongly decided. The appeal process allows a higher court to decide whether or not to review a case. The higher court can change or overturn a ruling.

The provincial judiciary systems also have a wide range of courts of specific jurisdiction. County or district courts have jurisdiction to hear smaller disputes and lesser criminal offences. Probate courts settle the estates of deceased persons. Family courts handle marital disputes and matters involving children. Small claims courts allow persons to represent themselves rather than using lawyers in suits involving claims for damages up to certain maximum dollar values. The procedures are more informal, with the judge assisting to clarify points at issue.

Federal Courts

The federal courts decide civil suits brought against the Crown in federal affairs. Cases mainly involve revenues of the Crown, ships and navigation, and some matters arising out of federal legislation, such as copyright and patents. There is a separate tax review board for cases involving taxation.

Supreme Court of Canada

The Supreme Court is the highest court in Canada. It decides whether or not to hear appeals from provincial appellate courts and from the federal courts. Since the passage of the Charter of Rights and Freedoms in 1984, the importance of the Supreme Court as the final interpreter of Canadian law has grown immensely.

ISSUES IN BUSINESS 4.3

HOW THE LAW IS CHANGING BUSINESS

POLITICIANS MAY ENACT LAWS, but it is always up to the courts to interpret them. Even when politicians don't legislate on certain matters, courts still must set the rules of proper conduct. As the English jurist Sir William Blackstone wrote more than two centuries ago, courts "are the depositories of the law, the living oracles." This perception of the courts' role is just as accurate today—especially in the realm of business conduct. As we continually modify the way we do business and the kinds of deals we structure, it falls to our courts to redefine constantly what the law really says.

Consider the Charter of Rights and Freedoms, since its entrenchment in our constitution. Already, courts have used it to curb or expand government intrusion in business in matters ranging from commercial speech and economic freedoms to the rights of unions. Courts have also widened or restricted the scope of permissible corporate conduct. In employment law particularly, Canadian courts in recent years have effectively strengthened the rights of employees vis-à-vis their employers, handing down a spate of wrongful dismissal decisions. They've even spawned novel legal doctrines. In the case of *Queen* vs. *Cognos* Inc., for instance, Ontario's Court of Appeal confirmed a lower court's conception that a company could "wrongfully hire" someone if it innocently misrepresented a job. Though Queen lost the case because of an employment contract

(continued)

that protected the company, the recognition of wrongful hiring shows nevertheless how the courts do not shy from charting new territory.

If recent court decisions in the area of competition law withstand appeals, they could seriously whittle the power of the federal government to regulate mergers and curb misleading advertising.

In April of 1990, Quebec's Superior Court handed down a double-barrelled judgment in *Alex Couture Inc.* vs. *Attorney General of Canada.* The case concerns Quebec City–based Alex Couture's acquisition of Lomex Inc., a Montreal meat rendering company. The federal Bureau of Competition Policy argued that the deal would reduce competition in the industry, and sought an order from the Competition Tribunal to dissolve it. Alex Couture took the matter to Quebec's Superior Court. The decision struck down the federal Competition Act's merger provisions on the grounds that they contravened the charter, and declared the tribunal invalid. The judgment is not final, of course, even in Quebec. The matter won't be settled until Quebec's Court of Appeal, and probably the Supreme Court of Canada after that, passes judgment. In fact, the federal Competition Bureau is emphatic that business cannot use the judgment to ignore its power to regulate.

The lesson from the Supreme Court of Canada's decision in *Lac Minerals Ltd.* vs. *International Corona Resources Ltd.* in 1989 was this: before accepting confidential information, make sure you get a clear agreement on what your rights and obligations are. If you don't, and if you turn those secrets to profit, the other party could successfully sue you for everything you've gained.

The case involved the Page-Williams gold mine in Northern Ontario. From drilling tests done on neighbouring land, Corona, a junior mining company, believed the Page-Williams property held a vast pool of gold reserves. Corona approached Lac, a senior mining company, with its results, in the hope of striking a joint venture to buy the property and exploit it. Lac, however, used Corona's information to buy the property for itself. Corona sued.

All five Supreme Court of Canada justices held that Lac had committed a breach of confidence. Despite the fact Lac and Corona had struck no official partnership, Lac had ignored an unwritten code that mining companies exchanging vital information should deal fairly. But an even more significant aspect of the Court's decision is the way it chose to compensate Corona. Rather than making Lac pay for Corona's loss, a majority of three to two opted to make Lac give up what it had gained—the mine itself. This was surprising since no Canadian court had ever invoked such a remedy in a case of simple breach of confidence. Courts have used the remedy only when a fiduciary, or non–arm's-length, relationship existed between parties. In the Lac case, the Supreme Court, by a three-to-two majority, found there was no such relationship.

Donovan Waters, University of Victoria law professor, says the Court's motivation in breaking with precedent was to ensure the mine went to the party that had every expectation of getting it, in this case, Corona. In the future, says Waters, "I'm inclined to think that restitution will be ordered in those cases where the nature of the injury to the defendant is such that he will only be put right if he gets the property in question."

Source: Reprinted from Christian Allard, "How the Law Is Changing Business," *Canadian Business*, August 1990, pp. 43, 44, and 46.

Questions for Discussion

1. List new legal interpretations made by the courts that are mentioned in this article. Explain why you think the interpretations are important for business?
2. Do you agree with the decision the Supreme Court made to compensate Corona Resources?

BUSINESS REVIEW 4.3

---

1. What is the relationship of tort law to agency?

2. A client has refused to pay you for goods worth $800, claiming the goods were defective, but when you try to reclaim the goods, the client says they were thrown away. You decide to sue. In which branch of the court system would you pursue this suit?

DEVELOPING YOUR BUSINESS SKILLS

SAVE COURT COSTS: RENT A JUDGE

Given the high cost of court cases, corporations are seeking a kinder, gentler-on-pocketbook way of settling their differences.

Mediation—very popular south of the border, where it's known as Rent-a-Judge—offers a faster, cheaper, and more private way of resolving grievances. Unlike arbitration, another form of alternative dispute resolution, it's not binding and leaves open the possibility of resuming dealings with your opponent in a civilized fashion.

Although private mediation has been around for decades, it's only recently that top retired judges have become available for mediation. For example, in British Columbia there is former B.C. Supreme Court justice Tom Berger and Nathan Nemetz, formerly chief justice of the B.C. Supreme Court. But the trend is strongest in Ontario, where more judges seem to be retiring earlier, and a serious backlog in the courts has encouraged a trust company, a major brokerage firm, and various multinationals to seek mediation. One recent case, for example, involved a spat between an insurance company and several large corporate tenants. The disputed sums so far have ranged from $50,000 to $20 million. The judges charge about $300 per hour. A full day's hearing costs $2,000 or $2,500. Most conflicts are resolved in a few hours, although a very complex case can take as long as four days. Compare that with up to three years for a case, with appeals, in the regular court system and you'll appreciate the savings.

Richard Holland, formerly with the trial division of the Supreme Court of Ontario and now with Toronto law firm Genest Murray DesBrisay Lamek, explains that the key to mediation success is privacy and informality. "All of us take off our jackets and sit around a common table in a regular office," says Holland. "We talk about the case fully and frankly, with no notes taken. And we come to a mutually satisfactory solution that is signed in front of me."

Corporations in Ontario seem to be responding to the savings; one Toronto firm specializing in mediation and arbitration services, the Private Court, keeps three judges on its commercial dispute resolution roster. The only obstacle is that some lawyers may be reluctant to inform clients about a cheaper method if it cuts into their fees. But those who have experienced mediation are enthusiastic. "It's the way to go," says Holland.

Source: Reprinted from Miguel Rakiewicz, "Want to Save Court Costs? Rent a Judge," *Canadian Business*, December 1991, p. 17.

(continued)

Question for Discussion

1. Two businesses have decided to pursue a dispute through mediation rather than by going to court. How do the skills required to achieve success in mediation differ from those required for success in a court case?

INTERACTIVE SUMMARY AND DISCUSSION QUESTIONS

1. Can women best serve women's legal interests? Consider the career of Elizabeth Lennon presented at the beginning of the module.

2. Many Canadian corporations are utilizing in-house lawyers at an increasing rate. What are the reasons for this movement?

3. A real estate agent met a colleague for drinks at a bar after work, and became quite intoxicated. As she left the restaurant, she crashed her company car into the side of the building, damaging an exit extensively. Is the real estate firm responsible for the actions of their agent? What are the legal issues to be considered in this case?

4. Two sisters living in Prince Edward Island were awarded $120,000 in damages by a jury because they were burned extensively when a commercial dryer in a local shopping centre laundromat caught on fire. Only a week previously, a newly developed lint filter had been installed in the dryer, and the manufacturer claimed that their dryer was never built to handle the new type of lint filter. What legal issues are to be considered in this case?

5. Copyright law has become an increasingly complex and yet popular field in business law. What are some of the current events which have led to the large number of cases and specialization in this area of law?

6. The Charter of Rights and Freedoms has been used by the courts to curb or even expand government intrusion in business matters ranging from speech and economic freedoms to the rights of unions and conduct of corporations. Trace and discuss recent cases and rulings presented in this text to illuminate the situation.

7. An upholstery cleaning firm refused to accept a cheque endorsed by Pierre Boyer. The cheque was originally from Heidi Brink for the exact amount of the account—$53—and payable to Mr. Boyer. He endorsed the cheque to the upholstery cleaning company, including the notation "without recourse." Why do you believe the cleaning firm refused to accept this cheque for the correct amount?

8. Explain what you believe to be major differences between tangible and intangible personal property. Cite recent business incidents or examples to support your answer.

9. What sorts of issues would be best suited for resolution by a "Rent-a-Judge"? Be specific in your answer.

CASE 4.1

CLASS ACTION

A NEW ONTARIO LAW could become a powerful tool for challenging the powers that be. The Class Proceedings Act, which came into effect in January, makes it easier for individuals with a common grievance to join together to sue for damages.

Already, a group of Canadian war veterans has shown how it may open this new legal avenue. The Bomber Harris Trust has filed a multimillion-dollar lawsuit for group defamation over the CBC Television documentary *The Valour and the Horror*. Until now, group defamation lawsuits have been all but unheard of in Canada.

(continued)

But defamation law is just one area where the new act may bring changes. For consumers, it may prove a weapon to sue over false advertising or faulty products. One large such suit has been filed on behalf of up to 40,000 women who received silicone-gel breast implants, which the plaintiffs say caused physical harm to the women. Another suit has been begun by owners of condominiums against a builder in Mississauga, just west of Toronto. For those who purchase securities, it could be used to sue over misrepresentation in a company's published financial information. For farmers, Native people and environmental activists, it may be used to sue corporations that have polluted their land.

The result, says lawyer Edward Belobaba, will be a new type of consumer movement where citizens will sue the education system if their children aren't meeting certain standards, or to sue municipal governments if their streets aren't safe.

Mr. Belobaba, who sat on a government advisory board that helped develop the legislation, sees a citizens' consumer movement as a democratizing force. It will be less interested in winning monetary damage awards than in seeking improvements in services.

"It may be empowering of the middle class that has been shut out of the Canadian political system," said Mr. Belobaba. The act may, in other words, continue the process of shifting political power to the courts, a process that has gained momentum since the Canadian Charter of Rights and Freedoms took effect in 1982.

In a class action, individuals bring a lawsuit on their own behalf and that of others who have suffered a similar wrong. While always permitted to do so, those who tried faced large barriers.

Financially, lawyers now will be able to work on contingency fees, meaning they get paid only if they win; groups will also be able to apply to the Law Foundation of Ontario to pay their lawyers' costs.

Procedures have been changed to make it easier for one person to represent an aggrieved group. For example, the group cannot be disqualified if some members are seeking more damages or have somewhat different interests than others.

Quebec has had a class-action law since 1978, but Toronto lawyer Garry Watson considers Ontario's law more liberal than Quebec's (or the U.S. class-action law).

Class-action suits improve access to the courts because the risk is shared. No one would sue for $1,000 when lawyers' fees might be tens of thousands of dollars. But large groups would be able to take on such suits.

The new law provides that groups launching class actions be approved, or certified, by a judge from the Ontario Court, General Division. Certification can't be withheld because the number of people in the class isn't known. As a result, the lawsuit over the breast implants (between 20,000 and 40,000 women had implants) became possible.

The war veterans' lawsuit would not have been possible before because, in defamation law, the statements complained of must be directed at the individual bringing the suit; when umbrella organizations attempted to bring a defamation suit on behalf of a group, the courts often found that the umbrella organization itself had not been defamed. (A group such as women or Jews might be too broadly based to sue for a group defamation; but a particular women's group or a religious congregation, or even members of a profession, might be able to sue as a group.)

Source: Reprinted from Sean Fine, "Group Grievances Now More Easily Aired in Court," *The Globe and Mail,* August 9, 1993, p. A9.

Questions for Discussion

1. Name three groups the new Ontario statute described here might assist. For whom might it cause difficulties?

2. Why do you think the law provides that groups launching class actions must be approved by a judge?

CASE 4.2

WHO DISCRIMINATES AGAINST WOMEN LAWYERS? LAW FIRMS DO!

MOST WOMEN LAWYERS say they've been victims of sex discrimination on the job and earn less money than male lawyers, and that work-related stress and gruelling hours are driving many of them out of the profession.

Those are some of the findings in a Law Society of Upper Canada survey of 1,583 lawyers and their attitudes to the practice of law.

While the results won't surprise lawyers who know the profession is no different from any other business, some are leery of the law society's aggressive plans to improve the "quality of life" in law firms.

Recently, governing benchers unanimously endorsed all 50 recommendations in a report calling on the law society to prod law firms to narrow the income gap and encourage better working conditions with job sharing, sabbaticals, part-time employment, and liberal parental leave policies—measures some lawyers, including women, feel could do more harm because they'll create resentment.

The survey asked lawyers called to the bar in the past fifteen years about the hours they worked, job security, income, opportunities for advancement, and how it all affects their personal life.

It found both men and women feel a legal career makes excessive demands on family lives, but focussed mostly on how women view law. Seventy percent of the women said they experienced actual or perceived discrimination at work, versus 6 percent of men.

The survey found women wield little power in law firms. About 44 percent of men say they play a role in policy making, versus 25 percent of women.

While women have been entering law in greater numbers each year, many are also leaving. In the past fifteen years, 30 percent of those called to the bar have been women. But 37 percent of lawyers leaving law are female.

Bencher Fran Kiteley, head of the Women in the Legal Profession Committee, which designed the survey, says it's not all gloom and doom.

"There are people who are happy to be lawyers," she says. "But they want to combine those skills with a lifestyle that does not require 1,800 or 2,000 docketable hours a year."

The society hopes to steer law firms into a gentler and kinder way of life by encouraging them rather than requiring them to change.

Some aren't so sure the society will keep its distance. For example, it endorsed a policy stating "quality of life" in law firms is a matter of public interest since it affects quality of legal services. The fear is the society will want to meddle in law firm management, something Kiteley denies will happen.

It is believed that women can often overcome discrimination by simply doing "a good job," and it's only a matter of time before the old guard changes.

Source: Reprinted from Michael Crawford, "Women Lawyers Aren't Happy," *The Financial Post*, May 16, 1991, p. 12. Reprinted with permission from Michael G. Crawford.

Questions for Discussion

1. Under which law can the situation described above be located? Fully explain the violation.

2. Are the law firms acting responsibly? What must they do to correct this problem?

NOTES

1. Canadian Press, "Bruised Shins Led Soccer Player to Bright Idea," *The Toronto Star*, August 5, 1993, p. D9.

2. Joseph J. Joyce, "How to Select and Protect a Trademark," *Product Marketing*, May 1979.

3. Laura Ramsay, "Copyright Protection Keeping Lawyers Busy," *The Financial Post*, July 9, 1991, p. F6.

4. Rate A. Howell, John R. Allison, and Nate T. Henley, *Business Law: Text and Cases*, 2nd ed. Hinsdale, IL: Dryden Press, 1981, p. 503.

5. Michael Crawford, "War Zone of Bankruptcy Battles Is Getting Bigger and More Profitable," *The Financial Post*, December 13, 1990, p. 18.

PHOTO CREDITS

MODULE
◆ SOC ◆

THE SOCIAL RESPONSIBILITY OF BUSINESS

THE FOCUS OF THIS MODULE

1. To describe how social responsibility should be integrated with general business policy

2. To discuss means of regulating social performance within the individual firm, across the industry, or through government regulation

3. To examine business's responsibility to employees, to associates, to investors, to customers, and to the community at large

4. To define sustainable development and observe how business has taken environmental protection, pollution control, and energy use into account in the past and the changes it is now making

5. To consider the responsibility business can and should take for the overall economy

6. To define the following terms:

KEY TERMS

social responsibility	non-renewable resources
stakeholder	renewable resources
consumerism	global warming
ecology	inflation
sustainable development	demand-pull inflation
pollution	cost-push inflation

IN EARLY JULY 1992, just a few days in advance of the news story, the alarm bells began ringing at Marion Merrell Dow Canada. The Montreal-based company, one of Canada's largest producers of pharmaceuticals, had just been informed that Health and Welfare Canada would be issuing warnings about health risks associated with its best-selling antihistamine, Seldane. Around the world, 83 people, including 13 in Canada, had suffered "serious adverse effects" after using the over-the-counter allergy remedy.

Clearly, Merrell Dow was facing a potential gigantic public-relations headache. Seldane has been available in Canada since 1983, and millions of allergy sufferers have taken the drug regularly with no side-effects. But company researchers, working with U.S. and Canadian health officials, recently discovered that Seldane, taken either with certain other drugs or by users with heart or liver conditions, could be linked to serious heart problems. Merrell Dow, whose major business is health care, was being tied to a series of sudden deaths (none of them in Canada). If the "problem" went uncontained, it could quickly mushroom into a crisis, eroding public confidence and possibly Merrell Dow's financial future.

"We knew it was a delicate situation for us," company president Kirk Schueler said. "We had a major issue concerning the public's safety to confront and we didn't have much time to pull a strategy together."

Merrell decided to beat the Feds to the punch by issuing their own warning about Seldane. They identified users at risk and the nature of that risk. They released media bulletins. They set up a toll-free telephone number staffed by health professionals, and within five days, "informational" advertisements, with Schueler as the spokesman, hit the airwaves. Letters also went out to doctors and pharmacists giving the company's side of the story. And although Seldane lost its "over-the-counter" status in Ontario, the company headed off a federal government initiative to have the antihistamine reclassified as a prescription drug. Now, Seldane is sold "behind the counter." This provincial classification requires no prescription, but the user must request it by name from the pharmacist.

"The immediate objective of our strategy was to bridge the information gap that existed with the public," said Gary Handelsman, Merrell Dow's vice-president (corporate affairs). "We had to be forthcoming with information about who was at risk and how serious the danger was."

Despite the stop-gap nature of its plan, Merrell Dow, and its U.S. parent, actually followed a prescription that has become almost standard for firms facing a public crisis. When bad news breaks, it's essential for the company to get its side of the story out fast.

When Exxon Corp. and Perrier Group faced their own embarrassments (the 1989 *Valdez* oil spill and the 1990 contaminated mineral water, respectively), the public damage each company incurred was compounded by initial explanations that were either inaccurate or incomplete. A Perrier recall in Canada cost the company $15 million in lost sales and clean-up expenses, and market share was never fully recovered. Initial reports blamed a worker. And Exxon's contested clean-up eventually cost the firm $2.5 billion U.S. Delaying or withholding information not only exposes the firm to being tried and sometimes convicted in the media but it can also lead to a total loss of control of the situation.

For Merrell Dow, the stakes are huge. Before the scare, Seldane led the "non-sedative antihistamine" category, with sales of between $25 million and $30 million, or about 35 percent of the Canadian market. And since the health scare broke, Merrell Dow has already changed its packaging and the product "monograph," which describes who should use the antihistamine.

Schueler said his firm's own research indicates that Seldane has in fact weathered the public-relations storm. "The consumer surveys we've commissioned indicates that we've turned the corner," he said. "The public understands the problems we've been facing and they trust us to do what's right."

Source: Excerpts from Bob Papoe, "Merrell Dow Quick Study in Dealing with Seldane," *The Montreal Gazette,* September 3, 1992, p. C2. Reprinted with permission from The Toronto Star Syndicate.

MERRELL DOW'S REACTION to the information that its best-selling allergy medication was causing health problems was swift and sure. The company wanted to let the public know who was at risk and what the risks were before the announcement came from Health and Welfare Canada. Not only did it have public safety in mind, it wanted people to know that, as a member of the Canadian community, the company was concerned and prepared to take responsibility for its actions.

Managers are not just managers but also members of society, and know that at work they must not lose sight of the importance of **social responsibility,** the duty to ensure that their company considers the effects of their decisions on the life of the community as a whole as well as on the company. This duty includes operating in an environmentally safe manner, maintaining fair employment practices, and offering adequate product information to consumers. It also leads to less obvious considerations, such as restoring the land after laying a pipeline through open countryside, helping employees deal with the psychological and economic impact of a company relocation or downsizing, and communicating honestly and openly with investors and consumers, as Merrell Dow did in the Seldane incident.

Social responsibility involves everyone in an organization, from senior executives to support staff. And it is rarely bad for business. Within the firm, a common ethical philosophy shared by all employees helps create a community and encourages co-operation and sensitivity, which in turn may lead to higher productivity. Outside the firm, consumers' respect for coherent responsible behaviour may lead them to patronize the firm and thus bring greater profits.

Translating a policy of corporate responsibility into action is not straightforward. Without clearly enunciated overall guidelines, the company may drift from its policies as it pursues other, seemingly more immediate, goals. To build trust in the larger community, the company must be seen to follow up on its commitments. Many organizations have developed and implemented codes of conduct for their employees to ensure that their public statements of purpose are followed up every day. Exhibit 5.1 shows the code of conduct for the Edmonton Telephone Corporation.

social responsibility
Consideration of the effects of corporate decisions on the life of the community as a whole as well as on the company

---

EXHIBIT 5.I • EDMONTON TELEPHONE CODE OF CONDUCT

The Edmonton Telephone Corporation (the "corporation" or "ED TEL") is proud of the honesty and dedication upheld by its employees when conducting the corporation's business. The manner in which employees carry out their jobs is a reflection on ED TEL as a whole.

While employees are generally aware of the corporation's business practices, there may be times when employees find themselves in situations which require some guidance.

To provide this guidance, the corporation has a Code of Conduct. While this code cannot possibly cover every situation, it will provide ED TEL employees with guidance on conduct expected by the corporation.

From a corporate perspective, ED TEL expects its employees to conduct themselves in a manner that supports and promotes its mission and goals and its most deeply held beliefs, values and commitment to a Total Quality environment.

OUR MISSION . . .

"To understand and fulfil our customers' communication and information needs in a superior and profitable manner."

Supporting our mission, the corporation's goals are:

1. To provide outstanding customer value through service, products and price.
2. To support and develop committed employees working together as a team.
3. To meet financial objectives resulting in profit.
4. To support an ethical and responsible culture.
5. To provide an advanced telecommunications system.
6. To actively pursue market opportunities.
7. To be a good corporate citizen.

ED TEL is proud of its reputation for conducting its activities in a fair and businesslike manner. This reputation has been built on a foundation of total commitment to quality and service through a team effort. To preserve and strengthen this foundation, the corporation has the following expectations of its employees.

VALUES

The corporation views its employees as the messengers of its corporate philosophy. In order for our customers to be secure in the knowledge that they are receiving excellent value by doing business with ED TEL, the customers must know that they are dealing with honourable people. Therefore, the corporation expects all employees to maintain the highest degree of integrity in this conduct. The corporation views all employees as professionals and expects their conduct to reflect its trust, including, but not limited to:

- an honest day's effort,
- completion of all tasks in a professional manner,
- avoidance of unnecessary absenteeism and,
- avoidance of carrying on personal business during working hours.

(continued)

All employees are expected to refrain from any activity or conduct that might adversely affect the corporation including, but not limited to:

- harassment,
- discrimination,
- physical abuse,
- insubordination,
- conduct in violation of federal or provincial legislation,
- consumption of alcohol or any illicit substances such that might affect the employee's ability to perform work-related duties.

CUSTOMER RELATIONS

The nature of our business often requires that employees enter into our customers' private property. In order to protect the trust that our customers have conferred on employees in these instances, ED TEL expects its employees to follow certain procedures when on a customer's premise.

Employees are expected to:

- present their identification cards if requested,
- provide service to customers as efficiently, courteously, and quickly as possible,
- ask and receive permission before removing, using, or borrowing items from a customer or the customer's representative,
- respect a customer's property at all times and leave the premises in the same condition as they were found, removing all service-related debris and equipment.

Source: Excerpts from "The Code of Conduct," Edmonton Telephone Corporation, Edmonton, Alberta, 1992. Reprinted with permission from the Edmonton Telephone Corporation

But being socially responsible is a dynamic process. Legal, social, technological, and political changes mean that what were the right things to do ten years ago are no longer adequate today. Business people must be alert to all changes in the world around them for more reasons than simply to make a profit. Recognizing incremental change that calls for new approaches is often more difficult than recognizing more sudden events in the business environment.

When, because of unwillingness to act or simple ignorance, industry fails to maintain current standards of social responsibility, the public will react. The sanctions, both formal and informal, that society can bring to bear will soon bring the matter to the attention of management.

REGULATING BUSINESS BEHAVIOUR

How do businesses become aware that their behaviour is not, or is no longer, accepted as responsible? And how are changes brought about? There are three basic approaches to establishing regulations for business behaviour.

The first, and most immediate, comes from within the individual firm itself, exemplified by formal codes of conduct and a willingness to change behaviour as circumstances change. For example, when evidence grew that chlorofluorocarbons (CFCs) were contributing to the destruction of the ozone layer, companies like McDonald's

NEVER LET IT BE SAID WE DIDN'T SEE THE FOREST FOR THE TREES

In 1989, Lever Brothers reformulated its premier brand, Sunlight Laundry Detergent, as a 100 percent phosphate-free product. This is a significant investment considering that Sunlight accounts for approximately one-third of Lever's total sales. Lever Brothers recognizes their corporate responsibility to minimize any adverse effects on its company's products by responding proactively to environmental concerns in anticipation of government legislation.

immediately ordered their packaging suppliers to reformulate their fast-food containers to eliminate CFCs.

The second approach is agreement on regulations across the industry so that all firms within the industry follow similar rules of conduct. Such agreement ensures that no firm gains a competitive edge through some form of irresponsible behaviour. (This usually proves counterproductive over the long term in any case, because when it is discovered, the public outcry leads customers to turn against the offending firm.) The advertising industry has rules that all its members follow about advertising to children. Doctors, lawyers, engineers, and accountants are members of what are known as self-regulating professions and govern their own conduct through even more formal mechanisms.

All business people are aware that, if voluntary means of regulating behaviour fail to produce acceptable standards, the government will step in with regulatory legislation. Many managers prefer self-regulation, because it is more flexible and allows them to react faster to changing conditions. But all agree that there are many times when government regulation is necessary and welcome. It is, for example, helpful to know and be able to emphasize that worker and product safety requirements are backed up by law. To return to a problem mentioned earlier, eliminating CFCs from food containers was relatively easy, and with a few industry leaders taking a stand, government regulation was hardly necessary to ensure success. But finding alternative refrigerants to freon (a CFC) in refrigeration and air-conditioning units is a much more complicated and expensive procedure. In 1987, governments of industrialized countries agreed to phase out the use of CFCs by 1995 and without the spur of government regulation it is highly unlikely that industry would meet the goal of eliminating the use of freon by the deadline. By 1993, it appeared that ending the destruction of the ozone layer was a worldwide success story. Measurements indicated that some CFC levels in the Arctic may have already peaked and others will do so before the turn of the century. It is, however, likely to be as much as 50 to 100 years before the ozone-damaging chemicals are washed out of the upper atmosphere.[1]

WHAT ARE THE SOCIAL ISSUES FACING BUSINESS?

No business can operate in isolation from society. All issues that face society are also the concern of business. With some, the policies of individual businesses can have a direct effect. With others, any one business is only a small part of a much larger puzzle. For discussion purposes, we can divide these issues into three areas: issues that affect people, issues that affect the environment, and issues that affect the economy. Of course, these issues overlap, and action in one area may affect, positively or negatively, aspects of another.

How Business Treats People

Economist Milton Friedman, who bases his views on those of the eighteenth-century theorist Adam Smith, believes that a company has no responsibility except to maximize profit.[2] Accordingly, the object of managers should be to pay as little as possible for raw materials, labour, and related production costs, and sell as much as possible to its customers for as high a price as possible. Many business people would agree with the profit-maximization goal, but argue about the best way to achieve it.

In the long run, society will not allow an organization to continue to hold economic power if it acts irresponsibly. Workers may strike; governments may tighten regulations; injured parties may bring lawsuits; consumers may boycott the company's profits. These groups, among others, are a company's **stakeholders,** who have varying interests in the company's performance. As these stakeholders are equally important to the company, it is responsible business practice to take their interests into consideration.

stakeholder
Any group with an interest, or stake, in a company's performance

Responsibility to Employees

The way organizations treat their employees is often put in terms of "people versus profit," as if profit-driven priorities leave little time for accommodating personal needs. But many human resource managers today say that this is a vast oversimplification. Treating people as people is often the route to increased productivity.

Although employees are hired to fulfil specific functions, they don't perform best if treated like cogs or replacement parts. Managing with memos, policy manuals, and sales quotas alone will not achieve a company's purposes—and when dissatisfied staff leave in droves for more human workplaces, the turnover interferes with the smooth operation of the enterprise. Similar problems exist in the public service when rigid procedures make civil servants feel like grades or classifications rather than people with genuine talents and needs.

Much workplace dissatisfaction is directly related to the job and how employees are expected to carry it out. The greatest experts on how to do a job are the people who actually do it, a fact that has often been ignored in the past. Today the trend is toward participatory management, with workers participating in decisions that affect them. This can lead to (or cancel) changes that affect a whole area of production, or simply make the work easier for a few employees with special needs. Companies are also realizing that their workers are a vast resource that can be mined for talent through retraining and upgrading opportunities.

Responsibility to employees includes equity in hiring practices as well as among employees already on the job. Employers are realizing that cutting off opportunities on the basis of ethnicity or gender only decreases the talent pool from which they choose new employees or promote existing ones. Developing Your Business Skills discusses how one pharmaceutical company is learning to change its former rigid hiring practices and to deal with its employees' human needs.

An area that has been neglected for far too long is the provision of employment opportunities for persons with disabilities. In the past, many companies have refused to consider hiring people for whom the company would have to make changes, even in such simple matters as installing a wheelchair ramp, moving an office to the ground floor, or redesigning the requirements of a job to allow for typing or voice communication rather than writing. Even now, as Issues in Business 5.1 shows, attitudes are slow to change.

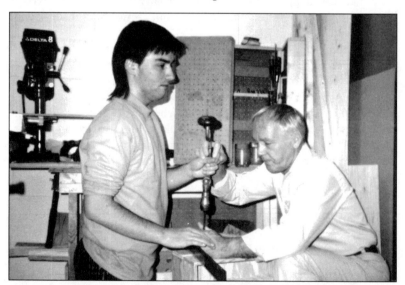

This visually impaired student is learning the necessary skills to work as a carpenter. The Canadian National Institute for the Blind is one of many organizations that help to prepare people with disabilities for a wide range of careers. Many universities and colleges are also working to adapt traditional classrooms to the needs of students with disabilities. It is now the responsibility of prospective employers to be willing to find suitable and fulfilling positions for persons with disabilities.

Responsibility to the firm and to its employees is a careful balancing act. Nearly every day managers must make judgements in situations that are not black or white. There will never be a policy manual that can provide answers to every question. The management of employees is rarely straightforward. Hiring and firing decisions, making salary adjustments, and being able to justify promotions and transfers are all areas that require fair treatment of employees as well as concern for the priorities of the organization. But what should a manager committed to increasing the representation of women and visible minorities among supervisors do when a vacancy arises and all the candidates are equally qualified? Should the manager choose a candidate on the basis of gender or ethnicity, or a white male who has more seniority?

Individual employees within an organization must also be aware of their responsibilities toward each other as well as to the organization as a whole. This sort of personal ethical behaviour can contribute greatly to a firm's success. The situation where one executive keeps important information from a peer so as to enhance his or her own chances for promotion and to lessen the advancement opportunities of the other manager may be all too common, but it is counterproductive. No one functions well in an atmosphere of distrust.

DEVELOPING YOUR BUSINESS SKILLS

WARNER-LAMBERT WALK THE TALK

Sherran Slack scans her employee population distribution chart with a reasonably satisfied eye. Five months into her job as Warner-Lambert Canada Inc.'s vice-president of human resources, she has mastered enough historical facts to make the case that affirmative action is working at the company.

Since 1975, when Warner-Lambert decided International Women's Year was an opportune time to start an affirmative action program, women, who make up 43 percent of the firm's 1,594 employees, have grabbed a growing share of management jobs. Now they hold 44 percent of supervisory positions, compared with 18 percent in 1975. And counting Slack, who was recruited last summer from pharmaceutical maker Eli Lilly Canada Inc., 8 of 52 senior managers at the company are female. You could argue that is too few—but 15 years ago there weren't any.

Warner-Lambert sells everything from cold remedies and mouthwashes to a battery of sophisticated prescription drugs, and through its Adams brands division, Chiclets, Bubblicious, and Trident gum as well as Clorets and Rolaids. Starting in the 1950s, when then-chairman Frank Cleary began preaching that corporate success depended on employee commitment and co-operation, Warner-Lambert has developed a strong reputation for enlightened personnel policies. Says one management consultant: "Warner-Lambert is always mentioned as a leading-edge company."

Partly responsible is the Warner-Lambert creed developed by head office in Morris Plains, N.J., in 1985. Dozens of major companies have creeds or codes of ethics. What makes Warner-Lambert different is that it delivers on its promises—at least to employees. Slack, sounding at times like a lay minister for some new secular spiritual movement, says every employee partakes of a three-hour discussion about the creed and how it applies to them. Moreover, she says, "People are invited to challenge us if we don't walk the talk. We're strongly committed to the

(continued)

individual and to being a good corporate citizen. We think this is consistent with being a profitable business."

Slack has inherited a common-sense approach to human resources management, which begins with recruiting good people and follows through with basics such as health and vacation benefits and insurance. "Along with that, you want to provide a positive working environment," Slack says. "And you have to show you're concerned about the employee's mental and physical well-being. You need to ensure that people will actually get their benefits. Then you provide training and development."

This approach means affirmative action, for minorities and the handicapped as well as women. It also means applying the principle of equal pay for work of equal value. Yet what is so striking about Warner-Lambert is the sheer scope and diversity of its employee benefit plans. It can arrange for its employees to get counselling on everything from substance abuse and family conflict to personal finances and even sexual performance. On top of that, there are scholarship programs for employees' offspring, and assistance in retirement planning. After they have retired, former employees are welcome participants in company-sponsored outings and community projects.

Does it work? Well, Warner-Lambert, with 1989 sales of roughly $300 million, is consistently profitable (its officials won't get more specific). The company admits that it is not the highest-paying pharmaceutical or candy maker in the country and has no unions in its plants or offices, but its employee turnover is about 7 percent a year, low for its industry. It has also been able to weather plant closings, such as the 1981 shutdown of its Schick razor facility in Toronto, with remarkably little employee distress or recrimination.

Mostly, says Slack, the payoff is happier, more productive workers who realize that responsibility is a two-way street. "You're more successful," she says, "when employees get the opportunity, and the obligation, to fulfil their career objectives."

Source: Adapted from Charles Davies, "Strategy Session 1990," *Canadian Business*, January 1990, pp. 51–52.

Question for Discussion

1. How does Warner-Lambert show its responsibility to its employees?

ISSUES IN BUSINESS 5.1

AN ADAPTABLE WORKFORCE

THE BARRIERS ARE beginning to be torn down, but the 3.3 million Canadians with disabilities still face complex problems in their everyday lives, not the least of which is how they are perceived in society.... "There's a generosity of spirit but a paucity of action," said Carolann Reynolds, who operates Challenge Media Productions Inc. and produces TVO's *Challenge Journal,* an acclaimed series that examines all of the aspects of disabilities.... "Government has had to adopt policies and legislation to ensure that things really do change. Employment equity is a perfect example. The idea is there but the implementation hasn't quite made it....Attitudes are changing, but more often than not, when the real challenge is right in front of you, it doesn't happen as easily as one would hope."...

Sadly, able-bodied people see a person who uses a wheelchair or a person who is blind and don't see beyond the chair or the white cane. Yet a physical impairment does not mean mental impairment—a fact that is often forgotten. But things are changing for people with disabilities.

(continued)

Technology is helping; governments are coming around and society as a whole is, too. There are more job opportunities for people with disabilities and a realization by governments that it is more beneficial to society to make sure a person with a disability has a job instead of a handout. That's why many businesses now consider people with disabilities to be an adaptable workforce—willing and eager to adapt to new jobs just as they have adapted to their new physical challenges.

John Southern, of People United for Self Help, said the recognition that persons with disabilities are out there, that they need jobs and better service, is a help because some things are being done.

Employment equity is a hot issue in the disabled community, and one that's linked directly to several problems. Persons with disabilities are often denied the opportunity for sufficient education to get a job and advance in a career. And a qualified worker can't take a job without finding accessible housing, and attendant services, and special transportation....

Laurie Beachell, national co-ordinator of the Winnipeg-based Coalition of Provincial Organizations for the Handicapped, said that quality vocational training that's integrated and flexible is in short supply across the country.

"A lot of the programs don't have the funds to provide appropriate accommodation," Beachell said. "By that I mean everything from interpreter service, to materials in alternate media, to attendant services on the job site, not just the ramp in the door and accessible washrooms. Educational facilities, be they technical, vocational, or universities, are still sadly lacking in accommodating needs of disabled persons and removing barriers to their participation."

The result of inadequate education and training shows up in statistics published by the federal Status of Disabled Persons Secretariat. Nearly 60 percent have an annual income of less than $10,000, and only 6.3 percent earn more than $35,000....

Nancy Leeman, director of human resources for the Canadian Bankers Association, said the percentage of persons with disabilities who work in the banking industry has increased from 1.9 in 1987 to 4.5 in 1990.

"It doesn't sound like a lot, perhaps, but because there are a number of real problems in finding job-ready candidates, because persons with disabilities face problems getting into the labour market, it has made the process slower than we would have liked," Leeman said.

"But the process is far too slow for me," said Southern, who is blind. "People tell me things can't happen overnight but I've been involved in the disability movement in Canada for 15 years and we've made precious little advances."...

There are people who have finished an MBA and then run into so many barriers and frustrations trying to get into the system that they've given up looking for work.

The only way to grapple with such attitudes is to first acknowledge that they exist and then attempt to change them. Many corporations, such as the CBC, Bell Canada, Petro-Canada, and the Royal Bank, have begun to provide diversity-awareness courses for all employees, whether they work in the corner suite or the mailroom. Other companies have decided that the only way to achieve integration is to reward those managers who practise outreach and punish those who don't. Says the TD's Jim Lawson: "We felt that the only way to meet our expectations was to institutionalize the ways and means. That's why we've made employment equity part of the job-performance criteria of each and every senior manager. If one of our VPs doesn't show proof that he's hiring and promoting people from diverse groups, he'll get hit where it counts—in the pocketbook."

Without question, there's a payoff for those employers who do choose to make the effort. The bottom line is that the company benefits when you start to reach out. Not only are you putting yourself in a good position to deal with the future, but it's been the experience that the majority of people with disabilities are highly motivated, hard-working employees.

(continued)

Source: Excerpts from "Attitudes," *The Globe and Mail,* September 18, 1991, p. C-1. .

Questions for Discussion

1. What can government regulation do to ensure greater employment equity for people with disabilities?
2. What can employers do to ensure employment equity?
3. What can people with disabilities do?

EXHIBIT 5.2 • EMPLOYER REPORT CARD

When it comes to hiring the disabled, who gets good marks?

E for Effort

No firms yet rate an A for outreach to disabled people. But some corporations are working hard to improve their performance. Here are some of the most deserving:

IMPERIAL OIL LTD.   Two years ago, Imperial began to study all its business practices with the intention of weeding out entrenched discriminatory habits.

THE ROYAL BANK.   The Royal provides managers with discrimination awareness training. This summer, 700 employees participated in a seminar on disability issues.

THE BANK OF MONTREAL.   As well as co-sponsoring a one-year, community college skills-upgrading course for individuals with hearing impairments, the bank is working with the Canadian Hearing Society to tailor the society's newly developed management training program for in-house use with deaf employees.

AMERICAN EXPRESS CANADA LTD.   American Express has begun to participate in employment events targeted to people with disabilities. This year, for example, company management reps as well as employees with impairments staffed a booth at People in Motion, a week-long job fair in Toronto for the disabled.

TORONTO-DOMINION BANK.   Two years ago, the TD hired Patti Fuhrman-Thompson, a 41-year-old consultant who happens to be blind, as a full-time employment-equity watchdog and disabled-rights advocate.

IBM CANADA LTD.   IBM recently produced a video on how business should deal with diversity. Big Blue makes it available to other businesses on request.

ROGERS CABLESYSTEMS LTD.   In affiliation with the March of Dimes, Rogers has begun to provide telephone and customer-service training and job opportunities to individuals with mobility restrictions.

(continued)

The D List

Public pressure, employment-equity legislation, and demographics have inspired even the most complacent firms to start taking action. But there are still many companies and industries that are resisting progress.

THE MANUFACTURING AND RESOURCE SECTORS.   According to Joe Coughlin, a long-time activist who co-hosts the CBC's *Disability Network*, these areas are hotbeds of hidebound thinking. "These sectors have traditionally been bastions for white males," he says. "It's hard to shift them around to the idea that anybody different—women, minorities, or people with disabilities—could do the job equally well."

HEALTH CARE.   Advocates acknowledge that it's not easy to integrate the disabled into health care jobs. But they don't think there's been much trying. "I know of people who have been told 'You can't be a nurse' or 'You can't be an occupational therapist' because they were disabled," says Vic Willi, executive director of Toronto's Centre for Independent Living Inc. "But, the idea of accommodation has never been tested in these professions to my knowledge."

THE EDUCATIONAL SYSTEM.   Activists say that, while change has begun in this area, it's too little and too late. "This is one of the most critical areas," says Willi. "Although part of your job as a teacher may be to mouth words about integration of the disabled and other groups, kids aren't stupid. When the teacher isn't disabled and they've never seen one who is, they get the message very quickly."

THE FEDERAL GOVERNMENT.   The employer most often cited as being among the poorest performers is the federal government. Advocacy groups complain that its record of hiring people with disabilities is dismal.

Source: Reprinted from Shona McKay, "Willing and Able," *Report on Business Magazine*, October 1991, p. 61. Reprinted with permission from Shona McKay.

Responsibility to Business Associates

"Conflict of interest" is a term we hear most often in relation to politicians who may find themselves able to influence affairs to suit their own private interests or those of their friends and supporters. Business organizations, and their employees, must be conscious of similar unethical behaviour. For example, most business relationships are built on a spirit of professionalism and mutual give and take. When friendship enters the relationship as well, it may be important to recognize what an associate from another firm mentioned in confidence as a friend and what may be considered legitimate competitive information. Is a gift from a supplier a sign of appreciation or a bribe to obtain favours in the future? Can it be both? Because this issue can become confusing, many companies today do not allow their employees to receive any gifts, or at least provide strict guidelines to control possible excesses. Good managers encourage ethical business practices by being role models whose decisions are consistent with these guidelines.

Responsibility to Investors

Throughout history there have been financial scandals. The financial health of firms has been misrepresented, numerous land swindles have been perpetrated, savers have lost millions of dollars due to embezzlement, and non-existent assets have been reported to the financial community.

Each of these types of financial abuse has been dealt with by the government, so that we now have a comprehensive, well-developed set of laws regulating financial affairs. But business management has also moved to a higher level of ethical behaviour. Firms are now more alert to financial misconduct by their personnel. Professional organizations and societies such as the Canadian Institute of Chartered Accountants have also worked to improve financial ethics.

Most members of the general public give little thought to how small companies and large corporations are managed. They do, however, expect all firms to be trustworthy in handling money. Pension funds, money market accounts, and bank accounts are invested for people in companies they have probably never heard of. Therefore, investors and pension contributors have especially high ethical expectations of bankers, stockbrokers, and pension fund managers to administer the money entrusted to them wisely and honestly. And all corporations have a responsibility to treat the investments made by shareholders seriously. There is no law against managing a company's assets so poorly that shares drop in value from ten dollars to ten cents, but the public regards such behaviour as unethical—as well as extremely poor business.

Responsibility to Customers

Since business is the provision of goods and services that customers want, responsibility to those customers is central to all commercial activity. Conversely, those same customers may be the first victims of dishonest or unethical business practices. For example, the aggressive door-to-door or telephone sales representative is unlikely to remind customers that the law allows them to withdraw from unsolicited sales contracts within a specified period. Customers complain of other merchandising practices they regard as shoddy: awkward package sizes that make it difficult to compare prices across brands; poor design; sloppy construction; misleading advertising; poor after-sales service.

consumerism

The demand that businesses give proper consideration to the broad needs of consumers in the design, manufacture, and sale of their products

Consumerism is the demand that businesses give proper consideration to the broad needs of their ultimate customers—consumers—in the design, manufacture, and sale of their products. Whether businesses like it or not, they are finding that, when a few consumers have identified problems with a product or service, it won't be long before there is a widespread outcry. The objective of the consumer movement is to create an informed public and to apply pressure on irresponsible businesses by way of boycotts, lobbying, publicity, and consumer education.

Since the emergence of the consumer movement in the 1960s, organized consumer groups have sprung up all over the country. Some are local or regional; some are concerned with particular products, such as automobiles or children's toys; others, like the Canadian Consumers'

Loblaw Companies Limited actively attempts to anticipate the needs of its customers. The President's Choice G.R.E.E.N. products are a well-developed range of all natural and environmentally friendly products, including cereals, paper products, and pet food. These products and many other specialty lines draw customers to Loblaw stores and improve the Loblaw corporate image.

Association, are national in scope and interested in the quality of all consumer goods and services. Consumer education is now a standard part of the curriculum in most schools. Thus consumerism has created a more informed class of shoppers who know, or know how to find out, what features are desirable in a particular product and what are inessential frills, and are ready to investigate the relative merits of rival products.

The consumer movement has given impetus to consumer protection laws covering everything from sales practices to the licensing of workers in the repair industry. At the federal level, the Consumer Affairs division of Industry and Science Canada is the main government agency concerned with consumer complaints and products. It administers four major acts:

1. Hazardous Product Act. This act gives the government the right to ban outright or to regulate sales, distribution, labelling, and advertising of potentially dangerous products.
2. Consumer Packaging and Labelling Act. This act defines how ingredients, weight, and so forth are described on the labels of consumer products.
3. Food and Drug Act. The main purpose of this act is to protect the consumer from injuries, fraud, and other deceptive practices relating to food and drugs.
4. Weight and Measures Act. This act regulates weighing and measuring devices to ensure their accuracy and defines the measuring units that may be used in trade (for example, units of the metric system).

Comparable agencies operate in each of the provincial governments. The Combines Investigation Act prohibits price fixing, price discrimination, resale price maintenance, and some mergers and monopolies.

Deceptive advertising, fictitious sales, and provision of misleading information to consumers are criminal offences under this act.

Issues in Business 5.2 examines consumer protection and how Canadians can help insure that the products or services they buy will be reliable.

ISSUES IN BUSINESS 5.2

CONSUMER CHAMPIONS

WHEN LYSE AND Réjean Villeneuve of St. Basile le Grand bought a new 1989 Ford Tempo, they thought they had a good car—one that would work well for a long time.

But less than two years later the car began to make "horrific" noises when it was started and it began stalling. The problem was diagnosed as a faulty fuel pump and it cost $276 to replace. The same thing happened to many other owners of Ford Tempo and Mercury Topaz cars. Their cars stopped or stalled for no reason—even in warm weather. Hundreds of owners complained to Ford of Canada, which responded with goodwill payments to cover the cost of new fuel pumps and labour.

But the settlements did not satisfy the Quebec government's Consumer Protection Office, which oversees a network of legislation—regarded as Canada's best—protecting the public from unscrupulous operators in a number of fields including health clubs, prearranged funerals, and car repairs—areas formerly fraught with fraudulent practices. So on July 3, the Consumer Protection Office sent a letter to Ford of Canada reminding the company of its obligations under Quebec consumer laws and demanded compensation for all Ford owners—not just those who complained.

"It was a stiff letter. It really shook them [Ford] up." said Phil Edmonston, who in 1969 organized the Automobile Protection Association to wage war against the manufacturers of cars that rusted prematurely. He is now the Chambly member of Parliament who serves as consumer affairs critic for the New Democratic Party.

Six weeks later, on August 13, Ford agreed to replace faulty fuel pumps on any or all of the 132,000 1988–89 Ford Tempo and Mercury Topaz vehicles registered in Canada. Consumers who shelled out between $135 and $508 each for parts and labour when fuel pumps malfunctioned will be reimbursed. Moreover, those who have not yet had fuel pump problems are protected.

"The Consumer Protection Office really has clout," said Edmonston.

The letter to urge Ford into action is just the latest in an impressive list of accomplishments of the Consumer Protection Office. "We did exactly what we are here to do and the industry understood," said Georges-André Levac, director of communications for the office.

In addition to providing the best warranty and credit protection in Canada, Quebec is the only province to offer consumers recourse to law through class action suits, he said.

While its clout is based on law, the Consumer Protection Office is not a court. Its duty is to advise and assist consumers. Nevertheless, the office plays a large role in shaping consumer legislation.

According to Levac, the office initiates changes whenever consumer laws are ignored or when buying trends make new legislation necessary. "Today we have very different consumers than we had 20 years ago." They know their rights and they file receipts and other supporting documents, he explained.

But as the Consumer Protection Office celebrates its 20th anniversary with a justly deserved reputation as Canada's toughest consumer watchdog, it is coming under fire for not

(continued)

keeping up with the times. Automobile Protection Association president George Iny said the Consumer Protection Office is inadequately monitoring car repair centres. Office investigators look for garage practices that were rampant in the '70s. "Today, most garage crimes are economic," he said. Overbilling for time is an example.

And despite having some of the best consumer-protection laws in North America, many Quebeckers do not know their rights or how to exercise them, critics say. Consumer education, a responsibility of the Consumer Protection Office, is severely lagging, said Brian Barbieri, professor of marketing at Concordia University.

Consumers "need clear instructions on where to go, when," said Marie-Andrée Amiot, who once headed the Association des Consommateurs du Québec. "The Consumer Protection Office is no longer ahead of its time....it has lost its fire."

And communications need to be updated, said Emily Reid, a financial counsellor. Glossy leaflets detailing consumer rights have little impact on people in the video age. "We need zippy ten-second clips that hit home," she said.

In another example of its shortcomings, the office ended publication of the English-language magazine *Protect Yourself*, which tests and rates consumer products, in March 1991 after piling up a $350,000 deficit (the self-financing French version, *Protégez-vous*, continues to be published).

According to Edmonston, Quebec has the best consumer legislation in Canada.

Source: Adapted from Nancy Durnford, "Consumer Champions," *The Montreal Gazette*, August 22, 1991, pp. F1–F2.

Questions for Discussion

1. What is the relationship of consumer watchdog groups like the Automobile Protection Association and government offices like the Consumer Protection Office?

2. Do you think that the Consumer Protection Office is doing an adequate job of consumer education?

Responsibility to the Community

A major stakeholder for any enterprise is the community in which it does business. The community should not be confused with customers, who are also stakeholders with more specific interests.

Responsibility to the community involves helping to make it a good place to live and work. It can include contributing to cultural events, participating in charity drives, and ensuring that a company's operations do not inconvenience its immediate neighbours. Many large firms have public affairs departments that explain company policy to the community and also keep a watchful eye on trends that their companies should be aware of and may need to adjust to. In smaller firms, this is part of the job of every manager.

Special interest groups within the community often force attention on areas of social responsibility that have been ignored, whether intentionally or not. Even though business executives often wish such groups would just go away and let them get on with the job, they realize that the concerns are often valid, and really do need to be dealt with. More and more often, businesses are finding responsibility to the community means responsibility to the environment.

BUSINESS REVIEW 5.1

1. Choose three types of businesses. For each, describe two areas that require decision making on the basis of social responsibility. Is government regulation warranted or do you think the business is capable of regulating itself?

2. Describe socially responsible actions that a local business has taken in response to consumer demand or the pressure of special interest groups within the community.

HOW BUSINESS TREATS THE ENVIRONMENT

Until well into the twentieth century, the prevailing attitude was that humanity could take what it wanted from land and sea and discard anything that it regarded as waste, and that the world would go on as before. For most of history, there was little evidence to the contrary. But since the Industrial Revolution of the nineteenth century, technological changes and medical advances have altered the balance between humanity and the rest of nature. We now have the ability to extract far more non-renewable resources from the earth; we use processes that produce waste that nature cannot easily break down; our population has multiplied and those of us in the industrial world use vast quantities of energy, much of it from non-renewable resources.

ecology
The relationship between living things and their environment

Ecology is the relationship between living things and their environment. We now know that much of modern industry—indeed of our entire way of life—in the so-called developed nations of the world rests on exceedingly shaky ecological foundations. Those businesses that do not recognize the challenges when problems are identified will eventually be forced to do so, whether by popular outcry, government legislation, or the collapse of the resources they have, perhaps unwittingly, been abusing. A stark example of this last point is the disappearance of much of the cod stocks from the Grand Banks, which is at least partially blamed on the modern fishing industry's ability to locate a school of fish by sonar and net the entire school in huge seines that stretch from the surface to the ocean floor, and its failure to ensure that smaller fish can escape in order to grow and breed. In other words, we have developed the technology to achieve the immediate purpose of catching the fish but not that required to sustain the stock for the future.

sustainable development
Development that meets the needs of the present without compromising the ability of future generations to meet their own needs

Business, as well as government and private individuals, is now examining its responsibility to this second challenge. The World Commission on Environment and Development calls it **sustainable development**: development that "meets the needs of the present without compromising the ability of future generations to meet their own needs."[3] While the goal seems almost self-evident, the path to achieving it is not. It is so much easier for us to avoid spending on pollution controls and waste management now in order to maintain this year's profits than to look ahead 200 years, or even as far as 5 or 10 years.

Keeping the World Clean

Pollution, or the contamination of the environment, is caused by almost all commercial activity. Some industries are more obviously to blame than others, but in the end, nearly all businesses depend on the products of the worst polluters. People have been conscious of air and water pollution for a long time, and governments have legislation in place to prevent the worst excesses.

Sometimes what seems like a satisfactory solution is no cure at all. For example, in 1972, Inco Ltd. completed a giant chimney stack at its Sudbury refinery to combat air pollution, and air quality around Sudbury improved significantly. But the sulphur compounds that no longer fell on the city hadn't disappeared; they were merely being spread over a wider area. In fact, they remained in the atmosphere longer, allowing more of the chemicals to combine with water vapour to form sulphuric acid and to fall as acid rain. More recent attempts at controlling air quality aim at catching the pollutants at the source. Roy Aitken of Inco put the company's position this way:

If you think you can ignore the environment and stay in business you've got your head in the sand. We've not only cleaned up, we've made ourselves more efficient in the process. Everything we do is designed to support a sustainable approach to our growth.... Society is demanding it—and rightly so. We're going to have to absorb the cost. It may mean margins will be squeezed a little bit and the distribution of benefits will be squeezed.[4]

Water pollution is a major problem in heavily industrialized areas such as the Great Lakes basin. As much as possible, "zero discharge" of harmful chemicals is now the rule. But downstream, the St. Lawrence River, the environment for several pods of beluga whales, remains highly polluted from chemicals and untreated municipal sewage. The whales are dying, and scientists who have performed autopsies on the carcasses believe that environmental pollution is the chief cause.

The paper industry is undergoing great changes because of concern about pollution. Pulp and paper mills are notorious polluters. In 1970, a paper mill at Dryden, Ontario, was found to be a source of mercury in the English–Wabigoon river system after a large number of residents at the Grassy Narrows and Whitedog reserves downstream from the plant came down with Minamata disease, caused by mercury poisoning, because they lived on contaminated fish. Although the provincial government ordered the mill to cease dumping mercury immediately, the river waters did not improve until the paper mill ceased using mercury in 1976. Meanwhile, the Native people had lost not only their health and one of their main sources of food, but also what had been a thriving tourist industry based on sport fishing.

Once the problems caused by pulp and paper mills became widely known, the industry began to look for new processes that would cause less damage. Consumers, book and magazine publishers, newspapers, and other businesses spurred them on by demanding paper products that were manufactured in less harmful ways. (Customers

pollution
The contamination of the environment

are also expecting more paper products to be made from recycled paper, which creates yet another challenge for the paper industry.)

Land pollution is often hidden, and many businesses fail to recognize it as a serious problem. Only when a plant closes down is the state of the soil it sits on revealed. Poor containment practices can lead to the need for extremely expensive clean-up procedures, and the courts are beginning to refuse to allow owners of polluted sites simply to abandon them.

Reducing Waste

For the industrially developed nations, the twentieth century has been an era of abundance. New techniques, new materials, and mass production have put more of everything onto the market. To a large extent, commercial success has been built upon waste. We expect consumers to buy new cars every few years; to give up wearing clothes when they go out of fashion instead of when they wear out; to replace old appliances with newer, more convenient models; and to throw away vast amounts of packaging, used mostly for the convenience of the retailer.

Much of the waste that ends up in our rapidly filling garbage dumps is what is called post-consumer waste, as if the consumer were responsible for it. In fact, the major responsibility lies with business, which chooses not only the materials it uses in its products but also those it wraps them in with little regard for whether they will biodegrade, break down through natural processes, when they are thrown away. Germany and the Netherlands now require manufacturers to take back any unwanted packaging from items they sell, which is one way of impressing on industry exactly how much packaging it is forcing on the consumer.[5]

The problem of waste is addressed by the environmental "3 Rs"—*Reduce, Reuse, and Recycle*. Business has chosen mostly to look at the third option, recycling. For example, soft drink manufacturers have contributed to "blue box" programs, which allow consumers to direct used cans, glass and plastic bottles, and newspapers to plants that will reconstitute them into new products. Environmentalists would prefer more attention paid to reducing—as in printing smaller newspapers—and reusing—as with returnable bottles. There is no consensus as to which processes are actually the least damaging in the long run.

Many enterprises these days are basing their businesses on innovative ways of using waste materials. In Halifax, the Ecology Action Centre and the Halifax Adult Services Centre came together to recycle waste plastic drums into composters for domestic use. The Canadian Waste Materials Exchange matches generators of industrial waste with potential users. As a result, over 200,000 tonnes of waste are exchanged regularly between producers and users. And companies such as Mother Parker's Foods in Mississauga, Ontario, have reduced the waste they send to landfill by as much as 85 percent by going back to what would have been normal practice 50 years ago: Mother Parker's sells used jute bags, corrugated cartons, and scrap metal, and gives away wooden pallets and scrap timber. Table 5.1a and b show that Canada has a long way to go in the efficient use of materials to avoid waste.[6]

TABLE 5.1A • AMOUNTS OF MUNICIPAL WASTE, SELECTED COUNTRIES, 1989

Country	Amounts (1000 tonnes)	% increase	Amounts per Capita (kg/cap.)	% increase
Canada	16,400	2.5	625	-1.7
USA	208,760	17.3	864	16.2
Japan	48,283	16.3	394	14.5
France	17,000	13.3	303	11.3
W. Germany	19,483	0.5	318	0.2
Netherlands	6,900	11.7	465	9.0
United Kingdom	18,000	5.9	357	4.9

Source: Adapted from "Amounts of Municipal Waste (a), Selected Countries, 1974–1989," *OECD Environmental Data*, 1991: Compendium, OECD, Paris, 1991.

TABLE 5.1B • DISPOSAL OF MUNICIPAL WASTE

Country	Year	Total Collected (1000 tonnes)	Mechanical Sorting	Composting	Total	% Energy	Landfill	Others
Canada	1989	16,400	82	.	1,416	7.1	13,448	160
USA	1986	178,000	82	.	15,000	7.1	138,705	160
Japan	1987	44,810	82	53	32,616	27.4	16,486	1,454
France	1989	17,000	15	1207	6,970	67.0	7,684	1,139
W. Germany	1987	19,483	15	429	5,942	67.0	12,917	195
Netherlands	1988	6,900	205	345	2,555	72.0	2,790	5

Source: Adapted from "Disposal of Municipal Waste, Selected Countries, late 1980s." *OECD Environmental Data*, 1991 Compendium, OECD, Paris, 1991.

Issues in Business 5.3 describes one firm that has capitalized on its strong environmental reputation.

ISSUES IN BUSINESS 5.3

THE BODY SHOP

ONE SUMMER, The Body Shop store windows displayed information about the danger of ozone layer depletion on behalf of Friends of the Earth, a non-profit environmental group based in Ottawa. The stores sold $30,000 worth of Protect the Ozone T-shirts and gathered 20,000 signatures on a petition seeking federal government action. The following summer, a membership drive and T-shirt campaign on behalf of World Wildlife Fund Canada raised $45,000.

Such campaigns have made The Body Shop—a chain of franchised and corporate-owned personal care stores—a national standard bearer for corporate social consciousness. And, according to the owners of the Canadian franchising rights—Margot Franssen; her husband, Quig Tingley; and her sister Betty-Ann—sales are booming.

The Body Shop's products, which include everything from facial cleansers to wooden foot massagers, are all made from natural, biodegradable ingredients. They are packaged in mostly recyclable containers, are sold without benefit of advertising, and are not tested on animals.

This alone would rank The Body Shop high on the admittedly short list of the world's practising eco-capitalists. But what makes the company unique is its policy of giving time, money, and display space to non-commercial causes. For four months of the year, store windows are given over to campaigns run from head office in conjunction with environmental and human rights groups.

These are not risk-free undertakings. A campaign on behalf of Amnesty International that showed human rights abuses in graphic detail outraged many shopping mall managers. But there is a payoff. "People want to shop in stores that support their value systems," says Franssen. Her words are borne out by the company's astonishing growth. In its first year, ended in December 1980, sales were $175,000; ten years later, they were nudging $50 million.

The cost of opening a franchise store has risen over the years to $190,000 from $75,000. But most Canadian outlets have profit margins of 20 to 25 percent, and given the average growth of sales, says Tingley, the total investment is likely to be paid back in two years or less. "As far as the Royal Bank is concerned," he says, "we're very profitable."

Franssen first heard of The Body Shop in 1979, when a friend gave her a gift basket of the products. She went to England and met Anita Roddick, The Body Shop's founder, and her husband. Impressed by their insistence on running a profitable business that made a social contribution, Franssen made a verbal deal giving her exclusive Canadian franchising rights.

With her sister's help, Franssen opened her first store in Toronto in 1980. Three years later, Tingley quit his job as a bond trader to manage the growing firm's financial operations. Since then all three have lived the business 24 hours a day.

Success has allowed them to apply their values to internal operations. With the Don Mills, Ontario, head office, warehouse, and manufacturing facility strained beyond capacity, they are considering moving out of the Toronto area to someplace—say central Ontario—where workers could afford to buy homes. As Franssen says, "It's the only right thing to do for employees."

Source: Adapted from Charles Davies, "Strategy Session 1990," *Canadian Business,* January 1990, p. 55.

Questions for Discussion

1. Why does The Body Shop give time, money, and display space to causes seemingly unrelated to the business of selling personal care items? Do you think this is good business practice?

2. As The Body Shop does not advertise, how do potential customers find out about it?

Using Energy Wisely

The industrial advances and tremendous growth in production that occurred in the twentieth century were largely made possible by the availability of cheap and abundant sources of energy. Canada has been particularly fortunate, having large resources of oil and natural gas and some of the best hydro-electric facilities in the world. This has given Canada a competitive advantage in many industries, such as aluminum smelting, that require large amounts of energy. It has also protected the economy to some extent from the price shocks that have occurred periodically since the oil-exporting nations of the Middle East quadrupled prices in 1973.

It has also meant that Canadian consumers and Canadian industry are the biggest users of energy in the world. Some of our energy usage is attributable to the climate and the difficulties of transportation in a large and thinly populated country, but a great deal of it is simple inefficiency. While the rest of the industrialized world has been learning to make do with less energy, or has always used less, Canada has continued on in the old, wasteful ways.

There are numerous reasons for Canadian industry to reduce energy use, some purely economic, others matters of social and environmental responsibility. The economic reasons include not only the cost of the energy we use, but also the fact that if we do not design energy-efficient products, they will not be competitive on the world market. More importantly, we must realize that fossil fuels such as oil and gas are **non-renewable resources**: when we have used them up, they are gone forever. Estimates of the number of years' supply at present rates of consumption vary widely, but all experts agree that the resource is finite. If we want future generations to benefit, we should be as economical as possible in our own use of energy.

Though it is true that hydro-electricity is a **renewable resource** that will last as long as the rains fill our rivers and lakes, not all electricity is generated from water. Some generators are powered by coal or oil—non-renewable resources. Nuclear generators are suspected by many to pose dangerous risks in operation and especially in case of accident. Over the past years, we have begun to realize that even hydro-electricity comes at its own environmental costs. No dam can be built without destruction of habitat for plants and animals and the dislocation of communities that live nearby.

We have also realized that the immense consumption of energy over the past century has changed the atmosphere that surrounds us. The process of burning carbon-based fuels such as oil, gas, coal, and wood creates carbon dioxide in the atmosphere, and this traps heat in a "greenhouse effect" that may increase temperatures at ground level by as much as 2–3°C by the mid-twenty-first century. Such **global warming** would likely affect the growing patterns of plants; melt glaciers and polar ice, leading to a rise in sea levels and the flooding of some coastal communities; and disrupt many other natural processes.

Government and the Environment

There are few aspects of the environment of Canada that are not covered by at least one government department and quite comprehensive

non-renewable resources
Natural resources that do not regenerate over time: once used, they are gone forever

renewable resources
Natural resources that grow again or recur through natural processes

global warming
A possible rise of 2–3°C in the world's temperature from heat trapped by larger amounts of carbon dioxide in the atmosphere created by the increased use of carbon-based fuels

legislation. At the federal level, environmental protection is spread among several major departments. Environment Canada and Oceans Canada are responsible for dozens of different acts affecting water, wildlife, clean air, fisheries, inspection, forestry, freshwater fish, migratory birds, ocean dumping, whales, Pacific fur seals, and international rivers. Other environmental protection mandates are spread among other government departments. Agriculture and Agri-food Canada regulate animal health and parasites. Energy, Mines and Resources Canada controls mineral extraction processes and chemical uses. Labour Canada regulates industrial hygiene and safety. External Affairs and International Trade Canada deal with international air and water pollution. The provinces handle similar responsibilties.

In 1992, government representatives from around the world met in Rio de Janeiro to discuss the state of the global environment in what came to be known as the Earth Summit. Presentations from many groups were heard about the effects of environmental degradation on their ways of life. One presentation that was warmly received came from four young girls from British Columbia. Their eloquent plea for the natural world and the future of their generation and those that will follow should not be forgotten.

BUSINESS REVIEW 5.2

1. Name an industry that has shown responsibility toward the environment, and describe the changes it has instituted to improve its environmental record.

2. Name an industry that, in your opinion, has not shown adequate responsibility toward the environment, and suggest ways in which it might discharge its responsibility.

HOW BUSINESS PRACTICE RELATES TO ECONOMIC ISSUES

The responsibility of business toward the overall economy is perhaps the most difficult to define. Maximizing profit, at least in the short term, may involve astute business practices that may in the long term be seen as counter to the economic health of the region or the country. But the issues are not nearly as clear cut as they are in the cases of social or environmental responsibility, where individual action can be seen to be valuable. In economic matters, there is little that one firm can do to change economic patterns. Yet economic responsibility is important, and companies and managers can lobby to influence government's economic policies.

inflation
A decrease in the purchasing power of a nation's currency, which is felt as rising prices

Inflation: An Issue Still with Us

Inflation is defined as a decrease in the purchasing power of a nation's currency—in other words, as rising prices. Inflation has often been a critical economic problem for both consumers and businesses. The two traditional types of inflation are demand-pull and cost-push. **Demand-pull inflation** occurs when there is too much money relative to products available. If consumer demand for a product is greater than its supply, the price of the item tends to go up—economists describe this as too much money chasing too few goods. **Cost-push inflation** results from rising costs (labour, raw materials, interest rates, and the like) that are passed on in the price of goods and services to the consumer.

Canada has not experienced the *hyperinflation* that occurred in Germany after the First World War and even today in parts of the former communist bloc and South America. Hyperinflation, a rise in prices so rapid that a loaf of bread can cost more in the afternoon than it did in the morning, is nearly always demand-pull in nature and a sign that economic system is not producing the goods that people need. Hyperinflation is usually related to wars or other social upheaval. But the slower, seemingly inexorable, cost-push inflation that Canada is familiar with has its own effects.

The overall effect of inflation is to redistribute wealth from lenders to borrowers. In the 1970s and 1980s, when inflation was generally higher than 5 percent each year and sometimes as much as 10 percent, it made a lot of sense to borrow in order to make purchases, because even though borrowers had to pay interest, they could be fairly sure that they would be paying back the money in dollars that were worth less. This led to a large demand for goods—and, for a while at least, plenty of jobs. But at the same time, people were seeing their savings worth less and less each year. Pensioners who contributed to pension plans years before were repaid with dollars that bought far less than they had expected.

Interestingly enough, at the time of the Gallup poll when 30 percent of respondents mentioned inflation as the greatest problem in Canada, the actual annual rate of inflation was less than 2 percent. The rate had been pushed down by the Bank of Canada, which pursued a policy of high interest rates to increase the cost of borrowing, thus restoring the balance between lenders and borrowers. Also, cost-push inflation is often halted by a recession as during the early 1990s. Because consumers are less willing to buy, producers cut their profit margins in order to achieve sales. Whether the rate of inflation is likely to increase again is a matter of debate. Some analysts say that it is inevitable; others that the Bank of Canada would once again institute policies to counteract it.[7]

Unemployment

No one can be unaware that unemployment is a major social and economic problem in Canada today. Unemployment is a concern for business for purely practical reasons: unemployed people have little money to spend on industry's products; people who fear that they may lose their jobs are also reluctant to buy goods and services they do not absolutely need. The social costs of unemployment are illustrated in the statements of unemployed workers in Exhibit 5.3.

demand-pull inflation
Inflation caused by demand for products that exceeds supply

cost-push inflation
Inflation caused by a rise in operating costs that is passed on in the price of the product

EXHIBIT 5.3 • VOICES OF THE UNEMPLOYED

ANDRÉ PRITCHARD, 21, restaurant worker: "Its a feeling of being useless. You spend your days at home or out trying to find a job. Everybody says, 'We don't need you,' or especially in the restaurant business, 'We want to hire a girl.' I'm bored. … I want to do something with my life. I have goals. And if I want a wife and kids later on, I need to start making money."

HAZEL McBEATTY, 63, social-services worker: "I'm not an old 63 and I'm not ready to stop. My dad stopped at 80, so I'm going to keep trying. In July, my UIC runs out and then I'll have zilch. It's that inward feeling of insecurity that's so hard. … I'm at peace because I know the Lord will provide. But it's not knowing when or where I'm supposed to be."

CLARENCE VOKL, 41, architect and city planner: "The hardest thing is knowing that as long as the market is bad, there will be very little happening in my field. Architecture is directly linked to the economy: if nobody is building, there is no work. It would be a lot easier to handle if I was on my own, but I have my parents to look after, so that's difficult."

REGINA BOURBONNAIS, 25, medical lab technologist: "I went through a three-year college program and they kept telling us this is where the jobs are. Only two or three grads from my year are working full time. I climb the walls, I'm so bored. … Not knowing is hard: I would just like to know I have this job, I make this much money, and I work these days, so I could plan my life a little."

Source: Adapted from Terrance Wills and Michell Lalond, "Six Faces of the Unemployed," *The Montreal Gazette*, April 11, 1992. p. 1.

Various reasons are cited for the high rate of unemployment. Products, production processes, and even entire industries have become obsolete. New technology can allow one worker to do work that used to take dozens to accomplish. The relatively high cost of labour in Canada makes it more efficient to set up plants in Asia, Mexico, or the "right to work" states in the United States where there is no minimum wage and safety standards may be more lax. The Free Trade Agreement and the North American Free Trade Agreement encourage these trends. Because of the recession, people aren't buying, so companies have to let workers go. Canadian workers don't have the right skills. All these viewpoints have some validity; none is the whole truth.

No one company can solve the problem of unemployment, but it is in everyone's interests to contribute to the solution. And there are things that can be done. For example, consider the statement that "Canadian workers don't have the right skills." It is true that skilled workers laid off from the declining manufacturing industries don't have a background in high technology, but companies that make this complaint often want highly specialized workers with expertise in the specific software programs on precisely the computer system the company is using. In a rapidly changing job market, such people may not exist anywhere. Perhaps the company should consider training candidates itself. In the past, North American industry has taken little responsibility for training workers, relying on the educational system to do it for them. Where the schools failed to meet specific needs, the practice has been to turn to immigrants from countries that do have adequate job training and apprenticeship programs. Business should be working with government to ensure that educational institutions provide relevant general training—and be prepared to undertake specific training of their own workers themselves.

BUSINESS REVIEW 5.3

1. What problems are caused by high rates of inflation? What are the risks and benefits of lower rates of inflation for business and individuals?

2. What responsibilities should business take toward the overall economy with regard to unemployment? Discuss.

THE SCORECARD ON SOCIAL RESPONSIBILITY IN BUSINESS

In the same way that more exacting guidelines on using advanced technologies are a response to new understandings in the field of biomedical ethics, social responsibility in business is a response to complex and rapidly changing conditions in the marketplace. As the concept of social responsibility is more finely delineated, we become able to evaluate progress in this complex but interesting field.

In the past, business people lacked guidelines for handling tough ethical questions, and often drifted when it came to action. Even now, the major weakness continues to be consistent implementation. Sometimes business leaders use their influence unethically, causing politicians to break the public trust. Sometimes individuals doing business in developing countries have put personal gain ahead of the spirit of joint co-operation. Business practices in the public service are not always above reproach. Sometimes information concerning the mismanagement of municipal tax money is concealed from taxpayers. (Of course, there are also taxpayers who try to avoid paying their fair share in taxes to various levels of government.) However, continuing education of employers and workers in all types of business and the support of such associations as the Better Business Bureau and the Consumers' Protection Agency have created a system that, overall, works very well. These agencies, supported by business people and concerned citizens, set standards and encourage businesses to adopt the principles of social responsibility because it makes good business sense to win the trust and respect of consumers.

All firms must remember that social and environmental responsibility can be properly exercised only by firms that show good economic responsibility. Issues in Business 5.4 discusses the fate of one company whose managers did not understand that management must be different when borrowers cannot rely on inflation to wipe out their financial obligations.

ISSUES IN BUSINESS 5.4

PATERNALISM AND CORPORATE IRRESPONSIBILITY

JUST INSIDE THE front gate of the sprawling Kemtec Petrochemical Corp. refinery in east-end Montreal stands a large scoreboard marking the number of accident-free work days at the complex. The tally shows more than 280 days without incident—a good record in the danger-prone petrochemical business. But just beneath, someone with a wry sense of humour has inserted a "0" where the total number of employees is normally shown.

Kemtec's workers are the most recent victims of entrepreneur Bernard Lamarre's crumbling business empire. Since the end of July, about 300 of them have lost their jobs. Last week the Quebec government stepped in to meet the payroll after Kemtec's bankers stopped paying a skeleton staff still working at the site. The employees, abandoned by their employer and the banks, had been working for nearly a week without pay to guard against a possible explosion.

Beneath Kemtec—and much of the east end—lies an oily cocktail of heavy metals and other petrochemical waste. And no one, it seems, wants to be stuck with the estimated $100-million cost of cleaning it up.

The refinery's predicament has become a potent symbol of Mr. Lamarre's paradoxical legacy. For years, he could virtually do no wrong as he spread his personal and corporate largesse. He loved Montreal, and Montrealers loved his grandiose schemes. When image-conscious Montrealers had all but lost hope of seeing their roofless Olympic Stadium topped, Mr. Lamarre was there to talk politicians into spending $155 million for the original retractable roof. In the 1960s, he built the Métro, Montreal's efficient subway system. A decade later, his Groupe Lavalin conceived and built the Ville Marie expressway to whisk traffic under the heart of the city. One of Mr. Lamarre's last contributions was a 51-storey showcase office tower—the city's tallest.

Kemtec was a gift of sorts to the politicians who helped his engineering firm win many lucrative contracts over the years. In 1987, Mr. Lamarre turned an abandoned Gulf Canada refinery into Kemtec, vowing to save hundreds of jobs in Montreal's depressed east end. The 60-year-old engineer also showered the Université de Montréal's École Polytechnique with money. And Lavalin hired its graduates by the hundreds. Likewise, profits from the Groupe Lavalin business empire supported hospitals and promising Quebec artists.

But Mr. Lamarre's free-spending days are over. Gutted of its prized businesses, his once-powerful empire is teetering on the brink of collapse. Mr. Lamarre has dropped from public view. Now the life of "Le Monsieur," as he was affectionately known by employees, is undergoing a little revisionist history. Politicians and a once-fawning local media have suddenly turned against him. They now say he was self-serving and corporately irresponsible, more worried about his image than doing the right thing.

There has been a painful realization that Mr. Lamarre's legacy has come at a hefty price, a price Montreal and Quebec taxpayers will likely wind up paying. In his wake lies a trail of defaulted

(continued)

government loans, angry creditors, and a potentially dangerous environmental mess. The tent-like stadium roof is in tatters, polytechnic graduates have one place less in which to work in the city after the forced merger in August of the Lavalin Inc. engineering firm with rival SNC Group Inc., and the office tower no longer belongs to Mr. Lamarre.

But nowhere is Mr. Lamarre's hasty retreat being felt harder than in the east end, a bleak area of aging and abandoned plants. Serge Baril, head of Kemtec's union, says working for Mr. Lamarre was like being adopted as a five-year-old orphan only to be beaten by one's stepfather. Says Mr. Baril, "Lavalin abandoned us."

Source: Reprinted from Barrie McKenna, "Workers Reassess Generous Grandfather," *The Globe and Mail*, September 20, 1991, p. A3.

Questions for Discussion

1. Was Bernard Lamarre acting responsibly when he proposed and financed his grandiose schemes? Present arguments both for and against the proposition.

2. What responsibilities do you believe Groupe Lavalin has for the employees of Kemtec Petrochemical Corp. and for the environmental damage Kemtec has contributed to? In your answer, bear in mind that Lavalin did not take over the refinery until 1987.

INTERACTIVE SUMMARY AND DISCUSSION QUESTIONS

1. Sherran Slack, the vice-president of Human Resources for Warner-Lambert Canada, in discussing and defending the affirmative action policies developed in response to recent events, stated: "People are invited to challenge us if we don't walk the talk. We're strongly committed to the individual and to being a good corporate citizen. We think this is consistent with being a profitable business." Do you feel there is a relationship between being socially responsible and being a profitable business? Discuss.

2. Canadian business has been challenged to drive toward a new era of environmentally sound economic development and to adopt a strategy that "meets the needs of the present without compromising the ability of future generations to meet their own needs." What do these two statements mean to you? How will they be met?

3. What needs to be done in the short term and also in the longer run to help manage Canada's complex energy problem in balancing gas, oil, and electricity?

4. Comment upon how you feel Mr. Bernard Lamarre managed the Kemtec Petrochemical Corp. dilemma in Montreal from a corporate ethics viewpoint. What should not have happened?

5. What do you feel are critical ethical and social problems for the late 1990s facing the following organizations?
   (a) automobile manufacturers
   (b) detergent manufacturers
   (c) corporate lawyers
   (d) real estate developers
   (e) pharmaceutical firms selling AIDS prevention/cure products

6. Why have Canadians with disabilities suddenly become an adaptable and important resource for contemporary corporations to consider in their planning?

7. Why are the owners of The Body Shop being called "practising eco-capitalists"? Is this a new breed of owner or is it a new attitude on behalf of some entrepreneurs driving toward the year 2000? Explain.

8. Look around your neighbourhood and select three important social issues facing a number of the businesses you are aware of. How have these organizations taken on this challenge? Also, how have local, provincial, and federal government agencies responded to these issues?

CASE 5.1

GOOD BEHAVIOUR AND THE BOTTOM LINE

IS IT PREDICTABLE that a beer company that believes it should promote women into management will make more money than one that doesn't care? Max Clarkson, former dean of the University of Toronto's management school and current director of the faculty's Centre for Corporate Social Performance and Ethics, thinks so.

Clarkson remembers the days in 1985 when he was analyzing data on two major Canadian brewers' attitudes toward female managers. Molson Breweries admitted it wasn't making much progress promoting women; Clarkson figured this was understandable in a macho industry and gave Molson credit for trying. But executives of the other company, Carling O'Keefe Breweries of Canada Ltd., were not even aware that equal opportunity for women was an issue. "That's when I realized I was definitely on to something," Clarkson says. "Because it was predictable that Carling was not going to do as well as Molson."

Carling, in fact, did so poorly that two years later it was absorbed by Molson. And just what was it that Clarkson was on to? Further confirmation of his pet theory—namely, that it pays to be good. During eight years of research, he has devised an elaborate system for rating companies according to their performance in such areas as labour and customer relations, environmental protection, and product safety. He, his associates, and his MBA students have applied it to 60 companies in Ontario and Quebec and found that, within industry groups, those that get the highest marks on a series of issues related to ethics and social responsibility also, over the long term, make the most money.

At first glance, this doesn't make much sense. A company's job is to make a profit. What does awareness of trendy social issues have to do with the bottom line? Who cares about the gender of a brewer's managers as long as the beer is cheap and good?

Well, says Clarkson, if a company's executives are totally clueless about such a well-publicized, if peripheral, issue, they are probably clueless about a lot of other things as well. To be blunt, they are probably not very bright, and people who are not bright tend to make dumb decisions. And when you're selling a product that depends as heavily on marketing strategy as beer does, you are in deep trouble if you are not aware of what's happening in the outside world.

Clarkson believes that employees, customers, suppliers, governments, and even competitors of a company have a stake in it. Management's job is to balance the stakeholders' often conflicting needs, and, when it succeeds, healthy profits are the inevitable by-product. What surprises Clarkson is that some people think these ideas are revolutionary. Successful companies have "known these things for years," Clarkson says.

What his thinking has been up against, however, is the notion popularized by U.S. economist Milton Friedman in the early 1960s that the only business of business is to make money and that the social responsibility of management extends no further than obeying the law. But Friedmanism is now on the wane. Under increasing pressure from consumers, lobby groups, shareholders, and governments, corporations may now be ready to take a fresh look at the code Clarkson champions.

He and his team see themselves as social scientists, not moralists. Still, Clarkson admits he can't explain scientifically why ethical companies are more profitable. All he knows is what his data reveal. During the 1980s, for example, his students investigated three large banks and discovered that the Toronto-Dominion Bank and the Royal Bank of Canada had better employment equity records than did the Bank of Montreal. Similarly, BMO had no retirement or termination counselling

(continued)

while the TD had a good program in place. In short, BMO didn't treat its people particularly well. And financially, it was the worst performer of the big banks during most of the decade.

By the same token, good behaviour can forestall a lot of grief. When Imperial Oil Ltd. of Toronto allowed gas to get into the sewer system in Timmins, Ontario, a few years ago, it immediately took responsibility for any costs of remedying the problem, until claims were settled by insurance companies. The incident, according to Clarkson "was off the front page in 24 hours."

Source: Excerpts from Daniel Stoffman, "Good Behavior and the Bottom Line," *Canadian Business*, May 1991, pp. 28–29.

Questions for Discussion

1. Comment on the statement that corporations who do not place business ethics as a top priority do not perform as well as those who do. Can you support this view?

2. Discuss the various stakeholders of the corporation who need to be concerned with the firm's ethical behaviour and their role in this.

CASE 5.2

OIL ON TRIAL

THE CASE AGAINST: The petroleum industry is a leading target of environmentalists, who point out that fossil-fuel combustion produces carbon dioxide—a greenhouse gas. Some activists have called for national targets to reduce carbon emissions. But Petro-Canada and other large oil companies have resisted such measures. The Canadian Petroleum Association—to which Petro-Canada belongs—has issued an environmental report that argues that there is not enough scientific information about global warming to justify targets.

According to Petro-Canada's director of environmental affairs, Michael Robertson, the company played a major role in drafting the CPA report. He added that Petro-Canada is examining its operations to find ways of cutting greenhouse emissions, but that the issue is complex. "Maybe an all-out strategy of CO_2 reduction is not the best way to go," says Robertson. "Certainly, there is no simple solution."

In conjunction with other major gasoline retailers, Petro-Canada argued against a federal plan to prohibit sales of leaded fuel as of December 1, 1990. Previously, Ottawa had said that the prohibition would take effect in 1993. Petro-Canada vice-president Robert Foulkes said that the company's "early resistance" to the amended deadline was "based on timing and cost." But once it became clear that Ottawa would not back down, Petro-Canada moved swiftly to remove leaded gasoline from its pumps. It also ran television commercials publicizing its decision.

The environmental group Probe International has criticized Petro-Canada's participation in oil exploration in Ecuador. To reach a remote drilling site, the company built a 9-kilometre road through the rain forest. Ecologists insist that the road will give rise to further development in the area, driving out Native groups. According to Petro-Canada, police guard the road to stop settlers from moving in.

Petro-Canada has repeatedly violated the Ontario environment ministry's guidelines for industrial discharges. In 1986, the ministry said that the company's refineries in Mississauga and Oakville were "areas of concern" because waste water from the plants contained toxic substances. Two years later, officials reported that the two refineries exceeded guidelines for industrial discharges during 13 of 96 inspections.

(continued)

THE CASE FOR: Several of Petro-Canada's recent advertising and promotional campaigns have focused on the environment. Last year, the Calgary-based company raised $218,000 for the Canadian branch of the World Wildlife Fund. The money was channelled into a program aimed at saving some of Canada's 195 endangered species. Currently, Petro-Canada is running a promotional campaign aimed at raising about $200,000 for a tree-planting program organized by Scouts Canada.

In 1989, Petro-Canada spent $37 million on environmental activities, including expenditures on refinery waste-water treatment plants and storage improvements at the company's refineries and terminals. The company says that it will spend $40 million over the next five years to guard against leakage from underground fuel-storage tanks.

As well, Petro-Canada says that it has developed a chemical treatment for the pulp-and-paper industry that is free of contaminants, which can turn into cancer-causing dioxins. And the company is building a plant in Edmonton that it says will produce a fuel additive that increases gasoline performance without causing additional harm to the environment.

Commentary: Most of the money that Petro-Canada spends on environmental concerns is devoted to corporate-image campaigns or ways to avoid environmental disasters such as oil spills. But, in future, rising public concern about global warming may pose a far greater challenge to the petroleum industry—particularly if Canada bows to international pressure to limit carbon emissions. Said Robertson: "Petro-Canada does not reject the idea that global warming is an issue, and one that we are playing a role to solve." But he added, "The solution has global ramifications." And, along with other oil companies, Petro-Canada will continue to run the risk of controversial accidents. In an era of acute concern about the environment, the oil industry can be an easy target. But with the demand for oil and gas continuing unabated, the companies can only hope to minimize the risks.

Source: Reprinted from "Oil and Image," Case Study, *Maclean's*, September 17, 1990, p. 63.

Questions for Discussion

1. Is Petro-Canada a good corporate citizen? Support your answer by citing examples of what environmentally conscious corporations are doing in this regard.

2. Is Petro-Canada disregarding the rigid requirements needed to be a good corporate citizen? Support your answer by citing examples of what you believe they should not engage in.

NOTES

1. Stephen Strauss, "Study Finds Hope for Ozone Layer," *The Globe and Mail*, August 26, 1993
2. Milton Friedman, *Capitalism and Freedom* (Chicago: University of Chicago Press, 1962).
3. World Commission on Environment and Development, *Our Common Future*, United Nations, 1987.
4. Bertrand Marotte, "Some Businessmen Say Ticket to Profit in the Future is Green," *Montreal Gazette*, October 19, 1990, p. A8.
5. *The Globe and Mail*, August 25, 1993
6. "Environmental Protection: The New Order of Business," *Royal Bank Reporter: To Conserve and Protect*, Spring 1990, pp. 19, 21.
7. George Vasic, "Learning to Navigate at Lower Altitudes," *Canadian Business*, September 1992, p. 27.

PHOTO CREDITS

MODULE

◆ MGT ◆

THE MANAGEMENT PROCESS

THE FOCUS OF THIS MODULE

1. To describe the management hierarchy in a large corporation and outline the duties of supervisory, middle, and top management

2. To discuss the technical, human relations, and conceptual skills required to varying degrees at all levels of management

3. To examine the interpersonal, informational, and decisional roles managers are required to undertake at various times

4. To consider how an organization's mission, goals, and objectives define managers' jobs and set standards for all employees

5. To describe the management functions of planning, organizing, leading, and controlling, and how they are interrelated

6. To discuss the steps in the decision-making process

7. To define the following terms:

KEY TERMS

management	objectives
management hierarchy	planning
supervisory managers	strategic planning
middle managers	tactical planning
top managers	organizing
technical skills	leading
human relations skills	autocratic leader
conceptual skills	democratic leader
mission	free-rein leader
mission statement	controlling
goals	decision making

FOR SHEER MIND-NUMBING boredom, it's hard to beat the work that's carried out at Revenue Canada's taxation centre in Winnipeg. The centre is a factory for processing an endless flow of millions of individual and corporate tax returns, as well as other tax-related forms—an unlikely place to go in search of workplace excellence. Yet the centre has managed to consistently lead the federal civil service in innovative management since the early 1980s.

It has implemented a number of pilot programs later adopted across the country. One of them reduced the tax reassessment process to four weeks from twelve. What's more, most people *like* working at the centre—the number of grievances filed are precious few, especially considering that employees are members of a union affiliated with the highly militant Public Service Alliance of Canada. "A lot of people have realized that it's easier to try to get along and work together than it is to fight and make everything an issue," says Reid Corrigall, who has been director of the centre for the past six years.

To help supervisors understand employees, Corrigall has carried on the centre's policy of holding two or three workshops annually that focus on values, motivation, and behavioural problems. And workers are involved in such substantive matters as setting production standards in certain departments. There is an undeniable sense of community, a sense of ownership among the staff. "We try to co-operate and get the employees involved in the decision making rather than being just chess pieces that you move around and tell what to do," he says. He expanded on the management workshops, which now range from outdoor adventure-training exercises designed to build trust, to seminars aimed at creating a better understanding of employees with disabilities.

Corrigall brought in stress management sessions for the entire staff. He also took a greater role in supporting the recreation association, which attracts employees at every level in social activities inside and outside the building. It's all predicated on a simple principle: if people could occasionally have fun on the job and meet or exceed their quotas, what harm could be done?

Still, there's no denying the "let's-get-on-with-it" attitude that pervades the building. It accounts for the enthusiasm for undertaking pilot projects. It also accounts for a widespread feeling that Winnipeg stands apart from more conventionally disciplined federal offices. "I've spoken to people in a lot of other government offices. It's just different here. We have a different attitude," says Arlene White, a former part-time employee who is now chief of operation services, one rung down from Corrigall. "We've never said, 'no.' We've always said, 'why not?'"

Source: Excerpts from Michael Ryval, "Reid Corrigall: Born Again Bureaucrats," *Canadian Business*, November 1991, p. 71. Reprinted with permission from Michael Ryval.

Good management skills are necessary in all types of organizations. Hospitals can be very busy places, with doctors, nurses, other hospital staff, and patients all requiring co-ordination. Designated areas of the hospital are established to act as central controlling areas where information can filter through to ensure that efficiency is maintained. Thus, hospital staff must be good managers in addition to having health professional skills.

G OOD MANAGEMENT REQUIRES more than understanding the principles of management. It requires the knack of recognizing how to fit them to an organization's special circumstances, whether that organization is a government department, a non-profit corporation, a giant multinational, or the corner grocery store. Yet the core principles remain the same.

MANAGEMENT AND MANAGERS

In any organization, **management** is the process of planning, organizing, leading, and controlling its various resources in order to meet its goals. Although many managers have a technical background, their role as managers is to see that things *get* done rather than to actually *do* them. In a one-person operation, of course, seeing that things get done probably includes the doing, but in a large organization, management may not only involve supervising production workers, but also managing the supervisors. We tend to think of managers as managing people, but it is equally important co-ordinate all the factors of production efficiently and effectively. Figure 6.1 indicates the management process for a business enterprise.

The principles of management work virtually anywhere: administrators of hospitals, community colleges, government agencies, and charitable and volunteer organizations have similar responsibilities to

management
The process of planning, organizing, leading, and controlling the various resources of an organization, in order to meet its goals

FIGURE 6.1 • MANAGING THE FACTORS OF PRODUCTION

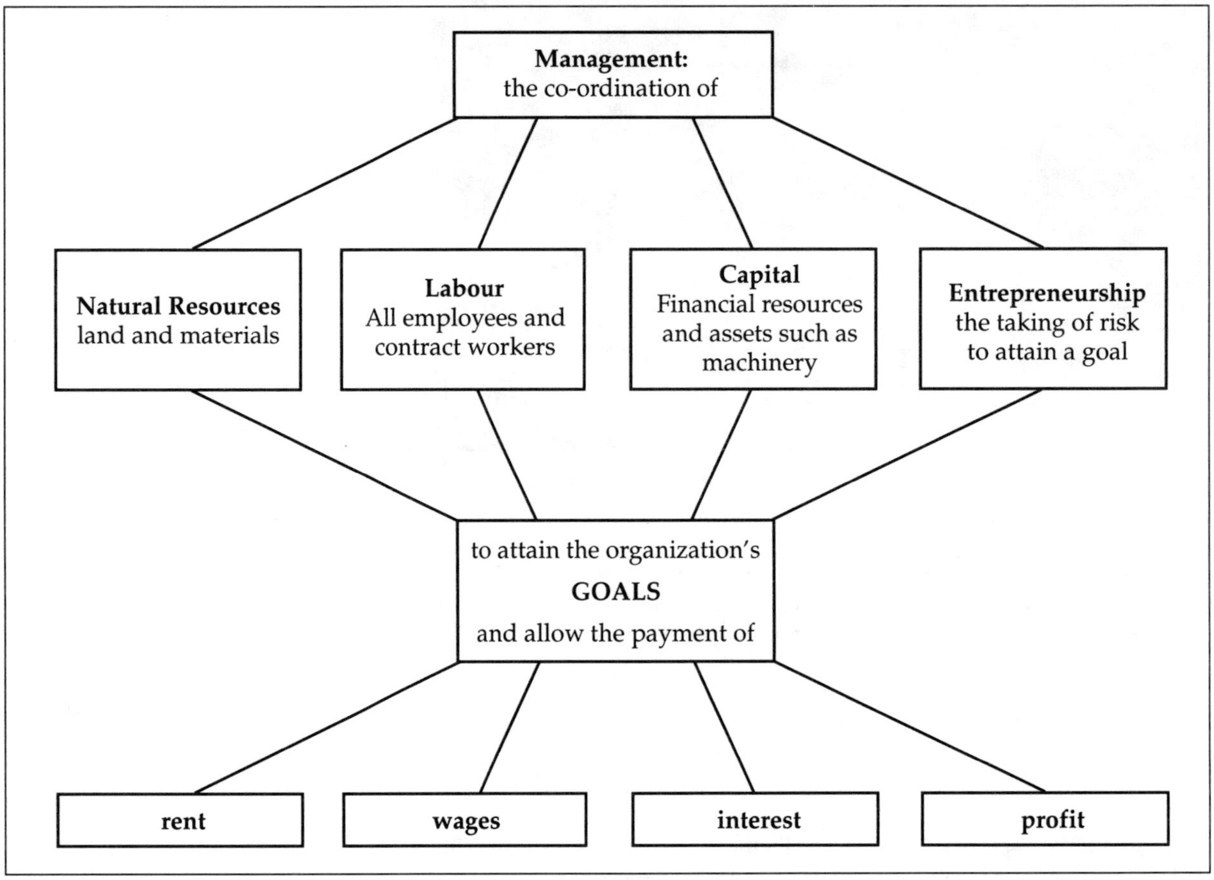

```
                    Management:
                   the co-ordination of

  Natural Resources    Labour          Capital        Entrepreneurship
  land and materials   All employees   Financial      the taking of risk
                       and             resources      to attain a goal
                       contract        and assets
                       workers         such as
                                       machinery

                   to attain the organization's
                          GOALS
                   and allow the payment of

     rent           wages           interest          profit
```

those who work in profit-oriented businesses. The goals of organizations differ, and probably the greatest differences within them stem from whether the aim is to make a profit or to provide a public service, but in all settings, success or failure depends on how basic management principles are applied.

Levels of Management

In a large organization there are several levels of managers within the **management hierarchy**. Management is usually divided into three categories: supervisory, middle, and top management. At Revenue Canada's taxation centre in Winnipeg, for example, supervisors work with the employees who process the tax returns. Arlene White, as chief of operation services, is part of middle management. Reid Corrigal, as director, can be considered top management.

Supervisory managers are those directly responsible for employee performance and productivity. Supervisory managers have the important task of running a smooth operation "on the front lines." They oversee the level of production on a daily (and sometimes hourly) basis. Their focus is on action and meeting short-range, concrete objectives.

management hierarchy
The various levels of management within an organization, usually divided into three categories: supervisory, middle, and top management

supervisory managers
The level of management directly responsible for employee performance

Supervisory managers must work closely with plant operators to oversee the day-to-day operations of the business. The reviewing of schedules and control charts is done on a regular basis by the supervisor to determine if the process needs to be adjusted. Supervisory managers and operators discuss their observations and come to an agreement on what adjustments should occur. The supervisory manager is directly responsible for meeting the daily production objectives.

Middle managers typically have titles such as plant manager and department head. Their responsibility is to plan and implement detailed procedures to meet the long-range goals of the organization. Middle managers are usually in charge of a particular section of the organization or of a service, such as payroll management, that affects all sections. They are skilled in making decisions such as determining the number of salespeople for a given territory, how to start up and manage a new branch, how to budget for and select new equipment, or how to evaluate and improve employee performance.

middle managers
The level of management responsible for planning and implementing procedures to meet the organization's long-range goals

Top managers include the president, vice-presidents, and other key executives. Their priority is the development of long-range plans for the oganization as a whole. For example, the introduction of new products or the decision to enter foreign markets overseas is the responsibility of top management. Top managers keep an eye out for changes in the external environment. In addition, they assess the impact of changes in government regulations or taxes and pay attention to the organization's role as a good corporate citizen in the communities where it operates. Top managers must avoid the temptation to lose sight of long-range goals by devoting too much time to immediate problems, crises, and short-term objectives better handled by managers lower in the hierarchy.

top managers
The level of management responsible for the development of long-range plans for the organization as a whole and representing its interests in the community

This description applies to the management hierarchy in a large corporation. Smaller operations will have fewer managers and a less extensive hierarchy, but the same tasks must be carried out. Managers will often serve at more than one of the levels as described here—and will need all the appropriate managerial skills.

Managerial Skills

What makes a good manager? A manager needs skills in three basic areas: in operational techniques, in human relations, and in grasping concepts. How much emphasis a manager places on each of these areas depends on the specific job and the manager's position in the hierarchy.

technical skills

An understanding of, and proficiency in performing the tasks associated with a particular job

Technical skills are the understanding of and proficiency in performing the tasks associated with a particular job, such as drafting, manufacturing, or accounting. Technical skills are needed to supervise the work of those actually doing the job, to discuss its requirements with the workers or with other managers, to instruct sales personnel in the technical specifications of a new product, and to ensure the availability of appropriate tools for the department. Recently, many managers have been expected to understand the usefulness and limitations of computer systems in their technical area and for the organization as a whole. Technical skills are most important for supervisory managers, but middle and top managers also need some understanding of the technical aspects of tasks the organization is involved in if they are to make realistic plans and set attainable goals.

human relations skills

The ability to work effectively with and through other employees, providing direction and leadership to subordinates and conveying information to other managers

Human relations skills, often called social or "people" skills, are the ability not only to get on well with others but also to work effectively with and through them, providing direction and leadership when needed to subordinates, working well as a group member, and conveying necessary information to other unit managers and to senior management. Communication is the "glue" in all organizations. One aspect that is often overlooked by junior managers is the ability to communicate effectively with their own superiors. Human relations skills are required by all managers, especially as they move up the hierarchy.

FIGURE 6.2 • THE MANAGEMENT HIERARCHY AND MANAGEMENT SKILLS

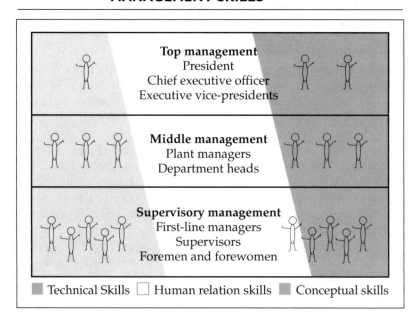

Top management
President
Chief executive officer
Executive vice-presidents

Middle management
Plant managers
Department heads

Supervisory management
First-line managers
Supervisors
Foremen and forewomen

■ Technical Skills ☐ Human relation skills ■ Conceptual skills

Conceptual skills are that special ability to see details beneath the surface and at the same time keep in mind the "big picture." This requires not only understanding the responsibilities of each unit or department but also grasping the complex interconnections among the various parts of the organization and the position of the organization in the outside world. Conceptual skills are very important for top managers who must interpret information in the context of a changing environment and make difficult, sometimes risky, decisions in planning for the future. Managers who reach the top of their firms may have started out using their technical expertise in a specialized area, such as engineering, but their success at the higher levels is largely determined by their ability to appreciate the contributions of all departments to the overall goals of the organization—from human resources to finance, from manufacturing to sales, and from research to public relations.

Figure 6.2 indicates the relative importance of each of the three types of skills at the various levels of the hierarchy. A real advantage possessed by those with strong conceptual and human relations skills is their ability to transfer these skills to different settings. This strength gives a top manager the flexibility to move easily into a senior position in another company or industry. It is also not unusual for high-ranking government employees to change careers by moving into the private sector. Compared with those who only have technical backgrounds in specialized areas, people with strong conceptual and human relations skills are clearly more mobile and more sought after as leaders in both government and industry. Issues in Business 6.1 discusses the skills required by a chief executive officer in the 1990s. Developing Your Business Skills features Bob Lunney, who has applied management theory in his position as chief of the Peel Regional Police (Peel is a rapidly growing community near Toronto).

conceptual skills
The ability to see each part of the organization in a unified whole and to judge what goals are realistic in a changing environment

---

ISSUES IN BUSINESS 6.1

THEY WALK ON WATER

COMPARED WITH EVEN a few years ago, finding the right CEO is a corporate search for the Holy Grail. The perfect CEO is difficult to describe, rare to find, and even harder to hire. The reason isn't a dearth of candidates from which to choose. It's simply that the job suddenly got tougher. Fiercer competitors, flatter management pyramids, fast-changing technology, and tougher business conditions all conspire to make the CEO's job more demanding than before—and, therefore, irresistible to the few who can handle it.

In the no-nonsense '90s, marketing geniuses, financial wizards, and other corporate specialists are still in demand. But according to many headhunters surveyed by *Canadian Business*, the overwhelming demand these days is for CEOs who are strong not just in one area of corporate expertise but in almost all of them. Call them leaders, or visionaries, or Renaissance men or women, what it boils down to is inspired generalship.

(continued)

Today, the first job description to change as the result of changing business conditions is that of CEO. Companies now consider the position too demanding to be filled by narrow-gauge experts, no matter how awesome their expertise. A legendary talent in corporate finance, for instance, might work wonders for the company's balance sheet, but will he be able to crack badly needed markets in Japan or Europe? A superbly skilled engineer might get projects built on time and on budget, but will he be able to attract people in a tight labour market?

True leaders can do all of these things and more. Increasingly, this multifaceted quality is what companies are looking for in their next CEO. According to the country's top executive head-hunters, the specifications they are being handed demand nothing less than visionary leadership. Or, in the words of Compton, "the one who walks on water."

Shaping these specifications are some very challenging business conditions, all slamming the corporation at the same time. The result is that the real task for today's CEO is not to manage a company so much as to transform it. Indeed, the ability to master change is the No. 1 requirement executive recruiters now receive from companies shopping for a new CEO. "Change has overwhelmed the evolutionary forces in most corporations," says Herman Smith, president of executive search firm Herman Smith International Inc. "They want change now and demand a CEO who can hit the ground running."

As business increasingly shifts to longer-term perspective, companies are putting far more emphasis on human resources and team building. For the CEO, this means that, instead of barking orders to a second-in-command, he or she now works directly with far more people—listening, persuading, and gently steering the team toward consensus.

U.S. studies indicate that as many as 20 percent of new CEO appointments now go to out-siders, compared with only 7 percent in the 1960s. And a recent Canadian study of 300 senior executives (presidents, vice-presidents, and directors general) conducted by Sobeco found that 71 percent expected to join another company within the next five years. It is estimated that the ratio would have been more like 30 percent a decade ago.

Many of today's CEOs are finance- and control-oriented appointees of the early 1980s. Increasingly, companies want their successors to be builders who can develop new products, pen-etrate new markets, and create new teams of skilled people. "Downsizing the company is an enervating experience, and there are an awful lot of tired CEOs out there. Now, everyone seems to be looking for a CEO who can really make things happen."

Source: Excerpts from Randall Litchfield, "They Walk on Water," *Canadian Business*, September 1990, pp. 46, 47, 49. Reprinted with permission from Randall Litchfield.

Questions for Discussion

1. What are regarded as the most important skills for chief executive officers in the 1990s? How has the situation changed from the early 1980s?

2. What changing business conditions must the new CEO be expected to meet?

DEVELOPING YOUR BUSINESS SKILLS

CHIEF BOB LUNNEY: PEEL REGIONAL POLICE

Chief Bob Lunney likes to pop downstairs to the squad room of Ontario's Peel Regional Police headquarters from time to time to watch his officers change shift. The sergeant might order them to "be careful out there" as they head for their patrol cars. But Lunney doesn't have to say a word. The whole force, and everybody else, got his message long ago: "Go out and give good customer service."

"I want you to think of me as a CEO," he once said to a bemused marketing expert. "I have a staff of 1,400, I run a 400-vehicle fleet, I do market research, and I try to deliver the right products in the most efficient, cost-conscious way." Products? Market research? Does this sound like a public servant talking? Yessiree. "I regard us as being in the police business. I know we have public and legal responsibilities, and there are transcending issues," says Lunney. "Nevertheless, effective management is at the source of good policing and a good police organization."

Lunney tries to put his money where his mouth is. As a public servant, he can't think about increasing the bottom line, but that doesn't stop him from being motivated by expenditure control. His budget, which grew a healthy 20 percent a year in the late 1980s to $94 million by 1990, increased only $5 million last year, and Lunney realizes he may have to make do with less in the future. He admits that's a tough challenge in a region like Peel, 680,000 citizens strong and growing at the rate of 20,000 "new customers" a year.

After doing a stint with the RCMP and heading up forces in Edmonton and Winnipeg, Lunney knew the first place he had to look to cut costs at Peel. "Over 85 percent of our budget is salaries," he says. "So it's the person-hours that we have to maximize." Lunney combed through the organization to identify every position that didn't require the skills of a highly trained police officer. Soon he had civilians taking over such chores as entering police reports directly into the computer over the phone, a job civilians could do more cheaply and efficiently, and a task that cops loathe. And he boosted morale by investing in information technology to further streamline the administrative process. One time- and labour-saving device he bought was a document imaging system. Now records go right into the central computer instead of having to be microfilmed the old-fashioned way.

Lunney has earned some fans at the board level. "In an organization where resources are always taxed, he can focus people's energies and get the whole system working at full efficiency," says Miles Obradovich, Toronto lawyer and chairman of the Peel Police Services Board. "He's created a real vibrancy."

Trimming administrative costs was only one step for Lunney. Now he had his highly skilled workers doing more real policing, but were they delivering what people wanted? Lunney found out that there was a big appetite for improved emergency response and crime prevention, but that other services weren't in demand. "Regulatory law enforcement isn't making it anymore," he says. "People wouldn't ever notice if we didn't do it. Perhaps we should spin it off to the private sector."

Lunney has a message for those who say you can't do anything unless you can change the whole system. "The trap is in feeling powerless," he says. "You've got to relax and start to think creatively."

An avid student of management theory, he maintains that public servants can use sound

(continued)

business principles within the system. "You've got to watch what's happening in the private sector, what the buzzes are out there. Learn from what they're doing in the way of organizational configuration and cost-cutting. That's the way to go." One concept he loves is on-time delivery, which he's applying to the force's in-house shoe store. Soon the shop that stocks 400 pairs of boots will order when there's a need and reduce costly shelf time. Now if only the chief could apply the on-time delivery principle to dealing with citizens in distress.

Source: Reprinted from Wendy Trueman, "Chief Bob Lunney: Born Again Bureaucrats," *Canadian Business*, November 1991, pp. 64, 65, 67. Reprinted with permission from Wendy Trueman.

Question for Discussion

1. List examples of the technical, human relations, and conceptual skills Bob Lunney uses in his work.

Managerial Roles

Henry Mintzberg of McGill University observed and recorded the day-to-day activities of managers and characterized these activities as fitting into three major categories: interpersonal relationships, the transfer of information, and decision making. Within these categories he identified ten specific roles that a manager may be called upon to perform. The categories and roles are outlined in Table 6.1.

TABLE 6.1 • MINTZBERG'S MANAGERIAL ROLES

Category	Role	Description
Interpersonal	Figurehead	Performs ceremonial and symbolic duties: greeting visitors, signing legal documents
	Leader	Directs and motivates subordinates: training, counselling
	Liaison	Maintains contacts both inside and outside organization through mail, phone calls, meetings
Informational	Monitor	Seeks and receives information on the organization and its external environment
	Disseminator	Forwards information to other members of the organization; sends memos and reports, makes phone calls
	Spokesperson	Transmits information on the organization through speeches, reports, memos
Decisional	Entrepreneur	Initiates projects, identifies new ideas, delegates responsibility to others
	Disturbance handler	Takes corrective action during disputes or crises; resolves conflicts among subordinates; adapts to crises brought about by external changes
	Resource allocator	Decides who gets resources: scheduling, budgeting, setting priorities
	Negotiator	Represents department during negotiation of union contracts, sales, purchases, budgets

Source: Adapted from Henry Mintzberg, *The Nature of Managerial Work* (New York: Harper & Row, 1973), pp. 92–93, and Henry Mintzberg, "Managerial Work: Analysis from Observation," *Management Science* 18 (1971), pp. B97–B110. © 1973 by Henry Mitzberg. Reprinted by permission of HarperCollins Publishers, Inc.

Though all managers perform all these roles to some extent at various times, the proportion of time managers spend in any of them depends on the work they are assigned to do. For example, the leader role is most required at lower levels. Entrepreneur and disturbance-handler roles come into play at all levels of the hierarchy, whereas most of the other roles are most often exercised by upper management.

BUSINESS REVIEW 6.1

1. Describe the skills that are required for managers to be successful.

2. What are the ten managerial roles that have been identified by Mintzberg? Give a brief example of a manager performing each of these roles.

MISSION, GOALS, AND OBJECTIVES

Managers in any organization need to know what the organization's **mission** is—its reason for existence. This is usually articulated in a formal **mission statement** that declares in broad terms the organization's field of endeavour, its intended markets, and its philosophy of business. Without such an understanding, management, and the organization as a whole, will drift and operate at cross-purposes. For example, if a company's mission is to produce utility furniture at budget prices for a mass market, a purchasing manager should not be looking for delicate weaves and fancy velvet upholstery materials. Having a well-understood mission is so important to success that even if a company does not draw up a mission statement, the provincial and federal governments insist on a statement of purpose in a business's articles of incorporation.

To fulfil its mission an organization needs to set goals. **Goals** are detailed descriptions of what the organization as a whole hopes to achieve within a stated period of time. Peter Drucker identifies eight areas in which goals should be set.[1] Our furniture company might have the following goals for the next five years:

1. *Market standing:* to place its products in all major budget department stores, lumber stores, and hardware store chains, and to double its market share in Canada; to expand to test locations in the United States and in Asia.
2. *Innovation:* to develop techniques to streamline furniture components to make many of them interchangeable for greater efficiency in the plant and for the convenience of customers.
3. *Productivity:* to increase production by 50 percent with a minimally larger workforce.
4. *Physical and financial resources:* to modernize the plant in British Columbia and establish production facilities in New Brunswick to serve the eastern market, both to be financed by corporate bonds and a new share offering.
5. *Profitability:* to maintain profits at their present level for the next

mission
An organization's reason for existence

mission statement
A formal statement of an organization's field of endeavour, its markets, and its philosophy of business

goals
Detailed descriptions of what an organization as a whole hopes to achieve within a stated period of time.

two years, with the understanding that they will be lower in the third and fourth year of the period when the new production facility is tooling up but that they will return to present levels in the fifth year.

6. *Managerial performance and development:* to train present and newly hired first-line supervisors in the new techniques and for increased responsibility; allow middle management to shrink through attrition; and broaden responsibilities of remaining managers.

7. *Worker performance and attitude:* to encourage craftsmanship through apprenticeship programs operated with local community colleges; to reduce work-related accidents in each and every year; to introduce an employee profit-sharing plan when the new facilities come onstream.

8. *Public responsibility:* to use raw materials from local sources where possible; to increase the proportion of waste products that are reused or recycled from 40 percent to 95 percent; to develop a special workshop where for a nominal cost the company's standard furniture can be adapted to meet the needs of people with disabilities.

objectives

Specific, often measurable, results that divisions and departments must achieve if an organization is to meet its overall goals

Objectives for the various divisions and departments within the organization are based on these goals. **Objectives** are specific, often measurable, results that the various parts of the organization must achieve if the organization is to meet its overall goals. For example, the design department at the furniture company will have to redesign products to ensure that the interchangeable components work well in every application. The manager will need to ensure that this objective is met early in the five-year planning period so that the production managers can assess the adjustments to the production process that will be required and have them in place at the appropriate time. The vice-president of finance must prepare a prospectus for the new share offering. When the New Brunswick facility is ready, the human resources department must be ready to transfer some managerial employees from the parent operation and to hire workers and other managers locally. Improving productivity may involve setting specific numerical targets for each shift.

Objectives as Standards

Goals and objectives are not only definite statements of what the organization wants to accomplish, they are also a tool for managers to evaluate performance. If the department is not reaching the standards set by the objectives, managers can take corrective action either within the department or by enlisting the support or co-operation of other departments.

Regularly checking performance against objectives may occasionally lead to reassessment of those objectives. Organizations must be alert to changes that make goals unattainable—or that create opportunities to set even more ambitious goals.

Goals and Profits

It is generally accepted that the overall goal of any business is to make money. Why, then, should a business concentrate on anything else? Peter Drucker points out that too tight a focus on the next balance sheet leads to short-term thinking that may blind management to the health of the entire firm and to future risks and opportunities. Profits and coherent goals and objectives are two sides of the same coin.

As illustrated in Figure 6.1, profits make a firm's owners happy. They give investors confidence and make additional growth possible. They maintain good relationships with suppliers. They provide wages for employees and resources for employee training and development. They allow the firm to improve products to achieve greater customer satisfaction and to build better relations with the wider society. And long-term profitability is achieved through attending to the needs of all these stakeholders—owners, investors, suppliers, employees, customers, and society.

BUSINESS REVIEW 6.2

1. Mission, goal, and objective all mean roughly the same in everyday speech. Explain how each term is used in the context of business.

2. Peter Drucker popularized the concept that objectives can be used as standards for performance 40 years ago in a classic text, *Management for Results*. Using the example of the furniture company (or another organization of your choice), show how objectives might be used as standards in three specific departments.

MANAGERIAL FUNCTIONS

Success in business is never accidental. It is accomplished by careful management of resources to achieve specific goals. The manager's job is to co-ordinate raw materials, trained personnel, equipment, and entrepreneurial ideas.

Analysts say that all managers perform four basic functions: planning, organizing, leading, and controlling. (Sometimes they break these functions down into more specific responsibilities such as staffing, communicating, co-ordinating, motivating, innovating, and evaluating.) The four functions are all equally important and, of course, they are interdependent. In a real business situation, managers are performing—or thinking about—all activities all the time, becoming experts at developing procedures for leading and controlling while they are planning and organizing. Though the basic management functions are performed at *all* levels of the management hierarchy, top and middle managers devote more time to the planning function, and supervisory managers spend more time on the leading function.

Planning

Planning is the development of goals and objectives and defining courses of action to achieve them. Managers must plan in order to use resources without wasting time and energy. Planning includes many considerations, such as how a project is to be initially financed, which

planning
The development of goals and objectives and defining courses of action to achieve them

resources are required and when, what the various stages are in the project, and which people need to be involved at each stage. A good plan is a carefully designed and detailed sequence of events and actions.

However, a plan is never complete. Managers must always be ready to change their plans. Businesses do not operate in isolation. Legal, political, social, and economic influences may have dramatic effects on organizations and the markets they serve. Organizations themselves change. Managers must be prepared to adjust their plans in response to both the external environment and the state of their own operations. Paying close attention to the world outside the organization and conditions within it helps managers to fine-tune their plans before minor problems become major crises.

strategic planning
Development of overall goals and of long-range strategies to achieve them, including allocation of resources

Strategic planning looks at the "big picture," the overall goals of the organization, and development of strategies to achieve them, including allocation of resources. Strategic plans have a major influence on a company's course of action over several years. Managers must never lose sight of organizational goals, without which their plans would have no focus or direction.

tactical planning
Planning the implementation of specific aspects of strategic plans with a focus on the immediate or near future

Tactical planning looks at the practical issues of implementation once strategic plans have been developed. Tactical plans focus on narrower, shorter-range objectives in the present and near future in order to implement overall strategic plans.

Strategic planning is typically performed at the highest level of the organization, while tactical planning is typically performed at middle and supervisory levels. Although there are clear differences between strategic and tactical planning, the two processes must be coordinated and integrated. Strategic planners must be realistic and not lose sight of practical constraints. Tactical planners must not get bogged down in detail and lose sight of organizational objectives.

Organizing

organizing
Assigning tasks and resources to accomplish those tasks to departments and individuals

In the process of **organizing**, managers bring together human and material resources in an effective structure to accomplish organizational objectives. Factors to be considered in organizing work into manageable units include: a complete inventory of activities and required resources involved at each stage of the project; logical groupings for the various activities and the assignment of the activities with the necessary resources; appropriate departments, positions, or individuals.

Organizing also includes anticipating long-term staffing needs according to organizational goals and objectives. Such advance preparation can identify people already in the organization capable of assuming responsibility for certain tasks, or bring competent people into the organization as they are needed.

One approach to organizing that has become common is for management to delegate specific organizing tasks to task forces or teams of employees, often including non-management workers, who bring a different perspective to the problems. Issues in Business 6.2 discusses one company's use of teams to organize work.

ISSUES IN BUSINESS 6.2

TEAM PLAYERS

JOHN BATY KNOWS a thing or two about corporate task forces. A twelve-year veteran of Consumers Packaging Inc., Baty left the Toronto head office in January 1991 to head up the human resources department at the company's glass container plant in nearby Bramalea. The plant had been a chronic underperformer in recent years. Nearly every aspect of its operation needed improvement. To do that, Baty and his colleagues set up a number of special committees at the plant—communications teams, he calls them—to solve various problems. There are twelve teams in all, and Baty sits on all of them, playing the role of "facilitator."

Now, such a network may seem extreme for one plant (and a good indication of the complexity of Baty's job). But special teams and task forces are increasingly common in Canadian companies. In theory, the mandate of these task forces can vary greatly, from simple fast-track product development to a complete corporate restructuring. The task force's field of action can be narrow (confined to a single department, for example) or almost frighteningly broad (such as improving customer service in every aspect of a company's operation). Responsibility for supervising such projects can be vested in teams as small as two or three, or handed to committees of a dozen managers. Task forces of varying sizes, with various mandates, can even be sprinkled throughout an organization, from head office down to a local service department.

In practice, however, the Consumers task-force project mirrors current management trends in two important respects. First, it is an innovative response to the need to improve a plant's performance in the face of intense domestic and foreign competition. Consumers, for example, has seldom used task forces in the past. Instead, it has tended to hand problem-solving assignments to particular senior managers—which sometimes had the effect of absolving everyone else of responsibility for the problem.

Second, the Consumers program, however exceptional in its scope and ambition, is part of a larger corporate purpose. Thanks to the current vogue for "leadership" and "vision" among CEOs, committees such as those at Consumers are convened not to design a broad course of action, but to determine the details of a strategic vision already sketched at the top.

At Consumers' Bramalea plant, for example, each of the twelve teams is free to determine its own agenda. "The only thing we demand is that they meet once a month and keep detailed minutes," says Baty. Well, that's not quite all. The team must somehow find ways to improve the plant's performance according to eight key indicators already designated by senior management. These criteria range from general indices of productivity and profitability to measures of some of the plant's specific problems, such as absenteeism. Further, the indices must improve within a very specific time frame—by the end of this year, when new goals will be set as part of a continuing process of improvement.

Within this new context, the success of a corporate task force is still primarily a function of the tractability of the problem at hand. But other, subtler criteria also come into play. Context is perhaps the most important. Who decided to have a task force in the first place? What is the project's relationship to the company's strategic vision? Is the CEO behind it, or is it just the pet brainchild of an ambitious vice-president? William Band, partner with the Coopers & Lybrand Consulting Group in Toronto and head of the firm's Centre for Excellence in Customer Satisfaction, says simply: "I'm convinced that unless senior management is committed, positive change won't happen."

(continued)

But even an initiative from the top comes with no guarantee. If the CEO lacks the support of his executive team, task forces attempting change may find themselves stymied by indifferent or hostile VPs.

Baty offers a checklist to task-force success. "First," he says, "there has to be a real performance gap—that is, a quantifiable shortfall between the existing situation and the corporate ideal. Second, that performance gap must be generally recognized. People who don't believe there is a problem are hardly going to be able to help solve it. Third, the team must have the ability to solve the problem."

Baty is quick to stress that "ability" means several things: "It can encompass the skills of the individual members of the task force, and also the level of support the team enjoys among senior management." Nothing, for instance, can be more vital to a task force's success than adequate time—how much of a team member's own time has been freed for the job during the day or week and how long the team has been given to finish its assignment.

The biggest obstacle to task-force success, however, can be internal dissension. Organizational conflict is often built into the problem itself. In fact, it may be the problem. At Consumers' Bramalea plant, one of the first steps to improving performance was correcting a drastic drop-off in productivity during shift changes. The plant's efficiency is measured in terms of the percentage of total output represented by acceptable glass containers. During the twice-daily shift changes, output would drop by as much as 30 percent.

The problem was exacerbated by a conflict between what the plant's people call the "hot end" and the "cold end" of the production line. The hot end forms the bottles and jars that make their way down the line to the cold end, where they are packed for shipment to Consumers' clients. The cold end, meanwhile, is responsible primarily for quality control. The packing room's performance is measured on an index of customer complaints and returns, and the cold end's automated equipment rejects defective bottles. The trouble is, workers at the hot end receive bonuses based on rejection rates—the fewer the defects, the fatter the bonuses—leaving employees at the hot end of the line wondering if their buddies at the cold end are being too fussy.

In Consumers' case, the task forces helped crystallize the realization that the shift changes had become pretty sloppy. The teams—composed of managers, supervisors, and employees from both ends of the line—managed to correct the problem by instituting a mandatory communication system during shift changes. Outgoing employees now must inform their replacements of the status of the line and any problems encountered in the previous twelve hours. Incoming teams at both the hot and cold ends of the plant communicate with each other, to ensure that their understanding of the line's status jibes.

It was not an acrimonious process— "no yelling or screaming," says Baty. "Each side readily acknowledged the lack of discipline during shift changes and readily agreed to do what was necessary to fix the problem. And the shift change shortfall already has begun to improve.

"Our results from January and February were pretty much as usual," says Baty. "But in March we almost hit all of the eight performance criteria we'd been targeting for January of next year." Was he surprised? "Yes and no. Our teams worked awfully hard the past three months to get us out of the hole. At first I wondered if the March results weren't something of a fluke. But April and May were also good months."

"You know," says Baty, "If you go into these programs expecting that you'll get ideas that will make you a million dollars, you're wasting your time. It's a question of small wins. It's getting employees to focus on those little things you can do a little bit better that can make all the difference in the world."

Source: Excerpts from David Evans, "Team Players," *Canadian Business,* August 1991, pp. 29–31. Reprinted with permission from David Evans.

(continued)

Questions for Discussion

1. Why are teams and task forces so popular today? What are the benefits realized by firms utilizing them?

2. What factors contribute to success in the use of teams to organize work?

Leading

Planning and organizing set the stage and assign roles. **Leading** is the direction and motivation of employees to meet the goals and objectives of the organization. While leading, managers assign tasks, clarify procedures, give direct orders, correct errors, and assist employees to avoid similar errors in future. Work will be best accomplished if the leader establishes an atmosphere where workers are truly motivated to achieve the tasks assigned.

Leading, or directing as it is sometimes called, quite logically is most time-consuming at the supervisory level where managers are working to achieve tasks with production workers and other non-management employees. Leading is the human relations aspect of managing.

What makes a good leader? Research that has concentrated on isolating leadership characteristics has identified three major traits—empathy, self-awareness, and objectivity in dealing with others. Table 6.2 examines these three traits and the sort of questions leaders are continually (if subconsciously) asking themselves.

Leaders have differing approaches to leadership. For example, **autocratic leaders** make decisions unilaterally. They do not believe in consultation and they do not welcome comments, suggestions, or any

leading
The direction and motivation of employees to meet the goals and objectives of the organization

autocratic leader
A leader who make decisions without consulting subordinates

TABLE 6.2 • TRAITS OF A GOOD LEADER

A good leader should possess
1. *Empathy*, the ability to place oneself in another's position
   "How does the worker view this new rule?"
   "Will the worker be able to see its value if I explain it this way?"
   "Whom does the worker trust, and whom does he or she fear?"

2. *Self-awareness*, knowledge of oneself
   "What are my strengths? My weaknesses?"
   "What do my people think of me?" "Do they consider me fair and objective?"
   "Am I too gruff in dealing with others?"

3. *Objectivity in interpersonal relations*
   "Am I objective in dealing with my subordinates, or do I react too emotionally?"
   "Do I maintain a detached view in reacting to subordinates' behaviour?"
   "Can I be empathetic and objective at the same time?"

FIGURE 6.3 • CONTINUUM OF LEADERSHIP STYLES AND BEHAVIOUR

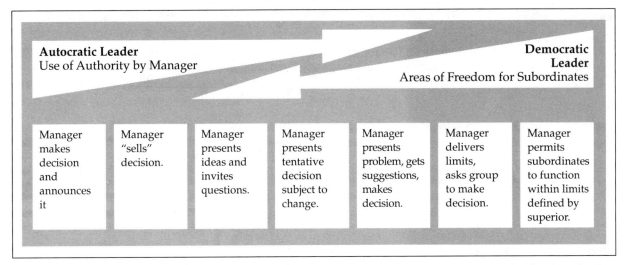

Autocratic Leader
Use of Authority by Manager

Democratic Leader
Areas of Freedom for Subordinates

| Manager makes decision and announces it | Manager "sells" decision. | Manager presents ideas and invites questions. | Manager presents tentative decision subject to change. | Manager presents problem, gets suggestions, makes decision. | Manager delivers limits, asks group to make decision. | Manager permits subordinates to function within limits defined by superior. |

Source: Reprinted by permission of the *Harvard Business Review.* An exhibit from "How to Choose a Leadership Pattern" by Robert Tannenbaum and Warren Schmidt (May/June 1973). Copyright © 1973 by the President and Fellows of Harvard College; all rights reserved.

democratic leader

A leader who involves subordinates in decision making

free-rein leader

A leader who believes in minimal supervision, leaving most decisions to subordinates

other form of input from others. They like to tell people exactly what to do and how to perform. In direct contrast, **democratic leaders** encourage the involvement of their subordinates. They welcome input and listen to feedback, and they prefer to reach consensus on issues, even if it takes more time. An extreme form of democratic leaders are **free-rein leaders**, who believe in minimal supervision, leaving almost all decision making and problem solving to subordinates. Figure 6.3 illustrates the continuum of leadership styles and behaviour.

The best leadership style, of course, varies with the circumstances, changing according to the characteristics of the leader, the followers, and the situation. Some leaders simply will not encourage or even allow subordinates to participate in decision making. And some followers do not have the ability or the desire to assume such responsibility. The actual work environment may be the deciding factor. If the situation requires an immediate solution, there may be no time to consult subordinates. But when there is no urgency, the involvement of an entire staff may provide a solution that workers can feel is their own.

Managers are increasingly moving toward a more democratic style of leadership. They find that workers involved in decision making tend to be more interested in the overall organization and may be more motivated to contribute to organizational objectives than those not so involved. Of course, force of circumstance may require autocratic leadership. For example, if there is to be a 10 percent reduction in staff, those subject to being laid off are not likely to be consulted on who should go.

We now accept that one ideal style of leadership does not exist. Management professor Fred Fiedler has concluded that effective leadership is determined by the kind of power the leader holds, the complexity of the responsibilities to be carried out, and the profiles of the workers involved in getting the job done. Interestingly, one of his key findings is that leaders who stress task accomplishments are quite successful in both extremely straightforward and extremely complex situations but in moderately difficult situations leaders who place more emphasis on participation and consultation are apt to be most suitable.

Controlling

Controlling is the ongoing evaluation of performance to determine whether a project is on schedule and meeting its objectives. Whereas planning is mostly ideas on paper, controlling measures the success of the planning stages by evaluating results. Controlling is a process that can be described in three basic steps:

controlling
The ongoing evaluation of performance and correction of deviations from standards

1. Setting standards,
2. Collecting information to discover any deviations from standards,
3. Taking corrective action to bring any deviations into line.

The temperature control system shown in Figure 6.4 provides a good illustration of the controlling function. First, the objective of a temperature setting, say 20°C, is established. Then information about the actual temperature in the building is collected and compared with the objective, and a decision based on this comparison is made. If we assume it is winter, when the temperature drops below 20°C, the decision is to activate the furnace until it reaches the desired level. If the furnace drives the temperature too high, the decision is to turn off the furnace and allow the outside temperature to cool the building back to 20°C.

Controlling is perhaps the most neglected of the functions of management because people tend to be reluctant to change carefully

FIGURE 6.4 • A TEMPERATURE CONTROL SYSTEM

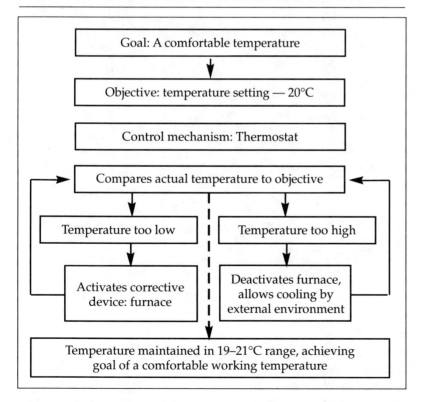

Goal: A comfortable temperature

Objective: temperature setting — 20°C

Control mechanism: Thermostat

Compares actual temperature to objective

Temperature too low

Temperature too high

Activates corrective device: furnace

Deactivates furnace, allows cooling by external environment

Temperature maintained in 19–21°C range, achieving goal of a comfortable working temperature

worked out plans. But businesses occasionally experience deviations from organizational goals. If there are changes in profitability, return on investment, or in market share, managers may have to step in and adjust price structure, locate different sources of raw materials, change methods of production, or recommend a new package design. These kinds of decisions are based on the availability of accurate control information: sales records, production cost figures, financial data, or additional market research. A timely and useful management information system includes analysis of present information—and the possible revision of plans. Thus the process of management is a cycle of functions (planning—organizing—leading—controlling) in a continuing effort to meet organizational goals.

Figure 6.5 represents the varying proportions of time managers spend on each function according to their managerial level. Managers at the top spend more time planning than do supervisory managers, who in turn devote more time to leading and controlling than do managers at the top. Time management itself, of course, is an essential part of any manager's job.

Electronic organizers are designed to help managers with time management. These portable organizers hold schedules, telephone numbers, and memos to allow managers to organize both business and personal data. Organizers can also be connected with other computers and printers. It is important that managers be able both to manage their time and quickly access important information. A good time management system often makes the difference between good managers and poor managers.

FIGURE 6.5 • THE MANAGEMENT HIERARCHY AND MANAGEMENT FUNCTIONS

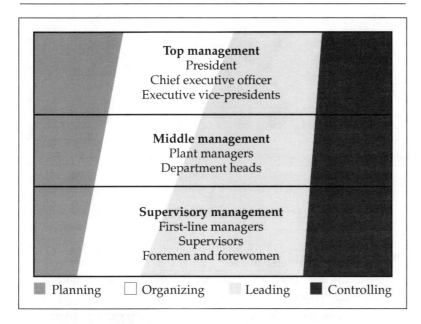

Top management
President
Chief executive officer
Executive vice-presidents

Middle management
Plant managers
Department heads

Supervisory management
First-line managers
Supervisors
Foremen and forewomen

■ Planning   ☐ Organizing   Leading   ■ Controlling

MAKING DECISIONS

Any manager will tell you that all management functions involve making decisions: Should we plan to serve our international customers from Canadian plants or set up production facilities closer to the market? Should we assign our financial resources to allow for delivery by air, which is expensive but efficient, or should we tie up inventory, and therefore money, in ground transportation? Should we allow workers to arrange their own coffee breaks or should we insist on set times? Does the slip in sales mean we should retrain our sales staff, rush the new model into production, or reduce prices—or all three? Efficient decision making solves present problems and anticipates future opportunities.

Decision making is the process of recognizing a problem or opportunity, developing and evaluating possible courses of action, choosing and implementing the chosen alternative, and evaluating the effectiveness of the decision. Figure 6.6 shows a five-step process managers go through in order to reach a decision. The first and final steps are probably the most critical. If the need for a decision is not recognized at the right time, the problem may mushroom or the opportunity be lost. Without appropriate analysis of feedback on the effectiveness of the decision, there will be no accurate information on which to base future decisions.

decision making
The process of recognizing a problem or opportunity, developing and evaluating possible courses of action, choosing and implementing the chosen alternative, and evaluating the effectiveness of the decision

FIGURE 6.6 • STEPS IN THE DECISION-MAKING PROCESS

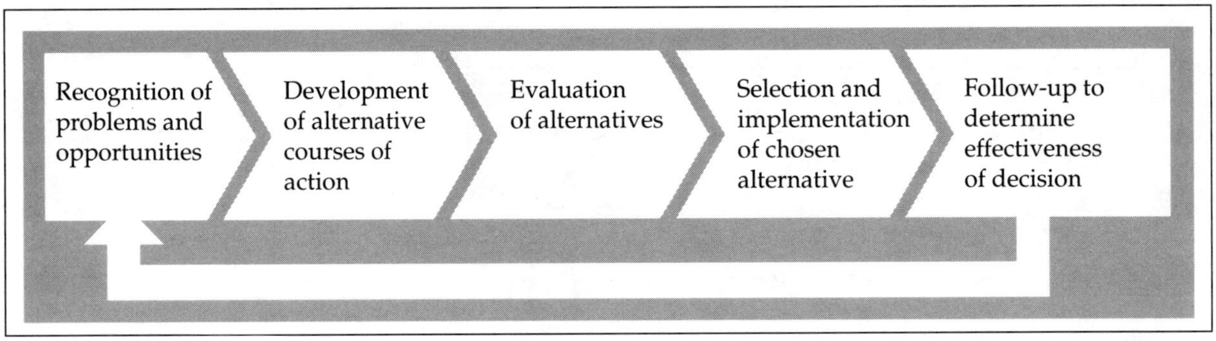

Recognition of problems and opportunities → Development of alternative courses of action → Evaluation of alternatives → Selection and implementation of chosen alternative → Follow-up to determine effectiveness of decision

---

BUSINESS REVIEW 6.3

1. Running a household is a management position. Give examples of how a homemaker might exercise the functions of planning, organizing, leading, and controlling.

2. Consider a decision you have made recently. Explain the process you used to arrive at the decision in terms of the five steps illustrated in Figure 6.5.

INTERACTIVE SUMMARY AND DISCUSSION QUESTIONS

1. At what level of the management hierarchy would you place each of the following positions?
   (a) executive vice-president
   (b) foreman of steel plant
   (c) Minister of Regional Development
   (d) branch manager of a bank
   (e) head of department in large firm
   (f) dean, School of Business Administration

2. Contrast Bob Lunney, Chief of the Peel Regional Police, as described in Developing Your Business Skills with the skills required for managerial success. Relate his performance with the three critical skills.

3. Classify each of the following plans as either primarily strategic or tactical. Defend your answer.
   (a) registrar's office system for processing student requests for dropping and adding classes

   (b) IBM's development of the relatively inexpensive PC jr computer
   (c) retail store manager's decision about the number of men's dress shirts to reorder
   (d) hospital's procedure for admitting new patients
   (e) Canadian Pacific Airline's decision to relocate corporate headquarters in Quebec City
   (f) student's choice of a college/university

4. Relate the steps in the controlling process to the following:

   Although Air Canada has established the performance standard that at least 85 percent of its customers at an AC flight counter shall be waited on within five minutes, airport construction has reduced the available space of their flight counter at one terminal and limited the number of company personnel who can physically be available to assist customers. Construction is scheduled for completion in 90 days.

5. Give an example of strategic planning *and* tactical planning for each of the following:

Strategic   Tactical

(a) off-campus bookstore
(b) General Motors of Canada
(c) *Frank* magazine
(d) local apartment complex
(e) Pizza Hut

6. In Issues in Business 6.2 you discovered how a corporate task force at Consumers Packaging Inc. reflected current management trends. Why does this technique work so well? Would you recommend using one for an organization needing to solve problems?

7. Identify the three basic leadership styles and cite an example of an instance in which each would be appropriate.

8. Brisebois et Frères, a small electronics firm situated in eastern Ontario, has long observed St. Jean Baptiste Day as a paid holiday for its employees, 60 percent of whom live in Quebec. Mr. Jacques Brisebois, the directeur genérale, has noticed that St. Jean Baptiste Day will occur on a Tuesday during the next year. He is wondering whether the Monday of that week should be declared a company holiday instead in the attempt to compact the weekend and first working day. Using each of the steps in the decision-making process, describe how you would help Mr. Brisebois make this critical decision.

CASE 6.1

A DAY IN THE LIFE OF A CEO

BY THE TIME Purdy Crawford is asked what it takes to be a corporate leader, it seems almost an afterthought.

Crawford has been working for more than eleven hours today. He has dealt with hundreds of items, including Imasco's share price and the fat content of the hamburger patties that U.S. subsidiary Hardee's Food Systems Inc. sells. Yet as he makes plain, leadership isn't about the mastery of details so much as the corporate sweep. "I think you've got to be prepared to make some tough decisions," he snaps. Short pause. "But if I left Imasco tomorrow, it wouldn't skip a beat. It's got good people and good succession."

Imasco—a consumer products and services company with a retail orientation—is a challenge to run. Imperial Tobacco Ltd., which generates 42 percent of Imasco's $5.7-billion sales and 48 percent of its $692 million in operating profit, faces a declining market as smokers continue to butt out. Crawford expects compensatory growth from Imasco's holdings in U.S. fast food (Hardee's and Roy Rogers restaurants, a recently acquired chain of chicken outlets in the eastern states), pharmacies (Shoppers Drug Mart Ltd. in Canada and Peoples Drug Stores Inc. in the United States), and financial services (through Canada Trust Co. and Canada Trustco Mortgage Co.). All these businesses, however, operate in highly competitive and shifting markets. Among them, they throw off more than enough problems and prospects to fill Thursday, April 12.

7:50 a.m. Crawford enters Imasco's 21st-floor corporate offices. As a spring blizzard fills the Montreal sky, he writes down his schedule for the day and some reminders on two pieces of lined paper. These he will keep in front of him the whole day.

Crawford's office is in a corner facing south and east with a view that takes in Place Ville Marie, the Jacques Cartier bridge, and the Eastern Townships beyond the St. Lawrence River. Although he has a custom-made beechwood desk, he spends most of his time seated at a small circular table near the windows, hands on the arms of his chair, legs outstretched and crossed, waiting for intelligence.

8:10 a.m. Roy Schwartz, senior vice-president, legal and corporate development, arrives to give Crawford his morning update. There's more ground than usual to cover because Crawford has

(continued)

been away for two days, one of them at Hardee's headquarters in Rocky Mount, N.C. Schwartz barks out a London Stock Exchange quote for Imasco's major shareholder, BAT Industries PLC. BAT, which holds 40 percent of Imasco, is—on April 12—the subject of a long-running takeover bid. The possibility that Imasco will be sold or broken up in the wake of a successful takeover both intimidates and galvanizes management.

Schwartz also has news about the valuation of some western Canadian real estate assets; a rumour that one of Imasco's lead underwriters may be for sale; and word that approval of the Roy Rogers purchase may be forthcoming from the U.S. Federal Trade Commission later today.

8:30 a.m. Crawford and Schwartz are joined for the day's main planning meeting by Ray Guyatt, chief financial officer and treasurer, and Torrance Wylie, executive vice-president.

Crawford steers the conversation to plans to convert the Roy Rogers restaurants into Hardee's units. He wants Guyatt and his staff to provide a new operating earnings analysis for the two fast-food groups combined to reflect revised sales targets for Roy Rogers he heard the day before.

The other main talking point at the meeting is the company's ownership of Canada Trust, held through Imasco Enterprises Inc. Two days ago, Crawford was at Canada Trust's executive committee meeting in Toronto where CEO Merv Lahn assured him of good first-quarter numbers. Those numbers are a major component of Imasco's first-quarter results, due to be released at the company's annual meeting in Montreal on May 1. "If we can get them this afternoon we can tie things down," Guyatt says. "The shareholders should be happy."

As the meeting closes, Wylie reminds his colleagues that the long-awaited legislation reregulating financial services may be introduced in the House of Commons within the month. He'll call his Department of Finance contacts after the long weekend to get a better fix on the timing. The legislation may require Imasco eventually to reduce its stake in Canada Trust to 65 percent from 98 percent.

9:40 a.m. In his role as chairman of the board of regents of Sackville, N.B.'s Mount Allison University, Crawford meets with the school's newly appointed interim president, Sheila Brown. Brown is also a candidate to become permanent president, so Crawford is trying to gauge her potential and attitudes to such things as the need for balance between teaching and research. But they spend most of the meeting negotiating her new pay and benefits package.

11:20 a.m. This is the first real gap in Crawford's day, a chance to make phone calls, look at mail, and contemplate longer-range issues such as the plan to consolidate Canada Trust's results, which would give a more accurate picture of the parent company's overall size.

12:00 p.m. Peter McBride, vice-president of public affairs, arrives to brief Crawford on an interview he's scheduled to do after lunch with Dow Jones Canada Inc. reporter Pierre Goad. McBride has prepared a five-part rundown of areas about which Crawford may be questioned, as well as three pages of quick facts on Imasco's performance.

12:10 p.m. Crawford holds court in the small cafeteria two floors below his office. Over salad and yogurt, he kids with his executives and picks up bits of information. The meal is a casual extension of the earlier morning meetings.

1:15 p.m. Back in his office, Crawford meets briefly with Wylie, who wants to know if Crawford can make a trip to Ottawa later in the spring to lobby for speedy passage of the financial services legislation. Crawford agrees to go.

1:35 p.m. Guyatt joins Crawford for the Dow Jones interview. The session goes pretty much as anticipated and Crawford is impressed with how well Goad has done his homework on the company's operations. The reporter stresses Imasco's earnings outlook and the effect of the uncertainty about the takeover bid for BAT. Crawford reiterates the value of sticking to your own business and creating shareholder value.

3:10 p.m. Twenty minutes after the end of the Dow Jones interview, Crawford resumes his place at the circular table to discuss plans for the May 1 annual meeting with McBride, Schwartz, and corporate secretary Rod MacKinnon. "It's a hell of a day," McBride chirps as he hands out a

(continued)

detailed script for the annual meeting extravaganza. "It's horrible," mutters Schwartz, contemplating plans for a seven-hour marathon that will begin with an early-morning directors' meeting and end with the chairman's address to shareholders. Crawford and his team review a host of details, including the location of corporate logos and product displays, arrangements for simultaneous translation, and the possibility that anti-smoking activists will show up. "Your speech is more buoyant this year, more promotional," McBride tells Crawford. "Give me a look," Crawford laughs. "I might want to rewrite it."

3:35 p.m. Crawford and Wylie place a call to Annette Verschuren, vice-president of corporate development, who's in Imasco's Toronto office for the day. Imasco is a member of the SkyDome consortium, and Verschuren is attempting to work out royalty and licensing problems that subsidiary UCS Group has encountered with the Blue Jays Baseball Club and Stadium Corp. For good measure, Verschuren mentions that the Association of Tennis Professionals is pushing Imperial Tobacco to sponsor a second Players Tennis Tournament in the SkyDome. Since the first one had poor attendance and lost money, Crawford is non-committal; Imperial Tobacco will make the final decision.

4:10 p.m. Crawford begins to tie up the day's loose ends and prepares for the question-and-answer session at L'Ecole des Hautes Etudes. The go-ahead from U.S. regulators for the Roy Rogers purchase hasn't come through yet, so Imasco will temporarily put the funds raised for the deal into money-market instruments. There are a few small, last-minute decisions Crawford must make before leaving. One is to beg off attending an awards ceremony later in the month at which Imasco will be honoured for its Montreal Job Creation Initiatives Inc., a five-year, $7-million program that will create 1,000 permanent jobs in the city. Wylie will represent the company instead. Crawford also opts to skip a dinner that L'Ecole des Hautes Etudes has planned after the question-and-answer session. Instead, he will travel to his family's country home outside Toronto for the Easter weekend; he'll be on the road until 1:00 a.m. to preserve a family tradition. Leadership, it seems, is also about inner drive and boundless energy.

Source: Reprinted from Vaune Davies, "Coping with Indecision," *Canadian Business*, May 1990, pp. 91–92. Reprinted with permission from Vaune Davies.

Questions for Discussion

1. Identify the managerial roles developed by Mintzberg that describe what Purdy Crawford does in his job.

2. Is Crawford involved in tactical or strategic planning—or both? Cite examples to support your answer.

CASE 6.2

COPING WITH INDECISION

PAUL SZABO WAS thrilled when he was offered a job at the U.S. head office. At 34, he was the youngest marketing director ever at General Products Canada, a branch office of a consumer products multinational. The transfer meant only one thing: the company was grooming him for a top position in international management. But within three months of starting the new job, Szabo was miserable. The problem was the vice-president he reported to.

Richard Frain was a 40-year-old corporate bureaucrat who had worked his way up through the ranks by keeping his nose clean and avoiding controversial decisions. Szabo was used to quick

(continued)

decision making at the Canadian office. There he had reported to the confident, competent senior vice-president of marketing, a man known for spotting a good business idea and approving it on the spot. Under his guidance, Szabo had built his career on a series of bold and innovative new marketing programs.

But Frain was a completely different animal. "Any time I ask him to make a decision, he says, 'Let's dig deeper into this,' and asks for 30 or 40 more pages of irrelevent data," Szabo complained to his wife. "I can't get anything done."

Szabo was convinced that the line of frozen dinners he was in charge of would be more profitable at a lower price. He and his five product managers spent weeks preparing charts and graphs to justify the new pricing strategy. But Frain kept waffling, asking for more information. His latest request—for an analysis of summer weather patterns that might affect shopping habits—was absurd.

Frain was terrified of tinkering with the status quo. He refused to update the frozen dinners' 1960s-style packaging, even though the dinners had been reformulated for microwave ovens. And when Szabo recommended a coupon program in March, Frain nixed it because they had always run coupons in April.

Frain measured progress not by results, but by hours spent in the office. He arrived at 7:00 every morning and shuffled his memos, charts, and graphs until 8:00 or 9:00 at night. Worse yet, he expected the same dedication from his hirelings. Anyone who tried to slip away earlier was intercepted with a snide "Going home?" This was intolerable to Szabo, who had three small children and faced an hour-long commute.

Szabo tried to reason with Frain. He politely explained that the department was taking a big risk by avoiding decisions. Market share was slipping, and changes to the product's pricing and promotion were vital. But Frain wasn't buying it. "You have to be more patient, build a better case," he told Szabo. Then the zinger: "Didn't they teach you to do your homework up there in Canada?"

Szabo's two best product managers eventually quit, burned out by marathon sessions analyzing pointless data. "That's it. I've got to talk to the division president," Szabo told his wife. "Frain is driving all the talent out of the company." But she urged caution: "If the president sides with Frain, and Frain finds out you've gone over his head, you'll probably have to leave the company. Are you prepared for that?"

Szabo hesitated. He wasn't. He had worked too hard for too many years to jeopardize his chances at an international career with General Products. Why should the president take his word over that of Frain, a twelve-year veteran of the company? After all, if Frain had survived this long, he had to be doing something right. What is Szabo's next move?

Source: Excerpts from Charles Davis, "Leasons in Leadership," *Canadian Business*, June 1990, pp. 62,63, 128 Reprinted with permission from Canadian Business ©1993.

Questions for Discussion

1. What process would you suggest Paul Szabo utilize to solve his problem? What are the steps he should take at this time?

2. Discuss Szabo's expectations of the job, his supervisor (subordinate relationships), and his communication style as all three affect this problem.

NOTES

1. Peter F. Drucker, *The Practice of Management* (New York: Harper and Bros., 1954), pp. 65–83.

PHOTO CREDITS

MGT 3   Photo courtesy of The Calgary General Hospital

MGT 5   Courtesy of Dow Chemical Inc. photo taken by Wayne Windjack

MGT 20   Sharp Electronics of Canada Limited

MODULE

◆ ORG ◆

ORGANIZATIONAL STRUCTURE

THE FOCUS OF THIS MODULE

1. To define organization in terms of its key elements

2. To describe factors that influence the structure of an organization

3. To describe the major forms of departmentalization

4. To discuss delegation in terms of authority, responsibility, and accountability and the degree of centralization of decision making within an organization

5. To explain how a manager's effective span of control may vary

6. To describe and evaluate six approaches to organizational structure

7. To discuss the importance of informal lines of communication within an organization

8. To define the following terms:

KEY TERMS

organization	span of control
hierarchy of organizational objectives	centralization
	decentralization
departmentalization	Parkinson's Law
product departmentalization	line structure
geographic departmentalization	functional structure
customer departmentalization	line-and-staff structure
functional departmentalization	matrix structure
process departmentalization	committee structure
delegation	horizontal organization
responsibility	organizational chart
authority	doughnut-shaped chart
accountability	grapevine

THE EXECUTIVE FLOORS of Petro-Canada's Calgary headquarters can hardly fail to impress the casual visitor.

Whether it is the huge modern paintings in the spacious, atrium-like reception foyer, the sweeping mountain view from the board-room, the chance to peer down at the top of the Calgary tower, or the gleaming chrome and lucite fixtures in the executive secretaries' wash-room, everything about the working surroundings of some of Canada's highest-paid public servants suggests luxury and grandeur.

The opulence extends to the private offices of the crown oil and gas corporation's new president and chief operating officer, Jim Stanford.* But here, the taxpayer vexed by the apparent lavishing of public money on executive perks in a company that claims to be cutting administrative overheads would do well to keep indignant thoughts to himself.

According to one of Stanford's closest colleagues, Petro-Canada products chief Barry Steward, the striking paintings and elegant soap-stone and bronze sculptures adorning the president's office come mostly from Stanford's personal art collection.

Soft-spoken and articulate, cultured and courteous, the silver-haired oilman talks enthusiastically about his Canadian painting and sculpture collection and about his passion for the arts in general.

In many ways, Stanford is a man of surprises: certainly, it is unusual to find that a one-time petroleum engineer who has built his profes-sional reputation in the oil and gas production business is also a dedicated patron of the arts. Even more surprising is that the second-in-command of the corporation many Calgarians still love to hate as a symbol of federal oppression is one of the oil and gas industry's most trusted and popular executives.

"He's amiable, effective, well-liked, and a real pro. He's a man who has a great deal of respect in the industry," says Ian Smyth, president of the Canadian Petroleum Association.

Though applauded, the federal energy minister's decision to appoint Stanford president was a surprise to some.

For one thing, Petro-Canada has recruited most of its top executives from outside. Stanford, the first Petro-Canada president to be pro-moted to the job internally, has been with the company since 1978.

Stanford is an operations man who studied petroleum and mining engineering at the University of Alberta and Loyola College in Montreal. His oil-patch credentials were established during a nine-teen-year stint as an engineer and manager for Mobil Oil Canada Ltd. After joining Petro-Canada, he ran its oil and gas production and fron-tier energy operations for several years.

But Stanford does have a finely tuned array of negotiating skills—something he will need as Petro-Canada edges toward privatization.

"He's charming. And he has a wonderful grasp of the issues," says John Shaw, executive director of the Calgary Philharmonic Orchestra, an organization to which Stanford has volunteered hundreds of hours of his personal time.

Right now, Stanford says Petro-Canada is taking up most of his mind and a good part of his heart. His task, he says, is to turn the company into a lean, efficient organization.

While Petro-Canada's CEO is responsible for the company's overall strategy and focus, Stanford says his job is to operate Petro-Canada in a way that follows the CEO's vision. In particular, he is concerned with the nuts and bolts of asset rationalization and cost cutting.

He has also reorganized the company's huge workforce, bringing in a new management system designed to "cut through bureaucracy, root out inefficiencies," and "bring into the business a sense of small-company entrepreneurship."

At Stanford's prompting, small teams of workers are being given direct responsibility for specific areas of operations. They work out plans for improving the efficiency of their "value centres," bringing their ideas directly to senior managers, including Stanford.

The reorganization has dramatically improved staff morale and productivity, Stanford says. "I have people who are managers of value centres coming to present to me their strategies for next year. The depth of understanding those people have for their business is greater than I have ever seen before."

*In January 1993, Petro-Canada rewarded both the organizational ability and leadership skills of Jim Stanford by promoting him to the position of CEO.

Source: Reprinted from Tamsin Carlisle, "Petro-Canada President a Man of Surprises," *The Financial Post*, June 4, 1990, p. 18.

D O ORGANIZATIONS ALWAYS work the way they are intended to? Do they run smoothly and efficiently? The task of chief operating officers like Jim Stanford is "to organize the organization"—and, if necessary, to reorganize it.

Wherever we go—to a family party; to church, mosque, or temple; to work; or to join in a softball game—we run into some form of organization. An **organization** is an intentional structure in which people interact to accomplish goals and objectives. Businesses, for example, are organizations in which people work together to provide goods and services to customers in order to make a profit. Other organizations bring people together in different ways for different purposes. But the definition of organization includes three interwoven key elements: structure, human interaction, and goal-directed activities.

Organizing the structure of a small business is fairly simple. The owner–manager of the local dry-cleaning firm employs a few people to take in clothing, launder and dry-clean it, and return it to customers and receive payment. The owner usually handles purchases of detergents, plastic wrappers, and other materials; assigns jobs to employees; and personally directs the operation of the business.

organization
An intentional structure in which people interact to accomplish goals and objectives

But larger companies require a more complex organizational structure, as shown in Figure 7.1. Employees hold more specialized positions, and entire departments are devoted to a single task. If it is to run smoothly, a sales force or an accounting department needs more supervision than one salesperson or solitary bookkeeper.

INFLUENCES ON THE ORGANIZATION'S STRUCTURE

Whether a business is a hardware store, an architectural office, or an appliance manufacturer, it has a clear mission that is accomplished by people working together in a formal structure. The hardware store sells home repair supplies through its structure of a manager and assistant manager; salespersons with specific knowledge of paints, tool maintenance, and the use of various building products; cashiers; and a part-time bookkeeper. The architectural office designs and supervises the construction or renovation of buildings through its structure of architects, town planning experts, landscape designers, site supervisors, an office manager, drafters and model builders, receptionists, and accounting and clerical workers. The appliance manufacturer produces stoves, dishwashers, refrigerators, and washing machines through its structure of research and development department, purchasing department, several production departments, quality control department, marketing department, human resources department, payroll and accounting department, public affairs department, and legal department. Each of these departments has its own internal structure.

How is an organization's structure arrived at? First, managers must identify the work that needs to be done to accomplish the organization's goals. Then the work load must be analyzed and divided into individual jobs. Qualified workers must be hired and grouped to work together according to their activities. A co-ordinating mechanism must ensure that employees pull together rather than at cross-purposes. Finally, the structure must be monitored and adjusted to ensure its continued effectiveness.[1]

FIGURE 7.1 • AS THE NUMBER OF EMPLOYEES WORKING IN A BUSINESS GROWS, SO DOES THE NEED FOR ORGANIZATION

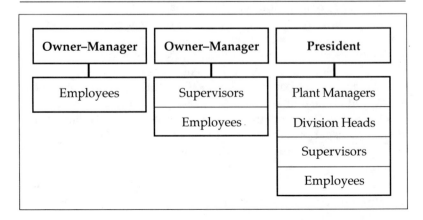

A clear structure allows employees to know where they fit into an organization. Employees who know what tasks they are expected to perform, who they report to, and how their contribution fits into the overall goals of the organization tend to be more committed and more productive. Employee morale is important to the operation of any business.

A Hierarchy of Goals

A company needs more specific goals than are described in a mission statement such as "XYZ Company provides quality goods at prices the average family can afford." The idea of routinely maintaining and repairing production equipment may be implicit in this statement, but it is certainly not going to be clear to the person who works with the machine—nor does it state whose job it is to maintain the equipment. Broad goals are very important, but they are only a first step. When they are broken down into specific objectives, it becomes clear to both managers and workers how all necessary activities are distributed among the various workers.

Well-structured companies operate according to a **hierarchy of organizational objectives.** A typical hierarchy, such as the one in Figure 7.2, shows how overall long-term goals are translated into precise, specific objectives for individual workers. The broad goals of profitability, sales, market share, and service are methodically broken down into clear objectives for each division, each factory, each department, each group of employees, and each individual employee. The number of levels in a hierarchy is determined by a company's size and complexity. Consider what the hierarchy of objectives for Bell Canada Enterprises would look like compared with that for your local independent grocery store.

hierarchy of organizational objectives
A progression from the overall mission and goals of the organization to the specific objectives for individual employees

Grouping People to Achieve Goals

The process of identifying the work that needs to be done to accomplish the organization's goals and dividing the work load into individual jobs leads to logical groupings, or departments, of workers who are performing the same task or working on the same project. **Departmentalization** is the subdivision of activities into appropriate units within the organization to allow specialization and increase efficiency. Major departments in most businesses consist of production, marketing, and finance. A marketing department may be headed by a vice-president of marketing in a medium-sized firm, and include sales representatives, advertising experts, and market researchers. In a large firm, each of these groups of specialists may be a separate department.

Departments can be organized on the basis of product, geography, customer, function, and process. Maclean Hunter subdivides its organizational structure on the basis of **products**—the *Financial Post* division, the Business Magazines division (*Photo Canada, Canadian Interiors, Canadian Aviation*), the Consumer Magazines division (*Maclean's, Chatelaine, Flare*). The Bay is subdivided on a **geographical** basis by regions of the country, as are CN and Canadian Pacific. Many sporting-goods stores subdivide on a **customer** basis, with a wholesale operation serving school systems and a retail division serving other

departmentalization
The subdivision of activities into appropriate units within the organization

product departmentalization
Subdivision of work according to type of product

geographic departmentalization
Subdivision of work according to regions served

customer departmentalization
Subdivision of work according to market segments

functional departmentalization
Subdivision of work according to functions performed

process departmentalization
Subdivision of work according to manufacturing process

customers. Oil companies are sometimes divided on a **functional** basis, with departments in exploration, production, refining, marketing, and finance (though Petro-Canada uses geographic departmentalization). Machinery manufacturers may departmentalize on the basis of **process**—cutting, heat-treatment, forming, assembly, and painting—all these activities being included in one or more departments.

As Figure 7.3 indicates, a number of different bases for departmentalization may be used within the same company. Each form of departmentalization has benefits and drawbacks and different forms may be used at different levels of a company. Figure 7.3 shows how a firm might departmentalize functional, geographic, and customer-related activities. Top management must consider the advantages and disadvantages of each possible subdivision of activities.

FIGURE 7.2 • THE HIERARCHY OF ORGANIZATIONAL OBJECTIVES

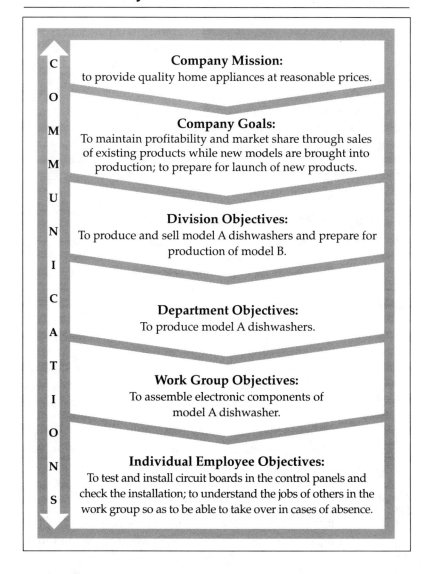

COMMUNICATIONS

Company Mission:
to provide quality home appliances at reasonable prices.

Company Goals:
To maintain profitability and market share through sales of existing products while new models are brought into production; to prepare for launch of new products.

Division Objectives:
To produce and sell model A dishwashers and prepare for production of model B.

Department Objectives:
To produce model A dishwashers.

Work Group Objectives:
To assemble electronic components of model A dishwasher.

Individual Employee Objectives:
To test and install circuit boards in the control panels and check the installation; to understand the jobs of others in the work group so as to be able to take over in cases of absence.

FIGURE 7.3 • AN ORGANIZATION USING SEVERAL BASES FOR DEPARTMENTALIZATION

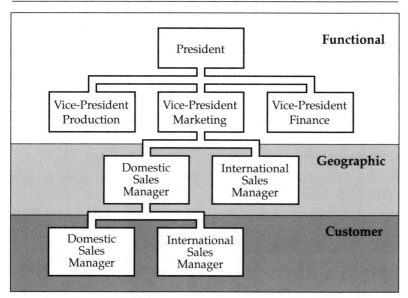

Delegation

"If you want something done right, you must do it yourself." Though the maxim sounds fine in theory, managers know that they cannot do the work of their entire departments. Yet one of the most difficult managerial skills is that of **delegation**, or assigning authority and responsibility for activities to subordinates.

The easy part of delegation is giving instructions. More difficult for many managers is handing over **responsibility**, the duty to take charge of the assigned activity, in the full expectation that it will be duly carried out. Even more difficult is granting the subordinate the **authority** to perform the activity, the power to make the required decisions. Once an activity has been delegated, the subordinate is accountable to the manager for its performance. **Accountability** includes not only the actual performance but also the liability associated with reporting and justifying the outcome to the manager. A manager who is reluctant to grant authority must realize that subordinates cannot be held fully accountable if they do not have adequate authority to act.

Perhaps one of the reasons many managers find delegation so difficult is that they themselves are accountable to their own superiors for the actions of their subordinates. One of the first tasks for any manager, therefore, is to select and train subordinates who are capable of accepting the appropriate responsibility and authority.

Span of Control

The president of a large corporation cannot directly supervise the work of every employee, which is why large firms are departmentalized. The number of people a manager actually supervises (and delegates activities to) is known as the **span of control**. The optimum

delegation
Assigning authority and responsibility for activities to subordinates

responsibility
The duty to take charge of an assigned task

authority
The power to make the decisions required to perform an assigned task

accountability
The liability to report and justify to the manager the outcome of a delegated task

span of control
The number of people a manager supervises

number of employees whom a manager can effectively control depends on the type of work they do, their skills and training, the manager's own abilities, and the lines of communications within the organization. For example, when employees work at similar, routine tasks, supervisors do not need to be closely involved and can control a fairly large number of people. At the top management level, it has been widely accepted that four to eight is probably a good number of subordinates, because the subordinates themselves have widely different areas of responsibility, such as finance, marketing, or production. On the other hand, more modern theories of management suggest that as employees at this level are highly skilled at their jobs and appropriate lines of communication are set up, a wider span of control is possible.

Degree of Centralization

The amount of authority delegated to subordinates does not always equal the amount of responsibility. In some organizations, subordinates are expected to refer all or most decisions to higher levels of management. With a strategy of **centralization** of decision-making authority, top management believes it can effectively control and co-ordinate company activities.

In other firms, the tendency is toward **decentralization**, or allowing lower levels of management a great deal of decision-making authority. This practice allows middle and supervisory managers more flexibility and means that the company can react faster to immediate situations. It also saves time for top managers, who can focus their attention on long-range strategic matters. Decentralization means the firm must have good lines of communication—and a great deal of confidence in the people who fill lower management positions. IBM has a reputation for being a highly centralized company, but it has recently decentralized its operations into strategic business units to increase effectiveness and efficiency. The president and CEO of IBM Canada, Bill Etherington, under whom the changes were made, had this to say:

> "We made more changes in 75 days than we made in 75 years. We were faced with two alternatives—do this slowly or go more quickly to get in front of the wave. The main criticism of the company has been we tended to make incremental changes when the industry is moving at exponential rates. We had to get in front. . . . Our customer satisfaction has improved and revenues are going up. We've broken some of the old paradigms in the business, and the employees feel less entitled, and more that they need to earn their way."[2]

Another type of decentralization is strategic business units where companies sell senior management a percentage stake in one of the company's divisions. This allows managers to participate in the company as owners. Issues in Business 7.1 discusses how Royal Trustco restructured and introduced strategic business units, in the form of a management buy-in system. Issues in Business 7.2 discusses some factors that may affect executives' views on centralization in the future.

centralization

The practice of retaining decision-making authority in the hands of top management

decentralization

The practice of allowing lower levels of management a great deal of decision-making authority

ISSUES IN BUSINESS 7.1

MANAGEMENT OWNERSHIP AT ROYAL TRUSTCO

WHEN TOM TUCKER turned 61 in 1987, he decided to retire early and start his own business. Not that he had any complaints about his career with Royal Trustco Ltd., which culminated in the vice-presidency of the property investment services division, Builders Capital Ltd. "I just wanted to prove to myself that I could be a success without a big corporation behind me," he says.

Today, Tucker is still sitting behind the same desk. Loath to let 35-plus years of real estate expertise walk out the door, Royal Trustco decided to sell Tucker and his two former colleagues—Peter Emmings and Rob Hawkins—a 20 percent stake in the division and make them partners.

Tucker, Hawkins, and Emmings wanted the chance of returns that only ownership can bring, and were willing to take the accompanying risks. Royal Trustco wanted the enthusiasm and commitment that comes when a manager puts his or her own cash into the business. "That's the important thing—thinking and acting like an owner," president and CEO Michael Cornelissen says. "That's a totally different mindset than an employee's."

Since 1987, Royal Trustco has sold equity positions of up to 25 percent to managers of six domestic divisions, ranging from the Western Canada retail banking operations to specialized services such as pension fund management, and is now preparing to do the same in its five major international divisions. Fifteen company executives have borrowed more than $5 million to buy equity in their divisions, for an average personal debtload of more than $300,000—not including the money most of them owe for mandatory Royal Trustco stock purchases.

Most divisional owner–managers have participated willingly, preferring to give up secure base salaries for a share of their division's profits and the equity value they think they can create. A few, however, had to be pushed. Cornelissen imposed ownership on one group of executives. They'd made an investment that cost the company $2 million and admitted they probably wouldn't have made the deal with their own money. "They struggled a bit," Cornelissen recalls, "but we told them if they weren't willing to take the risk, we'd find other managers who would."

To understand Cornelissen's enthusiasm for management ownership, you must know his background. He spent seven years in the Edward and Peter Bronfman investment empire before moving to Royal Trustco after Edper's Trilon Financial Corp. bought a majority stake in the stagnant trust in 1983. He found a big hidebound bureaucracy. Twelve management layers stood between the customer and the president's office, and a vast pool of executives were accustomed to being rewarded on the basis of seniority rather than performance. "Those who didn't get caught making decisions tended to filter to the top," Cornelissen says.

Cornelissen wanted to change all that. He'd brought with him from Edper a belief that senior management should participate in the risks taken by shareholders. Now, instead of raises, Royal Trustco directors, vice-presidents, and senior vice-presidents get loans to buy the company's stock at a 10 percent discount. Cornelissen himself owes more than $2 million for his Royal Trustco shares.

The management buy-ins launched in 1987 apply the same principle at the divisional level. But the rewards are linked to the operating results of executives' own divisions rather than to increases in the value of shares in the parent company. Most of the company's owner–managers take on debt of as much as 100 percent of whatever is set as the entry price of their divisional shares. Royal Trustco underwrites the loans for the buy-ins; interest is payable twice a year whether or not there are any earnings to share. Says Tucker: "We're on the hook, in every sense of the word."

(continued)

Divisional buy-ins will not work for every company. A corporation must have or implement (as Royal Trustco did) the culture and streamlined operations to support the aggressive risk-taking style of owner–entrepreneurs.

Nor can all operating units be turned into semiautonomous subsidiaries, although the concept can be stretched to fit even service departments, if they can bill internal or external clients. In general, however, it is easier to implement management partnerships in clearly defined profit centres. Royal Trustco's Quebec corporate and retail trust services, for example, were ripe for a management buy-in. Given the province's unique financial services regulations, Royal Trustco's Quebec management was running what amounted to an independent subsidiary even before the entire Quebec unit was spun off into a separate corporate entity, with a new board of directors, in July 1989. Negotiations for a management buy-in of Royal Trust Co. (Quebec) should be finalized next month.

One problem Royal Trustco faced in structuring divisional partnerships was establishing entry prices that both managers and the company were happy with. Many of the divisions are fee-based investment services with no hard assets other than their partners' ability to generate earnings. In the end, the company found it did not matter what multiple was used to value those earnings, as long as the formula was the same at both entry and exit from the partnership. "If you think you're coming in cheap, then you're going to go out cheap when you cash in your chips," says Lee Bentley, vice-chairman of investment services. "If you overpay going in, you'll get a bonus going out."

The company also found that the way in which different parts of a division's business were valued was more important than the cash price. It applies higher values to recurring than nonrecurring earnings, ensuring that partners will concentrate on building for the long term.

Royal Trustco is not the only financial institution giving its executives the chance to be owner–entrepreneurs. Canadian insurance companies have known for years that the best way to keep talented pension fund managers happy is to give them a stake in the business. And most of the chartered banks that have taken over brokerage firms have allowed management to keep substantial minority interests. Ken Hugessen, a director and executive compensation specialist at William M. Mercer Ltd., believes financial institutions no longer have much choice in the matter: "If they want the best, most aggressive talent around, they have to give managers a piece of the action."

Tom Tucker is living proof that equity ownership is the best way to retain such talent. At 64, he is working longer, harder hours and enjoying it more than ever. He plans to stay on the job into his 70s, he says, "Or until the grim reaper, or my grim partners, push me out."

Source: Reprinted from Vaune Davis, "Restructuring: Bureaucracy Busting," *Canadian Business*, March 1990, pp. 89–91.

Questions for Discussion

1. What are the advantages and disadvantages of a management buy-in system?
2. Management buy-ins will not work in every company. Why?

ISSUES IN BUSINESS 7.2

HOW IMPORTANT IS THE BOSS?

THE BOSS IS no longer the most important person in the corporate structure.

In fact, the customer is. And if bosses are not honest about accepting this, they will watch their companies fail.

This was the disturbing word—at least for bosses—presented yesterday to a group of senior executives by management consultant Ron Farmer.

"Companies are not stable anymore," Farmer, a director of the international consulting firm McKinsey and Company, said.

"The recession, ruthless competition, globalization, and free trade have guaranteed this. Top managers or CEOs have to create new organizations which can compete in the new business environment. If they don't, their companies will not be around in the next generation."

The nub of Farmer's theory is that the traditional, hierarchical organization is out of date—even dangerous in the modern competitive world. The pyramid structure with "a man in charge" is lowering productivity and costing companies money because they've lost sight of their real goals, he argued.

"Everybody from the hourly worker at the bottom to senior management spends most of their time trying to please the boss," Farmer said, "Everybody is looking up when they should be looking out—at the real power in the business, the customer."

The solution to this stagnant structure is to simply throw it out, he argued. "We're talking about whacko, off-the-wall brainstorming here," Farmer told his somewhat shocked audience. "The idea is to get rid of the pyramid structure and create a flat, horizontal structure that gets orders in one door and products out another door and doesn't care about the guy on top."

Source: Reprinted from John Davidson, "The Corporate Structure Must Change," *The Montreal Gazette*, November 28, 1991, p. F-3.

Questions for Discussion

1. How do Ron Farmer's theories affect your views about delegating authority and responsibility?
2. Is it really possible "to get rid of the pyramid structure and create a flat, horizontal structure that . . . doesn't care about the guy on top"?

How Much Growth Is Necessary?

As the size and complexity of an organization increase, the tendency is to add still more supervisory personnel and specialists. When managers become aware that their effective span of control is limited, the addition of new managerial levels seems the most obvious solution. However, unless such new positions can be clearly justified, there may be surprisingly little benefit to production and efficiency.

British historian–philosopher C. Northcote Parkinson has explained this tendency as **Parkinson's Law:** "Work expands to fill the time available for its completion."[3] He points out that organizations tend to continue hiring more and more employees regardless of how much work actually has to be done. In one dramatic illustration he showed how growth in the British navy continued unchecked for

Parkinson's Law
"Work expands so as to fill the time available for its completion."

many years. At its most powerful in 1914, it was managed by 2,000 admiralty officials. By 1938, this number had grown to 3,569, and by 1954, when the British navy had a whopping 33,788 admiralty officials, this once-proud fighting force had become "practically powerless." In another useful example, Parkinson wrote about the growth of the British Colonial Office from 372 to 1,661 officials from 1935 to 1954 at a time when the British Empire was actually shrinking.[4]

Why do organizations tend to add employees at a rate faster than that at which the work to be done is increasing? Parkinson attributed unnecessary growth to selfish managers who wanted to build personal empires by having vast numbers of subordinates, and to paperwork necessitated by the hiring and managing of these extra employees.[5] Parkinson's Law is practical advice for top management as it evaluates the need for proposed new positions—and it is advice that has been taken one step farther as many businesses such as investment banking firms have "downsized" since the late 1980s.

BUSINESS REVIEW 7.1

1. How does an organization's size affect its structure?
2. Explain how the key elements of an organization—structure, human relations, and goal-directed activities—are related to departmentalization, delegation, span of control, and degree of centralization within an organization.

DESIGNING THE ORGANIZATION'S STRUCTURE

Any group working toward common goals is an organization. Business organizations can be classified according to the nature of their internal authority relationships. When managers make structural decisions—for example, at what level decisions should be made or to what degree standardized rules are established for employees to follow—they are engaged in organization design. Organization design is part of the organizing function, which also encompasses job design, the creation of authority relationships, and the staffing of the organization.

In the pages that follow, six forms of organization design or structure will be discussed: line, functional, line-and-staff, matrix, committee, and horizontal organization. The line structure is the oldest and simplest and is frequently used in smaller organizations. The functional form uses specialist managers entirely responsible for their own fields within the operation. It has been superseded by the line-and-staff form which uses specialists to assist line officers. This form is commonly used in medium- and large-sized firms. Matrix and committee forms of organization exist in many firms but are typically used for only parts of the organization within a line-and-staff structure rather than as the sole type. The sixth type, the horizontal organization, is becoming more popular in the turbulent environment of the mid-1990s.

Line Structure

A **line structure** is based on the direct flow of authority from the chief executive through levels of subordinates. For example, in the archetypal army, the general initiates an order which is passed down the line through the colonel, major, captain, lieutenant, and sergeant to the lowly private who actually carries it out. The Roman Catholic Church has used a line structure throughout its history, as illustrated in Figure 7.4.

A line structure is straightforward. The chain of command is clear, and buck passing is difficult. Managers can make decisions quickly because they only need consult their immediate superiors. The weakness in a line structure is that managers are completely responsible for various activities. For example, the production manager may be in charge of maintaining machinery, ensuring secure packaging of finished goods, overseeing product safety, and completing employment records and pension contribution forms, as well as making certain that production quotas are met. Such a manager has no choice but to try and develop expertise in a variety of areas. This is easier said than done.

The line form does not allow for the development of specialized units. In medium- and large-sized companies it can mean that executives devote time that should be spent on planning to day-to-day administration and paperwork. Small grocery stores, florists, office supply retailers, and small law firms can use a simple line structure very effectively. The CBC, Eaton's, and Canadian General Electric cannot.

line structure

An organizational structure in which authority flows in a direct line from the chief executive to subordinates

---

FIGURE 7.4 · LINE STRUCTURE USED BY THE ROMAN CATHOLIC CHURCH

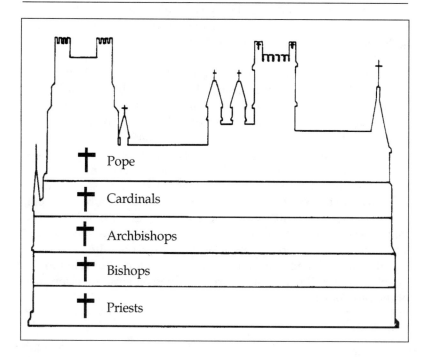

In an orchestra, the conductor is responsible for combining the activities of the strings, the woodwinds, the brass, and the percussion instruments. This direct communication between the conductor and the various independent groups of musicians creates a unified and harmonious effect. Thus, an orchestra may be considered an example of a line structure.

Functional Structure

functional organization

An organizational structure in which specialists have authority over specific work activities

The **functional organization** structure was developed in the early 1900s by Frederick Taylor, the "father of scientific management." Taylor was attempting to overcome the basic weakness of the line structure—the assignment of too many duties to a single manager. He broke down the work of a single supervisor into components and placed one supervisor in charge of each individual activity.[6]

Workers become responsible to specialists in various areas such as repair and maintenance, routing, inspection, training, and time and credit. A functional structure does not necessarily increase the number of managers: it simply groups them differently. In a line structure, each supervisor occasionally is responsible for training. In a functional structure, a specialist is placed in charge of all training. Thus a functional structure is based on a direct flow of authority for each work activity or function, as illustrated in Figure 7.5. The major problem with the functional form is that it creates a situation where workers have more than one boss at the same level. Even though each boss should possess authority only in the area of specialization, overlap and conflict are inevitable. And when problems occur, it is extremely difficult to locate the person responsible. With too many bosses, production may be slowed rather than speeded up, and disciplinary problems may be difficult to handle. The functional form no longer exists in most organizations, but it led to the development of line-and-staff forms to overcome the shortcomings of the pure line form.

FIGURE 7.5 • FUNCTIONAL STRUCTURE

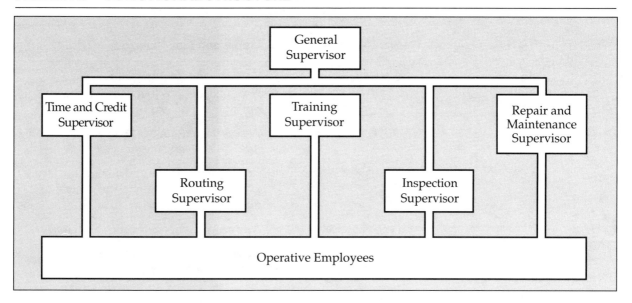

Line-and-Staff Structure

Combining the strengths of the line and functional organizational forms leads to a **line-and-staff structure**. Authority flows directly through *line* departments, which are responsible for organizational decision making, and *staff* departments provide specialized technical support. Figure 7.6 represents a typical line-and-staff organization in which employees interact with a line manager for ongoing supervision and with staff personnel for specialized assistance. Straightforward communication with experts in functional areas helps line managers make informed decisions rapidly and effectively supervise widespread activities.

line-and-staff structure

An organizational structure in which staff departments provide specialist support to line departments

FIGURE 7.6 • LINE-AND-STAFF STRUCTURE

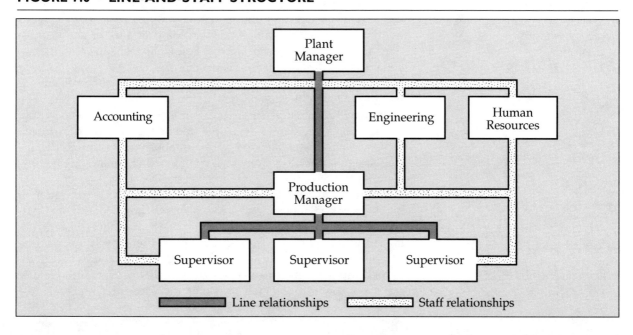

TABLE 7.1 • SOME STAFF MANAGERS AND THE LINE MANAGERS THEY ADVISE

Staff Manager	Duties and Line Managers Advised
Controller	Performs financial analyses and makes recommendations to the president and other high-level executives.
Advertising Manager	Assists the marketing director in developing the firm's advertising strategy.
Director of Research	Collects information and advises the firm's president, vice-president, and general managers.
Legal Counsel	Advises top management on legal matters.
Director of Engineering	Advises top managers on technical and engineering matters.

In a typical modern business, there are differences between line managers and staff managers, especially in terms of authority relationships. Although staff managers have line authority to provide direction in their own departments, their primary function is to recommend and advise line managers and not to give them direct orders. Note also that senior executives have line authority over staff departments. Table 7.1 lists a few staff managers and their activities.

Matrix Structure

matrix structure

A project management structure in which specialists assigned to a project are responsible to a project manager but remain within their functional departments

In recent times, the importance of research and new-product development has led some organizations to adopt the **matrix structure**. The matrix is a project management form that functions within a standard line-and-staff structure to bring together specialists who are best qualified to manage and contribute to specific projects. Many organizations use this structure, including Canadian Marconi, Procter and Gamble Canada, Canadian General Electric, Bell Helicopter, and the International Aviation Transportation Association (IATA) of Montreal, Quebec.

Because this structure is designed to tackle specific problems or projects, the identification of such projects is followed by the selection of a team whose members have the appropriate skills. General Motors Corporation's decision to develop a line of economical, front-wheel-drive compacts was followed by the establishment of project teams consisting of specialists from design engineering, finance, marketing, research and development, and information services.

Figure 7.7 represents the set-up of a typical matrix organization. It highlights a dual reporting structure in which those working on a project follow guidelines established by the project manager (the horizontal authority) without leaving their permanent positions in their functional departments (the vertical authority). In other words, individual employees have two bosses rather than one. In order to reduce the confusion and potential problems this structure can create, the

Canadian Marconi Company is a leading North American–based high-technology corporation that designs and manufactures products for both the defence and the commercial markets. The research and development divisions are important components of the corporation. The matrix structure allows groups of specialized individuals to work together to solve specific design and production problems, under the leadership of a project manager.

project manager usually has overall authority over the project and reports to the general manager rather than to the functional managers.

The matrix structure offers flexibility and allows the use of the most appropriate people and other resources for individual projects. The project manager, however, needs to pay careful attention to the importance of team building among project members with different specializations so they will be comfortable working with one another and for more than one boss. As a rule, matrix teams are temporary. For the duration of the projects, project managers normally take over decision-making responsibilities from line managers for salary adjustments and promotion recommendations for team members.

FIGURE 7.7 • A MATRIX STRUCTURE

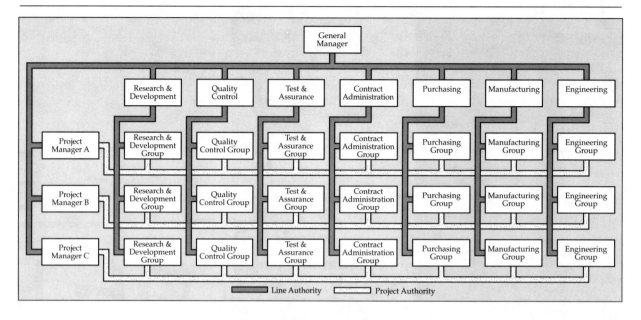

Committee Structure

When authority and responsibility are jointly shared by several people instead of one manager, the result is a **committee structure**. This structure is not used for an entire organization but as part of the regular line-and-staff structure.

For example, a new-product committee might include top management representatives from marketing, finance, manufacturing, accounting, engineering, and research to make decisions when introducing a new product. This approach improves morale by including all departments affected by new-product decisions and allows for vital input at the important planning stage from key people in the areas of production, marketing, and finance.

Committees do have drawbacks. Decision making can be slow and lack imagination because committee members tend to work toward compromise instead of choosing the best possible decision. Committee members must be careful to put the interests of the entire company ahead of those of their individual departments.

The Horizontal Organization

Perhaps the most radical approach to organizational design has come to be known as the horizontal organization.[7] Multinational companies especially are finding that their competitive advantage can come from many sources: cost advantages come from rationalizing research and development and production on a worldwide basis; on the other hand, sales can be increased by tailoring products to local market conditions. Finding the right balance between sources of advantage depends not only on strategic decisions but also on whether the organization is structured to allow it to happen.

In the **horizontal organization**, linkages between geographically dispersed units form and reform in the pursuit of specific opportunities

committee structure

A structure in which authority is shared by several people rather than held by one manager

horizontal organization

An organization in which linkages among units form and dissolve for competitive advantage rather than according to the vertical hierarchy that will contribute to the corporation's overall competitiveness. Marketing plans are shared across national borders to discuss collaboration; production plants are built to supply one product on a world scale; sales representatives will look at all company sources for a product rather than feeling bound to the local production facility.

Naturally the traditional vertical hierarchy cannot disappear entirely; corporations that have successful horizontal structures have developed approaches that allow vertical and horizontal approaches to coexist. In Developing Your Skills in Business, Thomas A. Poynter and Roderick E. White discuss guidelines for the horizontal organization.

Advantages and disadvantages of each type of organizational structure are summarized in Table 7.2.

TABLE 7.2 • COMPARISON OF VARIOUS ORGANIZATIONAL STRUCTURES

Forms of organization	Advantages	Disadvantages
Line	1. Simple and easy for both workers and managers to understand 2. Clear delegation of authority and responsibility for each area 3. Quick decisions 4. Direct communications	1. No specialization 2. Overburdening of top executives with administrative details
Functional	1. The benefits of specialization 2. Expert advice available for each worker 3. Reduced managerial workload	1. Workers having more than one boss 2. Discipline breaking down unless authority is clearly defined 3. Possible conflict due to overlapping of authority
Line-and-Staff	1. Specialists to advise line managers 2. Employees reporting to one superior	1. Conflict between line and staff unless relationships are clear 2. Staff managers making only recommendations to line managers
Matrix	1. Flexibility 2. Provides method for focusing strongly on specific major problems or unique technical issues 3. Provides means of innovation without disrupting regular organizational structure	1. Problems may result, since this approach violates the traditional unit of command (one boss for each individual) principle 2. Project manager may encounter difficulty in developing cohesive team from diverse individuals recruited from numerous parts of the organization 3. Conflicts may arise between project managers and other department managers
Committee	1. Combined judgement of several executives in diverse areas 2. Improved morale through participation in decision making	1. Committees slow in making decisions 2. Decisions that are the result of compromises rather than a choice of the best alternative
Horizontal	1. Ability to react to changing world conditions to achieve cost advantages 2. Ability to tailor products for local markets 3. Sharing of information, research, and development across national boundaries	1. May appear risky and chaotic 2. Requires new approaches to avoid reassertion of vertical hierarchy 3. Results cannot be evaluated at the local level

DEVELOPING YOUR BUSINESS SKILLS

MAKING THE HORIZONTAL ORGANIZATION WORK

In our research we identified five activities needed to create and maintain a horizontal organization. They are:

1. *Creating Shared Values*

   Collaborative decision making is not possible unless an organization has shared decision premises or a set of business values. Instilling the members of an organization with shared values that will lead to common decision premises is often viewed as an act of personal, charismatic leadership by the CEO. And, although personal leadership is an important factor, value infusion needs to be a much more broadly based socialization process.

   Some firms have in fact established "educational institutions." Matsushita, better known for its Panasonic and Quasar brands, has an overseas training centre in Osaka, Japan. Managers and supervisors from around the world come to this centre to learn specific skills, but more importantly they are exposed to the Matsushita history and philosophy, in theory and in practice, to which the first few weeks of study are devoted. Only after this phase is complete do the trainees visit Matsushita facilities in Japan to see how the philosophy works in the field.

2. *Enabling the Horizontal Network*

   There seems to be a natural tendency in any organization for vertical relationships to (re)assert themselves, but successful horizontal organizations counter this in several ways. To offset the inclination of senior executives to emphasize vertical relationships, headquarters executives often have dual or multiple responsibilities. Typically one responsibility would be for a geographic area, another for a global product—a sort of reverse matrix structure. Instead of one subordinate's having two bosses, each with a different orientation, each boss has several subordinates with different orientations. In addition, these executive assignments are rotated regularly among senior managers at world headquarters.

3. *Redefining Managers' Roles*

   A horizontal network requires skills, attitudes, and approaches at the senior corporate management level that are different from those in conventional vertical organizations. Fundamentally, senior managers must create, maintain, and defend an organizational context that promotes lateral decision making oriented toward the achievement of competitive advantage worldwide. Their primary role is to facilitate these processes, act as referee when required, and, except for unique circumstances, avoid becoming involved in the substance of decisions.

   This process role, as opposed to a substantive role in decision making, is counter-instinctive for many managers who rose to the top because of their decisiveness and action orientation. They need, however, to learn to influence decisions and actions more indirectly, by inculcating members of the organization with corporate values, encouraging appropriate horizontal relationships, and facilitating lateral processes.

4. *Assessing Results*

   Assignment of performance responsibility and accountability for results within horizontal organizations is problematic. The people involved in horizontal collaborative efforts change over time, and their individual contributions are difficult to measure. Hence, rewarding the overall outcomes associated with individual performance is almost impossible. The use of typical summary measures of performance based on individual geographic or business unit results can actually impede the establishment of the horizontal organization. . . .

   A big part of the local general manager's job is forging the link between local actions,

(continued)

worldwide advantage, and overall results. An effective general manager within a horizontal organization needs to be familiar enough with the business, close enough to the action, and involved enough in decision making to ensure subordinates see the whole picture and act accordingly, even when locally reported results may suffer. . . .

5. *Evaluating People*

Meaningful assessment of people in the horizontal organization is based upon their demonstrated willingness to collaborate for the overall good of the enterprise. The horizontal organization has a number of characteristics that make this approach easier to use. The strong set of shared business values and operating premises are used as a template against which people are assessed; those who do not share and promote them are not likely to do well in the horizontal firm. Evaluating executives in terms of their acceptance and application of a common set of beliefs is particularly appropriate for international management, because of the shortcoming of orthodox vertical measures for evaluating people. . . .

The horizontal organization is costly and risky to the uninitiated. These five activities offset the chaos and lack of accountability that could result. . . . The horizontal organization leads to greater costs than the traditional vertical organization, but its flexibility and adaptability offer important benefits. This internal flexibility is extremely valuable when the firm is confronted with highly unpredictable technological, financial and marketing environments. In a vertical organization, the traditional approach of a senior manager in world headquarters, that is, determining the sources of advantage and then changing organizational elements in response, becomes impossible in the face of substantial uncertainty and complexity. But, under the horizontal organization, the individual subunits scattered around the world play a major role in positioning themselves to the overall advantage of the corporation. The specific business strategy followed by the company is, to a large extent, the outcome of a collaborative process, not senior executive dictate.

The horizontal organization is a solution worthy of consideration by a larger number of multinational corporations. It can allow Canadian, U.S., and European companies to compete successfully without having to give up all their local market capabilities, as they move toward a more global approach.

Source: Excerpts from Thomas A. Poynter and Roderick E. White, "Making the Horizontal Organization Work," *Business Quarterly*, Winter 1990, pp. 73–76. Reprinted with permission of Business Quarterly, published by The Western Business School, The University of Western Ontario, London, Ont., Canada. Winter '90 issue.

Question for Discussion

1. Explain how the role of a manager in a horizontal organization differs from that in a traditional organization in each of the five activities cited by Poynter and White.

Organizational Charts and Organizations

The past few pages have contained a number of generalized organizational charts. An **organizational chart** represents visually the formal lines of authority and levels of responsibility in an organization. It shows all employees not only the relationships of the various units to each other and who reports to whom but also how everyone's work contributes to the company's overall operation. Frequently referred to as a blueprint, the organizational chart gives a view at a glance of staff relationships, line authority relationships, and permanent committees.

The organizational chart assists managers to co-ordinate activities

organizational chart
A visual outline of formal lines of authority and responsibility in an organization

doughnut-shaped chart
An organizational chart in a circular format to represent how work actually flows

by identifying clearly the various areas of responsibility and authority. However, organizations are dynamic, and charts must be updated from time to time.

Most organizational charts are pyramid-shaped, broadening as they extend downward from the board of directors or president. But as described in Issues in Business 7.3, they rarely represent the way work actually flows. Some firms therefore, have adopted the "**doughnut**" chart to illustrate their structure, as recommended by Robert Townsend, a former president of Avis. In *Up the Organization*, a satire on business practices, Townsend argues for organizational charts that reflect the activities of a modern business:

In the best organizations people see themselves working in a circle as if around one table. One of the positions is designate chief executive officer, because somebody has to make all those tactical decisions that enable an organization to keep working.[7]

The doughnut design is made up of concentric circles, in which the centre ring consists of top management. The second ring is composed of important staff personnel, such as legal, human resources, research and development, and information processing, whose services are used by all departments. The third ring consists of managers of functional areas, while remaining rings comprise department and other supervisory managers. Figure 7.8 shows the construction of a doughnut-shaped organizational chart.

FIGURE 7.8 • A DOUGHNUT-SHAPED ORGANIZATIONAL CHART

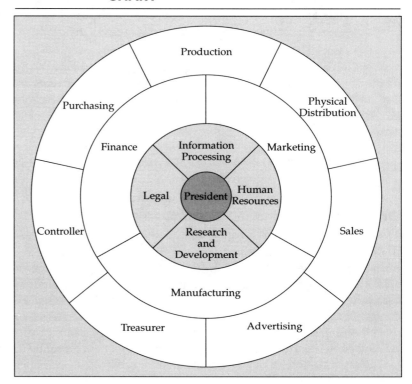

ISSUES IN BUSINESS 7.3

CHARTING WORK FLOW

ASK MOST MANAGERS to describe how their organization works and the first thing they will do is draw a picture that looks somewhat like a traditional organizational chart.

This "org chart" is a handy tool for describing reporting relations within an organization. It shows who reports to whom and what they are responsible for. But while an org chart describes reporting relationships, it does not describe how work actually gets done—how products or services get produced, delivered, and sold to customers.

In many organizations, the flow of work, from initial sales contact to final invoicing, proceeds across the organization, rather than up and down. As a result, employees are more often in contact with their counterparts in other departments than with superiors or colleagues in their own department.

So, although organization charts are a useful tool, trouble can arise when managers start to think of their organization as a collection of separate—or even competing—vertical functions and begin to manage accordingly.

Unless controlled, this can create what is known as a "silo" mentality, where each functional leader runs his or her own function as an independent fiefdom without regard for the negative effects on the rest of the organization.

For example, the sales department's numbers may look good if it has booked a lot of orders this month. However, if the products can't be manufactured on time, neither the organization nor the customer has benefited.

These kinds of problems may just be a result of poor communication between departments. But it might be the consequence of siloism, where the sales department is so fixed on making its own numbers that it doesn't care about any problems in manufacturing.

Either way, problems often arise as work flows across the so-called white space between departments, and managers at the top of each silo spend a lot of valuable time resolving difficulties with the heads of other functions.

According to consultants Geary Rummler and Alan Brache, many companies have found that great opportunities for performance improvement lie in functional interfaces—those points at which a baton is being passed from one department to another.

Rummler and Brache have just completed a book called *Improving Performance: How to Manage the White Space on the Organization Chart.* The two authors have studied how some leading companies like IBM, Ford, Boeing, and Motorola have used a practice called process management to improve the way they manage the flow of work.

Process management involves four simple steps:

1. Identifying the key processes. Each business should identify what its core processes are. What are the key products or services the business makes or does?
2. Charting each process. For each identified process, a chart should be drawn up showing the steps and the involvement of different departments. Take the airline industry, for example. What are the steps between selling a ticket and the passenger reaching a destination?
3. Identifying "disconnects." Using the chart of key processes, find the major interfaces between departments, or the points where one department's work depends on that of another. Identify critical interfaces and where there are the most errors or misunderstandings.

(continued)

4. Giving someone responsibility for the process. Many problems never get resolved because no one has responsibility for them. They just "fall between the cracks." Give ownership to someone and task them with finding ways to improve the interface.

Process management can be used to tackle any work process that crosses organizational boundaries, ranging from the ordinary (like how to expedite travel expense claims) to the most complex (like how to improve on-time delivery of new products).

"Most managers don't understand, at a sufficient level of detail, how their companies get products developed, made, sold, and distributed," say Rummler and Brache. Process management is a technique for analyzing what a company actually does and finding out how to do it better.

Source: Excerpts from Peter Larson, "Organizational Chart Provides Eye on Internal Relations," *The Montreal Gazette,* June 10, 1991, p. 6. Reprinted with permission from Peter Larson.

Questions for Discussion

1. What does a traditional organizational chart show? What does it fail to show?
2. Apply Rummler and Brache's concept of process management to a business you know and sketch a chart of the key processes required.

The Informal Organization

An organization is more than a collection of titles linked together by reporting relationships; it is also a group of people who talk to each other in the course of their work, gossip over coffee and lunch, meet on the bus or share car pools, and find mutual interests both inside and outside the workplace.

These relationships can cut across departmental lines and also bridge levels of responsibility. The company softball team may include operative employees, secretaries, programmers, supervisors, and the head of the finance department. The lunchtime crowd at the big table in the corner by the window may ebb and flow with clerical workers, junior managers, warehouse workers, and machinists. And the conversation will inevitably, at least part of the time, be about the organization.

grapevine
The informal communication network within an organization

If management respects this informal communication network or **grapevine**, it can be of immense value. It has been found that everyday information transmitted through the grapevine is largely accurate,[8] though at times of stress, stories may become exaggerated or distorted. Often the information can contribute to the smooth operation of the business, for example, when it answers questions that management did not think would need to be addressed. As the grapevine works by word of mouth, it also is faster to disseminate information than the official written communications of management. If managers are aware of the existence of the grapevine and how it works, they can use it to supplement official channels of communication and to counteract exaggerations or false rumours. At the same time, they must realize that it is almost impossible to manipulate the grapevine to hide the truth.

BUSINESS REVIEW 7.2

1. Describe a type of business that might be run with (a) a line structure; (b) a functional structure; (c) a line-and-staff structure.

2. For one type of business, describe aspects of the operation that might be run with (a) a matrix structure; (b) a committee structure.

3. What advantages can be gained by thinking of a business as a horizontal organization?

INTERACTIVE SUMMARY AND DISCUSSION QUESTIONS

1. What impressed you about the manner in which Stanford, president and chief operations officer of Petro-Canada, reorganized and restructured the giant crown corporation?

2. Explain what the hierarchy of organizational objectives is and what use it is to managers in complex organizations.

3. Give examples of firms that should employ each of the major forms of departmentalization listed below. Support your response.
   a) product
   b) geographic
   c) customer
   d) functional
   e) process

4. The typical professional sports team is owned by a wealthy individual who enjoys being involved with a particular sport. The owners usually make the major policy decisions, but a hired general manager handles other managerial duties. This person oversees facilities, equipment, vendors, and personnel matters, as well as usually having responsibility for player personnel decisions such as trades, new-player drafts, and assignment of players to minor leagues. The field manager, or head coach, is in charge of matters concerning players. Other personnel employed by professional teams include physicians, assistant coaches, trainers, equipment managers, secretaries, scouts, and ticket sales personnel. Draw an organizational chart for a professional sports team. Describe the strengths of this organizational structure.

5. The horizontal organization has been presented as a special structure for a firm to consider under certain circumstances. If they do decide to adopt this form, what are the five activities needed to create and maintain this structure? The first one is to create shared values. Describe briefly what you see as the meaning of this activity, and of the remaining four.

6. The organizational chart is quite useful, but trouble can begin when managers start to think of their organization as a collection of separate—and even competing—vertical functions and begin to manage these boxes accordingly. What problems are caused by this management perspective? What can be done to correct it?

CASE 7.1

MANAGING WITH NO MIDDLE

LABATT BREWERIES OF Canada's new Blue commercial opens like this: a cellular phone–toting yuppie struts up to a bar. He makes some calls, tries a line on a few women sitting nearby, and bombs. Although in business suits, the women spurn Mr. 1980s Archetype and turn to talk to a group of

(continued)

casually dressed men. The pitch is a sign of the times, and then some—because this ad says plenty about the new managerial life at the revamped Labatt's.

Since the beginning of the year, the venerable brewer eliminated its regional directors, rewrote its strategy, and shed about 120 managers. And now in Labatt's new world order, the swagger-up-to-the-bar management style doesn't cut it. As George Creelman, Labatt's new Saskatchewan general manager, is learning, he must assimilate the 1990s ethos for managing with fewer managers. That means dispersing real responsibility, guiding the staff as a coach rather than a boss, and keeping an eye fixed on corporate goals. His job is like driving a car without shocks, Creelman says: "You feel every bump."

The concept of the horizontal organization—where reporting lines stretch across departments and multidisciplinary teams supplant the boss's authority—is now part of mainstream thinking about bloated corporate structures. Information technology created redundancies everywhere. The consulting boom reflected the realization that some tasks, from data processing to product design, are better left to independent experts. The middle managers' worth came down to one question: did they add value? Let's just say we can add this corporate animal to the endangered species list.

During Labatt's corporate makeover, the 27-year veteran got the nod to be general manager for Saskatchewan. Creelman clearly relishes the fact that all aspects of the provincial operation eventually cross his desk. "I'm responsible for profit in this province," he asserts. "I can't hide from that."

As Creelman discovered, managers in a corporate glass house walk a fine line: with the added accountability, they must know more about their turf, yet they must be willing to delegate, and not just in name. The changes wrought at Labatt in Saskatchewan reflect the application of two objectives: a determination to manage the operation according to set strategy, and a desire to place direct responsibility at the employees' feet.

But delegation is just half the story. The disappearance of regional directors "eliminated a lot of information paperwork, because you're going to talk one on one." If Creelman wants to find a new plant manager inside Labatt, he'll get on a conference call with the nine other production managers to dig up a candidate. Before, head office would have given him a shopping list of names. Creelman now meets with the managers of finance, human resources, sales, quality control, and the brewmaster every Friday morning—no exceptions. Unlike the old regional monthlies, which he refers to as "who gives a damn" meetings, these are practical and timely. "We're not going to have them for the sake of having them."

As Labatt discovered, there is an umbilical link between management style and corporate structure. For the senior manager, a horizontal company is a very different creature from its vertical cousin. Spans of control increase, while the amount of time managers can devote to their staff decreases. Fewer supervisory layers, as Creelman acknowledges, means more personal exposure, especially for underachievers. Managers who are empire builders won't last. And customer service is the bottom line. "If you're not doing it for the customer, then why *are* you doing it?"

The concept of the flat organization is gaining acceptance among executives accustomed to neat pyramids. Typically, flat companies push decision-making and budgetary authority far down to reduce bureaucracy and encourage initiative at the customer-service level. The so-called cross-functional management team—comprised of managers from departments such as sales, marketing, R&D, and production—is a prominent player. Compensation is based on merit, not seniority.

"If you're waiting for things to go back to normal, forget it. This *is* normal." Senior managers must reconcile themselves to a redistribution of authority. "CEOs feel like they're going to lose control" observes one consultant. In the flat organization, managers will have more ways of getting tasks accomplished because decisions will be made by teams rather than individuals. A manager's influence will cut across networks, and their external relationship will become crucial factors in his own power base.

(continued)

Creelman searches for a suitable way to describe managing in an organization that decided to push authority into corners it's never been in before. "The way to think about empowerment is that we're trying to get people to act at work the same way they would act at home," Creelman says. "It's like your dad let you take the boat out."

Source: Excerpts from John Lorinc, "Managing When There's No Middle," *Canadian Business*, June 1991, pp. 86, 87, 92, 94. Reprinted with permission from John Lorinc.

Questions for Discussion

1. What is the difference between Labatt's horizontal organization and a traditional vertical structure?
2. How is it possible for George Creelman to function as general manager with no middle management? What are the implications of this management structure for management?

CASE 7.2

STRUCTURING AUTONOMY

DR. BERNARD BADLEY faces a daunting task as president and CEO of Atlantic Canada's largest hospital: he is responsible for turning Halifax's 800-bed Victoria General Hospital into an autonomous institution after 130 years as an arm of the provincial government.

As well as peeling away layers of bureaucracy and instilling a new ethic of accountability into managers, he's got to cope with some lofty comparisons.

In the midst of a provincial royal commission on health care in 1988, one commissioner opined that "Christ himself couldn't run that institution the way it's set up."

Badley himself doesn't talk about his role—or his goal—in such lofty terms. Instead, the British-born physician speaks in precise sentences of doing the logical thing by *restructuring* the hospital.

"A government organization is fine to run a liquor commission or a highways department perhaps, but its not ideally suited to run an organization like this which changes every day," he says.

The biggest day of change in the hospital's history occurred in 1992. The date, dubbed VG day, will see Badley heading an institution suddenly unfettered by a lot of red tape. While the institution will still be government-funded and receive a broad mandate from the provincial Department of Health, it will be free to meet its obligations under its own managers.

Badley is quick to point out that this is nothing new for Canada. He says the VG actually stands out as the last major acute-care hospital in Canada operating under direct government control.

To reach VG day successfully he must get his staff of 3,500 full-time and 500 part-time workers thinking and acting less like civil servants and more like private-sector employees.

"There needs to be a different sort of mindset and philosophy in moving from a civil service environment to a more entrepreneurial situation," he says.

As a government agency, the staff are literally civil servants and depend on government departments to keep the hospital running—from purchasing to payroll, from employment staffing to electrical work. Hiring a secretary has to be approved by a functionary downtown and involves a union-scrutinized and lengthy hiring procedure.

Badley is hoping freedom from the mandarins will mean managers accept responsibility and stop blaming civil servants outside the hospital for delays in getting things done. . . .

(continued)

Badley's chance to head the hospital—and work for transition—came with the sudden resignation of an executive director. After Badley pushed some organizational changes, the hospital board changed his one-year tenure to a five-year contract.

But administration hasn't removed him from medicine entirely. "To retain my sanity I see patients one-half day a week," he says.

One of his first acts on becoming executive director in 1988 was to change senior management, bolstering it with four new vice-presidents with different responsibilities. The move also changed his title to president and chief executive.

Now, he sees one of his biggest tasks as selling the staff on the shape of things to come. It has not always been easy.

The leadership of the Nova Scotia Government Employees Union, which represents most of the workers, has been far from supportive. The union has been extremely critical of the process, claiming the changes mean a move to private health care, he says.

That attitude isn't matched by the rank and file, however. Instead, questions from unionized workers at hospital meetings have reflected concern and fear, not antagonism.

Their concerns are easily understood. While the government has promised the transition will not mean job cuts, Badley may be forced to make layoffs because of budget shortfalls.

Source: Reprinted from Michael Redmond, "Getting Hospital Free a Difficult Operation," *The Financial Post*, April 12, 1991, p. 8.

Questions for Discussion

1. What are some of the problems Dr. Badley should expect as he restructures the Victoria General Hospital and moves from a civil service culture to one of entrepreneurship?

2. What changes will Dr. Badley as CEO of Atlantic Canada's largest hospital have to introduce in attitudes to authority, responsibility, and accountability?

NOTES

1. Cliff Bilyea, director of Ancillary Services, Wilfred Laurier University.

2. Direct quote from Bill Etherington, President and CEO of IBM Canada Limited, as appearing in Laura Ramsey, "Etherington Brings New View to Big Blue," *The Financial Post*, April 31, 1992 Reprinted with permission from IBM Canada Limited.

3. C. Northcote Parkinson, *Parkinson's Law and Other Studies in Administration* (Boston: Houghton Mifflin, 1957), p. 2.

4. Parkinson, *Parkinson's Law*, pp. 7–11.

5. Parkinson, *Parkinson's Law*, pp. 4–7.

6. Frederick W. Taylor, *The Principles of Scientific Management* (New York: Harper Bros., 1916).

7. The material in this section is based on Thomas A. Pointer and Roderick E. White, "Making the Horizontal Organization Work," *Business Quarterly*, Winter 1990, pp. 73–76.

8. Keith Davis, *Human Relations at Work* (New York: McGraw-Hill, 1972), p. 134.

PHOTO CREDITS

MODULE
◆ PEO ◆

WHY PEOPLE WORK

THE FOCUS OF THIS MODULE

1. To explain the impact on business of scientific management theory and the human relations approach to management

2. To describe content theories of motivation, including the hierarchy of needs, two-factor, ERG, and acquired needs theories

3. To describe process theories of motivation, including equity, goal-setting, and expectancy theories

4. To contrast Theory X and Theory Y beliefs about the psychology of workers

5. To discuss the importance of morale to motivation and productivity

6. To identify quality-of-work-life concepts and programs, including management by objectives, job enrichment, flexible work schedules, and job sharing

7. To consider the effects of participative management techniques in a "Theory Z" organization

8. To learn the meaning of the following terms:

KEY TERMS

Hawthorne effect	equity theory
scientific management	Theory X
human relations approach to management	Theory Y
	morale
need	management by objectives (MBO)
motive	
hierarchy of needs	job enrichment
two-factor theory	job enlargement
ERG theory	flextime
acquired needs theory	compressed workweek
expectancy theory	job sharing
goal-setting theory	Theory Z

WHEN MARG BAILLE'S husband retired after a twenty-year career in the military, she decided it was time for a change too. The pert, cheery-voiced woman gave up her profession as a social worker and opened a small art gallery in Yellowknife. "It's something I always wanted to do," she said. "So I did it. I was always interested in art, but we moved around a lot with the military. Now we're settled."

Changing careers is becoming more and more common as the workplace evolves and people's goals and ambitions shift. The day is almost gone when someone just out of school would start with a company and remain until retirement. The company might fold or switch its production, or merge with someone else. Or the worker might simply decide it's time to do something else and move on. The motive could be boredom, a desire for more money, or simply to satisfy some long-buried ambition.

A study by the Economic Council of Canada showed that, over a five-year period, almost half of all workers changed jobs. People who 30 years ago might simply have dreamed a dream now seek to make it real. Where workers might once have toiled at unsatisfying jobs, many now chuck it and start anew. They might want to become writers or lawyers or sociologists.

Audrey McLaughlin, the leader of the federal New Democratic Party, is a case in point. In her life before politics, she raised a family, taught school in Africa, helped women in the Caribbean start their own businesses, worked as a social worker, and ran a mink farm. A decade ago, she tired of her life in Toronto: "I'm of the view you should do something different every ten years," she says. She decided on the Yukon after studying a map of Canada. "I bought a truck and sold my stuff and went."

The idea of work for work's sake is becoming tarnished, and job satisfaction and the quality of life—a vague term with as many meanings as there are people—are growing in importance for many men and women. . . .

When Michael Pahkala was laid off from a Saskatchewan potash mine, he decided to improve his prospects. He enrolled in the mining school at Queen's University. The wiry young man wants to be a mine supervisor instead of a miner: "I could see I could do their job just as well as they could, but they had a piece of paper and I didn't."

Monique Bourget is a 36-year-old Montreal secretary and a single mother. She's planning to start university this fall, seeking a degree in social work. "I want something better than typing, filing and taking dictation," she said. "I want something better and I know if you work at it you can get it."

She's probably on the right track. Statistics Canada forecasts that, in percentage terms, the growth in job openings for social workers will be three times the openings for mechanics in the next few years.

Andy Gwinn of Vancouver has a teaching degree, but wants a business degree. "I think I'll like business better than the classroom," he said.

The Statistics Canada forecasts say he'll probably be better off, as the demand for teachers slowly shrinks.

Training and retraining. Two or even three careers in a lifetime. These are likely to become commonplace.

Source: Excerpts from John Ward, "Trading Places," *The Montreal Gazette*, September 2, 1990, p. B6.

A NY COMPANY would be glad to have intelligent, involved people like Marg Baille, Michael Pahkala, Monique Bourget, and Andy Gwinn work for it. What motivates these people to the extent that they are prepared to start new careers? How can managers make best use of the talents and the interests of workers like these to the advantage of the organization?

Motivating workers to do the best job possible is part of the leading function of management. Sensitive and effective leadership requires an understanding of why people work, what they expect to achieve in their jobs, and the personal satisfactions they hope to obtain from them.

The traditional belief has been that workers work for money: "Your motivation is your paycheque," the harassed stage director replied to the actor who had asked what the motivation was for the move he was to make across the stage. Various studies over the course of the twentieth century have indicated that the actor had a valid point. People need to be involved if they are to perform their jobs satisfactorily.

THE HAWTHORNE STUDIES

In 1927, Elton Mayo led a research team in a study at the Hawthorne Plant of the Western Electric Company to discover whether improved lighting and other physical conditions would increase the productivity of workers assembling electrical relays. Groups of workers were asked to act as experimental subjects and as control groups. Then, various changes were systematically introduced in the experimental setting. Improved lighting had beneficial effects on productivity, as did better ventilation. Coffee breaks and snacks were introduced, and again output went up.

Eventually, the investigators became suspicious about the consistently positive effects of all these changes, and they began restoring the original conditions, even turning the lighting down gradually so that the workers did not notice it. The researchers discovered that productivity did not suffer. Even more baffling, output continued to rise even when the employees worked in lighting conditions similar to moonlight.

[Mayo and his colleagues] swooned at their desks. . . . Because of some mysterious X which had thrust itself into the experiment. . . this group of six women was pouring 25 percent more relays into the chutes. . .

What was this X? The research staff pulled themselves together and began looking for it. They conferred, argued, studied, and presently they found it. It wasn't in the physical production end of the factory at all. It was in the workers themselves. It was an attitude, the way the women now felt about their work and their group. By segregating them into a little world of their own, by asking their help and cooperation, the investigators had given their subjects a new sense of their own value. Their whole attitude changed from that of separate cogs in a machine to that of a congenial team helping the company solve a significant problem.

They found stability, a place where they belonged, and work whose purpose they could clearly see. And so they worked faster and better than they ever had in their lives. The two functions of a factory had joined into one harmonious whole.[1]

Hawthorne effect
A theory that simply paying special attention to workers will improve their productivity

scientific management
Development of precise procedures to improve productivity, for example, through time and motion study to perfect the efficiency of an assembly line

human relations approach to management
Examining workers as people and how their needs act as motivating forces that affect their behaviour

need
Something missing that the individual wants or requires

motive
An inner feeling that encourages a person to take some action leading toward satisfaction of the need

What Mayo and his team had discovered is now known as the **Hawthorne effect**: that simply paying attention to workers and treating them as valued contributors to the organization's goals is as important to productivity as other factors such as pay and working conditions. This was borne out by the fact that productivity also rose in the control group whose working conditions had not changed—except for the fact that they knew they were part of the study.

Before the Hawthorne studies, most management experts had concentrated on **scientific management**, which aimed at developing precise procedures to improve productivity through such techniques as time and motion study. Researchers examined the steps involved in completing a given task. They subdivided tasks into separate steps and allocated each step to a specialized worker who was to perform the set task at a controlled pace without variation. The objective was to perfect the efficiency of the assembly line—in short, scientific management considered workers as cogs in the machine.

The Hawthorne studies gave prominence to the human relations approach to management that had emerged at the end of the nineteenth century but that had been overshadowed by the more easily measured benefits of scientific management techniques. The **human relations approach** looked at workers as people, examining their needs as motivating forces that affect their behaviour as they try to satisfy those needs. Figure 8.1 illustrates the process. A **need** represents something missing that the individual wants or requires. A **motive** is an inner feeling (for example, a desire or a fear) that encourages a person to take some action leading toward satisfaction of the need. When the individual is persuaded to move (the root word for "motive"), the action he or she takes reduces the state of tension and the organism then returns to a relaxed state of equilibrium.

CONTENT THEORIES OF MOTIVATION

Content theories of motivation concentrate on the first element in the motivation process: people's needs. They are based on the idea that if managers understand people's needs, they will be able to design reward systems that will increase motivation.

FIGURE 8.1 • THE PROCESS OF MOTIVATION

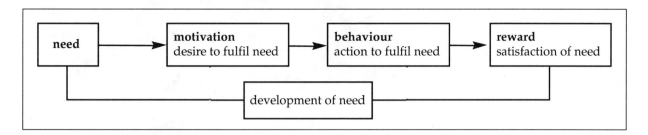

A Hierarchy of Needs

In 1943, psychologist Abraham Maslow formulated a list of human needs in the form of a hierarchy as illustrated in Figure 8.2. Maslow's **hierarchy of needs** was based on the thesis that lower-order needs had to be at least partially satisfied before a person began to think about higher-order needs. Maslow also pointed out that once a need is satisfied, it can no longer be used as a motivator; only needs the person still feels will seem important. He identified five types of needs, listed here in ascending order:

1. *Physiological needs* are the basic needs for food, clothing, and shelter. When a hungry person can think only of the need to find food, all other needs are temporarily put on hold. However, as soon as the physiological needs are at least partially satisfied, needs higher on the waiting list start demanding attention. In most industrialized countries, minimum wage laws, collective agreements, and welfare and pension arrangements provide most people with money adequate to satisfy their basic needs. Thus, today higher-order needs play a greater role in employee motivation.
2. *Safety needs* include job security, protection from physical harm, and avoidance of the unexpected. These needs are satisfied by guaranteed annual wages, group life insurance, the availability of unemployment insurance, medicare, and safety regulations in the workplace.
3. Once physiological and safety needs have been satisfied, people begin to consider their *social needs*. In the workplace, such needs include acceptance by the work group and other less formal social contacts.
4. When people feel they belong to the group, they begin to feel *esteem needs*, the desire to be valued and appreciated for their achievements and talents. *Esteem needs* lead people to work for promotions and to want recognition for their contribution to the organization.
5. *Self-actualization needs* are the needs to develop one's potential to the fullest, for what Maslow referred to as "peak experiences." The concept was expressed by Lao-tzu more than twenty-five centuries ago as "The way to do is to be." The Danish philosopher Kierkegaard believed that the aim of life is "to be the self which one truly is." Robert Louis Stevenson offered the suggestion that "to be what we are, and to become what we are capable of becoming, is the only end of life." Self-actualization can take many forms. The approximately 200 new entries in each revised edition of the *Guinness Book*

hierarchy of needs
A theory that people are motivated by a hierarchy of five categories of needs—physiological, safety, social, esteem, and self-actualization—and that as lower-order needs are satisfied they cease to have motivating effect

Emergency first aid training for all in-flight crew members ensures that everyone knows how to respond in the event of an emergency situation. This training allows the in-flight crew members to feel more secure in their respective positions and to be confident when helping passengers in need of first aid assistance.

of World Records represent individuals daring to accomplish what no person has done before. At work, self-actualization needs can be satisfied through promotion to challenging positions and other opportunities to be creative.

FIGURE 8.2 • MASLOW'S HIERARCHY OF NEEDS

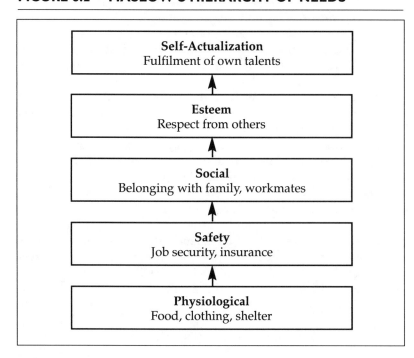

Basic physiological needs are largely satisfied in modern industrial societies and are no longer a motivating force. So for the most part are safety needs, though in times of recession, unemployment and the fear of unemployment mean that safety needs may still be a powerful motivator in some circumstances. (It is interesting to note that Maslow based his theory on observations made during the Depression of the 1930s, another time when unemployment was feared by many people.) It is the higher-order needs for belonging socially, esteem, and self-actualization that are most likely to be motivators in today's workplace.

Maslow's theory is illustrated by the earlier findings of the Hawthorne studies, which showed managers that workers could not be treated merely as machines that could be kept oiled by the incentive of money. The satisfaction of social and psychological needs were also powerful motivators. Managers now had to expand their perception of their employees and to develop new ways of motivating them.

Dissatisfiers and Motivators

In the mid-1960s, Frederick Herzberg developed a **two-factor theory** of motivation based on interviews with workers. He asked them about times when they felt dissatisfied with their work and times when they felt highly motivated. He discovered that the absence of what he called *hygiene factors*—good pay, safe working conditions, pleasant relationships with supervisors and other workers—created dissatisfaction. But putting these factors in place did not motivate the workers; it merely removed the sources of dissatisfaction. For workers to want to perform well, they needed *motivators*—they had to enjoy the work itself, feel a sense of achievement and responsibility, and know that their efforts were recognized.[2]

As illustrated in Figure 8.3, Herzberg's two-factor theory bears out Maslow's theory of a hierarchy of needs: Herzberg's dissatisfiers are the physiological, safety, and social needs that are filled for most people today. Only esteem and self-actualization needs seem to act as motivators.

two-factor theory
A theory that workers will be dissatisfied in the absence of hygiene factors such as good pay and safe working conditions and only motivated by the work itself, recognition, and achievement

Existence, Relatedness, and Growth

Alderfer's ERG **theory** is at the same time simpler and more complex than Maslow's hierarchy of needs. Alderfer suggests there are three categories of needs; *existence* or survival needs, *relatedness* or social interaction needs, and *growth* or personal development needs. Alderfer's research led him to the conclusion that movement through the hierarchy could proceed in both directions, reflecting the *frustration–regression principle*. In other words, a person who was unable to satisfy growth needs might well revert to concentrating on the satisfaction of existence needs by trying to make a lot of money or of relatedness needs by partying every night.[3]

ERG theory
A theory that humans have three categories of needs—existence, relatedness, and growth—and that if a higher-order need is frustrated, people may regress to satisfy lower-order needs

Acquired Needs

So far the theories we have looked at have concentrated on what the theorists have thought of as universal human needs. David

acquired needs theory
A theory that certain needs, such as those for achievement, affiliation, and power, are not inborn but acquired on the basis of life experiences

McClelland proposed that certain needs are not inborn but acquired. His **acquired needs** theory suggests that three such needs are for *achievement*, attaining high levels of success; *affiliation*, having warm personal relationships and avoiding conflict, and *power*, influencing and having authority over others. Early life experiences will determine which of these needs is most important to any particular individual. For example, children who are encouraged to do things and are praised for doing so will develop a need for achievement. They may often grow up to be entrepreneurs.

McClelland's theory suggests that people can be taught, even in later life, to develop certain needs. This finding has implications for employee training programs, which might aim at fostering a need for achievement in non-supervisory and lower-management levels or encourage the need for power to enhance performance of top-management candidates. The theory also holds a warning: by focussing on long hours and tireless devotion, companies can create damaging needs in their employees as discussed in Issues in Business 8.1.

Figure 8.3 compares the descriptions of human needs in various content theories of motivation.

FIGURE 8.3 • A COMPARISON OF CONTENT THEORIES OF MOTIVATION

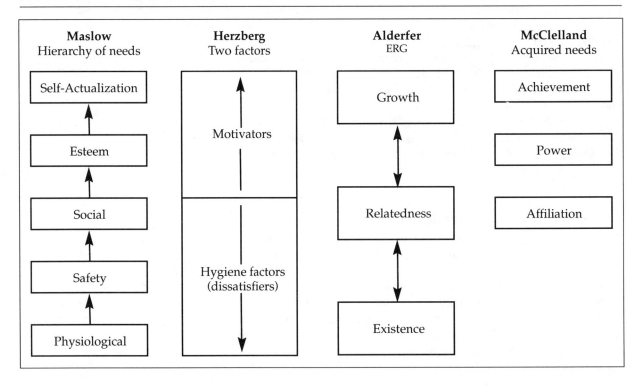

ISSUES IN BUSINESS 8.1

WORKAHOLICS

DURING THE success-oriented 1980s, "workaholic" was often a positive term used to describe fast-track baby boomers who earned their corporate reputations with long hours and a tireless devotion to detail. They carried bulging briefcases, worked late, and sacrificed their weekends in the hope of promotions, higher pay—and higher profits for their employers. But some psychologists now say that, for some people, the relentless pursuit of on-the-job perfection actually results in diminished productivity. Indeed, some experts say that eventually workaholics can lose their sense of control over their work and their lives. When that occurs, the person who is addicted to work can turn moody, become prone to rages, and alienate his or her family, friends, and colleagues. Said Barbara Killinger, a Toronto psychologist: "At their worst, workaholics are soulless—there's nothing inside, they have lost their integrity."

According to Killinger, who wrote *Workaholics: The Respectable Addicts*, published by Key Porter Books, workaholics are men or women who are addicted to working and who, as a result, experience personality changes. Yet despite the sometimes alarming consequences of the addiction, Killinger says that the problem is still widely misunderstood. She and other experts say that an increasing number of people are seeking treatment for workaholism. Because the addiction takes hold so slowly, Killinger said that co-workers and spouses tend to dismiss the early symptoms of workaholism—anxiety, irritability, and restlessness—as the temporary side effects of overwork.

At the same time, Kenneth Des Roches, an Ottawa-based employment counsellor with Peat Marwick Stevenson & Kellogg, a management consulting firm, says that employers sometimes make the problem worse by assuming that someone with workaholic attributes will be a model employee. By giving a workaholic more responsibility and prestige, says Des Roches, who regularly counsels individuals suffering from workaholism, employers can unwittingly push the workaholic too far. Still, Des Roches says that the main problem is the obsession itself. "People get a high from their work, and it becomes something of a vortex that they get caught up in," he said. "Before long, they need it, and they don't want to live without it."

Although the word "workaholism" has been in use for only about twenty years, psychologists say that the addiction has existed for much longer.... Bart, a recovering Vancouver workaholic who at one time juggled a full-time job and a private business during eighteen-hour days, told *Maclean's* that his addiction began in his childhood. Bart, 55, who asked that his last name be withheld, said that it was only by stopping work completely that he was able to deal with his workaholism. "Work is a way of avoiding your feelings, like booze or drugs," he said. "Work gives you the feeling that you're in control."

Killinger, who has studied workaholism for eight years, says that the classic workaholic starts off as a perfectionist who desperately needs the approval of others. Over time, she says, working becomes a compulsion and, finally, a single-minded pursuit of self-glorification that can lead to emotional problems and personality changes. Striving for power and control, workaholics suffer from chronic fatigue and guilt, are racked by fears, and sometimes even become incapable of distinguishing right from wrong. For her part, Susan Butt, a psychologist at the University of British Columbia in Vancouver, says that workaholics reach the crisis stage when they begin to lose control over their lives. When that happens to workaholics, says Butt, "they lose their sense of well-being."

(continued)

According to Killinger, workaholics are capable of lying, cheating, and, in extreme cases, violence if it serves their purposes. Increasingly bound to their work, yet feeling out of control, they may become impatient with their children and lash out at their spouses. "More and more," said Killinger, "I am realizing how much damage is done to the spouse."

According to Des Roches, companies and their employees have to recognize workaholism as a risk factor in order to prevent it from causing problems in the workplace. "Many companies are beginning to realize that being obsessed with work is counterproductive," he said. Individual employees, he added, must learn to work within realistic limits and not rely on work to feed their egos. Otherwise, the successes gained from overwork can ultimately lead to painful failure.

Killinger says that many work addicts can be cured if they get help early. Most important, she said, was for them to gain an understanding of their own feelings, and a realization of how their addiction has harmed their families and friends. "In most cases, what they have left behind is a pile of broken lives," she said. Killinger added that if workaholics can feel remorse for the damage they have done, then they can usually recover. But, for the minority of workaholics who are unable to do that, the future is likely to turn into a fast track to failure, both on and off the job.

Source: Excerpts from "Fast Track to Failure," *Maclean's*, June 17, 1991, p. 49.

Question for Discussion

1. Discuss how workaholism is a damaging need that can have negative consequences for both employee and the employer.

PROCESS THEORIES OF MOTIVATION

Rather than focussing on the workers' actual needs, process theories of motivation concentrate on the behaviour of workers as they attempt to meet those needs and how they decide whether they have succeeded in doing so.

Meeting Expectations

expectancy theory
A theory that motivation in the performance of a task is based on the relationship between effort and performance, between performance and outcome, and the value of that outcome for the individual

Expectancy theory, often associated with Victor Vroom, examines the thought processes and motivations of an individual approaching a task. It assumes that the person assesses the amount of *effort* that *performance* of a task is likely to take in relation to the desirability of the *outcome* that good performance will bring.

Several factors contribute to an individual's level of motivation. The first is *expectancy*, the individual weighing his or her capabilities and whether the effort involved will result in performing well. The next is *instrumentality*, the individual considering whether successful performance will lead to the expected outcome. Finally, there is *valence*, whether the outcome, or reward, is something valued by the individual. For high motivation, all three factors must be present.

Expectancy theory does not define needs or rewards; in fact, it emphasizes that they may be different for different people. James Bowditch and Anthony Buono give the following example to show how motivation operates:

Assume, for example, that there is a possibility of a reward (promotion, monetary bonus) for the preparation of a special report that must be well done and useful to management. The reward is important to the individual (high valence), so he or she is willing to work hard on the report. However, if the worker is unclear as to the type of report management wants, working hard may be perceived as wasting time. Since the effort involved on the report may require additional work hours which can cut into household responsibilities, the expectations of potential of marital discord could outweigh the potential reward, especially if what constitutes a "useful" report is unclear. Thus, the probability, linking the effort and performance together, will be relatively low. Even though it might be acknowledged that the individual worked hard and produced a quality report, the report may still not be useful to management (low instrumentality). Thus, getting the reward (valent item) may be perceived as unlikely, undermining the person's motivation to perform.[4]

Setting Goals

Goal-setting theory, put forward by E.A. Locke, suggests that the act of setting goals can itself be a source of motivation. A person will strive to achieve something that he or she has consciously decided to do. Furthermore, setting "difficult" (but not unrealistic) goals is a greater motivator than setting "easy" ones. Other factors that increase motivation are specific goals rather than vague or general ones, and the participation of the individual in setting the goals—if the manager simply says "Your goal is to increase sales by 25 percent this month," the sales representative is far less likely to feel motivated to achieve it than if the two have discussed and arrived at the specific target together.[5]

goal-setting theory
A theory that the act of setting goals can itself be a source of motivation

Is It Fair?

Equity theory focusses on people's perceptions of the way they are treated in relation to the way others are. J. Stacey Adams suggested that individuals strive to achieve a balance between the ratio of the inputs they bring to the job in the form of education, skills, experience, and effort and the outcomes they receive in the form of salary, recognition, or promotion and the inputs and outcomes of others.[6]

For example, assume that employee A is experienced and reliable, and has been with the firm for fifteen years, and that employee B is recently hired. If A sees B being promoted or being paid a higher wage, A would perceive this as inequitable and might complain to the boss, call in sick, or simply reduce the amount of effort put into work in order to restore the balance. B, who also would see the situation as inequitable, might work extra hard in order to justify the greater rewards. B might also try to restore the balance by suggesting that A receive the same or similar rewards. Both A and B may also try to regain equity by changing their perceptions: A may decide that B's rewards are not as great as they first seemed; B may come to believe

equity theory
A theory that people's perceptions of how fairly they are treated in relation to others affects their motivation

that he or she is more talented than previously understood. The discomfort of the inequity may also lead to one or both seeking new employment where they hope they will find greater equity.

Managers should strive to maintain equity in the eyes of employees. Those who see themselves as unfairly treated will have little motivation to perform well. The effect of inequity even on those who receive unexpected rewards may be confusion rather than greater motivation.

BUSINESS REVIEW 8.1

1. How did the Hawthorne studies help to shift attention from the physical concerns of scientific management to interest in the motivation of workers emphasized by the human relations approach to management?

2. What is the major difference between content and process theories of motivation? Which approach do you believe is more helpful in understanding the motivation of workers?

THEORY X AND THEORY Y

Douglas McGregor has described two theories about the psychology of workers that managers may hold. What he calls **Theory X** states:

1. The average human being has an inherent dislike of work and will avoid it if possible.
2. Because of this characteristic, most people must be coerced, controlled, directed, or threatened with punishment to get them to put forth adequate effort toward the achievement of organization objectives.
3. The average human being prefers to be directed, wishes to avoid responsibility, has relatively little ambition, and wants security above all.[7]

Managers who hold to Theory X concentrate on responding only to physiological and safety needs; higher-order needs receive no attention at all. It is true that there are employees in some firms who fit the Theory X model. The question for managers is whether these employees hold such attitudes in the first place or whether they have learned them from managers who focus on satisfying only the basic needs in Maslow's hierarchy. Organizations that work to satisfy social, esteem, and self-actualization needs as well have a good chance of seeing new behaviour patterns emerge.

Theory Y is based on a new and challenging assumption—that employees do not dislike work. Under supportive working conditions, they will show initiative and take on new responsibilities as a way of satisfying their higher-order needs. According to McGregor, the key points in Theory Y are:

Theory X
The belief that people dislike work and must be coerced to perform

Theory Y
The belief that work is natural and that, under proper conditions, people will seek out responsibility and use imagination and intelligence to solve problems

1. Workers do not inherently dislike work. The expenditures of physical and mental effort in work are as natural as play or rest.
2. Employees do not want to be rigidly controlled and threatened with punishment. They will exercise self-direction and self-control in the service of organizational objectives to which they are committed.
3. The average worker will, under proper conditions, not only accept but actually seek responsibility.
4. The capacity to exercise a relatively high degree of imagination, ingenuity, and creativity in the solution of organizational problems is widely, not narrowly distributed in the population.
5. Under the conditions of modern industrial life, the intellectual potential of the average worker is only partially utilized.[8]

McGregor believed that most managers hold to Theory X with its emphasis on external control and continual supervision. He felt, however, that Theory Y was really more representative of the modern work force in companies that foster decentralization, delegation, and broader job responsibilities in the interest of effectiveness and productivity.

Morale

What managers believe about workers and the way they treat them can have a great effect on morale within an organization. **Morale** is the attitude that workers have toward the company and the degree of enthusiasm they bring to their work. When morale is high, dedication to common organizational goals unifies the group.

morale
The attitude that workers have toward the company and the degree of enthusiasm they bring to their work

Many offices take part in charity fundraising campaigns, like the United Way, both to contribute to a good cause as a group and to raise employee morale. A positive office morale leads to higher productivity and enhanced company dedication. Participating in charity events is a good way to promote a good sense of camaraderie that will contribute to a happier workplace for all employees.

Low morale occurs when managers and employees disagree on key issues. The symptoms are absenteeism, employee turnover, poor co-operation, and strikes, and the result is predictable: decreased productivity.

Though managers are aware of the need for high morale, they often fail to understand the factors that lead to it. One study asked managers and employees to rank the importance of ten factors believed to have an effect on morale. Table 8.1 presents the ranking from the viewpoint of both groups. The managers emphasized the lower-order needs of money and job security, but the employees' ranking tells a different story.

Maintaining high morale is not simply a matter of keeping employees happy. Offering a shorter workweek, longer vacations, more coffee breaks, subsidized lunches, and carpeted offices do not improve morale. Morale is highest when employees obtain satisfaction directly from the work itself and are motivated to do it well. This naturally leads to increased productivity.

BUSINESS REVIEW 8.2

1. Think about your most recent boss/supervisor. Would you describe her or him as a Theory X or a Theory Y manager? Why do you feel this person has selected this management approach?

2. The survey in Table 8.1 was conducted nearly 50 years ago. Do you think attitudes of managers and employees have changed much over the last half-century. Why or why not?

TABLE 8.1 • MANAGERS' AND EMPLOYEES' ASSESSMENT OF FACTORS LEADING TO HIGH MORALE

Manager ranking	Employee ranking	Morale item
1	5	Good wages
2	4	Job security
3	7	Promotion and growth with company
4	9	Good working conditions
5	6	Interesting work
6	8	Management loyalty to workers
7	10	Tactful disciplining
8	1	Full appreciation for work done
9	3	Sympathetic understanding of personal problems
10	2	Feeling "in" on things

Source: Adapted from Lawrence Lindahl, "What Makes a Good Job," *Personnel*, January 1949, p.265. Reprinted by permission of publisher, from. PERSONNEL, January, 1949 © 1949. American Management Association, New York, All rights reserved.

IMPROVING MOTIVATION IN TODAY'S WORKPLACE

The workplace has progressed a long way from the days of scientific management when it was believed that the simpler a job was, the more efficiently it would be completed. Few managers today subscribe to the theory of job simplification. They know that boredom leads to "the blue-collar blues." Experience has shown that the quality of life in the workplace suffers when workers cannot take responsibility for controlling their pace, cannot take initiative or make judgements, and are given no incentive to move beyond a minimal skill level. Workers in this situation tend to lose the desire to participate willingly in achieving the goals of the organization.

When workplaces are rigidly managed and tasks narrowly defined, boredom is not the only undesirable consequence. Workers are not encouraged to be flexible. New engineering technologies in the factory and new information systems in the office demand a work force that has the skills and motivation to adjust, change, and evolve as the need arises. This has become more important as foreign competition has caused the disappearance of vast numbers of manufacturing jobs in the automobile and steel industries.

Current efforts to restructure the workplace are discussed within the framework of the quality of work life (QWL). This is a process in which each and every employee in the organization is actively encouraged to participate, not only through work in the normal sense, but also through meaningful contributions to defining both the overall organizational environment and the specific jobs for which they are responsible. This process, as described in Developing Your Business Skills, challenges management to treat workers as mature, individual adults with important and valuable input. A QWL program ties in the goals of the organization with those of workers: job enrichment, flexible work schedules, and participative management.

DEVELOPING YOUR BUSINESS SKILLS

STANDARDIZED PRODUCTION OR WORKER INPUT?

Many of the world's most successful companies are reorganizing management and manufacturing to give workers great input into determining and achieving the enterprise's objectives. Call it decentralization, teamwork, or quality circles, it is something more Canadian companies should consider.

In the traditional approach, company objectives are thought best achieved through standardized production that provides little scope for individual input. Labour is a cost to be minimized. That approach has been considered useful for high-volume production of basic goods, but is badly out of date—especially where innovation and quality are paramount.

The new approach sees workers as the company's most important resource. Recognizing the importance of the group dynamic, involving workers in decisions about objectives, seeking and rewarding their ideas on problem solving and improvements can pay big dividends for both workers and management. Workers feel a sense of identity with the process. They are given

(continued)

greater control over what they do and how much they earn. More highly motivated workers are absent less frequently and are less adversarial in labour–management relations.

An essential element in implementing such a program is the early involvement of employees in the planning process, so they will be as committed to its success as management itself.

The intellectual origins of this approach have been traced to Norwegian thinker Enar Thorsrud, and it was implemented in the late 1960s at the Kalmar Volvo plant in Sweden. The concept was introduced into the United States in the 1970s, but didn't really catch on until the 1980s. The Japanese took over this Western "social technology" and have become, according to Peter Drucker, "the most thorough practitioners of decentralization in the world."

One of the first companies in Canada to introduce such a reorientation was the Shell Chemical plant in Sarnia in 1978. Production at the plant is organized around six shift teams of nineteen people. New workers are selected by the workers themselves. Skills diversification is encouraged; workers who succeed in reaching a certain level of competence in six of the plant's ten skills classifications plus two maintenance skills earn the plant's top salary. Those salaries are higher than those earned by those doing comparable jobs in other companies in the industry.

The new GM–Suzuki plant in Ingersoll, Ontario, in operation since April 1989, has borrowed Suzuki's teamwork approach in Japan. Each area of production is done by a small group of eight to fifteen people. Workers are encouraged to become multiskilled. Their suggestions on resolving problems or making improvements are encouraged by both financial rewards and management commitment to immediate feedback. This approach is seen to be the most effective way of consistently producing quality automobiles, something U.S. car manufacturers now recognize as key to Japanese success. Northern Telecom is one of the Canadian firms considering this type of managerial and manufacturing reorganization, based on self-directed work teams piloted at its Morrisville, North Carolina, plant.

All businesses, even in the same industry, can't be lumped together in terms of production techniques and problems. But more direct involvement by workers in decision making and forward planning can mean improved productivity, better quality, and a healthier bottom line. In an increasingly competitive world, it's an approach that commends itself to Canadian management.

Source: Excerpts from "Worker Involvement Can Have Big Payoff." *The Financial Post.* April 11, 1990, p. 14.

Question for Discussion

1. Why might workers feel motivated to do well in the companies discussed here?

Management by Objectives

management by objectives (MBO)
A strategy whereby employees participate in setting goals, which are then used as a standard for evaluation of performance

Management by objectives (MBO) is a technique advocated by Peter Drucker as long ago as the 1950s. Drucker described it this way:

The objectives of the district manager's job should be clearly defined by the contribution he and his district sales force have to make to the sales department, the objectives of the project engineer's job by the contribution he, his engineers and draftsmen make to the engineering department. . . . This requires each manager to develop and set the objectives of his unit himself. Higher management must, of course, reserve the power to approve or disapprove his objectives. But their development is part of a manager's responsibility; indeed, it is his first responsibility.[9]

Management by objectives uses goal-setting theory in a strategy that aims at increasing motivation by directly involving employees in determining their own goals. Once goals have been agreed on by employees and management, they become the standard by which employees know their performance will be evaluated.

Management by objectives is a five-step program. Figure 8.4 represents the order of the five steps in standard MBO programs:

1. Individual employees review projects, timetables, and goals with the manager.
2. The employee and the manager agree on short-term performance goals.
3. The subordinate and the manager meet regularly to discuss progress toward the goals.
4. Progress is measured and compared with goals at fixed intervals.
5. At the end of the time period for the project, manager and the subordinate jointly evaluate the work accomplished, and new projects and goals are set.

The underlying principle is that goals should be identified by manager and subordinate together so that they have a common understanding of what the subordinate is to do and the expected level of performance. Objectives should be explicit and expressed as much as possible in numerical terms—for example, increase recycling of scrap materials by 50 percent or increase sales of portable computers by 15 percent. The objectives provide the employee with both guidelines and a clear set of responsibilities directly related to organizational goals. The time period within which the objectives should be met will vary according to the nature of the project, but a term of about six months is usually the most effective. During periodic discussions on whether interim objectives have been achieved, subordinates should be free to approach management with questions to clarify details and suggestions about the project. When one set of objectives has been met, discussions begin on new objectives.

FIGURE 8.4 • THE MANAGEMENT-BY-OBJECTIVES PROCESS

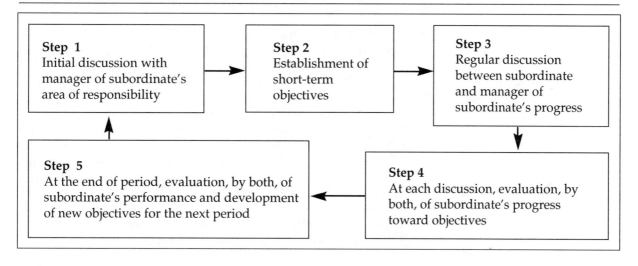

Management by objectives has many advantages. It raises employee interest and enthusiasm through active and ongoing participation. Employees involved in setting objectives understand exactly what needs to be accomplished and know in advance how their performance will be evaluated. Morale tends to improve when employees and managers communicate freely and openly. Employees can relate their own performance to the goals of the organization. MBO allows managers to see how employees approach their jobs, thus making decisions about salary adjustments and promotions fairer.

MBO can be used at every level of the organization. The president can begin the process by setting a clear course for the entire organization. At each successive level, the president's goals can be translated into more and more detailed objectives that ultimately provide every employee with clear, operational guidelines.

Management by objectives takes effort and requires serious planning if it is to be successful. It requires communication between managers and subordinates that may be uncomfortable for some people. However, once the parties have adjusted to the concept, they usually want to participate.

In many organizations, change, both internal and external, means that the objectives of employees must also change. Managers must not approach MBO in a spirit of rigidity. They must also realize that results can be more difficult to measure accurately than the five-step MBO program might suggest.

JOB ENRICHMENT

Job enrichment improves motivation by relieving boredom. Most assembly line jobs have common characteristics: mechanically controlled work pace, repetitiveness, minimum skill requirements, predetermined tools and techniques, and minute subdivision of the product that, therefore, requires only surface mental attention.[10]

job enrichment
Allowing workers to plan work, control details, upgrade skills, and exchange jobs

Job enrichment allows workers to plan their work, giving them the responsibility to work out details and providing opportunities to upgrade their skills and even exchange jobs with other employees. Herzberg suggests that job enrichment should improve worker motivation by emphasizing both individual and company needs:

[It] seeks to improve both task efficiency and human satisfaction by means of building into people's jobs. . . greater scope for personal achievement and recognition, more challenging and responsible work, and more opportunity for individual advancement and growth. It is concerned only incidentally with matters such as pay and working conditions, organizational structure, communications, and training, important and necessary though these may be in their own right.[11]

What kind of job enrichment techniques produce results? Chrysler was an early experimenter with the technique, giving assembly line workers the chance to road test cars to help spot defects.

In one assembly plant, Chrysler formed a workers' "damage committee" to check welding operations of car bodies. One worker wrote management after his week of moving around the department. "Since that week, I see metal damage, missing welds, and forming fits I never noticed before. This. . . gives me a whole new outlook on body building...a sense of real satisfaction. . . using my eyes and mind instead of just my hands."[12]

On the other hand, Volvo, the Swedish automobile manufacturer, undertook a challenging experiment in 1971 to achieve job enrichment through **job enlargement**, or increasing the number of tasks performed by a single worker. The monotonous, slow-moving assembly line disappeared, parts were brought to an individual working site, and teams of about seven workers collaborated to assemble the entire car. However, work proceeded too slowly, and productivity went down. Currently, Volvo employs a modified assembly line system.

job enlargement
Increasing the number of tasks performed by individual workers

General Foods Corporation tried a groundbreaking job enrichment experiment at a new manufacturing plant designed to process and package Gaines dog food products. Workers were free to work out their own schedules.

Three teams were created: one to take charge of all aspects of processing the various products, another to handle packaging and shipping, and a third to provide the usual office support. No individual held any particular job. Team members rotated responsibilities on a regular basis. For example, a packaging and shipping worker would switch from using the forklift one day to bagging "Gravy Train" the next. The least-popular jobs were automatically rotated among all members of the team. Responsibilities usually assigned to management, such as screening and hiring new team members and drawing up procedures, were handled by the teams, even though this required special training. For example, team members could not make personnel decisions without first becoming familiar with government policies related to hiring. From the viewpoint of the senior managers (who were not given reserved parking spaces), success depended largely on maintaining worker enthusiasm through ongoing training and keeping channels of communication open and running smoothly.

During the first years of the plant's operation, total employment tripled, but the policy of job enrichment continued. In 1981, Randy Castelluzzo, General Foods' manager of personnel services, summarized the benefits of the "experiment": "higher product quality, lower operating costs, little absenteeism, and productivity per worker averaging 15 to 20 percent higher than similar, conventionally managed plants."[13] This classic experiment has had a major impact upon organizations in North America.

Job enrichment, like the implementation of MBO programs, has enjoyed both success and failure. After introducing job enrichment programs in nineteen areas at AT&T, management reported that nine were outstandingly successful, one was a complete flop, and the remaining nine were moderately successful.[14] A series of interviews with assembly line workers in an "unenriched" television plant revealed that they did not view their jobs as either frustrating or dissatisfying.[15] One research project even discovered that some workers prefer routine jobs because it gives them more time to daydream or talk with their fellow employees without hurting their productivity.[16]

Although job enrichment programs continue to be relatively rare, their accomplishments in a number of industries and in companies of varying size indicate their merits. Even though they are not always successful, their numbers will undoubtedly grow during the 1990s. More and more managers are recognizing that such programs allow an integration of individual and company goals.

Flextime and Alternative Work Schedules

flextime
A flexible scheduling system for working hours whereby employees set their own arrival and departure times

Flexible work schedules allow companies to acknowledge that workers have needs and goals outside the work environment. Often referred to as **flextime**, such work schedules are arranged by employees to choose their own arrival and departure times and still meet the demands of their work. In Europe, the idea of flextime is very popular. Around 40 percent of the Swiss and 25 percent of the German labour forces follow some kind of flexible work schedule.

The Royal Bank has made flexible work schedules available to its employees. Like many other businesses, the Royal Bank recognizes their employees' need to balance their work and family obligations. A flexible schedule allows employees to respond to childcare needs without compromising their work commitments. Family supportive programs, like flexible hours, have obvious mutual benefits for both the employee and the employer in terms of less stress and less absenteeism.

FIGURE 8.5 • THE FLEXTIME CONCEPT

7 A.M.	**Fringe time**
8 A.M.	Employees work additional hours
9 A.M.	during this period or after 3:30 p.m.
10 A.M.	
11 A.M.	
12 A.M.	**Core time**
1 P.M.	Employees work 5 to 6 hours during this period (with optional 30-minute to one-hour lunch).
2 P.M.	
3 P.M.	
4 P.M.	
5 P.M.	**Fringe time**
6 P.M.	Employees work additional hours during this period or before 9:30 a.m.
7 P.M.	

In North America, flextime arrangements are not yet as common as they are in Europe. Most of the 12 percent of the labour force taking advantage of this approach are in the finance and insurance industries and in the federal government. It occurs less frequently in the manufacturing sector, but experiments in scheduling are being carried out in all major industries.

Most flextime arrangements specify a period each day when all employees are expected to be on the job. Meetings and other work that requires communication among employees take place during these "core hours," which may extend from 9:30 a.m. to 3:30 p.m. Employees choose to work the rest of their workweek in the "fringe hours" before or after the core period. Many people find these morning or evening hours ideal for uninterrupted work. Figure 8.5 shows this common form of flexible work schedule.

Many organizations using flextime ask their employees to specify which hours they intend to work and to keep more or less to that schedule. Supporters of the concept believe it has great motivating value because the flexibility gives people more freedom to organize other aspects of their lives. It also relieves transportation systems at peak periods. Many suggest that productivity improves when workers participate in creating their own schedules.

Flextime arrangements are not always straightforward. Continuous production or assembly line work requires workers to be present at fixed times. Production and supervisory problems can arise if key people are not always available. Flexible work schedules may also lead to increased energy consumption.

compressed workweek
A scheduling system whereby the hours of a normal workweek are completed in less than five days

Compressed Workweek

Compressed workweek schedules allow employees to complete the hours of a standard five-day workweek in fewer days. For example, a regular 40-hour week can be arranged into four days, which reduces energy and transportation costs and gives employees more time for personal obligations and other private activities. Compressed work-weeks are popular in hospitals and other settings requiring round-the-clock attendance. However, compressed workweeks do not work for everyone. Some employees working a ten-hour day may be more productive while others may simply become overtired. The compressed schedule may also lead to the temptation to "moonlight," which may ultimately harm quality of life as well as productivity.

job sharing
An arrangement that divides the responsibilities of one job between two people

Job Sharing

Job sharing is another approach that gives employees more control over their lives. In this arrangement, the responsibilities of one job are divided between two people. Although rare in industrial settings, job sharing is fairly common in retailing and clerical positions where sharing the workload can be accomplished without loss of productivity.

STYLES OF MANAGEMENT AND MOTIVATION

Over the past few years, it has become fashionable to contrast North American styles of management with those of Japan—to the advantage of the latter. No one in North America advocates a complete shift to the Japanese approach because cultural differences make it impossible. However, William Ouchi has developed what he calls Theory Z, or participative management, an approach that combines the two styles of management in a workable format for companies on this continent. **Theory Z** suggests that a high quality of work life and workers who are committed because they participate in organizational decisions are the key to increased productivity. Table 8.2 shows the adaptations of the two management styles that Ouchi recommends.

Theory Z
An approach to management suggesting that a high quality of work life and workers who are committed because they participate in organizational decisions are the key to increased productivity

TABLE 8.2 • THEORY Z: COMBINING JAPANESE AND NORTH AMERICAN MANAGEMENT STYLES

Typical Japanese organizations	Theory Z organizations	Typical North American organizations
Lifetime employment	Long-term employment	Short-term employment
Slow evaluation and promotion	Unhurried evaluation and promotion	Rapid evaluation and promotion
Non-specialized career path	Moderately specialized career path	Specialized career path
Implicit, informal control	Implicit, informal control with explicit measures and objectives	Explicit, formal control
Collective decision making	Collective decision making	Individual decision making
Collective responsibility	Individual responsibility	Individual responsibility
Holistic concern for workers	Holistic concern for workers and their families	Concern only for aspect of workers' lives that affect job

Source: Adapted from William C. Ouchi and Alfred M. Jaeger, "Type Z Organizations: Stability in the Midst of Mobility," *Academy of Management*, 3 (1978), pp. 308–14.

For example, North American businesses—and North American workers—are unlikely to accept the idea that a person should spend a lifetime working for one employer. The needs of both the company and individual may change. But, for both, thinking of employment in somewhat longer terms may be beneficial. With slower evaluation and promotion, individuals' career paths need not be entirely confined to the special skills and functions for which they were first employed, but new and previously undiscovered talents can be allowed to develop. The explicit rules and objectives common in North American companies may be limiting if not tempered by implicit respect between manager and employee. Similarly, reaching decisions together will lead to greater commitment to goals and objectives. On the other hand, the fact that individuals are held responsible for specific objectives means that buckpassing is minimized. Knowing that workers have lives beyond working hours helps management react with sensitivity to personal considerations, which is likely to lead to greater productivity and commitment.

WHY PEOPLE WORK: CONTINUING STUDIES

It is interesting that most research into motivation has examined the manufacturing environment. As Issues in Business 8.2 makes clear, in an economy such as Canada's that is moving from a manufacturing base to a services base, the morale and motivation of office workers are of prime concern—and represent an area in which we seem to be ahead.

Our understanding of the motivation of people at work has come a long way since the Hawthorne studies revealed that money and working conditions were not the sole factors affecting productivity. Improving the quality of work life to discover the right mix of motivational techniques that lead to high productivity and an alert and eager work force will continue to be a focus for management. The same approaches will not work under all economic conditions, in all industries, or even within all companies within the same industry; yet, though the social chemistry will vary, managers must always be aware of the needs and motivations of employees.

ISSUES IN BUSINESS 8.2

MISSING MOTIVATORS

An INCREASING NUMBER of Canadian office workers think working life is becoming less fun, more exhausting and, well, more work.

A recent study shows that more workers than ever before (nearly 30 percent) say the quality of working life has worsened, while job security and opportunities for advancement are disappearing.

However, their dissatisfaction pales beside the unhappiness of Japanese office workers, found to be the least satisfied in the industrial world.

(continued)

These are some of the findings of a global survey on office environment issues commissioned by Steelcase Inc., a major designer and manufacturer of office furniture based in Grand Rapids, Michigan, which has been surveying workers' attitudes since 1978.

The latest poll was conducted by the research firm Louis Harris & Associates Inc. in the first six months of 1991. It included interviews between January and April with more than 6,000 secretaries, clerks, and other office workers, as well as managers, senior executives, and interior designers in fifteen countries.

"The study has been tracking a fair number of questions since 1978 to follow the quality of working life," says Linda Rumbarger, Steelcase's supervisor of marketing research.

The recession is being blamed for the fairly dramatic increase in the number of Canadian office workers who feel the quality of working life has worsened in the past ten years: 29 percent of workers now say the quality of work life has worsened, compared with 18 percent in 1989. And only 39 percent report being very satisfied with their jobs, compared with 45 percent in 1989.

As well, office workers in Canada are more likely than those elsewhere to feel they are working as hard as they can (60 percent in Canada, compared with fewer than 25 percent in Japan and about 50 percent in the United States and Europe).

The recession has also battered the concept of risk taking. Only 18 percent of Canadian office workers now say they are encouraged to take risks, compared with 27 percent in 1986.

Overall, the survey found U.S. office workers were the most satisfied with their jobs (43 percent), compared with 28 percent in the European Community and only 17 percent in Japan, the least satisfied.

"Many of us think of the Japanese as leaders in total quality management and participative management, but that doesn't seem to have transferred from the factory floors into the offices of Japan," says Lou Harris, chief executive officer of the survey research firm.

Rumbarger adds that "a lot of what has been written about Japanese management styles is about what goes on in factories. The production concepts involving team work and communication don't look as true of the office in Japan."

Canadian executives were found to be more in touch with how office workers feel than senior managers in any other country.

"They seem to be on the same wavelength with what characteristics office workers are looking for in their jobs," says Rumbarger.

The implication is that Canadian managers know what their workers want to make them happier—they just aren't able to do anything about it.

Japanese executives are least aware of what's important to their office workers' "frustrated aspirations," with wide gaps between what Japanese office workers aspire to and what they actually encounter.

Japanese executives significantly underestimate the importance office workers attribute to a host of characteristics. These include the company's sensitivity to balancing job and family needs, ethical management practices, recognition of an employee's contribution and good pay and benefits.

So-called aspiration gaps—the difference between the percentage of workers who say a characteristic is very important and the percentage who say it exists in their current job—is also widest among Japanese workers. These areas include:
- Being encouraged to work in teams: Japan's office workers report a 50-percentage-point gap, compared with 14 points in Canada and the United States and 25 points in the E.C. countries.
- Being able to contribute significantly: Japanese workers reported a 45-percentage-point gap, compared with 12 points in the United States, 15 points in Canada, and 18 points in the E.C.

(continued)

- Having a challenging job: Japanese workers reported a 48-percentage-point gap, compared with 17 points in the United States, 18 points in the E.C., and 19 points in Canada.

Rumbarger said the Canadian statistics have a margin of error of plus or minus 6 percent, and are accurate 95 percent of the time.

The U.S. statistics, which were drawn from a larger sample, have a margin of error of plus or minus 3 percent.

Accuracy for the statistics of the other countries surveyed ranged from plus or minus 3 percent to plus or minus 6 percent, as sample sizes varied between countries.

Source: Reprinted from Laura Ramsay, "Japanese Workers World's Unhappiest," *The Financial Post*, November 20, 1991, p. 35.

Questions for Discussion

1. What impact does a recession have on the level of satisfaction of the North American office worker?

2. How can you explain the lower level of satisfaction in Japanese office environments as compared with manufacturing environments? Cite the various factors contributing to this

---

BUSINESS REVIEW 8.3

1. List motivational techniques used to improve the quality of work life and explain which techniques you yourself would find most satisfying.

2. Do you think Theory Z management is possible in today's economic climate? Explain.

INTERACTIVE SUMMARY AND DISCUSSION QUESTIONS

1. The opening vignette introduced a number of people who changed careers at varying points in their lives—some even into late adulthood, others into remote occupations having little to do with their prior training and experiences. Explain the motivation for this phenomenon by examining Herzberg's motivators and dissatisfiers.

2. Based upon Maslow's hierarchy of human needs, which needs are being referred to in the following statements:

a) "The new General Motors labour agreement will guarantee the jobs of at least 80 percent of all GM workers through 2000."

b) "This is an entry-level job here at Tip-Top Clothiers, and we pay minimum wage for the first six months."

c) "We have just organized a company hockey team. Why don't you try out Thursday afternoon after work?"

d) "Jean won our Employee of the Month award this month because of her/his exceptional performance."

e) "We pay a 20 percent bonus for employees who work the midnight shift."

3. In Issues in Business 8.2 you discovered that many Canadian office workers are experiencing less fun on the job and becoming more exhausted while feeling that the quality of work life has decreased. In spite of these findings, the Japanese in similar studies perceive work as even more negative and pessimistic. Contrast the Canadian with the Japanese work culture to explain these findings.

(continued)

4. How would you identify the basic needs of a "workaholic" in relation to McClelland's socially acquired needs theory. Support or reject each of the three needs described in relation to what you now know about the pattern and motivation of a "workaholic."

5. Describe the five steps in a basic MBO program. Utilize these steps and apply them to design an MBO program for the successful completion of this course or a related business course you are taking at this time.

6. In the October 1980 issue of *Business Horizons*, J. Clayton Lafferty, president of Human Synergistics, made the following statement: "When a three-engine Boeing 727 flying at 40,000 feet loses all three engines at once (under normal circumstances the plane could glide for over 130 miles) the captain has ample time for quickly consulting with his copilot and flight engineer to get their ideas about the cause and remedy, and to discuss emergency procedures with the flight attendants. However, if a similar power loss occurred at 500 feet during a takeoff climb, the captain would be ill-advised to practise such participative techniques."

   Relate this statement to the participative approach to management and point out the perceived strengths and possible problems with this approach.

7. "Many of the world's most successful companies are reorganizing management to give workers greater input into determining and achieving the enterprise's objectives. Call it decentralization, teamwork, or quality circles, it is something more Canadian companies should consider." Support this statement with your understanding of what is currently happening in Canada and the United States, or even what you believe should be happening.

CASE 8.1

WHEN YOU JUST CAN'T GO TO WORK

EVERYONE, AT ONE time or another, has come down with a bout of psycho-social illness, the severity of which prevents us from working. In layperson's terms, absence from work due to psycho-social illness is a mental health day.

Fortunately, most of us rarely get truly sick. Scores of diseases have been eradicated from North America, thanks to medical ingenuity, and the real killers—cancer and heart disease—are rarely used as excuses for a day or two's absence from work. But despite improved health, absenteeism because of illness and disability is increasing.

According to Carol Ann Curnock, whose company, Path Consulting, assists employers with absence management, absenteeism to a large extent is not so much the result of illness as it is of poor management.

"Absenteeism increases when people don't have an incentive to come to work," Curnock said. "If you're a person who loves your job, nothing stops you from working. If you hate it, a hangnail is too much to bear."

She believes good management practices can make the difference between enthusiastic high attendance and apathetic, low attendance.

"Absenteeism is most commonly found in bureaucracies, in high-volume, low-control jobs or in jobs that aren't linked to people," Curnock said.

"Not surprisingly, people working in commissioned jobs or highly creative jobs have extremely low absenteeism rates."

Figures from Statistics Canada show that in 1990 (the latest available figures) absenteeism is highest in health and social services (14.3 days a year) and financial institutions (11.7). During an

(continued)

average week in 1990, 8 percent of public servants and 7 percent of manufacturing employees were absent from work for all or part of the week.

Senior-level employees are not away as much as their subordinates, "but not, as many people think, because they're more 'responsible.' The more senior you are, the more feeling of control you have over your work environment and the more ego you have invested in it," Curnock said.

Monday and Friday are popular sick days and, as Curnock points out, also favoured by employees with drinking problems.

Dealing with absenteeism is a delicate issue, as evidenced by the emergence of consulting firms like Curnock's. Regarding employees who tax employers' patience with their regular absences, Curnock said: "Look, some people need a good kick and some need help."

As illnesses like anxiety and depression increase, taking their toll on short- and long-term disability programs, employers are looking for ways to minimize the effect on their operations.

"One of the problems is that we tend to think in black and white about illness; Either you're sick or you're not. When an employer expects to see an employee back on the job in three months, she doesn't stop to think about what makes that person able to work on Monday morning and not the preceding Friday? Sickness isn't like that."

Source: Excerpts from Katherine Gary, "Poor Management Can Spawn Absenteeism," *The Financial Post*, January 23, 1993, p. S18.

Questions for Discussion

1. Explain the problem of absenteeism using Herzberg's two-factor theory and expectancy theory.
2. Would you recommend QWL programs, job enrichment, and/or flexible work schedules to help correct this problem? Explain your reasoning carefully.

CASE 8.2

AIR CANADA'S THEORY Y CEO

CLAUDE TAYLOR HITS the deck early, in time to catch CTV's *Canada AM* at 6:30.

He's on the road by 7:00, so he can listen to the CBC news in his car.

Then, as soon as he arrives at Air Canada's downtown headquarters, the chairman of the country's largest airline heads straight for a computer terminal to find out what all that weather and world turmoil did to his airplanes.

Were flights disrupted? Were they late? Is there a jet stranded in some airport somewhere around the world?

He laughs and feigns frustration at the thought. It's tough running a business where so much depends on elements you can't control.

But it's also fascinating.

"Every morning is kind of exciting, because you know something is going to be different from yesterday."

Things do change quickly. Last summer, PWA Corp., owner of Air Canada's archrival, Canadian Airlines International, had just taken over Wardair and reduced the industry to two major airlines.

The fierce fare wars, which had been a boon to consumers but sapped the airlines' profits, were gone. The future looked bright for the airlines.

But on this grey January morning, Taylor is talking about turbulence. Last month's bitter weather caused costly delays and cancellations. Now fuel costs are rising, and the weakening economy means fewer people will be flying.

(continued)

With the dimmer outlook for profits, Air Canada's stock has been sinking in recent weeks, from $13 at the start of the year to $10.25 yesterday.

Seated in his 26th-floor office in the Air Canada tower in downtown Montreal, the affable Taylor is being frank about Air Canada's prospects for 1990. But he dismisses with good humour any attempt to answer the other nagging question about the airline's future. At 64, after roughly eight years as president and six years as chairman, is he ready to pack it in?

"There are days when I wish I could," he quips. Then, in a terse businesslike tone, he says that question will be answered by April 26, the airline's next annual meeting.

The decision is bound to be tough.

One staff member described Taylor as very much a "hands-on chairman," which is probably not surprising since he and the airline have been together since youth.

Taylor recalls how his first job paying real money—25 cents an hour—involved lugging buckets of water to the construction crews building air training strips in his native New Brunswick in the 1940s.

Musing aloud, he wonders, if he had to do it over again, if he would spend his whole career in one industry. But then he quickly points out how exciting it has been to be in on the building of an industry from the ground up.

Stock analyst Frederick Larkin of Bunting Warburg Inc. said Taylor has done "a tremendous job." Taylor's major accomplishment, Larkin said, was convincing the federal government to turn the airline into a private company answerable to shareholders, a process that was completed last spring with the second and last issue of Air Canada stock.

"In the process, he has put together a very capable team," Larkin said. "I don't see any problem with the transition at all."

The walls of Taylor's meeting room are decorated with editorial cartoons about the privatizing of Air Canada, and his attitudes sound far more in tune with a businessman than a civil servant.

To him the change was essential. In the increasingly competitive airline industry, he believes, Air Canada could not have survived shackled by government bureacracy and subject to political whim.

"We literally stood the risk of becoming another Via Rail," he said. "Other airlines would have made it unnecessary for us to exist."

To him, Air Canada crossed the river to a point of no return when it was privatized, although the decision still remains controversial in consumer circles.

However, the arrival of the airline's 38 new Airbus jets, which begin showing up later this month, will bolster efficiency since they can carry passengers and cargo, he said. Air Canada is also looking into cost-cutting equipment, such as automated ticketing and vending systems.

Taylor believes his airline is well positioned—"better than the other guy"—to face the year ahead.

Source: Reprinted from Sheila McGovern, "Air Canada's Hands-On Boss," *The Montreal Gazette*, January 24, 1990, pp. F1 and F2.

Questions for Discussion

1. It has been said that Claude Taylor is a people-type executive. Describe his style in terms of McGregor's Theory Y.

2. Describe Mr. Taylor in terms of McClelland's socially acquired needs theory.

NOTES

1. Stuart Chase, *Men at Work* (New York: Harcourt, Brace and World, 1941), pp. 21–22.
2. Frederick Herzberg, *Work and the Nature of Man* (Cleveland, OH: World Publishers, 1966).
3. C.P. Alderfer, *Existence, Relatedness, and Growth* (New York: Free Press, 1972).
4. James Bowditch and Anthony Buono, *A Primer on Organizational Behavior* (New York: John Wiley & Sons, Inc, 1985), p. XX. Copyright ©1985, 1990 by James L. Bowditch and Anthony F. Buono. Reprinted by permission of John Wiley & Sons Inc.
5. E.A. Locke, "Toward a Theory of Task Motivation and Incentives," *Organizational Behaviour and Human Performance* 3 (1968), pp. 157–89.
6. J. Stacey Adams, "Injustice in Social Exchange," in L. Berkovitz, ed., *Advances in Experimental Social Psychology*, 2nd ed. (New York: Academic Press, 1965), pp. 267–69.
7. Douglas McGregor, *The Human Side of Enterprise* (New York: McGraw-Hill, 1960).
8. McGregor, *The Human Side of Enterprise*.
9. Peter Drucker, *The Practice of Management* (New York: Harper and Bros., 1954), pp. 128–29.
10. Charles R. Walker and Robert Guest, *Man on the Assembly Line* (Cambridge, MA: Harvard University Press, 1952), p. 19.
11. William J. Paul, Jr., Keith B. Robertson, and Frederick Herzberg, "Job Enrichment Pays Off," *Harvard Business Review*, March–April 1969, p. 61.
12. "Workers Don't Give a Damn? Chrysler Thinks They Do, If—," *Ward's Auto World,* June 1972, p. 43.
13. Interview with Randy Castelluzzo, manager of personnel services, General Foods Corporation, May 1981, reported in Steven Appelbaum, M. Dale Beckman, Louis E. Boone, and David L. Kurtz, *Contemporary Canadian Business*, 3rd ed. (Toronto: Holt, Rinehart and Winston, 1990), pp. 205–6.
14. Robert N. Ford, *Motivation through the Work Itself* (New York: American Management Association, 1969).
15. M.D. Kilbridge, "Do Workers Prefer Larger Jobs?" *Personnel*, September–October 1960, pp. 45–48.
16. William E. Reif and Peter P. Schoderbek," Job Enrichment: Antidote to Antipathy," *Management of Personnel Quarterly*, Spring 1966, pp. 16–23.

PHOTO CREDITS

MODULE

◆ HRM ◆

HUMAN RESOURCE MANAGEMENT

THE FOCUS OF THIS MODULE

1. To define human resource management and the responsibilities it entails

2. To describe human resource planning for the future needs of the organization

3. To differentiate among job analysis, job description, and job specification

4. To describe the various steps in the hiring process

5. To consider how human rights legislation affects the work of the human resource department

6. To describe various forms of employee training and development and to follow typical movements of employees within the organization

7. To discuss the motivational factors of various compensation programs and employee benefits as part of compensation

8. To learn the meaning of the following terms:

KEY TERMS

human resource management

human resource planning

human resource forecast

job analysis

job description

job specifications

hiring from within

discrimination

pay equity

employment equity program

harassment

on-the-job training

apprenticeship

mentor

assessment centre

performance appraisal

promotion

seniority

lateral transfer

separation

layoff

dismissal

wage

salary

(continued)

time wage

piecework

commission

bonus

profit sharing

employee stock ownership

    plan (ESOP)

employee benefits

workers' compensation act

Canada Safety Code

HER NAME IS JOAN Crawford. And yes, she's heard all the jokes. "I get them all—the shoulder pads, wire hangers, 'Mommy Dearest.' But I have endured," deadpans Crawford. "People do remember my name —it does have that going for it."

There's much more to Crawford than a famous name. Vice-president of human resources at Thomas Cook Group (Canada) Limited, Crawford has never done things in halves. When she joined Thomas Cook, the company was in the throes of major upheaval, having just entered into a joint venture with Eaton's Travel Ltd. It meant a swelling of the company's ranks from 100 to over 500 employees, and its branches growing nationwide from 14 to over 80. At the same time, Midland Bank Canada, owners of Thomas Cook Traveller's Cheques, were divesting their interests in Canada, which meant that segment of the business was to come under the Canadian company's umbrella.

As a result, Crawford found herself facing a merger of three companies in her first week on the job. "Along with my one colleague, we had to set up an HR department and pull it all together," recalls Crawford. "We were also both new to the company so we had to get up to speed quickly."

It wasn't a case of simply piggybacking on existing programs, she says, but analyzing what each company had, and creating an entirely new strategy and policies catering to three different corporate cultures. "All the HR issues had to be contended with—market analysis, benefits, compensation policies, you name it." Even with related experience behind her—at General Trust she helped handle a District Trust merger—Crawford says it was a formidable challenge. "I knew what the issues would be. I'd been there. But we had only three months to put everything in place."

Communicating with their employees during that time helped keep the ship afloat, Crawford says. They presented "integration newsletters" to employees on an ongoing basis. "We were merging three distinct cultures. A lot of people were wondering what was going to happen to them. Even if you reassure them, change of this magnitude can be traumatic. You have to manage it very carefully." Also important during the merger of national companies, says Crawford, was ensuring that their field personnel were included in the loop and not made to feel isolated.

She looks back on those months with real pride—and a wipe of her brow—but admits an extra month would have given her more manoeuvring room. "It was too short a period of time to effect that many changes, to give employees enough time to digest them, and get their input."

Barely on their feet, rumblings of change were heard again. Thomas Cook began negotiations to buy the retail foreign exchange business of Deak International. The acquisition added another 30 branches to Thomas Cook's Canadian network, along with 220 employees. In the Deak integration, Crawford had the luxury of time to map out strategies and to talk to employees about what the changes mean to them. She travelled across Canada holding meetings with various staffs of Deak, what she calls a priceless opportunity. "It's a chance to meet with them, answer their questions and detail new plans. I feel really good about it."

Crawford visits as many branch locations each month as time permits. Employees are happy to see her, says Crawford, and she fields every question conceivable. The one question she *never* gets, she says, is "Why are you here?" The get-togethers are part of an attempt to break down the "we–they" mentality, she explains. "It helps us appreciate what the people in the field are up against when the customer walks in the door.". . .

Crawford characterizes her management style as highly participatory. She admits she's very demanding, but adds "I'm probably more demanding on myself than anyone. I've come up the ranks, I know what it's like out there." Her door is always open, and she prides herself on being accessible. "I admire the people I work with and value their opinions. I've learned not to expect perfection. But I feel I can demand excellence and it's my job to help them get there—with guidance and training."

She intends to stay in HR. "I love HR here because of the way we have positioned ourselves within the company. We're not regarded as just a support function that people pay lip service to. We've integrated ourselves within the business and all our programs and the tools we give managers are put together with their commercial objectives in mind.". . .

Source: Excerpts from, "On the Front Lines of HR" *Human Resources Professional*, January 1991, pp. 6–7. Reprinted with permission by Faulkner & Gray, Inc., 11 Penn Plaza, New York, NY 10001.

J oan Crawford is well aware of the importance of human resource management to any company. HR at Thomas Cook helps its four major business lines—leisure travel, business travel management, traveller's cheques, and foreign exchange—achieve their commercial objectives, provides professional advice to managers regarding government legislation and legal issues, and offers cost-effective in-house expertise in a variety of areas. "We make sure everything we do adds value to the operation," she says.[1]

People are an organization's most important resource. No matter how plentiful the natural resources, how up to date the facilities, how limitless the access to capital, and how brilliant the entrepreneurial idea, no organization will accomplish its goals without the hard work and dedication of people with the right skills and talents, carefully directed and sensibly controlled. At the same time, people who are not working to potential can also be the reason for inefficiency, loss of productivity, and possible bankruptcy. The strategic management of its human resources is recognized by every organization as critical to success.

WHAT IS HUMAN RESOURCE MANAGEMENT?

human resource management
recruitment and training of employees, assessment of future personnel needs, and the maintenance of a positive working atmosphere

Human resource management is a vital function, whether it is carried out by the owner–manager of the local carpet cleaning service or by a specialized staff department such as Joan Crawford's at Thomas Cook. It includes not only recruitment and training, but also the assessment of future personnel needs and the maintenance of a positive working atmosphere to motivate employees toward the achievement of organizational goals.

Human resource management, of course, can never be entirely confined to a single department within an organization. All managers are to some extent responsible for assessing their future personnel needs, selecting employees, training and motivating them, and evaluating their performance. In a large organization, a human resource department works with others to plan levels of staffing to meet organizational goals; ensure consistency in employee recruitment and selection; assist in training, development, and counselling; administer salaries and benefits; handle labour relations issues; and ensure compliance with government regulations. Table 9.1 outlines the responsibilities of the human resource function as they would be handled by a staff department in a large organization. It shows clearly how the department, of necessity, is involved in the entire operation.

TABLE 9.1 • RESPONSIBILITIES OF A HUMAN RESOURCE DEPARTMENT

Responsibilities	Shared with
Planning levels of staffing to meet organizational goals	Top management, department managers
Recruitment and selection of personnel to fill required positions	Department managers
Training and development	Department managers, outside experts
Reassignments and promotions	Top management, department managers
Employee counselling	Department managers, medical personnel
Ensuring compliance with government health and safety, employment, and taxation regulations	Accounting department
Administering salaries and benefits	Accounting department
Labour relations	Top management, union executives, shop stewards
Layoffs, retirements, resignations, and dismissals	Top management, union executives, shop stewards
Enabling a satisfying and motivating working environment	All employees

In the description that follows, we will be discussing the human resource function as if it were being handled by a staff department that serves other parts of the organization. The activities described, however, are part of the human resource function, whether it is handled as part of the responsibility of a top management employee, a single human resource specialist, or an entire department.

HUMAN RESOURCE PLANNING

An organization's goals are the guidelines it uses to assess its future needs for resources—including human resources. **Human resource planning** is the development of a strategy to meet those needs, with the objective of having the right number of people available with the right skills at the right time. This may require increasing or decreasing the overall size of the staff through hiring, reassignment, retraining, layoffs or early retirement, or any combination of these.

Human resource planning starts with a careful inventory and analysis of current human resources, looking at current needs and whether the present match between people and jobs is appropriate. This inventory is the basis for a **human resource forecast,** in which the skills employees currently have, and can easily acquire, are compared with the organization's projected needs. The forecast, in turn, is the starting point for planning the personnel changes and special training required to prepare for the future. The object is to provide current employees with appropriate training and to recruit new personnel who will be able to serve the organization in the future as well as perform the tasks that need to be done now. Figure 9.1 shows the various steps involved in human resource planning.

From the point of view of an employee, the day-to-day activities of the human resource department start with the selection and hiring process. It is important to realize, however, that when an organization wishes to fill a position, the first place it looks for candidates is among people already employed there. Issues in Business 9.1 examines the planning aspects of "hiring from within."

human resource planning
The development of a strategy to meet the organization's future needs for employees

human resource forecast
An analysis of the number of employees and the skills they will require to meet future needs

FIGURE 9.1 • STEPS IN THE HUMAN RESOURCE PLANNING PROCESS

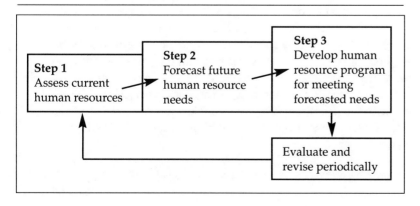

ISSUES IN BUSINESS 9.1

SUCCESSION PLANNING

As DEMAND GROWS for top executives with broadly based managerial backgrounds, more companies are adopting formal succession planning, which exposes promising managers to broader reaches of the corporation.

This is partly in response to the growing demand for CEOs with experience across a variety of corporate disciplines. But there's another reason why corporate cross-pollination is increasingly popular: managers are demanding it.

Michael Stern, president of executive recruiting firm Michael Stern Associates Inc., says that this is why Procter & Gamble Inc.—a company with a reputation for keeping senior managers slotted into particular specialties—is such fertile ground for headhunters. He says, "We've recently placed two marketing people out of P&G into Pepsi-Cola for this very reason."

The attraction of Pepsi-Cola Canada Ltd. may be that it does let its managers move around. In fact, they don't get a choice. As part of a multinational, Pepsi-Cola Canada has sent 20 percent of its 140 employees on international assignments since 1987. In addition, promising managers are frequently given assignments in areas outside their expertise. David Thacker, Pepsi's vice-president of personnel (recently returned from a stint in the U.K.), says, "When we see good management skills developing, we give people assignments outside of their area where they can be backed up by technical expertise."

Co-ordinating everything is Pepsi's human resource plan, a people "overlay" of the business plan. As the business plan changes, so do the human resource requirements, and Pepsi can forecast the skills it will need to develop to meet its objectives.

To Thacker, this is the core of Pepsi philosophy. He says, "We are in the business of building businessmen who build the company. The payout is that good succession planning brings broader sets of talents to bear on increasingly complex problems."

At Imperial Oil Ltd., succession planning starts with the corporate maxim "Imperial never appoints outsiders to senior management positions." Instead, the company recruits on campus; "grounds" people in a particular area of the business such as upstream, downstream, or finance; then exposes the promising to general management and staff positions. Grant Nuttall, vice-president of executive development and organization, is keeper of the master plan that tracks Imperial's 15,000 employees and 200 executives. He says, "As we bring people along, we give them cross-functional responsibilities that test their line management and co-ordinating abilities. To make it to senior management, they have to be broad."

Although the opportunity is open to everyone, Nuttall says that the vast majority of Imperial employees find their level in the organization and stay in their disciplines. It's the leaders who move up, and the company tracks their careers in five- to seven-year time frames. By the time they are two or three positions away from a possible CEO candidacy, the scrutiny is intense. Says Nuttall: "When we move people around, it isn't for the fun of it, because it is very costly. We do it to grow people and we only do it with the promising few. For every key job, the aim is to have three or four candidates. We lost a treasurer and a controller all in one year. They died. How else do you plan for that sort of thing?"

Source: Excerpts from Randall Litchfield, "They Walk on Water," *Canadian Business*, September 1990, p. 48.

(continued)

Questions for Discussion

1. What are some of the key reasons why organizations have adopted more formal succession planning for promising professionals?
2. What techniques do Pepsi-Cola and Imperial Oil use to implement succession planning?

THE RIGHT WORKER FOR THE JOB

Matching people to jobs is an important responsibility. The costs of having an introverted salesperson, an overly assertive customer service representative, or a secretary in the accounts department who cannot spot numerical errors would be a drain on any firm. The selection process is in itself expensive, including the costs of recruitment, interviewing and testing, medical examinations by company doctors, and training programs, but because making the wrong decision can be an even greater expense, successful companies tend to invest heavily in this process. Inefficient employees not only are unproductive but waste money.

What *Is* the Job?

Before even beginning to look for a person to fill a particular position, the human resource department must know exactly what the job entails. To acquire this information, three tools are used: job analysis, job description, and job specification.

Job analysis is a detailed and methodical study of all the steps and all the processes involved in performing the job. It usually starts by turning to the experts—asking those who perform the job now to list what they do. Though this will give a broad outline, it is rarely sufficiently accurate; people become so familiar with their jobs that they may overlook certain procedures because they are "too obvious" to be mentioned. So managers and outside analysts are often called in to observe workers and record what they see happening. The workers' contribution is still necessary, however, because they can report on the thought processes they must go through, and the factors that they must remain aware of, which are not readily apparent to the outside observer.

From the job analysis, a job description and job specification are drawn up. The **job description** is a written document listing the objectives and overall responsibilities of the job, the tasks performed, the relationship of the position to other positions in the organization, and the working conditions. Exhibit 9.1 shows a typical job description. The **job specifications** lists the qualifications required: education, experience, special skills, and specific requirements of the position such as freedom to do shift work, or ownership of a car.

The practice of job analysis started in factories but is now a routine procedure in retail stores, banks, and many offices. Human resource departments maintain a file of job descriptions and job specifications for all the jobs within an organization and update them as necessary— when new machinery or a new product is introduced or the needs of the organization change. This information is the basis for choosing applicants to fill available job openings.

Job analysis
A detailed and methodical study of all the steps and processes involved in performing a particular job

job description
A list of the objectives and overall responsibilities of a job, the tasks performed, the relationship of the position to other positions, and the working conditions

job specifications
A list of the qualifications required for a job including education, experience, special skills, and other requirements

EXHIBIT 9.1 • A JOB DESCRIPTION

BREVARD GENERAL HOSPITAL
Job Description

Job title:	Job analyst	**Job code:**	166.088
Date:	January 3, 19--	**Author:**	John Doakes
Job location:	Human Resources Dept.	**Job grade:**	
Supervisor:	Harold Grantinni	**Status:**	Exempt

Job summary   Collects and develops job analysis, information through interviews, questionnaires, observation, or other means. Provides other personnel specialists with needed information.

Job duties   Designs job analysis schedules and questionnaires.
Collects job information.
Interacts with workers, supervisors, and peers.
Writes job descriptions and job specifications.
Reports safety hazards to area manager and safety department.
Verifies all information through two sources.
Performs other duties as assigned by supervisors.

Working conditions: Works most of the time in well-ventilated modern office. Data collection often requires on-site work under every working condition found in company. Works standard 8 a.m. to 5 p.m., except to collect second shift data and when travelling (one to three days per month).

The above information is correct as approved by:

(Signed)   _____   (Signed)   _____
                    Job analyst   Department Manager

Source: Reprinted from Werther, Davis, Schwind, Das, *Canadian Human Resource Management*, Third edition Toronto McGraw-Hill Ryerson 1990, p 152.

Avoiding Discrimination in Job Specifications

Numerous laws—both federal and provincial—have been passed to prohibit the use of job specifications that contain irrelevant require- ments that might limit employment to able-bodied people, to those from one ethnic group or to one sex. Of course, necessary physical requirments such as strength may, in practice, bar persons with certain disabilities and many women from consideration for some jobs.

The issue of sexism is one most people are familiar with. In many countries, women are widely employed in occupations that some would label "men's jobs." For example, 90 percent of the physicians in

Russia are women; so too are 70 percent of the overhead crane operators in Sweden. Women are now being hired in greater numbers to fill organizational positions. A reason for this event is that the federal government, through the Advisory Council for the Status of Women, has set mandatory guidelines requiring that a proportion of women must work on federally funded projects.

One result of job specification laws is the elimination of sex distinctions in the "positions available" sections of newspapers. A second result is the change in job titles. An Employment and Immigration Canada document entitled *Canadian Classification and Dictionary of Occupations* includes a *Manual of Sex-free Occupational Titles*.

Looking for Candidates

When a position becomes open, the first step is to create, or update, the job description and job specification to make sure they are a proper guide to what the job entails and to the qualifications for it. The human resources department then decides where to search for candidates.

Hiring from within, common practice in many firms, gives first consideration for any openings to present employees. The advantages of a hiring-from-within policy are twofold: it is less expensive and time-consuming because the human resource department can check quickly the information it already has on file to establish which employees might be suitable for the position, and it contributes to morale by letting employees know that the organization values their skills and their loyalty and will reward those attributes with promotion when appropriate.

hiring from within
Giving first consideration for any job openings to present employees

If no qualified employees are discovered within the firm, and better-qualified people are believed to be available, the firm must search outside. Sources that may bring good candidates for consideration include the placement offices at universities and colleges, advertisements in newspapers and professional journals, Canada Employment Centres, private employment agencies, vocational schools, and labour unions. Employees may also recommend candidates—and every human resource department has a file of unsolicited applications from people who would like to work for the company. Firms looking for candidates for senior or highly specialized positions frequently engage the services of executive recruiting agencies or advertise in the "careers" section of *The Globe and Mail Report on Business* or *The Financial Post*.

The employee selection process is illustrated from the point of view of the candidate in Figure 9.2.

Creating the Short List

When the firm has an adequate pool of candidates, the screening process begins in order to shorten the list. The first step is often to have applicants complete a company application form that sets out in a consistent manner the type of work desired, and details of the applicant's formal education, technical and professional skills, work experience, and personal references.

FIGURE 9.2 • STEPS IN THE EMPLOYEE SELECTION PROCESS

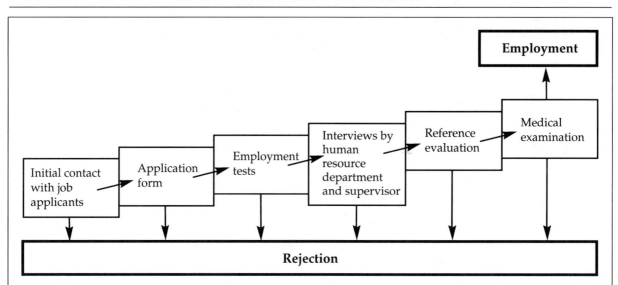

Aptitude and Attitudinal Testing

Qualified applicants may be asked to take a series of tests that act as an objective measuring tool. Psychologists and professionals have developed a wide variety of standardized tests to measure particular aptitudes and abilities required for specific types of jobs. Less common but also used by some companies are personality tests that are designed to determine what kinds of attitudes applicants may bring to the job. These can be used to assess whether the applicant has appropriate attitudes for the requirements of the job itself, but also how long the applicant might stay with the firm, and other more subtle but equally important factors. Many people believe that properly administered scientifically valid tests can objectively eliminate unsuitable candidates and can predict which applicants have the potential to succeed at various levels in the organization. Others say that most tests are "culturally biased" and may unfairly eliminate people who are excellent candidates.

The Job Interview

The interview is usually an applicant's first face-to-face contact with the company. Skilled interviewers can evaluate the applicant's attitudes toward others, self-perception, values, and priorities, to name a few issues. The human resource department may conduct a preliminary interview, but the line manager to whom the new employee will be reporting should take part at some point during the interview stage. The line manager, with the advice of the human resource department, usually has the final say in the selection of the successful applicant.

Only when candidates have done well at the interview stage will the department follow up by contacting the candidates' references.

The last hurdle is, in most cases, a purely technical one: the company medical.

The Company Medical

Managers need to know if applicants can handle the physical demands of certain jobs. Companies also need to be aware if an employee has a particular disability at the time of hiring, as protection against liability should the employee claim the disability was acquired on the job. Medical examinations, therefore, are becoming more and more common. Some countries—France, Belgium, and the Netherlands for example—require pre-employment physical examinations by law.

Welcome on Board

When, at last, the new employee is hired, the company will conduct some sort of formal or informal orientation program. This is the joint responsibility of the human resource department and the department in which the employee will work. Orientation is likely to include a tour of the building and a meeting with the department head and the new employee's immediate supervisor.

The human resource department explains company policy on such matters as vacation, sick leave, breaks, and lunch periods, and describes the employee benefits package and any options available. The supervisor introduces the new employee to fellow workers and helps the new person to begin smoothly by explaining the job to be done and how it contributes to the overall operation of the department and the organization.

Proper orientation is critical to the morale of the new employee. The first few days are extremely important in helping office and factory workers, sales representatives, technicians or anyone to feel comfortable and welcomed. A well-designed orientation program lets the new employee integrate into the organization effectively. The human resource department takes care of the paperwork and procedural matters, but it is up to the immediate supervisor and workmates to make the new employee feel part of the team.

BUSINESS REVIEW 9.1

1. What are the basic functions of the human resource department? Which of these responsibilities do you feel would most likely be shared with line departments?

2. You have just been assigned the task of recruiting and selecting a new management trainee for your department. What steps would you follow to find the best candidate?

EMPLOYMENT AND HUMAN RIGHTS

Human resource departments are probably most aware of the provisions of human rights legislation at the employee selection stage, though human rights issues pervade most aspects of the their work. At no time may a company practise **discrimination** in hiring, compensating, promotion, or dismissal on the basis of sex, race, religion, physical condition, national origin, age, or other issues irrelevant to performance on the job. Court decisions in the early 1990s mean that sexual orientation has been added to the list.

Human rights legislation affects employment practices in every jurisdiction of Canada, starting at the federal level with the Charter of Rights and Freedoms and the Canadian Human Rights Act, administered by the Canadian Human Rights Commission. Each province and territory has its own human rights code or act that prohibits discrimination in employment, administered by a human rights commission or council. Provisions vary slightly from jurisdiction to jurisdiction, sometimes only in wording. For example, discrimination may be prohibited on the grounds of "ancestry," "national origin," or "ethnic origin," which all have similar meanings. The main thrust is the same: to insist upon fairness for all people.

Each human rights statute specifies the grounds upon which individuals should not be recognized as being different. Table 9.2 lists these issues for each of the thirteen Canadian jurisdictions. Each statute prohibits discrimination on the basis of race, religion, marital status, and sex.

Pay Equity

Probably the oldest human rights concern is "equal pay." This was originally perceived as requiring employers to pay men and women the same amount for doing exactly the same work. Early efforts addressed the practice of giving different job designations to men and women who performed essentially the same functions, for example, calling men "janitors" and women "cleaners" in order to justify different pay scales. As little as twenty or thirty years ago, it was common practice, even in office environments, to offer men and women widely divergent starting salaries. Most companies now regard such practices as unfair, and for the most part they are illegal.

Attention has now turned to **pay equity**, or "equal pay for work of equal value." This is a more complicated issue as it requires employers to compare and weigh the value of work in vastly different areas. Sometimes this produces some strange anomalies. For example, Ontario nurses (mostly female) were incensed when their work was equated with that of pastry cooks (mostly male).

Employment Equity

Another difficult problem human resource departments must face is how to make up for discrimination in the past, not only in pay but also in hiring procedures and promotion. **Employment equity programs** improve opportunities for groups that have previously suffered from discrimination, but the courts have declared that such programs are

discrimination
Hiring, compensating, promotion, or dismissal on the basis of issues irrelevant to performance on the job

pay equity
Equal pay for work of equal value

employment equity program
A deliberate structured approach to improve work opportunities for women, minorities, and people with disabilities by removing barriers to their advancement (sometimes called affirmative action program)

TABLE 9.2 • EMPLOYMENT: PROHIBITED GROUNDS FOR DISCRIMINATION*

Prohibited grounds	Federal	British Columbia	Alberta	Saskatchewan	Manitoba	Ontario	Quebec	New Brunswick	Prince Edward Is.	Nova Scotia	Newfoundland	N.W. Territories	Yukon
Race or colour	●	●	●	●	●	●	●	●	●	●	●	●	●
Religion or creed	●	●	●	●	●	●	●	●	●	●	●	●	●
Age	●	[19-65]	[18+]	[18-64]	●	[18-65]	●	●	●	●	[18-65]	●	●
Sex (incl. pregnancy or childbirth)	●	●1	●	●	●2	●	●	●	●1	●	●1	●1	●
Marital status	●	●	●	●	●	●	●3	●	●	●	●	●	●
Physical/mental handicap or disability	●	●	●	●	●	●	●	●	●	●	●	●	●
Sexual orientation	●4	●		●	●	●	●	●1		●	●1		●
National or ethnic origin	●			●5	●	●6	●	●	●	●	●	●5	●
Family status	●	●		●	●	●	●3			●		●	●
Dependence on alcohol or drug	●	●1	●1	●1	●1	●1		●1,7	●1	●1			
Ancestry or place of origin		●	●	●	●	●		●				●5	●
Political belief		●		●			●	●	●	●			●
Based on association				●	●			●	●				●
Pardoned conviction	●	●					●	●	●	●	●		●
Record of criminal conviction		●					●						●
Source of income				●8	●					●			
Place of residence												●	
Assignment, attachment, or seizure of pay											●		
Social condition/origin							●				●		
Language							●						

Harassment on any of the prohibited grounds is considered a form of discrimination

Threatening, intimidating or discriminating against someone who has filed a complaint, or hampering a complaint investigation, is a violation of provincial human rights codes, and at the federal level is a criminal offence.

This chart is for quick reference only. For interpretation or further details, call the appropriate commission.

* Any limitation, exclusion, denial or preference may be permitted if a bona fide occupational requirement can be demonstrated.

1. complaints accepted based on policy
2. includes gender-determined characteristics
3. Quebec uses the term "civil status"
4. pursuant to a 1992 Ontario Court of Appeal decision, the Canadian Human Rights Commission now accepts complaints on the ground of sexual orientation.
5. defined as nationality
6. Ontario's code includes "citizenship"
7. Previous dependence only
8. defined as "receipt of public assistance"

Source: Canadian Human Rights Commission, August 1993. Reproduced with Permission.

legal. Employment equity, sometimes called affirmative action, does not necessarily involve quotas but is a deliberate structured approach to improve work opportunities for women, minorities, and people with disabilities by removing barriers to their advancement. Some consider that employment equity programs constitute "reverse discrimination" against those groups no longer favoured—primarily white males.

Assisted by both landmark legal decisions upholding equality in every work force and employment equity legislation, qualified and capable women have earned their rightful place in so-called non-traditional job areas. Beginning with women's pioneering efforts at the turn of this century and up to the present, patriarchal obstacles and prejudices have been and continue to be proven false.

Companies often voluntarily develop employment equity programs to correct earlier discrimination practices and also to avoid any future infractions. The existence of such a program helps guard against both intentional and unconscious discrimination. The federal government requires that companies in its jurisdiction have employment equity plans, and the provinces have similar requirements, as shown in Table 9.3.

Equal employment opportunity legislation and employment equity plans affect the activities of human resource departments in the following ways:

1. Job descriptions cannot contain irrelevant requirements that are intended only to exclude certain individuals.
2. Human resource plans must state the firm's employment equity commitment.
3. Performance evaluation cannot contain biases intended to discriminate against special individuals.
4. The recruitment process cannot exclude any prospective applicants and must attract all.
5 The selection process cannot use screening mechanisms that are not related to the job.
6. Compensation must be related to performance, skills, and seniority and must not discriminate against individuals in special classifications.
7. Training must be available to all individuals without regard to factors external to the work.

Developing Your Business Skills discusses the need for special training so that women and other disadvantaged groups can follow up on the opportunities that should be open to them.

TABLE 9.3 • EMPLOYMENT EQUITY COMPLIANCE LEGISLATION

	The laws	Who must comply	Deadlines & targets	Status reports
Federal	Employment Equity Act	Crown corporations Federally regulated companies with 100 or more employees	Yes	Yes
	Contractors program	Government suppliers with contracts of $200,000 or more, and 100 or more employees		
Yukon	Yukon Human Rights Act	All sectors	Yes	No
NWT	Policy only	Public service	No	No
BC	BC Human Rights Code	All sectors	No	No
Alberta	Policy only	Public service	No	No
Sask.	Policy only	Public service	No	No
Manitoba	Manitoba Human Rights Act Collective agreement	All sectors Public service	Yes	No
Ontario	Ontario Human Rights Code Government policy Proposed Employment Equity Act (by NDP when in opposition)	All sectors Public service Public sector (utilities, etc.) Businesses with payrolls of more than $300,000	Yes Yes	Yes, annually
Quebec	Quebec Charter of Rights and Freedoms Contract compliance program	Public sector (utilities, etc.) Government suppliers, subcontractors with contracts of $100,000 or more, and 100 employees or more		Yes
	Act to Secure the Handicapped in the Exercise of their Rights	Businesses with 50 employees or more	Yes	
NB	Policy only	Public service	No	No
NS	NS Human Rights Act Government policy	All sectors Public service	Yes	No
Nfld. & Labrador	Newfoundland Human Rights Code Government policy on appointment of women	All sectors Board and commissions	Yes	No

Source: Reprinted from John Southerst, "What Price Fairness," *Canadian Business*, December 1991, pp. 67–70, 72, 74.

DEVELOPING YOUR BUSINESS SKILLS

TRAINING FOR EQUITY

Women have advanced farther and faster as middle managers in Canadian banking than in any other workplace traditionally dominated by men.

At 47 percent, they're surging ahead of some underrepresented minorities to approach parity —which, some demographic experts would argue, tilts the balance toward reverse discrimination.

However, statistics being what they are, this gain becomes less impressive in context:

- For one thing, other groups specified in the federal Employment Equity Act—visible minorities, aboriginals and the people with disabilities—are making gains faster than women in most non-banking industrial categories.
- For another, senior positions in banking are still largely reserved for men, although women hold 73 percent of all jobs.

Clerical and supervisory posts in the banks are crowded with women, and their lot is no different from that of minorities in the lower ranks of the labour force. Even though the doors of corporate advancement have been thrown open by policy decisions at the top, women and disadvantaged groups can't move up any faster.

Their shortcoming isn't sex-related. It isn't physical, mental, or racial. It's a readily correctable problem of know-how. To speed their advance toward employment equity, they need access to educational and skills-improvement programs that don't exist yet.

However, a few pioneering models are being put in place by some organizations, particularly those under federal regulation or providing contract services to Ottawa and provincial governments.

In studies of three employment sectors—banking, railways, and utilities—the Conference Board of Canada has shown that opportunity in itself is no longer the main problem. The next wave in the drive to equity will require major investments in skills enhancement and a harder line on affirmative action all along the line, from classrooms to executive offices.

One example of the harder line being adopted by management is contained in a letter sent by Sam Horton, Ontario Hydro's senior vice-president of human resources, to the presidents and deans of engineering schools across Canada. It says, among other things:

"As one of Canada's largest employers of engineers. . . we can't afford to employ engineers who are reluctant to work with and for women and men of all races. We have plenty of bigotry and chauvinism in the workplace without continuing to import it each year with new university graduates. It's time to stop the cycle."

When Hydro began to attack the issue of employment equity by establishing an affirmative action department in 1984, the emphasis was on hiring and promoting women. Today, it covers all groups experiencing job discrimination.

Hydro quickly discovered it was not enough to decree respect for human rights. Policies and practices had to be developed, built into the management structure, and communicated to and understood and followed by all employees. This was followed by educational programs and the redesign of work systems and places.

The percentage of women in Hydro jobs is still less than half that of women in the general labour force, partly because they are only beginning to enter the trades and technical training fields in force.

Hydro's goal is to increase female representation to 33 percent by 2000. The proportion of aboriginals, minorities, and people with disabilities will be raised until it reflects levels in the population as a whole.

Hydro's zero-tolerance of sexual harassment has been adopted by such organizations as the

(continued)

Toronto Transit Commission and the Ontario government's human resources secretariat. Scholarships are available to help aboriginals and other minorities acquire the qualifications needed for Hydro jobs.

At Canadian National, as at Hydro, the progress of women is slower in technical areas than in administration and management. Women apply for only 10 to 12 percent of openings in non-traditional occupations.

The major emphasis of CN's equity program is an insistence on measurable affirmative action at all levels of management. Just seven years after establishing its employment equity department, in 1990 CN appointed Louise Piche as vice-president, human resources.

Her task is twofold: "To recruit and develop the representation of women, natives, the disabled and visible minorities; to create a work environment that gives all people the opportunity to reach their full employment potential.". . .

Apprenticeship and work experience programs help women and minorities acquire new work skills. Among the methods used to promote equity are scholarships, management development, work experience, and awareness training.

The banking system, which employs 180,600 workers, far more than CN and Hydro combined, is ahead of both in its commitment to achieve change through training.

The Canadian Bankers Association reports that the major banks have been steadily increasing their investment in training for ten years. . . .

A Statistics Canada survey in the late 1980s showed that the Canadian private sector spent $1.4 billion on formal training. The banks, which employ only 1.3 percent of the work force, spent $130 million, or 9 percent of the total.

Source: Excerpts from James Purdie, "Formal Training: A Key Part of Employment Equity," *The Financial Post*, October 7, 1991, p. 42.

Question for Discussion

1. Why has it been difficult for women and other disadvantaged groups to develop appropriate work skills?

Harassment

In school corridors, in locker rooms, and at the workplace a long-standing tradition exists: harassment of anyone who is "different." The form of harassment we hear most about is sexual harassment, but the difference may also be a matter of skin colour, physical size, age, clothing, religious practices, physical disability, or sexual orientation. Harassment is an immature form of bullying and deplorable in any setting. In the workplace, it is illegal.

The Canadian Human Rights Commission describes **harassment** as including any verbal abuse or threats, unwelcome invitations, leers or other offensive gestures, posting suggestive pictures, or unwelcome physical contact. More often than not, harassment goes on out of the public eye, with a supervisor harassing an immediate subordinate or a small group of workers harassing another at the same level. However, turning a blind eye to harassment is not good enough. Issues in Business 9.2 discusses the responsibility of management to ensure that harassment, particularly sexual harassment, does not occur. Figure 9.3 demonstrates how Canadian organizations are attempting to deal with the problem of sexual harassment.

harassment
Verbal abuse or threats, unwelcome invitations, leers or other offensive gestures, posting suggestive pictures, or unwelcome physical contact

ISSUES IN BUSINESS 9.2

AN ABUSE OF POWER

CANADIAN COURTS AND human rights tribunals treat sexual harassment as a serious and offensive form of employment discrimination.

While explicit sexual harassment laws in Canada are relatively recent and still evolving, this area of employee relations is a growth industry.

The Supreme Court of Canada and human rights tribunals are sending strongly worded messages to the executive suite. The message is this: sexual harassment is a serious offence—most particulary, it is an abuse of power. Those with power—employers—are not only required to stop sexual harassment, they ought reasonably to know about it and are also expected to prevent it. While these standards of due diligence may appear severe, savvy employers have committed substantial resources to attain and exceed these standards.

The power to deal effectively with sexual harassment resides in the boardroom.

Prevention starts at the top with executives who set the pace by word (a strong, plainly worded corporate policy that leaves no one in doubt and is fully communicated) and by deed (executives do as they say—no inappropriate conduct or comments, in or outside the boardroom).

Executives also have the power to make it clear that the workplace extends to all places where the business of the company is conducted—for example, company-sponsored events such as awards dinners and conventions, and social activities, such as the annual Christmas party or golf tournament.

Most importantly, executives have the power to allocate resources for the kind of employee-relations initiatives necessary to ensure the working environment is free of harassment. This means establishing both credibility and trust throughout the organization.

This will require money and patience. Corporate policies and procedures are meaningless unless both male and female employees are provided with the necessary guidance and human relations skills to resolve sexual harassment disputes between themselves without having to resort to either the company's internal procedures or a human rights tribunal.

Sexual harassment is a business issue. Protracted disputes are costly. The highest cost of all is damage to an expensively earned reputation. Canadian executives will not want to flunk the course.

Source: Reprinted from Belinda Morin, "Harassment Also a Canadian Issue," *The Financial Post*, October 18, 1991, p. 13.

Questions for Discussion

1. Is it fair to expect executives to be able to stop harassment that occurs in personal conversations among employees?

2. Judging from the information presented in Figure 9.3, do you think Canadian organizations are paying sufficient attention to the issue of harassment, the harassers, and the victims of harassment?

FIGURE 9.3 • FIGHTING SEXUAL HARASSMENT AT WORK

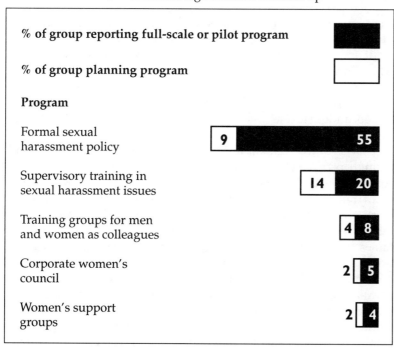

How Canadian organizations measure up

% of group reporting full-scale or pilot program ■

% of group planning program □

Program

Formal sexual harassment policy — 9 | 55

Supervisory training in sexual harassment issues — 14 | 20

Training groups for men and women as colleagues — 4 | 8

Corporate women's council — 2 | 5

Women's support groups — 2 | 4

Source: 1991 survey of 437 public and private organizations by Towers Perrin management consultants, and the Hudson Institute Montreal, *The Montreal Gazette*, October 19, 1991, p. B-5. Reprinted with permission of the Hudson Institute and Towers Perrin.

BUSINESS REVIEW 9.2

1. Explain the difference between the concepts of equal pay, pay equity, and employment equity.

2. You work at an employment agency and have been asked to provide candidates for an office manager's position in a small company. You have taken down the job description and job specification over the telephone and promise to send along some people the next day. Just as you are about to hang up, the general manager says, "I hope you'll find someone we can be comfortable with. You know we're a cohesive little ethnic group here, and we hope the ladies you send us will fit in nicely." What do you do?

DEVELOPING EMPLOYEES' SKILLS

The human resource department is responsible not only for hiring workers but also for co-ordinating the on-the-job training, classroom training, and management development programs needed to develop and maintain a productive work force.

On-the-Job Training

on-the-job training
"Learning by doing" under the guidance of an experienced fellow worker

New employees often receive **on-the-job training** on a formal or informal basis. This "learning by doing" typically takes place under the guidance of an experienced, knowledgeable, and patient fellow worker who can provide specific pointers and general advice. On-the-job training is usually the most efficient approach for relatively simple jobs.

In the past, most Canadian firms did not train new recruits in the skilled trades such as welding, plumbing, machine shop work, and carpentry but relied on immigrants with previous training to fill their needs. Now human resource departments can no longer find enough people who have the necessary training and experience.[2]

apprenticeship
A long-term combination of on-the-job and classroom training used in the skilled trades

Apprenticeship combines long-term on-the-job training with classroom training for these more sophisticated skilled trades. Apprentices work as assistants to skilled workers who are responsible for teaching them the practical aspects of their craft while theoretical training continues on a part-time basis at local community colleges. Some jurisdictions are experimenting with high-school-level apprenticeship programs, such as the School Workplace Apprenticeship Program (SWAP) in Guelph, Ontario. The Guelph program provides teenagers with valuable skills, and local industry with a pool of badly needed workers. "We've done a poor job of recruiting kids to the trades in the past," says Larry Pearson, executive vice-president of Linamar Machining. "Now we're going into the schools to show people at an early stage that they can earn money and feel good about making things with machines." At Linamar, "we have youngsters running machines—milling metal, drilling, and tapping holes. They do real work, deal with real people, and they love it.[3]

Classroom Training

For certain types of training, removing the learners from the day-to-day pressures of the job is important if they are to gain a firm grasp of new knowledge and skills. The classroom provides an environment where employees can meet new information, ask questions, and feel free to proceed at their own pace. They learn the theory before practising the skills on the job, so when they actually start to work with them they are not working by trial and error. If "errors" would be expensive, prior training may yield considerable savings in time and materials.

Classroom training tries to ensure that workers and their skills development are at the centre of every activity. After all, the company wants the employee to acquire and perform new skills, not simply learn how to describe them. Various techniques include lectures with question periods, group problem solving, simulations, films, audio-visual aids, programmed instruction, and training under expert guidance on the equipment workers will use in their new jobs.

A recent approach is computer simulation training (CST), which offers the student control over the learning pace and the advantages of interactive learning, participation, and positive reinforcement. CST programs range in sophistication from off-the-shelf courses in generic

Union Gas is a good example of a contemporary Canadian business that places great value on and makes serious investments in its most vital asset—its human resources. Union Gas created an education centre for both management and labour in order to enable them to upgrade their current skills, to learn new technologies, and to develop practical strategies adapted to their areas of speciality.

topics, through support courses with custom software packages, to flight simulators used by pilots to master a new type of aircraft and simulation of operating-room conditions for surgeons. Employees who are unfamiliar with computers, however, may bring negative attitudes or even be fearful of this approach to training.

Management Development Programs

Management development programs were first used about 40 years ago to broaden the knowledge and upgrade the skills of current managers and to identify and develop those with further management potential. Management development programs usually take place away from the workplace. Some large companies such as General Motors and Loblaws have set up their own training facilities for current and future managers. McDonald's trains new managers at its well-known Hamburger University.

On-the-job approaches to management development include job rotation and mentoring. Job rotation gives junior executives temporary assignments in a large number of departments so they can gain insight into departmental activities and the overview that top management needs in setting organizational goals. Mentoring matches a junior executive with a senior executive who acts as **mentor,** advising the junior on managerial strategies and offering support as he or she advances within the organization.

Management development programs need to be tailored to various managerial levels. Supervisory-level managers profit from training that develops technical and human skills. Middle managers need opportunities to expand their conceptual and analytical skills. Training for top managers emphasizes broad-spectrum conceptualization and long-term strategic planning—seeing the entire forest, now and in the future, and trusting subordinates to take care of the trees.

mentor
A senior executive who advises a junior in managerial strategies and offers support as he or she advances within the organization

Assessment Centres

The assessment-centre approach uses hypothetical situations to discover hidden talent and management potential.

assessment centre
A program that simulates real business-world situations to assess how individuals will react under stress and to predict their management potential

Though the name implies a place, an **assessment centre** is really a program that simulates real business-world situations. Groups are asked to solve problems through unstructured discussions with no assigned leader to determine how various individuals handle challenging assignments. In the "in-basket" simulation, for example, participants assume the role of manager and find themselves dealing with customer complaints, telephone calls from senior executives, personnel conflicts, and poor interdepartmental communications. Meanwhile, trained assessors judge their responses.

Research has shown that the assessment-centre concept, which was first used during the Second World War to find capable undercover agents, is effective in predicting how individuals will perform under stress. Among others, Bell Canada, Canadian General Electric, Sears Canada, and IBM Canada are some of the companies that use this strategy for measuring management potential. Assessment centres are also used to assist companies such as the brokerage firm Merrill Lynch in recruiting salespeople.

Performance Appraisal

Periodic evaluation of an employee's work is a valuable tool for training as well as a means of obtaining information useful to management. **Performance appraisal** compares actual performance with what has been expected. It helps management assess whether expectations have been realistic and whether further training is required. It is also the basis for transfers or terminations. Performance appraisal is used in many contexts outside the business world—such as in assessing whether or not someone is competent to drive a car and in evaluating students' performance through examinations and assignments and instructors' effectiveness through student evaluations.

performance appraisal
Appraisal of an employee's actual performance to expected performance in order to assess the need for further training, compensation, promotion, transfer, or termination

Performance appraisals provide feedback for employees. Employees need to know how their performance compares with expectations if they are to use their strengths to advantage and work on areas of weakness. Managers can use information from appraisals to recommend salary adjustments, arrange promotions, and make decisions about training requirements, transfers, and promotions. Appraisals can be a valuable source of employee motivation when managers identify and reward outstanding workers with praise, salary increases, or promotions.

Of course, the methods used for appraisal must be objective and aimed at acquiring information that is truly relevant. Line supervisors, who perform the actual appraisal, can work with human resource specialists to design fair evaluation forms and techniques that will allow comparison across the organization.

One of the chief advantages of the management-by-objectives approach is that it provides the employee with specific information on how performance will be evaluated. Because the employee participates in goal setting, there is little uncertainty about what constitutes satisfactory performance. Occasionally, however, workers feel that they have been unfairly appraised or that performance standards are too high, and they may wish to discuss their objections with a human resource specialist.

Employee Counselling

Employees who are having personal problems will become less efficient workers. Some may wish to discuss their problems with their supervisor, but human resource departments have found that trained specialists may be better able to help workers with family, financial, or other kinds of problems.

Most human resource departments also offer assistance with day-to-day work problems; for example, they may help to arrange car pools, adjust an employee's schedule by fifteen minutes to allow him to pick up a child from daycare, or arrange a transfer to lighter duties for an employee who is pregnant.

When employees must be laid off, the human resource department may offer counselling on other job opportunities and retraining possibilities. Pre-retirement counselling explains company pension plans and benefits and also what the retiree can expect from government plans.

EMPLOYEES ON THE MOVE

Employee turnover means an organization is a continually changing entity. Not only are employees constantly being hired, they also move upward or laterally within it, and leave it.

A **promotion** is an appointment to a position of greater authority and responsibility—and brings with it an increase in salary. Promotions are usually based on performance, but some companies follow a tradition of awarding promotions based on **seniority**, the length of time an employee has worked for the organization. Many labour unions also believe promotions should be based on seniority. At lower levels of an organization, where technical skills may be more important than conceptual skills, seniority may indeed be a valuable factor, but most managers prefer to use it only as a "tie-breaker" between otherwise equally qualified candidates.

A **lateral transfer** is a movement to a different position of the same status and salary level. The judicious use of transfers allows organizations to utilize available talents where they are most needed and also to satisfy employees' aspirations by moving them to positions they find more interesting.

Promotions and transfers may pose problems when they require movement to other locations. When a company moves an employee, it also has to move the employee's family, and this may mean that a spouse must leave a paying position. Many human resource departments also act as employment agencies in order to assist the spouse of a valued employee find a new job in a new city.

Separation occurs when employee and employer part company through resignation, retirement, layoff, or dismissal. Employees may resign to go to a better job, to leave an organization where they have been unhappy, or for any number of personal reasons. Traditionally in Canada, workers have retired at the age of 65, but the federal govern-

promotion
Appointment to a position of greater authority and responsibility

seniority
Status achieved by length of service with an organization

lateral transfer
Movement to a different position of the same status within an organization

separation
Departure of an employee from an organization through resignation, retirement, layoff, or dismissal

ment and the provincial governments of Manitoba, Quebec, Prince Edward Island, and the Northwest Territories refuse to allow compulsory retirement solely on the basis of age. The Supreme Court of Canada, however, has declared that a compulsory age of retirement is a justifiable infringement on human rights because it opens up opportunities for younger workers. Present economic conditions have given rise to the phenomenon of early retirement, usually encouraged by organizations that are downsizing and would prefer to retain younger employees rather than highly paid senior workers.

Layoffs occur when business is poor and fewer employees are needed to maintain lower levels of production. Layoffs may be temporary, with the employees called back at a later date, or permanent. Some unions negotiate partial wages and continuation of benefits during temporary layoffs. Layoffs are generally planned so that workers with seniority are the last to be affected, or, to look at the issue from the point of view of recently hired workers, "last in, first out."

Dismissal is the unpleasant but sometimes necessary process of discharging, or firing, an employee. The cause may be with the employee—incompetence, persistent inattention to work rules, or excessive absenteeism—or with the employer—permanent layoff because of the elimination of jobs as a result of downsizing or the closing of entire facilities. When an employer dismisses an employee, it must be sure that proper procedures are followed and that the employee has had due warning that his or her behaviour is unacceptable. Figure 9.4 illustrates typical warnings and penalties that, if unheeded, may lead to an eventual dismissal.

Failure to follow and to document such procedures may leave a company open to a charge of wrongful or unjust dismissal. Adjudicators and courts recognize that workers are stakeholders in the organizations they work for, that they have valid interests that cannot be abrogated at the employers' whim. Statements about due process in employee handbooks are being regarded as contractual obligations (which means human resource departments must be extremely careful in drawing these up, consulting with lawyers when necessary). Promises made during job interviews or when the employee is hired may be seen as binding. If one employee is dismissed and others merely reprimanded for the same type of offence, a court may deem the dismissal unjust and order reinstatement.[4] Dismissal, even for

layoff

Temporary or permanent dismissal of employees not needed to maintain lower levels of production when business is poor

dismissal

The discharge of an employee for incompetence, inattention to work rules, or absenteeism, or because of the elimination of jobs within an organization

FIGURE 9.4 • TYPICAL PENALTIES FOR VIOLATING WORK RULES, IN ORDER OF INCREASING SEVERITY

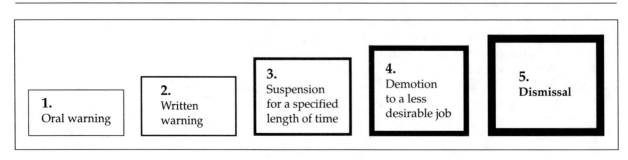

1. Oral warning
2. Written warning
3. Suspension for a specified length of time
4. Demotion to a less desirable job
5. Dismissal

cause, is no longer an easy process. No organization wants to be dragged through the courts in a wrongful-dismissal suit, which is time-consuming, expensive, and embarrassing. Most jurisdictions, however, allow employers to dismiss an employee without stating a cause during an initial three-month probationary period.

EMPLOYEE COMPENSATION

Developing and maintaining a fair compensation system is a delicate task. If salaries and other labour costs are a large component of the final price of a product, these costs must be kept low enough for the company to remain competitive. At the same time, the company is also competing for employees with other organizations requiring the same skills. Inadequate salaries lead to high employee turnover, poor morale, and low productivity. Compensation within the organization must also be kept equitable: if employees believe that others are being unfairly rewarded for lower levels of effort and skills, they will reduce their own level of productivity until they feel the balance of work and rewards has been restored.[5]

A compensation policy, therefore, must consider the company's ability to pay, rates paid by others competing for the same human resources, and the productivity of its workers. Other concerns are government legislation concerning compensation and the cost of living that employees have to cope with.

What Is Each Job Worth?

A comprehensive job evaluation can establish the relative worth of jobs within an organization. A job evaluation examines such factors as the skills required for each job; the formal education, training, and experience expected; the complexity of the job itself; strength and other physical requirements; working conditions; decision-making responsibilities; and the importance of the job to the organization's mission. Points are assigned to each criterion to develop a monetary scale. While human resource experts develop and conduct the job evaluation, it is top management that uses the scale to establish a pay range for each job and the actual compensation for the employees who perform it. A range is needed because it is the jobs that have been evaluated, not the employees. A valued and trusted employee might be paid at the top of the range for a particular function whereas an untried beginner whose productivity is expected to be lower would start farther down the range for that job.

Approaches to Compensation

Methods of compensation depend on the work setting and the type and conditions of work and which approach is most likely to motivate employees.

The most common forms of compensation are wages and salaries. Although the terms are often used interchangeably, they have slightly different meanings. A **wage** is paid on the basis of the number of hours worked or per units of production. A **salary** is a fixed payment usually made monthly or biweekly, and expressed in terms of an

wage
Compensation on the basis of the number of hours worked or per units of production

salary
Compensation made as a fixed monthly or biweekly payment and expressed in terms of an annual amount

annual amount. Office staff, managers, and executives, whose work cannot easily be assessed according to hours worked or units produced, are paid salaries.

Assembly line workers, maintenance workers, and some sales-clerks are usually paid **time wages.** These are easy to calculate and to administer and are seldom misunderstood. Time wages encourage a satisfactory level of performance but provide no motivation for exceptional performance. Governments set minimum hourly rates for time wages to ensure that employees are not exploited by being paid wages that will not meet the basic cost of living.

Wages for **piecework** are paid on the basis of units of output produced by an individual or by the entire department. Piecework encourages quality production because no payment is made for defective goods. The piecework approach is often criticized, however, because those who set the rates do not always take into account the length of time the work actually takes, and workers may end up being paid considerably less than they would on a time basis. Piecework wages are being used more and more for workers who work at home. Garment makers and order takers for fast food deliveries are often homeworkers paid on a piecework basis.

Commissions, a percentage of sales earned by salespeople, are a form of piecework wages. In retail stores, commissions tend to replace hourly wages in stores or departments that sell more expensive items such as electronic equipment, automobiles, or household furniture or appliances. Insurance sales representatives, real estate agents, and others who work on telephone or door-to-door sales are usually paid on a commission basis. Commissions provide an obvious incentive and also allow workers to structure their own work schedules.

Some companies combine a low hourly wage with piecework or commission payments as an additional incentive.

Bonuses are payments in addition to wages or salary paid to workers as a reward for especially good work. They act as an incentive to maintain or increase productivity.

Profit sharing distributes a percentage of the profits of a good year to the employees, who contribute to generating them. Profit sharing helps employees feel they are a valued part of the corporate family, encouraging loyalty and smoothing relations between management and labour.

An **employee stock ownership plan (ESOP)** encourages employees to buy shares in the company so that they are working for themselves as owners and share in the gains and losses. ESOPs are a useful incentive if the shares are bought in small amounts, perhaps through a payroll deduction scheme. Some companies, however, have used ESOPs aggressively to gain commitment from management personnel, arranging loans so that executives could buy large blocks of shares. This may be a dangerous technique when the company itself is on a shaky footing. The 1993 collapse in the value of shares of Royal Trustco and of Bramalea left many executives with huge debts incurred in the boom years to buy shares that are now virtually worthless.

Pay for performance is a motivational concept that can incorporate a number of these approaches to compensation as described in Issues in Business 9.3.

---

time wage
Compensation on the basis of the number of hours worked

piecework
Work compensated on the basis of units of output

commission
A form of piecework compensation whereby salespeople receive a percentage of the sales they make

bonus
A payment in addition to wages or salary made to workers as a reward for especially good work

profit sharing
Distribution of a percentage of profits to employees who contribute to generating them

employee stock ownership plan (ESOP)
A plan that allows employees to buy shares of stock

ISSUES IN BUSINESS 9.3

PAY FOR PERFORMANCE

MOST EMPLOYEES ARE paid for their time or the number of hours they work. In this case, pay is not contingent upon levels of individual performance. What, then, motivates employees to perform even to acceptable levels?

Employees can be motivated by their boss, by co-workers, or by the non-financial rewards of work, such as intrinsic satisfaction derived from the job. This section deals with an alternative approach to motivating employees: pay for performance.

Pay for performance means that an employee's pay is contingent upon some level of performance specified by the organization. In its *Compensation Planning Outlook 1990* survey, the Conference Board of Canada found that performance-pay management, combined with variable compensation, was a significant priority for many organizations.

There are three basic approaches to pay for performance. The first is *merit pay*, in which pay increases are based on subjective evaluations of employees' performance. In determining merit pay for individual employees, superiors usually fill out performance evaluation forms. The second approach makes promotion to higher-paying jobs contingent upon superior performance. Again, superior performance is usually judged by the employee's boss, using a system of performance appraisal. This approach is most commonly used for white-collar, professional, and managerial employees. As a pay-for-performance method, promotions have two major disadvantages. First, employees compete against one another for promotions, which may reduce co-operation among employees. Second, a high level of performance may not lead to promotion because such opportunities are limited. Many Canadian organizations are likely to have fewer promotion opportunities in the 1990s than in the past because they have become leaner organizations with flatter structures, because successful early retirement programs mean fewer retirements, and because high unemployment means lower turnover.

The third approach to linking pay to performance is to make pay directly proportionate to criteria such as the number of units produced, sales volume, or the profitability of the organization. This type of system is called an *incentive pay system* because the level of monetary reward associated with different levels of performance is specified in advance.

If linking pay to performance is to be used in motivating employees, the work situation must meet five conditions:

1. The jobs must have the potential for meaningful performance variation.
2. Employees must have—and *believe* they have—the ability to perform at higher levels.
3. Employees must be motivated by money.
4. Employees must perceive an equitable pay–effort bargain.
5. Employees must perceive that the system is fairly administered.

Source: Reprinted from Thomas H. Stone and Noah M. Meltz, *Human Resource Management in Canada*, Third Edition, (Toronto: Holt, Rinehart & Winston of Canada Limited, 1993), p. 570.

Questions for Discussion

1. What are the strengths and the weaknesses of each approach to motivating employees through pay for performance?
2. Describe a job you have held recently. Which approach to pay for performance would have best motivated you?

employee benefits

Financial and non-monetary elements of compensation for employees and their families such as pension plans, dental and drug insurance, sick leave, and severance pay

Employee Benefits

An important part of any compensation package today is the benefits employees and their families receive that go beyond their paycheques. **Employee benefits** are financial and non-monetary elements of compensation such as subsidized meals, pension plans, dental and drug insurance, disability insurance, life insurance, sick leave, relocation allowances, severance pay, post-secondary scholarships for children of employees, and corporate social and recreational programs. Few employees realize that the benefits organizations provide add up to about one-third of total payroll costs, as shown in Table 9.4.

Because needs vary from family to family, some organizations let employees choose from a "cafeteria" of benefits. Employees also contribute to many benefits through payroll deductions.

Many organizations do not allow part-time workers to take advantage of company benefit plans, and no jurisdiction has yet addressed this inequity. It has been suggested that this is one reason part-time work is becoming more and more common—paying a wage with no additional benefits is much cheaper. Pressure is being placed on governments and human resource departments to find ways to extend at least partial benefits packages to part-time workers.

Occupational Safety

The importance of safe working conditions has received a great deal of attention in recent years. Accidents, whether they occur in the factory, the laboratory, the office, or the parking lot not only cause suffering for injured workers but can result in heavy costs to the employer who may lose an experienced employee, suffer from poor morale among other workers, and be subject to increased insurance premiums. Provincial workers' compensation acts and the Canada Safety Code help provide for a safe working environment.

TABLE 9.4 • AVERAGE EMPLOYEE BENEFITS

Cost as a percentage of gross annual payroll

Overall	**33.5**		
Vacations	6.0	Pension plans	3.6
Holidays	3.6	Welfare plans	5.0
Coffee breaks, rest periods	3.6	**Pension and welfare plans**	**8.6**
Bereavement, jury duty	0.2		
Other paid time off	0.5	Severance and savings	1.3
Paid time off	**13.9**	Bonus and profit sharing	2.9
		Cash benefits	**4.1**
Unemployment Insurance	2.3		
Workers' compensation	1.6	**Other noncash benefits**	**1.5**
Canada/Quebec pension	1.4		
Legally required payments	**5.3**	**Overall employee benefits**	**33.4**

Source: Reprinted from Peat Marwick Stevenson and Kellogg, "Employee Benefit Costs in Canada," 1989.

Workers' compensation acts provide compensation for workers who are injured in accidents at their work. A provincial compensation board administers the act in each province. Employers contribute to workers' compensation funds at rates based on their total annual payroll and on the safety record of their particular industry. For example, a mining company will pay a higher rate than an advertising agency. The benefits falling under this legislation include protection against industrial accidents, first aid and hospitalization costs beyond those paid by medicare, rehabilitation services, cash benefits for the period of disability, and for a pension for life in the case of permanent disability. Workers' compensation programs are not preventative; they come into effect only after accidents have happened.

The Canada Labour Code, proclaimed in 1978, includes the **Canada Safety Code** of 1968. The safety code spells out the basics of industrial safety programs and makes regulations to handle occupational safety problems in various industries and related occupations. The provinces are responsible for the administration of the program. Safety inspectors with powers and responsibilities laid down by the Canada Labour Code usually inspect industrial firms yearly. Each province sets occupational health standards with regard to smoke, chemicals, gases, and other forms of pollution associated with industrial activities. The code requires all employers to operate their businesses in a manner that will not endanger the health and/or safety of employees. Employers must also enforce reasonable procedures designed to prevent or reduce the risk of injury on the job.

The key element in these government programs is the commitment of business to co-operate in good faith and enforce all safety procedures.

workers' compensation act
Provincial legislation that provides compensation to workers for work-related injuries

Canada Safety Code
Occupational safety regulations in the Canada Labour Code administered by the provinces

---

BUSINESS REVIEW 9.3

1. What type of training programs did you participate in at your last or current job? Would further training have been useful to you in performing your functions?

2. What type of compensation did you receive in that job? Was it appropriate and did it motivate you to perform well?

HUMAN RESOURCES IN THE FUTURE

As the world changes, so do an organization's needs for human resources. Employees of the future will need different skills from those of the past, or even those of today. As stakeholders in the organizations they work for, they will be making different demands of their employers and the human resource personnel who represent them. Human resource departments will find themselves dealing more with white-collar workers doing their jobs from computer terminals in their homes, which will save the employee travel time and the employer office space but demand a new style of management. Workers will

The work force of the near future will better approximate and reflect Canadian society regardless of an individual's sex, age, sexual orientation, race, physical condition, or religion. As more and more "non-traditional" workers enter the labour pool, the market will accommodate more single-parent households, stay-at-home professionals, and working retirees (as depicted above), to name but a few examples.

want different hours, transferable pension plans, early retirement, contract work. Human resource experts see the changing motivations of employees, not as threats to the smooth running of the organization, but as opportunities.

INTERACTIVE SUMMARY AND DISCUSSION QUESTIONS

1. The opening vignette describes the role of Joan Crawford as vice-president of human resources for Cook Travel. What accounts for her success in this position?
2. Would you recommend major organizations follow succession planning in developing and retaining their home-grown talent? Discuss fully.
3. Do you feel the current Employment Equity Act should be changed or allowed to remain intact? What modifications would you recommend and why?
4. What are the responsibilities of employees in sexual harassment cases? Why is this such a critical human resource problem?
5. Give an example of a job in which each of the following employee compensation alternatives would be most appropriate:
   a) piecework
   b) commission
   c) salary
   d) time wage
6. Describe fully the type of compensation plan you would recommend for each of the following:
   a) professional athlete
   b) musical instrument repairer
   c) real estate salesperson
   d) assembly line worker in microwave oven factory
7. Describe the typical benefits offered to employees of a large organization. What special types of benefits might each of the following firms offer their employees, and what problems do you feel would occur with each type?
   a) Royal Bank
   b) Bell Canada
   c) Air Canada
   d) The Bay
   e) Domtar

CASE 9.1

GUESS WHOM YOU CAN'T FIRE

IT PROBABLY WASN'T surprising that the Canadian Imperial Bank of Commerce concluded that Jacqueline Chayer wasn't an ideal employee. Although she'd been with the bank for five and a half years and her on-the-job performance was satisfactory, the bank had a few reservations about her off-hours associations. As a federal labour adjudicator was later to point out, the police had burst into her apartment and found five men dividing the $6,403 cash proceeds of a robbery that had taken place half an hour earlier at a nearby CIBC branch. They were suspects in another robbery at the same branch, where two employees had been wounded by blasts from a sawed-off shotgun. And, according to the adjudicator's decision on the case, one of the suspects had lived with Chayer, who had posted bail for him after he'd been charged in yet another robbery. And Chayer's roommate seemed more than conversant with the bank's security procedures. The bank asked Chayer to resign voluntarily, "failing which it would be obliged to fire her."

The bank's behaviour may seem reasonable, but not according to the Labour Canada adjudicator who reviewed the case. Chayer, who had worked as an accounting supervisor, appealed her firing under a little-known section of the Canada Labour Code. The adjudicator ruled that the bank did not show "just cause" for the firing. Chayer hadn't done anything wrong herself, and therefore the adjudicator ordered the CIBC to give her back pay. "The only reason why I am not ordering reinstatement," wrote the adjudicator, "is that such an action was not requested."

The unjust-dismissal legislation, covering non-unionized, non-management employees in federally regulated industries such as banks and interprovincial transportation and telecommunications companies, was added to the Canada Labour Code in 1978 with the best of intentions.

(continued)

The process seems relatively straightforward. A fired employee lodges a complaint with Labour Canada; if the complaint is judged worthwhile, Labour Canada contacts the employer and asks it to state its reasons for the firing. (If the case gets to adjudication, those reasons will form the basis of the employer's case, although instances of employee wrongdoing that later come to light may be added.) A Labour Canada inspector, who has the right to see all the relevant documents, reviews the case and tries to get the two parties to come to an agreement—a process that usually takes about three months. If the parties still can't agree, the case goes to an adjudicator, who will either uphold the dismissal or order the employer to reinstate and/or compensate the employ. . . .

So, what makes unjust dismissal so alarming to employers? First, according to the legislation, the individual complainant ought to be given the benefit of the doubt whenever possible—which means the proceedings are weighted in favour of the employee. And unlike wrongful-dismissal suits, the company must prove it had "just cause" to fire the employee.

Adjudicators for unjust-dismissal cases are chosen by Labour Canada, usually from a pool of provincially selected government mediators, labour lawyers, and professional labour arbitrators. Unlike judges, adjudicators don't have a long history of legal precedent upon which to base their rulings. Nor do they necessarily pay attention to the precedents that do exist. . . .

Judgements by adjudicators may be disputed. Either side can ask for a judicial review by the Federal Court of Appeal. However, such reviews can be expensive and are not always successful, and the grounds for one are limited. The adjudicator must have exceeded his jurisdiction, made a "patently unreasonable" judgement or one against "natural justice"—both sides must have the chance to be heard, for instance. (The Chayer decision was appealed and sent back to the adjudicator, for example, because the court felt one of the CIBC's reasons for dismissal did indeed provide just cause. The bank claimed that confidence in its employees was necessary, and that it had lost confidence in Chayer.) If it's a case of just not agreeing with the decision, judges won't touch it.

Given the pitfalls of arbitration, many employers prefer to settle. Fighting through arbitration can cost between $5,000 and $10,000—or more if the case drags on. Then there's the drain on management's time and morale. And the ultimate terror—reinstatement. Even if the adjudicator doesn't award reinstatement, the meter of back pay is always ticking. Small wonder that 75 percent of the roughly 600 complaints annually are resolved before they ever get to adjudication, and another 10 percent before the adjudicator's report.

Avoiding unjust dismissal can be as simple as improving employee relations. The fact that the CIBC had four times the number of unjust-dismissal cases in the early 1980s than it has now may have been partly its own fault. . . . As part of an overall drive to make employee relations more professional, the CIBC's legal and human resources department now makes sure that all managers are well informed about the possibility of unjust-dismissal cases and how to prevent them. There's no denying that while good employee relations practices can cut down the number of cases, there will always be employees who are eager to hold their employers to ransom with the threat of reinstatement and financial awards. But it's reassuring to note that roughly half of the cases are either decided in favour of the employer or dismissed for lack of jurisdiction. Reinstatement—the most feared result—occurs only in about 15 percent of the decisions.

Source: Excerpts from Diane Forrest, "Guess Whom You Can't Fire," *Canadian Business*, November 1991, pp. 97, 98, 100.

Questions for Discussion

1. Why is the threat of reinstatement "the ultimate terror" for management in cases like that of Jacqueline Chayer?

2. In general, is the process of reviewing unjust dismissal fair and reasonable? Discuss from the point of view of (a) an employee and (b) an employer.

CASE 9.2

CAUGHT IN THE WEB OF WORTH

TO UNDERSTAND HOW the red tape of pay equity can hammer even the best-intentioned company, consider the sad case of the Consumers' Gas Co. Ltd.

When pay equity became law in Ontario in 1987, the Toronto-based utility didn't think it would have any problems. The company had been evaluating jobs for twenty years and, says Consumers' compensation director John Brugos, "Men and women in the same pay grades were getting the same amount."

So far, so good. But then the Energy and Chemical Workers Union's Local 513, representing Consumers' inside workers, jumped into the act. It didn't agree that equality ruled—even though it had helped management develop the job evaluations.

The two sides were soon butting heads over whether the company's evaluation system applied only to the inside clerical workers or whether it could also fairly evaluate the jobs of the predominantly male outside workers—labourers, gas technicians, and fitters—who earned more and belonged to a different local.

The problem was that, although the two locals had each negotiated pay equity for men and women through their collective agreements, Ontario's legislation opened the door to comparisons outside the bargaining unit. If Local 513 could make sure the higher-paid outside workers' jobs scored low enough on their evaluations to be equal to inside scores, the inside workers could win pay equity increases. It wanted new evaluations.

"We told them from the beginning those evaluations were to apply to the whole company," says Brugos. But Local 513 national representative Dave Moffat says differently: "When we developed the system, it was on the basis it would apply solely to clerical workers."

Local 513 called in a review officer of the Ontario Pay Equity Commission to mediate the dispute. He specified amendments to the evaluation plan. But that didn't solve the dispute. The union appealed to the pay equity tribunal, which scheduled twenty days of hearings. But after twelve days of paying lawyers, consultants, shop stewards, and managers to attend, the two sides suspended the hearings and sat down to negotiate. After two weeks, they signed an agreement that gave *every* man and woman in Local 513 a pay equity increase averaging 3 percent. In return, Consumers' doesn't have to evaluate outside jobs and can still use the original job evaluations for inside positions.

Moffat says the cost of fighting it out at the tribunal was prohibitive—"A couple of hundred thousand dollars. And it wasn't finished." Brugos says Consumers' costs were comparable. While everyone walked away with something, he says, the result was not pay equity for women: "Somebody once asked me for a copy of my plan. I said no, because it really isn't a textbook model for what pay equity is supposed to be."

Source: Excerpts from John Southerst, "What Price Fairness?," *Canadian Business*, December 1991, pp. 67–70, 72, 74.

Questions for Discussion

1. Was the solution to the dispute in which every man and woman was awarded a pay equity increase averaging 3 percent equitable? Defend your answer.

2. Why are the views of labour and management concerning equity in conflict? What are these views? How can they be resolved?

NOTES

1. Tricia McCallum, "On the Front Lines of HR," *Human Resources Professional*, January 1991, pp. 6–7.
2. Jerry Zeidenberg, "Extra Curricular," *Canadian Business*, February 1991, pp. 66–67.
3. Zeidenberg, "Extra Curricular," pp. 66–67.
4. Diane Forrest, "Guess Whom You Can't Fire," *Canadian Business*, November 1991, pp. 97, 98, 100.
5. Equity theory of motivation as discussed by J. Stacey Adams, "Injustice in Social Exchange," in L. Berkovitz, ed., *Advances in Experimental Social Psychology*, 2nd ed. (New York: Academic Press, 1965), pp. 267–69.

PHOTO CREDITS

HRM 14   Shell Canada Limited

HRM 21   Union Gas Limited

HRM 30   Industry, Science and Technology, Canada

MODULE
◆ LR ◆

LABOUR RELATIONS

THE FOCUS OF THIS MODULE

1. To discuss the history and development of labour unions

2. To outline the major laws that affect labour–management relations

3. To describe the collective bargaining process and the use of conciliation, mediation, and interest arbitration in achieving a collective agreement

4. To discuss a union's use of strikes, picketing, and boycotts and management's use of lockouts and strikebreaking as tools of last resort in achieving an acceptable agreement

5. To describe union–management relations during the course of a collective agreement and the process of settling grievances

6. To consider present concerns of labour unions and the future of the union movement in Canada

7. To learn the meaning of the following terms:

KEY TERMS

labour union	interest arbitration
craft union	strike
industrial union	picketing
collective bargaining	lockout
closed shop	grievance
union shop	wildcat strike
Rand formula	work to rule
bargaining unit	grievance arbitration
mediation	featherbedding

AFTER HER FIFTH FIVE-HOUR shift on the Public Service Alliance of Canada picket line in front of the Government of Canada Custom House building in downtown Vancouver, Jean Allan hurried home to phone her bank manager. She wanted to discuss the possibility of delaying her $280 monthly car payment on the 1987 Nissan Sentra that she acquired a year ago. Tired, nursing a bruised back and elbow from being knocked down one day and pushed up against a wall the next in a confrontation with picket-line crashers, the president of the 30-member PSAC Union of Solicitor General Employees Local 20086 had been too busy during the first week of the nationwide strike to attend to all the details of her domestic affairs. But after seventeen years as a single parent—her daughter, Melanie, is now nineteen and a community college student—the 40-year-old Allan is accustomed to juggling her books. The salary from her job as a parole office clerk for Corrections Canada in Vancouver —$25,000 a year, $300 take-home a week—has never been quite enough. Said Allan: "You learn to rework your budget very well. I know it's very important, but I can't afford house insurance. I save all year to pay my car insurance. You learn to do without."

Allan says that she could earn more in the private sector or in other work—"My brother is a welder; maybe my father should have taught me how to weld too," but she has set her sights on a career with Corrections Canada. Since joining the service in 1985, after spending seven years as an accommodations co-ordinator for the University of Alberta in Edmonton, Allan has studied criminology part time at Simon Fraser University, taking one course a semester. She is now in her third year of the four-year course. "I've been scratching away, little by little, at the criminology degree that I need to reach my goal of becoming a parole officer," Allan explained. "I want to stay in Corrections." But like tens of thousands of PSAC members, Allan did not hesitate to join the picket line when the strike began early last week. "This has been building for a long time, and there is more at stake than just wages," she said in an interview. "We have been dealing with downsizing, with contracting out." Claiming that a cabinet minister's tax-free allowance amounted to more than her annual salary, she added: "You know something is seriously wrong."

Allan says that she is not convinced that the strike will solve her problems, or those of her fellow workers. But she added: "We don't know how else to get the point across. We are on the inside. We see how the money is spent, how it is wasted. The public knows, too, that the spending priorities of this government are out of line." And last week, earning $125 in strike pay, the five-foot, one-inch native of Dauphin, Manitoba, had to rethink her own spending priorities. Said Allan: "If the strike goes on much longer, I might just have to do without a car.". . .

Allan says that in three years, when her daughter graduates, she may be able to take some time off to study full time herself. Until then, she will work to keep both their dreams alive. Last week's events have cast a cloud over that future. Yet, said Allan, "We have to pull together or we won't accomplish anything. But who knows if it will be resolved by this government waking up?"

At week's end, as the Treasury Board president announced that he will table back-to-work legislation in Parliament this week, Allan and the entire PSAC membership braced for what may well be an escalation of the confrontation. "It will be the law," Allan acknowledged. But, noting PSAC president Daryl Bean's threat last week to defy such a law, Allan said that she will support the union leader. "If he goes to jail, I'll definitely stay out," she said. "There's no way in hell that I'd go back in. A lot of others feel that way, too." Saying that she was "born in Manitoba, raised in Saskatchewan, worked twelve years in Alberta, and now that I'm out here, I can't go much farther west," Allan has chosen her place to make a stand.

Source: Excerpts from Hal Quinn, "A Striker's Defense," *Macleans*, September 23, 1991, p. 36.

"WEATHERING A STRIKE" is a term usually used about employers who have to survive the effects of their workers walking off the job. Jean Allan's story is typical: it indicates that strikes are no less devastating for the workers involved. As Allan says, sometimes workers "don't know how else to get the point across." But strikes are a last resort; no labour union wants to inflict such pain on its members; the workers themselves are usually saddened by the need to inflict such pain on their employers.

WHAT IS A LABOUR UNION?

A **labour union** is an association formed by workers to negotiate in the collective interest with employers, especially in matters of wages and working conditions. In Canada, there are two types of labour unions—craft and industrial. A **craft union** is a labour union composed of workers in one skilled trade, such as carpenters, electricians, machinists, and printers. These unions include the United Brotherhood of Carpenters and Joiners and the International Union of Operating Engineers. An **industrial union** is made up of workers from one industry, including, therefore, members with a wide variety of skills and responsibilities. The Canadian Automobile Workers, the United Steelworkers of America, and the Amalgamated Clothing and Textile Workers Union are industrial unions.

LABOUR UNIONS: A HISTORY

The Industrial Revolution, which began in the 1700s, dramatically and permanently changed most conditions of work—where it happens, how it is organized, who does it, and how it is paid for. The large factory replaced the cottage system of production where family units worked together and to some extent controlled their own working conditions and the price they received for their labours. An entire new technology based on the use of steam and machinery rapidly increased efficiency and output.

The rewards of the Industrial Revolution, however, went almost entirely to the owners of the means of production. Formerly self-employed producers now found themselves dependent on factories for work. When business was poor, the factories closed, and with no unemployment insurance, those let go found themselves homeless, destitute, and living in poorhouses.

labour union
An association formed by workers to negotiate in their collective interest with employers

craft union
A labour union composed of workers in one skilled trade

industrial union
A labour union composed of workers who have various skills and responsibilities but who work in one industry

Working conditions were not a priority for most factory owners. Workdays were long. At the end of the nineteenth century, the average workweek was 60 hours long, half as long again as today's standard of 40. In the steel and other industries, workers put in 72 or even 84 hours a week—seven 12-hour days with few breaks. Safety standards were almost non-existent. Noise, poor lighting, fatigue, and danger were facts of life for the average factory worker. Owners often preferred to hire children, whom they could pay next to nothing, but who had to help out their families. In 1889, eight-year-old children in a Montreal textile mill worked six days a week, from 6:00 a.m. to 6:00 p.m., for $92 a year. In the coal mines of Nova Scotia and Manitoba, small boys worked for 60¢ a day on their hands and knees in shafts and tunnels too small for a grown man to enter. Even at the beginning of this century, young children continued to work in factories without protection from exploitation.

Strength in Numbers

A worker negotiating alone had no power to improve wages or working conditions. The employer could simply turn around and hire someone else. Only when workers acted together could they hope to improve their situation. When the first "friendly societies" of workers were formed, employers argued, often successfully, that such associations were illegal because the law prohibited "restraint or any activities that prevented a company from carrying out its business." Union organizers were often jailed for conspiracy. Membership in a union often meant dismissal and blacklisting. In Canada, it was not until the 1870s that the government finally passed legislation, modelled on British laws of 40 years earlier, removing barriers to unionism.

Instead of disciplining workers with beatings, fines, and imprisonment, employers grudgingly began to bargain with unions about hours of work, job security, reasonable wages, and sanitary working conditions. During this century, the gulf between labour and management has narrowed, and fairer wages and safer conditions have resulted in a more productive work force. The joint interest that employers and employees have in their corporations was recognized when Douglas Fisher, the leader of the United Auto Workers, was invited to join the board of directors of Chrysler Corporation. Inco opens its books to the United Steelworkers of America twice a year so that the union is aware of the company's financial position.[1]

Development of Labour Unions in Canada

To a large extent, the development of unionism in Canada was a reflection of the development of industrial relations in the United States. The growth was, however, considerably slower. An agriculturally based society, a scattered population, little industrialization, and poor communication in Canada sharply limited the scope of labour organizations.

Until the mid-nineteenth century, unionism was limited to small, loosely knit local organizations among a small number of skilled craft workers in a few major urban centres. The first union recorded was in Montreal in 1827 among the boot and shoe workers.

Encouraged by the rapid progress of trade unionism in both the United States and Great Britain, unions developed more rapidly during the 1850s to 1870s despite their shaky legal status. Increased mobility between Canadian and American workers also led local organizations to join international unions.

The depression of the mid-1870s to mid-1890s and the growth of manufacturing combined to create inhuman working conditions. This stimulated the growth of unions and led to the establishment in 1886 of an umbrella organization, the Trades and Labor Congress (TLC). In many cases, these unions were affiliated with their American counterparts, thus forming international unions. The first half of the twentieth century saw unionism in Canada grow by leaps and bounds: membership went from 50,000 in 1900 to 250,000 in 1919 to 912,000 in 1947. The conservative TLC and the equivalent body in the United States, the American Federation of Labor (AFL), were made up almost entirely of "craft" unions serving skilled workers. They largely ignored the needs of the unskilled and semi-skilled workers. To meet these needs, other groups, including "industrial" unions serving all workers within an industry, were formed. After a period of dispute with the TLC and various attempts to consolidate, these organizations, which often had broader social and political objectives, came together in the Canadian Congress of Labour (CCL) in 1939. The same year, the Congress of Industrial Organizations (CIO) was formed in the United States. The rivalry between AFL-TLC and the CIO-CCL persisted for almost twenty years, until 1955 when the AFL and the CIO were united under the presidency of George Meany. The following year, the Canadian groups came together as the Canadian Labour Congress (CLC).

The Winnipeg General Strike, in 1919, began as a result of labour–management disputes over union recognition and collective bargaining rights in both the metal and the building trades in the city of Winnipeg. A general strike was called in which more than 20,000 workers province wide participated, including civic and government employees. The strike was a landmark because it aided in establishing new industrial-based unions in the Prairie provinces.

TABLE 10.1 • UNION MEMBERSHIP IN CANADA 1901–1990

	Number of Union Members (000s)	Percentage of Non-farm Work Force
1901	50 (est.)	not recorded
1911	133	not recorded
1921	313	16.0
1931	311	15.3
1941	462	18.0
1951	1,029	28.4
1961	1,447	31.6
1971	2,231	32.4
1981	3,487	36.7
1990	4,031	36.2

Source: Excerpts from Labour Canada, Bureau of Labour Information, Director of Labour Organizations in Canada, 1990/91, Table 1, Ottawa, Canada, p. XII. Reproduced with permission of the Minister of Supply and Services Canada, 1994. Adapted from Statistics Canada, *Historical Labour Force Statistics*, Catalogue 71–201, various years. Reproduced by authority of the Minister of Industry, 1994.

Note: Readers wishing further information on data provided through the cooperation of Statistics Canada may obtain copies of related publications by mail from: Publications Sales, Statistics Canada, Ottawa, Ontario, K1A 0T6, by calling 1-613-951-7277 or toll free 1-800-267-6677. Readers may also facsimile their order by dialling 1-613-951-1584.

TABLE 10.2 • THE TEN LARGEST UNIONS, 1990

	Membership (000s)
1. Canadian Union of Public Employees (CLC)	376.9
2. National Union of Provincial Government Employees (CLC)	301.2
3. United Food and Commercial Workers International Union (AFL-CIO/CLC)	170.0
4. National Automobile, Aerospace and Agricultural Implement Workers Union of Canada (CLC)	167.4
5. Public Service Alliance of Canada (CLC)	162.7
6. United Steelworkers of America (AFL-CIO/CLC)	160.0
7. International Brotherhood of Teamsters, Chauffeurs, Warehousemen and Helpers of America (AFL-CIO)	100.0
8. Social Affairs Federation Inc. (CNTU)	94.6
9. School Boards Teachers' Federation (CEQ)	75.0
10. Service Employees International Union (AFL-CIO/CLC)	75.0

Source: Excerpts from Labour Canada, Bureau of Labour Information, Directory of Labour Organizations in Canada 1990/91, Table 4, Ottawa, Canada, p. XV. Reproduced with the permission of the Minister of Supply and Services Canada, 1994.

The Canadian Labor Congress represents about 60 percent of Canadian workers. The Confederation of National Trade Unions and the Congress of Democratic Trade Unions are Quebec-based organizations that have similar functions and purposes.

Union membership grew by leaps and bounds at the turn of the century and after the First and Second World Wars. Another great spurt came when unions became legal in government service during the 1960s. In the 1980s, the service industries have provided large numbers of new members. This growth is shown in Table 10.1. The ten largest unions in Canada and their affiliation are shown in Table 10.2.

After the formation of the CLC, a trend began in which Canadian unions broke away from their American counterparts because social and political conditions, and therefore workers' interests, were different in the two countries. A prime example of this was the formation of the Canadian Auto Workers in 1985 when the Canadian branches of the United Auto Workers disagreed with the American branches over whether to accept profit sharing and lump-sum payments instead of annual percentage increases in pay. Inflation rates in Canada were running much higher than in the United States, and Canadian workers were afraid the lump-sum compensation system would erode the value of their wages over time. By 1990, members of national unions made up 62 percent of CLC membership, and members of international unions only 38 percent.

The Canadian Labor Congress includes 59 percent of Canadian union members. Other significant umbrella associations include the Quebec-based Confederation of National Trade Unions; the Canadian Federation of Labour, a breakaway group from the CLC that represents building trades unions; and the international AFL-CIO. These associations each represent about 5 percent of union members. (Many other AFL-CIO unions also belong to the CLC.) About 22 percent of Canadian union members have no affiliation beyond their own union or local organization.

LABOUR LEGISLATION

The right of workers to form unions and to use collective bargaining to negotiate contracts with employers is now firmly established and regulated by law. Judicial decisions over the years have given the federal government jurisdiction in labour relations matters only over the federal public service, crown corporations, airlines, most railways, communication companies, and federal government agencies. The public service accounts for 5 percent and federally regulated industries for approximately 10 percent of the labour force. All other organizations fall under the jurisdiction of the provinces.

The Canada Labour Code and provincial employment standards acts regulate minimum wages, the minimum age for employment, hours of work, overtime pay, vacations with pay, statutory holidays, and maternity leave. Other forms of legislation prohibit discrimination in employment on the basis of race, ethnic origin, colour, religion, and sex. The Canada Labour Code and the labour codes of each province reflect the same general policies with regard to labour unions: the right of employees to form and join unions; protection against unfair labour practices by either employers or employees; the right of employees to strike and of employers to lock out employees when no agreement can be reached.

Legal Designations of the Workplace

Labour legislation recognizes unions' right to arrange with employers long-term security for the union through various designations of the workplace. These arrangements affect the powers of both the union and management.

A **closed shop** is a business with an arrangement that all workers must be hired through the union "hiring hall" and remain members of the union while they are employed. Only if no union members are available may management look beyond union ranks, and even then, workers must become union members before being hired. For the union, the closed shop is a form of security. If all workers are members of the union, no one will undercut union workers by accepting poorer wages or working conditions than those negotiated by the union. Closed shops are usually negotiated by craft unions in the construction industry where the skills of union members are needed but only on a temporary basis. While management does not have complete control over who is hired, the union hiring hall is a convenient source of skilled labour.

If only union members can be hired, however, some qualified workers may be excluded. The guaranteed membership also opens up the possibility that union leaders may become irresponsible and not act in the best interests on their members. Criticisms of the closed shop have led the United States to ban it. In Canada, the closed shop is legal where both parties have agreed to it, but outside the construction industry it is very rare today.

A more common designation is the **union shop**. In a union shop, the employer may hire qualified workers whether they are members of the union or not. Once employed, however, workers who are not members must join the union within a specified time limit. About 40 percent of workers in Canada are protected by some type of union shop arrangement.

Another arrangement is called maintenance of membership, whereby no one is forced to join the union but those who are already members or who do join must remain members.

Dues Checkoff

Legislation at both the federal and the provincial level requires an employer to "checkoff" union dues from an employee's wages, when the checkoff is part of the collective agreement—or, if there is no collective agreement, when the employee has agreed to it. This ensures the union has the financial capacity to represent its members.

About half of all collective agreements include no union security clause. In an arbitration award handed down in 1946 following a strike of employees of the Ford Motor Company in Windsor, Ontario, Supreme Court Justice Ivan Rand set up a system now known as the **Rand formula** that has served as the basis for many union–management agreements in Canada. Instead of a closed or union shop, Rand provided for the compulsory checkoff of union dues from the wages of all workers under the agreement. This allowed workers who, for

closed shop
A business where all workers must be hired through the union and remain members of the union while they are employed

union shop
A business where the employer may hire any qualified workers, but those who are not members of the union must join within a specified time limit

Rand formula
A system devised by Justice Ivan Rand whereby, instead of a closed or union shop, employees participate in the compulsory "checkoff" of union dues from their wages

personal, political, or religious reasons, did not wish to join a union to remain non-members. But as all workers benefited from the union contract, they were all to contribute to union funds.

BUSINESS REVIEW 10.1

1. Why were labour unions needed in the nineteenth century? Do you think workers need unions and collective bargaining today?

2. What is the role of the government and legislation in protecting the rights of unions and workers?

JOINING THE UNION

When workers decide they want to work collectively to improve their working conditions, they must either form a union or (more likely) join an existing one that they feel will represent their interests. They may then ask the employer to recognize the union voluntarily or apply to the labour relations board for certification. In most jurisdictions, 55 percent of eligible workers must sign up to join a union before the labour relations board will certify it. Once the union is certified, management must recognize it as the bargaining agent. The board will consider whether the employees included in the application constitute an appropriate **bargaining unit**. Management may request to have certain employees, such as supervisory staff, excluded from the unit or even that other employees performing similar functions should be included.[2]

The ground is now set for the negotiation of a first contract. This is usually the most difficult as management–employee relations were probably poor in the first place or workers would not have felt the need to form the union. Management may also have tried to prevent the signing up of union members to avoid certification. Feelings may run high, and neither side may be experienced in the art of negotiation. Strikes are more likely to take place at the time of union recognition or first-contract negotiations than at any other point in union–management relations. In the sections that follow, we will discuss the collective bargaining process in the less emotional context of contract renewal.

REACHING A COLLECTIVE AGREEMENT

The primary objective of labour unions is the improvement of wages, hours, and working conditions for their members. This goal is achieved primarily through **collective bargaining**, a process of negotiation between management and union representatives for the purpose of arriving at mutually acceptable wages and working conditions for employees.

Union contracts, or collective agreements, typically cover a one-, two-, or three-year period. They are often the result of days, weeks, or even months of discussion, disagreement, compromise, and eventual agreement. Once agreement has been reached between the representatives of the union and management, union members must vote to accept or reject the contract. If the contract is rejected, union representa-

bargaining unit
A group of workers the labour relations board certifies as having sufficient common interests to bargain collectively for labour contracts

collective bargaining
The process of negotiation between management and union representatives to arrive at mutually acceptable wages, hours, and working conditions

The collective bargaining process seeks to maintain the balance of power between labour and management, so that they can solve their differences. When grievances arise between an employee and management, a union official usually supports and assists the griever during the grievance process. The collective bargaining process facilitates discussion between labour and management regarding the terms and the conditions of employment.

tives may resume the bargaining process with management representatives, or the union members may vote to strike to obtain their demands.

Negotiating Units

The number of union groups and employers participating in the bargaining process can vary considerably. Although several arrangements or patterns are possible, usually collective bargaining to reach contract or agreement occurs between representatives of workers at a single plant and a single employer. In cases where the participants represent workers at many plants and one employer, the resulting set of agreements legally binds all plants of the employer. For example, the terms and conditions agreed to by both the International Brotherhood of Electrical Workers and Westinghouse Electric apply uniformly to all Westinghouse plants without exception. Sometimes coalition bargaining occurs, as when two or more unions acting together negotiate with an employer. Coalition representatives have the expectation that together they will have greater bargaining strength than any one of them alone. In some situations (for reasons of fairness, equity, and standardization), the appropriate pattern is industry-wide bargaining where a national union, such as the Communication Workers of Canada, would meet with several employers in the industry to negotiate a collective agreement.

It is preferable, from the viewpoint of management, to avoid coalitions of unions if possible and to bargain with each local union individually. Just as there is strength in numbers, experienced manufacturers see smaller, unaffiliated unions as being less powerful.

FIGURE 10.1 • THE BARGAINING ZONE

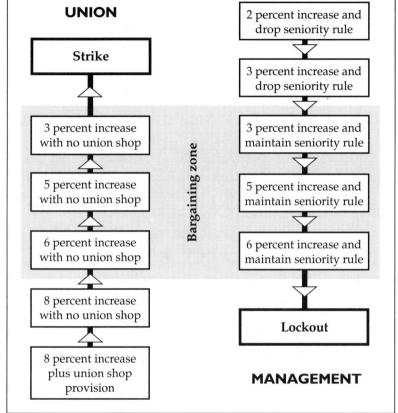

The Bargaining Zone

The standard issues in any collective bargaining are wages, work hours, benefits, union activities and responsibilities, grievance handling and arbitration, and employee rights and seniority. Negotiations follow a predictable outline. Union and management both set out their initial positions, such as the Canadian Auto Workers' position in Issues in Business 10.1. These are followed by proposals and counterproposals, and eventually a compromise is reached. Figure 10.1 shows the process of negotiation over a single wage issue and two security issues—a union shop provision and a seniority rule. From the union's perspective, the best outcome would be an 8 percent wage increase based on increases in productivity and in the cost of living and the addition of a union shop provision. Management intends to begin negotiation with an offer of a 2 percent wage increase and the elimination of current seniority rules.

As Figure 10.1 shows, the initial demands of each party will ultimately result in a "final" offer from the union representative of a 6 percent pay increase and removal of its demand for a union shop. Management's "final" offer will be a 3 percent increase and an elimination of seniority rules. However, if the union is forced below its 3 percent wage increase demand, a strike will occur. Management's outer boundary in the bargaining zone is a 6 percent wage increase and maintenance of present seniority rules. These are the maximum terms it will accept without closing the operation by locking out the employees. The solid areas indicate the range of possible terms within the bargaining zone. The negotiations should fall within this zone, with the final agreement dependent upon the negotiating skills and relative power of management and union representatives.

Once ratified by the union membership, the contract becomes the legally binding agreement for all labour–management relations during the period of time specified. Collective agreements typically include such areas as wages, industrial relations, and methods of settling labour–management disputes. Some are only a few pages in length, while others run more than 200 pages. Table 10.3 lists topics typically included in a collective agreement.

TABLE 10.3 • TOPICS USUALLY INCLUDED IN A COLLECTIVE AGREEMENT

Union activities and responsibilities
Dues collection
Union bulletin boards
Union officers and shop stewards

Wages
Job evaluation
Wage structure
General wage adjustments
Wage incentives
Time studies
Shift differentials and bonuses
Pay for reporting and calling in

Hours of work
Regular hours of work
Vacations
Holidays
Overtime rules
Rest periods
Leaves of absence
Sick pay

Insurance
Dental, drug, and life insurance
Pensions
Supplemental unemployment benefits

Employee job rights and seniority
Seniority regulations
Transfers
Promotions
Layoffs
Recalls

Grievance handling and arbitration

Discipline, suspensions, and discharge

Health and safety

ISSUES IN BUSINESS 10.1

SPREADING THE WORK

IN RECOGNITION OF the "jobless recovery," the Canadian Auto Workers union has tabled an ambitious set of contract proposals aimed at spreading the available work at the Big Three auto companies among more employees.

(continued)

"There has to be a more equitable way of sharing the jobs that we have," CAW president Buzz Hargrove said yesterday after opening negotiations with General Motors of Canada Ltd.

More time off with pay, improved pensions, early retirement incentives, and an innovative proposal that would allow senior employees to "grow into retirement" through reduced work-weeks—with a pay top-up—are major features of the CAW bargaining agenda presented to GM yesterday.

The opening proposals are designed, in part, to deal with the mixed blessing of new investment in the Canadian auto industry—modern plants produce far more with far fewer workers. They require the auto companies to maintain larger work forces if work hours were reduced, while pension incentives would preserve jobs for younger employees. . . .

"We intend to bargain responsibly and we intend to bargain tough," said Mr. Hargrove, who is also seeking "substantial increases" in wages.

Bill Tate, vice-president of personnel at GM of Canada, said yesterday that the CAW's opening proposals appear to be "extremely rich"; that current auto industry pensions are generous; and auto workers already get more paid time off the job than workers in most other industries. GM's focus in the negotiations will be "on cost containment and operational flexibility."

However, he did say there might be "some merit" in the union proposal "that work could be shared by retiring employees and people who are laid off."

While on the surface there appears to be a wide gulf between the two parties, the past three years have forced them into a close working relationship.

Restructuring, shutdowns, and the reorganization of work have meant daily contact between the two. They do not always agree on the best way to do things, Mr. Tate said, but "the relationship is quite professional."

Indeed, there was no wild or provocative rhetoric from either side yesterday, although Mr. Hargrove and Mr. Tate, at separate news conferences, stated their cases strongly.

Mr. Tate said that while there has been slow but measured growth in the U.S. auto markets, "we believe that improvement is somewhat fragile" and markets in Canada remain soft.

There are twelve GM plants in Canada, including four assembly facilities.

In 1990, about 36,500 CAW members worked at GM plants in eight communities, the union said in a background document distributed yesterday. In 1993, about 27,727 work in seven communities—a van plant in the Metropolitan Toronto municipality of Scarborough closed in May, with a loss of 3,000 jobs.

Mr. Tate said yesterday "the good news" is that GM will require 700 new workers when it starts operating a third shift at its Oshawa, Ontario, truck plant late next month.

GM has paid about $150 million in the past three years to supplement the unemployment insurance benefits of its laid-off workers. Replenishing that fund will be a major issue in negotiations, Mr. Hargrove said.

The CAW says that as a result of restructuring, investment, and reorganization of work, the productivity of Canadian auto workers has improved by more than 30 percent an hour per worker over the past few years. that "productivity dividend" should be shared with the workers—in the form of higher wages and reduced work time—as well as with shareholders, the union argues.

Assemblers, who make up the largest job category at the Big Three auto makers, now earn $20.48 an hour, and are generally scheduled to work 40-hour weeks.

Source: Reprinted from Virginia Galt, "CAW Focussing on Job Sharing," *The Globe and Mail*, July 14, 1993, pp. B1 and B12.

(continued)

Questions for Discussion
1. What are the main features of the Canadian Auto Workers' opening bargaining position?
2. What do you think management's opening position is likely to be?

Both parties realize fully that it is usually to their mutual advantage to reach an agreement. But what happens if union and management cannot agree? At this point, several approaches are available to see if a resolution can be reached.

Conciliation

In most provinces, before a work stoppage can occur, a government conciliator must meet with union and management representatives to establish what the points of disagreement are and to report to the government on the likelihood of a settlement being reached. Once that report has been filed, a "cooling off" period of seven to fourteen days must elapse before the union may strike or the employer may lock workers out.[3] In Quebec, conciliation is voluntary because it was believed that the compulsory procedure was often treated merely as a technical formality before exercising the right to strike.[4]

Mediation

mediation
The use of a neutral third party to advise and assist in reaching an agreement between the union and management

In most cases, **mediation** is a voluntary procedure, with union and management deciding together to bring in a neutral third party to advise and assist in reaching an agreement. It may occur before a strike or lockout takes place or as part of the attempt to settle a dispute when a work stoppage is already underway. Occasionally, the government will impose mediation if it feels that a work stoppage would damage the public interest. Mediators are usually non-government professionals such as lawyers, retired judges, academics, or other community leaders skilled in the art of negotiation and resolving conflict.

Mediators do not make decisions but try to help the union and management representatives to find common ground. Usually, they meet representatives of each side separately before bringing them together with suggestions and advice for reaching a compromise. Obviously, mediators must not have a vested interest in the outcome or a preference for either side. Without impartiality, one or both sides would lose confidence in the mediation process. This is especially true if the mediation is imposed by government. Sometimes, a mediator will insist that work be resumed as a gesture of good faith before mediation efforts begin.

Arbitration

interest arbitration
The process of bringing in a third party who takes submissions from the two sides in a contract dispute and comes to a legally binding decision

Arbitration is the process of bringing in a third party who takes submissions from the two sides and comes to a decision. When arbitration is used to settle contract disputes, it is known as **interest arbitration** and the arbitrator's decision is legally binding. Interest arbitration may be carried out by a single, impartial arbitrator or by an arbitration board made up of one nominee from management, one from the union, and an impartial chair.

In the private sector, arbitration is rare, and when it occurs, it is usually *voluntary*, with both parties agreeing that it is the best way to settle their differences. The government may impose *compulsory arbitration* to prevent or end prolonged strikes affecting major industries.

Compulsory arbitration occurs most often in the public sector in cases where workers do not have the right to strike. The provinces vary considerably as to which of fire fighters, police, teachers, hospital workers, and other public servants they allow to strike.

Conventional arbitration procedures allow the arbitrator to choose from the positions put forward by the parties or to modify them as seems appropriate. One problem with conventional arbitration is that, if the parties expect their dispute to end in arbitration, they have little incentive to bargain and make concessions when an arbitrator is likely to choose a position midway between the two. *Final-offer arbitration* requires the arbitrator to choose one position or the other, either on an issue-by-issue basis or on a total-package basis. The theory is that this will encourage the two sides to present positions that are as reasonable as possible.[5]

Tools of Power

The last resort for the union in achieving an acceptable contract is the strike. A **strike** is the total withdrawal of services by members of the bargaining unit until the dispute is settled. Most collective agreements are achieved through negotiation, but occasionally unions will demonstrate the strength of their convictions by walking out before attempting mediation or arbitration (which may then be used to end a strike rather than prevent one).

This ultimate weapon is used in fewer than 10 percent of all contract negotiations. Union representatives can often exert sufficient pressure on management simply by threatening a strike that will stop production. They also have to consider the effect of a strike on their members. When workers strike, they immediately lose all wages and benefits, which is why unions try to build up strike funds to provide their members with subsistence living for the course of the strike. Without strike pay, many workers would be forced to return to work before concessions had been made by management.

Striking workers often **picket,** or walk back and forth at the entrance to a store, factory, or office, to bring public attention to their cause. By virtue of the Criminal Code, picketing is illegal, except for the purpose of communicating or obtaining information. Some provincial labour codes permit picketing only when the workers are legally on strike or have been locked out. Signs carried by union members outside the plant are intended to inform the public that a labour problem exists and also to give other companies the message to not deal with the picketed firm. Emotions can run high on a picket line. Picketers who block access to the workplace are commiting an illegal act. Sometimes, employers obtain court injunctions to limit the numbers of picketers and lessen the possibility of violence.

strike
The total withdrawal of services by members of the bargaining unit until a dispute is settled

picketing
Walking at the entrance of a workplace to inform the public of the union's dispute with management

Picketing, in front of the worksite, is common during a strike. Workers will often carry either signs or banners to inform passers-by of their grievance and to encourage people to boycott the products or services of the picketed firm. Sometimes strike demonstrations can become confrontational and dangerous. During the Winnipeg General Strike of 1919, two strikers were killed and twenty people were injured.

lockout

The refusal by management to allow workers to come to their jobs, thus depriving them of their wages until a dispute is settled

For management, the tool equivalent to the strike is the lockout. A **lockout** is the refusal to allow workers to come to their jobs, thus depriving workers of their wages until the dispute is settled.

Lockouts are much rarer today than in times past. They are usually only used when a strike by members of one bargaining unit has partially shut down operations and non-striking employees cannot operate efficiently. For these other workers, a lockout is a temporary layoff. Management may gamble that these locked-out workers will put pressure on their striking colleagues to return to the bargaining table, but this can backfire if they sympathize strongly with the strikers' cause. The lockout in response to a strike is sometimes also used as a management tactic to gain further concessions by preventing striking employees from returning to work when they have decided to end their job action.

Sometimes, management employs substitute workers—"scabs" or "strikebreakers" to the union—to perform strikers' jobs. This procedure has been illegal in Quebec since 1977, and in Ontario since 1993. Only management personnel may perform the functions of union members during a strike. Because the use of strikebreakers raises the ire of the striking workers, the Quebec provisions have been considered instrumental in lessening the chance of violence on the picket line—and also in shortening the length of strikes. Quebec employers in general have learned to live with the provisions, whether they like them or not. The reaction from the business community when the changes were proposed in Ontario is described in Issues in Business 10.2.

ISSUES IN BUSINESS 10.2

BUSINESS LOOKS AT A NEW LAW

NOVEMBER 8, 1991: The battle between business leaders and Ontario's NDP government escalated yesterday with the release of proposed labour-law changes that would ban the use of strikebreakers and ease union certification.

"We're going to fight the whole package," vowed Linda Ganong of the Canadian Federation of Independent Business. "There's no need for this. It's so tilted in favour of unions, there's no fairness, no balance here at all."

She noted recent studies that indicate the changes could cost 500,000 jobs and up to $20 billion in investment over five years.

Paul Nykanen, vice-president of the Canadian Manufacturers' Association, echoed Ganong, warning that the changes would tilt the balance of worker–management relations in favour of unions.

Labour minister Bob Mackenzie released a discussion paper with roughly 40 recommended changes that retreat somewhat from organized labour's demands.

The recommendations include banning replacement workers during strikes, allowing low-level supervisors to unionize, encouraging a pro-union stance at the Ontario Labour Relations Board, and easing unionization of workers in the retail and service sectors.

Mackenzie linked the proposed reforms, which are to be subject to extensive discussion and consultation before legislation is introduced in the spring, to just those issues.

"The government believes that giving a meaningful voice to employees through an improved collective bargaining process will make for greater industrial peace and improved efficiency," Mackenzie said. "Such a result can play a major role in Ontario's economic renewal. I don't see it as a payoff [for unions]."

Source: Reprinted from Geoffrey Scotton, "Ontario Unveils Labor-Law: Business Leaders Promise a Scrap," *The Financial Post*, November 8, 1991, p. 6.

Questions for Discussion

1. Do you feel the results of the labour law on business in Ontario will be as drastic as business representatives believed in 1991?

2. Is the labour minister right when he suggests that these provisions will make for greater industrial peace? Discuss fully.

BUSINESS REVIEW 10.2

1. What are the major factors affecting the bargaining power of each party in the collective bargaining process?

2. Trace the process of negotiating a collective agreement, including legal requirements and voluntary procedures that may help the two parties reach an agreement.

WHEN A CONTRACT IS IN PLACE

Once negotiators have agreed to a contract and it has been ratified by union members, it is a legally enforceable document that governs the relations of workers and management, specifying the rights and obligations of both parties. The contract is for a fixed period—usually one, two, or three years—and cannot be reopened, except with the consent of both parties. Unions may wish to reopen a contract when high inflation is eroding their wages. Management may want to do so when business is poor or technological change renders work rules specified in the contract inefficient. Only if the reasons are compelling to both parties is a contract likely to be reopened.

Like all rules, terms of a contract are open to disagreement. Management may not like the way union members interpret a particular clause. More often, workers may feel management is abusing its power. In either case, the party that feels the injury may file a **grievance**, or complaint that the other party is violating a provision of the contract.

grievance
A complaint by the union or by management that the other party is violating a provision of the contract

Wildcat Strikes

In dealing with a grievance, courses of action are much more circumscribed than they are in negotiating a contract. In the first place, except in Saskatchewan, there is no right to strike or lockout for the duration of the contract. If employees are angry enough, this may not prevent **wildcat strikes**, but these can bring fines or imprisonment. Wildcat strikes are usually short and unauthorized by the union; workers often strike merely to publicize the perceived injustice, and management rarely asks the courts to impose legal sanctions. The prevalence of wildcat strikes in Canada has dropped considerably since the 1970s, when they made up a quarter of all strikes. Experts consider that the development and increased use of new grievance arbitration procedures has contributed substantially to the decline. However, only grievances on matters that are actually covered in the contract can be submitted to arbitration, so unexpected events that affect the working situation may still lead to strikes.[6]

wildcat strike
An illegal strike, usually without the approval of union leaders, taking place while a contract is in effect

Work to Rule

A less drastic protest than a wildcat strike is **working to rule**, which has the advantage that workers remain meticulously within the law. Workers follow the contract work rules, operating procedures, and any company regulations to the letter as they work. For example, workers will read all instructions before starting a job they know perfectly well how to do; if the coffee break is supposed to start at 10:30, they will stop work in the middle of a job that might take another minute or two to complete and then check every step already done when they return. Work to rule can slow production considerably. The technique is sometimes used to spur on lagging contract talks when one agreement has expired, as well as during the life of a collective agreement.

work to rule
The meticulous following of work rules and operating procedures in order to slow down production

Grievance Procedures

How grievances are handled reveals the state of the relations between union and management. These points of friction are the major source of contact between union and management after one set of contract negotiations, and the way they are resolved will influence attitudes during the next set.

Most contracts set out a formal grievance procedure following a specific series of steps, as illustrated in Figure 10.2. Most grievances arise over issues such as transfers, work assignments, seniority, and

FIGURE 10.2 • A TYPICAL GRIEVANCE PROCEDURE

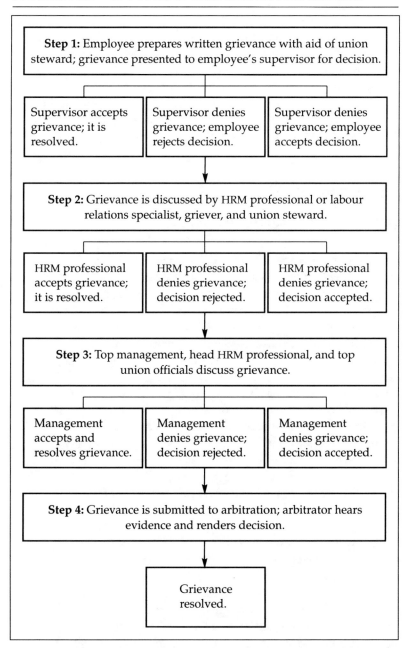

Source: Reprinted from Thomas H. Stone and Noah M. Meltz, *Human Resource Management in Canada*, Third Edition (Toronto: Holt, Rinehart and Winston of Canada Limited, 1993), p. 744.

grievance arbitration

The process of bringing in a third party to interpret specific clauses in the collective agreement in order to settle a union or management grievance

dismissals. The rules usually require a worker who feels unfairly treated by management to "obey now; grieve later"—taking the complaint to the shop steward, a worker who is an official representative of the union empowered by the contract to handle grievances on workers' behalf. The shop steward takes the grievance to the worker's immediate supervisor, and many times, the issue is resolved then and there. If not, the grievance is brought to higher levels of management and union officials. A similar process takes place if management has a grievance over some union practice or a particular worker; management will bring its complaint to the shop steward and take it through higher levels of the union, as necessary. If the parties cannot settle the grievance, they may take it to arbitration. **Grievance arbitration** is different from interest arbitration in that it is concerned with the interpretation of specific clauses in the collective agreement rather than deciding what those clauses should be. Although grievance arbitration has been an extremely successful process, some people feel it is time to take another look at the process, as discussed in Issues in Business 10.3.

ISSUES IN BUSINESS 10.3

ARBITRATION IS NO LONGER CHEAP

SINCE CANADA'S FIRST substantive labour laws came into effect after the Second World War, what has helped keep most collective agreements intact and union–management tensions from boiling over has been the option to send disputes to arbitrators—a theoretically cheap, quick, and binding alternative to the courts.

But in recent years, there's been an explosion in the number of labour arbitrations and increasing complaints from both sides about raising costs and delays rivalling those of the courts.

"For unions, it isn't working nearly as well anymore," says Michael Lynk, a staff legal counsel at the national office of the Canadian Union of Public Employees in Ottawa.

CUPE's disputes, mostly dismissal matters, are taking an average of ten to sixteen months to be resolved. With lawyers and arbitrators charging up to $2,000 a day, it's not unusual for each side to spend $15,000 and more for a three- to six-day hearing.

That's multiplied many times over in other workplaces. Peter Barnacle, an Ottawa lawyer with Nelligan/Power who edits a national reporting series on arbitration decisions, says there are about 4,500 major cases decided each year now in the private sector alone.

Most are heard by a small pool of certified arbitrators that Barnacle estimates at fewer than 40 people. "In some cases," he says, "you're looking at a year to get before some of the more popular arbitrators."

And cases are also more complex, with many lawyers now raising Charter of Rights arguments. "The one-day hearings are becoming a thing of the past, let's put it that way," says Barnacle.

Some lawyers, particularly in unions, say it's time for governments to overhaul the process. And that may happen. In summer 1991, the Ontario Law Reform Commission is expected to recommend major changes to the entire structure for settling workplace disputes.

The report is based on a study by Queen's University labour law professor Bernard Adell, who examined the growing myriad of tribunals overseeing minimum employment standards, occupational health and safety, human rights, and labour relations.

(continued)

Adell also looked at arbitration, where he found strong support in some sectors for a government role, particularly in paying the costs and supplying arbitrators since the law requires grievances be arbitrated.

He also feels governments will have to address how much power arbitrators should have. These days, arbitrators are being asked to apply not only the collective agreement, but also legislation, such as human rights codes, particularly in cases involving disabled workers or religious objectors.

And Adell suggests the right to arbitrate should be expanded to non-unionized workers. "Unorganized employees generally have inferior terms and conditions of employment compared to organized employees," he says, noting they now have no alternative but the courts.

While Adell couldn't reveal his final recommendations, some lawyers believe he favours creating an omnibus tribunal to handle all workplace matters, even arbitrations.

If so, the idea will run into opposition. Christopher Riggs, a Toronto lawyer at Hicks Morley Hamilton Stewart Storie who represents management, says the arbitration system is generally working well.

"From the management perspective, one of the strengths of the present system is that it maintains the right of the parties to choose their own arbitrator," he says. "The parties can get arbitrators who they use on a regular basis and are familiar with the relationship of a company and its trade union and their problems. That's a distinct strength and it's independent of government."

As for concerns over delays, Riggs says companies and unions can use the collective agreement to come up with any number of mechanisms to fast-track cases. And he also finds it hard to swallow union complaints over costs, noting that a primary reason members pay dues is so that the union can enforce the agreement.

"The proposition of David and Goliath is a bit misleading in these things," he adds. "In many cases, it will be a small employer facing a well-financed union."

Still, CUPE's Lynk thinks more has to be done to make the system cheaper and quicker. One option, he says, would be eliminating the use of lawyers—something already done by the railways, where company and union representatives meet with a lone arbitrator.

The chances of getting lawyers out of the arbitration business are slim, but Barnacle is confident that unions and management would prefer to keep the system out of government hands.

"I think the system itself is a good one," he says. "With all its faults, it's still a hell of a lot cheaper and quicker than civil court."

Source: Excerpts from Michael Crawford, "Time to Reform Labor Arbitration," *The Financial Post*, June 13, 1991, p. 10. Reprinted with permission from Michael Crawford

Questions for Discussion

1. Why is the present grievance arbitration system under review?
2. What changes would you recommend to improve the system for both unions and management?

CONCERNS FOR ORGANIZED LABOUR

Labour unions have done well for their members and for all of society. Without them, the average worker would be a lot poorer and be working under far poorer conditions. The money that has gone into union members' wage packets has brought prosperity to the many businesses that provide goods and services to the general public. The existence of unions has helped pull up the incomes and working conditions of non-unionized workers who have expected better treatment simply because they see the advances that unionized workers have achieved. But the union movement faces continual challenges. Among them are technological change and the changing nature of the work force.

Technological Change

When new technologies are brought in, secure jobs can disappear overnight. In the past, unions have tried to use work rules to stem the tide. For example, when diesel locomotives replaced steam engines on Canadian railways, the fireman who had stoked the furnace of the old steam engine was no longer necessary, but the unions insisted that this worker be retained. Such restrictive work practices are known as **featherbedding**. (Many professional associations resist the substitution of cheaper labour than their own with similar restrictive work rules; for example, doctors have tried to keep midwives from delivering babies, and lawyers to keep law clerks from appearing in court to represent clients.) As described in Developing Your Business Skills, more modern approaches call for labour–management technological change committees and special retraining programs for workers affected by technological change.

featherbedding

The inclusion of restrictive work practices in a labour contract to maintain employment levels for union members, often in the face of technological change

DEVELOPING YOUR BUSINESS SKILLS

CO-OPERATION KEY TO COMPETITIVENESS

Currently, Canadian unions and management are recognizing the importance of working together to tackle technological change and global competition, says a Conference Board of Canada study.

"Labour and management are realizing they can't keep beating each other up," said Ruth Wright, author of the study by the Ottawa-based research institute. "It's destructive in helping us compete. We need to move away from confrontation to dialogue."

The study surveyed 28 major Canadian unions and 58 unionized employers.

Its findings show management is giving employment security and communication a higher priority in managing technological change. For example:

- More than 90 percent of the respondents said they offered retraining to employees affected by technological change.
- More than 75 percent of organizations communicate changes through union representatives.
- About 60 percent of the organizations have joint union–management committees to deal with technological change.

The study found, however, that unions are more likely than management to say technological change leads to a decrease in job satisfaction, downgrading of jobs, and increased stress.

And, while the study shows unions and management are improving their channels of communication, Canada is still far behind countries such as Germany and Japan.

Germany—which Wright describes as a model of progressive labour relations—gives labour strategic involvement in how companies are run and policies set at the national level.

In contrast, North American unions operate from the shop floor up, creating a greater tendency to "drop the tools and walk," Wright said.

(continued)

But companies are hammering out mechanisms for resolving disputes. For example, Inco Ltd. and the United Steelworkers of America (both participants in the Conference Board study) have forged a strong relationship despite dramatic job cuts and rapid technological change.

The reason is that Inco has given the union a voice, said David Campbell, president of local 6500 in Sudbury, representing 6,300 workers. Twice a year, Inco opens its books up to the USWA, which in turn raises its concerns with management. There is also a joint environmental committee with equal representation from labour and management.

Similarly, British Columbia Telephone Co. (another participant in the study) has a joint union–management committee to introduce a new technology and resolve disputes that arise from it.

"It keeps parties talking and trying to resolve issues rather than coming to loggerheads," said a company spokesperson.

Source: Reprinted from Erik Heinrich, "Labor, Management Team Up," *The Financial Post*, July 3, 1991, p. 5.

Question for Discussion

1. Should management keep labour representatives informed of, or even give them a voice in, upcoming technological change? Why or why not?

A Changing Work Force

Unions now represent approximately one-third of the non-agricultural paid work force. Though union membership has increased in terms of numbers, recently labour unions have grown little in terms of the proportion of workers who are members.

In the past, union strength has been derived from workers in traditional blue-collar occupations and industries. The prospect of increasing union membership from these sources is bleak. Membership has levelled off because there are almost no new blue-collar industries to organize. Most employees of the automobile, steel, paper, mining, transportation, and many manufacturing industries are already union members. Some companies still resist unionization, but the period when there were millions of non-unionized industrial workers is over. In fact, the strength of the blue-collar sector is decreasing and will likely continue to do so in the future. As factories become more automated, the demand for blue-collar workers will decrease. At the same time, many labour-intensive manufacturing industries are pulling out of Canada, and taking hundreds of thousands of jobs—and potential union members—with them.

Unions are likely to increase their efforts to recruit white-collar workers and agricultural labourers. Of white-collar workers, only public employees are unionized on a large scale. Workers in some large retail stores are beginning to organize. Agricultural workers have not joined labour unions largely because many of them come from outside Canada on temporary work permits. Also, organizing is difficult among workers who move from job to job. In contrast, many agricultural workers in the United States are now union members. If unions continue to be attractive primarily to blue-collar sectors, it is likely that union membership has peaked.

BUSINESS REVIEW 10.3

1. How does interest arbitration differ from grievance arbitration?
2. Cite factors affecting the future of organized labour.

LABOUR AND MANAGEMENT: FUTURE RELATIONS

As employment in goods-producing industries continues to decline, the stereotype of the blue-collar industrial worker becomes less valid. For nearly half a century, the dominant pattern of bargaining over wages, hours, and working conditions has been set by the blue-collar unions. In the near future, eight of every ten workers may be employed in providing services rather than goods, particularly in information-processing industries such as finance, education, and communications.

The new workers will be better educated than their predecessors. They are likely to have little patience with bureaucracy, whether union or management. They will also be more militant on the issues of environmental concerns, flexible working patterns, and shared decision making. The future of organized labour will be greatly affected by its responses to these workers.

INTERACTIVE SUMMARY AND DISCUSSION QUESTIONS

1. Discuss fully the history and development of labour unions in Canada.
2. Fully explain the process of collective bargaining as it relates to the concept of bargaining zones.
3. Strikes, both legal and wildcat, are a sign of poor management. Discuss.
4. Discuss why some critics feel it may be time to reform the arbitration process in Canada.
5. Describe the major tools of the union and management. Recommend cases in which such may be employed.
6. Request a copy of a recent collective bargaining agreement from a local organization. Next, divide the class into labour and management bargaining teams and conduct a simulated bargaining session for the next contract to be negotiated. Your professor will assume the role of moderator and will also establish all rules needed for this bargaining experience.

CASE 10.1

THE WESTAR LOCKOUT

A HIGH-STAKES waiting game has begun in the stand-off between Westar Mining Ltd. and about 1,100 members of the United Mine Workers of America union who were locked out yesterday from their jobs at Westar's Balmer mine.

The southeastern B.C. mine, the biggest coal producer in the province, is teetering on the brink of financial failure. The lockout halted production and idled about 1,300 employees.

(continued)

The next move, Westar president Peter Dolezal said, is up to the union. "I hope the employees change their minds before it's too late."

Westar made good on its long-standing lockout threat only hours after UMW members voted 62 percent to reject a company contract offer.

The offer contained a pay freeze for two years, with a possible increase of up to 5 percent in the third year. Westar demanded a series of changes to workplace practices that management estimated would save $6 million a year.

Management wants to scrap the contract provision that allows each employee to not show up for work for up to seven days a year without having to telephone in or explain the absences. Management claims that no-shows can undermine daily production plans, halting operation of major equipment and costing an estimated $1.4 million a year.

Management also wants to end a rule limiting warranty repair work allowed offsite, and wants the right to assign workers to different job areas so that it—and not the union—can choose which subcontractors work at the mine.

Westar estimates it can save $1.5 million a year in lost production time by having workers take their 70-minute break period in three blocks, instead of the current four, each 12-hour shift.

"You can't keep a mine operating that's highly uneconomical at today's prices and costs without doing something about the costs," Mr. Dolezal said.

"They are looking for a cheaper labour force and we aren't willing to go along with that," union official Gary Taje said yesterday. "But we're taking the high road. We have no pickets up. We're willing to work. We aren't striking yet."

Mr. Dolezal would not say how long Westar would wait for a union change-of-heart before shutting down the mine. "It depends how far the company's position can support it."

It would appear to be not very far. The dispute has complicated already delicate and protracted negotiations between Westar and its bankers over the rescheduling of the mine's crippling $330-million debt.

In a day of ironies, the lockout came just before Westar announced a net loss of $6.4 million for the first quarter of 1992, on earnings of $129.2 million. The loss for the same period last year was $9.9 million.

Westar also said it failed to make a $4.7 million payment of its debt principal that was due on April 30. It has asked its lenders—including the Bank of Montreal and the Royal Bank of Canada—for more time. As of yesterday, the banks had not replied.

May 1, International Labour Day, is a holiday at the Balmer mine under a long-standing contract perk. More than 200 workers booked for a holiday shift on overtime were told to go home when they arrived at the mine.

Coupled with $4 million of other cost cuts, the $6 million in contract savings were described by the company as an essential step in the debt refinancing bid.

Westar has said that without refinancing, including more than $75 million in new working capital, the mine can't survive.

Source: Excerpts from Robert Williamson, "Westar Locks Out Workers," *Report on Business Magazine*, May 2, 1992, p. B3.

Questions for Discussion

1. What factors is the union refusing to acknowledge in this dispute. What factors is management refusing to acknowledge? What do you think will be the result of this lockout?

2. Is Westar justified in locking out its workers? What other approaches to dispute resolution could Westar have used instead? Which would have been the most effective?

CASE 10.2

PEACE BREAKS OUT ON THE SHOP FLOOR

As THEY HEADED into bargaining talks last fall, union and management brass at two of Rockwell International of Canada Ltd.'s Ontario plants took an unusual step.

They wrote to the plants' biggest customer, Chrysler Corp., saying they would try their best to sign a new agreement three months before the old one died.

The parties then delivered on that pledge, wrapping up a deal 3½ months before the existing contract ran out in March 1993.

For the 160 hourly workers at Rockwell's coil springs factory in Milton, just west of Toronto, it was a further sign that the mood had changed in this former hotbed of labour–management conflict. The Canadian Auto Workers local—along with its sister local in Chatham—has now signed four consecutive contracts before the pacts in force have expired.

"We're the only supplier for Chrysler and we don't want to lose that customer," says Guido Tonin, chairman of the CAW plant committee at Milton. "If we lose Chrysler, we've lost our jobs."

Because of sentiments such as these, early signings have become the trend in auto parts plants. Managers and CAW locals seek alternatives to strikes, once a prominent feature of industrial relations.

The reasons: changing economics, work methods, and plain fear. Overcapacity means there's plenty of competition for work. With auto makers committed to just-in-time deliveries of parts to their assembly lines, suppliers who can't maintain flows don't keep the contract....

A company executive points out, "If you go on strike, you're never going to get that customer again. Striking is no longer an option."

Tom Johnson, president of the CAW local at Rockwell's Milton plant, doesn't disagree: "I don't know about big companies, but it's certainly true for smaller ones."...

It's normal for a supplier to finish making a batch of parts only 60 or 90 minutes before they are needed at a nearby car maker's plant. there is little inventory to draw from in case of a shortfall. If there is a problem, "there's an enormous amount of pressure on everybody to find a solution," says a CAW representative.

Managers are learning that consulting and communicating—building trust, in effect—are keys to keeping those supply lines open. Workers recognize that a grasp of the business, and its various jobs, is in their own interest as well as the company's.

Rockwell's Milton plant is a striking case study of the new labour relations. Back in the 1970s, it suffered from industrial relations that were as poor as any in the industry. . . .

John Gates, who came off the shop floor to become industrial relations manager, remembers it as a time of "adversarial relations—them and us. They [the union] were militant. We got harder nosed."

Meanwhile, the plant was becoming less competitive and wasn't making any money. Operations were cluttered by rigid classifications and working rules.

Faced with demands for a big wage hike at the March 15, 1980, contract deadline, Rockwell took a strike. It lasted eight months. Salaried staff continued to make coil springs—enough to keep a few customers happy in a recession that had crippled car sales.

"Through those eight months we all changed," Mr. Gates says. "You could see we were starting to come to grips with reality. I changed—I started to feel much more vulnerable."

After an agreement was signed, only the most senior one-fifth of the CAW workers were called back. The early months were not pleasant. "It was difficult to look each other in the eye," Mr. Gates says.

(continued)

Relations gradually improved. One reason, Mr. Gates says, was that management started to let people make decisions on the shop floor. In an environment where supervisors called the shots and workers did as they were told, that was an important step.

For this to work, personal communication had to improve. Ironically, this was easier to do in what had become a much smaller work force. Through the early 1980s, the Milton plant did little hiring.

The plant today has a yawning generation gap. Forty percent of workers have been there at least 29 years, putting them a step away from retirement. The other 60 percent have worked for five years or less.

The demographics have a big impact on the business. For one thing, pension issues are high among bargaining priorities. Also, because long-serving employees with critical know-how (such as changing dies and setting up machines) are near retirement, they are increasingly involved in training replacements and creating a job manual. Spending on training has doubled in the past three years. . . .

Mike Savilo, who became plant manager in 1989, believes in creating a climate in which good things happen. Formal plant meetings are scheduled six to ten times a year, but it's a day-to-day open-door policy that makes things tick.

Canvassing for weekend overtime, for example, may be done by a supervisor or perhaps the union's plant chairman, or both. If they can't agree on manning, they will find Mr. Gates—or someone in management—to talk it through to a swift resolution. Similarly, line workers will take a problem directly to Mr. Savilo if they think middle managers are slow to respond.

The best recent example of co-operation, both sides say, was in determining how the Milton plant might bid for—and deliver on—a big chunk of new work that General Motors Corp. had put up for outside bids.

In the past, the bid for the GM contract might have depended on plenty of overtime, which often starts well but falters as human stress builds. This time, the union suggested hiring 50 more people and running the plant seven days a week.

It turned out Milton didn't get the GM contract. Yet the seven-day agreement can be put in place whenever an opportunity arises. Meanwhile, it serves to underline the new flexibility in a workplace where hardened positions once dominated.

Source: Reprinted from Timothy Pritchard, "Peace Breaks Out on the Shop Floor," *The Globe and Mail*, July 6, 1993, p. B18.

Questions for Discussion

1. Why was it important to both management and workers at Rockwell to sign the collective agreement early?

2. Give evidence of the understanding workers and management each have of the needs of the other.

NOTES

1. Erik Heinrich, "Labour, Management Team Up," *The Financial Post*, July 3, 1991, p. 5.
2. John C. Anderson, "The Structure of Collective Bargaining," in John C. Anderson, Morley Gunderson, and Allen Ponak, *Union–Management Relations in Canada* (Don Mills, ON: Addison-Wesley, 1989), pp. 210–11.
3. John C. Anderson and Morley Gunderson, "Strikes and Dispute Resolution," in Anderson, Gunderson, and Ponak, *Union–Management Relations in Canada*, p. 307.
4. Jean Boivin, "Union–Management Relations in Quebec," in Anderson, Gunderson, and Ponak, *Union–Management Relations in Canada*, pp. 425–26.
5. Anderson and Gunderson, "Strikes and Dispute Resolution," pp. 308–309.
6. Anderson and Gunderson, "Strikes and Dispute Resolution," pp. 292–93; Anthony Giles and Hem C. Jain, "The Collective Agreement," in Anderson, Gunderson and Ponak, *Union–Management Relations in Canada*, pp. 328–29.

PHOTO CREDITS

MODULE
◆ GLO ◆

BUSINESS IN A GLOBAL ENVIRONMENT

THE FOCUS OF THIS MODULE

1. To explain why companies should pay attention to the international market

2. To discuss various reasons for businesses to "go international"

3. To consider various ways that companies can take part in international business

4. To examine the basic conditions required to get started in international business

5. To explain some macroeconomic factors that affect a country's trade picture

6. To discuss the importance of international business to Canada

7. To learn the meaning of the following terms:

KEY TERMS

globalization

indirect international trade

direct international trade

licensing

international joint venture

direct investment

free trade area

tariff

revenue tariff

protective tariff

import quota

embargo

exchange control

dumping

friendship, commerce, and
  navigation (FCN) treaties

International Monetary Fund (IMF)

General Agreement on Tariffs and
  Trade (GATT)

multinational corporation (MNC)

customs union

common market

balance of trade

balance of payments

exchange rate

devaluation

revaluation

floating exchange rate

countertrade

absolute advantage

comparative advantage

Ricardo theory

EATING BIRTHDAY CAKE at 19 of the firm's 29 manufacturing plants around the world is a "broadening" exercise. Nevertheless, that is how Wayne McLeod, president and CEO of CCL Industries Inc., celebrated his company's 40th birthday. The Toronto-based company produces labels and containers for consumer goods, as well as a range of brand-name household and personal care items for multinationals like Nabisco and Procter and Gamble.

In the past two years, his determination to survive free trade and conquer foreign markets has spurred CCL to expand from its domestic base into an international operation with 5,200 employees across North America, Mexico, England, and Australia.

Little did CCL know that, on its first birthday, the Free Trade Agreement (FTA) would be "the worst and best thing that ever happened to us [in 40 years of doing business]," said Mr. McLeod. "It forced us to become more focussed and much more aggressive to survive."

Indeed, the FTA forced CCL to become larger or face going out of business. Before the agreement, large manufacturers of brand names such as Javex detergent or Arrid antiperspirant found it more economical to use companies like CCL to serve the smaller Canadian market. With the FTA in place, it became possible for these companies to serve the Canadian market from their U.S. facilities.

Mr. William Chisholm, an investment analyst, said about CCL: "They had carved out a niche as the cost-effective Canadian manufacturer for marketing companies, but they now have to duplicate that role in a North American context to survive."

CCL is not only surviving but growing. The company has attained the critical size to compete internationally. CCL has grown into the largest North American manufacturer of pressure-sensitive labels and antiperspirants. It is now a major force in the global aerosol-container industry. It is exploring partnerships in countries like Germany and India. The growing private-label products for huge retailers such as Kmart and Wal-Mart will provide more areas for expansion.

Clearly, CCL management is looking forward to more birthday celebrations, in many more countries.

Source: Adapted from Deidre McMurdy, "Packaging for Growth," *Maclean's*, August 12, 1991, p. 31.

THE PERFORMANCE OF companies such as CCL Industries shows the benefits of becoming involved in the international marketplace. For those which produce goods and services for a specialty market, selling abroad enables the firm to work at more efficient volumes. For example, a producer of environmental monitoring equipment finds opportunities not only at home but in the United States and Southeast Asia.

CAE Inc., based in Montreal, Quebec, is a leader in the development and production of electronic simulation training systems and devices for commercial airlines, the military, and space agencies. Shown above is the flight deck of a simulator built by CAE Inc. for Singapore Airlines. CAE Inc. operates both throughout Canada and internationally, alongside the aerospace electronic groups in the United States and Europe.

Marketing in other countries also exposes management to new ideas and methods of doing business. This can make the firm more efficient at home and abroad. For example, Canadian bankers find that they can learn new dimensions of international banking and finance from studying Hong Kong banks. The Canadian garment industry regularly turns to Europe for new clothing designs. The North American automobile industry has been vastly improved through competition with Japanese automakers.

Few firms, in fact, can avoid international competition. Firms choosing to operate only in Canada usually must face strong international competitors striving for a share of the local firm's own home market. The broader base of the international competitor often makes it a stronger opponent than the domestic firm, much to the local firm's distress.

So many Canadian firms have found success in the international market that Canada is consistently among the top seven trading nations of the world. Canada's exports account for more than 30 percent of our Gross National Product. Every day finds more Canadian companies enjoying new opportunities and profits. Nevertheless,

globalization

Focussing the resources and goals of an organization on global opportunities in marketing and production

there is a consensus that Canadians—and Canadian companies—need to do more. The emphasis today is on more than trade. Companies are focussing their resources and goals not only on looking for markets around the world but also on developing production facilities in the most efficient locations, wherever they may be. This trend toward **globalization** is altering the map of world business.

THE GLOBAL CHALLENGE

In boardrooms across the country executives are considering where to build the factories of the future. Will it be Windsor, Ontario; Seoul, South Korea; Minneapolis, Minnesota; Chiang Mai, Thailand; or Richmond, BC?[1] The view of business has changed. The concept of exporting or importing from or to our country is evolving into a global view of the world. A garment may be designed in Winnipeg, partially manufactured in Malaysia, and finally made ready for the market in Montreal. Computers and cars are made of parts manufactured in many parts of the world.

The concern is with total efficiency and opportunity wherever it is found. It is clear that Canada cannot compete with cheaper labour countries in certain types of manufacturing. On the other hand, we may be more able to perform other business activities such as sophisticated marketing planning, or those based on information technology. Firms are learning to manage and think in a global context.

The process of broadening business horizons is illustrated in the recognition of nations that freer trade between them is desirable. In 1993, the North American Free Trade Agreement (NAFTA) was signed. It provided for a gradual elimination of obstacles to trade between Canada, the United States, and Mexico. This trend is also exhibited in the finalization of a fully integrated common market in Europe that took place in 1993.

NAFTA and its predecessor, the Canada–U.S. Free Trade Agreement, have forced many firms to think on a continental rather than a Canadian basis. Moreover, many have utilized the stimulus of the agreement to formulate global strategies. Gillette, for instance, has closed plants in Montreal and other parts of the world to centralize operations in Boston, where the company had unused plant capacity.

On the other hand, Du Pont Canada invested heavily in plants in both Canada and the United States, each of which could be world-competitive. Other foreign companies have set expectations that their Canadian subsidiaries will serve specific market niches on a global basis.[2]

These examples show that the marketplace has changed. The Canadian economy and Canadian companies will suffer or benefit from the realities of global competition. It is to business's advantage as well as Canada's if firms recognize and respond to these challenges and opportunities.

ENTERING THE WORLD MARKET

Firms usually decide to enter the international market when they see market opportunities for their products abroad and anticipate increased profits because larger volumes will lead to economies of scale. Such expansion will make the business more competitive in its domestic market as well.

Some managers particularly enjoy the challenge of making an international venture work. For example, Gary Stieman, president of Gemini Fashions of Canada, found that in addition to providing a great deal of additional sales, customers in other parts of the world were prepared to buy merchandise at times that fitted into Gemini's normal production valleys. This made the operation more competitive and profitable. "An extreme example," says Stieman, "was Australia, where we had some large customers. Because their winter season was different from ours, we were able to extend our winter production by as much as ten days by producing Australian orders for winter wear at the tail end of our domestic order production." Stieman cautions that "it takes effort, time, investment, talent, and luck to achieve success in the export market. It is there for those who are willing and able to pay the price."[3]

Sometimes unfavourable conditions at home, such as competitive pressures, declining domestic sales, or overproduction, stimulate consideration of international opportunities. Competition may come not only from other companies in the home market but also from foreign companies expanding their markets. If domestic opportunities are limited, a company may look to markets abroad. Overproduction may force a company to look to other markets to take up the excess supply. Issues in Business 11.1 discusses the challenge of developing a global marketing strategy.

ISSUES IN BUSINESS 11.1

GLOBALIZATION GETS TOUGHER

WHAT DOES IT take to compete in an era of global business?

Canadian businesses have tended to rely on the notion that as long as their products satisfied national markets then they were fine. Now they face competition from all sides, and they must change their strategies if their companies are to survive. "We have to think more globally and less parochially as a country, because we no longer have those nice sweet protective trade barriers that we benefited from for so long," said Denis St. Amour, president of Drake Beam, Morin Canada Inc., a human-resources management firm in Montreal.

According to Mr. St. Amour, Canadian firms will have to sharpen their tactics in a number of ways:

- To be exceptionally sharp and be prepared to compete toe-to-toe with American and other overseas competitors
- To adapt product and strategy to changing world markets
- To provide products that are the best that can be marketed
- To understand your customer's concept of satisfaction
- To be adaptable in responding to customers' needs across time zones

Source: Adapted from Bruce Gates, "Globalization of Business Means Canadian CEOs Must Be Sharper," *The Financial Post*, May 4, 1992, p. S21.

(continued)

> **Question for Discussion**
> 1. Mr. St. Amour's tactics sound good. However, how could a firm adapt to make some of these changes come about? Using a company that you are familiar with, suggest a *realistic* way for the company to start to implement each item from Mr. St. Amour's list above.

MODES OF INTERNATIONAL ACTIVITY

Firms can participate in the international market in a number of ways and to a lesser or greater extent. The lowest level of participation is indirect exporting and importing; the highest levels are international joint ventures and foreign production and marketing.

Indirect Exporting and Importing

indirect international trade
Exporting and/or importing only through other domestic companies that trade internationally

A company involved in **indirect international trade** does not attempt to buy or sell in other countries. However, some of the companies it does business with will be involved in exporting or importing. For example, a supplier produces and sells parts to Monarch Pumps, which markets its products in many countries. Similarly, the supplier buys from a Canadian distributor some components to include in his product that are made in Germany. Although the supplier has no direct contact with foreign firms, it is a vital part of the international market.

Direct Exporting and Importing

direct international trade
Exporting and/or importing directly to markets and from suppliers in other countries

Some companies are more committed to **direct international trade.** They may produce in Canada and then seek to export a portion of their output to foreign markets. For example, the developer of a software program for the management of trucking distribution companies markets the product in both Canada and the United States, and considers which other countries would have similar needs. Conversely, an oil company imports crude oil from Venezuela or the Middle East to refineries in Montreal in order to sell the finished product in eastern Canada.

Triple E, a Canadian recreational-vehicle manufacturer, is involved in both importing and exporting. The firm directly imports certain components from the United States and other countries. It also exports its RVs directly to Europe, as well as selling them in Canada.

Licensing

licensing
The granting of authority to produce and sell a product developed in one country in another

Licensing allows a producer in another country to manufacture and sell a product for a fee paid to the licensing company. For example, the Canadian inventor of a commercial trash compacter displays her product at a trade show. Among the visitors to her booth is a Japanese businessman. Impressed with the product, he offers to produce and sell it in Japan under licence. The licence agreement gives him the know-how and rights to produce the compacter in Japan, at a set fee per unit. This saves the Canadian business a great deal of hassle, but normally the return is quite low, and it may be difficult to maintain patent control.

Joint Venture

In an **international joint venture,** a company sets up a business in a foreign market by going into partnership with a local enterprise. Such an arrangement allows for the sharing of financial risk and reduces the problems inherent in doing business in a foreign country because the partner can supply knowledge of local marketing and production practices. A joint venture requires a much greater commitment of resources than importing and exporting or licensing. General Motors and Suzuki, in Ingersoll, Ontario, and Honda and Rover, in Britain, are examples of international joint ventures.

international joint venture
A partnership of firms from different countries, often to set up a local business in a country foreign to one of the partners

Foreign Production and Marketing

Direct investment in another country requires the greatest commitment to international endeavour. In such an enterprise, a firm invests in facilities, staff, and marketing programs in a foreign market without a local partner. If the enterprise is successful, the rewards will not have to be shared, and the business can operate freely without the need to make decisions jointly with a foreign partner. Canadian auto-parts manufacturer Magna has such an operation in Mexico.

direct investment
The ownership and management of production and/or marketing facilities in a foreign country

Multinational Enterprise

A company that handles its own foreign production and marketing might be, or could become, a **multinational corporation (MNC).** An MNC produces and markets in several countries; it has a world orientation rather than to any one country. Thus, it chooses to produce components in whichever country happens to be the best for the job. Similarly, marketing strategies are often interrelated between countries, and may follow a common theme.

multinational corporation (MNC)
A corporation that produces and markets goods and services in several countries according to where opportunities are best

Alcan Aluminum is a multinational corporation headquartered in Canada, but its products can be found around the world. The company has branches in many world markets. With approximately 80 percent of its sales originating outside Canada, the company must think in global rather than domestic terms.

STARTING INTERNATIONAL OPERATIONS[4]

Before deciding to "go international," a company needs to ensure that it has the following elements: a strong senior-management commitment, adequate resources, a viable product, and strategic planning.

Management Commitment

Developing and implementing a strategic plan for an international venture requires a substantial investment of corporate resources (financial and human) for a considerable period before any profits are seen. Therefore, it is crucial that senior management be committed to an international venture before embarking on such an exercise.

Adequate Resources

Prior to making any decision to export, a thorough review of the firm's domestic performance and capabilities should be made. For example, sales profit margins and prices should be compared with those of the industry. If competitors are already exporting, this is a positive sign that there may be a good opportunity.

The company's own resources should be thoroughly assessed. Does it have the financial and human resources to research foreign markets? Does it have the production capacity to ensure prompt deliveries when orders come in? Reliability is one of the most essential requirements for success in selling internationally.

Viable Product

The exportability of the product should be determined by considering the following factors:

- Who will use the product?
- Who will make the purchasing decisions in the foreign country?
- Will the product be purchased throughout the year or on a seasonal basis?
- From whom is the product being purchased now?
- Will there be a requirement for product modification in order to adapt to specific market nuances, or regulations? What will this cost?
- Is the product easy to ship? Are there any special handling costs?
- Is the product competitive on the basis of price, quality, and delivery?

STRATEGIC PLANNING FOR EXPORT

Export strategy should be part of overall corporate strategy. The company must be clear about its expectations from an international venture as well as fully aware of its own limitations. For example, if the company is not prepared to spend the time and money to research the market, and adapt and produce the proper type and quantity of products, then it should not be considering the export market.

Once management decides to examine the feasibility of an international venture, it should begin by scanning possible markets. Countries first considered would normally be those that are geographically close, similar in language and culture, or familiar to company officials. The preliminary scanning would include factors such as market size, political and economic stability, competition, distribution, and profit potential. This initial survey would provide management with the information to select the four or five most likely markets for further analysis. Such an analysis would consider the market, the product (already discussed), the price, distribution, and marketing communications. A few examples of the relevant issues for each factor follow.

The Market

- What are the tariff barriers, import quotas, and internal taxes for the product?
- What is the size and the sector of the market purchasing the product?
- What is the long-term potential, based on future growth for each sector?
- Who are the major competitors and what is their market share?
- Is the market politically and economically stable?

The Price

- What is the profitability at various pricing levels?
- Can the pricing match or better the competition and still have a healthy profit margin?
- If pricing cannot match the competition, can it still sell because of product superiority, ability to deliver, and after-sales servicing?

Distribution

- What methods of distribution are available in the country, and which is the most reliable and cost-efficient?
- What markups are normally sought by intermediaries in the industry?
- Who are the main importers; what are their reputations, capabilities, and financial strengths?
- What types of carriers are needed? What are the transportation costs? How frequent and reliable are the various methods of transportation?
- Is there an agent capable of providing satisfactory technical services?

Marketing Communications

- What are the types and costs of advertising in the individual markets, and which are best suited to the needs of the product?
- What are the advertising practices of competitors? What percentage of their gross profit goes into advertising and what media do they advertise in?
- Where and when do trade fairs and exhibitions take place, and what opportunities exist for participating in them?

Some of this information is available from provincial business and trade departments as well as the federal Department of Foreign Affairs and International Trade. After gleaning as much information as possible in Canada, it is very important for the business person to make a trip to the target country to size up the situation.

After an analysis that takes the foregoing factors into consideration, the business will then be in a position to decide whether it should proceed. Such an appraisal also provides the groundwork for developing the company strategy necessary to enter the foreign market. It is a challenging task. However, those who proceed in a systematic fashion generally find that going international is quite worthwhile.

BUSINESS REVIEW 11.1

1. List and discuss the main motivations that lead companies to participate in the international market.

2. Review the various ways that companies can be involved internationally.

THE INTRICACIES OF INTERNATIONAL BUSINESS

Businesses that expand to an international focus discover an array of complications that do not exist, or that they are unaware of, on the domestic scene. Many of these factors may seem to have little to do with day-to-day business, but ignoring them is likely to lead to failure.

Social and Cultural Factors

Buying preferences differ from country to country, and hold many surprises for the unwary. Canadians are used to winning quick contract approval on the basis of presentation of the "best" deal. They are sometimes surprised that in many other countries, such as in Asia and Mexico, agreement is as much dependent upon first developing a good personal relationship. Bureaucracy slows operations in Malaysia, whereas in Hong Kong the frenetic pace of business forces the firm to be quick and aggressive in order to survive.

Products in one market do not always meet the needs of foreign consumers. China's popular White Elephant brand of batteries has a

The Asian market has become increasingly attractive to many Canadian businesses. Trade with Asian countries, particularly with Hong Kong, Japan, South Korea, and Taiwan, has increased enormously in recent years. Canada tends to export raw materials to Asia, while importing finished manufactured goods. The obvious challenge for Canadian businesses is to expand exports to include Canadian-made finished products.

very negative connotation in Canada. Washing machines made in North America do not sell well in Germany because consumers there have different expectations and standards for the product.

Similarly, ways of conducting business differ across national borders. Developing Your Business Skills offers a list of important considerations for business people wanting to do business in Japan. All in all, cultural sensitivity and awareness are important business skills. For example, body language differs from one culture to another, and it is easy to convey the wrong message while travelling abroad. U.S. president George Bush flashed what he thought was a V-for-Victory sign to a crowd in Australia—the equivalent of North American's single-finger salute. In South America, what we in the Northern Hemisphere regard as an "okay" sign—thumb and forefinger forming a circle—has the same insulting meaning. In Arab countries, the sole of one's shoe should never face another person, and the left hand is considered unclean and should not be used to hand an object to someone.

Comfortable speaking distances also vary. In North America, talkers tend to stand at arm's length. Some Europeans and South Americans feel comfortable about 25 centimetres apart. A Canadian is likely to back away from a South American, who will then come closer, as both strive to maintain their comfort levels.[5]

DEVELOPING YOUR BUSINESS SKILLS

FACTORS TO CONSIDER IN DOING BUSINESS IN JAPAN

There's no doubt about it: they do things very differently in Japan, and anyone who wants to break into that market is well advised to do a little homework first. Here are some useful tips for doing business successfully and surviving, from Westerners who've found out the hard way how to operate:
- *Building relationships.* The Japanese like to set up relationships and get to know you before they sign a contract. This means that, at a first meeting, they are likely to discuss general topics, such as the state of the world economy. They may even take you out to a restaurant or to the golf course, a very fruitful place for meetings. One place you're unlikely to go is home with them to meet the family.

   Once things feel more comfortable, they'll start to talk business. From this fact follows the advice that it's better for the same people to do the negotiating—even if it takes several years—as did Northern Telecom Inc. negotiations for an important contract.
- *Business cards* translated into Japanese are appreciated. Cards are exchanged at the beginning of a meeting—remember to present yours Japanese-side-up, and to wait to see whether they wish to shake hands or bow. Do not write on cards you have just been given as this is considered highly impolite.
- *Scheduling meetings.* It is important to set up appointments in advance because the Japanese don't like "cold" calls—part of their credo of no surprises. But because many people commute long distances from their offices, it's difficult to fit in more than three meetings a day. Breakfast gatherings are not popular, nor are after-work get-togethers unless they invite you.

(continued)

- *Negotiations*. One feature that can be bewildering is being confronted by a phalanx of negotiators. It helps to sort out who's who by arranging the business cards always exchanged at these meetings to reflect the seating order. What's even harder is figuring out who's the head individual, who often may be the person who says nothing. Equally, the silent one could be a neophyte who is at the meeting only to gain experience and is expected to say nothing.

  The slowness of Japanese decision making (the famous consensus) can be frustrating for the Western business person who is used to jetting in and out and arriving at decisions quickly in between. However, it probably evens out in the end, as once a contract has been signed, most of the hard work is over.

  During negotiations, don't take silence as a criticism. It may simply be that your suggestions are being considered and evaluated before a reply is made. There's probably no need to sweeten the deal by adding concessions you may later regret. Similarly, listen to everything that is said to you before responding. A sentence that starts off, "Yes…" may well contain a "but" farther on.

- *Using an interpreter*. Find out if an interpreter is needed. If so, hire your own. This can be arranged by your hotel. Make sure he or she is briefed thoroughly on any difficult technical terms you might be using and knows something about your line of business.

  When conducting a meeting through an interpreter, speak slowly and clearly. Break your thoughts down into simple but self-contained sentences so that what you say can be translated point by point. If you are going to be involved in hard negotiations that last all day, you will probably need two translators who will work in shifts.

- *Getting around*. Before automatically taking a cab, consider the easy and extremely efficient train and underground system. Your hotel will give you directions, or should you decide to take a cab, write out your destination in Japanese and instruct the driver. Be warned, however, of Tokyo's extraordinary address system, aptly described as blindman's bluff. Few streets have names, although some of the biggest have recently been labelled.

Source: Adapted from Araminta Wordsworth, "How to Conduct Business the Japanese Way," *The Financial Post*, June 9, 1984, p. S7.

These examples suggest the importance of social and cultural factors in the success of international business. Business managers who want to operate in an international market must learn to adapt to new circumstances.

ECONOMIC AND POLITICAL BARRIERS TO TRADE

Tariffs

tariff
A tax, or duty, levied on imported goods

revenue tariff
A tariff levied for the purpose of raising funds for the government

protective tariff
A tariff levied to protect domestic industry from foreign competition

Tariffs, or taxes, imposed upon imported goods, can be significant barriers to trade. Tariffs may be levied per kilogram, litre, or some other unit; on a commodity, per item; or as a proportion of market value. Tariffs serve two purposes. **Revenue tariffs** are primarily a source of funds for the government. **Protective tariffs** raise the price of imported products to protect domestic producers. Issues in Business 11.2 examines the reasons countries have used protective tariffs and suggests arguments for and against the practice.

ISSUES IN BUSINESS 11.2

THE PROS AND CONS OF TARIFFS

VERY FEW ECONOMIC choices—maybe none—can be explained in clear black–and–white terms. Tariffs as protection against lower-priced imports raise an issue of some dispute.

Consumers would benefit from the lower-priced competition. It means more choices and lower prices. But business people would probably see things differently. They would see potential business going to foreign competitors, meaning lower sales, less revenue, and hence less profit or a loss. Workers at domestic companies trying to compete with these cheaper imports might become unemployed if enough business was lost to foreign competitors.

Tariffs have the effect of raising the price at which foreign companies must sell their products to make a profit, which gives domestic firms an advantage. The issue of tariff protection is a crucial one. Here are some of the points made on either side of the debate.

Major Points of Those Arguing For Tariff Protection:
- Tariffs are necessary to protect jobs. If people buy lower-priced imports, domestic production falls and some workers will lose employment.
- Tariffs are necessary to protect certain businesses (if not entire industries) from lower-priced imports. Some industries may be in the early stages of development and need the chance to grow without foreign competition. Other countries may be able to produce more cheaply because of lower wage costs, cheaper resources, etc. As such, they may be able to underprice domestic producers and put them out of business.
- Tariffs help broaden the areas in which domestic industries can compete. This can increase business opportunity and jobs.

Major Points of Those Arguing Against Tariff Protection:
- Tariffs raise prices for consumers.
- Tariffs protect inefficient industries—those that can't compete on equal terms with foreign producers. They should be forced to compete or allowed to fail. If they fail, the resources invested can be redirected to a business that can compete. Companies that can compete more effectively and employ more workers should be supported.
- Levying a tariff encourages other countries to retaliate with their own tariffs. This hurts the sales of exporting firms. Production and employment fall, and opportunities for economies of scale are lost. Hence, prices of goods produced at home rise.

Question for Discussion
1. How do these arguments apply to Canada's participation in the Free Trade Agreement with the United States and the North American Free Trade Agreement with the United States and Mexico?

Non-Tariff Barriers

import quota
A limit on the amount of a commodity permitted to enter a country

Tariffs are only one kind of deterrent to trade. Non-tariff barriers, often euphemistically called "trade restrictions," include, for example, **import quotas,** which specify maximum amounts of commodities that may enter a country. Trade restrictions such as these are imposed to protect domestic industry and workers and to maintain foreign currency reserves. Often simply the threat of trade restrictions such as import quotas will cause an exporting nation to impose "voluntary export quotas." For example, the Japanese agreed to limit the number of automobiles shipped to Canada in the face of such a threat.

embargo
A ban on importing or exporting products from a certain country

The most extreme form of import quota is the **embargo,** which is a virtual ban on trade with a certain country. Embargoes are often imposed to achieve political objectives. In the early 1990s, Canada joined other countries in an embargo of strategic and other goods to Serbia in order to achieve compliance with United Nations attempts to bring peace to the region.

exchange control
Government restrictions on the amount of foreign currency that may be bought or sold

Governments can also influence foreign trade through currency exchange controls. **Exchange control** uses a mechanism such as a central bank or government agency as the only clearinghouse through which foreign currency may be bought or sold. Businesses are thus allowed to expand foreign trade or forced to restrict it according to the availability of foreign currency as set by government policy. When money is not available to spend abroad, firms are forced to buy from within the country or to try to barter their products for foreign goods. India uses a similar approach to keep capital within its borders. It restricts the amount of money any individual or business may take out of the country.

dumping
Selling a product in a foreign market for a price below that charged in the domestic market

Many countries, including Canada, try to protect domestic industries from what they regard as unfair business practices by foreign traders. For example, dumping is viewed as a threat to economic systems. **Dumping** is selling a product in a foreign market below the selling price for the same product at home. If foreign goods sell in Canada at prices substantially lower than those offered by local producers, the result will be lost jobs for Canadians. The Anti-Dumping Tribunal investigates any complaints related to dumping. The tribunal has the power to impose extra duties and tariffs in order to protect Canadian employment.

Dumping is a difficult charge to prove. Not only are firms reluctant to make data available, but accountants on the pro and con sides can show significantly different interpretations. Furthermore, dumping complaints can take a long time to resolve. Although Canada remains committed to a free-trade philosophy, pressures exist to protect basic industries from unfair foreign competition, sometimes from firms actually owned by foreign governments. Another worry is that dumping complaints may lead to extensive trade warfare.

In an age of declining tariffs (because of agreements such as NAFTA), trading partners such as the United States are more frequently charging others with dumping. This legitimizes the imposition of protective tariffs. It seems certain that the question of dumping will remain a vital public issue as long as countries suffer from relatively high unemployment, economically threatened industries, and related economic ills.

Government policy and public opinion on imports have varied over time. Relatively high unemployment usually leads to calls for higher tariff walls and severe import restrictions to protect Canadian industry and its employees. This economic protection argument has been voiced by both corporate management and labour union executives.

National and International Law

Companies doing business abroad are subject to a legal environment with three components: the law of their home country, that of host countries, and international law. The home country will have regulations, tax laws, and import–export requirements that will affect dealings abroad. Local legal requirements in host countries may be quite different from those at home. For example, candy commercials in the Netherlands must contain tooth decay warnings. Some countries have strict domestic content requirements in goods offered for sale. Managers must be familiar with aspects of local legislation that affect their industries. Broader-reaching international conventions and agreements govern the behaviour of business and relationships among countries.

INTERNATIONAL AGREEMENTS AND ECONOMIC ALLIANCES

International law is the product of various agreements between countries. Canada has entered **friendship, commerce, and navigation (FCN) treaties** with various countries that define business relationships such as the limits to business activity in one another's domestic markets and reciprocal tax arrangements. Wider agreements set standards in such areas as international air travel and communications, product quality, and patents and trademarks. The definition of territorial waters as extending 200 nautical miles from the borders of a country is an international law established by such a treaty. When disputes arise on the interpretation of FCN treaties such as the one over precise delineation of the boundaries between the United States and Canada on the Grand Banks, they may be taken to the World Court in The Hague for resolution.

friendship, commerce, and navigation (FCN) treaties
Treaties that include business relationships in partners' domestic markets, reciprocal tax arrangements, etc.

One important treaty negotiated among 44 countries in 1944 through the United Nations established the **International Monetary Fund (IMF).** The Fund watches over the international financial capability of nations and maintains a large pool of financial resources that it makes available to member countries to enable them to carry out international monetary co-operation. Participation in the Fund has given countries liquidity (i.e., money or a means of payment) beyond the reserves of gold or foreign exchange. This greatly facilitates trade and investment between nations.

International Monetary Fund (IMF)
A fund established to make loans to countries to allow them to trade on the international market

General Agreement on Tariffs and Trade

Despite the existence of barriers to trade as discussed earlier, most countries want wider trade.

In principle, most countries believe that more trade is a good thing. The **General Agreement on Tariffs and Trade (GATT)** is an international trade pact among more than 90 countries that together generate about

General Agreement on Tariffs and Trade (GATT)
An agreement among most world trading nations that reduces tariffs and other barriers to trade

The Uruguay Round of GATT was settled in 1993 after seven years of negotiation and numerous disagreements regarding the amount of tariff protection and subsidies that should be given to the agricultural sector. Canada's economy, which significantly depends on its natural resource exports, including agricultural products, had much at stake in the resolution of the agricultural-subsidy issues at the GATT table.

85 percent of the world's trade. In this accord, tariffs have been gradually negotiated downward through a series of negotiation "rounds" (the Geneva Round, Dillon Round, Kennedy Round, Tokyo Round, and Uruguay Round). The effects on tariff levels have been significant. For example, tariffs on most industrial goods are generally less than 8 percent in the most advanced Western countries. The most recent round, the Uruguay Round, faced real obstacles to agreement, especially in the area of agricultural subsidies, but was finally settled in late 1993.

Although overall the trend has been toward reducing tariffs, predictable demands have been made for protecting any industries threatened by sluggish economic periods and local industry problems. In numerous instances, the successes of GATT in reducing general tariff barriers have been undermined by a multitude of restrictive trade practices and agreements that have sprung up outside the framework of GATT. These include such restrictions as quotas, "voluntary" export restraints, and similar measures. This development is often described as "managed trade," and now covers a broad range of industries, including textiles, clothing, steel, automobiles, machine tools, and consumer electronics. There seems to be a growing consensus that such restrictions have put the multilateral trading system at risk. The developed countries show a growing understanding that the best route to improved competitiveness is through positive adjustment within an open international trading system. The Uruguay Round of GATT struggled over several years with these problems and opportunities. The decisions are not easy, because while there is agreement that freer trade is necessary, international industries cry out for protection.

Sylvia Ostry said when she was Canada's ambassador for Multilateral Trade Relations, "Canada's ability to compete in a rapidly changing and increasingly tough world environment depends to a large degree on open trade. In many industries, our domestic market is too small to permit optimum plant size and product specialization. That is why we are deeply concerned with maintaining and enhancing the GATT system."[6]

Regional Economic Alliances

The end of the Second World War saw the beginning of a new era of international economic activity. The result has been the formation of multinational economic alliances. Overall, these partnerships tend to be based on one of three possible models—the free trade area, the customs union, and the common market.

The **free trade area,** as the name implies, permits trade without tariffs, and theoretically, without trade restrictions. The North American Free Trade Agreement (NAFTA) between Canada, the United States, and Mexico is one example. Another is the European Free Trade Area (EFTA) between Austria, Finland, Iceland, Liechtenstein, Norway, Sweden, and Switzerland.

If a **customs union** format is used, members operate within a free trade format, but trade with non-member countries includes a compulsory uniform tariff applied to non-members.

Within a **common market** or economic union, the members not only have a customs union but also plan to allow capital, labour, and products to flow freely among members and remove all differences in government trade rules. The European Community (EC), often referred to as the Common Market, is the most developed example of an economic union. The EC and EFTA have special trade relations as well.

free trade area
An agreement to permit trade without tariffs among the member countries

customs union
A free trade area that includes an agreement to impose uniform tariffs on goods from non-member countries

common market
An agreement among members to allow capital, labour, and goods to flow freely, maintain a customs union, and co-ordinate government trade rules

TABLE 11.1 • TRADING BLOC COMPARISON

	Asia	NAFTA	EC/EFTA	World
Population (millions)	1,620	360	358	5,206
Percentage of world's	31.1	6.9	6.9	100
GDP ($ trillion)	3.853	5.864	5.532	19.982
Percentage of world's	19.3	29.3	27.7	100
Exports ($ billions) total	656	509	1,320	2,902
Percentage of world's	22.6	17.5	45.5	100
Imports ($ billion) total	561	636	1,360	3,046
Percentage of world's	18.4	20.9	44.6	100

Source: OECD
NAFTA = North American Free Trade Area (Canada, Mexico, United States)
EC = European Community (Belgium, Britain, Denmark, France, Germany, Greece, Ireland, Italy, Luxembourg, Netherlands, Portugal, Spain)
EFTA = European Free Trade Area (Austria, Finland, Iceland, Liechtenstein, Switzerland)

Source: *Canada and the World* 57, No. 9, April 1992, p. 15. Reprinted with permission of *Canada and the World*, Waterloo, Ontario

The trend toward the development of multinational economic communities continues. They will contribute significantly to international business activity in the future. Consequently, both the demands and exciting possibilities of economic integration will have a noticeable effect on how businesses are managed and operate within the new and larger context. Table 11.1 depicts NAFTA and EC/EFTA as trading blocs and compares their magnitude in relation to Asia and the world. NAFTA and EC/EFTA each has only 6.9 percent of the world's population, but the largest percentage of the world's exports. Asia is a region to watch. Other evidence shows that its economic performance is growing rapidly. Its large population base combined with its growth will make it an economic powerhouse. Furthermore, discussions are being held concerning the formation of formal economic alliances within Asia.

Readers wishing further information on data provided through the cooperation of Statistics Canada may obtain copies of related publication by mail from: Publication Sales, Statistics Canada, Ottawa, Ontario, K1A 0T6, by calling 1-613-951-7277 or toll free 1-800-267-6677. Readers may also facsimile their order by dialling 1-613-951-1584.

ISSUES IN BUSINESS 11.3

ASIA *IS* KEY TO OUR QUALITY OF LIFE

"I PREDICT THAT BY the end of this decade more than 70 percent of all world trade will be with or among the economies along the western shore of the Pacific," says Graeme McDonald, president and CEO of the Asia Pacific Foundation of Canada.

There are a number of factors which make this prediction believable. First, Japan's current expansion, the "Heisei Boom," is characterized by massive capital and R&D investments. It is massive because neither the United States nor Europe has invested as large a portion of its GNP in these critical areas over the past 25 years.

Another factor is IPIZ (integrated production and investment zone). This refers to the principal Asian economies that carry on a higher proportion of their trade with one another than do the countries comprising the European Community. Japan is at the zone's centre. Canada could try to make sure that this IPIZ extends to Vancouver (and on to St. John's).

Third, productivity improvements are driven largely by a focus on innovation and on quality. These days the strongest innovation and quality paradigms are in Asia.

Canada is a trading nation. One in every four jobs is directly related to an export industry. Since the IPIZ is currently the dominant area in trade, then it seems logical that the Canadian economy can become stronger by dealing with these economies.

Or does it?

Canada's biggest trading partner has been the United States. In 1990, the United States had $394 billion in foreign trade. Canada also has longstanding social and cultural connections with Europe. Europe also has huge trade potential. For example, Germany surpassed the United States as a trading nation for the first time that year, with $421 billion (U.S.) in foreign trade. France, Britain, and Italy are also trading nations larger than Canada. Therefore, because of better knowledge of European culture and ways of doing business, Canada could do extremely well emphasizing trade with Europe.

(continued)

Source: Adapted from Graeme McDonald, "Asia Is Key to our Quality of Life," *The Financial Post*, May 6, 1992, p. S2.

Question for Discussion

1. Why is there such a great focus on Japan when any of these large European trading nations might offer ample trading growth for Canada? Is the Asian focus appropriate?

BUSINESS REVIEW 11.2

1. Review the important considerations in doing international business.

2. How do multilateral and regional trade agreements affect international business?

MACROECONOMIC FACTORS

Companies that operate globally must be aware of larger economic considerations than the state of their own profits. The overall economic situation of the countries in which they do business is an important factor in planning future activities. A country's economic health is indicated by factors that are described in such terms as balance of trade and balance of payments, and changes in the exchange rate for its currency.

INTERNATIONAL TRADE TERMINOLOGY

The Balance of Trade

The difference between the value of the goods imported and exported from a particular country is known as its **balance of trade.** A country has a favourable balance of trade when the value of its exports is greater than the value of its imports because this tends to mean that new money enters the country and strengthens the economic system. Conversely, when the value of imports exceeds that of exports, the country has an unfavourable balance of trade as money moves out of a country's economy. Canada usually has a positive balance of trade in goods (more exports than imports). Figure 11.1 shows the fluctuations on a monthly basis for 1991 and 1992 and the overall trend of the trade balance. The total trade balance for 1992 was +$9.5 billion.[7]

balance of trade
The difference in value between a country's exports and its imports

The Balance of Payments

The balance of trade is only part, though an important part, of a country's **balance of payments**—the difference between total payments made to and total receipts from other countries. When receipts exceed payments, the country has a favourable balance of payments. When payments exceed receipts, it has an unfavourable balance of

balance of payments
The difference in the flow of money into and out of a country, affected by trade, tourism, foreign aid, etc.

FIGURE 11.1 • CANADA'S TRADE BALANCE

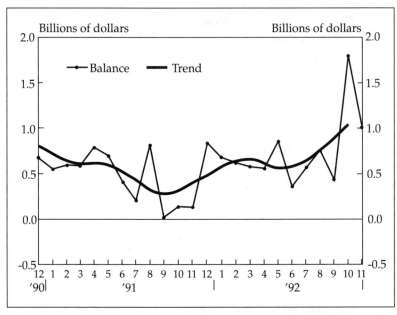

Source: Statistics Canada, Catalogue 65-001P, December 1992, p. 1. Reproduced by authority of the Minister of Industry, 1994.

payments. The balance of payments may be unfavourable even when the balance of trade is favourable, and vice versa. Other economic activities, such as tourism, military obligations, payment from foreign investments or to foreign investors, and foreign aid, influence a country's balance of payments.

The Exchange Rate

In the past, it was customary to express the value of a country's currency according to the *gold standard,* or the amount of gold a monetary unit would buy. As international business increased during the twentieth century, it became more useful to think in terms of an **exchange rate,** or the value of one country's currency in terms of that of another. The American dollar has been accepted as the universal basis of comparison.

Exchange rates can be set by the government. Sometimes a government may decide to devalue its currency, that is, to lower its value in relation to other currencies. **Devaluation,** it is hoped, will mean lower prices for that country's goods in other countries, thus increasing exports. It can stimulate tourism, because visitors from other countries find that travel, goods, and services are cheaper. Residents of the country, on the other hand, will find goods imported from other countries more expensive and will turn to domestic products. Devaluation is usually employed as a desperate measure when a country's economy is in trouble. It rarely, however, provides the miraculous cure that is sought. Exports may increase marginally, but if the quality of goods is not what the international market requires, buyers will still turn else-

exchange rate
The value of one country's currency in terms of that of another

devaluation
Reducing the value of a country's currency in relation to other currencies

where, for example, to goods from Japan and Germany. Indeed, the value of the **revaluation,** or the decision to adjust the value of the currency upward, is a less typical occurrence. The Australian government once revalued its dollar to attract cheaper imports in an attempt to combat severe inflation caused by domestic producers' raising prices.

A government can legislate devaluation or revaluation only if it maintains a *fixed exchange rate.* Problems with fixed exchange rates arise when the international market considers a currency over- or undervalued and begins to discount the value of goods and services implied by the artificially fixed currency. The ruble in the old Russian regime was vastly overvalued by the Communist state. Most countries today work on a **floating exchange rate** determined by international market conditions. This still allows the government to influence exchange rates to some degree through various monetary policies, such as influencing interest rates, as well as some fixed policies.

In recent years, Canada's dollar has fluctuated from a value of $0.75(U.S.) to $0.92(U.S.) and back to $0.75(U.S.) again. Exchange rate changes like these can have considerable impact on trade flows as Canadian goods become cheaper or more expensive for people in Germany, Japan, or Switzerland. As the value of the Canadian dollar fell in the early 1990s, the incidence of "cross-border shopping" by Canadian residents looking for bargains in the United States dropped accordingly.

COUNTERTRADE

Many countries from the former Communist bloc and less developed countries wish to buy goods and have goods to trade, but no foreign currency. Companies wishing to do business in such countries sometimes use **countertrade,** accepting goods for their products instead of money, and then sell the goods themselves in other markets. For example, in recent years Spar Aerospace has sold Brazilian-made Volkswagen Beetle spare parts in the United States and mangoes in Toronto.

This practice of international bartering has grown considerably in the past few years. It is estimated that it now affects approximately 10 percent of world trade.

A typical countertrade agreement requires the seller to also purchase something from the buyer. For example, Versatile Farm Equipment might sell sugar cane harvesters to Cuba from their plant in Australia. However, in order to get the business, Versatile could be required to purchase an equivalent value of sugar from Cuba. Versatile would then have to use an agent to sell the sugar to another country before it could receive remuneration in the form of currency. Countertrade is a common feature of East–West trade. It is not always easy to implement, and adds extra work to consummating a deal.

Countertrade was the key that unlocked a major export deal in Europe for one Ontario manufacturing company. In Poland, Vulcan Equipment secured a $1 million order for tire repair equipment with a countertrade deal for coal through a Danish trading house. The coal

revaluation
Raising the value of a country's currency in relation to other currencies

floating exchange rate
An exchange rate determined by international market conditions

countertrade
Accepting goods for products instead of money and then selling the goods themselves in other markets

was sold in Denmark and funds were then released to Vulcan. Normal after-sales service and training were arranged by the company on a regular commercial basis.

WHY INTERNATIONAL BUSINESS?

We all know that international trade has grown steadily throughout the ages and has grown by leaps and bounds in the twentieth century as transportation and communications have become easier and cheaper. But is this really a good idea? Would it not be better for countries to maintain at least some degree of self-sufficiency?

The Argument for Self-Sufficiency

When a country is committed to self-sufficiency, it insists on producing to meet as much of its needs as possible within its borders. Israel is one such country. The former Soviet Union attempted to produce all essential goods to avoid any dependence on non-communist countries. Sometimes countries aim for self-sufficiency in certain specific commodities. For example, Canada focusses on the development of energy sources as a long-term strategic goal.

The motive for self-sufficiency is usually more political than economic. Countries that consider military and economic reprisals from other countries a real danger are likely to emphasize nationalism and self-reliance. They see the possible economic advantages of purchasing abroad goods that are difficult to produce at home as contributing less to national welfare than the non-economic advantages of overall self-sufficiency.

The Argument for Specialization

New Zealand has a climate and terrain ideally suited to raising sheep, while Hong Kong's estimated 6 million people live in a small area that has become one of the most urbanized territories in the world. Hong Kong is a world trader as well as a source of foreign exchange for the People's Republic of China. Kuwait has rich oil fields but few other industries or resources.

By doing what it does best, each country is able to exchange goods it does not need at home for goods it cannot produce as efficiently. This leads to a higher standard of living than the country would have if it tried to be self-sufficient. This does not mean that the country need have an **absolute advantage** in the goods it produces—that it can produce them better or more cheaply than any other country in the world or if it holds a monopoly with respect to a particular product. Indeed, such a situation is extremely rare. What the country does need to exploit is **comparative advantage** in the goods it produces—those that can be produced relatively more cheaply than other goods per unit of input.

It makes sense for countries to devote their resources to the production and export of goods that give them the most comparative advantage or the least comparative disadvantage. It is also to be expected that countries will concentrate on importing goods that give them the least comparative advantage or the greatest comparative disadvantage.

absolute advantage
Being able to produce a class of goods better or more cheaply than another country

comparative advantage
Being able to produce one class of goods better or more cheaply than other goods

How could a country benefit from trade with another country that has absolute advantage in producing products? The key to the answer is comparative advantage. The theory of comparative advantage was initially developed by the British economist David Ricardo, back in the early 1800s. The **Ricardo theory** illustrated that two countries can benefit from trade (even if one country is better than the other at producing all items) if each country specializes in its areas of comparative advantage. The reason is that, if each specializes in producing those goods and services in which it has the greatest comparative advantage, both will achieve the most economic output per unit of resources spent on producing the goods.

Ricardo theory
A theory that countries will benefit from trade if each specializes in its areas of comparative advantage

Warren J. Keegan illustrates the concept by citing the example of the famous impresario Billy Rose, who was also the world's fastest typist. He faced a decision: "Should I do my own typing or should I pursue a career as a typist?" The answer to both questions was no, because even though he had an absolute advantage as a typist over all other typists in the world, his *comparative* advantage was as an impresario.[8]

Therefore the theory of comparative advantage concludes that a country can be successful in trading if it specializes in the production of those goods and services in which it has a comparative advantage. The effect of trade is to make each country better off than it would be without trade.

In Canada, export commodities tend to be those in which the country has a comparative advantage. Being an industrialized nation with good natural and agricultural resources, Canada tends to export manufactured items, food products, and natural resources such as wood (see Table 11.4). By contrast, countries with low-cost labour and less developed technology often specialize in products that require a significant amount of labour such as shoes and clothing.

Specialization can produce odd situations. For example, Cherry Valley Duck Farms, a British firm, has a long-term contract to provide Peking ducks to the People's Republic of China. The British ducks grow and breed faster than their Chinese counterparts, so they will be used to upgrade the local variety of Peking duck. Water-poor Saudi Arabia once spent $1 million on a feasibility study on hauling Antarctic icebergs to one of their ports. The Saudis and other Middle Eastern nations found it more practical to buy fresh water from Japan: tankers bringing oil to Japan are loaded with water for the return trip.

Specialization and trade benefit countries by enabling more production and generating more income. They also benefit the world economy because they result in economies of scale and can help to lower prices.

CANADA'S TRADE PICTURE

The tables that follow provide an overview of the extent of Canada's trade in merchandise, its principal trading partner, and the commodities it imports and exports.

Merchandise trade, both exports and imports, has grown steadily, as shown in Table 11.2. Canada has had a positive balance of trade in each of the years reported. It dipped to only $3,510 million in 1989, but rebounded in subsequent years.

Table 11.3, Merchandise Trade by Principal Trading Areas, shows that the United States accounts for the vast majority of Canada's exports and imports. A total of 77.62 percent of exports are to the United States, and 70.65 percent of imports are from the same country. The next-largest exports are to the European Community and Japan (5.22 and 4.53 percent, respectively). These same two areas account for the next-highest imports as well.

The same table shows the balance of trade by trading area. Here, the importance of the United States to Canada is more striking. It is the only principal trading area with which we have a positive balance. This balance is large enough to make up for the negative balance with the other areas and leave Canada with an overall positive balance of trade.

Tables 11.4 and 11.5 provide an overview of the type of goods that we export and import. Canada's largest export group is automotive products (24.14 percent). This is followed closely by machinery and equipment and industrial goods and materials (19.96 and 18.71 percent, respectively). Note that agriculture and fishing products and energy products are each about half the size of the largest export groups, but forestry products is the fourth-largest category of exports.

In the case of imports, the largest grouping is industrial goods and materials (31.08 percent). Automotive products is the next-most-important category (22.81 percent), which gives Canada a modest positive balance of trade in automotive products.

A large portion of Canada's exports are manufactured goods, which is an advantage because more jobs are normally created in manufacturing than in most natural-resource extraction.

Canada needs its positive balance of merchandise trade to counteract a generally negative balance in investment income and services. Because of Canada's high government debts to overseas lenders and the high proportion of Canadian industry owned by foreign interests that take their profits out of the country, the balance of payments (the combined balance of trade and investment income and services) is negative.

TABLE 11.2 • MERCHANDISE TRADE OF CANADA

1992	Customs basis		
	Exports	Imports	Balance
1986	120,670	112,511	8,159
1987	125,087	116,239	8,848
1988	138,498	131,172	7,326
1989	138,701	135,191	3,510
1990	148,912	136,245	12,667
1991	145,660	135,365	10,295
1992	162,121	147,866	14,255

Source: Statistics Canada, Catalogue 65-001P, December 1992, p. 13. Reproduced by authority of the Minister of Industry, 1994.

TABLE 11.3 • MERCHANDISE TRADE BY PRINCIPAL TRADING AREAS

1992   Balance of payments basis, seasonally adjusted

	Year to date total ($ millions)	%	Change over previous year ($ millions)
Exports to:			
United States	122,288	77.62	14,671
United Kingdom	3,065	1.95	52
EC excl. U.K.	8,227	5.22	–196
Japan	7,135	4.53	322
Other OECD*	3,236	2.05	753
Other countries	13,599	8.63	2.19
Total	157,549	100	15,821
Imports from:			
United States	104,610	70.65	10,876
United Kingdom	4,023	2.72	–278
EC excl. U.K.	9,446	6.38	–217
Japan	8,839	5.97	154
Other OECD*	4,532	3.06	84
Other countries	16,613	11.22	1,495
Total	148,063	100	12,115
Balance with:			
United States	17,678		3,794
United Kingdom	–958		330
EC excl. U.K.	–1,219		21
Japan	–1,705		168
Other OECD*	–1,296		–1,276
Other countries	–3,014		–1,276
Total	9,487		3,706

*Series not seasonally adjusted
— does not meet criteria for seasonal adjustment.
Note: EC includes: Belgium, Denmark, France, Germany, Greece, Ireland, Italy, Luxembourg, Netherlands, Portugal, Spain and the United Kingdom. Other OECD includes: Austria, Finland, Iceland, Norway, Sweden, Switzerland, Turkey, Australia, and New Zealand. (The EC countries, United States, Japan, and Canada are also members of the OECD.)

Source: Statistics Canada, Catalogue 65-001P, December 1992, p. 14.
      Reproduced by authority of the Minister of Industry, 1994.

TABLE 11.4 • EXPORTS BY COMMODITY GROUPINGS

1992   Balance of payments basis

	Year to date	
	Value ($ millions)	% of total
Agricultural and fishing products	14,856	9.43
Wheat	4,177	
Other agricultural and fishing products	10,679	
Energy products	15,674	9.95
Crude petroleum	5,954	
Natural gas	4,756	
Other energy products	4,964	
Forestry products	21,286	13.51
Lumber and sawmill products	7,980	
Woodpulp and other wood products	4,851	
Newsprint and other paper and paperboard	8,455	
Industrial goods and materials	29,476	18.71
Metal ores	4,129	
Chemicals, plastics, and fertilizers	7,531	
Metals and alloys	12,009	
Other industrial goods and materials	5,807	
Machinery and equipment	31,450	19.96
Industrial and agricultural machinery	6,176	
Aircraft and other transportation equipment	6,511	
Other machinery and equipment	18,763	
Automotive products	38,834	24.14
Passenger autos and chassis	17,786	
Trucks and other motor vehicles	10,205	
Motor vehicle parts	10,043	
Other consumer goods	3,873	2.46
Special transactions trade	3,340	2.12
Unallocated adjustments	–441	(0.28)
Total	157,549	100

Source: Statistics Canada, Catalogue 65-001P, December 1992, p. 15. Reproduced by authority of the Minister of Industry, 1994.

TABLE 11.5 • IMPORTS BY COMMODITY GROUPINGS

1992   Balance of payments basis

	Year to date	
	Value ($ millions)	% of total
Agricultural and fishing products	9,731	6.57
Fruits and vegetables	3,251	
Other agricultural and fishing products	6,481	
Energy products	6,374	4.30
Crude petroleum	4,072	
Other energy products	2,302	
Forestry products	1,386	0.94
Industrial goods and materials	27,105	18.31
Metals and metal ores	6,579	
Chemicals and plastics	9,284	
Other industrial goods and materials	11,241	
Machinery and equipment	46,020	31.08
Industrial and agricultural machinery	11,367	
Aircraft and other transportation equipment	5,071	
Office machines and equipment	7,995	
Other machinery and equipment	21,587	
Automotive products	33,776	22.81
Passenger autos and chassis	11,679	
Trucks and other motor vehicles	3,699	
Motor vehicle parts	18,398	
Other consumer goods	18,932	12.79
Apparel and footwear	3,915	
Miscellaneous consumer goods	15,017	
Special transactions trade	4,075	2.75
Unallocated adjustments	664	0.45
Total	148,063	100

Source: Statistics Canada, Catalogue 65-001P, December 1992, p. 16.
    Reproduced by authority of the Minister of Industry, 1994.

BUSINESS REVIEW 11.3

1. Explain the concepts of absolute advantage and comparative advantage.
2. Discuss Canada's current trade picture. Comment on the proportions of exports to each trading area.

CANADIAN BUSINESS OR GLOBAL COMPETITION?

A Canadian business person might read the numerous concepts in this chapter and conclude that business within Canada is enough of a challenge in itself. This is a big country with many opportunities without looking beyond our borders. Many firms have done this successfully.

However, today's trends are increasingly making confining operations to Canada a less desirable option. The facts of globalization have created a situation where the local business is competing with international competitors right in the home market. The economies of scale that such international competitors bring to the market can make it very difficult for the firm with a small localized market base.

On the other hand, the fact that so many Canadian firms have been successful in the international marketplace is a great incentive to others to become involved. The opportunities for the firm are multiplied many times. International business is exciting and can be very rewarding. The issue is not one of ability, but one of vision.

INTERACTIVE SUMMARY AND DISCUSSION QUESTIONS

1. In the vignette at the beginning of this module, CCL Industries found that the Free Trade Agreement (FTA) was "the worst and best thing that ever happened" to them. Explain what Mr. McLeod meant, and apply the logic of this statement to the situations of other Canadian companies. Outline the pros and cons of the FTA for Canadian business.

2. Globalization is a trend that is altering the map of world business. Explain how this is happening.

3. Four main direct modes of going international were discussed in this module. Find examples of four companies in your community that represent these practices.

4. The multinational corporation is a special case of a firm practising foreign production and marketing. Explain.

5. There are a number of important factors to weigh before attempting to market internationally. Suppose that, after graduation, you join a business that is thinking about going international. You are assigned the task of developing an outline of things the firm should consider. What items would be included in this outline?

6. From the example list of important factors suggested for business people wanting to do business in Japan, draw some conclusions as to some factors to consider when doing business in any foreign country.

7. Differentiate between a free trade area, a customs union, and a common market.

8. The exchange rate can make a significant difference in the price of Canadian goods perceived by buyers in another country. Give an example of this with the exchange rate of the Canadian dollar being low in terms of the U.S. dollar, and with it being high. What will happen to trade in each case? Does your conclusion apply to cross-border shopping?

9. If it costs less to produce two products in Canada than in Australia, it still might benefit the two countries if there were trade between them with these products. The reason for this is the concept of comparative advantage. Explain how this can be.

10. Explain how Canada can have a positive balance of trade, and yet a negative balance of payments.

CASE 11.1

FINDING VIABLE BUSINESS OPPORTUNITIES IN UKRAINE

LLOYD DYCK HAS vivid memories of the decision of Ukraine's parliament to break free of the former Soviet Union in the summer of 1991. Calls immediately started pouring in to his company, Brett-Young Seeds Ltd., from Canadians acting on behalf of distant relatives in Ukraine and proposing deals to buy pedigree seed.

"You'd come in every morning and have five or six fax orders on your desk," recalls Dyck, chief executive officer of Brett-Young. "They were going to buy boat loads of grain, but when you asked how they were going to pay for it they wouldn't know what to say."

The eagerness to establish business ties between Ukraine and Canada was understandable. Over one million Canadians trace all or part of their lineage to Ukraine, and many believed the "Old Country" would be the first free-market success story to emerge from the former Soviet Union. Ottawa's decision to be the first government to recognize the new country seemed to signal the dawn of a new era.

Ukraine's rich agricultural land is one of its key assets, and the inefficiency of state-run collective farms made that sector a natural target for Canadian agri-business. But like Dyck's naive would-be customers, the realities of business have clashed with expectations. Today, the stories coming out of Ukraine are of political gridlock, runaway inflation, corruption, poverty, and despair. "Independence was a very monumental event for Ukrainian Canadians," says George Chuchman, an economics professor at the University of Manitoba. "I think a lot of that sentimentality has melted away or been tempered."

Chuchman is a frequent visitor to Ukraine and is bullish on its long-term prospects, but many business people are pulling back. Among that number are several members of Agri-Tec Canada Inc., a consortium of Western Canadian agri-businesses set up to sell Canadian expertise in agriculture abroad.

The problem encountered by Dyck's company—a member of the Agri-Tec consortium—was the constantly changing cast of characters it had to deal with. "We had numerous people we made contact with, negotiated with, then you find a month later they're gone and you have to start all over again," Dyck says.

Many potential partners or customers in former Soviet states don't seem to understand some of the basic language of business, says Al Roberts of Roberts, Sloane and Associates Inc., a Winnipeg engineering firm and Agri-Tec member. They consider a company that's only barely breaking even to be a success without giving any thought to its ability to generate a return on investments.

Another Agri-Tec member, Central Canadian Structures Ltd., has been active for several years in both Russia and Ukraine but is also scaling back. A general contracting firm, Central Canadian, has extensive experience in the kinds of storage and processing systems used to handle grain, feed, fertilizer, and other bulky dry goods.

Those systems would have a very short pay-back period in a country like Ukraine, where upwards of 30 percent of its grain crop is allowed to spoil. "Unfortunately, the Ukrainian economy is not really in shape to support that kind of infrastructure [investment]," says Ossama Abouzeid, senior vice-president of Central Canadian.

Part of the problem is the lack of hard currency and lack of incentive for farmers and farm managers to become more efficient, says Abouzeid. "People can't seem to see that grain that rots because of poor storage could be saved and sold abroad to earn much-needed foreign exchange," he adds. These days Central Canadian has adopted a wait-and-see attitude and has limited itself to building projects funded by agencies from outside Ukraine.

(continued)

But the picture is not as bleak as it seems, Chuchman says. He admits the problems are many. Former Communist bosses remain in place; government's timid approach to reform has failed; the amount of red tape is frightful; and graft and corruption are widespread. "You hear all these bleak stories, but if you go there you find economic activity going on everywhere," Chuchman says. "People are coping."

Coping takes a variety of forms. In summer, large cities nearly empty as people head to the country to tend to their gardens. As a result, most people have a large enough store of produce to see them through the winter, he says. With inflation running around 70 percent a month and the karbovanet currency nearly worthless, businesses take to large-scale bartering—like the man Chuchman met who was starting a furniture factory in western Ukraine. "He needed foam rubber for cushions," Chuchman recalls. "So he lined up some lumber and shipped that to a firm in central Ukraine in exchange for foam."

Still Chuchman is quick to say that the government's reluctance to apply free-market "shock therapy" has been a failure, and he is critical of what he describes as its current retreat to policies from its old command economy.

Ukrainians need only look at neighbouring Poland to see the benefits of market reform, Chuchman notes. Workers in Poland, which underwent rapid privatization and other difficult reforms, earn twenty times what the average government worker in Ukraine makes. As a result, Poland now attracts large numbers of Ukrainians as migrant workers, he says.

Source: Adapted from Glenn Cheater, "Agri-businesses Proceed with Caution," *The Financial Post*, January 8, 1994, p. 12.

Questions for Discussion

1. It appears that firms in the Agri-Tec consortium have adopted a wait-and-see approach to doing business in Ukraine. Do you agree with this?

2. Evaluate the pros and cons of the following for doing business in Ukraine:
   a) licensing
   b) export
   c) joint-venture
   d) wholly owned subsidiary

3. On the basis of the discussion above, can you suggest other business opportunities in Ukraine?

4. "Doing business in other countries is always subject to dangerous and often uncontrollable conditions. The situation found in Ukraine just happens to be a bit more extreme. That is why Canadian firms should really concentrate on making it in the home market." Discuss.

CASE 11.2

CANADA'S FAVOURITE BAR

CANADA'S TOP chocolate-bar maker is trying to take a share of the huge American market. "Canada's favourite bar" is prominently displayed on the U.S. packaging of Crispy Crunch. "That is often enough to persuade people to try the bar," said Howard Bateman, Neilson's vice-president of strategic development.

(continued)

Neilson's move south is the latest step in the company's efforts to become more competitive. Founded in 1894, Neilson has historically been Canada's leading manufacturer of candy bars. Over the past two decades, sales of chocolate bars have levelled off in Canada. In an effort to maintain efficient production levels, the company acquired the Canadian subsidiary of Cadbury Schweppes in 1987 to become the largest manufacturer in the Canadian chocolate business. The Canada–U.S. Free Trade Agreement forced Neilson's next move. Under the 1989 pact, both countries agreed to eliminate tariffs on chocolate-bar exports over ten years. The time was right to tackle the tough but potentially lucrative U.S. market.

The company faced major challenges in vying for a significant portion of the $6.8 billion that Americans spend each year on candy bars. "But to survive in the U.S. market, we had to become more efficient," said Arthur Soler, Neilson's president. The U.S. market is dominated by multinational corporations whose products are a well-entrenched presence on store shelves. "It's a fantastic opportunity," said Mr. Soler.

Neilson's first response was to replace the 75-year-old method of producing Crispy Crunch bars. Thirty-pound lumps of sugar had been hand-tossed and stretched between pairs of employees to give the candy bar its light and flaky filling. This method was time-consuming and labour intensive. Neilson invested $3 million in German-made machinery which stirs and spins the toffee before extruding it in a long, thin ribbon that is flattened, sliced, and coated with chocolate.

The next step was to introduce a Japanese-style production process known as "continuous improvement," designed to encourage ever higher levels of quality. This strategy gives each of the 870 workers the right to stop the production line at any time if they notice a problem. In addition, newly installed machines monitor the quantity, temperature, and consistency of the ingredients to ensure uniformity in the candy bars that roll off the production line.

The next step in trying to ensure Neilson's future was the decision to export. In January 1990, Neilson executives agreed to base their marketing efforts outside Canada on two of their most popular brands—Crispy Crunch and Mr. Big.

In addition to the United States, Neilson began selling the bars in Southeast Asia, where Mr. Big has been renamed Bang Bang. New Zealand and Hong Kong were the next export destinations.

But the challenge of marketing Neilson's products in the United States was far from easy. The number of large retail chains in the United States is far greater than in Canada. "In Canada, we have to make maybe 20 key sales calls," said Howard Bateman. "Down there, there are maybe 20,000."

To avoid having to establish its own U.S. sales force, Neilson formed a partnership with Pro Set Inc. of Dallas, the largest producer of trading cards in the world. Pro Set's 2,500 sales representatives stay in close contact with convenience-store owners and other clients, so it made sense for them to sell another, non-competing product.

The alliance appears to be succeeding. The 7-Eleven convenience-store chain, which has 6,500 U.S. outlets, agreed to carry Crispy Crunch and Mr. Big for one year. And Wal-Mart Stores Inc.— the largest retailer in the United States—agreed to sell the bars for a three-month trial period.

Neilson's proven track record in Canada has made entrance to the American market much easier. To build brand awareness, Neilson plans to begin airing two of its four Canadian television commercials, in which a man and a woman pilfer each other's candy bars, on U.S. television.

Competition in the United States was so severe that announcements about the next market to be covered by advertising had to be guarded. If competitors knew in which cities Neilson would be introducing its products, opposing sales forces would buy up the products in these markets. This would have distorted sales results and prevented Neilson from assessing how effective their sales ads had been.

Source: Adapted from Barbara Wickens, "Sweet Success," *Maclean's*, December 16, 1991, pp. 26.

(continued)

Questions for Discussion

1. In what way does tackling the U.S. market make Neilson more competitive?

2. Suggest social trends/factors that might have caused the stagnation in sales of chocolate bars in Canada over the past two decades.

3. Analyze the steps taken by Neilson to penetrate the U.S. market. Comment on all aspects of the program discussed.

4. This case described a sales strategy for the U.S. market. How might these steps differ when Neilson Ltd. entered the Asian market? the New Zealand market? the other markets approached by Neilson?

5. Mr. Big was renamed Bang Bang in Asia. Why? What might be an alternative name for the Crispy Crunch bar in Asia?

NOTES

1. David Estok, "Firms Restructuring for a Global Market," *The Financial Post,* January 9, 1989, p. 11.

2. Estok, "Firms Restructuring for a Global Market," p. 11.

3. Myron Love, "Gemini Shines in the Western Sky," *Style,* March 25, 1986, p. 144.

4. This section is adapted from Geoff Nimmo and Michael MacDonald, *Export Guide: A Practical Approach* (Ottawa: Department of Foreign Affairs and International Trade), pp. 3–4.

5. Adapted from "Social Studies, A Daily Miscellany of Information: Body Language," *The Globe and Mail,* April 20, 1992, p. A14.

6. Sylvia Ostry, "In Praise of GATT—and a Warning on the Long Term Implications of Protectionism," *The Financial Post,* March 9, 1985, p. 48.

7. Catherine Harris, "Exports to Aid Anemic Recovery," *The Financial Post,* February 20, 1993, p. 7.

8. Warren J. Keegan, *Global Marketing Management* (Englewood Cliffs, N.J.: Prentice Hall, 1989), p. 25.

PHOTO CREDITS

MODULE
◆ INF ◆

INFORMATION IN THE ELECTRONIC AGE

THE FOCUS OF THIS MODULE

1. To identify major sources of information for management decisions

2. To describe the evolution of computers in processing and transmitting information

3. To discuss the role of computers in management

4. To define the difference between quantitative and qualitative data and between primary and secondary data

5. To outline the marketing research process

6. To identify methods of collecting primary data and when each might be used

7. To learn the meaning of the following terms:

KEY TERMS

spread sheet analysis

word processing

universal product code

debit card

networking

interactive voice
technology (IVT)

quantitative data

qualitative data

transaction processing
system (TPS)

management information
system (MIS)

marketing research

secondary data

internal data

external data

primary data

census

sample

probability sample

AS LONG AS people have conducted business, they have kept records for future reference—on clay tablets, on parchment, on paper. They have also processed the facts that these records contain into manageable information—with the aid of tally sticks, abacuses, slide rules, and calculators. Pen computing is only one of the more recent ways business people can gain access to existing information and record and process new facts.

Information is the basis for all management decisions. The day-to-day course of activities will provide much essential information about the organization itself, its employees, and the efficiency of its operations. A study of the firm's accounts provides a scorecard of the financial transactions that have occurred so that managers can understand the current position on which they will build future plans. Marketing research is used to answer such questions as "How will consumers like our new product?," "Where should we locate the new franchise?," and "What are people's attitudes to our advertising?"

Reams of data are available from within the organization, from public sources, from the organization's everyday contacts in the external environment, and from its more formal research efforts. But a mass of facts is no use until it is organized into an understandable form. Only when a manager is able to find and use relevant data do they become useful business information.

The compilation and analysis of data to provide useful information have always been part of business. Business people today, however, have a tool that has given them access to more data and speeded up the process of analysis to a degree that would have been unbelievable even 50 years ago. That tool is the electronic computer.

COMPUTERS IN MANAGEMENT

If the processing of information is difficult and limited, the kinds of analyses available for management decision making are severely restricted. Imagine the problem of analyzing by hand a survey of 1,000 automobile owners' preferences and buying behaviour. If and when you got through all the manual organization and tabulation of data, your information would be outdated and you would need another survey. The task is trivial for a computer. And managers have found many other invaluable applications of computer technology to virtually every corner of a business.

The Transition of Information Processing

The transformation of business from the manual era of pencils, hand calculations, and mechanical tabulating machines to the computer era was accelerated by war. In 1944, IBM Corporation, working closely with the U.S. Navy, built the Mark I, the first real computer. This electromechanical computer—14 metres long and 2.5 metres high—was controlled by punch cards and paper tapes and could perform both arithmetic and logical operations.

The first truly electronic computer was developed two years later. It was called ENIAC (Electronic Numerical Integrator and Computer). By using vacuum tubes rather than the Mark I's electronic relay switches, the ENIAC's calculating speed was increased 1,000 times. In 1954, General Electric became the first business organization to buy a computer (the Sperry UNIVAC I).

More than a decade ago, *Scientific American* suggested that if the aircraft industry had evolved as spectacularly as had the computer industry over the previous 25 years, a Boeing 767 would cost $500 and would circle the globe in 20 minutes on 20 litres of fuel.[1] Since then, computer technology has become even more powerful, cheaper, and more convenient—consider laptop and hand-held microcomputers. With such progress, it is no wonder that the computer has become *the* essential business tool. Its underlying technology has been adapted to applications as diverse as analyzing huge research studies to controlling a production line, or sending information from office to office or around the world in an instant.

Survival in the Third Wave

In *The Third Wave*,[2] Alvin Toffler describes the development of society as coming in three waves. During the first wave, the agricultural age from 8000 B.C. to A.D. 1700, the majority of people worked the earth as farmers, living primarily off what they produced and trading for or purchasing only a few items they did not produce.

The second wave, the industrial age, changed all that with the introduction of different forms of energy and machinery. This wave brought with it bureaucracy and the hierarchical management style that still predominate. Standardization, specialization, and maximization are common goals of the second wave. Order, discipline, and assembly line mentality are other familiar characteristics.

The third wave, the information age, began about 1950 with the advent of the computer. It has grown at an increasing rate since then. In fact, business expert Tom Peters, in an address to the Commonwealth Club in San Francisco, has suggested an actual date for the transition:

The end of the Industrial Revolution can literally be dated to a day in January 1992 when the total stock market value of the Microsoft Corporation surpassed the total stock market value of the General Motors Corporation.

This was the pivotal moment when the "intangibles" of "software, brainware, and knowledge" surged past the "hardware of tangible assets" of the industrial age.[3]

Toffler colourfully suggests that second-wave leaders today are like passengers on the *Titanic* squabbling for deck chairs—a dying fraternity trying to hold on to their position and power while their world sinks under them. Toffler reminds us that most of our current institutions were designed *before* the airplane, the automobile, the factory, and the computer.

Managers who will survive in the third wave have a different perspective. They see information, and the ability to understand and manage it, as the foundation to wise decisions. They have adapted to the computer, which is embedded in every aspect of personal and business life. Beyond this, they have developed the ability to access, understand, and work with information stored in databases. These managers have the interest and ability to regularly work with a personal-computer terminal.

The computer has become a personal productivity tool for them. They regularly and easily turn to stored databases, and have the skills to access the data, as well as to apply relevant analyses to get the most out of such information. Suppose Mara Janessa, a recent college graduate, has been assigned the task of reviewing the package sizing for a line of salad dressings sold by her company. She turns to her computer (always turned on) and from the menu on the screen selects the database that records all sales of that product line, by store type, city, and province. The database also contains details of pricing and profit information by package size. Calling up one or more pre-established models, she inputs the foregoing information. Now she is able to ask "what if" questions—What would be the effect on profits if we consolidated package sizes from five to three? If we eliminated two package sizes, are there any locations where accepted purchase patterns would be disrupted (for example, small package sizes for seniors)? And, based on the model, she is able to forecast the effect of various proposed changes. Within twenty minutes, she has done a thorough analysis of seven options and has a report with recommendations printed out for others in the department to consider.

The foregoing scenario is an example of what is currently unfolding before us. We are in an information age based on computer technology that has been incorporated into the fabric of life. The routine use of the ubiquitous computer, as seen on *Star Trek: The Next Generation*, is not far away.

BUSINESS APPLICATIONS OF COMPUTERS

The information processing systems that managers are beginning to use are evolving from the current basic business applications of the computer, such as accounting, data analysis, word processing, production, and transfer of information, that are routine in many organizations.

Accounting

One of the earliest and most widespread uses of computers in business has been storage and processing of numerical records. In repetitive work such as payroll accounting, inventory management, and billing, the speed and accuracy of the computer have been put to good use. The computer's memory can also assist management by supplying data on performance. For example, it can report on sales for each geographic region, for each product and brand, and for each type of customer.

Data Analysis

The speed of the computer has opened the door to new research methods in the laboratory and in marketing research. The availability of highly sophisticated software enables complex analyses of enormous masses of data, allowing researchers to ask questions that were inconceivable earlier. Thus, the main challenge for the user is to understand the strengths and limitations of the statistical procedures available.

Spread sheet analysis is a special business application that has found universal use in management. An electronic spread sheet is created that allows the manager to array numerical information in

spread sheet analysis
A computer application that allows one to arrange related numerical information in columns and rows and to demonstrate the result of manipulation of certain figures

columns and rows, and then to apply mathematical operations to the data. For example, once a column of figures is listed, simple commands are available to add, subtract, or otherwise manipulate the figures.

The features of such electronic spread sheets allow the manager to ask "what if" questions by means of a few key strokes. For example, in a spread sheet portraying next year's budget projections for product A, you could ask, "What would be the effect on our returns of cutting price by 5 percent?" By changing one number, you would be able to recalculate the entire budget almost instantly.

Word Processing

The volume of written communications is massive, and costly. There is always a need for more efficient methods of handling communications such as routine letters to customers, reports, and business proposals needing specific modifications for a particular client. These activities can be handled faster and more efficiently by the use of word processing systems.

Word processing is the use of computers to store, retrieve, view, edit, and print text material. By inputing information into a computer using word processing software, the operator can easily revise sentences, correct errors, and print out individual letters or reports, as needed. Personalized letters designed to respond to customer inquiries, to remind credit purchasers of overdue accounts, or to notify an entire address list of potential customers of a new product can be created by combining stored names and addresses, sentences, and paragraphs.

word processing
The use of computers to store, retrieve, view, edit, and print text material

Production

Computers have also taken over many production jobs that formerly were performed by hand. Continuous-process operations, such as petroleum refineries, are often run entirely by computers. At each stage of the refining process, information on pressure of flows, temperature, and the like is fed into a computer. This information is then used by the computer to send instructions to machinery that will change the temperature, increase or decrease the pressure, or take whatever action is needed to control the refining process.

Automobile manufacturers use hundreds of computers in their production operations. Each automobile can have as many as 12,000 component parts, and computers are used to make certain that the right part is in the right place at the right time. Other computers test the engines, fuel injection systems, brakes, and other machine parts. The automobiles themselves will have computers to operate such systems as cruise control.

In other industries, computers are also at work, monitoring glass-manufacturing plants, blast furnaces, paper machines, pulp digesters, nuclear power plants, and warehouse inventory.

Retailing

In many stores, the cashier punches in a bunch of numbers that seem to bear no relation to the price of the item. This is the **universal product code**, and it enters the price and inventory number into a computer, enabling the retailer not only to give you an itemized receipt but

universal product code
A series of numbers and electronically scannable bars that identify a product and its price, used to record sales and maintain inventory

also to know immediately its sales and inventory position. Supermarket scanner checkout systems that read the numbers on a series of bars are even more efficient (and more expensive—costing between $100,000 and $150,000 per store). Despite the costs, the increase in efficiency makes it worthwhile.

A more primitive version of computer inventory control is still used in many clothing stores. A complicated price tag is attached to suits dresses, and sportswear, showing the price but also including several punched holes and numbers. When the article of clothing is sold, the salesperson tears off the tag and deposits it in a special box. The tags are actually computer punch cards identifying the article of clothing and its cost and colour as well as the store and department. At the end of the day, these tags are collected and taken to the computer centre. Processing them allows inventory in the store to be controlled automatically. When inventory reaches a certain level, new shipments can be made to stores, minimizing the possibility of running out of popular items.

debit card
An encoded card that allows purchases to be deducted directly from a customer's bank account

The **debit card** is another piece of computer technology that is finding its way into some retail stores. A customer can "swipe" his or her card through a device at the checkout counter and enter his or her personal identification number on a special key pad. As soon as the number is entered, the amount shown on the cash register is debited directly to the customer's bank account and credited directly to the retailer's account. This process saves the customer having to carry much cash; writing a cheque; or using a credit card, which can lead to heavy interest charges if the account is not paid off promptly. And, of course, the retailer does not have to deposit the cash, process the cheque, or wait for payment by the credit card company.

Transfer of Information

Most business information now resides within computers, allowing easy analysis, formulation, and production of information for further business decisions. If this information is needed elsewhere, why should it be transferred to paper and re-entered in another machine? For many years, computer manufacturers deliberately made their machines incompatible with others in the hope of ensuring customer loyalty. Having discovered that modern uses of the computer mean that incompatibility leads only to customer frustration, the computer industry has now largely overcome compatibility problems between computers and other connecting hardware.

Within organizations, local area networks (LAN) connect various types of computers and enable information to be readily transferred by means of electronic mail. Any member of an LAN can instantly alert all other users—"There will be a department meeting tomorrow at 9:00 a.m."

networking
Transferring information electronically from one computer to another, either within an organization through a local area network (LAN) or between organizations and cities, or around the world

Between organizations, **networking** figures more and more prominently in company plans. It is becoming increasingly easy to sit down at your computer, press a few keys, and transmit information from one city to another, or around the world, in a matter of seconds. For example, Peter Maurice, president of Canada Trustco Mortgage Co., has said, "With our system I can sit at my cottage and access almost all of the information at Canada Trust."[4] This author communicated regularly by computer with his secretary in Canada while visiting Australia. Networking is here, but its development is not yet complete. As business reaches around the globe, the demand for easier access to more networking facilities is also growing.

More and more organizations are installing computers as part of their telephone systems. **Interactive voice technology (IVT)**, or "voice mail," not only allows a computer to answer the phone and store incoming calls but also enables system members to send and receive messages to and from other system members. Thus, voice memos replace paper memos.

Customers can speed the process of getting to the right person or department when they call a company using IVT. Customers are offered a menu of responses by the computer, each keyed to a number on the key pad of a touch-tone telephone: "Press one for your account balance, two for your record of payments...," and so forth. Operators can take more time to handle non-routine calls.

Many university and college students have also benefited from IVT when registering for courses. Frustrated students no longer have to shuttle between buildings when they discover that admissions to a desired course are closed. The entire process can be done through interacting with the computer on the telephone. Almost all major universities in Canada either have or are shopping for a system. "I can't think of a single innovation that had such a happy impact on campus," said Hugh King, associate registrar of schedules at the University of Alberta.[5]

interactive voice technology (IVT)
A computerized telephone system that answers, directs, and stores incoming calls and enables members to send and receive messages within the system

TYPES OF INFORMATION AND INFORMATION SYSTEMS

Computers and well-designed software can help managers organize data into useful information in a number of areas. Accounting, production processes, and inventory control are only some of the more obvious. If the proper data have been recorded, managers can also gain access to information that answers many questions. Computers, however, cannot substitute for managerial decision making, as the following list of typical business questions makes clear.

1. Is machine No. 3 about to break down again?
   How much has it cost to repair it in the last six months?
   Is it really worn out or does its operator not know how to use it properly?
   Is it receiving proper maintenance?
   Is it worth repairing or should it be replaced?
   If replacement is the answer, should the same model be ordered or is there a machine available on the market that is better suited to the job?
2. Is the order department communicating adequately with the warehouse?
   What is the proportion of returned merchandise?
   Why is it returned?
   Is the problem design flaws in the product? unrealistic expectations created by sales representatives or advertising? damage during shipping?

3. What contingency plans should we make to counter the possibility of decreased productivity in the accounting and human resources departments while their facilities are being renovated?

How disruptive will the process actually be?

How many offices and workstations will be affected at any one time? Should we expect employees simply to put up with the noise and confusion as best they can?

Should we rent space in a nearby office building and move the entire department into temporary quarters?

How much will that cost? Is it feasible to ask some members of the department to work at home during the renovations?

What extra equipment will they need? What will be the cost of providing them with computers, fax machines, and/or modems?

Will they be able to perform adequately without regular supervision or face-to-face contact with other employees?

What distractions will they face in the home environment?

While the computer can provide answers to some of these questions, others require a different sort of approach. A computer can assist in decision making by handling **quantitative data**, facts that can be expressed in terms of numbers. It cannot, however, deal with more nebulous **qualitative data**, which can be analyzed only through judgement and experience. And, of course, the most important factor in management is knowing which questions to ask.

Computer hardware and software have evolved from the starting point of **transaction processing systems (TPS)** that reduce clerical work by carrying out routine functions, such as billing customers, placing orders, and recording receipts and payments, through to **management information systems (MIS)** that assist decision making by summarizing changes in accounts receivable, inventory levels, loans outstanding, cash on hand, customers, product lines, profitability of particular divisions, quality of materials, and employee turnover. Software designers continuously refine programs to make information analysis and presentations easier to assist in strategic decision making. For example, easily understandable data analysis, charts, and graphs can be produced by most programs.

MARKETING RESEARCH

Business information is important in all aspects of the enterprise. Perhaps the most fundamental information is that which concerns the

quantitative data
Facts that can be expressed in terms of numbers

qualitative data
Facts that cannot be expressed in terms of numbers but must be analyzed through judgement and experience

transaction processing system (TPS)
A computer system that handles routine functions such as billing, ordering, and recording receipts and payments

management information system (MIS)
A computer system that collects and organizes information to assist managerial decision making

---

BUSINESS REVIEW 12.1

Discuss the similarities and differences between

a) manual and electronic data systems

b) data and information

c) quantitative and qualitative data

d) transaction processing systems and management or executive information systems

organization's mission or reason for existence and the goods or services it supplies to the clients who need them.

How does a business know whether its marketing plans are likely to be successful? Marketing research has become an indispensable tool for many organizations in ensuring business success through positive market response to their offerings. **Marketing research** is the systematic gathering, recording, and analysis of data about problems relating to the marketing of goods and services. After the research problem has been defined, the marketing research process starts with a search of secondary data. This step is followed by the collection of primary data, then all data are analyzed and normally presented in a final report.

marketing research
The systematic gathering, recording, and analysis of data relating to the marketing of products

SECONDARY DATA

Secondary data offer an extremely important source of management information. **Secondary data** are data that have already been collected for other purposes. They are therefore an inexpensive and fairly readily available source of information. **Internal data** are data generated within the organization. A tremendous amount of useful information is available from financial records. Data can be obtained on changes in accounts receivable, inventory levels, loans outstanding, cash on hand, customers, product lines, profitability of particular divisions, or comparisons of sales by territories, salespeople, customers, or product lines. These records provide important insights into business operations. And because they are collected on a regular basis, these data can be added to the firm's management information system (MIS) at a low cost.

secondary data
Data that have already been collected for other purposes

internal data
Data generated within the organization

Although much of the internal information is financial, other kinds of information input are also available. The human resource department can supply data on employee turnover and on worker attitudes and suggestions. Quality control can supply information on the quality levels of materials purchased and the rejection rate of the firm's products. Customer complaint letters can serve as another information input.

External data are data generated outside the firm by sources other than the company itself. Although considerable amounts of secondary data are available internally, even more are available from external sources. So much is available at little or no cost that the information manager faces the problem of being overwhelmed by the sheer quantity.

external data
Data generated by sources other than the organization itself

Government Sources

The various levels of government are the nation's most important sources of secondary data; one of the most frequently used is census data. Although Statistics Canada spends large sums in conducting each census of population, as well as other statistics, the information is available for use without charge at local libraries, or it can be purchased on computer tapes for a nominal fee. The census of population is so detailed that population characteristics for large cities are available by city block. Data are available on age, sex, race, citizenship, educational levels, occupation, employment status, and income.

Statistics Canada also collects and publishes data on finance, commerce, manufacturing, construction, primary industries, transportation, employment, education, culture, health and welfare, and prices.

To help users find the right information the agency produces a guidebook, the *Statistics Canada Catalogue*. Businesses can subscribe to its publications in their particular area of concern. Firms may also subscribe to CANSIM (Canada Socio-Economic Information Management System). CANSIM uses government statistics and other data to create a computerized database that provides much significant information for business decision making in such matters as overall size and regional distribution of the market, and trends in various segments. Developing Your Business Skills discusses the services that Statistics Canada provides to help business people turn the agency's data into valuable business information.

Provincial and city governments are still other important sources of information on employment, production, and sales activities within a particular province or city.

Private Sources

A number of private organizations provide information for business decision makers. Trade associations are excellent resource centres for their members. They often publish journals or newsletters containing information on production costs and wages in the industry and suggestions for improving operations. Advertising agencies continually collect information on the audiences reached by various media such as magazines, television, and radio.

Several national firms offer information to businesses on a subscription basis. The A.C. Nielsen Company collects data every 60 days on the sales of most products stocked in food stores and drugstores. The Conference Board of Canada publishes the *Handbook of Canadian Consumer Markets. The Financial Post* publishes an annual *Survey of Markets,* which provides extensive demographic and business data on provinces, cities, and counties. *Sales and Marketing Management* magazine publishes an annual *Survey of Buying Power,* which provides detailed information on population, income, and retail sales in cities

DEVELOPING YOUR BUSINESS SKILLS

USING STATISTICS CANADA INFORMATION

A trip to one of the Statistics Canada Regional Offices in St. John's, Halifax, Ottawa, Toronto, Winnipeg, Regina, Calgary, Edmonton, or Vancouver can be like a trip to a nicely laid out, price-smart retail operation: one generally leaves with more goodies than originally intended. It's best first to purchase the current Statistics Canada catalogue. This guide briefly describes publications on statistics ranging from demographics to sales of running shoes. The 1993 Statistics Canada catalogue is available for $13.95 plus GST.

The *Daily* is the official release vehicle of StatsCan data and publications. At a glance, it provides highlights of newly released data with source information for more detailed facts. It contains schedules of upcoming major releases and announces new products and services. A subscription costs $120 per year, or $0.90 per issue.

(continued)

The Infomat is published every Friday, runs six to eight pages, and complements *The Daily*, providing more in-depth analysis that focusses on recent trends. A subscription costs $125 per year, or $2.50 per issue.

Canadian Economic Observer, Statistics Canada's flagship publication for economic statistics, presents a monthly summary of the economy and major economic events. A statistical summary contains a wide range of tables and graphs on the principal economic indicators for Canada, the provinces, and the major industrial nations.

A major StatsCan effort is the *Canada Yearbook*. A Herculean feat of compilation, it is targeted at schools, universities, and businesses with library facilities. There is no area of Canadian endeavour not measured or documented in this tome. The 1994 *Canada Yearbook* cost $59.95 plus GST. *Canada: A Portrait*, more general in scope and not as large, costs $34.95.

If your eyes tire after scanning the multitude of information, the telephone is a useful alternative. There is no charge for data gathered by phone, so long as the request is for data that are readily accessible and brief. You are welcome to visit the Reference Centre, which is open to the public. The automated telephone service also provides recorded information on labour force, population, and the consumer price index.

When the information is more difficult to track down and assemble, the agency's cost-recovery plan kicks in. The minimum charge for researching and supplying relevant information is $30 per hour.

For more detailed needs, a StatsCan consultant can plug you into the Canadian Socio-Economic Information Management System (CANSIM). You can gain quick access to customized information on complex economic or demographic data and have it downloaded onto your own system. For example, an *ad hoc* retrieval would cost approximately $40 and up.

Regional offices offer another service. They will prepare an official letter on behalf of anyone hammering out a salary contract or moving arrangement with an employer. It will confirm changes in the consumer price index, for example, to support a pay increase. In the eyes of most Canadians, when StatsCan puts its name at the bottom of a page of information, the debate on its accuracy ends there. An official letter costs $30.

Source: Adapted from Evan Thompson, "The StatsCan Catalogue," *Canadian Business*, December 1988, p. 130.

and counties for each Canadian province and each state in the United States. Moody's, Dun & Bradstreet, and Standard & Poor's provide financial information about companies on a subscription basis.

PRIMARY DATA

Secondary data provide a useful background of information and may even provide most of the answers to a particular research question. Often, however, a marketing manager will have more specific questions that can be answered only through new research. **Primary data** are facts collected for the first time. Most primary data are collected by one of three methods—survey, experimentation, or observation. The choice depends on information needed, costs, and time.

Considerable expertise is required in collecting primary data. Many firms have research departments staffed with specialists in designing questionnaires, training interviewers, developing representative samples, and interpreting the findings of the research study. Other organizations hire specialized research firms to handle specific projects.

primary data
Data collected for the first time for a specific purpose

This resarcher for Market Research Associates is conducting a survey in a Halifax shopping mall. The researcher approaches volunteers in the mall to ask them specific questions prepared for the questionnaire. The data collected from this survey may, if properly analyzed, provide retailers with valuable information about the consumers in this particular shopping mall.

Survey Method

Three different techniques can be used in the survey method: telephone, mail, and personal interview. Each has its advantages and disadvantages.

The personal interview is the most expensive and time-consuming survey method. It calls for well-trained and well-paid interviewers and involves the expense of travelling to the respondents' locations. Still, the personal interview is typically the best means of obtaining detailed information, particularly because the interviewer can explain to the respondent any questions that are vague or confusing. The flexibility and detailed information offered by this method often more than offset the time and cost limitations.

Telephone interviews are cheap and fast for obtaining small amounts of relatively impersonal information, but they must be limited to simple, clearly worded questions. Because many firms have some sort of long-distance saving plan, a survey of suppliers' opinions on, say, a proposed payment plan could be conducted quickly and at little expense. Long-distance saving plans include 1-800 numbers that allow a firm to make unlimited numbers of long-distance calls for a fixed rate. Telephone interviews have two major limitations: (1) it is extremely difficult to obtain personal information from respondents, and (2) the survey may be biased because two important groups are omitted—those without telephones and those with unlisted numbers.

In order to develop a representative sample of all telephone subscribers, telephone researchers frequently resort to using random numbers. Here is how it might work. If, for example, a sample of 100 respondents was to be chosen from an area with a 269 phone number prefix, the researcher would develop a list of perhaps 125 four-digit random numbers. Such lists may be obtained from a relatively simple computer-programmed number-generator or from published lists of random numbers. The telephone interviewer would then dial the prefix and the first four-digit number on the list. If that number proved to be busy, the interviewer would simply move to the next number on the list.

Mail interviews allow the researcher to conduct national studies at reasonable costs. Personal interviews with a national sample may prove too costly, but mail interviews allow the researcher to reach each potential respondent for the price of postage. Costs can be misleading, however, because the rate of return of questionnaires in such a study may average only 15 to 25 percent, depending on the length of the questionnaire and on respondent interest. Unless additional information is obtained, through a telephone interview or other method, from those not responding, the results could be biased; there may be important differences between the characteristics of the non-respondents and those who took the time to complete and return the questionnaire.

Companies using mail questionnaires to collect data often try a variety of techniques to increase response rates. Some firms include research questions on warranty cards. TI Corporation received a 60 percent response to its questionnaire to shareholders by printing the questions on the back of dividend cheques. Others use a coin to attract the reader's attention.

Questionnaires are used to record responses from mail and telephone surveys as well as personal interviews. Considerable care should be taken in designing the questionnaire in order to minimize confusion in the respondents. Most researchers pretest questionnaires to detect and correct problems before administering the questionnaire.

Experimental Design

Information from all the foregoing methods can be influenced by extraneous variables, such as the surroundings in which the data were gathered (e.g., receiving a request for a telephone interview when eating dinner), or the interviewer's interpretation of an answer.

Researchers may design experiments to attempt to overcome these problems. An experimental design might assess price sensitivity through simulating purchases of various items in a laboratory using a given amount of money. Such experiments are difficult to set up in a realistic manner, and to control. Where they can be used, however, the information obtained may be some of the most reliable primary data available.

Observation Method

The *observation method* involves studies that are conducted by actually viewing the actions of the respondents either directly or through mechanical devices. Researchers sometimes watch the pattern grocery shoppers travel in a supermarket. Traffic counts are used to determine the best location for a new fast-lube station. The A.C. Nielsen "People Meter" is used to calculate the national television audience. This device not only records when the television set is turned on and what programs are being viewed, but can also indicate which member of the household is watching.

The A.C. Nielsen People Meter is a method of determining television viewership. Respondents indicate their viewing preferences through the use of a remote control unit. The viewing records are stored in a microcomputer and transmitted over the phone lines to the Nielsen computers. Thus, the Nielsen client audience data are available on a daily basis for prime-time programming. This information allows advertisers and television broadcasters to make more informed decisions that may lead to better television program-

SAMPLING IN MARKET RESEARCH

When gathering information, the decision maker is trying to develop an understanding of the entire population being considered. Procter and Gamble may want to know what all mothers think about diapers. The Liberal party may wish to know what most Canadians think about the unemployment insurance system. Information is rarely gathered from all possible sources, however, because the costs are too great. (If all sources are reached, the results are called a **census**.) Instead, the researcher selects a representative group called a **sample**. If the sample is chosen in a random way so that every member of the population has a known chance of being selected, it is called a **probability sample**. Probability samples are also used in quality control to give production control engineers a means to assess the overall quality of the work. A random selection of student names from the list at the registrar's office will provide a probability sample of students at a college or university.

It is common to hear of a Gallup research report that says "88 percent of Canadians think that the government should. . ." Then we

census
A survey of all possible sources of data

sample
A representative group from which data are gathered

probability sample
A representative group selected randomly to give every member of the population an equal chance of inclusion

discover that this finding was based on interviews with a sample of 1,000 Canadians, and the accuracy rate is 95 percent plus or minus 4 percent. How can a sample this size represent 27 million Canadians? Statisticians can prove that a truly random sample yields estimates of the population that cluster toward its true values. And the sampling error of this process can be estimated mathematically.

ISSUES IN BUSINESS 12.1

INFORMATION: PRIVACY OR PIRACY?

USE AND OWNERSHIP of information is now a major concern. Who owns what, and who has the rights to use it?

Arguments about privacy, ownership, and even free trade have taken on new life in the information age.

Over the past two decades, governments have passed laws on the use and abuse of computers. But none has yet come to grips with the underlying problem: how to devise rules on what is and is not acceptable in the way information flows between people.

Are information users pirates stealing valuable privacy from their victims?

Classified documents and private papers kept in a locked file are protected from theft by the law of trespass. But classified documents kept in a computer can be read by someone who never even leaves home.

In the developed world, the majority of people earn their living by dealing in ideas. Stealing a car means that the thief has something which the owner does not: namely, the car. "Stealing" an idea means that the "thief" and the "owner" both have exactly the same thought.

Ideas, unlike cars, can be dismantled in intriguing ways. A computerized list of the names of the vicars of the Church of England would in itself pose no big risk to privacy. However, the same list cross-indexed with a list of the mail-order customers of Sleaze-O-Rama would be a high privacy hazard.

Information is slippery stuff. Questions of how to control its flow have always been controversial. The use and abuse of information through modern information technology raises old questions about privacy but in new forms.

Source: Adapted from "Computers and Privacy," *The Economist*, May 4–10, 1991, pp. 21–23. Copyright ©1991. The Economist Newspaper Group, Inc. Reprinted with permission. Further reproduction prohibited.

Questions for Discussion

1. How much scope should marketers have when data collected by them in computers can be so easily transferred and rearranged to suit the purposes of the "pirates" using this information?

2. Can anyone really own an idea?

3. Should the use of the computer to cross-link names and purchasing behaviour be controlled?

4. Should governments restrict the flow of information across borders?

COMPARING SECONDARY AND PRIMARY DATA

The use of secondary data offers two important advantages over the use of primary data: lower cost and less time for collection and use. Even though some secondary data may require fees paid to the firm involved in the data collection, the cost is invariably less than if the user-firm has to collect the data itself. A considerable amount of time must be spent in determining information needs, identifying sources of data, preparing collection instruments, training researchers, and collecting and interpreting the data—all activities that are performed in obtaining primary data.

But the use of secondary data is subject to a number of important limitations. First, the information may be obsolete. The data provided by the 1991 Census of Population are already obsolete in many areas as substantial population shifts have occurred since then. Second, most secondary data were originally collected for a specific purpose, and the way they have been classified may not provide appropriate information for a decision maker with a different problem. For example, a retail merchant who is deciding whether to open a new store in a shopping mall may require information on household income for a 10-kilometre area, but the only available data may have been collected on a county basis. In still other cases, available facts may be of doubtful accuracy. Errors in collecting, analyzing, and interpreting the original data may make the information inaccurate. In all such instances, a firm may be forced to collect primary data. Even the accuracy of the 1991 census has been questioned on the grounds that data were not obtained from all members of the population.

BUSINESS REVIEW 12.2

1. Discuss the advantages and disadvantages of using secondary data.
2. Why should the marketing researcher start with a review and analysis of secondary data?
3. Discuss the advantages and disadvantages of using primary data.
4. Discuss the pros and cons of the three primary-data collection methods.

INTERACTIVE SUMMARY AND DISCUSSION QUESTIONS

1. Alvin Toffler suggests that humanity has experienced three economic and social "waves." Discuss the implications of graduating from a university or college in the information era.

2. Interactive voice technology (IVT) involves a talking computer and your telephone. Suppose you are assigned the task of making the most out of such a system being installed in a department store. Suggest the ways the store, its employees, and its customers can maximize the benefits of this technology.

3. Information for decision making is made more effective through the use of the computer. Describe some of its applications in spread sheet analysis, production, and retailing. Interview information managers at one or two companies to see which of these applications they are using, and which other applications they consider to have good potential.

4. Review the use of the computer in the transfer of information, discussing the implications of the increasing use of electronic networking in business.

5. Three main sources of information are the day-to-day course of activities, marketing information, and marketing research. Under what circumstances would the use of each be appropriate?

6. Differentiate between primary data and secondary data in market research.

7. Three methods of collecting primary data are the use of the questionnaire, the carefully designed experiment, and the observation method. Give an example of when each might be used.

8. In "probability sampling," every member of the population has a known chance of being selected at random as a sample participant. Select a probability sample of 30 from the "A" names in the white pages of the phone book. What decision did you have to make to ensure that the sample was viable? Have you any concerns about the nature and quality of the sample you have drawn?

CASE 12.1

BEDFORD FURNITURE INDUSTRIES INC.

BEDFORD FURNITURE INDUSTRIES INC., like many Canadian manufacturing companies, realized it needed drastic action to become competitive and stay competitive. The need to cut inventory costs and to improve customer service led the company to consider electronic data interchange (EDI).

EDI links a company's computer system with those of its clients, enabling the parties to send out and receive data needed to do business. What was formerly done by courier and mail is done electronically. One of EDI's greatest benefits, its proponents say, is that it vastly improves turn-around times for manufacturers and retailers. It can save between 10 and 20 percent a year in the cost of sending documents, and shave off as much as 40 percent from an order-cycle time.

"When you're delivering the same day, every minute counts," said Allan Snow, data processing manager for Bedford Furniture Industries Inc., a Toronto manufacturer and distributor of bedding and upholstery products.

The PC-based EDI system cost Bedford less than $10,000 to install, and it has played a key role in the company's switch to just-in-time delivery, which cuts its inventory costs and enables it to deliver products to the customer exactly when needed.

(continued)

Snow said the turnaround time now is within the same day from the time it receives an electronic order to the time it makes the delivery. The old way could take up to three weeks.

In addition, EDI can be used for electronic funds transfer (EFT) and an electronic advanced shipping notification, often called a bill of lading, which will streamline the delivery and billing process by eliminating the need for invoicing. EDI/EFT gives more detailed billing information immediately.

Harvey Gellman, a founding partner with Toronto computer consulting firm CGI-Gellman, Hayward, said, if implemented properly, EDI is a "great idea, [because] once you've got data electronically captured, it makes more sense to send it electronically than to have it rekeyed and printed for sending."

Source: Adapted from Bruce Gates, "Reducing Costs Electronically," *The Financial Post*, April 13, 1992, p. S28.

Questions for Discussion

1. How does the information system described in this case assist Bedford Furniture to become competitive?

2. How does electronic funds transfer (EFT) help make a company competitive?

3. What disadvantages will those Canadian companies who are not using EDI or a similar system have when competing with companies using EDI?

4. In what other ways could EDI benefit a company?

CASE 12.2

CAMBRIAN CONSULTING

MARC LAURENCE, president of Cambrian Consulting, had just read an article that greatly intrigued him. His management consulting firm, headquartered in a small city near Toronto, had experienced steady growth over the past eight years. The firm was known for its awareness of the development of new technology, and for the creative ways that technology could be used in business applications.

Once the consulting firm figured out useful business applications of a technology, it approached organizations which could benefit, and sold them on having Cambrian help them to apply it. It had been some time since a promising new idea had presented itself. However, Mr. Laurence thought that the technology reported in the following article had great potential business applications:

The information era is helping to put criminals behind bars even more quickly than before.

Edward Escubedo, president of Comnetrix Computer Systems Inc., a Mississauga, Ontario–based software company, has developed a specialized program that will make it faster and easier for police to store and retrieve mug shots and written descriptions of thousands of individuals.

The program, formally known as the Repository for Integrated Computer Imaging, Identification of Mug Shots (RICI), is designed to be used by police officers who have little or no computer experience. Using a keyboard, an officer simply types into a desk-top terminal all of the available information about a suspect's appearance. The computer then searches its databank to select the individuals who most closely match that description, displaying their photographs on a video screen.

(continued)

The Metropolitan Toronto Police force plans to install 24 interconnected work stations throughout the metropolitan area at a total cost of $200,000. That way, investigating officers in the field will have direct access to photographs of suspects as soon as they are arrested, rather than having to wait as long as two weeks for a mug shot to come from police headquarters. Officers in each of the force's 18 divisions will also be able to use the computer network to compile electronic lineups of physically similar people, eliminating the need to line individuals up behind one-way glass so that witnesses can identify suspects.

Inspector Alvin Thompson of the York Regional Police force noted that one strong feature of RICI is its ability to share mug shots with other forces. "Instead of tying up someone in the lab, developing the photo, we'll just push a button and have it come up on the colour printer." If both forces are equipped with RICI, the information can be transmitted electronically in seconds over a telephone line.

Other law-enforcement agencies are seriously considering installing the RICI system in their crime-reduction programs.

Information comes in various shapes and sizes. The use of the RICI system is an example of how an information system has found an irrevocable place in our society. It will not be too long before we wonder how the police forces across Canada have ever managed without the ease of transferring information as provided by RICI.

Source: Adapted from Barbara Wickens, "Making Crime Pay," *Maclean's*, January 13, 1992, p. 30.

Questions for Discussion

1. Suggest to Mr. Laurence some ways that the RICI system might be adapted to assist industries other than crime prevention?

2. How might the transfer of information available through linking RICI systems be of assistance to the police force? To a corporation?

NOTES

1. Hoo-Min D. Toong and Amar Gupta, "Personal Computers," *Scientific American* Offprint, December 1982, p. 3.
2. Alvin Toffler, *The Third Wave* (New York: Morrow, 1980).
3. Alexander Besher, "Focus Changes from Rim to the Interconnected Globe," *The Times Colonist*, February 27, 1993.
4. Susan Gittens, "Networking Know-How Strained to Meet Corporate Data Demands," *The Financial Post*, November 14, 1988, p. 51.
5. Howard Druckman, "Chatter Boxes," *Canadian Business*, November 1988, p. 199.

PHOTO CREDITS

MODULE

◆ OP ◆

OPERATIONS MANAGEMENT

THE FOCUS OF THIS MODULE

1. To explain the concept of operations management

2. To demonstrate how productivity serves as a measure of performance

3. To describe the four key production processes

4. To explain the process of planning production

5. To examine the issues that affect levels of inventory and approaches to inventory management

6. To discuss the management of the various inputs to the production process

7. To discuss the management of the outputs of the production process

8. To examine the focus on quality in operations management

9. To learn the meaning of the following terms:

KEY TERMS

competitive priorities

job shop

batch processing

assembly line

line flow

continuous flow

bill of materials (BOM)

routing sheet

   planning (MRP)

manufacturing resource

   planning (MRP II)

capacity

materials requirement

fixed cost

variable cost

cycle inventory

pipeline inventory

anticipatory inventory

buffer inventory

just-in-time inventory control (JIT)

total productive maintenance (TPM)

quality

The contribution of Professor Ian Stuart in developing this module is gratefully acknowledged.

WHETHER IN A service industry such as a fast-food restaurant or a manufacturing industry such as an automobile factory, operations must meet the needs of a changing market. Operations departments in fast-food plants are manufacturing new products to keep up with such consumer demand. Salads and low-fat frozen yogurt are replacing traditional favourites like french fries and ice cream. McDonald's introduced its McLean Deluxe with twelve grams less fat than the Quarter Pounder. Harvey's is competing with a product containing only ten grams of fat.

The raw materials used to produce McDonald's McLean burger have been combined in a unique fashion to meet demand for health-conscious foods and yet maintain the succulent flavours and quality of the traditional fast-food hamburger. "Fat tastes good," said Michael Goldblatt, assistant vice-president for Nutrition and Product Development, McDonald's. The process of creating the McLean results in a product that simulates the taste and juiciness of fatter meat by adding cornstarch, salt, natural beef flavour, and water to lean beef.

Source: Adapted from John Daly, "A Low-Fat Attack," *Maclean's*, July 8, 1991, p. 48.

MANAGING THE OPERATIONS function so that a firm can meet shifting consumer demands is a significant challenge. In the fast-food industry, or in the production of steel, electronic equipment, or a new approach to college texts such as this one, operations management plays a key role.

WHAT IS OPERATIONS MANAGEMENT?

Operations management is concerned with the production process that transforms all an organization's resources, or *inputs*—purchased raw materials and components, labour, capital, information, and energy—into its products, or *outputs*—manufactured goods or delivered services. This production process is often referred to as the transformation or conversion process. The principles of operations management were developed for the most part within the manufacturing context, but are also applicable in service industries. Thus, just as managing the manufacturing of a car falls within the realm of operations management, so too does the management of a city bus service or a French restaurant. The operations function is depicted in Figure 13.1.

The output of a manufacturing organization is visible, but the output of a service organization is sometimes less so. For example, the output from the post office is delivered letters and parcels; that of the city bus service is transported passengers. Operations management is concerned with the effective and efficient management of all inputs and the process required to deliver the output.

FIGURE 13.1 • THE OPERATIONS FUNCTION

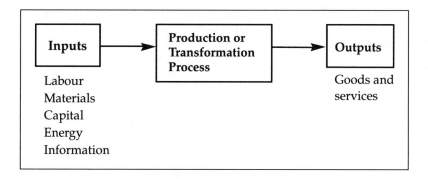

OPERATIONS MANAGEMENT AND PRODUCTIVITY

A broad measure of performance in operations management is the productivity growth of the economy. Usually economists report this measure of efficiency by calculating the ratio of output value to labour-hour inputs. A comparison of this ratio with those of prior years indicates the productivity growth of the economy as a whole. The use of such a broad economists' measure focussing only on labour productivity may be misleading at the level of the individual firm, especially in a capital-intensive field such as nuclear-power generation. As indicated in Figure 13.1, the operations manager would also be interested in capital productivity, energy productivity, and materials productivity. Nonetheless, such a broad measure does provide us with a notion of how well Canada's economy is performing.

Table 13.1 indicates that, while productivity grew in other countries during the twelve years covered, it remained static in Canada. (The Canadian economy as a whole grew over this period, but the labour input grew at the same rate as the output of goods and services.) Economists believe that inattention to operations management, particularly in the service sector, contributed to this poor performance. The lack of productivity growth means that the cost of goods and services has remained the same, and this indicates that the standard of living has remained the same. Negative productivity growth, as experienced in some of the former Communist bloc countries, leads to higher costs and, ultimately, a lower standard of living.

TABLE 13.1 • PRODUCTIVITY GROWTH

Average annual percent growth 1979–1990			
Japan	2.0	Italy	1.4
France	1.8	Germany	0.8
Britain	1.6	United States	0.2
		CANADA	0.0
All OECD countries			0.8

Source: Adapted from OECD Economic Survey: Canada, 1991, 1992.

Productivity and Competitiveness

Effective and efficient operations management is critical to reversing this disturbing trend. However, the need to improve productivity goes beyond raising the standard of living. The economic realities of the 1990s include a breakdown of economic barriers between countries.

Robert Hillier, senior vice-president of Campbell Soup Co. Ltd., a subsidiary of the U.S. giant and one of the largest food companies in Canada, stated that international trade and, in particular, the Canada–U.S. Free Trade Agreement have "changed the rules for success, and we are no longer competitive." As trade barriers came down, the Canadian food-processing industry found it was saddled with "higher costs right across the board. Competition is ferocious in this business." Even the well-established companies had to struggle to survive.[1]

Campbell Soup, like many Canadian companies, is well aware of the increasing competitive pressure that Canadian business faces. As globalization of business increases, Canadian manufacturers and service delivery firms will not survive unless they are competitive in cost and quality with foreign firms. A strong and vibrant manufacturing and service base will ultimately depend on how well the transformation processes are managed.

APPROACHES TO THE PRODUCTION PROCESS

The choice of production process depends not only on the type of good being manufactured or service being delivered but also on the firm's overall **competitive priorities**. Is it the firm's goal to be a low-cost producer? Is it aiming at high quality? Does it want the flexibility (e.g., customized service or volume variation) to react speedily in a changing market? Does it stress the level of service it offers its customers? It is almost impossible for the firm to excel on all four dimensions. Inevitably, some trade-offs will be made when choosing an overall approach to production operations.

In manufacturing, production processes fall into four basic types: job shop, batch processing, assembly line, and continuous flow. The same classifications can be applied to many service industries. The choice of production process should be consistent with the company's priorities, as we will see.

The Job Shop

The oldest and most direct approach to production is the job shop. A **job shop** produces goods or services according to a customer's specifications, usually in very small quantities. Job shops go back to the craft-based industry of the medieval era and even earlier. Most job shops today are small businesses such as neighbourhood hairstylists, custom machine shops, and desktop printing services, but large enterprises such as many construction firms and shipbuilding yards also operate as job shops.

In a job shop, production rarely precedes a firm customer order. Orders may come from repeat clients or one-time walk-in customers, or through a bidding process in which several shops may compete to meet specific requirements on the basis of criteria such as price, speed of delivery, and quality.

competitive priorities
The bases on which a firm competes: cost, quality, flexibility, and/or service

job shop
A production process in which goods or services are produced according to the customer's specifications

DEVELOPING YOUR BUSINESS SKILLS

FLEXIBILITY IN MANUFACTURING PROVIDES NEW OPPORTUNITIES

Linamar Machine Ltd. and its twelve subsidiary companies used to focus on aerospace and military contracts. When these began to look less promising in the era of glasnost, chairman and CEO Frank Hasenfratz and president Larry Pearson decided the precision manufacturer already had much of the quality requirements to serve the auto industry as well.

That is when the company began a program of continuous improvement, or in the lexicon of Japanese management, *kaizen*. With a steering committee of five drawn from management, quality, cost, delivery, and technology, Linamar zoomed in on a twelve-point agenda ranging from transportation costs to employee satisfaction. The result, says Pearson: "A much more dynamic company." After the change, new revenue and profit levels were set.

One way that Linamar stays flexible—"responsive to customers," as Pearson puts it—is by putting limits on the growth of its subsidiary companies. Plants are limited to 200 employees and 70,000 square feet because managers should know workers on a first-name basis. Mid-sized plants located close to one another can also share workers and managers when one business starts to expand more quickly.

Linamar can also move quickly to accommodate temporary booms without losing valuable changeover time. Whole production lines can be uprooted and reconstructed for a three- or four-month contract, then moved again for the next one. The key is that the equipment must be close together to keep workers talking to each other and to trim time lost between tasks to a minimum.

What Pearson calls the backbone of Linamar's quality improvement program, however, is statistical process control (SPC). SPC nails down in numbers and decimal points exactly how the manufacturing process will go. But it also states explicitly who will take measurements and when. What comes out of this process is a set of detailed operating instructions for each stage of the process.

That is crucial to the manufacturing quest for quality. "Without it," says Pearson, "the goals of your continuous improvement program may be hard to create, let alone for you to know whether you have improved them or not."

The Linamar experience is one indication that, ready or not, the new era of manufacturing is upon us. Great gadgets and clever processes won't save a plant that lacks a strategy to make the most of what it can do best and rid itself of the rest. "It's all the wrong idea if there is a big gap to close," says one observer. "And that is where much of Canadian manufacturing is today. It has a big gap to close." Adds Jim Locker from Raymond Industrial Equipment Ltd., "You've got to be the best. It's basically survival. If you don't seek to improve, you're dead."

Source: Adapted from John Southerst, "The Next Industrial Revolution," *Canadian Business*, June 1992, pp. 99–101.

Customer requirements often differ from job to job, dictating a lack of common pattern in the production process. As a result of this jumbled flow, the layout of the plant or office is often very different from that of a mass-production business. In many cases, equipment is arranged for the convenience of the operator rather than the efficient flow of the product through the production process.

Job shops use versatile, non-specialized equipment, allowing flexibility to meet changing customer requirements without the need for vast capital investment in new machinery. In most job shops, however, the average utilization rate of machinery tends to be very low, although frequently jobs must wait for equipment to become available. For example, the next time you visit the hairstylist, note how often the hair-washing area is idle. Not every customer requires this operation as part of the service, but lack of control over customer demands may also lead to delays when all the hair-washing equipment is in use.

Labour costs in a job shop tend to be high because workers must be paid during slow periods and work is slowed by the start-up time needed to learn the requirements of and to set up for each new job. Operations can often be improved by focussing on good scheduling rules and by improving the layout of the facility to balance movement of workers and of the product or service. In many cases, this balance can be achieved by segmenting the service to handle different customer requirements. For example, our hairstylist might consider a special arrangement for a standard shampoo and haircut.

The competitive priorities favouring job shop operations tend to be flexibility and quality rather than price or speed of service. For example, a custom tailor can provide garments that fit perfectly and match the individual's taste in fabric and style but cannot compete in price or speed of delivery with a retail clothing store. Despite its natural appeal to entrepreneurial instincts, the job shop is usually terribly inefficient. Costs are high because capital is often tied up in underused equipment. Purchases from suppliers tend to be erratic, so the shop fails to take advantage of quantity discounts. Individual jobs may be held up waiting for other equipment or workers to become available when too many special-order customized jobs arrive at the same time. Time is

First Choice Haircutters is a Canadian franchise that offers affordable and professional hair care. This neighbourhood hairstylist offers flexible services to meet the various needs of its customers. Its reasonable prices, good locations, and reliable services have enabled First Choice Haircutters to target successfully the whole family.

also wasted in moving the product from one location to another. Thus, the job shop may be an appealing place to work, but it can rarely deliver goods and services in a cost-efficient or timely manner. Excessive customization, a characteristic of job shops, causes inefficiencies in the transformation process and yields a higher-cost operation.

The Batch Operation

Benihana is a chain of Japanese steakhouses with an interesting approach to fine dining. Guests register for a table and are escorted for a brief stay in the restaurant's lounge area. Within 15 minutes, eight names are announced, and the entire group, often strangers to one another, are shown to the "teppanyaki" table. The menu choice is limited. Chicken, shrimp, or steak, or a combination of these, are offered. Side orders are unchanging (mainly rice, and bean sprouts and other vegetables). Everything is cooked on the grill in front of the customers. Within 45 minutes during peak periods (longer when business is slack), the entire table will have finished their meals and will be escorted, en masse, to the exit. The simple menu, the flamboyant yet basic cooking technique, and the batching of customers have yielded high profit margins for the Benihana chain of restaurants.

Benihana's approach to delivering service is an example of **batch processing**: guests move through the various courses of the meal in groups or batches. Many job shops evolve into batch producers if the product or service they offer triggers repeat orders. The size of the batch varies, often according to the capacity of some element in the production process (an output restriction in the process). For example, a batch of sweaters might consist of bundles of 30 to 40 units of the same colour because that is the number that can be knitted from one dye lot of yarn. A batch of beer depends on the capacity of the brewing kettles. Benihana uses a batch size of eight customers, with the lounge area serving as a staging area for the batch formation.

batch processing
A production process in which goods or services move through various stages of production in batches

Batch producers tend to narrow the product or service offering to a more limited range than do job shops. This allows the operations manager to begin to take advantage of economies of scale. For example, fixed costs (costs that do not vary over a range of production volumes) can be spread over a larger volume of production. Typical fixed costs encountered include machine set-up time (for example, rethreading the knitting machine or changing from one type of beer to another) or, in Benihana's case, cleaning the teppanyaki grill and restocking the food carts. Additionally, consistent and larger orders to suppliers yield significant cost benefits in purchasing and delivery. Finally, the higher volumes of production mean that equipment can often be specialized and automated, which can increase production speed or replace labour as a factor of production.

Batch production involves trade-offs. For example, because their products are necessarily somewhat standardized, batch producers, unlike job shops, can rarely produce to order. Individual customers will not wait for standard product offerings, so the batch manufacturer must have goods available in advance of customer orders. Doing so requires an investment in inventory and storage and a reliance on demand forecasts. Since any forecast is liable to error, the manufacturer may either overproduce, leading to excess inventory and possible obsolescence of the product stored, or underproduce, thereby running out of stock and being unable to fill customer orders in a timely fashion. In service settings, such as Benihana, poor estimates of customer volumes may lead to incorrect staffing and purchase planning. (A service cannot be stored in inventory, but maintaining spare capacity to provide the service is possible.)

Effective management in a batch operation requires the balance of myriad competing demands. For example, the trade-off between the fixed cost in set-up for a batch run must be balanced against the inventory costs associated with running larger batches. The possible loss of business associated with underproduction must be balanced against the cost of maintaining inventory to meet unforecasted demand. Finally, the efficiency associated with narrowing the product line must be balanced against the inability to accept small-volume customer orders with special requirements. The batch producer cannot afford to provide excessive customization.

Assembly Line and Continuous Operations

The last two basic types of production process, the assembly line and continuous flow, are responsible for the mass production that has allowed industrial societies to achieve a high standard of living. They will be discussed together. In an **assembly line**, the product travels along a line of workers, each of whom performs one specialized task toward the assembly of the final product. A similar approach is used in many industries that do not involve actual "assembly"—for example, an airline has reservation clerks, ticket takers, baggage handlers, waiting area personnel, aircraft maintenance workers, pilots, and cabin crew who have their own specialized tasks in transporting the passenger. These wider applications of what we know as the assembly line concept are sometimes referred to as **line flow**. In a **continuous flow** operation, such as an oil refinery, electricity generating station, or sewage treatment plant, the product is not divided into individual units but flows continuously so that the individual activities that make up the production system are closely linked. Usually, continuous flow operations are highly mechanized and the workers are more involved in reading dials and regular maintenance than in actual production.

In both the assembly line and continuous flow processes, the individual tasks and activities that make up the process system are closely linked so that the product appears to flow through the plant on a somewhat continuous basis. In a car assembly plant, there might be up to 1,500 separate workstations. Starting at initial welding for a car frame, a visitor can walk through the plant and watch the steel begin to resemble the finished product. The slowest operation will dictate the speed of the entire line: every step in the assembly process is carefully planned and managed to eliminate any serious imbalances in the time required to complete it.

assembly line
A production process in which the product travels along a line of workers, each of whom performs one specialized task toward the assembly of the final product

line flow
An enlargement of the assembly line concept to describe any operation in which individual workers perform specialized tasks in succession toward the production of a good or service

continuous flow
A production process in which the product flows continuously so that the individual activities that make up the production system are closely linked

TABLE 13.2 • JOB SHOP PRODUCTION VERSUS THE ASSEMBLY LINE

Minutes of effort to assemble	Job shop Fall 1913	Mass production Spring 1914	Percent reduction
Engine	594	226	62
Magneto	20	5	75
Axle	150	26.5	83
Final assembly	750	93	88

Source: Womack, J.P., D.T. Jones, and D. Ross, *The Machine That Changed the World*, Harper Perennial, 1990, p. 29.

In manufacturing settings, the product normally travels along a belt, linking the activities in sequence. The moving assembly line was, perhaps, the most notable contribution that Henry Ford made to mass production. The dramatic impact that Ford's assembly line had when it was introduced is shown in Table 13.2.

Most continuous flow operations, as well as large-scale assembly lines, require relatively few workers, but the scale (production volume) and capital investment in such operations are enormous. With so much capital at stake, it is easy to understand why a key management emphasis is maintaining continuous plant production. For example, a steel plant will rarely shut down except for planned maintenance. Surprisingly, an income statement analysis reveals that less than 10 percent of expenses relate to direct labour in most continuous operations. In contrast, well over 60 percent of expenses relate to purchased components and raw materials. Capital and purchasing productivity are key performance criteria in such operations.

Cost, consistent quality, and fast service are competitive priorities for most mass-production operations. The *throughput time*—the time it takes a product to move from the beginning to the end of the manufacturing process—is so short that marketing demands can be met, for the most part, on a demand basis. Demand patterns are generally predictable. However, the variety of product is extremely limited, and once the highly specialized technology has been introduced and the mass-production operation is tooled up, there is little flexibility in basic product design. As Henry Ford said, the customer could have a Model T in any colour as long as it was black.

A major problem with the emphasis on efficiency and mass production of a limited variety of product is that it has yielded jobs that many workers find monotonous and boring. High absenteeism and employee turnover have posed significant problems in high-volume operations.

The pursuit of efficiency, therefore, has its price. The decision to use dedicated facilities geared toward high-volume production of a limited variety of products is a strategic one that requires careful attention. Issues in Business 13.1 considers the advantages and disadvantages of a more flexible manufacturing process.

ISSUES IN BUSINESS 13.1

FLEXIBLE FACTORIES A BOON FOR SOME INDUSTRIES

THE SUPERMARKET CHECKOUT counter on which you balance your *National Enquirer* while waiting to be shocked by the grocery bill takes about a month to make using conventional methods. However, Oston Ltd. can whip one through its Peterborough, Ontario, plant in about three days, using flexible manufacturing.

Flexible manufacturing is a catch-all phrase that, in its broadest sense, refers to any manufacturing line that can be reprogrammed to perform different movements with a few keystrokes. A line also can be made flexible by moving machines in or out of it, or by repositioning them.

Each order for a checkout counter is essentially a custom job, produced in small numbers, so Oston's flexibility has enabled it to speed up production.

"We could see the demand for more product variety was coming," says Oston president Antero Laitila. "Customers want more and different things, and they want to get them fast."

Flexible systems enable manufacturers to cut the time it takes to switch lines from one product to another. That enables them to produce much smaller batches cost-effectively, and to improve quality.

Flexible manufacturing was imported from Japan. Like other Japanese business principles being applied in North America, it isn't for everyone. A company that bangs out the same widgets year after year has little need of a production line that can be reconfigured in a hurry.

At the same time, a line that is highly flexible can be slower than a dedicated line because it is designed for its ability to be rapidly changed rather than to push through a single item.

"The more flexible the manufacturing process, the less throughput you can get in and out," says Barrie Hawkins of Giffels Associates Ltd. in Toronto, which owns the Ontario Centre for Advanced Manufacturing.

"An engine manufacturer wants a dedicated line," he said. "With flexible manufacturing, you can do more types of products, but throughput won't be as high as it can be doing one product."

There are other drawbacks to flexible manufacturing. It's very expensive, and highly capital intensive. . . . It also takes a significant amount of investment in terms of engineering support and there are a lot of cultural issues to break through with people. Some employees view the flexible machines as threats to their livelihood and some employers use that threat to push their workers. . . .

However, given the proper incentives, . . . statistical process control training, group problem solving, and a positive attitude, people have a tremendous capacity to improve their performance. . . .

Northern Telecom spent about $6 million in 1985–86 to build a computer-integrated manufacturing line. It was to be the first step toward a so-called lights-out factory, which would be so automated it could run in the dark without human intervention.

The company developed fourteen manufacturing cells, each of which could add components to a circuit board, solder and inspect them, with little or no human assistance.

But what Northern Telecom found in building this incredibly sophisticated system is some machines work best with people—the cost of installing and maintaining them far exceeded the cost of paying a person to do the same job.

Northern Telecom learned that its greatest gains were achieved by integrating people and machines rather than striving for a lights-out factory.

Source: Excerpts from Geoffrey Rowan, "Flexible Factories a Boon for Some Industries," *The Globe and Mail*, February 22, 1990, p. B3.

(continued)

Questions for Discussion

1. What are some of the drawbacks of flexible manufacturing?
2. What are the advantages of having a dedicated production line?
3. Under what circumstances is flexible manufacturing an appropriate methodology?

PRIORITIES AND PROCESS

The production process depends on the task required by the firm's competitive priorities. Inflexible but cost-efficient line flow and continuous flow processes are most appropriate for high-volume, low-cost operations. Large product variety and highly flexible production methods demand job shop or small batch processing. Inappropriate choice of processes, such as trying to manufacture a wide variety of products on an assembly line, leads to poor productivity, unnecessary changeover costs, and the inability to compete. The major characteristics of the various production processes are summarized in the matrix shown in Figure 13.2.

Although this matrix was originally developed for manufacturing firms, it can be modified and used in the service sector when such criteria as service variety, customization, and customer contact are adopted as relevant terms. The matrix can be used to understand competitive positioning and the pros and cons of such positioning in terms of operations management.

FIGURE 13.2 • THE PRODUCT/PROCESS MATRIX

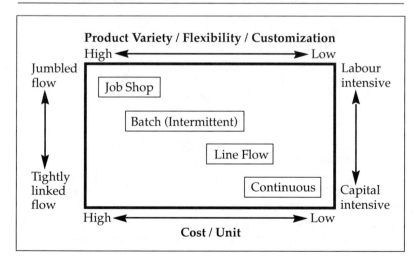

Source: Adapted and reprinted by permission of Harvard Business Review. An exhibit from "Link Manufacturing Process and Produce Life Cycles" by Robert H. Hayes and Steven C. Wheelright, January/February 1979. Copyright ©1978 by the President and Fellows of Harvard College; all rights reserved.

BUSINESS REVIEW 13.1

1. Position three varieties of urban public transportation within the product/process matrix: the taxi service, the bus service, and the subway system.
   a) Which system involves the greatest capital cost?
   b) Which has the highest level of fixed costs?
   c) Which system has the greatest flexibility?
   d) Which is the most labour intensive to operate?

2. Three services or goods where the product/process matrix might apply are education, film making, and restaurants. How does the choice of process match the apparent competitive priorities that lead to the placement of each enterprise?

PLANNING PRODUCTION

After a ten-minute wait in line, the man steps up to the desk at Consumers Distributing, clutching a slightly damp order form. It is a hot, humid, sticky Toronto evening, and he wants to buy a sixteen-inch electric fan. "We're all out," says the clerk, "but we have a twelve-inch model." A pause while the clerk checks the stock list. "Oh gee, we just sold the last one of those, too. Sorry." His anger adding to the day's heat, the customer stomps out, vowing never to return.[2]

This is the way it used to be in 1987. Henri Roy, the then incoming chairman, CEO, and president, admitted that, at any one time, Consumers did not have 20 percent of the items listed in its Canadian catalogue. And that was only an average. If an item was seasonal—a fan in the summer, a popular toy at Christmas—chances were that the customer could forget about being able to purchase it there. This situation has an enormous negative impact for a company whose product catalogue is a promise of availability.

The consequences of poor demand forecasting can be devastating. Managing the operations process requires a reasonably accurate forecast of demand and times at which such demand is likely to occur. Operations managers must work closely with those in marketing to ensure that demand forecasts are as accurate as possible since the costs of making too many or too few products or of having excess or insufficient capacity in a service setting can be high. Demand forecasts are usually based on past sales and, for new products, on marketing research data.

Assessing Materials and Timing Needs

Using the forecast of demand volumes and timing, the operations manager can begin planning for production. Many pieces of information are required for this task, but the most important are known as the bill of materials and the routing sheet.

FIGURE 13.3 • ASSEMBLY OF A SIMPLE PRODUCT

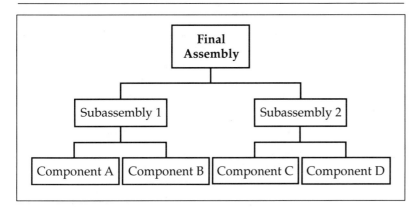

The **bill of materials** (BOM) lists the raw materials, components, and subassemblies that are required to form the finished product. The BOM is a measure of the product's complexity because it indicates what is required for each subassembly before final assembly can be accomplished. A schematic representation of the subassemblies and components required to assemble a fairly simple finished product is shown in Figure 13.3. Final assembly cannot start until subassemblies #1 and #2 are completed. In addition, these subassemblies cannot be completed until the required components are manufactured or purchased from suppliers.

The lead time necessary for the purchase or manufacture of components and the building of subassemblies must be planned for so that the final product can be assembled according to forecasted demand. The second important piece of information the operations manager needs, therefore, is provided by the routing sheet. The **routing sheet** lists the various activities that must be performed at a certain stage of operations, often including the time required for each. Thus, it is a measure of the complexity of the process. A typical routing sheet is shown in Figure 13.4. According to this sheet, a batch of 1,000 would take 50 hours of processing time, and 20 minutes for setting up equipment. The set-up time is incurred only once per batch, regardless of the batch size, so, if only 100 units were included in the batch, the total time required would be 5 hours, 20 minutes. Ten such batches would therefore take 53 hours, 20 minutes. Time estimates on the routing sheet are normally based on work-measurement studies by industrial engineers within the plant or on times cited in reference books or film studies of work activities.

The BOM and routing sheet are used to plan production by giving operations managers estimates of the timing and quantity of resources (labour, machines, materials) that will be required in order to meet forecasted demand. Later, the BOM and the routing sheet can be compared against actual experience for performance appraisal.

Developing a Schedule

The actual scheduling of production and the allocation of resources are usually referred to as the production planning process. As the

bill of materials (BOM)
A list of all raw materials, components, and subassemblies required for a unit or batch of a product

routing sheet
A sequenced list of the activities needed to perform an operation, often including the time required for each

FIGURE 13.4 • ROUTING SHEET FOR A SIMPLE PROCESS

Subassembly 1

Operation #	Task	Time required per unit (seconds)	Set-up per batch (minutes)
00	Machine face	60	15
10	Grind	30	—
20	Polish	20	—
30	Drill hole	25	5
40	Insert nut and bolt	15	—
50	Tighten	10	—
60	Inspect	20	—
		180	**20**

materials requirement planning (MRP)

Planning, often with the help of a computer program, to ensure that the bill of materials required for a product is available when needed

manufacturing resource planning (MRP II)

Computer programs that help the operations manager plan all aspects of production—materials, labour, scheduling, quantities, warehousing, etc.

capacity

The maximum output possible, said of a machine or a facility

complexity of the planning task grows (for example, because many products are involved or the BOM is very complicated), companies will often resort to a computer to assist with the planning of production. **Materials requirement planning (MRP)** programs help ensure that the bill of materials is available when needed. IBM has developed and uses a more sophisticated program known as MRP II—MRP here stands for **manufacturing resource planning**. MRP II systems break down a factory's master production schedule to tell managers how many individual parts are needed to make the product and what subassemblies must be done, what labour is required to do them, and what time is required. At IBM Canada, every part that goes through the plant is barcoded and can be traced from start to finish. This information is connected to all plant databases. Thus, the purchasing department knows what is needed, and IBM's engineering design system, costing system, and warehousing system can use the information for planning. "I couldn't deal with the 30,000 to 40,000 parts we have here without an MRP system," said Eugene Polistuk, IBM plant manager.[3]

IBM is clearly a frontrunner in developing production plans using the sophisticated MRP II tool. But, despite the advances in planning tools, the production plan is only as good as the demand forecast and the ability of managers to adhere to the schedule provided by the plan.

Production scheduling requires a balancing of conflicting demands. If a plant is to operate at full **capacity**, producing the maximum output possible, set-up times must be minimized. Therefore, in car assembly plants, painting is usually planned to move from lighter to darker colours to reduce cleaning times. In bottling plants, changes in bottle sizes are minimized because they are very time-consuming. Changing a flavour line, however, requires less set-up time, so operations managers will schedule batches of several flavours in the same-sized bottles and only then go through the expensive process of changing bottle size. (Breweries, which used to provide beer in "pint" and "quart" bottles, now use only one size of bottle.) Such scheduling obviously has an impact on the timing of delivery of raw materials, work force requirements, and availability of the final product. A computer planning system, such as MRP II, can be used to inform suppliers when materials will be needed and marketers when orders will be filled.

MANAGING INVENTORIES

Most manufacturers produce more than one product. From the discussion so far, it might seem that production runs should be as long as possible in order to minimize the set-up costs involved in switching over production of one product to another. Imagine, for example, a food processor that manufactures peanut butter and jelly. Changing from peanut butter to jelly production might involve significant cleaning of equipment, jar size changes and filling adjustments, line speed adjustments, and carton packing modifications. This set-up cost is a **fixed cost** incurred with each changeover regardless of the volume produced, as distinct from the **variable cost** of materials and labour incurred for each unit produced. One might minimize set-ups by running very large batches of jelly. However, large batches will result in high levels of inventory, which ties up working capital and storage space, requires insurance against the possibility of theft, and runs the risk of spoilage. On the other hand, smaller batch sizes will result in excessive set-up costs. The trade-off decision, assuming that demand is known and that the only two relevant cost factors are inventory and set-up, is illustrated in Table 13.3. Of the options presented, a batch size of 250 cases is the logical choice to balance set-up costs and holding costs.

fixed cost
A cost that is not dependent on the length of a production run, for example, factory rent, set-up time

variable cost
A cost that varies in direct proportion to the length of a production run, for example, materials

Uses of Inventory

The operations manager is responsible for choosing optimal or near-optimal batch sizes for production. (In the illustration in Table 13.3, the

TABLE 13.3 • SET-UP COSTS VS. INVENTORY COSTS

Assumptions:	Annual demand for peanut butter	10,000 cases
	Maximum batch size	2,000 cases
	Set-up cost per run	$100
	Inventory cost per case per year	$ 25

Batch size (cases)	# Set-ups per year	Average* inventory	Set-up $ cost	Inventory $ cost	Total $ cost
100	100	50	10,000	1,250	11,250
200	50	100	5,000	2,500	7,500
250	40	125	4,000	3,125	7,124
500	20	250	2,000	6,250	8,250
1,000	10	500	1,000	12,500	13,500
2,000	5	1,000	500	25,000	25,500

* The inventory reaches a maximum of the batch size and a minimum of zero for an average inventory of ½ times batch size.

cycle inventory
An inventory level based on the trade-off between set-up costs and inventory costs

pipeline inventory
An inventory level maintained to ensure customer demand can be satisfied in the period between ordering a new supply of a product and its delivery

anticipatory inventory
Inventory built up in anticipation of seasonal peak demand

buffer inventory
Inventory maintained to cope with unexpected demand or problems in the production process

just-in-time inventory control (JIT)
An inventory control system under which suppliers deliver parts and materials to the factory floor just as they are needed in the production process, and finished goods are not produced until demand for them exists

optimal batch size is actually 283 cases, which will give a total set-up and inventory cost of $7,071.07, but 250 cases is a reasonable choice.) An inventory level calculated this way is referred to as a **cycle inventory**, balancing fixed set-up costs with variable inventory-carrying costs.

An operations manager who fails to understand the various functional reasons for maintaining inventory may be tempted to reduce inventory size indiscriminately. **Pipeline inventory** is a level of inventory needed to satisfy customer demand during the time between ordering new product to be manufactured and the delivery of that product. Reducing lead times from suppliers and the time taken by the production process reduces the need for pipeline inventory.

In a goods-producing environment, the forecasted demand for the final product can differ dramatically from the actual production plan. Because supplies, labour, and plant capacity are not easily increased or decreased quickly, operations managers often choose to produce stock, building an **anticipatory inventory** in advance of peak demand requirements, thus allowing a manufacturing facility to run smoothly and efficiently. For example, a toy manufacturer will make sleds in summer and fall, and wading pools in winter and spring. Inventory may also be built up at the input end of the production process when the purchasing manager takes advantage of special prices on materials

Buffer inventory is inventory maintained to handle uncertainties in demand, in the production process (when machines fail or workers are absent), or in supply (when bad traffic conditions delay delivery trucks). Buffer inventory can be extremely expensive because it is non-productive, and in recent years operations managers have worked to reduce the need for it by improving demand forecasts and reliability of machines and suppliers. It is better in the long run to correct the problem itself than to drown its impact in a "sea of inventory."

Types of Inventory

We often think of inventory solely as *finished goods inventory*, but operations managers must also be concerned with two other types of inventory: *materials inventory*, which is the inventory of inputs from suppliers, and *work-in-progress inventory*, which includes all goods going through the production process.

All inventory represents capital—capital that is unavailable for other purposes. It also requires warehousing and maintenance. And as pointed out earlier, if the goods do not sell, the materials, labour, and other inputs may all go to waste. For these reasons, operations managers try to keep inventory levels as low as the demands of cycle, pipeline, anticipatory, and buffer inventory allow.

Just-in-Time Production

In recent years, companies have increasingly taken a "just-in-time" approach to inventory control. Under **just-in-time (JIT)**, suppliers deliver parts and materials to the factory floor just as they are needed in the production process, thus reducing materials inventory—and the space required to accommodate it—dramatically. Ideally, the same

The just-in-time inventory system allows Ford Motor Company of Canada Ltd. to assemble cars exactly to the specifications requested by customers across Canada. The basic idea of just-in-time inventory is to trade off higher expenditures for reduced inventory costs. Yet another advantage of the just-in-time method is that it allows Ford to respond quickly to changes in market conditions.

approach is followed in production: if possible, goods are produced only in response to actual customer demand, thus reducing finished goods inventory. Thus, just-in-time production is as much a management philosophy as an inventory management technique (some refer to the philosophy as Big JIT and to the inventory control technique as Little JIT).

Ford Motor Co. of Canada Ltd. began implementing JIT at its Oakville, Ontario, plant in 1988. After two years, 130 of the 1,456 parts used there were delivered just-in-time. To start with, Ford focussed on bulky parts and materials supplied by trucks that were shipped at least every second day. Ford is working to increase the JIT portion of its supplies, but some parts, such as body metal, engines, and transmissions, are still best shipped by rail, and thus cannot easily be scheduled to arrive just-in-time.[4]

Ford has found JIT to be a difficult but valuable pursuit. Reducing inventories to expose problems has proven successful for many. Based on analysis of the trade-offs between inventory and set-up costs, such as that in Table 13.3, a manufacturer would logically move toward JIT production if set-up costs could be reduced or if the cost of inventory were to grow dramatically. Avon Canada Inc. is a good illustration of the efforts to reduce set-up costs to make smaller batch sizes a profitable venture. Any machine at Avon's factory, twenty minutes' travel west of Montreal, that cannot be retooled within a half-hour is a relic. Over the past four years, Avon has converted its production processes from long marathon runs to quick hundred-metre sprints. Everything that is produced—from cosmetics to jewellery—is churned out in small batches.

Since shortening its runs, Avon has reduced inventories by 25 percent, which has freed up cash to increase such activities as marketing and sales.[5] The smaller batches mean goods reach the market faster and the company can respond more alertly to changing tastes.

Many companies now consider inventory to be "evil," hiding problems that exist in the production process and in supplier quality. Continuous improvement of product quality, which is receiving increasing emphasis, is made easier by removing inventory as much as possible so that problems and their causes are made visible and can be rectified.

There is a risk in adopting JIT production (and supply) approaches to manufacturing and service delivery. The lack of any inventory in the system means discipline and adherence to standard production and delivery times is essential. Any deviation from the plan can lead to a complete halt in production because necessary parts or materials have not arrived. In a time flow system with high fixed costs, such a shutdown can be extremely expensive. For example, a ten-day strike at General Motors' Lordstown, Ohio, metal stamping facility had a domino effect on assembly plants from Baltimore to Oklahoma City because the JIT approach meant they had no inventory to use when supply was disrupted. By not stockpiling parts, GM saves factory space and money, but the risk can be enormous.[6]

Just-in-time is a made-in-Japan solution developed by people unused to labour trouble. In North America, many companies have found that the benefits from reduced working capital and the improvements in the production process necessary to implement JIT have exceeded the costs and associated risks. Just-in-time has great merits for a company that has a stable market for a predictable and limited variety of products.

THE SERVICE PLANNING ENVIRONMENT

Many services cannot be produced until they are actually used. A bus company cannot carry passengers in the early hours of the morning if they do not appear until rush hour. The service cannot be stored, so many service industries do not have the option described earlier to smooth out production volumes.

The service provider has two basic options. It can take aggressive action to level the actual demand. For example, telephone companies offer discount prices for phone calls made at off-peak times of the day or week primarily as a demand management technique. This utilizes idle capacity, and the volume of peak capacity required can be reduced. The other option is to store excess capacity to handle peak requirements. (For example, a supermarket may have banks of cash registers and use only a few of them most of the time, bringing in extra cashiers at peak demand times.) Many service providers use a combination of both approaches to avoid as much as possible tying up capital in resources that are idle for all but the peak demand times.

BUSINESS REVIEW 13.2

1. Check your understanding of the following production planning terms and how they fit the process:
   a) demand forecasts
   b) bill of materials and routing sheet
   c) production scheduling
   d) goods-producing versus service-providing production planning
   e) just-in-time production

2. Examine your refrigerator and medicine cabinet and classify the inventory of each by function and form, as explained in this section.

MANAGING INPUTS

Three key inputs to the production process are capital equipment, labour, and purchased parts/materials. The relative importance of these inputs will vary according to the type of process. For continuous and line flow processes, purchases and capital costs dominate the statement of income and expense. In job shops and, to a lesser extent, batch manufacturers, labour will represent an important expense item.

Equipment Maintenance

Machinery is a capital cost, and idle machinery is a waste of capital resources. For plants operating on a just-in-time basis or using continuous process technology, planned maintenance can greatly improve productivity. In Japan, often an award given for quality improvement (the PM [Preventative Maintenance] prize for the implementation of total productive maintenance) is considered to be the most prestigious industrial prize.

Total productive maintenance (TPM) is the complete elimination of equipment breakdowns through activities carried out by all employees. Like the disruption of supply in a JIT plant, a machine problem within a line or continuous flow production plant can lead to the shutdown of the entire operation. Proper maintenance allows the plant to operate at full capacity.

The objective of preventative maintenance is to improve the reliability of each machine and thus the system as a whole. A planned maintenance program is usually less expensive than equipment duplication, or repair after failure. It is, therefore, a cost-effective method for improving productivity.

Obviously, there is a trade-off between the costs of maintenance frequency and the probability of failure. The cost of failure is the output lost. Careful gathering and analysis of data about past machine failures can be used to determine the optimal frequency of maintenance for various machines. In the example shown in Figure 13.5, maintenance should occur about once every three weeks to minimize total costs.

total productive maintenance (TPM)
The complete elimination of equipment breakdowns through regular maintenance so that the plant can operate at full capacity

FIGURE 13.5 • MAINTENANCE VS. FAILURE COSTS

Annual basis

Assumptions: Maintenance cost = $100
Failure cost = $500

Maintenance frequency	Probability of failure	Maintenance cost*	Failure cost**	Total cost
Weekly	0.1	$5,200	2,600	7,800
Every 2 weeks	0.3	$2,600	3,900	6,500
Every 3 weeks	0.5	$1,733	4,333	6,066
Monthly	0.9	$1,200	5,400	6,600

* Number of maintenances per year x cost per maintenance
**Number of maintenances per year x probability of failures x cost per failure

Labour Management

A key concern for the operations manager involves the trade-offs associated with the pursuit of the efficiencies achieved by the division of labour. The benefits that accrue from dividing a task into discrete work elements have been well known since Adam Smith described the concept in *The Wealth of Nations* more than 200 years ago. However, when workers get bored with monotonous tasks, the quality of the output may deteriorate, morale may sink, and absenteeism may rise.

Operations managers have tried, with some success, to maintain the positive work environment of a job shop with batch and line flow processes through job enlargement and job enrichment programs. A garment factory asks workers to assemble a complete sweater instead of just knitting the sleeve. The new General Motors Saturn plant in Tennessee gives workers additional job responsibilities such as proposing and implementing quality-improvement ideas, purchasing materials and supplies, and managing job assignments. Such efforts have been effective in many companies. Issues in Business 13.2 shows how a Ford electronics plant developed a harmonious operation with labour through job enrichment and, at the same time, achieved superior productivity and quality.

ISSUES IN BUSINESS 13.2

THE SOLID STATE FACTORY

IMAGINE AN AUTO industry plant where high-tech robots and other computer-controlled machines do virtually all the physical work, but where the unionized shop-floor work force hasn't been decimated by the automation. The workers check quality and keep the gadgetry

(continued)

humming for the day's near-perfect run. And, just as importantly, they plan—everything from shift and production schedules to innovative wrinkles that will lower defects and costs and raise output. Such is the nature of Job One at the Ford Electronics Manufacturing Corp. plant in Markham, just north of Toronto.

A unit of Ford Motor Co. of Detroit, this showcase factory contains no vast production lines for cars or trucks. Its products are intricate electronic units that control dashboard displays, audio and temperature systems, and safety devices such as airbags and seatbelts. At the core is a well-organized team structure that puts most decision making and quest for innovation into the hands of workers. The culture, says plant manager John Barkley, "makes us more inclined to try something new, to take risks."

"This is the No. 1 plant in (Ford's) electronics division mainly because of our ability to react to technological change," boasts Rod Reynolds, president of Local 2113 of the International Machinists and Aerospace Workers union, which represents 1,100 hourly employees, three-quarters of whom are women. Markham's star status among Ford's nine electronics plants in four continents is getting wide recognition. It recently nabbed Ford's Total Quality Excellence award, adding to its Q1 (top-quality manufacturing) designation. It is among the finalists in the federal government's 1992 Canada Awards for Business Excellence.

Every day, the factory assembles four million components and solders nine million joints to make 35,000 circuit boards for vehicle control devices. Ninety-five percent of production is exported—not just for Fords in North America, Europe, and Asia, but also for Mazdas and Volkswagens.

A typical electronic unit is built on a printed wire board, to which various components (such as microchips or transistors) are glued and soldered, and brackets or other housings are affixed. Over the past few years, this exacting work has been done with increasing speed and quality, and with lower costs, as a result of the conversion to teamwork.

Among the achievements: a steady reduction in "manufacturing cycle time," the time it takes to make a typical control unit. From twelve days in 1988, it has dropped to seven in 1989, two in 1990, four-fifths of a day in 1991, and half a day in 1992. Inventory has been cut by 50 percent over five years, generating cash flow savings of $8 million. Production costs have been trimmed by 5 to 8 percent a year, half of it passed on to customers. Even the floor space required is down 20 percent, meaning new products won't require plant expansion.

A prime catalyst for these gains is Charles Szuluk, a former IBM manager, who demanded breakthroughs that would make Ford highly competitive in auto electronics. Management had been thinking about team concepts for some time, but hadn't figured out how to implement them. With Detroit's encouragement and Mr. Barkley's arrival from head office two years ago, teamwork became central to the plan of attack. The union local has supported the thrust toward teams and continuous improvement. Hourly workers have felt good about sharing real control and about their accomplishments. "But the bottom line," Mr. Reynolds says, "is that Ford will keep the plant open if we're the best."

In pursuing that goal, the Markham facility puts a lot of effort into education, which has become a "business within a business," says Margaret Seelen, who is in charge of training. Eleven people work at instruction full time, and 30,000 paid employee hours have been devoted to it in the past year. When 120 people were recently called back from layoff, they were each given 40 hours of reorientation. Supervising it all is an advisory board, including people from management, the unions, and the training unit.

On the shop floor, each team of seven to twenty members is responsible for a specific product line. All workers belong to at least one team, and the results of their labour has been impressive.

(continued)

One group has cut defects in installing surface mount devices, such as integrated circuits, on printed wire boards. In 1990, the seventeen members began working with equipment suppliers to get defects down to 200 parts per million from 3,500. By the first quarter of 1992, the fault rate was lowered to 60 parts per million.

Another team oversaw the first installation of inert-gas wave soldering machines in Ford's electronic plants. These new machines—a response to environmental regulations—do not use ozone-depleting freon or other toxic elements. Five were installed over thirteen months in 1990–91. When the first machine was set up, the soldering defect rate was 720 parts per million, almost ten times higher than with the old system. By March 1992, the spoil rate was down to 27 per million, thanks largely to the team's development of a new fluxing system and more maintenance.

Although the work force is expected to grow 30 percent by 1995, the salaried head count is to rise by two to 237. Management layers have already been cut to four from six, and a supervisory layer will disappear over the next few years. Some managers may not applaud this trend, but Mr. Reynolds, the union president, is supportive. He says the current management group has credibility and has given workers confidence, although he cautions against "the impression that we're in bed with the company."

The machinists' union organized the plant in 1966. While they have not gone on strike, he says, grievances used to run at more than 100 a year. Currently, there are two grievances; neither is seen as serious.

Source: Timothy Pritchard, "The Solid State Factory," *The Globe and Mail*, September 22, 1992,

Question for Discussion

1. Outline various factors that have produced the success found in the Markham plant.

Purchasing Management

Long considered merely a clerical function, purchasing has recently received a lot of attention as a possible source of both productivity and quality improvements. Purchasing has been described as the right quality in the right volume from the right supplier at the right time at the right price. Much of the recent emphasis on purchasing is a result of the move to just-in-time production, which necessitates reliability and high-quality inputs. Additionally, a high proportion of sales income goes to the purchase of materials in many industries, as illustrated in Table 13.4. The proportion tends to be particularly high in those that utilize a continuous process.

North American firms have had to rethink the way they select their suppliers and the way they manage the relationship between suppliers and purchasers. The change is illustrated by the two extremes presented in Figure 13.6.

The traditional approach is still common and is appropriate where purchase price dominates in the selection of suppliers. The purchasing process is somewhat routine, often involving a tender and bids from various suppliers to meet detailed specifications for performance, including delivery and volume. For numerous small-dollar-value purchases, such as office supplies or routine lab supplies, the purchaser may select a supplier under a *systems contract*, which makes the supplier responsible for yearly supplies of forecasted volume of a broad

TABLE 13.4 • MATERIALS COST AS A PERCENTAGE OF SALES INCOME

Industry	Purchased materials ($ millions)	Sales ($ millions)	Materials as a percentage of sales
Petroleum and coal products	161,291	179,135	90.0
Food and kindred products	197,274	301,562	65.4
Textile mill products	32,258	53,276	60.5
Chemicals and allied products	101,696	197,311	51.5
Fabricated metal industries	70,490	139,580	50.5
Furniture and fixtures	14,764	31,294	47.2
Electric and electronic equipment	83,079	192,731	43.1
Tobacco products	6,626	18,507	35.8
Printing and publishing	39,103	111,885	34.9

Source: Adapted from D.W. Dobler, D.N. Burt, and L. Lee, Jr., *Purchasing and Materials Management,* Fifth Edition, New York: McGraw Hill, 1990, p. 12. Copyright ©1990, McGraw-Hill. Reproduced with permission of McGraw-Hill.

range of products. The advantage of a systems contract is that individual purchases by users do not require separate purchase orders, so much of the paper burden for routine, low-value items is removed from purchasing's shoulders, leaving more time and resources for high-dollar-value items. Traditionally, the main reason for choosing a supplier has been the lowest price for goods and services on a short-term basis.

Increasingly, however, firms are adopting an approach in which

FIGURE 13.6 • A COMPARISON OF PURCHASING STRATEGIES

Traditional approach	Supplier partnership
Primary emphasis on price	Multiple criteria including quality and management philosophy
Short-term contracts	Longer-term contracts
Evaluation by bid	Intensive and extensive evaluation, including site visits
Many suppliers	Restricted list of suppliers
Improvement benefits distributed based on relative power	Improvement benefits shared
Occasional improvements	Continuous improvements
Problems the supplier's responsibility to correct	Problem jointly solved
Information kept private	Information shared
Clear delineation of business responsibility	Responsibility a joint concern

they treat their suppliers as business partners rather than as adversaries in a bidding war. The partnership approach is particularly useful when the criteria for the choice of supplier are multi-dimensional, with supplier quality and on-time delivery being of prime importance. Choosing the right supplier requires an extensive investigative effort to identify those suppliers who are willing to improve their process and product quality on a continuous basis. This narrows the sources of supply and entails careful management of the relationship with each supplier. Under the traditional bidding process, doing good work does not guarantee the supplier the next job if another company comes through with a better price. In a partnership arrangement, suppliers lose contracts only if quality and willingness to improve are not maintained. Joint problem-solving teams attack any quality and process problems that surface. For the partnership to succeed in the long run, benefits from problem solving and quality improvements must be shared equitably. For example, if the joint problem solving can yield a cost reduction of 5 percent, only part of this reduction is passed on to the purchasing company. The contrast with the traditional power-based, adversarial approach to supplier selection makes adapting to purchasing partnerships difficult for some purchasing managers. As indicated in Issues in Business 13.3, General Motors, like many other high-volume producers, has recognized the importance of purchasing components and supplies at the best possible price by maintaining good relationships with suppliers.

ISSUES IN BUSINESS 13.3

GM'S "WARRIORS" ON A MISSION

HE SAYS HE is just another team member, but J. Ignacio Lopez de Arriortua is shaking up suppliers to giant General Motors Corp. as never before, first with a fearsome mystique and now with some real gains to brag about.

In an interview in Toronto, Mr. Lopez said Detroit-based GM is on the way to building a more competitive supply base, and not—as rumoured—by demanding unreasonable price cuts and tearing up contracts. GM's annual purchases top $50 billion (U.S.).

"We've got the most powerful tool in the industry," GM's vice-president in charge of worldwide purchasing said, "and we're giving this free to our partners," company-owned and independent parts makers. That tool is PICOS, which stands for Purchased Input Concept Optimization with Suppliers. That awkward acronym forms the Spanish word for mountain peaks, no accident since Mr. Lopez is a Basque Spaniard.

In the past four and a half months, following his move to Detroit from GM Europe, 200 engineers in global purchasing have conducted 101 week-long PICOS seminars in specific work areas of U.S. supplier companies, Mr. Lopez said. Average gains, by his reckoning, are 65 percent in productivity, 52 percent less material on hand, 35 percent space saving, and 56 percent time reduction between orders received and delivered. The PICOS system was developed in Europe and implemented in countries with a range of industrial sophistication from Germany to Malta. The average result was a 50 percent improvement in productivity, Mr. Lopez said.

(continued)

"We need to know we have the best in quality, service and price ... but we are not breaking any contracts." Mr. Lopez isn't making public pronouncements about GM's cost-saving objectives either, but the industry rumble is that it's $100 million a week—about $5 billion a year—a chunk of which is already in hand.

Source: Excerpts from Timothy Pritchard, "GM's 'Warriors' on a Mission," *The Globe and Mail*, September 30, 1992, p. B6.

Questions for Discussion

1. Outline the reasons why GM has brought Mr. Lopez to North America.
2. What aspects of purchasing, other than price, is GM focussing on? Why are these aspects important?

MANAGING THE OUTPUTS

Distribution of the product often requires joint decision making between the marketing and operations departments. Matters such as warehouse location, distribution methods, and inventory service levels are important expense items. In some merchandising companies, the cost of distribution and warehousing exceeds 25 percent of sales, and such costs can easily exceed 10 percent of sales, even in a manufacturing environment. Distribution management primarily calls for marketing expertise, but some of the trade-offs involved will influence operations decisions.

Warehouse Policies and Distribution Costs

Operations managers must consider the location and number of warehouses, and inventory policies within each warehouse, in order to serve customers speedily without unnecessary transportation, handling, and inventory expenses. It is generally recognized that, as the number of warehouses decreases, the total volume of inventory required to maintain constant service levels to the customer also decreases. Two separate warehouses each might require 100 units of inventory to provide a certain level of customer service; one centralized warehouse might be able to supply the same number of customers with 140 units.

Distribution strategy, however, must take more into account than just inventory costs. A larger number of small regional warehouses may provide faster response to customer orders, leading to a reduction in pipeline inventory (inventory in transit to the customer).

Transportation costs are also a factor in planning warehouse locations. It may be more cost-efficient to ship goods in volume to a regional warehouse by train or transport truck and then use smaller vans from the warehouse for individual orders. But this transport plan must be watched carefully; if shipments to regional warehouses are too small, transportation costs will increase again. The costs of running a number of warehouses (rent, handling, etc.) must also be considered. The trade-offs among the costs of transportation, warehouse management, and inventory are represented in Figure 13.7. Clearly

FIGURE 13.7 • WAREHOUSE TOTAL COST STRUCTURE

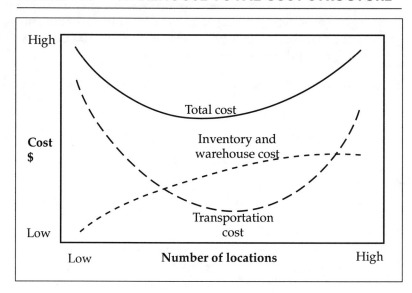

the decision on the number of locations to have, their size, and the inventory safety stock will be specific for each industry and company.

Decisions on location extend to the manufacturing plant as well as the warehouse. For example, it is typical for metal-can manufacturers to locate within close proximity to food processing companies to avoid expensive shipping of "air" (empty cans). On the other hand, cars are regularly shipped directly to distributors from a central facility (the manufacturing and assembly plant) because the cost of shipping is relatively small in relation to the value of the product and about half of all cars are produced with factory-installed options to meet a specific customer's order.

BUSINESS REVIEW 13.3

1. Discuss the management of the following inputs to the production process for a fast-food restaurant or another enterprise with which you are familiar.
   a) capital equipment
   b) labour
   c) materials

2. Visit a retail outlet and talk to the store manager. Find out and report to the class how the distribution centre fills up the store shelves (frequency and stocking volume). How might the concepts learned here help explain your weekly food-purchasing decisions?

QUALITY CONTROL AND QUALITY MANAGEMENT

Formal quality control measures go back to the 1920s, when Walter Shewart established sampling procedures to monitor quality of output at Bell Laboratories. During the last twenty years, quality has re-emerged as a critical issue in operations management. The emphasis now is on monitoring each stage of the production process to ensure that quality is designed and built into the product rather than on simply inspecting the output and discarding product that does not meet quality standards. Since 1985, in the United States, firms have competed vigorously for the Malcolm Baldrige award for total quality management. In Japan, the Deming prize, named after American statistician Edwards Deming, is the most coveted award. Figure 13.8 indicates some of the bases that companies are using to ensure continuous quality improvement.

Defining Quality

In a business context, **quality** is generally defined as conformance to customer expectations. Thus, the organization's efforts are focussed on understanding the needs of the customer, translating those needs into specifications for the manufacturing operation, and controlling the manufacturing process to conform to those specifications. The output of the production process is, therefore, only part of the concern in total quality management. No matter how good the production process, the output will not be fit for customer use if customer needs are poorly measured. Because the measurement of customer needs is usually a marketing responsibility, its discussion in this module will focus on the steps required to conform to specifications.

quality
In a business context, conformance to customer expectations by analyzing those expectations, preparing specifications accordingly, and conforming to them in the production process

FIGURE 13.8 • HOW QUALITY STRATEGIES STACK UP

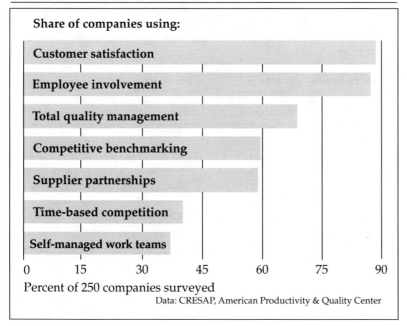

Share of companies using:

- Customer satisfaction
- Employee involvement
- Total quality management
- Competitive benchmarking
- Supplier partnerships
- Time-based competition
- Self-managed work teams

0   15   30   45   60   75   90
Percent of 250 companies surveyed
Data: CRESAP, American Productivity & Quality Center

Source: Reprinted from October 25, 1991 issue of *Business Week* by special permission, copyright ©1991 by McGraw-Hill, Inc.

Quality in the Production Process

A specification defines some target dimension (weight or volume, for example) and acceptable tolerances or deviations from that target value. For example, a bottling plant's engineers might specify that bottles be filled to a volume of at least 250 millilitres (ml), with an acceptable range up to 260 ml. In this case, the target value is 250 ml with a tolerance of 10 ml above the target value. It is then the responsibility of manufacturing to conform to these criteria.

No matter how good the machine or worker, some variations in the output will occur. The objective of statistical process control is to provide information to an operator if and when a machine begins to exhibit performance that goes beyond normal and acceptable variation. A useful method for controlling the process output is to chart measurements of samples of the output against identified limits. (How these limits are calculated is beyond the scope of this text.) A simple control chart is shown in Figure 13.9. A number of samples are measured at regular intervals, and each time the average measurement is plotted. The profile (plotted over time) can be used to assess whether the process is meeting specifications.

The chart is divided into zones to provide a basis for interpretation. Many rules are used in practice to determine whether the process needs to be investigated and perhaps adjusted. Typically, operators use three primary rules to decide whether the process has gone out of control:

1. If any one point on the chart falls outside control limits
2. If two of three consecutive points fall in the A zone
3. If four of five consecutive points fall in the A or B zone

The second and third rules help identify a gradual deterioration in the process; the first rule determines whether the output is acceptable. The manufacturing process charted in Figure 13.9 would be considered out of control toward the end of the run because two out of three sample averages fell in the A zone. The manufacturer should stop the

FIGURE 13.9 • A SIMPLE PROCESS CONTROL CHART

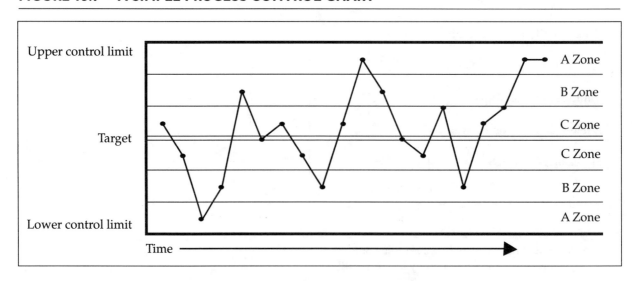

process and investigate why. Often, the problem can be traced to one of several causes—a new worker, a worn machine, a new supply shipment or supplier, or a change in operating procedure.

Process control charts can easily be adapted to service sector environments. "Proportion of defects" is commonly used where the measurement is made on a pass/fail basis (i.e., where there are no tolerances). For example, order-taking errors in a restaurant could be charted, and deviations from expected performance subjected to the same rigorous cause-and-effect analysis used in a traditional manufacturing setting.

Quality and Productivity

Identifying the cause and correcting the problem are two separate activities. In either a manufacturing or a service setting, the quality control process should lead, not to the fear of making a mistake, but to the desire for continuous improvement. And managers should look beyond equipment failure or poor work practices. Some of the most difficult problems require a change in management thinking. For example, eliminating the concept of multiple suppliers to avoid the unnecessary introduction of variances in supplies may cause major difficulties for traditionalists in purchasing. Edwards Deming has suggested that 85 percent of quality problems can be traced to poor management. Evidence gathered during the past decade indicates that increased conformance to specifications invariably yields improvements in productivity through reduced scrap, overtime, warranty, and product liability costs. In other words, quality is free.

MANAGING CHANGE

No business can remain static for very long. Customer expectations and preferences change rapidly. New enterprises are forming daily, trying to carve out market niches that erode an existing firm's business. International competition is fierce, and complacency makes easy prey of firms that are not cost- and quality-competitive. Operations management is no different. Change and continuous improvement are necessary prerequisites for those firms that wish to remain competitive.

Change often means the creation and adoption of new technology that can either expand production without a similar increase in inputs or maintain production with a decrease in inputs required.

However, this traditional economist's view of technology is giving way to the view that technology should increase flexibility so that a line flow production system can produce the variety possible in a job shop without the high costs. Many firms have adopted technologies that they presume will offer flexibility, such as computer-aided design and computer-aided manufacturing, or CAD/CAM (for fast product-design changes), and reprogrammable robots (for consistency and change), but all too often the new technology is used as pure automation and fails to use the flexibility it offers.

A second key area of change that operations managers need to focus on is the pursuit of continuous quality improvement. The never-ending pursuit of quality in conformance to specifications yields reduced production and customer dissatisfaction costs—leading to gains in market share, economies of scale, and superior corporate performance.

Continuous improvement is not an easy task. It requires efforts by individuals and problem-solving teams to determine the causes of variance in performance, devise methods to reduce the variance, implement solutions, and monitor the results. Once one cause has been corrected, the entire cycle must be performed over and over again. Obviously, such a continuous improvement process requires management commitment, a contribution from all workers, and the absence of fear that these efforts will lead to reprisals or job elimination.

INTERACTIVE SUMMARY AND DISCUSSION QUESTIONS

1. This module has discussed the key operations management process classifications (job shop, batch, line flow, and continuous) and their associated characteristics. Where does a McDonald's restaurant fit within the framework? A gourmet restaurant? The cafeteria at your college or university?

2. Each of the above processes is appropriate for certain tasks. Which would be more appropriate for a high-volume, low-cost operation? For operations with a wide variety of products and requiring high levels of flexibility?

3. How does the customer's changing tastes and preferences for products have an impact on the manufacturing facility?

4. Demand forecasting is an integral part of production planning. Explain.

5. Two important components of the production plan are the bill of materials (BOM) and the routing sheet. Explain how they are used.

6. Inventory serves a number of functions. These are implied in the different names given to it: cycle inventory, pipeline inventory, anticipatory inventory, and buffer inventory. Define each.

7. Just-in-time (JIT) production attempts to reduce batch sizes as much as possible. What is the rationale for this philosophy?

8. Why do JIT production systems rely heavily on process control procedures?

9. Total productive maintenance is an important concept in efficient production. What is the meaning of this concept?

10. The management of inputs involves capacity management, labour management, purchasing, and supplier partnerships. Outline how these are related.

11. Discuss ways in which the variability in products or services that you have purchased affects the way you view the companies providing the products and services.

CASE 13.1

HIGH TECH AND COMMON SENSE

A LONG LINE OF men and women shuffle grey-faced from a factory, bringing home not paycheques but layoff notices. At another plant, outdated machinery rusts, while the building itself invites the attention of a fire inspector. That's Canada's industrial sector, as glimpsed in the glare of newspaper headlines and film clips on the nightly television news. The reality? Manufacturing is very much alive, fighting harder and more successfully than ever to renew itself. Free trade and tough times have produced a flurry of innovation in factories, with everyone from top management down intent on producing far-higher-quality goods at far lower costs.

(continued)

Just how are they doing it? The smartest operators are using a combination of high tech and common sense. Yes, some of the new machinery looks like it could have been designed by the illustrators of Marvel comics. But no, it doesn't take a genius to put some of the most successful innovations into practice. "We've seen dramatic quality improvements just by putting people closer together," says consultant Peter Kreppenhoffer of Progressive Manufacturing Solutions in Kitchener, Ontario. "If one guy in a factory can talk to the guy upstream in a normal voice, you have a 20 to 25 percent reduction in rejects right there."

If necessity is the mother of invention, competition is surely the father of innovation. With the implementation of free trade, Canada's productivity lag became more evident, and manufacturers began cutting employees at the first whiff of recession. What was called for was radical surgery, according to Richard Hossack, manufacturing and logistics partner at Coopers & Lybrand in Toronto. "[Manufacturers] need to improve their costs by one-third, not 5 to 10 percent," he says, "and they need to improve delivery times by two or three weeks, not two or three days."

If that's so, they need look no farther for a model than Brantford, Ontario–based Raymond Industrial Equipment Ltd., a subsidiary of publicly traded Raymond Corp. of Greene, New York. Since general manager Jim Locker took charge of Raymond three years ago, his team has done nothing short of transforming it into a plant for the '90s. In fact, the 250-employee manufacturer is now so efficient that in two years it has collapsed the time to make a forklift truck to four days from fifteen. Along the way, it slashed inventory by at least 60 percent, cutting warehouse space in half and adding $7 million to cash flow. While Locker won't talk sales, he says market share has jumped 20 percent in a smaller recessionary market.

The factory's transformation to super efficiency began with a meticulously orchestrated switch to cellular, or synchronous, manufacturing. Raymond rearranged the plant into self-contained work cells, each doing one job: welding on one side, assembly on the other. After the various components of a forklift pass along three parallel production lines, they meet simultaneously in the middle for assembly. That's why the process is called synchronous. "The idea," says Locker, "is to shorten all delays and optimize value-added time."

Another achievement took place in the shop where forklift tractor bodies are welded. In 1989, the job took four men six hours to complete. Now, three men and two robots take just 35 minutes. The men change the tooling, reprogram the computer controlling the robots for different jobs, and operate the cranes that move the heavy truck bodies. Meanwhile, the robots do the welding.

Like many plants in the auto sector, Raymond has adapted the Japanese *kanban* system to its reconfigured production lines. *Kanban* systems ensure that workers make only as much of a component as the next station immediately needs. It's a simple way of synchronizing the factory and limiting the production of unnecessary parts. "You're balancing a shop," says Locker, "so that material isn't sitting around." Bottlenecks, where subassembly takes longer, get more manpower; a worker may handle several simpler tasks that take less time.

Compare that with the old batch system. A worker made as many parts as he or she could each day, because every part of the subassembly was done consecutively in batches. The parts then sat in stock for four or five weeks, until they were used up. Workers were constantly spending unproductive time storing parts in the warehouse, then hauling them out again as they were needed.

At Raymond, in a typical week in June 1989, 907 manufacturing orders were issued to the shop floor for different components, says Locker. In one week in June 1990, the shop floor handled a mere 60. All were for finished trucks. That's planning.

Locker says the next step is the paperless plant. Later this year, he plans to tie in Raymond's mainframe computer to the engineers' CAD/CAM stations and a personal-computer network on the shop floor. Engineering designs for each set of trucks will travel to the mainframe, which in turn will send synchronized orders to the shop floor. "It will eliminate the need for paper," says Locker. Efficiency is a concern productivity statistics show far too few bosses share.

(continued)

Manufacturing consultants say synchronizing production and improving plant layout should take priority for most factory rethinks. But some managers resist that idea. "They say they don't want [workers] talking to each other," says Kreppenhofer. "They'll waste time." But all too often he sees a press operator and a welder who've worked together twenty years without ever talking about how the work they do affects each other.

Great gadgets and clever processes won't save a plant that lacks a strategy to make the most of what it can do best and rid itself of the rest. As Locker puts it, "You've got to be the best. It's basically survival. If you don't seek to improve, you're dead."

Source: Excerpts from John Southerst, "The Next Industrial Revolution," *Canadian Business,* December 15, 1992, pp. A1, A6.

Questions for Discussion

1. Explain the plant layout Raymond uses for its synchronous production process.
2. What are the advantages of the *kanban* system?
3. Is Raymond using new technology efficiently?

CASE 13.2

SOMETHING SMELLY AT THE JEEP PLANT?

NEARLY 400 PEOPLE at Chrysler's Jeep facility in Toledo, Ohio, have been asked to stop using their anti-perspirants. The active perspirant ingredients include such elements as aluminum, zirconium, chlorine, and silicon, and have been found to cause marring of the Jeep paint surface.

In the paint line, the employees dress like scrub nurses, wearing white gloves, hairnets, and coveralls. However, small flakes of their anti-perspirants can filter through the protective material and deposit a tiny flake onto the vehicle. When the vehicle gets painted, the paint will flow away from the flake, leaving a small "crater" about the size of a baby's fingertip.

A little bit of paint marring may not sound like much but it's enough to send a car back for repairs that might cost thousands of dollars. Problems such as these have become more prevalent in the last fifteen years as paints have become more environmentally sensitive. The cause of the problem can be particularly difficult, somewhat like finding the needle in the haystack. Part of the problem is the intermittent nature of the defect. The problem can appear out of nowhere and disappear just as quickly.

The problem at the Toledo facility became very serious in 1990. There were times when every car seemed to have a crater defect, and some had as many as 20–50 craters on the roof and hood. The entire Jeep production line had to stop and the line workers were sent home for lack of work.

Other car facilities had experienced similar problems in the past and had traced the cause, in one case, to grease and oils from eating potato chips during worker rest periods. In another facility, one case of cratering was caused by an aerosol cleaner used on the glass of a vending machine near the paint line.

At the Toledo facility, sampling plans and control charts were used to try and identify the timing of more frequent occurrences. A number of problem-solving sessions were held, but to no avail.

Eventually, samples from the vehicles were examined at the University of Michigan's Electron Microbeam Analysis lab. The chemicals found turned out to be those from anti-perspirants that the workers were using.

(continued)

Getting workers to change their personal hygiene habits, however, has proven to be as challenging as identifying the actual cause of the cratering problem.

Source: Adapted from Tahree Lane, "Jeep Is Sure about Ban: It Puts 'Craters' in Paint," *The Toledo Blade*, December 15, 1991, pp. A1–A6.

Questions for Discussion

1. When the paint line experienced high levels of defects, why did the other workers have to go home?

2. How would your answer to question 1 "force" management to find a solution to the paint cratering problem quickly? Is this advantageous?

3. If you were responsible for finding the cause of the cratering problem, detail the various steps you might follow and, specifically, who would be in the best position to carry out your work steps.

4. You are the manager of production at the Jeep facility and you have just received the report from the University of Michigan. Detail the steps and actions you would take to implement a change in personal hygiene on the plant line. What issues do you think management had to face to solve their problem?

NOTES

1. Oliver Bertin, "Food Firms Feel Threatened as Trade Barriers Collapse," *The Globe and Mail*, May 19, 1990, pp. B1, B4.
2. Michael Salter, "Sorry, We're Out of It," *Report on Business Magazine*, September 1987, p. 67.
3. Geoffrey Rowan, "New System for Planning," *The Globe and Mail*, February 23, 1990, p. B5.
4. Patricia Lush, "Just-in-Time Pays Off for Auto Sector," *The Globe and Mail*, September 7, 1991, pp. B1, B2.
5. Anne Gibbon, "Ding Dong Avon Smalling," *The Globe and Mail*, August 18, 1992, p. B18.
6. John Saunders, "GM's Just-in-Time Delivery," *The Globe and Mail*, September 7, 1991, pp. B1, B2.

PHOTO CREDITS

MODULE
◆ MKT ◆

MARKETING: BRIDGING THE GAP BETWEEN PRODUCER AND CONSUMER

THE FOCUS OF THIS MODULE

1. To discuss some of the central tenets of marketing

2. To describe the breadth of marketing functions

3. To discuss the consumer focus of marketing

4. To consider elements that should be taken into consideration in developing marketing strategy and marketing plans

5. To explain the concept of the marketing mix and describe the elements of it

6. To learn the meaning of the following terms:

KEY TERMS

marketing research	marketing niche
financing	marketing plan
marketing	marketing mix
product orientation	product
sales orientation	pricing
market orientation	distribution
market segment	communication
target market	

DOUGLAS MASON WHISTLES cheerfully as he rummages through a file box near his desk on the nineteenth floor of a downtown Vancouver office building. This successful entrepreneur has every reason to be cheerful. His most recent business venture is a monster win.

Clearly Canadian Beverage Corp., which Mason launched in 1990, has succeeded largely on the strength of an astute marketing campaign that targets young, health-conscious consumers, primarily in the United States. Its main product is a carbonated sweetened soft drink available in six fruit flavours. To distinguish it from other carbonated drinks, Clearly Canadian is sold in a distinctive blue-tinted bottle. The

THINK CLEARLY™

Think of cold, refreshing waters and fresh, sweet fruit.
Now, drink that thought. And let the water take you there.
Clearly Canadian: Pure sparkling water imported from
Canada with natural fruit flavours.

Since its launch in 1990, Clearly Canadian Beverage Corporation has quickly expanded, creating three new flavours as well as two new products, Clearly Tea and Clearly 2, the latter of which is a 2-calorie drink in a distinctive 12-ounce can. Clearly Canadian targets young consumers, ages 13–34, in Canada and the U.S., advertising through cable TV (*MuchMusic*), regional and local TV (*Kids in the Hall, Beverly Hills 90210*) and consumer magazines (*Rolling Stone, Seventeen*).

company's advertising features scenes of British Columbia's snow-capped Rocky Mountains.

While working in the food-retailing industry, in 1984, Mr. Mason became fascinated by, as he puts it, "the amount of shelf space in grocery stores devoted to diapers and bottled water." He decided to start his own water company.

Originally Mason said he intended to market an alternative to Perrier, a French mineral water. "But our research showed that the soft drink market was 8,000 times the size of the water market," he added. "I thought, 'Why not have a combination? We'll have a mineral-water drink, but sweeten it.'"

Clearly Canadian is packaged to appeal to image-conscious consumers; the product sells for $1.39 in some Canadian stores—about 50 cents more than a typical canned soft drink. Said Glen Foreman, the company's chief operating officer: "We have created a white-table-cloth profile for Clearly Canadian."

Source: Adapted from Hal Quinn, "Canadian, Clearly," *Maclean's*.

THE ACCOMPLISHMENTS OF Clearly Canadian illustrate how careful marketing planning and execution have helped the business. If Douglas Mason had done no more than produce a fine product, most of it would still be sitting in a warehouse somewhere, and the company would likely be out of business.

Marketing is about the process of getting and keeping customers. No organization can exist for long without them. The initial enthusiasm surrounding a new business venture quickly turns to gloom if customers are not attracted. Furthermore, a reasonable number must purchase again and again to generate a reliable stream of revenue. Survival depends on a surplus of revenues (i.e., profits).

The key to success, therefore, is finding and keeping customers. This is done by learning about, understanding, and serving their needs. The more careful the marketing program, the better the chance of prosperity for the organization. Devising such a program is not a simple task. As indicated in Figure 14.1, it often requires specifically designed research as well as a careful analysis of more general trends and values in society.

Clearly Canadian is one company that understood the market. It targeted young, health-conscious consumers and produced a product attuned to their values and tastes. Then it developed a marketing program that was in harmony with such values and tastes.

Numerous bankruptcies bear witness to companies that ignored, failed to understand, or were unable to satisfy the real needs of the customer.

BRINGING PRODUCER AND CUSTOMER TOGETHER

The role of marketing can be illustrated, as in Figure 14.2, by visualizing a large gap between the producer and customer. They are separated by five conditions: perspective, time, space, needs or wants, and possession.

Perspective

The producer or supplier of a good or service has certain views about that product. The consumer may not even be aware of, or may fail to appreciate, its attributes.

Time

There is often a large gap between the planning stages of a product and when it is available. With goods, manufacturing may occur long

FIGURE 14.1 • HOW TO FIND AND KEEP CUSTOMERS

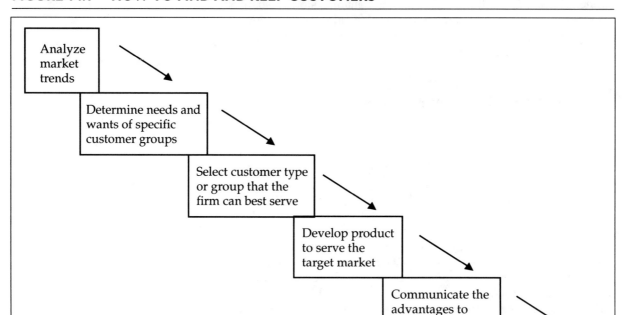

before consumers even think about buying (a service, such as dry cleaning or tax-return preparation, can be produced only when the customer purchases it). For example, Sony produces a Walkman some months before a student walks into a store in Thunder Bay to buy one.

Space

Similarly, the Thunder Bay customer seldom considers the many spatial aspects of the provision of a good that is produced in Asia. It is transported by land to a port, placed on a ship, and then transported to a central Canadian distribution point. The distributor opens a container filled with hundreds of Walkmans and ships five units to the bookstore at Lakehead University. Our student, who has been thinking about such a product (and probably comparing brands and prices), gets up on Wednesday morning and decides to purchase a Walkman that afternoon. She expects to find it waiting for her (instead of having to order it from Japan), and does.

Needs or Wants

The needs or wants of suppliers and customers are very different. The supplier's needs are to provide a good or service that will be attractive to enough customers to earn profits. The customer has a varied set of needs or wants that he or she wishes to satisfy, such as thirst, or to listen to music while jogging.

FIGURE 14.2 • MARKETING BRIDGES THE GAP BETWEEN PRODUCER AND CONSUMER

Possession

The producer of the good or service has the product and an infrastructure to produce it. Thousands of customers have money (or credit) to buy the product if they think it worthwhile. Possession of product and possession of money are exchanged, thus enabling the satisfaction of both the producer's and the customer's needs.

THE TOOLS OF MARKETING

Nothing will happen in business, nor will consumers have the goods and services they deem necessary, unless this gap is overcome. Marketing can be thought of as the actualizing force that bridges the gap between the producer and the consumer. Eight functions of marketing are the tools that accomplish this: marketing research, transporting, wholesaling, retailing, buying, advertising, selling, and financing.

Marketing Research

The business needs information about product performance, customers, the competition, and many other things. **Marketing research** is a systematic way of gathering and analyzing data that leads to intelligent decisions about products and efforts to market them.

marketing research
The systematic gathering, recording, and analysis of data relating to the marketing of products

Transporting

Transporting consists of the many methods of getting products to consumers. The numerous steps to getting a Walkman or a bottle of Clearly Canadian from the factory to a customer in Thunder Bay, Ontario, Ucluelet, British Columbia, or Morin Heights, Quebec, require many different transportation modes. The efficient interconnection of these modes requires sophisticated organization. This task is often called physical distribution.

Wholesaling

When a ship lands in Vancouver with thousands of Walkmans, how does the campus bookstore in Thunder Bay get the five Walkmans that it wants? How does E.D. Smith in Ontario get its canned foods into the thousands of small and large retail outlets in Canada? For many products, wholesalers act as intermediaries in the marketing channel between manufacturer and retailer. Often found in regional locations, they buy large quantities from many manufacturers and break that bulk down into smaller packages to supply to retailers. Because they represent many different food products, it is efficient for them to call on retailers, representing and delivering all the product lines they carry.

Retailing

Retailing is one of the most visible marketing functions. Retailers accumulate an assortment of products to sell to the specific groups of customers they are trying to serve. Only the largest, such as department stores, are able to develop an assortment comprehensive enough to serve most customers.

Distribution through wholesalers and retailers is not universal. Many producers do not use wholesalers, taking their own products direct to the retailer. Some, such as automobile manufacturers, use their own exclusive retailing establishments rather than allow stores to sell their products alongside those of competitors.

Buying

Wholesalers and retailers are businesses in their own right, wishing to acquire the products that will meet their customers' needs. As a result, they encounter a daunting task in choosing the items that they will stock and promote. Buyers are specialists in these organizations who know their customers' needs and select products that will serve those needs and will bring profits to their organization.

Advertising

Many people confuse advertising with marketing, but it is only one aspect of the marketing function. Advertising is used to inform existing and potential customers about goods and services. It is also often used to try to persuade customers of the advantages of using a particular brand. Advertising is non-personal: it uses the mass media to reach a wide audience.

Selling

Personal selling is the most immediate aspect of marketing communications. Sales people call on customers, or meet the public, when the potential sales response warrants the expense, and when the sales message can be made most persuasively through person-to-person contact. Each contact costs much more than an advertising message, but direct communications provides information specific to the customer's needs and is thus more persuasive. Selling is another function that is often confused with marketing.

Financing

Consumers and business organizations do not always have the resources to pay cash in full at the time of purchase, but may be ready to cover payments over a period of time. Students finance the purchase of cars, families have house mortgages, and business firms purchase inventory and equipment on credit. The provision and management of credit to facilitate the purchase of goods and services is known as **financing**. Financing is a vital part of marketing as it allows buyers to make purchases when needed and sellers to maintain a steadier flow of sales and production.

financing
The provision and management of credit to facilitate the purchase of goods and services

MARKETING DEFINED

Marketing is much more than sales or advertising. All the functions of marketing must be performed in the generation of trade for virtually all business organizations.

The official definition of **marketing** (adopted by the American Marketing Association) is "the process of planning and executing the conception, pricing, promotion of ideas, goods and services to create exchanges that satisfy individual and organizational objectives." This definition implies that marketing applies to not-for-profit organizations as well as to business organizations.

Religious groups, charities, arts organizations, and government services benefit from the application of marketing thinking to their organizations. For example, a church-based, privately run school such as Trinity Western University in Langley, British Columbia, needs to market its services to both students and potential supporters.

marketing
The process of planning and executing the conception, pricing, promotion of ideas, goods, and services to create exchanges that satisfy individual and organizational objectives

---

BUSINESS REVIEW 14.1

1. Explain the nature of the "gap" between producers and consumers.
2. What are the functions of marketing, and how do they help to bridge the gap?
3. Explain how the definition of marketing applies to not-for-profit organizations as well as to business.

ORIENTATION OF MARKETING EFFORTS

Companies manifest three different approaches to their marketing efforts. Some are *product oriented*, some are *sales oriented*, and others are *market oriented*. It is often suggested that these orientations are a series of "eras" through which marketing has passed. However, as Ronald A. Fullerton has pointed out,[1] there is little historical support for the concept of this progression. Rather, a firm's orientation depends more on the skills of its top management than on the development of marketing theory and practice over time.

Product Orientation

product orientation
A concentration on the production of goods and services rather than on advertising and sales or the needs of the market

In a firm with **product orientation**, the emphasis is on the product itself rather than on the consumer's needs. In this case, market considerations are ignored or de-emphasized. Ralph Waldo Emerson is quoted as saying that, if you build a better mousetrap, the world will beat a path to your door. A product-oriented firm stresses production and assumes that a good product will sell itself. Such a strategy is very limiting, for it assumes that the world knows about the product and that the tastes and values of the producer are the same as those of the market.

An example of firms with a product orientation is the North American auto makers in the 1970s and early 1980s. They did not realize how badly their cars were out of phase with what customers wanted until Japanese car makers began to take large shares of the market.

Sales Orientation

sales orientation
A concentration on advertising and sales of the product rather than on the needs of the market

A firm with a **sales orientation** still concentrates on the product, but recognizes that the world will not beat a path to its door to purchase its product. Thus, it invests in an aggressive, high-powered sales orga-

Being aware of social trends such as the rise in environmental concerns helps manufacturers to meet consumer needs. Increasingly, because of environmental issues, manufacturers of deodorants like Gillette Canada Inc. are not only offering multiple fragrances but also different forms. The stick form is considered more environmentally friendly than the aerosol spray. Now consumers have the choice between brands, fragrances, and forms.

nization, and an advertising program. However, as we have seen, selling is only one component of marketing. Some consider that IBM's huge losses in the early 1990s were partially attributable to the fact that the company has been too sales oriented.

Market Orientation

Many firms have discovered the limitations of product and sales orientations. They understand that there is no point in building a better mousetrap if the world does not want one. They have found that it makes a great deal of sense to pay careful attention to understanding customer needs and objectives, and make the business serve the interests of the customer rather than trying to make the customer buy what the business wants to produce. **Market orientation** is thus an organization-wide focus on providing chosen groups of customers with products that will satisfy their needs. The satisfaction thus achieved will bring about repeat business and long-run profits. The phenomenal success of McDonald's restaurants around the world is attributed to the fact that this company serves the needs of certain market segments extremely well.

market orientation
A concentration on the needs of a chosen group of customers in order to supply them with products to satisfy those needs

UNDERSTANDING THE CUSTOMER

The key to effective marketing lies in locating customers that the organization can serve better. Some customers may not be purchasing at all because the goods or services they want are not currently available. Others may be buying products that only partially meet their needs and they may be willing to switch quickly to new products that offer greater satisfaction. Potential or unsatisfied customers like these should be the targets of market-oriented companies.

Market Segmentation

No marketer can devise a program to satisfy all consumers. Even Coca-Cola, with its range of products and extensive distribution, cannot do so. Thus, other firms, such as 7-Up and Canada Dry, have emerged to serve other customer groups. The fact is that, in most markets, there are several relatively homogeneous groups, or **market segments.** They are sometimes defined by demographic characteristics, such as age or sex. At other times, behavioural (frequent as opposed to infrequent buyers) or social (home-oriented buyers) attributes are used to identify a market segment.

market segment
A relatively homogeneous group of potential customers defined by demographic or behavioural characteristics

Careful analysis of customer needs within various market segments leads to business opportunities. An analysis of how competitive products serve each segment leads to the choice of target markets with good sales potential. A firm's **target markets** are market segments with similar values regarding a product category that the firm aims to serve.

target market
Market segments that have similar values regarding a product category and that a firm aims to serve

Identifying and serving target markets is an important and useful marketing tool. Increased technological sophistication allows business to link up with various databases and "remember" buying behaviours. The question of how far businesses should take such applications is raised in Issues in Business 14.1.

ISSUES IN BUSINESS 14.1

TARGET MARKETING: TURNING BIRDS OF A FEATHER INTO SITTING DUCKS?

WHOLESALERS AND RETAILERS are no longer content to advertise in the mass media, spending millions of dollars for messages that may fall on deaf ears. Manufacturers want to target customers directly and try to lock them into consistent buying patterns. The only way to accomplish this successfully is to know everything about the customers.

When customers reach the sales counter at Casual Corner or August Max clothing stores, the clerks ask them for their telephone number, which is then entered into the cash register.

We are conditioned to provide information like this innocently, because we have been led to believe that it will help the merchant track us down if a cheque bounces or a credit card transaction is erroneous or invalid. But these stores have other uses in mind for the information. They are using a new computer software program called REACT, which links the phone number with the customer's identity, address, age, income bracket, dwelling type, and previous purchases in the store.

Combining this information with a description of the current purchases permits the stores to target customers by mail, telephone, or in-store marketing to purchases for which the customer is known to have a high interest (to be vulnerable?). Some refer to this as "targeting by taste."

REACT people stress that the information is kept confidential and that providing the telephone number is purely voluntary. A customer is told, they say, that the phone number is requested for marketing purposes.

But is that an acceptable explanation?

Source: Adapted from Robert Ellis Smith, "Target Marketing: Turning Birds of a Feather into Sitting Ducks," *Business and Society Review* Winter 1991, No. 76, pp. 33–37.

Questions for Discussion
1. Do you think the reasons for extracting personal and private information from customers should be made clear to them at the time the request is made?
2. What rights do you think the consumer has in this form of target marketing?
3. What rights do you think the retailer has to "target by taste"?
4. Are there ways to make this procedure more appropriate for both the consumer and the retailer?

ANALYZING CONSUMER BEHAVIOUR

Since the key to marketing success is satisfied customers, it is important to develop an understanding of their needs and wants, as well as their likely response to marketing efforts. Consumer behaviour is a large and complex area, part of the even larger subject of human behaviour in general. And, just as psychology has not plumbed the depths of human behaviour, so analysis of consumer behaviour has many limitations. Nevertheless, a great deal is known about the consumer decision process.

Several general models of consumer behaviour can help a business to respond better to needs and to influence decisions. For example, the Engel, Blackwell, and Miniard Consumer Decision Process Model has four components: information input, information processing, decision process stages, and variables influencing the decision process.[2]

Information Input

Many types of information enter into a consumer's decision process to purchase a product. This information comes from many sources, such as personal observation, discussions with friends, sales people, and the mass media.

Information Processing

An individual screens out most of the many incoming stimuli. Some factor in one's active memory determines whether the mind will process the stimulus or not.

Decision Process Stages

In making a purchase decision, individuals are considered to pass through the following steps: recognition of a problem, search for the most appropriate solution, evaluation of alternative solutions, purchase decision, purchase act, and post-purchase evaluation.

Variables Influencing the Decision Process

Many factors influence the purchase decision process. These may be grouped in three categories: social influences (e.g., culture and family), characteristics of the individual (e.g., motives, values, lifestyle, and personality), and situational influences (e.g., atmosphere, urgency of purchase, and availability).

A full explanation of the concepts presented in this model would require an entire book. This brief outline is presented here to show that there is a great deal of research that can help the firm to make intelligent analyses of customers in each market segment and their likely response to marketing efforts.

Developing Your Business Skills discusses the importance of assessing consumer demand and market opportunities by examining **marketing niches**—highly specific market segments that can be targeted and served through specialized marketing plans.

marketing niche
A highly specific market segment that can be targeted and served through a specialized marketing plan

---

DEVELOPING YOUR BUSINESS SKILLS

NICHE MARKETING

Niche marketing is a term based on the concept of market segmentation. It denotes the development of a marketing plan to serve a very specific segment. The size of such a segment can vary from marginally economic to quite large.

Niche marketing fits current trends in consumer demand. Consumers will respond better to product offerings that serve their specific needs rather than accepting something made for the mass market.

The need for niche marketing is exemplified by the declining influence of department stores. Many are increasingly running into difficulties because competitors are more precisely serving market niches. Examples are clothing stores serving youth, high fashion, or non-standard sizes.

(continued)

As a result, marketers will be challenged to identify niches within society. This will require the use of sophisticated marketing research and analytical skills to uncover new market segments whose needs can be served more precisely through a niche strategy. For example, some have discovered that there is no such thing as a typical teenager. In addition, they must develop the ability to personalize products for (sometimes) quite small markets.

BUSINESS REVIEW 14.2

1. Explain why the central focus of marketing should be the needs of the customer.
2. According to Engel, Blackwell, and Miniard, what are the major components of the consumer decision process?

MARKETING STRATEGY

The business must do more than try to know as much as possible about the customer. To succeed, a marketer must know the customer in a context that includes the competition; government policy and regulation; and the broader economic, social, and political forces that shape the evolution of markets. From this perspective, a marketing strategy can be developed.

A firm's corporate strategy is the overall direction of the organization. Corporate strategy is the responsibility of the head of the organization, and includes inputs from all of the functional areas of the company, such as finance, production, and marketing.

Marketing strategy is the overall direction of the marketing efforts of an organization. It incorporates the entire marketing program within it, and focusses on developing a unique long-run competitive position in the market by assessing consumer needs and the firm's potential for gaining competitive advantage. Marketing strategy must be congruent with corporate strategy.

THE MARKETING PLAN

After a marketing strategy has been developed, a marketing plan must be generated as part of its implementation. The **marketing plan** is a tool of marketing strategy. It is defined as a program of activities that lead to the accomplishment of marketing strategy. Sometimes the marketing plan is referred to as the marketing program.

THE MARKETING MIX

Marketing plans are based on decisions about four elements: product, pricing, distribution, and communication. As shown in Figure 14.3, the combination of these four elements is known as the **marketing mix**.

Product is based on decisions about the product: the need for it, its development, uses, brand names, package design, and types of warranties. Product strategy will vary according to the stage of the

---

marketing plan
The program of marketing activities that support the organization's marketing and corporate strategy

marketing mix
The combination of four strategic elements—product, pricing, distribution, and communications—that form a marketing plan

product
An element of the marketing mix that involves decisions about the product: the need for it, its development, uses, brand names, package design, warranties, and the stage of the product life cycle

FIGURE 14.3 • THE MARKETING MIX

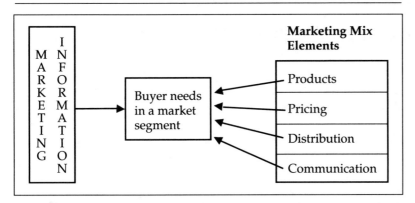

product life cycle (that is, whether the product is new, familiar, or verging on obsolete).

Pricing involves decisions concerning the methods of setting prices. In some market segments, competitive prices are extremely important. In others, a higher price will lend prestige and desirability to the product. Good consumer analysis is vital in making pricing decisions.

Distribution involves decisions about the physical attributes of goods and the selection and management of marketing channels. *Marketing channels* are the steps or handling organizations that a good or service goes through from the producer to the final consumer. Channel decision making entails selecting and working with wholesalers, retailers, and other intermediaries.

Communication requires decisions about the message to be delivered as well as when and how to use personal selling, advertising, and other promotional elements. There are many factors to consider in developing an effective marketing communications program.

The concept of the marketing mix helps the marketing planner. For example, Pizza Hut has successfully catered to market segments such as families and young adults. It has developed distinctive high-quality products of interest to each segment, priced them competitively (buy the second pizza for $5), and to ensure good distribution has located stores close to where its target markets live. Its communications strategy involves a continuous stream of mass-media advertising supplemented by occasional flyers delivered to the door.

The concept of the marketing mix is important because it emphasizes that decisions about one component of the mix must take into consideration each of the others. A good marketing plan uses mix elements in such a way that they complement and build upon one another to produce a plan greater than the sum of its parts. And, over time, there should be consistency to the mix.

Keeping up with trends is a significant issue for business. Companies need to seek new and flexible marketing strategies to cope with current social and economic trends or they will find themselves prey to competitive dominance. Issues in Business 14.2 considers four trends of consequence today.

pricing
An element of the marketing mix that involves decisions about the price at which a product is offered, depending on analysis of the target market and the stage of the product life cycle

distribution
An element of the marketing mix based on decisions about physical distribution and the marketing channels that take the product from producer to final consumer

communication
An element of the marketing mix requiring decisions about the message to be delivered as well as when and where to use personal selling, advertising, and other promotional efforts

ISSUES IN BUSINESS 14.2

TRENDS MARKETERS MIGHT RESPOND TO

Debit Cards: Debit cards allow instant deductions from the customer's chequing account. The system is handled by point-of-sale terminals situated at the checkout counter in retail stores. The cards facilitate purchases and could eliminate the use of cash, cheques, or credit cards.

Harried Two-Income Couples: Two-income couples will soon be demanding a return to the luxury of home delivery. With husband and wife busy with their careers, time is at a premium.

The Greying of North America: As a result of medical breakthroughs and declining birth rates, people over 65 now outnumber teenagers for the first time ever in North America. By the year 2000, 40 percent of adults will be over 50. These demographic trends will have enormous consequences for business in the years to come. "Woopies" (well-off, older people) represent a very attractive market.

Source: Adapted from Allan Cohen, "Marketing Trends and Changes," *Canadian Manager*, Winter 1990, 18–21.

Questions for Discussion
1. In what ways do debit cards represent advantages and/or disadvantages for marketing firms?
2. Suggest practical steps that marketers might consider to attract the various consumer groups discussed above.

INTERACTIVE SUMMARY AND DISCUSSION QUESTIONS

1. This module points out that marketing is the actualizing force which bridges the gap between producer and consumer. Explain.
2. Define each of the following functions of marketing: marketing research, transporting, wholesaling, retailing, buying, advertising, selling, and financing.
3. Show how the functions of marketing relate to the five components of the gap between producer and consumer: perspective, time, space, needs or wants, and possession.
4. This module shows that, for the organization to exist, it must get and keep customers. Explain.
5. Three approaches to marketing efforts are product orientation, sales orientation, and marketing orientation. Demonstrate the strengths and weaknesses of each.
6. This module explains the concepts of target markets and market segmentation. Define each

and show how the concepts relate to each other.
7. The Engel, Blackwell, and Miniard Consumer Decision Process Model has four different components: information input, information processing, decision process stages, and variables influencing the decision process. Provide some examples of each of these components.
8. Define the term "marketing strategy" and interpret the relationship between it and "marketing plan."
9. The vignette at the beginning of this module showed how one company, Clearly Canadian, developed a successful marketing plan. Part of a marketing plan is the marketing mix. Outline the elements of the mix for Clearly Canadian.
10. The marketing mix comprises four elements: product, pricing, distribution, and communication. Show how these relate to marketing strategy and the marketing plan.

CASE 14.1

LOCAL PIZZA SHOP FACES NEW COMPETITION

MCDONALD'S RESTAURANTS of Canada Ltd., with a long reputation for consistency and value in supplying hamburgers, has made a major departure from its previous product strategy.

Shifting consumer attitudes about healthy eating and an all-out price war being waged by rival burger chains forced McDonald's to change tack. It now wants to become known as Canada's largest pizza chain.

"McDonald's is simply giving consumers what they want and what they asked for," says Peter Beresford, the company's vice-president and national director of marketing. "We have always been a customer-driven company."

Extensive research has shown a swing toward pizza as a favoured food, he says. "Extremely positive" marketing trials in Winnipeg, Ottawa, and Kingston convinced the chain of this new product's inevitable success.

Burgers, which have taken a knocking because of their high fat content, are now being downplayed by McDonald's in favour of pizza, which is seen by nutritionists as a healthier alternative.

The fast-food industry is showing trends of product diversification. "The burger guys are selling pizza, the pizza guys are selling chicken wings, and the submarine guys are selling pasta dinners. It's an incredible cross-pollination." said David Menzies, assistant editor of *Canadian Hotel and Restaurant* magazine, which follows the fast-food business. He advised: "It's one thing to be all things to all people and expand your menu. But once you do that, there's a danger of losing sight of your original goals."

Source: Adapted from Randall Scotland, "McDonald's Confirms Pizza As Fast-Food King," *The Financial Post*, April 6, 1992, p. s25.

Questions for Discussion

1. What target market is McDonald's trying to reach with this new product?
2. From your knowledge of this company, identify the marketing mix used to satisfy this market. Would you recommend any changes to this mix?
3. Discuss the personal influences on consumer behaviour in this business situation.
4. Identify the types of marketing research used to develop McDonald's new strategy.
5. How does product diversification help McDonald's image and name? Does it have any disadvantages?

CASE 14.2

MARKETING GINGER ALE IN A COMPETITIVE ENVIRONMENT

"GINGER ALE HAS an image problem. Older people drink it. You mix it with rye or bourbon, drinks of a bygone age. Ginger ale is served in hospitals, not mod bars. Ask someone the last time they had a sip. As often as not, it was years ago, lying in bed with an upset stomach," writes Eben

(continued)

Shapiro in an article in *The New York Times* (May 3, 1992, p. 10) This fact fails to cheer the heart of those responsible for marketing ginger ale.

Ginger ale is part of a huge, and extremely competitive market. Teenagers are the biggest consumers of soft drinks. They drink approximately fifty percent more than the average consumer. The market is also undergoing a slow change.

This change can be seen in the growing spectrum of choices available to consumers. Colas have long held, and still maintain a dominant share. However, "New Age" beverages such as natural sparkling water represented by Clearly Canadian, and Koala Springs are growing in popularity. Adding flavours to such products has further increased their acceptance. These products serve a growing market preference for drinks that are lighter in taste and colour, as well as less sweet in taste. Ginger ale marketers are trying to have their product seen in this category. The market share held by New Age products is still small in comparison with the cola share — but it is growing.

Long established producers have responded to the new competition by introducing products with a new image. Pepsi has a clear cola, Chrystal Pepsi. Ginger ale manufacturers are bringing out new flavours such as raspberry and cranberry ginger ale in an attempt to attract younger drinkers.

Ginger ale sales jumped by 8.2 percent as a result. Nevertheless it still represents only about one percent of soft drink sales. Despite the fact that ginger ale meets changing consumer tastes, its image is not the same as other modern soft drinks with similar attributes. Shapiro quotes a market research firm executive, George Rosenbaum: "Of all the carbonated beverages I can think of, there is none that is more underdeveloped from a marketing standpoint."

Shapiro also quotes another consultant, Tom Pirko, who feels the low profile of ginger ale may work to its advantage: "You have a dead zone when a product is going out of fashion. Once you get into that dead zone, you can almost create a new product."

The growing popularity of lighter products seems to provide an opportunity for ginger ale, but low market share shows that the challenge is great. On the one had, the qualities of ginger ale would seem to match the new trend in consumer demand. On the other, people's perceptions of the product are not too positive. It appears as though ginger ale marketers must overcome a very significant image problem.

Questions for Discussion

1. Is the introduction of new flavours really a solution to the ginger ale "image" problem?

2. Who is the target market for ginger ale? Who should it be?

3. Using the consumer decision process model, analyze consumer decision making in choosing between ginger ale and cola.

4. From the evidence shown above, develop a plan for marketing ginger ale that will lead to the attainment of long-term market share.

NOTES

1. Ronald A. Fullerton, "How Modern is Modern Marketing? Marketing's Evolution and the Myth of the 'Production Era,' " *Journal of Marketing*, January 1988, 108–25.

2. James Engel, Roger Blackwell, and Paul Miniard, *Consumer Behavior*, 5th ed. (Hinsdale: Dryden Press, 1986), p. 559.

PHOTO CREDITS

MODULE
◆ PRI ◆

PRODUCT MANAGEMENT AND PRICING STRATEGY

THE FOCUS OF THIS MODULE

1. To differentiate between the concepts of goods, services, and products

2. To describe general patterns of consumer behaviour in the purchase of products in various categories

3. To explain the product life cycle, and some of the decisions to be made at the various stages of the cycle

4. To discuss product brands, brand identification, and brand loyalty

5. To explain the role of product management in keeping a company's offerings profitable

6. To explain the basic concepts of pricing

7. To consider the difference between pricing new products and pricing those that have many substitutes in the market

8. To consider that different pricing objectives can lead to a variety of pricing decisions

9. To learn the meaning of the following terms:

KEY TERMS

product	generic product
consumer products	demand curve
industrial products	supply curve
convenience products	equilibrium price
preference products	markup
shopping products	list price
specialty products	fixed costs
product life cycle	variable costs
brand	breakeven point
trademark	price lining
private brand	profit maximization

(continued)

target return goal	odd pricing
sales maximization	inflation
market share	skimming price strategy
psychological pricing	penetration price strategy

DAVE NICHOL USED to speak about Canada's best-selling cookie the way a soldier might a sophisticated piece of military hardware. "I have the ultimate retail weapon," said Nichol. "Anybody who loves this cookie has to shop in my stores."

Mr. Nichol was, until recently, head of product development for the Toronto-based food-retailing giant Loblaw Cos. Ltd. The Decadent Chocolate Chip Cookie, a calorie-laden confection, is part of the grocery company's "President's Choice" line of house brand products.

The strategy to introduce high-quality house brand products, ranging from cookies to snack foods, sauces, and frozen dinners, is based on hard economics. By offering the items under a store label, the company retains full control over distribution, advertising, and pricing of their store-label items.

Fickle grocery customers in both Canada and the United States have been attracted by the Loblaw's line of gourmet items. In 1991, Loblaw's house brands, which include Green and Club Pack, along with President's Choice and No Name, generated 20 percent of the firm's revenues and "a significantly greater" share of its profits.

Industry analysts say that Nichol has been helped by a gradual decline in consumer loyalty to existing brand name products. "People no longer think one brand is clearly the best," said Bradford Fay, project director of the New York–based Roper Organization Inc.

Loblaw's competitors are taking advantage of the erosion in brand loyalty by introducing their own brand products. Canada Safeway's brand name products include Empress, Lucerne, and Bel-Air.

And Loblaw's has launched a new line of high-fibre and low-fat products called "Too Good to Be True"—yet another attempt by this retailing giant to differentiate its stores from those of its competitors.

Source: Adapted from Diane Brady, "The Names Game," *Maclean's*, February 3, 1992, pp. 64.

Companies are built upon the sales of goods and services. You are not in business until you have something to sell. Thus, most companies pay a great deal of attention to the product components of the marketing mix. The special products developed by Dave Nichol and his Loblaw's staff produced a significant increase in sales for the company, and are a good example of the importance of developing and managing a stream of new products.

GOODS, SERVICES AND PRODUCTS

What exactly is a product? We refer to both goods and services as products, though we often think of these as distinct entities: goods as *things* that people want to own; services as *performances* that people want to have done for them.

But when consumers buy goods, they are often buying more than physical attributes. In the case of President's Choice cookies (a good), the physical attributes are the cookie, including its flavour and its packaging, and its non-physical attributes include the convenience of associated services offered in the store and the symbolic prestige gained by serving family and guests a recognized top-of-the-line snack. Similarly, when consumers take advantage of the service provided by a fine restaurant, what they are buying has both physical and non-physical dimensions.

Thus, a **product** can be defined as a bundle of physical, performance, and symbolic attributes offered to satisfy the wants of the consumer. The importance of products is so great that many companies become bound by product orientation to the extent that they forget that the real focus of business should be the needs of the customer.

In many instances, the non-physical benefits are the determining factor in choosing between one product and another. For example, a significant number of people choose to buy their groceries at high-priced supermarkets because they perceive the service to be better and find the layout more pleasing. Thus, it is possible for a marketer to "create" a superior product through the judicious addition of non-physical benefits to a particular good. The bundling of physical (tangible) and performance and symbolic (intangible) attributes is characteristic of a vast number of products. Products can thus be thought of as being on a continuum ranging from tangible-dominant (goods) to intangible-dominant (services).

One reason for differentiating between goods and services is that some aspects of the marketing of each differ. Lynn Shostack proposes that the approach of "opposites" be used when communicating about a good or service to your markets.[1] A service (intangible) should be promoted with tangible ideas and a good (tangible) with intangible ideas. For example, Revlon, which has a tangible product line, sells visions and images (hope), not cosmetics. By contrast, Air Canada emphasizes the type of plane and tasty meals rather than the transport of customers through the air.

product
A bundle of physical, performance, and symbolic attributes offered to satisfy the wants of the consumer

PRODUCT CLASSIFICATION

Because distribution and marketing communications differ widely according to the type of customer, products are often classified as consumer or industrial. **Consumer products** are those sold directly to the ultimate consumer. **Industrial products** are used in the production of other goods and services (which may, in turn, be sold to the consumer or to still other businesses). Sometimes, as in the case of pens, paper, hand tools, or cooking ingredients, the items are virtually the same, but because the customers and their needs are so different, the division is important from a marketing point of view.

consumer products
Goods and services sold to the ultimate consumer

industrial products
Goods and services used in the production of other goods and services

Consumer Products

Consumer products are often classified according to the amount of effort the consumer will make to acquire them and the risk that the

convenience products

Products consumers buy routinely and with little effort as the risk of a poor purchase is minimal

preference products

Products that consumers are prepared to make some effort to seek out

shopping products

Products that consumers are likely to buy only after evaluating competing offerings

specialty products

Products for which consumers will accept no substitutes

consumer perceives in making the purchase. The categories used are convenience products, preference products, shopping products, and specialty products. Figure 15.1 shows where each type of product falls in relation to the dimensions of the consumer's effort and risk. Each category of product demands a different marketing approach.

Convenience products are those that consumers buy routinely. They are not prepared to expend much effort as they perceive that the risks of making a poor purchase decision are slight. If one brand of milk, paper towels, or detergent is not available, another will do just as well.

Preference products are those that consumers are prepared to make some effort to seek out. They may go to the neighbourhood greengrocer for lettuce rather than buying wilted produce at the supermarket with the rest of their groceries or forgo purchase of a candy bar if their preferred brand is out of stock. The risk of making a poor purchase is somewhat higher, but consumers are unlikely to work hard to acquire the product.

Shopping products are normally purchased after the purchaser has shopped around, comparing competing products on the basis of various characteristics, including price. The risks of making a poor decision are significant enough that purchasers are willing to take time and expend effort to learn about and evaluate alternatives. Many clothing and furniture items, and cars, fall into this category.

Specialty products are important enough to certain buyers that they are unwilling to accept substitutes. They feel it is worth the effort

FIGURE 15.1 • CLASSIFICATION OF CONSUMER PRODUCTS

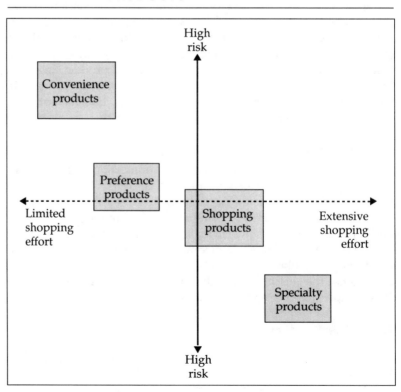

DEVELOPING YOUR BUSINESS SKILLS

TAILORING PRODUCTS TO FIT MARKET SEGMENTS

One of the most important marketing skills is to be able to develop products to fit specialized market niches. Canadian manufacturers produce a wide variety of beds. However, Simmons Canada Ltd. recently introduced another brand, Dr. Hard. This was specifically designed to serve the needs of Asian Canadians for mattresses that were closer to what they were used to back home. The company expects this bed to account for 20 percent of its sales.

Simmons Canada is one of a small but growing number of Canadian companies that are starting to develop new products and advertising strategies specifically for consumers from different cultures and backgrounds. Executives with those firms say that they have already found new and lucrative markets among the 3.2 million Canadians—about 13 percent of the population—whose mother tongue is neither English nor French, and whose product preferences are still strongly influenced by the prevailing tastes within their ethnic community.

A food-processing company, Best Foods Canada Inc. of Toronto, which makes Knorr brand soup mixes, initiated a three-step program to attract more Asian customers. First, Best manufactured limited amounts of Knorr soups and other products based on the same recipes employed in Hong Kong. Then the company applied trilingual labels—English, French, and Chinese—on shipments bound for Asian specialty grocery stores across Canada. The next stage was to sell the products in mainstream supermarkets.

The service sector also has found that it pays to tailor business to newcomers. The Canadian Imperial Bank of Commerce set up a specialized Asian Banking Group and special branches in Vancouver, Calgary, Toronto, and Montreal.

Having the insight to identify such special market niches, as well as the ability to produce appropriate products to serve such segments, is a reliable formula for success.

Source: Adapted from Barbara Wickens, "Cultural Cross Talk," *Maclean's*, October 28, 1991, p. 42.

---

to await delivery, or to travel the distance to the one store that carries the specific product. One man who specialized in making the "ultimate" cheesecake drove 750 kilometres from Winnipeg to Minneapolis to buy a cakepan that he felt would help him perfect his favourite dessert.

Industrial Products

Industrial products are those purchased by organizations to carry out production and distribution activities or to incorporate as an actual part of items produced. In the first category are facilities, equipment, supplies, and services. The second category includes raw materials, component parts, and materials such as sheet steel for auto bodies.

THE BIRTH AND DEATH OF PRODUCTS

Each year, thousands of patents are registered. However, only a few of the products patented find their way to the market. And, of those that do, most fail. There are many reasons for this: an ill-conceived product, the wrong target market, too high or too low a price, or poor marketing communications.

Other products are well accepted, but then are dropped in favour of something new and better. For example, you would not want to run a company supplying vinyl recordings of last year's hit songs. The compact disc has made the vinyl recording obsolete, and last year's hits are—last year's hits.

The life span of vinyl recordings extended over many years, but that of eight-track tapes was relatively brief. Lipton tea was introduced before 1923 and is still going strong. Ivory soap has been on the market for more than a century. On the other hand, a financial service can be rendered obsolete overnight by a change in a law or by a competitor who offers a better one.

Figure 15.2 shows a standard life cycle: sales are plotted on the vertical axis and the passage of time on the horizontal one. The standard **product life cycle** can be divided into four stages to help managers think about the marketing activities that are normally required at each stage. These are the introductory, growth, maturity, and decline stages. Profits tend to follow the shape of the product life cycle curve.

product life cycle

An ongoing series of stages in the life of a successful product: introduction to the market, growth, maturity, and decline

Ivory Soap, a product of Procter & Gamble Inc., was first sold in Cincinnati, Ohio, in October 1879. It came to Canada in 1916. A key reason for Ivory soap's longevity has been its approach in advertising which uses the image of a baby to emphasize the soap's purity. The slogan "99 44/100% pure" runs through its advertisements and is now a registered trademark.

FIGURE 15.2 • PRODUCT LIFE CYCLE AND PROFIT CURVE

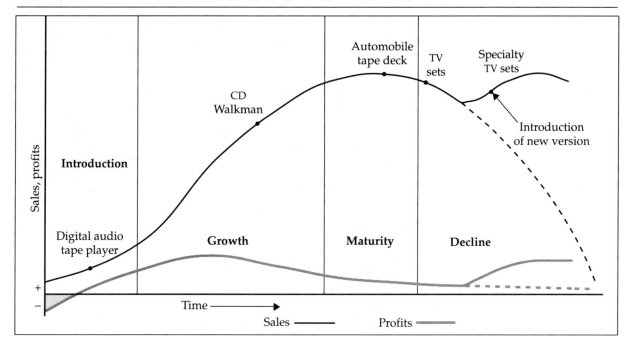

Because the life spans of particular products vary enormously, the actual shape of the curve varies considerably. Nevertheless, it is helpful to think about the managerial decisions that have to be made at each stage of the standardized product life cycle.

The *introductory stage* determines whether a product will succeed or fail. Initially, sales are slow because both consumers and distributors are unfamiliar with the new item or service. At this stage, considerable effort is required to inform and persuade potential customers to try the product and to persuade or develop appropriate distribution outlets to make the product available to the public.

It is quite common for companies to lose money on initial sales of new products because revenue does not cover the costs of new-product development and introductory promotional campaigns. However, investing in these start-up activities is essential to increase the chances of making long-term profits.

During the *growth stage,* sales increase at an accelerated pace as new customers join those who first tried the new product. Referrals and effective marketing communications can have great impact at this stage. However, many products disappear from the market if there is minimal or no growth. And, although increasing customer demand for a product can lead to profits, success will quickly encourage competitors to introduce similar products.

At this stage of the product life cycle, management must continue to extend distribution of the product. The focus of marketing communication gradually moves from explaining the product to emphasizing the advantages of this company's product over those of new competitors. Modifications and improvements are often made to the product to make it more competitive.

During the *maturity stage,* sales grow more slowly. Natural population growth aside, the potential market may be saturated to the point that most sales are replacement sales. Competitors will also have gained a share of the market. Marketing communications focus on reminding people of the brand and showing that it is better than competing ones. Price is often reduced, or special price promotions are used to get people to switch from other brands. Toward the end of the maturity stage, it is quite common for overall sales volume to diminish. The maturity period for many products can be quite long.

As volume drops off in the *decline stage*, one of two things usually happens: sales continue to decrease and the firm "milks" any remaining potential for profits, or it introduces an improved version of the same brand to replace the old one. This may lead to a new life cycle rising from the final sales level achieved with the previous product, creating an S-curve. This process is often repeated several times.

Some products have a short life cycle; others continue for generations; and still others experience a rebirth of interest periodically. Consider the reasons for the resurgence described in Issues in Business 15.1.

ISSUES IN BUSINESS 15.1

TROLLS STEAL HEARTS

THE LIFE CYCLE of some products never really seems to end. Trends often lead to the resurgence in popularity of items not considered essential or even of any importance. And yet, these trends can become a booming business once again. The lovable troll dolls are such a product.

For many parents, it's a stroll down memory lane. Not since the wild-haired troll dolls produced by Norfin and Russ Berrie Inc. first hit North America in 1968 have so many of them covered the walls of toy stores across the continent.

Trolls are one of the hottest-selling toys this season. The figures go to school, to the bathtub, and even to bed with a generation of kids whose parents are shocked to see their old toys back in the sandbox.

"We don't even know why this is happening today," said Sid Arronson, director of communications for Russ Berrie and Company Inc. Arronson noted the company reintroduced trolls to the market about every six years since its first success with the dolls, but "this [success] is beyond anybody's expectations [at the company] and certainly beyond anybody's previous expectations."

In 1991, Russ Berrie grossed $44 million on the trolls, an unanticipated rise from the company's 1988 gross of only $200,000.

The brightly coloured plastic dolls range in price from $1.50 to $30.00, and the smallest are only 3 centimetres high and cost $10.00.

Why are trolls so popular? Children like to collect things, and trolls hold appeal because they are cute and bright. "They are easy to pack around and they are a good solid toy," said Chris Munro, manager of Hallmark Card Shop at Hillside Mall, in Victoria, B.C. One fourth-grader explains the popularity this way: "It's their hair. No people's hair sticks up like that and it's those bright colours.'

(continued)

Troll-mania has caught on with adults as well. One store manager claims it's their appealing eyes, happy faces, bright colours, and affordable prices.

Source: Excerpts from Wil Hylton, "Trolls Steal Hearts," *Times-Colonist* and *Baltimore Sun*, April 28, p. C1.

Question for Discussion

1. Trends are complex to understand. Marketing strategies must be flexible to meet the quickly changing demand. The product and price have something to do with the troll's popularity. How could these combine with social changes to make the timing just right?

BRAND IDENTIFICATION

Although there are exceptions, almost every commercial product is identified as a brand with a special brand name and a trademark. A **brand** is a name, term, symbol, design element, or some combination of these, used to identify the product of one firm and to differentiate it from competitive offerings. A **trademark** gives the brand's identifying words or symbols legal protection. Elements protected by trademark may be used solely by the brand's owner. The trademark golden arches of McDonald's restaurants easily stand out among all other fast-food outlets, even to young children. Sunkist Growers, a co-operative, brands its oranges with the name "Sunkist." Brand identification and trademark protection are important matters that often involve critical strategic decisions for marketing managers.

A brand creates an image in the eye of the consumer. Simply the appearance of a recognizable brand symbol provides instant advertising for the product's manufacturer. The majority of casual shoppers who see the familiar dog-at-the-phonograph symbol know they are looking at the RCA trademark. They need no other information. Effective branding provides assurance of repeat purchases, and this can reduce the need to participate in certain types of price competition. Furthermore, if the consumer sees the brand as a guarantee of the product's quality, the firm can pay less attention to competitors and safely sell it at a substantial price premium. Achieving brand loyalty is an important aspect of marketing.

Brand Name or Generic Term?

Brand names cannot contain words in general use such as *television*, *automobile*, or *sunscreen*. These are generic words—words that describe a type of product—and they cannot be used exclusively by any company.

Conversely, if a type of product becomes generally known by a certain brand name, the name can be ruled generic, and the company that successfully developed the name can lose exclusive rights to it. The generic names *cola*, *nylon*, *kerosene*, *linoleum*, and *shredded wheat* were once brand names.

Some brand names that still have legal protection are viewed as generic by many consumers. Xerox is a brand name; yet many consumers use the name generically to refer to all photocopying processes. Legal brand names such as Aspirin, Formica, Kodak, Styrofoam, Kleenex, Scotch Tape, Fiberglass, Band-Aid, and Jeep are

brand
A name, term, symbol, design element, or some combination of these, used to differentiate a product from competitive offerings

trademark
The words, logo, or symbol or other designation registered as a mark to distinguish one company's products from others'

often used in everyday language, yet a person who asks for "a Kleenex" will quite likely be satisfied to receive "a tissue" made by a competitor.

If brand names are legally ruled generic, brand owners lose control over how they are used. To avoid this, companies are very careful to protect themselves by registering their brand names as trademarks and informing others that this protection gives them exclusive ownership. Coca-Cola Ltd., a Canadian subsidiary of The Coca-Cola Company, uses the trade-mark notice "Trade Mark Reg." under its trade-marks, i.e., inter alia, under "Coca-Cola," "Coke," "Coca-Cola Classic," "Diet Coke" and "Sprite" to give notice that these trade-marks are registered trade-marks of Coca-Cola Ltd. The company may also inform newspapers, novelists and non-fiction writers who improperly cite trade-marks in their text of the correct use. Companies of this sort face the task of retaining exclusive rights to brand names that are known throughout the world.

Private Brands

private brand

A brand established by a retailer or distributor rather than a manufacturer; sometimes called a house brand

Although brand names would logically be thought of as the property of manufacturers, there are exceptions. If a brand name belongs to a retailer or distributor, it is called a **private brand** (sometimes referred to as a house, distributor, or retailer label). Using one of these brands will associate the product with the retailer, not the manufacturer. Some examples are Viking (Eaton's), Life (Shoppers Drug Mart), and St. Michael (Marks & Spencer). President's Choice, a private supermarket brand, has become so successful that it is available across Canada, in 34 U.S. states, and in Bermuda.

"Coca-Cola" was registered as a trademark with the U.S. Patent and Trademark office in 1893, and in 1905 with the Canadian Trade-marks Office. The recognizable contour bottle was also granted registration as a trade-mark (a legal right given to few other packages) in Canada in 1929, and in 1977 in the U.S.

In addition to selling manufacturers' and private brands, some retailers offer consumers a third option—generic products. **Generic products** typically are packaged plainly, meeting minimum quality and labelling requirements. Little if any advertising is used to market them. As long as minimum quality standards are met, nothing else is needed. Generic products generally do not have individual brand names and sell at real discount prices in relation to manufacturers' and private brands.

generic product
A product offered for sale with no brand identification

PRODUCT MANAGEMENT

If you were the product manager for cassette tapes at Philips, would you be worried about the growing popularity of compact discs? The cassette-tape system won out over the eight-track tape in the 1970s. Is it now destined to share the fate of the eight-track system? The answer lies both in the wisdom of marketing decisions and in the evolution of technology. From the time a product category is introduced until it is removed from the market, many management decisions must be made to make it successful in the marketplace. Product management involves decisions about the development of products and their pricing distribution, and promotion in light of consumer needs and the actions of competitors. Many of these decisions are related to the stage that the product is at in its life cycle. For example, in the introductory stage, marketing communications emphasizes information about the product. During the maturity stage, the emphasis changes to more persuasive communications. Companies must have a stream of new products ready to enter the market. Competition and improving technology ensure that a firm cannot comfortably rely simply on existing products. A great number of new products must be continuously under consideration so that the "right" product will be ready at the right time.

Modifying Existing Products

A major aspect of product management is the modification of existing products. Modifications are often minor, but the spur of competition provides a continual incentive to improve. Over time, the improvement in products is often dramatic. Consider the difference between television sets when they were first introduced and today. Continual product modification can often keep a product alive and profitable. Tide detergent has undergone hundreds of modifications since it was first introduced, which has helped to keep it a leading product.

Eliminating Products

Despite careful management, some products gradually fall out of favour with customers. An important aspect of product management is assessing the profitability of each product, the likelihood of its acceptance in the future, and the time to eliminate it. Frequently, such assessment is more difficult than it seems. Decline often comes about gradually, and the precise moment to abandon a product may be hard to pinpoint. Sentimental attachment to certain products may lead to reluctance to let them go. Management must have a continuous and hard-headed assessment program to suspend the "dogs."

PACKAGING

It is difficult to think of many products without their packages. Packaging is more than protection for a product. It can be used for many purposes, such as enhancing the function of the product itself. For example, Saran Wrap is packaged in a box with a serrated edge for dispensing and cutting the wrap.

Packaging is also a powerful marketing tool and can be used to provide information. A box for a motion- sensor light shows a picture of the light. In addition, each feature is highlighted with text and an arrow. Beyond providing information, packaging can also offer persuasive messages to win consumers over. Product labels perform the same functions.

BUSINESS REVIEW 15.1

1. List the four consumer product classifications and the two broad categories of industrial products.
2. Should the distribution of convenience products be intensive or selective? Why?
3. Draw a standard product life cycle curve, including the introduction, growth, maturity, and decline stages. Think of different products that can be currently classified as being at each stage. Plot the position of each on the life cycle curve and write in the product name.
4. Choose a well-known brand product and list and describe various elements the brand owner has used to establish brand identification. Do you think the product has achieved brand loyalty among consumers?

PRICING

A man cleared a portion of land covered with poplar trees. He put up a sign saying Free Firewood and had no response. He then changed the sign to read: Firewood—$60 a Cord, and sold all of it within a few days. As the man discovered, price connotes value. Marketers of cosmetics and consulting services have discovered the same thing. Thus, there are psychological aspects to pricing.

There are, of course, cost elements to pricing. The price of an item must include the cost of producing it, plus some profit. Cost can be determined systematically (although doing so is not as simple as it might seem), but the final price must take into consideration many other factors as well, such as the size of the overall market, the market share the company plans to achieve, the company's social objective, the image it wishes to project, and the planned promotional strategy for the specific product. All of these factors affect one another in various ways. Pricing is a complex aspect of the marketing mix.

SETTING PRICES

Businesses sell their products in order to make a profit. It seems fairly simple to calculate what a product costs, sell it at a higher price, and retain the difference as profit. The problem is to establish what the higher price should be. If the price is set higher than what the market will bear, the product will not sell at all and the company's entire investment in the product will be lost.

Price determination is the result of input from several departments in the firm. Sales data are provided by marketing. Production cost data are generated by the accounting manager and verified by production and industrial engineering personnel. Sales projections can be worked out by computer analysts. Marketing departments supply calculations of how much they will spend on distribution and promotion. The financial department considers all these figures and also assigns a portion of the company's overhead to the product. All these data provide information on what the product actually costs. From there, marketing managers can consider supply and demand forecasts, conduct breakeven analyses, and use the results as a guide for setting prices according to the firm's normal practices—for example, price lining or markup.

Price determination can be looked at from a broad perspective, in order to see the "big picture" or from close-up, in order to inspect the fine detail. Economic theory examines the broad context, while cost-based pricing focusses on all the critical numbers. A further perspective is added when marketers relate economic theory to the realities of the marketplace in setting the actual price.

The Law of Supply and Demand

According to economic theory, if the objective is profit maximization, the market price will be set at the point where the amount demanded by consumers is equal to the amount supplied. More specifically, price will be set at the point of equilibrium where the amount of a product desired at a given price is equal to the amount suppliers will provide at that price. As shown in Figure 15.3, the effect of prices on buyers can be plotted along a **demand curve** to show how different price levels affect the amounts that will be demanded. Research clearly proves that, overall, increases in the price of a product are followed by decreasing sales. To take a straightforward example, if an industrial chemical costs $3 per kilogram, 5,000 kilograms might be sold. If the price increases to $4 per kilogram, sales might fall to 3,200 kilograms, and if customers are faced with another increase, to $5 per kilogram, sales could drop off to only 2,000 kilograms. Higher prices affect the market by encouraging customers either to switch to less expensive substitutes or to delay purchasing until the price is reduced.

If the price a product can command on the market is low, sellers will supply only a small quantity; as the price they can charge rises, they will want to supply more of the product. The effect of prices on sellers can be plotted along a **supply curve** (see Figure 15.3).

In theory, the simple intersection of the demand curve and the supply curve represents the **equilibrium price** for a particular product in the marketplace.

demand curve
A graphic representation of the quantity of a product buyers will demand as prices change, running from high price–low demand to low price–high demand

supply curve
A graphic representation of the quantity of a product sellers will supply as prices change, running from low price–low supply to high price–high supply

equilibrium price
The price at which the sellers' supply satisfies the customers' demand (the point of intersection of supply and demand curves)

FIGURE 15.3 • SUPPLY AND DEMAND CURVES

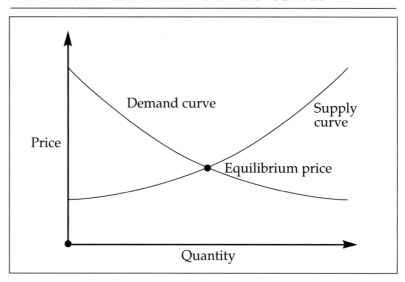

Practical Price Setting

Although this economic analysis is correct with regard to the overall market for a product, managers face the problem of setting the price of individual brands on the basis of limited information. Anticipating the amount of a product that will be bought at a certain price is difficult, so business has tended to adopt cost-based pricing formulas. While these are simpler and easier to use, executives have to be flexible in applying them to each situation. They first ask their marketing personnel to total all costs included in the introduction of a new product. Cost-based pricing is therefore based on an analysis of the total of production, transportation, distribution, and marketing expenses. The marketers then add on the **markup**—an amount that will cover expenses not yet included and a profit.

markup
An amount added to the cost of products to cover expenses and profit, usually calculated as a percentage of the final retail price

The amount may vary in accordance with the demand for the product. The total of this amount and the cost of the item determines the selling price. The *markup percentage on retail*, then, is the markup divided by the price of the item:

$$\text{Markup Percentage} = \frac{\text{Markup (Amount added to cost)}}{\text{Price}}$$

If a game in a toy store is priced at \$10, and its invoice cost (the amount the store has paid for it) is \$6, then the markup percentage is 40:

$$\text{Markup Percentage} = \frac{\$4}{\$10} = 40 \text{ percent}$$

The firm's markup should be related to its *stock turnover*—the number of times the average inventory is sold annually (using sales figures if the inventory is recorded at retail value, and cost of goods sold if the inventory is recorded at cost):

$$\text{Stock Turnover} = \frac{\text{Sales}}{\text{Average Inventory at Retail}} \text{ or } \frac{\text{Cost of Goods Sold}}{\text{Average Inventory at Cost}}$$

Markups are generally lower for products with high stock turnover figures (e.g, groceries) and higher for items with low turnover figures (e.g., jewellery).

Marketers must be flexible, willing to adjust their markups and prices according to the demand for their products. While costs are a useful place to start, market demand must be considered in arriving at an appropriate price.

Markups have been standardized to the point that manufacturers often calculate a final retail or **list price** based on what they charge retailers and the accepted markup percentage. Publishers, for example, often print the list price on the covers of books and magazines. In many areas, however, retailers must be flexible and willing to adjust their markups and prices according to demand. Often, stores offer a percentage discount on the list price. This decreases their own markup; however, the reduction may be necessary to stay competitive. Sometimes, lower prices increase demand, thus producing equal or greater revenue.

Breakeven Analysis

An important aspect of setting prices is to find what number of sales at what price allows the company to break even, sustaining no loss on its operation even if it does not make a profit. Breakeven analysis can be used to determine the relationship required to reach this point.

All operations have certain **fixed costs**, such as rent, machinery, and some salaries, that stay the same no matter how much of a product is produced and sold. Added to these are **variable costs**, such as materials, production workers' wages, and inventory expenses, that are directly related to the quantity of items produced. These costs can be plotted on a graph, as is shown in Figure 15.4.

It is then possible to plot revenue from sales at a certain price. The point at which the revenue line meets the total cost line is the **breakeven point**. If sales fall below that point, the company will sustain a loss. Sales beyond it bring the company a profit.

If the level of sales required to break even seems too high, the marketing manager may suggest raising the price. This would change the revenue line and lower the breakeven point. But the law of supply and demand must also be considered: the higher the price, the lower the demand. Another option would be to reduce costs, which is likely to affect quality. Lower quality is also likely to reduce demand.

The way prices can be manipulated in order to account for supply and demand and also aim for a breakeven point is illustrated in the airline industry, where pricing policies attempt to utilize both low and high prices for different target groups. Discount prices aim to attract people to purchase unused airline seat space. To remain profitable, an

list price
The selling price to a final buyer suggested by a manufacturer and based on the cost plus some markup

fixed costs
Costs that stay the same no matter how much of a product is produced and sold

variable costs
Costs that are directly related to the quantity of items produced

breakeven point
The point at which revenue from sales covers all fixed and variable costs

FIGURE 15.4 • BREAKEVEN ANALYSIS

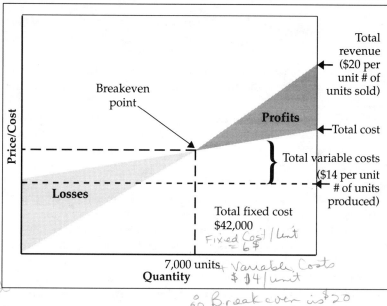

(handwritten notes in margin)

10,000 units 4.20
14.00
18.20
6o profet $1.80 unit

Fixed Cost / Unit = 6$

+ Variable Costs $14/unit

6o Breakeven is $20

airline must then cut services and other costs. This may annoy business travellers, who need to arrive at their destinations relaxed and ready to work. Business-class passengers are prepared to pay a higher price for extra benefits and services, but are not willing to pay the vast premiums that first-class passengers do. This juggling act with prices works well, except in times of recession when demand may fall below the airline's fixed costs.

Price Lining

The law of supply and demand and breakeven analysis provide a range of suitable prices for products. Within this range, other factors, such as convenience and ease of bookkeeping, will be brought to bear on the pricing decision.

Instead of setting prices for each product individually, a business might decide to offer merchandise at a limited number of prices. **Price lining**—offering products at a limited number of prices instead of pricing each item individually—is particularly common in retailing. For example, many clothing stores have $15, $25, $40, and $60 racks of shirts or pants. This strategy allows customers to decide what they are prepared to pay and then to concentrate on colour, style, and fabric available at that price. Price lining standardizes and streamlines inventory control; it eliminates the confusion that results from having to price each item individually; and it dramatically simplifies certain buying and production issues. The main disadvantage of price lining is the element of inflexibility it introduces. Buyers quite naturally identify sellers by their price lines. If costs change, retailers have difficulty continuing to offer the same items at the same familiar prices. When a business is forced to choose between raising prices and

price lining

Offering merchandise at a limited number of prices rather than pricing items individually

A current variation of a price lining retailer is Everything For A Dollar Store™, which started out in 1985, and now totals 33 stores across Canada. As the name implies, the store sells a variety of products, at $1.00 each. Everything For A Dollar Store™ follows two slogans, "See how much you can buy for a dollar" and "Everyday is a dollar day."

reducing quality, the clientele (especially regular customers) is not happy with either option. The usefulness of price lining therefore depends on careful analysis by marketing managers and careful implementation by retailers.

PRICES AND CORPORATE GOALS

An organization must consider many factors as it sets its pricing policies. Among these are its expectations for profit, the volume that it can efficiently produce, and matters that reflect on its corporate image.

Profitability Objectives

There is an important relationship between pricing strategy and profitability. As a first consideration, management focusses on the importance of

Profit = Revenue – Expenses

and, as a second consideration, on factors affecting revenue:

Total Revenue = Price x Quantity Sold.

A firm's decision to drastically increase prices can be unwise. Such increases can result in a disproportionate decrease in the number of units sold. For example, profits will increase if a 10 percent rise in price causes only an 8 percent decline in volume. On the other hand, it would be unprofitable if a 5 percent price increase caused a 6 percent reduction in sales.

On the surface, it seems quite reasonable to concentrate on **profit maximization** as a key objective and to develop a pricing strategy accordingly. However, achieving this objective is very difficult. In its

profit maximization
A pricing strategy aimed at achieving maximum profits

target return goal
A desired percentage of return on sales or on total investment

sales maximization
A pricing strategy aimed at gaining as many sales as possible

market share
The proportion of the target market for a product that a company serves

place, it has become more common for firms to focus on **target return goals** as a less complex profitability objective. Obviously, a company can continue to exist only if it earns a profit. The objective of target return pricing is to work toward achieving a profit target. For example, two possible options could be a 9 percent return on sales or a 20 percent return on investment. A profitability objective is usually expressed in this way—as a desired return on either sales or investment.

Volume Objectives

Pricing behaviour can also be described using the concept of **sales maximization**. In the application of this concept, management first establishes an acceptable minimum level of profitability and then puts resources into maximizing sales. The priority, therefore, is to expand sales rather than to focus on short-run profits.

Another volume objective is **market share**—the proportion of the total supply of a product or service controlled by any one firm or company. Management strategies tend to look at two different but related issues: the overall realistic market share the company could aim for within the entire industry and ways the company could expand (or at least maintain) its market share for particular products.

Increasing emphasis on market share objectives has become a useful and attractive idea to many companies. One reason is that there is a direct connection between corporate performance and market share statistics. Another reason is the likelihood that increased sales result in both higher profits and lower production costs. Each unit in a production run of 10,000 computers will be relatively cheap compared with its cost if production stopped after 500 units.

Other Objectives

Several objectives that do not directly pertain to profitability or sales volume are nevertheless quite important in making pricing decisions. These objectives include social and ethical considerations, status quo objectives, image goals, and product promotion objectives.

Social policy objectives examine the ability of potential customers to pay for the products and services being offered. For example, it is important not to overlook levels of income when making decisions about public transportation prices, retirement fund contributions, and walking-assistance devices for people with disabilities.

Status quo pricing objectives guide those firms that tend to follow the leader. By not trying out different pricing strategies and sticking with this secure approach, these firms are free to experiment in other competitive areas such as product design and promotion. Status quo pricing is standard policy in most oligopolistic markets controlled by a few firms.

Image goals can also significantly influence pricing strategy. For example, major department stores establish price structures that are consistent with the high quality of their merchandise—that is, with the image they promote to keep old customers and to attract new ones. On the other hand, discount outlets promote a different image: good value at low prices. Thus, pricing strategy can contribute in a very important way to a firm's overall image goal.

Finally, *product promotion objectives* often come into play in the pricing decision. In certain competitive situations, such as during the maturity stage of the product life cycle, a company might choose to use some special pricing strategy as a means of promoting the sales of a product. In such circumstances, special pricing could be more effective than spending a similar amount on advertising. Companies know that once they get a product into a consumer's hands, repeat purchases (even at a high price) will often occur.

PRICES AND CONSUMERS

Marketers know that consumers are price conscious and use this knowledge in their pricing strategies.

Price–Quality Relationships

Consumers often attribute quality to a product largely on the basis of its price. They tend to see products with higher prices as having better quality. This is especially true when buyers cannot discern quality simply by examining the product.

Not all firms want to signal that their product is of premium quality. They realize that many consumers wish to purchase in the midrange between "too low" and "too high." Others will always look for the cheapest products. Such attitudes must be taken into consideration when establishing prices for a selected target market. The choice will be related to the overall marketing strategy for the product.

Psychological Pricing

Experts in marketing believe that customers are naturally attracted to certain prices more than to others. This belief is the basis of **psychological pricing**, an approach that has been adopted in all parts of the world. The setting of image pricing goals, mentioned earlier, represents one form of psychological pricing.

Although more research is needed, it is believed that consumers consider odd-numbered prices to be better bargains. For psychological reasons, they seem to be more attracted to such prices as $29.95, $19.99, or $1.98 than to $30.00, $20.00, or $2.00. The retailers who initiated **odd pricing** claimed that such prices forced retail clerks to use the cash register to make change, thereby reducing the risk of money being pocketed by employees. This is no longer an issue, but odd-numbered pricing has become standard practice. Some retailers have now taken this strategy one step farther by experimenting with prices ending in 1, 3, 4, 6, or 7. Because prices ending in 95, 98, or 99 have become so common, they believe that a "new look," with such prices as $1.11, $3.22, $4.53, $5.74, $3.86, and $9.97, will be more effective in attracting the attention of consumers. In contrast, some retailers such as IKEA have turned the idea of psychological pricing on its head. They make a point of using full-dollar prices to indicate that they understand that the consumer is not easily manipulated. In a market where odd-number pricing is the norm, full-dollar prices are yet another form of psychological pricing.

Prices and Inflation

Inflation can be defined in terms of rising prices or the decreased purchasing power of a nation's currency. Consumers became accustomed

psychological pricing
The practice of pricing products at prices believed to be attractive to the consumer

odd pricing
The practice of pricing products at figures that are not round numbers

inflation
A decrease in the purchasing power of the nation's currency, which is felt as rising prices

to high rates of inflation in the late 1970s. The rise in consumer prices peaked in 1980 at an annual rate of over 12 percent, then began to decline. By the early 1990s, an inflation rate of less than 2 percent began to change perceptions.

When inflation was high, consumers were conditioned to further price hikes. Once inflation trended downward, this perception remained for a period of time. Now Canadians are more concerned with other economic issues than they are with inflation. What does this mean for marketers?

Consumers recognize that inflation is not the primary culprit in price increases any more. This suggests that buyers will be more sensitive to price hikes than they were a few years ago. Marketers must work to keep prices at reasonable levels if the nation's economic progress is to continue.

Even in times of low inflation, price changes may be necessary — because of fluctuating material costs, reduced demand, increasing unit costs, or simply the need for higher profits to satisfy investors. There are a number of approaches to increasing prices. The Issues in Business looks at one method that attempts to do so without customers realizing it.

ISSUES IN BUSINESS 15.2

INCREASING PRICES BY REDUCING PACKAGE SIZE

IN TODAY'S HOTLY contested consumer product market, there is increasing pressure on brand managers and planners to improve the "bottom line." Because of probable competitive response and possible consumer resistance, it is not always easy to implement a price increase to improve a brand's profit margin.

Caught in this situation, many managers have opted for reducing the size of their products while maintaining or increasing the price. Downsizing is an attractive pricing strategy for many reasons:

1. It can maintain a price point (commonly accepted price). Research shows consumers are aware of price points, but not of amount of contents.
2. It may increase margin and profitability. Sales are not affected in the long term as consumers forget that downsizing has occurred.
3. It could increase the frequency of purchase. If the new size is small enough, consumers may buy a greater number of units to achieve their quantity needs.
4. It responds to lifestyle changes. Health-conscious eating habits make smaller quantities more appealing to consumers.
5. It raises the price per unit of volume. Manufacturers attempt to bring price levels in line with the perceived product value.
6. It offsets raw material cost increases. For example, as chocolate becomes more expensive, manufacturers use less and sell a smaller candy bar.

It can thus be seen that there are some powerful incentives to consider downsizing. The way this could be done is to change sizes in such a way that the difference would not be noticed. Another

(continued)

alternative is for a manufacturer to lower price and cut the size more than proportionately. If down-sizing is accurately done, consumers may perceive that they are getting more for their money.

Source: Adapted from Anthony Adams, C. Anthony di Benedetto, and Rajan Chandra, "Can You Reduce Your Package Size Without Damaging Sales?," *Long Range Planning* Vol. 24, No. 4, pp. 86–96, 1991. Copyright ©1991, with kind permission from Pergamon Press Ltd., Headington Hill Hall, Oxford 0X3 0BW, UK.

Questions for Discussion

1. Is this method of maintaining profit margins for the manufacturer fair to the consumer?
2. Is this pricing strategy manipulation by the manufacturer at the consumer's expense? Is it any different from increasing price on existing packages?
3. How should the manufacturer advise the consumer of these changes?

Pricing decisions for existing products, or new ones that are very similar to those already on the market, are bounded by the expectations of the marketplace. There is normally little room to differ from the norm. A higher price would likely lead to a loss of sales. Equally serious, a lower price could invite retaliation by competitors, leading to a loss of profits and possibly sales as well.

PRICING NEW PRODUCTS

A product that is new to the world offers more scope in the pricing decision. However, pricing a new product is no less difficult. If the product is truly original, the marketer is free to set any price that the market will bear. The decision may be to set a price that will maximize profits. This is rare. Marketers are aware that buyers almost always have alternatives, such as finding other products that take different approaches to meeting their needs.

The price setter thus must follow the cardinal principle of marketing—understand the buyer's viewpoint. Look at the possible substitutes for the new product and determine the range of prices being charged to satisfy the need. Consider how well the product serves customers' needs compared with substitutes. This can provide some idea of the "superiority differential" of the product. Develop some estimate of the price–volume relationship. Decide whether the firm should aim at selling a high volume at low prices or a lower volume at higher prices.

Two major policies are often available to the marketer of the truly new product—a skimming price strategy and a penetration price strategy. Numerous considerations surround each of them.

The Skimming Price Strategy

Under a **skimming price strategy**, the firm sets a high initial price for a new product, then lowers it by stages. This strategy allows the firm to sell to several different categories of consumer and to obtain feedback from different sectors in the market. This technique is useful if price determines how the market is segmented. For example, if a small number of high-class customers would buy the product at $50, it is likely that

skimming price strategy
Introducing a product at a high price and lowering the price by stages, attracting different segments of the market

a larger group would buy it at $40, and an even larger group would buy it at $35. The sensitivity that consumers have toward price differences on calculators, personal computers, and VCRs has been tested quite successfully using a skimming price strategy. A skimming policy helps a firm recover quite rapidly the initial costs of putting a new product on the market, and the revenue generated can also support expansion into wider markets as the product's life cycle unfolds. However, the initial profits of this pricing strategy tend to act like a magnet to competitors. If they see opportunities to increase their own profits, they will introduce similar products, and this reaction exerts pressure on prices. For example, although ballpoint pens sold originally for about $20 after the Second World War, their average cost today is under $1.

The Penetration Price Strategy

penetration price strategy
Introducing a product at a low price to capture a large share of the market and to discourage competitors from introducing similar products

This strategy is the opposite of skimming. Using a **penetration price strategy**, a firm sets the price of a new product relatively low in comparison with competitors' offerings, with the object of capturing the market. Familiar examples of products that have been introduced with this pricing strategy are soaps and toothpastes. Penetration pricing discourages competitors because splitting up the market at a low price is not usually worth it, from a profit perspective. In addition, a firm that adopts this strategy can reduce costs quite substantially through large-scale production and marketing.

BUSINESS REVIEW 15.2

1. Describe some of the internal company concerns and external environmental factors that influence a company's pricing policies.

2. Explain some of the differences between setting a price for products that are new to the world and setting a price for a new "me too" product.

3. Differentiate between skimming and penetration pricing. Under what circumstances might each be appropriate?

WHAT PRODUCT? WHAT PRICE?

Deciding on the exact characteristics of the product a company will bring to the market is not a simple matter. It requires decisions not only about the apparent good or service being marketed but about many, perhaps invisible, aspects that have value for the consumer who makes the decision to purchase one company's product, another's, or none at all. The stage the product is in its life cycle will affect all the elements in the marketing mix.

The mechanics of calculating breakeven points, turnover rates, and the markups of everyone in the distribution channel are only part of the complex process of pricing. The company must consider its objectives not only for profitability but also for its social policies and image, the needs of the target market, and the entire promotion strategy for the product.

INTERACTIVE SUMMARY AND DISCUSSION QUESTIONS

1. Companies sell goods and services. These are referred to as *products*. But what is a product?
2. "Perfume is a product made up of certain physical characteristics, including various chemicals." Explain why this description of the product is much too limited.
3. "Goods companies sell *things* and service companies sell *performances*." Explain.
4. Consumer products are classified as convenience products, preference products, shopping products, and specialty products. What are the dimensions on which this differentiation is based? Define each product category.
5. Sometimes the same product is classified as an industrial product and a consumer product. How can this be?
6. Explain how the application of the elements of the marketing mix might change at each stage of the product life cycle.

7. Some of the objectives that affect the final pricing decision are:
   a) profitability
   b) market share
   c) social policy
   d) corporate image
   e) product promotion
   Give examples of where each might affect the pricing decision.
8. Markup is the amount added to cost for expenses and profit. If a CD player sells for $295 and the retailer paid $200, what is the retailer's markup percentage on retail?
9. The breakeven point is determined by dividing total fixed costs plus variable costs by the per-unit contribution of sales to these costs. How can breakeven analysis be used to help make a pricing decision?
10. In pricing, markup should be higher for products with low turnover, and lower for high-turnover items. Why is this so?

CASE 15.1

NICKERSON'S RESTAURANT

IT WAS A COLD, dark, rainy morning in Winnipeg. Mr. Nickerson was sitting at the Formica-topped table in his restaurant. Although it was almost noon, the lunch-hour crowd was passing him by. All morning he had had only a handful of customers. "This has to change," he said. "Business has been terrible. I know there is great potential out there. This town has such a high demand for places in which to eat out."

He glanced at the newspaper, and the following article captured his attention.

A New Restaurant Offers a Lot of Jiggle with Every Bite

A young entrepreneur, Mr. Charles Shamoon, in Greenville, Mississippi, had a vision last year. That vision is now a luncheon reality. Cherry-cola Jell-O salad is served as a main course. Jell-O--coated popcorn is quite popular for dessert. Other specialties include a layered strawberry trifle and pizza (actually strawberry Jell-O with a cookie-dough crust, with M&Ms or pieces of fruit on top). Mr. Shamoon's new restaurant, "Hello I'm Jell-O," is part of a trend that's beginning to congeal.

In the back-to-basics '90s, gelatin is not only served at trendy "home-style" restaurants. Jerry's Famous Deli—the Studio City, California, haunt of actors, producers, and teenagers—serves enough strawberry and cherry Jell-O in sundae dishes to unload 30 pounds of the dessert powder in a week.

(continued)

Trying to explain this trend is like—well, it's like trying to pin Jell-O to a wall. Some food experts say people are tired of exotic foods and now crave the simple, inexpensive fare they grew up with. "It's similar to the resurgence of meat loaf and mashed potatoes," said Ron Paul, a restaurant analyst. *Shopper Report*, a consumer trend newsletter, adds that people are sick of hearing about cholesterol and calories and just want "to have fun with food, to play with it."

Barbie Harris, an eighteen-year-old who frequents "Hello I'm Jell-O" with her friends, explains its success: "Everybody has Nintendo and certain ways of dressing. But Jell-O is different and that's what makes it cool."

Mr. Nickerson put down the paper. "That's it!" he exclaimed. "I'm going to look into Jell-O. That idea sounds exactly like what this city needs."

Questions for Discussion

1. Should Mr. Nickerson introduce this restaurant to Winnipeg or any other city in Canada?

2. Does this specialized restaurant represent a service or a good?

3. Jell-O is a brand name of Kraft Inc. Can you identify any problems Mr. Shamoon might have using this name for his restaurant?

4. Could Mr. Nickerson use another name to identify the specialized nature of his new restaurant? What would you suggest?

5. Do you think loyalty to the Jell-O brand could account for the restaurant's success?

6. What pricing strategy would you advise for products at the Jell-O restaurant? Why? What information would be needed to calculate the breakeven point in units at this price?

CASE 15.2

DUTAILIER INC.

ONE SMALL QUEBEC manufacturer, Dutailier Inc., has taken the rather unusual step of concentrating on the production and marketing of one product, a rocking chair.

For the first twelve years after Fernand Fontaine founded the company in 1976, Dutailier made living-room and bedroom sets as well as rocking chairs. The special-design rocking chairs proved to be increasingly popular. In 1988, the company eliminated all lines except the rocking chairs. "That was the turning point. Before that, we were like everybody else in the Canadian marketplace— trying to be all things to all people," said Pierre Cloutier, vice-president of sales and marketing.

Dutailier Inc. has improved upon the traditional rocking chair and has bet its reputation on the success of this one product. Traditional rocking chairs tend to scuff floors and provide an uneven ride—and the rocker must continuously propel himself. But Dutailier's Glider Rocker, which retails for between $150 and $600, depending on the model, eliminates those drawbacks. Its base stays in place while the chair itself moves smoothly back and forth with a minimum of effort.

(continued)

The Glider Rocker is available in 35 models, with 12 different finishes—from plain varnished pine to each season's most fashionably coloured lacquers. Shoppers can also choose from among 60 chair coverings, from printed fabrics suitable for the nursery to sophisticated Italian leathers. A recently upgraded computer system for managing distribution also monitors consumer tastes. As a result, the selection of finishes and fabrics is modified twice a year. Says Cloutier: "You create demand by producing a product that the consumer wants."

Headquartered in St.-Pie-de-Bagot, 50 kilometres east of Montreal, the company has developed a global vision. Seventy-five percent of the company's 3,500 customers are outside of Canada. Most exports go to the United States. In 1990, Dutailier began exporting to France and Britain, and has laid plans for marketing in other parts of the European Community.

Source: Adapted from Barbara Wickens, "Lessons in How to Survive," *Maclean's*, August 12, 1991, p. 32.

Questions for Discussion

1. How would you classify the Glider rocking chair?
2. At what stage is the rocking chair in its product life cycle?
3. Dutailier's price range seems to be quite wide for a single-product company. Does this make sense?
4. Describe the price–quality relationship of this product.
5. What are some of the risks involved in focussing on one product line? What are the benefits?
6. What do you think of the name chosen to described this specialized rocking chair? Does it convey all the attributes of the product to the consumer?

NOTE

1. G. Lynn Shostack, "Breaking Free from Product Marketing," *Journal of Marketing*, April 1977, pp. 73-80.

PHOTO CREDITS

MODULE

◆ DIS ◆

DISTRIBUTION

THE FOCUS OF THIS MODULE

1. To learn how distribution fulfils four of the marketing functions

2. To explain channels of distribution and the functions of various channel intermediaries or middlemen

3. To compare and contrast conventional channels and vertical marketing systems

4. To develop an understanding of the basics of wholesaling

5. To explain the normal evolution of retailing and describe various types of retailers

6. To describe the functions of physical distribution

7. To learn the meaning of the following terms:

KEY TERMS

channel of distribution

intermediary

wholesaler

retailer

broker

subjobber

industrial distributor

vertical marketing
  system (VMS)

scrambled merchandising

general store

department store

specialty store

convenience store

chain store

discount store

catalogue showroom

supermarket

hypermarket

vending machine

warehouse club

direct marketing method

intensive distribution

exclusive distribution

selective distribution

physical distribution

private carrier

contract carrier

common carrier

freight forwarder

CHIP AND PEPPER Wetwear Inc., the hip maker of tie-dyed clothes, has emerged from receivership recently with a new distribution plan. "This is going to freak you out!" Pepper said.

The founders of Chip and Pepper Wetwear, twin brothers Chip and Pepper Foster, began the company as teenagers. They sold their colourfully dyed clothes ten years ago from their family home in Winnipeg, and the back of their Jeep. It grew into a $14-million-a-year business before running into trouble. They attributed the company's recent problems to a lack of managerial ability in controlling its growth. "We were building houses and no one was holding them up behind us," Pepper said.

Chauvin International Ltd. offered them a plan. The company was founded by Morton Forshpan, a Montreal native now living in Los Angeles. Chauvin International distributes the B.U.M. Equipment line of casual clothing throughout the United States. He sees similar opportunities for the Chip and Pepper line. "This is essentially a carbon copy of B.U.M., but I am confident that it will be bigger because the brand name and the personality image are already there," Mr. Forshpan said.

This new distribution plan is exciting news for Chip and Pepper. "There's no other Canadian label that has penetrated the U.S. like we have . . .," said Pepper. "Chip and Pepper will remain actively involved. We will just be the managers," said Mr. Forshpan. This new plan is predicted to gross $30 million by the end of 1993, and reach annual sales of $200 million.

Source: Excerpts from Murray Wood, "Chip and Pepper Get Back on Track," *The Globe and Mail*, April 24, 1992, p. B3.

IT TAKES MORE than a flair for developing new products to build a successful enterprise. A financially sound distribution plan is also fundamental. Distribution is a component of the marketing mix that is much more complex than many realize. Possible approaches are many, and the competition is fierce.

Suppose you decide to buy a new mountain bicycle this afternoon. In order for it to be available it had to be bought by the retailer and stored, awaiting your purchase. Before that, a truck-load of bikes were probably bought from the factory by a wholesaler and transported to the wholesale warehouse nearer its retail customers. The wholesaler then sold three or four to each of a number of retailers. The set of activities that gets a product from the point of production to the point of purchase is known as distribution.

Distribution management deals with two major areas: the choice of marketing channels or channels of distribution that ensure that products reach the consumer, and the means of physical distribution, or the actual handling, movement, and storage of products. This module discusses channels of distribution and takes a brief look at some of the concerns in physical distribution.

THE MARKETING CHANNEL

A **channel of distribution** is a network of co-operating organizations that together transfer goods and services from the producer to the end-user. New channels and marketing institutions are constantly replacing older methods of wholesaling and retailing. An example of shifting distribution patterns in Canada is gasoline retailing. The number of service stations has dropped as a result of shifts in distribution methods by major oil companies. The valuable locations left when stations closed offer considerable marketing opportunities to other forms of retailing. Consumers now find garden shops, used-car dealers, fruit and vegetable sellers, animal hospitals, real estate offices, and fast-food outlets occupying these sites.

Hundreds of channels of distribution exist. The modes of distribution depend very much on the type of good or service in question. Canned food products, for example, are usually handled by both wholesalers and retailers before going to consumers. Some cosmetics and household supplies are not available in retail outlets and must be purchased directly from company representatives. The channel for a particular product is not set in stone. For example, the channel of distribution for motor oil now includes supermarkets as well as service stations because many car owners do minor maintenance at home and

channel of distribution
A network of co-operating organizations that together transfer goods and services from the producer to the end-user

Founded as Hamilton Tire and Rubber Limited on September 15, 1892, by John W. and Alfred J. Billes, Canadian Tire began as a garage auto parts depot. In 1927, the company was incorporated as Canadian Tire Corporation, Limited. It has become Canada's leading hardgoods retailer, specializing in automotive (e.g. motor oil, tires), leisure, and home products. It sells national brand names as well as its own housebrands, Mastercraft and Motomaster.

intermediary
(also called **middleman**)
A marketing organization between the producer and the end-user

wholesaler
A marketing organization that sells goods primarily to retailers for resale

retailer
A marketing organization that sells goods primarily to consumers for their own use

broker
An independent sales agent that negotiates sales between buyers and sellers; a broker does not take legal title to goods but may take possession of them

subjobber
A wholesaler that buys from other wholesalers to sell to its own set of customers

industrial distributor
A marketing intermediary that sells goods to industrial users

like to purchase supplies with the weekly shopping. Marketing managers must be sensitive to consumer needs and changing market conditions or they will be using inefficient distribution patterns.

Intermediaries (also called *middlemen*) operate between the producer and the consumer or industrial purchaser. Their distribution functions include buying, selling, transporting, and warehousing. The two main categories of intermediaries are wholesalers and retailers. **Wholesalers** sell primarily to retailers and to other wholesalers or industrial users; they do not sell significant amounts to ultimate consumers. **Retailers** sell products to individuals for their own use rather than for resale.

Other persons or firms also operate as intermediaries in many channels of distribution. **Brokers** are independent sales agents who negotiate sales between buyers and sellers. Brokers do not take legal title to goods (they do not buy them in order to resell them) and may or may not ever take possession of them. **Subjobbers** are wholesalers who buy from larger wholesalers and serve their own set of customers. The paperback racks in the local drugstore may well be filled by a subjobber. **Industrial distributors** are intermediaries for industrial goods.

The most typical channel configuration is manufacturer–wholesaler–retailer. The wholesaler "breaks bulk"—buying a large quantity and selling a more manageable, smaller quantity to each of many retailers. The wholesaler also bears the major responsibility for representing the manufacturer to each retailer.

As can be seen in Figure 16.1, there are many other ways of organizing the channel of distribution. Newspaper publishers deliver directly to consumers as well as through retail outlets. Large retail organizations such as Eaton's or Canadian Tire often buy directly from manufacturers because they can easily handle the same volumes as the manufacturer would normally ship to wholesalers. Such retailers are important enough that manufacturers find it worth while to serve them. Other intermediaries serve specialized needs when they can perform some channel activities more efficiently than other channel members can. Subjobbers provide quick local service because they are located close to buyers. Independent sales agents or brokers are industry specialists who can serve the diverse needs of both sellers and buyers at various levels.

Using Multiple Channels

The choice of channel of distribution is determined by the target market. If more than one type of market is targeted, it may be appropriate to use more than one channel. A multiple channel of distribution strategy has become increasingly popular in recent years.

For example, a manufacturer of power tools may decide to opt for several channels of distribution: (1) going through wholesalers to cover the needs of independent hardware and lumber outlets; (2) going direct to large chains such as Canadian Tire and Woolco; (3) going through distributors who serve the industrial market; and (4) using brokers to handle export sales. Because each type of channel of

FIGURE 16.1 • CHANNEL CONFIGURATIONS

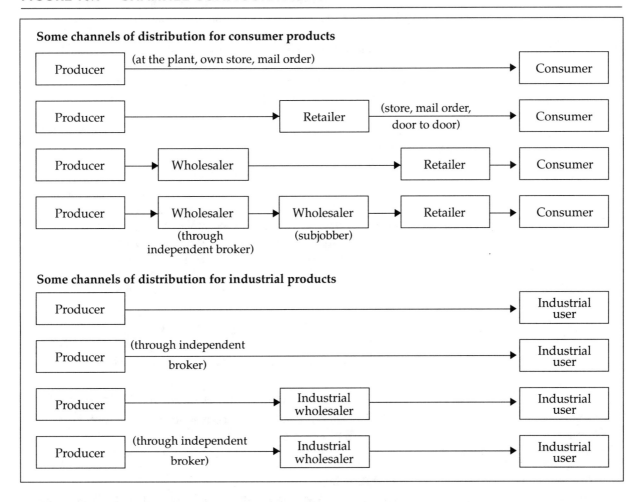

Some channels of distribution for consumer products

Some channels of distribution for industrial products

distribution solves a different set of problems, the choice of which to use is a critical marketing decision.

Conventional and Vertical Systems

Conventional marketing channels are made up of firms that deal with one another but remain independent. No one organization manages a co-ordinated network. Thus, channel members may participate or not, as they see fit. Members are free to operate in their own entrepreneurial interests. Usually this results in co-operation, but conflict can also occur. In contrast, a **vertical marketing system (VMS)** is a group of channel members organized to co-ordinate the efforts of each in a defined and co-operative fashion. The activities of the vertical marketing system are specifically co-ordinated and administrated in three types:

1. In a *corporate VMS*, one business organization owns the entire distribution system, managing its own manufacturing, wholesaling, and retailing functions. Color Your World manufactures its paints and sells them at its own stores. Beyond this VMS, the firm also has

vertical marketing system (VMS)
A group of members of a channel of distribution organized to co-ordinate their marketing efforts

franchised dealers and authorizes others as well to market its products. Tip-Top Tailors is another example of a corporate VMS.

2. A *contractual VMS* is, as the name implies, a group of channel intermediaries bound together by contract with defined roles and responsibilities. Many franchise arrangements would be included in this category. Canadian Tire acts as wholesaler to all its retail stores. The vast wholesaling capacity means that individual retail stores can supply a wide range of products quickly, even if they do not have specific items on their shelves. Conversely, the many retailers can support the wholesaling arm. The combined impact is considerable.

3. An *administered VMS* is less cohesive. It is co-ordinated by the power and persuasiveness of the channel manager. The channel manager is normally a large manufacturer or retailer. Manufacturers sometimes seek to exert channel leadership through producing a significant range of quality products, advertising them heavily, and providing significant merchandising support to retailers. Examples are Black & Decker in tools and appliances, and Michelin in tires. Large retailers such as The Bay and Wal-Mart also have the power to control the channels of distribution through their ability to purchase large quantities of a manufacturer's or wholesaler's products.

BUSINESS REVIEW 16.1

1. Draw a diagram illustrating various channels of distribution.
2. Describe the three types of vertical marketing systems.
3. Differentiate between conventional channels of distribution and a VMS.

RETAILING

To the consumer, retailing is the most visible link in the channel of distribution. The vast array of retail establishments is so common that we rarely stop to consider the extraordinary set of organizations that comprise the last link in the channel.

The 170,000 retail stores in Canada differ in many dimensions: size, layout, merchandise handled, amount of service, and lavishness of facilities, to name a few. Retailing comprises several different kinds of organizations, designed or evolved to serve specific market segments. They range from a small table or stall in a market with a few products, to the West Edmonton Mall with hundreds of stores, a waterway with submarines for shoppers to ride in, a recreation park with giant roller-coaster, and an indoor pool with a wave machine. Table 16.1 shows the largest retailers in Canada in various categories in 1992.

Evolution in Retailing

Most retail operations start small and remain that way. Nevertheless, to survive, all retailers must evolve to meet the changing demands of

TABLE 16.1 • LARGEST RETAILERS AND FOOD DISTRIBUTORS IN CANADA IN VARIOUS CATEGORIES (1992)

RETAILERS

Company and year end	Revenue $000	% change	Profit $000	% change	Return on capital (%) 1-year	5-year	Inventory turnover Current	Previous	Operating revenue per store $000
Department stores									
Hudson's Bay Co. (Ja93)	5,164,482	2	116,723	41	12.43	11.91	4.9	5.0	10,623
Sears Canada (De92)	3,974,600	–3	–90,900	–216	–1.62	8.07	6.0	6.0	36,309
Zellers Inc. (Ja93)	3,021,171	8	na	na	na	na	na	na	11,026
F.W. Woolworth Co. (Ja93)	2,143,355	3	4,151	123	4.48	14.21	3.9	4.1	3,855
Kmart Canada (Ja93)	1,244,354	1	6,476	258	8.02	10.33	4.0	4.1	8,763
Price Club Canada (Se91)	1,171,983	84	14,745	60	50.34	18.41	21.9	20.1	na
AVERAGE		9		–128	13.42	14.12	8.8	8.6	12,481
Clothing stores									
Dyles Ltd. (Fe92)	1,840,391	5	–55,430	–1,620	–6.25	1.86	6.8	6.5	1,187
Reltmans (Canada) (Ja93)	324,150	7	18,273	78	20.27	6.35	13.63	24.9	542
Château Stores of Canada (Ja92)	150,775	2	–5,349	–227	–16.93	4.64	8.3	10.0	867
Mark's Work Wearhouse (Ja92)	132,742	–26	–8,759	–38	–28.58	2.28	5.0	5.5	1,544
Pantorama Industries (Ja92)	113,221	–7	4,890	826	29.72	18.36	7.8	8.1	435
Dalmys (Canada) (Fe92)	106,735	–12	–16,495	–528	–50.41	–7.63	9.8	10.1	500
AVERAGE		–1		–357	–6.50	5.85	8.1	9.8	723
Specialty stores									
Canadian Tire Corp. (Ja93)	3,232,836	7	72,293	–43	10.86	19.46	9.5	10.3	7,599
Kinney Canada (Ja93)	660,216	4	–8,020	11	0.36	14.32	3.7	4.2	563
Groupe Ro-na Dismat (De92)	449,718	2	4,483	11	17.77	12.08	25.8	21.9	100
Big V Pharmacies (Se92)	430,700	9	na	na	na	na	na	na	na
Henry Birks & Sons (Oc91)	266,828	–31	–31,207	–1,576	–6.30	6.53	1.9	2.2	na
Leon's Furniture (De92)	266,320	0	10,412	–23	19.54	28.21	6.1	5.7	8,652
Peoples Jewellers (Mr92)	196,855	–7	–159,174	–4,703	–64.63	–6.11	1.6	1.8	713
Coles Book Stores (Ja93)	196,852	9	2,488	67	14.43	22.53	4.0	3.8	732
AVERAGE		45		–234	5.40	5.64	10.0	6.5	2,349

FOOD DISTRIBUTION

Company and year end	Revenue $000	% change	Profit $000	% change	Return on capital (%) 1–year	5–year
George Weston Ltd. (De92)	11,610,000	8	48,000	–48	8.73	14.32
Loblaw Cos. (Ja93)	9,226,100	9	79,800	–24	12.16	13.92
Univa Inc. (Ja93)	6,764,100	1	32,500	–34	11.27	11.24
Oshawa Group (Ja93)	5,021,900	8	41,800	19	9.62	16.22
Canada Safeway (Ja93)	4,360,400	0	45,500	–12	17.63	20.94
Great A&P Tea Co. (Fe92)	2,981,191	17	–5,197	–114	3.97	19.64
Westfair Foods (Ja93)	2,424,701	7	40,332	35	25.38	23.40
Métro-Richelieu (Se92)	2,308,619	4	13,101	39	10.64	8.41
AVERAGE		10		–257	9.16	14.67

Source: Report on Business 1000, July 1993, pp. 128, 130. Reprinted with permission from *The Globe and Mail*.

Listed in the *Guiness Book of Records* as the "largest shopping mall in the world," West Edmonton Mall covers a space of 5.2 million square feet (equivalent to 48 city blocks) with over 800 stores and services. The shopping and entertainment complex which has become a main tourist attraction for Alberta includes such lavish facilities as a waterpark, a miniature golf course and submarine rides. It cost a total of $1.1 billion (Cdn.) to build.

customers and counter the innovations of competitors. If they do not, their businesses will fail.

Many retailers that have had great success over time started off as very simple operations with low prices, basic fixtures, and few extra services. As time went on, services were added, store layouts were upgraded, and prices were raised to cover the added costs. For example, Kmart started as a very basic discount store but gradually followed the cycle described here.

As a retail institution moves in this direction, others see the opportunity to start a bare-bones low-price operation, and so the cycle is repeated. As shown in Figure 16.2, this evolving cycle from basic-service, low-price retailing to more elaborate offerings and high prices, and back again, is known as the *wheel of retailing*.

Another evolutionary characteristic of retailing is that one rarely sees a "plain" drugstore, gas station, or florist. Super Store is a grocery store that also carries hardware, automotive products, cameras, watches, and radios, as well as outdoor and yard-care products. Carrying products that are not directly related to the basic retail business is known as **scrambled merchandising**. Retailers find it creates opportunities for additional sales once a customer is in the store and believe it also attracts customers who otherwise would not enter the store to do so: a constant motive in retailing.

scrambled merchandising
The selling of merchandise that is not directly related to the basic retail business

FIGURE 16.2 • THE WHEEL OF RETAILING

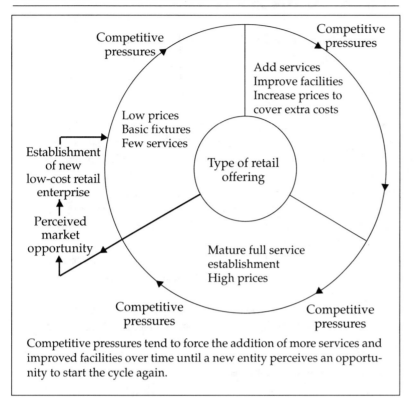

Competitive pressures tend to force the addition of more services and improved facilities over time until a new entity perceives an opportunity to start the cycle again.

Marketing Planning for Retailing

Retailing is "where the rubber hits the road" in marketing. Many quantitative decisions must be made concerning price, product turnover, and markups. As well, the ambience of the store, and many other psychological factors that affect purchase decisions, must be taken into consideration.

The process of developing a marketing plan for a retail operation is similar to developing a plan for a product. It commences with a careful analysis of customer needs in the proposed trading area and an appraisal of the strengths, weaknesses, and moves of competitors. This information is the basis for decisions about products to be carried, pricing strategy, and marketing communications.

One aspect of competition that has been the bane of Canadian retailers in recent years is cross-border shopping. In 1992, it was estimated that Ontario retailers alone lose $2 billion a year in sales when Ontario residents head to the United States to shop. Issues in Business 16.1 deals with how much governments should get involved in assisting Canadian retailers and how much responsibility the retailers themselves should bear.

ISSUES IN BUSINESS 16.1

COUNTERACTING CROSS-BORDER SHOPPING

IN SOME PROVINCES, the Retail Business Holidays Act restricts Sunday shopping to tourist areas and small stores. If this act were revoked by provincial governments, would Canadian retailers be better able to withstand cross-border competition?

In 1992, major retailers, such as the Hudson's Bay Co. and Consumers Distributing, threatened to defy the law and open on Sundays. Hudson's Bay claimed it lost $100 million a year in sales at its Ontario stores by not opening on Sunday. Ontario's shopping laws were finally changed to respond to the situation. But is Sunday shopping likely to put an end to cross-border shopping?

The value of the Canadian dollar, set by the Bank of Canada in accordance with government policy, is a major factor influencing the decision by Canadian consumers to spend money in the United States. As the Canadian dollar drops in value against the U.S. dollar, consumers more readily realize that not everything is cheaper in the United States.

On the other hand, perhaps if local retailers worked together and put more effort into telling the consumers about the good buys available in Canada, the discount-conscious shopper would be more inclined to spend in Canada.

Some facts are clear. Large amounts of business are being lost in Canada. This loss of business affects retailers and their employees directly. Such losses have negative ripple-effects in the rest of the economy.

Source: Adapted from Mark Evans, "Cross-Border Shopping Slows Down in March," *The Financial Post*, May 18, 1992, p. 3.

Questions for Discussion

1. Cross-border shopping is hurting retailers and the country. Should government bear the responsibility for helping retailers out?

2. What are some ways that retailers can counteract the cross-border shopping trend?

Types of Retailers

Because of the trend to scrambled merchandising, it is becoming more difficult to classify stores. Marketers, however, still find the categories discussed below useful in planning strategy.

General stores have always practised scrambled merchandising. Often the only retail outlet in a wide area, the general store has to meet customers' everyday needs: groceries, needle and thread to mend the clothes, a hammer and nails to fix the porch, a new saucepan, mittens and hats, first-aid supplies, fishing licences, birthday cards. Because the car has made it easier for people to travel farther to find a wider selection of merchandise, general stores are now few in number. They are found mostly in rural communities.

Timothy Eaton, the department store pioneer in Canada, opened his first store in 1869. **Department stores** not only stock many types of products under one roof but also provide a wide choice within each product. Large department stores can provide more than 200,000 items among many departments.

general store
A retailer that carries sufficient basic merchandise to meet customers' everyday needs, usually found in rural areas

department store
A retailer that carries a wide range of types of merchandise and a wide choice of products within each type

Specialty stores offer a wide selection in a specialized range of products, expert advice, detailed information for the inquisitive customer, and reliable services. They target a particular clientele (for example, skiers, hobbyists, photographers, adolescents, or men or women clothes shoppers). Such retailers are growing in importance as they are able to serve specialized consumer needs very well.

Convenience stores are just that—convenient. Usually located in high-density residential areas, they feature extended hours, rapid service, and often free parking. They sell high-volume products such as milk, newspapers, tobacco, and stamps. However, prices tend to be significantly higher than in other stores, especially on high-turnover items. Examples are Mac's Convenience Stores, Provisoir, and gasoline retailers.

Statistics Canada defines **chain stores** as those with four or more outlets, centrally owned and managed, that are in the same line of business. In addition to well-known department stores and supermarket chains, this category also includes hardware stores, automotive supply outlets, shoe stores, drugstores, and international chains such as Marks & Spencer, Smith Books, The Gap, and HMV.

Discount stores, popular since the end of the Second World War, offer lower prices and fewer services than other retailers. Their twofold objective is high-volume business and low operating costs. As time has passed, discount stores have naturally evolved to include more services. Consequently, there is now little difference between most discount stores and budget department stores such as Zellers.

Catalogue showrooms became popular in the 1970s. Potential customers visit low-overhead showrooms and browse through catalogues or receive catalogues by mail from which they select the merchandise they want. Because sales staff is kept to a minimum and orders are filled from inexpensive warehouses, prices are usually

specialty store
A retailer that offers expert advice on a wide selection of merchandise within a specialized range

convenience store
A retailer that is open for extended hours and sells high-volume products, usually located in a residential area

chain store
One of a group of four or more centrally owned and managed retail outlets

discount store
A retailer that offers a discount on the list price of merchandise but provides fewer services to the customer

catalogue showroom
A retailer that fills customers' catalogue orders from a warehouse-like back room, with only a small selection of available merchandise actually on display

Marks & Spencer is an international chain store that started out as Marks Penny Bazaars in England in 1884, and changed to its current name in 1894. Aside from the United Kingdom and Canada, there are Marks & Spencer stores in Belgium, France, Holland, Spain, and Hong Kong.

supermarket
A large self-serve retailer that sells grocery items and some general merchandise

hypermarket
A large-scale discount store that sells food and shopping goods

vending machine
A machine designed to sell various convenience goods without a sales clerk in constant attendance

warehouse club
A large retailer that sells sharply discounted goods, often in bulk, to club members; usually located in an industrial area

direct marketing method
In-home retailing to the customer through catalogues, person-to-person techniques, and television networks

lower. Consumers Distributing is one such firm. Growth of this type of retailing has dropped off with the advent of newer types of retailers.

Supermarkets sell mainly groceries but also a variety of other products such as kitchenware, school supplies, and even prescription drugs. They feature reasonable prices, good parking facilities, and self-service shopping in pleasant surroundings. Well-known supermarket chains are Provigo, Loblaws, Safeway, and Save-on Foods.

Hypermarkets are large-scale discount stores offering both food and general merchandise such as clothing and small and large appliances. Because each store is huge and uses advanced technology to reduce costs, customers can enjoy one-stop shopping at significantly reduced prices. A typical hypermarket is like a shopping centre in a single store. The Hypermarché Laval outside Montreal was the first to open in Canada. There are more hypermarkets in Europe than in North America, probably because large shopping centres, which service the same types of customers as hypermarkets, existed here before the hypermarket concept was developed.

Vending machines are an excellent method of retailing various types of consumer goods. Videocassettes, candy, soft drinks, ice, fruit, ice cream, chewing gum, sandwiches, coffee, milk, hot chocolate, and soup are all available through vending machines. Even entertainment has been packaged for vending operations, beginning with jukeboxes and pinball machines and progressing to the coin-operated video games found in a variety of settings today.

As the name implies, **warehouse clubs** are normally located in areas zoned for industry and warehouses. Members pay an annual membership fee of around $35 to shop for sharply discounted products. Merchandise is stored in metal racks, and customers must often dodge forklift trucks loading new supplies. Products carried range from popular electronic equipment to hardware and tools, toiletries, and food items. Often, products can be purchased only in large quantities, such as cases of canned goods or restaurant-sized jars. No services are provided. Examples are Price Club and Costco.

The price-saving technology of such establishments is now being adopted by other retail types. In the building supplies field, Aikenhead is an example. Similarly, The Business Depot provides office supplies.

In addition to these retail establishments, there are many different **direct marketing methods**. The emphasis in catalogue retailing has changed from the large general catalogue, which carried everything from clothing to patio doors (Sears). Instead, specialty catalogues, such as those issued by Lee Valley Tools, Marci Lipman, Tilley, and various gardening suppliers, are growing in number. TV shopping channels are another form of direct marketing. Beyond these methods is a wide range of in-home person-to-person techniques such as Tupperware parties and Avon and Amway sales.

The retailer is the last link in the channel of distribution to reach the consumer. A retailer's success depends on the ability to change and grow with consumer needs. The business skill required to manifest this understanding is that of repositioning the retail outlet. This involves great risks, a good deal of patience, and, sometimes, deep pockets, as illustrated in Developing Your Business Skills.

DEVELOPING YOUR BUSINESS SKILLS

KEEPING RETAIL STORES IN TUNE WITH CONSUMER TRENDS

Marks & Spencer Canada Inc. has come to be perceived by the Canadian consumer as a retailer with dowdy stores. The company has struggled in Canada while trying to replicate its parent company's success in Britain. It is attempting to reposition its image by expensive renovations, better merchandise displays, installing fitting rooms, and its first ad campaign.

Kmart Canada also has ambitious repositioning plans. With the battle heating up among discount retailers, the Toronto-based company aims to pick up market share by tempting new consumers with newly renovated stores, more brand name merchandise, and additional services.

The 1990–91 repositioning of Fairweather Inc., then a fashion retailer catering to the fickle teenage market, shows that an established retailer can change its spots. The first step was to take stock of existing customers. Research indicated that the chain was attracting women in their mid-twenties as well as the teenage market. This came as a surprise to company management. The company decided to focus on the older, more affluent crowd.

The next phase was staff training to ensure that the new direction was understood. Finally, an aggressive marketing campaign, which included hiring a public relations firm, drove home the message to consumers and the media.

Positioning a company's image to be in harmony with consumer wants is one of the most fundamental business skills the retailer must master.

Source: Excerpts from Mark Evans, "The Tricky Art of Changing Formats," *The Financial Post*, January 13, 1992, p. 3.

DENSITY OF DISTRIBUTION

The nature of different products greatly affects how widely they are distributed in a market area. If you wanted to buy Limoges china, you would be able to find it only in one or two select stores in any city. On the other hand, chocolate bars are found in hundreds of retail outlets. Distribution density depends on the importance of the product to the consumer and how willing the potential buyer is to look for it. There are three categories of distribution density—intensive distribution, exclusive distribution, and selective distribution.

The manufacturers of chocolate bars use **intensive distribution**. They know that customers will not go out of their way to look for a particular brand of chocolate bar and that, therefore, they had better ensure that it is available in every possible outlet. Other similar products are bread, chewing gum, newspapers, soft drinks, and other low-priced convenience products.

intensive distribution
The attempt to place a product in all available outlets

Limoges china is a specialty product. Since it is unique and of such high quality that a potential buyer will be willing to seek it out, it can be made available through **exclusive distribution**. The quality of the retail outlet, including the service it offers, is more important than density of distribution. The manufacturer can demand excellent service be supplied to buyers of its product in return for the right to be one of the few outlets that carries the product in a specific geographical area. Included in this service is adequate inventory level, and

exclusive distribution
Giving a member of the channel of distribution the exclusive right to sell a product or product line in a geographical area in return for the guarantee of a specified level of service

special efforts to display and promote the product. In exchange for an exclusive distribution arrangement, manufacturers expect to develop a close working relationship with their dealers and often split advertising expenses with them.

selective distribution
Giving a limited number of retailers the right to sell a product or product line in a geographical area

Televisions and electrical appliances are given **selective distribution**. Potential customers for such products are willing to shop around and compare brands, but to a limited degree. Selective distribution—an arrangement whereby a limited number of retailers are selected to distribute a firm's product lines—lies somewhere between intensive and exclusive distribution. As in the latter, manufacturer and dealer often work closely together on promotion and advertising.

BUSINESS REVIEW 16.2

1. Review the concept of evolution in retailing and supply some examples.
2. How does retail planning compare with marketing planning?

PHYSICAL DISTRIBUTION

Every day a huge fleet of trucks leaves the giant Canadian Tire warehouse in Brampton, Ontario. They keep the far-flung Canadian Tire stores stocked with merchandise carefully selected by the company's buying specialists—a challenging responsibility for physical distribution management.

physical distribution
The actual handling and movement of products from origin to final destination

Physical distribution is the actual handling and movement of products from origin to final destination and their storage at various points along the way. In alliance with various channels of distribution, the physical distribution system results in having a mountain bike awaiting your visit to a store in your home town. Quite a feat!

Physical distribution involves much more than putting some products on a truck or train and waving them on their way. Transportation is only one component of a physical distribution system. Other important ones are warehousing, inventory control, and order processing.

Transportation

private carrier
A company that transports its own goods

contract carrier
A company that hires out its vehicles for the exclusive use of a firm

common carrier
A company that moves products for several companies at the same time

Transportation modes are numerous, ranging from plane to pipeline. The distribution manager must consider not only the most appropriate mode of transportation to ensure delivery of the product but also the most efficient approach to ownership and control of the chosen transportation system. A company can act as its own private carrier or decide on a system using contract carriers, common carriers, or freight forwarders, or a combination of these. Companies that transport their own goods are **private carriers**. **Contract carriers** are transportation companies that hire out their vehicles for the exclusive use of a firm. Beaver Lumber Co. Ltd., for example, uses trucks owned by contract carriers to transport its merchandise to its stores. **Common carriers** are companies that organize a distribution route and move suitable

Reimer Express Lines Ltd., a "common" or "for hire" carrier, was founded in 1952 by Dr. D.S. Reimer who continues to be the head of the company. Reimer provides less than truck load (LTL) general freight service to shippers across Canada primarily along the routes between Montreal and Vancouver. It also offers international service between Canada and the U.S.

products for various companies at the same time. For example, Reimer Express, a general trucking company, is a common carrier. **Freight forwarders** contract for a portion of the space of other carriers and then sell it to many smaller producers. This service works well for companies that are too small to operate their own transportation system because the forwarder picks up and delivers to the carrier, then delivers at the other end. Large transportation firms, for the most part common carriers, are listed in Table 16.2.

freight forwarder

A company that arranges shipping, including pickup and delivery, through common carriers for companies with small shipments

TABLE 16.2 • TRANSPORTATION MODES

Company and year end	Revenue $000	% ch'ge	Profit $000	% ch'ge	Return on capital (%) 1-year	5-year	Assets $000	% ch'ge	Capital spending $000	% ch'ge
Canadian Ntnl Railway (De92)	4,069,550	–1	–1,005,242	–6,950	–16.39	0.05	7,051,580	1	333,851	40
Air Canada (De92)	3,501,000	–1	–454,000	–108	–6.34	2.30	4,810,000	–2	598,000	–40
PWA Corp. (De92)	2,901,286	0	–543,300	–236	–21.81	–2.98	2,461,900	–12	293,300	–45
Mobil Marine Transport (De91)	632,266	10	41,221	398	10.88	4.19	668,121	13	104,136	651
Via Rail Canada (De92)	546,056	–4	141	–51	0.23	0.08	866,436	–5	44,711	11
B.C. Transit (Mr92)	507,499	9	4,039	94	9.19	8.76	1,766,111	8	142,680	61
Trimac Ltd. (De92)	503,837	6	26,823	18	11.98	11.37	531,005	34	94,744	44
Canadian Pacific Express (De92)	419,500	–13	na	na	na	na	150,900	–17	na	na
Fednav Ltd. (De92)	337,000	15	3,810	6	5.77	10.13	361,002	5	na	na
AVERAGE		2		–217	5.87	7.94		2		5

Source: Report on Business 1000, July 1993, p. 124. Reprinted with permission of *The Globe and Mail*.

Warehousing

Goods normally have to be stored at various stages in the journey from producer to consumer. First, the warehousing function is performed at the manufacturing plant until a full order is ready for shipment, and then by the retailer until products are purchased by the consumer. In addition, warehousing may be required to store products for longer periods of time, or in order to break bulk at a distribution point in locations far from the supplier.

Inventory Control

Inventory control is an essential function in the distribution of products. It involves keeping track of shipments and stock in warehouses, and the maintenance of products in good condition through the distribution process.

Order Processing

Order processing involves the actual preparation of orders for shipment. It is a detailed and complex process. Efficient order processing can make a company more competitive and can help a company improve its customer service.

The physical distribution system comprises many parts. The numerous agencies involved work together to get products through the channels of distribution to consumers as efficiently as possible. Physical distribution costs are one area in which efficiency gains might increase profits, as discussed in Issues in Business 16.2.

ISSUES IN BUSINESS 16.2

PHYSICAL DISTRIBUTION AND COMPETITIVENESS

SINCE THE EARLY 1990s, many retailers have experienced serious financial problems. The sight of empty shops in malls, and boarded-up stores, is common. There are many reasons for this: unemployment, more-discerning customers, and poor management, to name a few.

However, some retailers are doing very well. Outlets such as Super Store, Costco, Price Club, and Byway are examples. A common characteristic of such successes seems to be lower prices.

Prices paid by retailers can be negotiated down only so far. Prices of goods sold can be lowered through smaller margins to only a limited degree. Thus, improving efficiency of operation is an important next step.

Question for Discussion

1. Think about the many components of physical distribution and suggest some ways that savings could be achieved through improvements to the system.

INTERACTIVE SUMMARY AND DISCUSSION QUESTIONS

1. This module says that distribution accomplishes four of the functions of marketing: buying, wholesaling, retailing, and transporting. Show how this comes about.

2. Change occurs constantly in channels of distribution. Give some important examples of such changes.

3. Both retailers and wholesalers act as intermediaries, or middlemen. Discuss how each performs this function.

4. In some channels of distribution, the product is sold directly by the manufacturer to the customer. In others, one or more intermediary is involved.
   a) Explain why this is so.
   b) Would the price of the product necessarily be lower if some of the intermediaries in a multiple channel were removed?

5. The three types of vertical marketing systems (VMSs) are corporate, contractual, and administered. Give examples of each type operating in your area. What circumstances might lead to the establishment of each of the three?

6. The module explains that evolution is a constant in retailing. Is this desirable? Explain the consequences of such evolution.

7. Three types of market coverage are intensive distribution, exclusive distribution, and selective distribution. Give examples of three products that would likely benefit from each type of distribution.

8. The principal components of a physical distribution system are transportation, warehousing, inventory control, and order processing. Using shirts as an example, explain these concepts. Do the same for the local newspaper.

CASE 16.1

EATON'S UPHILL CLIMB TO SUCCESS

DURING THE TOUGHEST retail climate since the Depression, George Eaton, president of the family empire, has made some dramatic changes to their stores' retail strategy. The chain was founded in 1869 by his great-grandfather, Timothy Eaton.

At a time when other retailers are promoting seasonal sales to lure consumer spending, George Eaton is discarding the Eaton's tradition of Trans-Canada sales in the spring and fall and instead is promoting "everyday low prices" and no sales. In its glory days, Eaton's had 50 percent of the Canadian retail market, excluding food and cars, and George hopes to regain some of this glory.

The idea has a compelling logic. The public is sceptical of claims of 50 or 60 percent off. Retailers devote considerable costs and resources to holding sales. Eaton's concluded consumers would buy the idea of low values on a daily basis. Market researcher Martin Goldfarb, whose research fed this strategy, said Eaton's, with its image of trustworthiness, is one of the few retailers that could pull it off.

But consumers are confused by conflicting messages in the marketplace. "It was a gutsy move because everyone today is responding to sales," said Peter Nygard, chairman of Nygard International Ltd. Efforts to dispel this confusion included heavier promotion of its everyday-value approach. "But it takes some time for the public to recognize the values," Nygard added.

Eaton's has reached for other weapons in its fight to support this risky strategy during a difficult market phase. It recently launched a Buy Canadian promotion, pledging to support Canadian industry through its purchasing policies. It's not a new idea—Eaton's has held such promotions in the past and tends to work closely with Canadian suppliers. But this time the message is being

(continued)

hammered home. It differentiates Eaton's from The Bay, which says it will import more U.S. merchandise to exploit the Canada–U.S. free-trade deal and to combat cross-border shopping.

Critics are sceptical that this plan will work. They maintain that country of origin is of significance to the consumer only if the prices and quality are competitive. But Eaton's campaign is just the surface of a much deeper strategy to develop closer links with about 250 key Canadian suppliers.

Eaton's wants to turn suppliers into strategic allies with unprecedented access to the stores' planning and information. "They want to eliminate the old-fashioned bureaucratic relationship," said Nygard, one of the designated suppliers.

A cornerstone of this new allegiance is information links through Electronic Data Interchange (EDI) systems. Eaton's, like many retailers, is turning to online processing of orders and invoices. The ultimate goal is instantaneous information exchange between suppliers and the store floors. Suppliers could determine which merchandise is moving and which isn't, then respond immediately. Eaton's is among the most aggressive retailers using this system.

George Eaton is also striving to put his mark on Eaton's conservative culture. Former managers said the company had suffered from low-flight management. It had shut itself off from fresh retailing ideas and invested inadequately in training.

George wants to shake up Eaton's with new ideas while maintaining its image of permanence and trust. He is trying to polish a tarnished commitment to value and service.

Source: Adapted from Gordon Pitts, "Striving to Lead Eaton Chain Back to Glory," *The Financial Post*, April 20, 1992, pp. S24–S25.

Questions for Discussion

1. Outline the steps George Eaton has taken to try to regain market share.
2. How successful do you think the "everyday value" campaign will be? Explain.
3. Evaluate George Eaton's strategy. What are the risks?

CASE 16.2

THE REPUBLIC OF BATA

MARTIN O'NEIL, PRESIDENT of Bata Canada, has left his imprint on a distinctive marketing campaign. . . . At a time when mall shopping has declined, Bata Canada, with most its stores in malls, needed to take bold steps to make their stores stand out from the rest. The "Republic of Bata" was born.

Declaring its 200 retail stores "independent republics . . . entirely independent of Canada's high prices," Bata promises its prices will be lower than, or the same as, those in the United States. Customers receive passports that entitle them to a free pair of shoes for every five pairs purchased. More than 200,000 passports have been handed out, and a million more will be printed.

The campaign is a dramatic change in communications strategy. Previous promotions used only in-store signs addressed to shopping mall traffic. The new "Republic" ads appear in all mass media, including flyer distribution.

"The Republic of Bata was a whole new concept in trying to generate a clearer distinction for ourselves in the mall. All the shoe stores were starting to look the same, so we decided we needed to do something totally different," said Martin O'Neill, president. Len Kubas, president of

(continued)

Kubas Consultants in Toronto, is enthusiastic about the new Bata approach. "By creating a powerful image, Bata will attract more traffic than it would by just lowering prices," he said. Another important aspect of the campaign, Kubas said, is that it has energized Bata's sales staff.

In addition to launching its new market campaign, Bata has revamped manufacturing processes at its plants in Batawa, Ontario, to make them more competitive with those of foreign rivals.

Bata claims to be "bringing Canadians to their feet" in an effort to put the boot to the cross-border shopping exodus.

Source: Adapted from Mark Evans, "New 'Republic' Delivers," *The Financial Post*, September 16, 1991, p. 12.

Questions for Discussion

1. Summarize the components of Bata's new strategy. How do they interact?
2. How does the fact that Bata owns its own factories, as well as shoe stores, affect the new strategic moves taken by the company?
3. Do you think that Bata's strategy will be successful in making its shoe stores distinctive from others in the mall environment?

PHOTO CREDITS

DIS 5   Canadian Tire Corporation, Limited   DIS 16   Marks & Spencer

DIS 11   West Edmonton Mall   DIS 18   Reimer Express Lines Ltd.

MODULE
◆ COM ◆

MARKETING COMMUNICATIONS

THE FOCUS OF THIS MODULE

1. To define the main elements of marketing communications

2. To explain the basic logic behind the concept of pushing and pulling marketing communication strategies

3. To consider various objectives that can be achieved through marketing communications

4. To describe types of advertising and when they are appropriate in a product life cycle

5. To review the nature and importance of the main advertising media

6. To describe various types of sales promotion

7. To differentiate among the three basic selling activities used by business

8. To describe the primary responsibilities of sales management

9. To learn the meaning of the following terms:

KEY TERMS

marketing
   communications
advertising
personal selling
sales promotion
pushing strategy
co-operative
   advertising
pulling strategy
positioning
product advertising
institutional advertising

direct marketing
narrowcasting
point-of-purchase (POP)
specialty advertising
sample
coupon
premium
trading stamps
promotion contests
order processing
creative selling
missionary selling

AS A SMALL company, how do you communicate the benefits of a new cosmetic when well-established giant companies are spending millions advertising their products? This was the problem faced by M.A.C.

Make-up Art Cosmetics (M.A.C.) was co-founded in 1985 by Frank Toscan, a photographer and former makeup artist, and entrepreneur Frank Angelo. Toscan became frustrated with the poor quality and limited range of colours available in the established line of cosmetics. He began by mixing new colours of cosmetics in his kitchen with the help of a high school chemistry book.

In an industry dominated by a handful of multinational giants, including Estée Lauder, Revlon, and Lancôme, M.A.C.'s road to success has been unconventional. Even its three-storey world headquarters, wedged between a Chinese fast-food outlet and a children's clothing store in downtown Toronto, is easily missed.

While other firms pump millions of dollars a year into advertising their beauty products, M.A.C. realized that they would have to find a different way of communicating with their target market. They did not have the resources to match the mass advertising efforts of competitors.

Instead, the company has relied on word of mouth and in-store promotions. Said Ted Nadel, a Montreal makeup artist: "M.A.C. is extremely smart about reaching people who set the trends." Industry analysts say that the use of M.A.C. products by prominent models and stars has contributed to the firm's success. M.A.C. started to build its reputation by participating in industry trade shows such as the Canadian Festival of Fashion in Toronto.

Another important part of their marketing strategy was the choice of a small number of exclusive retail outlets to carry the product. This reinforced the elite image of the product and transmitted a message of high fashion.

Among the users are Madonna, who uses M.A.C.'s fiery Russian Red lipstick. World-famous Canadian model Linda Evangelista is another user, as is singer Whitney Houston. "That's great word of mouth," commented one observer.

These celebrities, and especially their makeup artists, have been lured by the wide range of dramatic and unusual colours produced by Make-up Art Cosmetics. Said Kevyn Aucoin, a leading New York City makeup artist, "Everyone in the business considers M.A.C. to be the cutting edge."

Source: Excerpts from Diane Brady, "The M.A.C. Attack," *Maclean's*, August 26, 1991, p. 44.

M.A.C. IS A GOOD example of the fact that marketing communication can be accomplished in many different ways. The company's word-of-mouth communication strategy has certainly paid off. By its seventh year, the firm expected to have North American retail sales of $25 million, up $10 million from the previous year.

ELEMENTS OF MARKETING COMMUNICATION STRATEGY

Marketing communications is defined as all messages that inform, persuade, and influence the consumer in making a purchase decision. All organizations recognize that they must communicate with potential customers. Three main elements are involved in most marketing communication strategy: advertising, personal selling, and sales promotion.

Advertising is paid non-personal informative and persuasive communication to a mass audience. Advertising is the marketing communication method most people think of first, but it is not necessarily the most important element, as was seen in the case of M.A.C. **Personal selling** is direct person-to-person communication with the objective of influencing the potential buyer. **Sales promotion** involves coupons, displays, product sampling, demonstrations, and other activities designed to increase dealer effectiveness and stimulate consumer purchasing.

Pushing versus Pulling Strategies

The proportionate use of these three elements of marketing communications depends on whether the marketer tends to rely more on a pushing or a pulling strategy.

A **pushing strategy** places emphasis on the skill and effectiveness of a sales force. It is designed to gain sales for the product line or service through the efforts of intermediaries, or middlemen (wholesalers and retailers). Sales personnel "push" the product by persuading intermediaries to stock it and "push" it further to other intermediaries or to consumers. Intermediaries may be offered attractive discounts, advertising materials, and co-operative advertising allowances or incentives to carry products. **Co-operative advertising** is simply the sharing of local advertising costs between the producer and intermediary.

A **pulling strategy** places emphasis on advertising and sales promotion appeals to stimulate demand from potential customers. In response to this demand, retailers are motivated to carry the product and place orders with suppliers. Thus, effective advertising can "pull" goods through the channel of distribution. If the demand is maintained and the intermediaries and manufacturer continue to have supplies available, goods will keep flowing into the market without interruption.

In order to avoid the situation of achieving demand without having supplies available or having the shelves full with no demand from customers, pushing and pulling strategies are usually combined to some extent. The emphasis is usually on a pulling strategy, for example, the promotion of consumer products, whereas a pushing strategy is more effective in promoting industrial products.

marketing communications
All messages that inform, persuade, and influence the consumer in making a purchase decision

advertising
Paid, non-personal informative and persuasive communication to a mass audience

personal selling
Direct person-to-person communication with the objective of influencing the potential buyer

sales promotion
Coupons, displays, product sampling, demonstrations, and other activities designed to increase dealer effectiveness and stimulate consumer purchases

pushing strategy
A marketing strategy that emphasizes selling efforts to "push" a product through the channel of distribution to the ultimate consumer

co-operative advertising
The sharing of local advertising costs between a producer and channel intermediaries

pulling strategy
A marketing strategy that emphasizes advertising and sales promotions to stimulate consumer interest in a product and thus "pull" it through the channel of distribution

OBJECTIVES OF MARKETING COMMUNICATIONS

Marketers must consider their objectives in formulating an appropriate mix of elements in a particular marketing communication strategy. Is the strategy being used to provide information on a product or an organization? to position the product? to hold on to a current market position? to increase sales by expanding the market or reaching a particular target market?

Providing Information

The original purpose of advertising was simply to provide information on a product's availability. Town criers informed people that a ship had arrived with long-awaited cargo. As farmers and other colonists moved west, their source of commercial information became the local weekly newspaper in which the general-store keeper announced the goods that had arrived on the latest train.

In recent times, availability of goods has rarely been a problem, but providing information remains a very important objective for marketers. Advertising and personal selling are used to announce new products. Newspaper advertisements provide shoppers with information on which stores are featuring good prices on certain products. In the industrial market, customers need to be brought up to date on all changes in the technology of the equipment they use. This task largely falls to the industrial salesperson.

The primary focus of marketing communications is to provide *reliable* information on product availability, prices, and other relevant details. The messages marketing managers send have assumed an important educational function.

Product Positioning

A major marketing consideration is where to "position" a product in the minds of consumers relative to other products in the market. For example, Onkyo positions its stereo equipment as having extra high quality. The local 7-Eleven is positioned as having the basic foods you need, plus some specialty items, during hours in which other stores are closed. **Positioning** is a strategy that attempts to cultivate consumers' perceptions of the type and nature of a firm's product in relation to salient selection criteria and competing products.

positioning
Cultivating consumer perceptions of a product in relation to competing products

Frequently, positioning can be an effective strategy in cutting into the market share of a dominant product. The marketing of Scope mouthwash provides a good example of this. Claiming to replace "medicine breath" with "minty, fresh breath," it challenged Listerine, the mouthwash leader that promised control of bad breath. By cleverly comparing the two brands, Scope was able to focus consumers' attention on the leading brand's recognizable medicinal aftertaste. In response, Listerine repositioned its product as not only a mouthwash but also a reducer of dental plaque.

Increasing Sales

The ultimate objective of marketing strategy is to sell more product. Marketers sometimes set the objective for marketing communications as "increasing sales." The problem is that it is seldom possible to attribute sales to a particular advertising strategy, to a particular sales promotion, or even to personal selling. Realistically, in most situations many other components of the marketing mix also play a part in contributing to a sale.

Stabilizing Sales

It is common for firms to develop a promotional strategy with the specific purpose of stabilizing sales during a slow period. This could include providing incentives (such as paid vacations, appliances, and scholarships), cash bonuses, and a variety of promotional materials like calendars and pens to salespeople who meet certain objectives.

The effective application of marketing communication strategies in stabilizing sales can significantly contribute to cost savings. A company with a stable-sales situation can avoid production problems associated with peak periods and slow periods and use human and material resources more efficiently.

There is more to marketing communications than advertising. Each of the three distinct elements—advertising, sales promotion, and personal selling—must be considered in marketing communication planning. Let us look in more detail at each.

ADVERTISING

Advertising uses all media—newspapers, magazines, television, radio, direct mail, and outdoor advertising—to communicate the message to specific target markets and also to more widespread potential markets. Newspapers receive the single largest share of total advertising revenues. The leading national advertisers in Canada include the familiar names General Motors, Procter & Gamble, Labatt's, and Eaton's. However, the largest advertiser in the country is the Government of Canada. See Table 17.1 for a list of the top ten advertisers.

Advertising spending ranges greatly for different types of products, for example, from as low as 0.1 percent of sales in an industry like sanitary services to more than 10 percent of sales in the motion picture industry.

TABLE 17.1 • TOP TEN CANADIAN ADVERTISERS, 1993

Rank	Company	Expenditures
1	General Motors of Canada Ltd.	113,048,400
2	Procter & Gamble Inc.	84,499,500
3	The Thompson Group	79,159,300
4	BCE Inc.	53,972,900
5	John Labatt Ltd.	50,036,000
6	Eaton's of Canada Ltd.	47,135,900
7	Sears Canada Inc.	46,582,100
8	Government of Canada	43,928,700
9	The Molson Companies	42,873,600
10	Crysler Canada Ltd.	41,171,500

Source: copyright Nielsen Marketing Research Canada Limited (1994) All rights reserved

product advertising
Advertising created to promote a specific product

institutional advertising
Advertising seeking to emphasize the merit of an organization itself

Classifying Advertising

Most advertising is created to promote a specific product. This type is known as **product advertising**. The advertising for Coca-Cola, Becel margarine, and Saturn autos are examples. **Institutional advertising** seeks to emphasize the merit of an organization itself. Ford's "Quality Is Job One" message enhances the public's perception of the organization, and therefore the value of each specific product it produces. Other examples of institutional advertising are ads placed by the insurance industry ("Insurance is a good thing to have") and by the pork producers ("Pork is 26 percent lower in cholesterol").

Many advertisements combine the two approaches. For example, Nissan may create an advertisement to promote the Sentra, but the ad will also remind the reader or viewer that the company has one of the industry's best guarantees. Some companies, such as Benetton as described in Issues in Business 17.1, use advertising to shock—and thereby draw attention to social issues, the company, and its products.

Nothing but smooth sailing.

1994 Nautica Villager.

ISSUES IN BUSINESS 17.1

HAVE THE UNITED COLORS OF BENETTON GONE TOO FAR?

THE SOCIAL-ISSUE FOCUS of advertising campaigns is not a new one, but just how far do these companies have a right to go?

First it was a black woman breast-feeding a white baby; then an array of multicoloured condoms; then a nun and a priest kissing; then a new-born baby—blood-smeared—dangling from an umbilical cord.

Now Benetton, an Italian clothing firm which in the past two years has used these images in its worldwide advertising campaigns, has released an even more inflammatory advertisement: a picture of a dying AIDS victim. Has the company gone too far?

Britain's Advertising Standards Authority are calling the advertisement "obscene," "disgusting," and a "despicable exploitation of a tragic situation." Similar outcries have forced the firm to abandon the ads in some countries. Well-meaning newspaper publishers have published the ads with news stories describing the outrage of the advertising industry.

Benetton remains undaunted. In fact, the headlines they produce are precisely to the point. The company has turned courting controversy into a spectacularly successful marketing strategy. The "United Colors of Benetton" campaigns of the mid-1980s, which played on themes of racial harmony, helped turn the firm into a powerful global brand. But sales really rocketed when the ads took on other "social issues" (i.e., became intentionally incendiary).

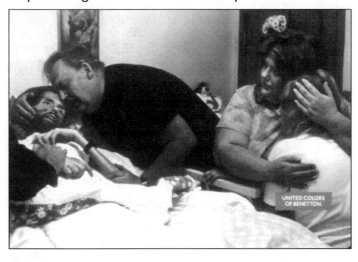

One advertising person from Benetton claims the campaigns are not designed to offend, but rather to "raise consciousness."

The AIDS ad has been criticized by one British AIDS charity as trying to profit from people's pain. However, American gay activists disagree, saying the advertisement gives the issue a higher public profile.

Source: Excerpts from "More Controversy, Please, We're Italian," *The Economist,* February 1–7, 1992, p. 72. Copyright ©1992 The Economist Newspaper Group, Inc. Reprinted with permission. Further reproduction prohibited.

Questions for Discussion

1. Is it appropriate for Benetton to have used consciousness-raising imagery based on someone's personal tragedy to attract attention to their products?

2. Why would Benetton engage in this type of advertising?

FIGURE 17.1 · RELATIONSHIP BETWEEN ADVERTISING AND THE PRODUCT LIFE CYCLE

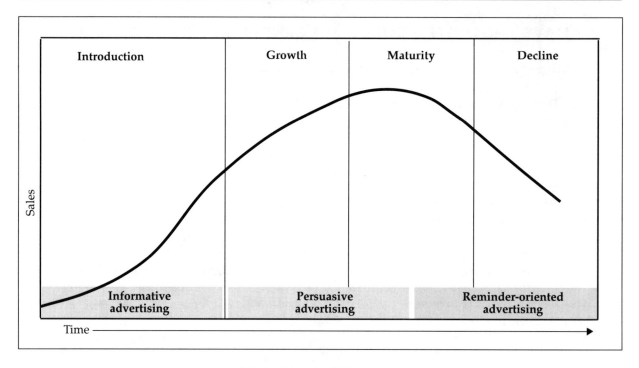

Advertising and the Product Life Cycle

Advertising strategy for a product varies according to its stage in the product life cycle (see Figure 17.1). During a product's introductory phase, informative advertising is a useful tool for building initial demand. The Australian Tourist Commission used an informative-promotion campaign to get young Australians to explore their country. The campaign was based on a free, youth-oriented booklet, *Australia—A Land of Things to Do*, that listed hostels, places to crash, surfing beaches, and the like.

During the growth and maturity stages of the product life cycle, persuasive advertising is used to develop a strong market share. By improving a product's competitive status, this type of promotion will help the firm secure its product in the market. "Save Money with a Carrier Heat Pump... Now!" is a persuasive advertising theme. The Milk-Bone advertisement reproduced on the opposite page is another example of persuasive advertising.

One type of persuasive advertising is comparative advertising, in which the advertiser's product is directly contrasted with a competing one. The specific competing brand is sometimes named in the comparison and often, the competing products are placed together into a generic group. For example, a Quaker advertisement compares nameless chocolate chip cookies with a Chewy Granola Bar, still partially wrapped in its packaging. The headline declares, "A Quaker Chewy

Granola Bar has 30% less fat, and that's the way the cookie crumbles."
When comparative advertising is used, it is a sign that the market is
very competitive.

Reminder-oriented advertising, as the name implies, is a useful
technique for reminding consumers of a product's value and importance. It is appropriate for the maturity and decline stages of the product life cycle as a way of reassuring the public that the product is still
available. Familiar products and brands that are marketed using
reminder-oriented advertising include soft drinks, sound-system
manufacturers, toothpaste, and oil companies. As Issues in Business
17.2 indicates, some advertisements for well-known products are trying to remind consumers of earlier advertising campaigns rather than
the products themselves.

A Quaker Chewy Granola Bar has 30% less fat,

and that's the way the cookie crumbles.

Did you know, gram for gram, an average Quaker Chewy Granola Bar has 30% less fat than the leading chocolate chip cookie?* That's a real difference. Our bars are made with Quaker oats, whole wheat, crisp rice, almonds, raisins and real fruit. So when it comes to your kid's lunchbox, you can count on Quaker goodness. Everytime.

Trust Quaker Goodness.

ISSUES IN BUSINESS 17.2

YOU MUST REMEMBER THIS

WITH LOYALTY TO brands eroding, and new brands more difficult to establish than ever, advertisers are casting a longing eye at the good old days. And advertisers of familiar products are hoping that consumers, jaded by today's barrage of advertising, will do the same.

With so many "baby boomers" (i.e., anyone born between 1946 and 1964) entering or already in middle age, companies are trying to catch their fancy by reviving the jingles most of them grew up with.

Coca-Cola has used Humphrey Bogart, Louis Armstrong, and other golden oldies to sell the "Classic" version of Coke. Campbell's soup is once again "Mmm, mmm good" (those words

(continued)

trigger a jingle in the mind of anyone over age 40). Alka-Seltzer has rerun a series of advertisements carrying the punchline "I can't believe I ate the whole thing." Such themes were so drummed into the first television generation that most baby boomers can still hear them in their sleep.

One running-shoe manufacturer, undeterred by the marketing muscle of Nike, Reebok, and Adidas, reintroduced "PF Flyers." This is the canvas sneaker worn by millions in the 1950s and 1960s. The company estimates that the thirty-something and forty-something generation will prefer these to the bulkier running shoes popular with teenagers.

At this rate, it may be only a matter of time before companies advertise products as "old" rather than "new and improved."

Source: Excerpts from "You Must Remember This," *The Economist*, February 1–7, 1992, p. 76. Copyright ©1992 The Economist Newspaper Group, Inc. Reprinted with permission. Further reproduction prohibited.

Question for Discussion

1. What is happening here? Is advertising creating trends or responding to existing social trends?

Advertising Media

Advertisers must have a clear understanding of the relationship between the amount spent on advertising and its impact on achieving objectives. However, having an adequate budget for advertising is not all that is needed. Selection of the best medium to promote a product is a critical decision, and each possible choice has benefits and drawbacks.

Newspapers account for almost a quarter of total advertising expenditure. They represent an important advertising tool with several advantages. They can focus on the specific interests and needs of a local population. The information they contain enjoys heavy exposure because people from all corners of a community regularly buy and read them. Newspapers also function as a reference source for many people when they plan their purchases, and advertisers can design strategy with this in mind. The disadvantages include the newspaper's short life span, the speed at which it is read, and the relatively poor reproduction quality.

A much smaller proportion of advertising funds is spent on *magazines*. In Canada, *Chatelaine* is read by more paid subscribers than any other magazine. The principal advantage of advertising in special-interest magazines is that it is a very efficient way to reach a target market. Other advantages include quality reproduction, long life, prestige, and the extra services that are offered to advertisers. The standard criticism of using magazines to advertise has been their limited flexibility compared with other media. However, this limitation may be largely eliminated as advertisers can place local advertising in regional editions of national magazines. Advertising in magazines is typically more expensive than in newspapers.

Taking in about one-sixth of total advertising revenue, *television* is an important advertising medium. In national advertising, television is the undisputed leader. It offers advertisers a variety of possibilities —coast-to-coast network ads, national spot ads, and local advertising, depending on the product and the market to be reached. Although the cost of using television is very high, the powerful impact of the medium on potential customers makes the expense worth while. The effects of mass coverage, "live" demonstration, and prestige represent additional benefits to advertisers. Television is particularly effective as it uses the visual appeals of print media in combination with the sound of radio. McDonald's is famous for a continuous series of outstanding commercials.

In Canada, *radio* accounts for about one-tenth of total advertising revenue, although in some countries radio advertising is forbidden or heavily restricted. Canada's sophisticated broadcasting system offers immediacy, low cost, practical audience selection, and mobility. The unavoidable disadvantage of radio is its highly fragmented audience. As well, because a radio message is only temporary, a great deal of repetition of messages is necessary.

The familiar billboard and other forms of *outdoor advertising* represent less than a tenth of all advertising. Outdoor advertising is a powerful medium for advertisers wishing to promote uncomplicated ideas quickly and repetitively. It is also used successfully to publicize local products. However, this form of communicating to the market is limited by the brevity of its messages. Public concern has also been expressed over the aesthetics of billboards and how they may often conflict with environmental priorities.

direct marketing
Advertising aimed directly at individual consumers through mailed catalogues, telephone solicitations, or videotapes

Direct marketing includes direct mail, catalogues, telemarketing, and videotape "brochures." In total, it is now the leading advertising medium. Direct mail is its largest component and it alone rivals newspapers in total advertising expenditure. Its growth in importance to advertisers can be attributed to the possibilities of selectivity, intense coverage, speed, flexibility, complete information, and personalization. However, direct mail is very expensive. And, as it relies entirely on mailing lists of potential customers, it depends heavily on the accuracy of those lists. Furthermore, many customers are resistant to direct mail, so the credibility factor must not be overlooked.

narrowcasting
Advertising on specialty cable television channels to reach specific markets

Marketing managers in many companies are now looking at a number of specialized media for marketing communications. One option is **narrowcasting**, which identifies a specific audience and reaches this narrow market with advertising on selected cable TV channels. For example, since cable channels are designed to specialize in sports, country music, and so on, advertisers can target their messages to these specific audiences. Other media possibilities include using movie theatres and airline screens for reaching truly captive audiences. Transit advertising is also a popular advertising tool.

Whether they are used as a stand-alone campaign or as part of a wider marketing communication strategy with several elements, these less traditional media options are being taken very seriously by marketing managers.

BUSINESS REVIEW 17.1

---

1. Differentiate between a pulling strategy and a pushing strategy. Suggest a situation in which a pushing strategy would be the one of choice.
2. List the four main objectives of advertising.
3. Show how advertising strategy might vary in accordance with the stage of the product life cycle.

SALES PROMOTION

Sales promotions are specific short-term inducements to buy, such as point-of-purchase displays, signs, gifts, trade shows, and coupons. The many forms of sales promotions can serve as a very valuable complement to advertising and sales management in the marketing communication strategy.

Point-of-Purchase Sales Promotions

Point-of-purchase (POP) promotional efforts place specific emphasis on the location and arrangement of products in the retail outlets in which they are sold. Displays, demonstrations, special packaging, samples, previously unadvertised discounts, and additional information are all forms of sales promotions designed to develop more interest in a product. Point-of-purchase promotions often enhance the desirability of purchasing one item by linking it to another item in the same retail location. The crowd of point-of-purchase displays around cash registers in many pharmacies is an example. Manufacturers compete for such favourable locations.

point-of-purchase (POP)
Sales promotions at the retail outlet through the location of the product, displays, demonstrations, samples, and unadvertised discounts

Specialty Advertising

Specialty advertising is a promotional technique based on giving both regular and potential customers an inexpensive but useful gift. These items, which tend to be such things as pens, rulers, calendars, and paperweights, are typically designed to cost less than $4 and include the firm's name, logo, and telephone number. Specialty advertising has been around for centuries. Artisans in the Middle Ages gave knights wooden pegs bearing the artisan's name on which to hang their armour. [1]

specialty advertising
Small gifts including a firm's name, logo, and telephone number

Trade Shows

Trade shows provide opportunities for manufacturers to promote their goods or services to audiences with specialized interests. Generally, trade shows are intended to attract retailers and wholesalers, rather than final customers. The interest of resellers in the channel of distribution is keeping up-to-date on new-product development and deciding which new lines they could profitably introduce. International trade shows bring together sellers and buyers from all over the world. Trade show locations and dates are regularly publicized.

Samples, Coupons, Premiums, and Trading Stamps

sample
Product distributed as a gift, usually in a small format

coupon
Paper, distributed in various ways, redeemable as a reduction in price on a subsequent purchase

premium
A gift, usually unrelated to the product purchased

trading stamps
Stamps, points, or "money" given to customers according to the value of purchases, redeemable for additional goods or services

promotion contests
Contests with spectacular prizes, designed to encourage potential customers to switch brands or try a new product

Samples are products distributed as gifts, often in a smaller, non-standard format. They are effective in promoting new or improved products, with the objective of stimulating or boosting sales. **Coupons** are circulated in many ways: through the mail, or in or on a package of the product being promoted or of a non-competing product, for example. They are redeemable in the form of a small price reduction on a subsequent purchase. They are frequently successful in attracting consumers to new or different products. **Premiums** attract customers by giving them bonuses. These tend to be small gifts and may be unrelated to the product (a T-shirt for buying some sports equipment, a plastic toy in a cereal box, and so on). Some retail establishments automatically give **trading stamps** to consumers according to the value of goods or services purchased; these stamps can be exchanged for additional merchandise once the consumer has accumulated a given number of them. Historically, they have been useful as a strategy for increasing loyalty to a particular company. Versions of this type of promotion are Club Z points, airline-mileage points, and Canadian Tire money. **Promotion contests** tend to offer spectacular prizes of cash or merchandise. Legal requirements are such that contests are usually designed for the promoter by an organization that specializes in such promotions. The lure of the contest encourages potential customers to switch brands or to try a new product.

PACKAGING

It is difficult to think of many products without their packages. Packaging was originally used simply as protection for the product, but it didn't take long for marketers to spot the communication potential of a package.

As a marketing communication tool, packaging falls partway between advertising and sales promotion. Packaging provides brand identification and valuable informative and persuasive messages. For example, the box designed for a motion-sensor light shows a picture of the light, with text and an arrow highlighting each feature. For unpackaged items, such as clothing, the product label performs similar functions. Messages on packaging must be skilfully composed, with careful attention paid to detail. Unsatisfactory instructions may deter consumers from making repeat purchases, and inaccuracy can have legal repercussions. It is also important that the marketer be able to communicate with customers in accordance with government requirements for truth in advertising. Developing Your Business Skills discusses the proper use of "green" terminology as stipulated by Consumer and Corporate Affairs Canada.

DEVELOPING YOUR BUSINESS SKILLS

"ENVIRONMENTALLY FRIENDLY" IN LABELLING AND ADVERTISING

1. Industry is responsible for ensuring that any representation made with respect to a product is accurate and in compliance with the relevant legislation. For example, the term "recyclable" will be interpreted to mean that the product is fully and universally recyclable. Therefore, industry should not make representations that a product is recyclable simply because the material it is made from is technically recyclable if the infrastructure for recycling the product does not generally exist.
2. Consumers are responsible, to the extent possible, for using appropriately the information made available to them regarding labelling and advertising.
3. Environmental representations that are vague, incomplete, or irrelevant, and that cannot be substantiated through credible information and/or test methods, should not be used. For example, vague expressions such as "green" or "environmentally friendly" are meaningless statements. These expressions should be made explicit by providing specific characteristics that set out the reason for the claimed benefit.
4. Representations should indicate whether they are related to the product or to the packaging material.

Source: Adapted from "Publication of the Guiding Principles for Environmental Labelling and Advertising," *Misleading Advertising Bulletin*, (Department of Consumer and Corporate Affairs Canada), January 1 to March 31, 1991, pp. 5–6.

Packaging has important point-of-purchase appeal. Cosmetics packaging, for example, is carefully designed to make the product look more attractive. The package format can provide a powerful message about the quality of the product. It can also enhance the function of the products, as the serrated edge on a box of plastic wrap does.

PERSONAL SELLING

Personal selling is face-to-face communication between a salesperson and a potential buyer. The idea of promoting products originated with this form of selling, which continues to be essential in many fields. Personal selling includes the work of sales clerks in stores, telemarketers, and sales representatives who call on potential customers. Personal selling is the most expensive form of marketing communication. A sales call, for example, is estimated to cost $200.

The role and function of the sales force have undergone many changes over the years. The image of the fast-talking, thick-skinned, glad-handing sales representative is passé. Companies have made significant changes in their sales forces. Managers now use formal, detailed job descriptions in building their team of salespeople. A high level of professionalism is considered critical. This requires having a technical understanding of a product, including a thorough appreciation of its limitations, as well as having a fine grasp of the skill of selling. Professional salespeople, indeed, often know more about certain aspects of their customers' business than the customers themselves do. In their function as advisers, they contribute valuable knowledge and insight into the decision-making process. The outcome of this kind of exchange is more likely to be satisfied customers using with confidence the products they purchase.

Selling Activities Categorized

Although it is possible to assign many different roles to salespeople, the three main ones are order processing, creative selling, and missionary selling.

order processing
Receiving and handling customer orders

Order processing includes receiving and handling orders that come through the channel of distribution. Order processors include route sales personnel for consumer goods such as bread, milk, and soft drinks. They are responsible for filling out forms and distributing copies, as necessary; updating inventory records; and making arrangements for completing each sale.

Sales jobs typically have at least some order-processing duties. In situations where customers' needs are quite obvious to both seller and buyer, this function represents almost the entire transaction. Consider Danny McNaughton's sales position in Belfast, Northern Ireland, during one period of civil unrest. McNaughton, while working for the Combined Insurance Company, sold 208 new personal accident income protection policies in a week, averaging one sale every twelve minutes of his working day.[2] Belfast residents readily acknowledged the need for McNaughton's product.

creative selling
Persuasive presentations used when a product's benefits are not obvious to the customer

Creative selling is persuasive presentation when a product's benefits are not entirely obvious or when the customer is undertaking a detailed study of alternative products before deciding on a purchase. Creative selling is particularly appropriate for the task of selling a new product, for example, because the item has no track record. In such a situation, winning those all-important initial orders requires a great deal of creativity on the part of the salesperson.

missionary selling
The building of goodwill through education and technical or operational assistance

Missionary selling does not necessarily include actual sales. Instead, the salesperson builds goodwill and sometimes educates potential customers by providing technical or operational assistance. For example, high-tech companies such as IBM and Xerox employ systems specialists who work closely with customers whenever the need arises. They contribute their problem-solving skills, sometimes even to situations where their employer's product may not be directly involved.

Clearly, there is a need for different types of sales positions, and the range of job descriptions can be quite wide. If the product is highly technical, the salesperson many be doing 55 percent missionary selling, 40 percent creative selling, and 5 percent order processing. However, it is common for many retail salespeople to be doing 70 percent order processing, 15 percent creative selling, and 15 percent missionary selling. Marketing managers frequently define and classify a particular sales job by considering the different emphasis given to each of these three tasks. Whichever role is primary determines how the sales position is classified.

Sales Management

Consider a management problem faced by Great-West Life Assurance. It has a field sales force of 900 representatives. The sheer size of this sales force triggers numerous questions about organization, personnel selection, training, motivation, supervision, and evaluation. But all sales forces, regardless of size, face similar problems, which must be solved if the sales force is to be truly effective and achieve the firm's promotion strategy objectives.

A company's sales function is supervised by multiple layers of sales managers. People are usually advanced to such positions from the field sales force. The sales management organizational structure follows a format similar to that shown in Figure 17.2.

Sales managers are required to perform various managerial tasks (see Figure 17.3). They must, for example, analyze the organization's sales personnel needs and recruit the appropriate number of candidates, who are then screened for eventual selection. Sales managers are closely involved in the training and development of sales personnel and in the organizational structure. Leadership and supervision are a natural part of the sales management role. Finally, sales managers must be involved in the evaluation of the sales forces and in making decisions on salaries, promotions, and dismissals. All sales management tasks are subject to the environmental influences that exist in competitive business surroundings.

FIGURE 17.2 • TYPICAL SALES MANAGEMENT ORGANIZATION FOR A LARGE COMPANY

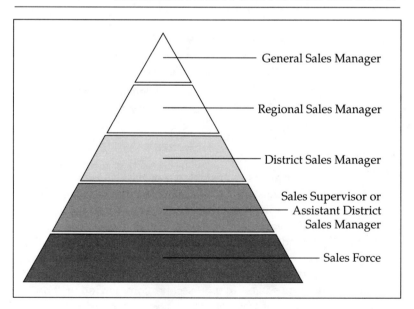

General Sales Manager

Regional Sales Manager

District Sales Manager

Sales Supervisor or Assistant District Sales Manager

Sales Force

FIGURE 17.3 • THE SALES MANAGEMENT TASKS

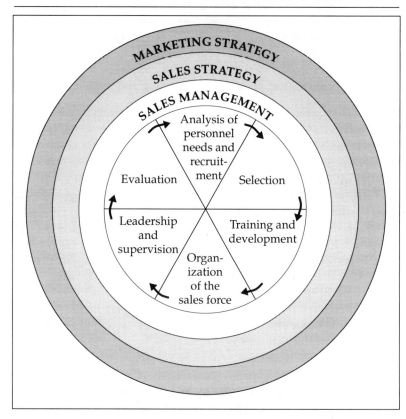

BUSINESS REVIEW 17.2

1. How does sales promotion differ from advertising?
2. Define each of the three types of selling: order processing, creative selling, and missionary selling.

WASTE OR MASTERPIECE?

Marketing communications is the element of the marketing mix that we as consumers are most exposed to. Some marketing communications are intrusive, badly designed, and plain stupid. The result of poor planning and execution, they are a waste of money.

On the other hand, some marketing communications are brilliant and might even be considered masterpieces. To be able to intelligently and empathetically solve a customer's problem through a sales call or to communicate a message—in a 30-second commercial, or through the transitory stimulus of a billboard or a newspaper advertisement—that is remembered and that changes behaviour is a remarkable feat. Such an accomplishment requires excellent analysis of market segments and consumers. It also demands relentless pursuit and intelligent execution of a marketing communication strategy.

INTERACTIVE SUMMARY AND DISCUSSION QUESTIONS

1. Marketing communications is defined as all messages that inform, persuade, and influence the consumer in making a purchase decision. What are the three main methods used in marketing communications?

2. Pushing and pulling are two basic strategies of marketing communications. Find and describe examples of each in your local business community.

3. The main objectives of marketing communications are providing information, positioning a product, increasing sales, and stabilizing sales. Under what competitive situations would you expect to see each used?

4. It is most realistic to set "communication" as the major objective of most advertising. Why is this so?

5. Advertising can be classified as *product advertising* or *institutional advertising*. Define, and provide illustrations of, each category.

6. "Advertising strategy for a product can vary according to its stage in the product life cycle." Explain the reasoning behind this statement.

7. Consider three advertising media: newspapers, magazines, and radio. Under what circumstances, and with what products, would you use each?

8. Sales promotion takes many forms. It includes specific short-term inducements to buy, such as coupons, point-of-purchase displays, signs, gifts, and trade shows. Explain how the many aspects of sales promotion serve as a valuable addition to advertising and sales management.

9. The three types of selling are order processing, creative selling, and missionary selling. Provide illustrations of each. Do all salespeople perform each of these tasks? Justify your answer.

10. Compare the sales management task illustrated in Figure 17.3 with the discussion of management you have encountered in other modules.

CASE 17.1

OLIVETTI

ALL ADVERTISING people have one quest in common. It is called the Big Idea—an advertising strategy that is so encompassing, original, and large that it becomes an integral part of the brand's being.

The partners of 360° Advertising Inc., in Toronto, Ontario, were striving toward this quest when a computer client walked in the door, which led them to create the Big Idea that served as a complete turnaround for the client.

The client, Olivetti Canada, had a problem. In the rest of the world, it was known as a marketer of sophisticated data processing with open-systems technology (i.e., a system that permits greater interplay between competing manufacturers' products and software). However, in Canada, Olivetti was better known as a typewriter manufacturer. It needed a new image.

At this time, other companies took the "product specifications approach" to computer advertising. This resulted in each claiming more, or new and improved, product features.

The president of Olivetti Canada, Mark De Simone, believed that Olivetti's image could be repositioned through a campaign designed to launch its new open-systems architecture.

The partners of 360°—the name refers to the firm's multidisciplinary approach to marketing—didn't believe this was enough. They drew heavily on their varied backgrounds to arrive at the Big Idea. Richard Clewes, founder, had worked for a computer firm in Toronto and had years of experience working at other ad agencies. Bruce Barr, the strategist, brought a different perspective to the Olivetti assignment, honed while working on the client side of the marketing business. Ron Vanderberg's past experience made him a part of 360°'s creative team. His stylistic contribution

(continued)

to Olivetti's advertising is evident in the typography he helped to invent to give the ads a look of their own.

In Olivetti's case, Clewes, Barr, and Vanderberg began by interviewing Olivetti employees, dealers, and customers. They wanted to develop an understanding of Olivetti's service quality, image in the industry, pricing competitiveness, and so on. The partners also dug up third-party background material to bolster these interviews. They scoured libraries and pored over trade journals to find out all they could about the computer industry sector, and where it was headed.

The team ended up with what Barr described as a thorough picture of the computer business, detailing where Olivetti stood versus its competitors, what the key industry issues were, and what 360° believed the client must do to succeed.

The company's image problems, combined with the turmoil in the industry and the fact that other computer firms had their own open systems, led the 360° partners to decide that a very large task was at hand. "We really thought the way to differentiate Olivetti in the marketplace was to focus on the issue of utility and empowering the individual," Barr said. The partners viewed the marketplace as chaotic—a battlefield of claims and counter-claims. They turned this pessimistic image around instead to view the marketplace as an area of incredible activity—highly positive and charged.

"We started thinking: when has there ever been a similar period?" Clewes recalled. "We realized there was, and it was called the Renaissance." Olivetti was well positioned to become a leader in this modern-day Renaissance, the 360° team said. It was the right time to position Olivetti as a company whose open-systems approach was in sync with the movement to more individual control and influence in the marketplace. The "Renaissance of the Computer" campaign was launched with fanfare across Canada during the 1991 World Series.

The symbol of this transformation was the Mona Lisa—a prominent figure of the Renaissance period whose quizzical smile has, for hundreds of years, led admirers to wonder at her thoughts. Mark De Simone likens the image to today's systems buyer: "What is it they [the customers] really want?"

After all the research that ended with the Renaissance idea, the 360° partners knew this was the Big Idea they had been waiting for. "Not only did the Renaissance take place in Italy, but what we really loved about the idea was that it was a position, from a marketing point of view, that no [North] American could make comfortable," said Vanderberg, the group's designer. "It became more and more evident to us that it was a situation of natural ownership [for Olivetti]."

Critics are not convinced the ad campaign fully explains the value of an open system or that Olivetti's ideas are so new. Nor do they think Olivetti has succeeded in altering attitudes about the company. One critic questions the advisability of linking the Renaissance of centuries ago to today's ultra-modern, high-tech computer industry.

But De Simone argues that the campaign has more than met its objectives. Sales revenues have increased by 20 percent. He gives credit to 360° Advertising Inc. for pushing Olivetti to take that leap of faith into doing something a little bit outside the traditional rules.

Source: Adapted from Randall Scotland, "Anatomy of an Ad Campaign," *The Financial Post,* March 2, 1991, p. S24, S25.

Questions for Discussion

1. What other factors might have caused the sales increase?

2. Evaluate the process followed by the advertising agency to develop the campaign strategy.

3. Evaluate the method chosen (the image of the Mona Lisa) to implement the strategy. Does it communicate the concept adequately?

CASE 17.2

MEADOWLANDS INVESTMENTS

MEADOWLANDS INVESTMENTS specializes in shopping centre developments. They are well financed, and have formulated a strategy of developing mid-sized shopping centres. These are modern facilities, with enclosed malls. The company has always been able to attract a large grocery chain, as well as a department store of the nature of Zellers or Kmart as anchors to create a good traffic flow.

In addition to these main stores, the malls have a variety of clothing stores, eating establishments, and service outlets. The developers also include a cinema complex in the mall.

Three new malls are in the completion stages in the lower B.C. mainland, suburban Toronto, and Halifax. Since each is relatively near to universities or community colleges, it is felt that such students might be an important target market. This was reinforced by a market study that described the nature of the student market.

A Current Profile of the Student Market

Today's university/college student is the quintessential consumer—educated, brand-selective, image-conscious, and somewhat materialistic. They're more concerned with their financial futures than were students of past generations, and are pursuing the degrees that will give them the most promising futures, the majors being business, marketing, engineering, and computer sciences.

According to Statistics Canada, full-time enrolment in Canadian universities in a recent academic year totalled 470,330 and in community colleges 319,360, a market segment of 789,690, the majority of which is between the ages of 18 and 24 years, comprising 5 percent of the adult population.

A survey for Campus Plus (Canadian University Press Media Services, Toronto, representing a network of campus newspapers across Canada) indicates an average personal income per

(continued)

Canadian university student of $5,809. Most are employed part-time (75 percent during the summer and 44 percent during the academic year).

Three out of five students reside away from their parents' home (64 percent of university and 40 percent of college students). This, of course, varies on a regional basis: Maritimes 74 percent, Quebec 50 percent, Ontario 62 percent, Prairies 59 percent, and B.C. 50 percent.

Their dorm rooms and off-campus apartments/rooms are in effect "mini-households," where students first enter the world of independent decision making, purchasing goods and services such as food, clothing, personal-care products, sporting goods, travel, and banking. They are more consumer-conscious than students in the past.

Almost nine out of ten look after their own food shopping (32 percent one to seven times a week and 27 percent two or three times per month); 95 percent prepare meals (78 percent three times a week or more); 65 percent do their own laundry; and 72 percent purchase their own personal-care products.

Almost half shop around to take advantage of specials/bargains, and 54 percent have redeemed coupons in the past three months.

One-fifth of the students spend between $500 and $1,000 yearly on clothes, and about half spend between $200 and $500.

Milk is a popular beverage with students (91 percent drink it daily), as are soft drinks (consumption of regular 80 percent, and diet 70 percent). The typical Canadian university student is as likely to be a regular drinker of liquor (60 percent) as beer (60 percent), and 75 percent quaff white wine on occasion.

Students take pride in their appearance: 91 percent use a deodorant/anti-perspirant, 75 percent hair conditioner, 57 percent medicated skin-care products, and 54 percent facial moisturizer.

Social life centres around frequent attendance at movies (97 percent), parties (92 percent), pubs/taverns (87 percent), and friends' homes (74 percent visit once a week or more).

And they're an active group: 86 percent swim, 85 percent bicycle, 69 percent jog or run, 55 percent play tennis and 40 percent squash/racketball, 51 percent go downhill skiing and 49 percent cross-country skiing. Photography is a popular hobby with 63 percent, and 40 percent own 35mm cameras.

In terms of mobility, 84 percent have a driver's licence, 32 percent own their own car/van, 40 percent have made one or more plane trips in the past year, and 40 percent have a passport. Slightly more than one-third have their own credit card(s).

Peer communication has consistently proven most successful in reaching this market, and print media, direct mail, and promotion help create a buzz on campus.

Because of their active lives, students are harder to reach by conventional advertising media. TV viewing is light (average hours tuned per week 10.6), as is radio listening (average hours tuned per week 14.2). However, seven out of ten students read a daily newspaper, and almost two-thirds read their campus newspaper.

Consumer magazines do not fare as well, with *Chatelaine* having 22.2 percent coverage, *TV Guide* 18.2 percent, *Maclean's* 16.3 percent, *Time* 14.9 percent, and *Flare* 8.6 percent.

Source: Adapted from Jo Marney, "Students—A Market Growing Up," *Marketing*, September 19, 1988.

Question for Discussion

1. Design a promotional campaign to attract university/college students to the new shopping malls. In your campaign, suggest appropriate target markets, advertising themes, and advertising media. The firm has allocated a budget of $40,000 for the campaign in each region.

NOTES

1. Walter Gaw, "Specialty Advertising," Specialty Advertising Association 1970, p. 7.

2. "Labor Letter," *The Wall Street Journal*, September 14, 1971.

PHOTO CREDITS

COM 6 Young and Rubicam Inc.

COM 7 Photo: T. Frare
Concept: O. Toscani

COM 9 Milkbone Advertisement reproduced with the permission of Nabisco Brands Ltd., Toronto, Ontario, Canada

COM 10 Courtesy of the Quaker Oats Company of Canada Limited

COM 21 Art Direction and Design: Ron Vanderberg
Copy: Richard Clewes

MODULE

◆ ACC ◆

ACCOUNTING

THE FOCUS OF THIS MODULE

1. To explain what accounting is and who uses accounting information

2. To explain the need for accounting standards and the role of the accounting profession in enforcing those standards

3. To differentiate between accounting and bookkeeping

4. To describe the accounting equation and the use of accounts

5. To outline the basic information included in financial statements

6. To describe how ratio analysis is used in making decisions regarding a business

7. To explain the importance of cash budgeting

8. To learn the meaning of the following terms:

KEY TERMS

bookkeeping	statement of changes in
journal	financial position
accounting	double-entry bookkeeping
assets	current ratio
liabilities	quick ratio
owner's equity	debt-to-asset ratio
balance sheet	inventory turnover
current assets	average hold period of inventory
liquidity	accounts receivable turnover
marketable securities	days sales in accounts receivable
fixed assets	cash conversion cycle
depreciation	return on sales
intangible assets	return on total equity
current liabilities	earnings per share (EPS)
long-term liabilities	share price–to–earnings ratio
income statement	budget

The contribution of Professor Paul J. Levie in developing this module is gratefully acknowledged.

ASK THE AVERAGE Canadian what Bombardier Inc. stands for and chances are you will still hear stories about the "Ski-Doo," the motorized box on skis that brought the Quebec company fame and fortune in the early 1960s. Ask Laurent Beaudoin, the organization's 54-year-old chairman and CEO, and he will tell you the sky's the limit—literally. Under his leadership, Bombardier has travelled far beyond its roots as the manufacturer of that most Canadian of vehicles, the snowmobile. Celebrating its 50th anniversary in 1992, the corporation employs 32,000 people in eight countries, has sales that exceed $3 billion, and its order book is valued at more than twice that amount. And although Bombardier continues to dominate the snowmobile industry, it has carved out an enviable niche for itself in the much larger rail and aeronautics sector. . . .

Laurent Beaudoin assumed control of Bombardier Inc. when his father-in-law, Joseph Armand Bombardier, died in 1964. Beaudoin was 26 years old at the time. From 1964 to 1974, sales skyrocketed, from $10 million to $132 million. The increase in sales was partly due to the company's expansion into the rail business when Bombardier Inc. won a substantial contract to manufacture cars for the Montreal subway system in 1974. The almost accidental foray into rolling stock would prove instrumental to the future of the company. "Ultimately, we have followed the example of the Japanese," explains Beaudoin. "We bought technology and know-how and then improved on the original." The contracts for manufacturing cars for the Montreal subway in 1974 and for the New York subway in 1982 really set Bombardier on track.

Along the way, the company bought the rights to the famous Pullman rail cars and acquired companies in the United States, France, Belgium, Great Britain, and Austria. In North America alone, it has reaped orders exceeding $2.5 billion for rolling stock and today controls 30 percent of the market. Through its acquisitions, the railway group of Bombardier recorded sales of $725.6 million for the year ended January 31, 1992, which makes it the second-largest division of the company and places Bombardier in tenth position worldwide. More than 96 percent of its transport equipment sales are made outside Canada.

Such figures pale, however, in comparison with the company's success in aeronautics. In 1986, Beaudoin responded to an offer from the Canadian government, which wanted to privatize the Montreal-based airframe manufacturer Canadair. By December of that year, it was a done deal and Bombardier has purchased the ailing company for $125 million. Also, in 1989, the company bought the Irish aircraft manufacturer Short Brothers PLC, and then, in 1991, acquired American Learjet Inc. The reason for getting into aircraft was logical for Bombardier. Beaudoin explains: "What does Bombardier do, essentially? It assembles metal parts. It welds. It uses professionals and trades that revolve around this key activity. If you look at it from this angle, you can see that there is not such a big difference between a railcar and an aircraft fuselage. For a welder or machinist, in fact, it is simply a question of millimetres or fractions of a millimetre." In 1991, the company's sales for the aeronautics sector reached $1.5 billion, with income before tax of $137.2 million. More than 96 percent of the company's sales were outside of Canada. From 1986 to 1991, the company rose in rank to the seventh-largest civil aircraft manufacturer in the world.

In addition to recreational/utility vehicles and aeronautics, the company is also active in the defence sector—to the tune of $366.2 million in 1991. Primarily through Canadair, Short Brothers, and Learjet, Bombardier now designs and produces surveillance systems and provides various support and maintenance services for military aircraft.

Bombardier's CEO has been wise enough to build himself a team of exceptionally talented and efficient managers. Beaudoin's self-confidence is strong enough for him to give the individuals he has chosen all the latitude they need to put their respective talents to good use. This is substantiated by the low turnover among Bombardier's key people.

The CEO makes no secret of his optimism. He continues on with the philosophy that transformed a little company into the rail and aeronautics giant it is today.

Source: Christian Bellavance, "Trains, Planes, and Snowmobiles," *CA Magazine*, November 1992, pp. 18–21. Reprinted with permission from *CA Magazine*, published by the Canadian Institute of Chartered Accountants, Toronto

Bombardier is a large and successful company that has grown from small beginnings. The evidence is in the numbers. Making sense of those numbers is the task of accountants. The role of accountants is frequently misunderstood by many people, including people in business. Accountants are often viewed as people who sit in offices apart from everyone else. They are viewed as being totally humourless individuals in beige suits with high-water pants that no one else would choose to wear.

While this description may be accurate in some cases, the majority of accountants in companies today do not fit this stereotype. Accountants in a modern business organization like Bombardier are essential for the success of the business. They are involved in all aspects of the company, from strategic planning all the way to the production floor. Accountants bring analytical and integrative skills to the management team and are always involved in any major decision.

WHO USES ACCOUNTING INFORMATION?

An information system is designed specifically to gather data about a business and then to summarize those data in a standardized format that will enable business owners, managers, and other users to make successful decisions. Accounting is the foundation of a business information system.

Owners and managers need to make decisions about a multitude of business activities, including the price to charge for a product, how much to pay employees, and how much to spend on advertising. In order to make these decisions, owners and managers must have accurate and up-to-date information. Good information leads to good decision making.

Checkpoint Systems developed an electronic tag that could be attached to library books and merchandise in retail stores to prevent theft. The company experienced tremendous growth over the years as product modifications resulted in increased market acceptance. But with growth came problems. Checkpoint's old accounting system was adequate for a small operation, but could not accommodate the company's rapid growth. The old system did not provide managers with the information they needed to spot trends, make pricing decisions, and control cash flows. As Jerry Klein, Checkpoint's vice-president of operations, stated: "Lacking timely data, the whole system had begun to collapse. Invoices lagged shipments by as much as 30 days; accounts payable ran 60 to 90 days." The business started to suffer. The importance of an adequate accounting system became obvious.

Accounting information is useful not only to owners and managers but to others as well. Revenue Canada wants to be certain that the business is paying its fair share of taxes. Bank managers use accounting information to decide whether or not to make a loan to the business, based on the business's ability to repay the loan. Labour unions want to determine if the business is making enough money to allow higher wages to be paid to its workers. New investors want to know what the business is worth before they decide whether or not to buy into it. Everyone who is affected by a business can be considered a user of its accounting information.

ACCOUNTING STANDARDS AND THE ACCOUNTING PROFESSION

In order to ensure that all users receive accurate information from the accounting system, accountants have developed standards for reporting. These standards are referred to as "generally accepted accounting principles" (GAAP) and apply all across Canada. Such standards ensure that accounting is done consistently among businesses. For example, if the owner of a shoe store in Halifax was interested in purchasing another shoe store in Vancouver, the owner could compare the financial statements of the two shoe stores and know that the same GAAP were used in the preparation of accounts for both stores.

There are two branches of accounting in Canada, private accounting and public accounting. Private accountants are employees of the business. The head of the accounting department is usually called the "controller" or "treasurer" and is considered part of the top management team. The controller or treasurer ensures that all of the bookkeeping and accounting functions of the business are carried out and that the financial statements at the end of the year are prepared in accordance with GAAP.

Public accountants are not employees of businesses; rather, they act independently. They are referred to as "auditors." Their role is to ensure that an organization's financial statements are in fact properly prepared in accordance with GAAP by conducting an audit of the statements. Companies that have bank loans or shares that trade on a stock exchange (for example, the Toronto Stock Exchange) are usually required to have an audit conducted annually. Many users feel that financial statements that have been audited are more reliable than those that have not been audited.

Most private and public accountants in Canada belong to one of three professional accounting bodies. Public accountants belong to the Canadian Institute of Chartered Accountants (CICA) or the Certified General Accountants Association of Canada. Private accountants belong to the Society of Management Accountants of Canada. Members are referred to as chartered accountants (CAs), certified general accountants (CGAs), and certified management accountants (CMAs) respectively.

The Canadian Institute of Chartered Accountants (CICA) is responsible for researching, setting and publishing the CICA Handbook from which the generally accepted accounting principles are derived. Members of all three accounting bodies are invited to comment on new standards as they are developed.

All three accounting bodies require their students to undergo rigorous examinations and to have practical experience before granting them their professional accounting designation. All accounting bodies ensure that their students have a thorough understanding of GAAP.

ACCOUNTING VERSUS BOOKKEEPING

"Bookkeeping" and "accounting" are not synonymous.

Bookkeeping deals with recording transactions in a systematic manner into a series of specially designed records called "journals." Every time the business makes a sale or pays for rent, the transaction is recorded by the accounting system. A **journal** is an accounting record that has been designed in order to record transactions with a minimum of effort. You keep a journal if you keep a chequebook record.

Accounting takes the information that bookkeepers have prepared and organizes this information into coherent financial statements. Therefore, bookkeeping is part, but only part, of accounting. Financial statements are prepared primarily for users that are external to the business, for example, shareholders, creditors, and government. Internal users, such as managers, often require other information that accountants can provide. The process of preparing information to assist managers in operating the company in an efficient and effective manner is frequently referred to as "management accounting." Management accounting is tailor-made to the needs of a particular manager and does not have to be governed by GAAP. The need for good management accounting is discussed in Issues in Business 18.1.

An accounting system has three main functions:
1. It determines what transactions carried out by the business are to be recorded in the system.
2. It records these transactions in a logical fashion (for example, bookkeeping, using journals).
3. It summarizes and communicates this information to the users.

bookkeeping
The systematic recording of business transactions

journal
An accounting record designed to record transactions with a minimum of effort

accounting
Organizing bookkeeping information into coherent overall financial statements

For example: (1) Suppose the business wrote a cheque for advertising. This transaction would affect the financial status of the firm and would be captured by the system. (2) The cheque would be recorded in a "cash disbursements journal"; and (3) the total of all the cheques written for advertising that were recorded in the cash disbursements journal would be summarized so that the owner or manager would know how much money had been spent on advertising during some period of time, usually a year. (The Jasper Ski Patrol, whose financial statements we will examine later in the module, spent $16,000 on advertising in 1994. The accountant would have calculated this total from entries in the cash disbursements journal.) The same approach would be used to keep track of sales that are made (in the sales journal) or cash that is received (in the cash receipts journal), and these journals would then be used to produce financial statements that summarize all of the year's activities in a standardized and logical format.

ISSUES IN BUSINESS 18.1

FIVE WARNING SIGNALS FOR BUSINESS

THERE ARE EARLY warning signals that can tell a business person whether or not the operation is heading toward failure. These have been put together by a Vancouver accountant named Donald J. Henfrey, who should know about these things. He is president of the Canadian Insolvency Association, and his firm, Henfrey Samson Belair Ltd., is one of Western Canada's leading trustees in receiverships.

Sad to say, his business has been brisk for several years. It may not be in his best interests to tell us how to avoid becoming one of his clients, but it is in the greater interest of the economy. A healthy economy generates plenty of business for accounting firms as well—and the business is more enjoyable to transact.

These are Henfrey's five warning signals:

One-man rule. "We've liquidated many companies which have a problem as a result of one-man rule," he says. This can be recognized when the owner and founder of the business works excessive hours, fails to hire competent staff, and fails to delegate. Such an individual becomes busier and busier until the firm's problems become overwhelming. One solution might be to find a partner to invest in the company, sharing both the risks and the load.

Cash-flow problems. These are cited by business people who think their companies are running at a profit—or would be, if only their customers paid the bills on time. Often, that reasoning contains a large element of self-delusion.

Inadequate accounting. This failure feeds the self-delusion. "When a company recognizes it has financial difficulties," Henfrey says, "one of the first things it does is fire the bookkeeper." This may reduce salary costs, but it also reduces the quantity and quality of vital information that management needs.

Inventory imbalances. When a business has invested in a product that then does not sell, it is an error to tie up expensive warehouse space and other costs just storing the dud. "Get rid of obsolete stock," Henfrey advises. "Get it out of your warehouse; get it out of your office; get it off your balance sheet."

(continued)

Failure to modernize. This is basic. One need only look to the American steel industry or British shipyards to recognize that poorly maintained or obsolete machinery and plants are unable to compete with modern facilities.

Source: *Skyword Magazine*, June 1984.

Question for Discussion

1. Henfrey lists inadequate accounting as one of the five warning signals that a business is in trouble. Explain how inadequate accounting might also contribute to the other four by failing to reveal specific problems.

THE ACCOUNTING EQUATION

A very basic concept used in accounting is the "entity." Each business organization, whether it is a corporation, proprietorship, or partnership, is considered a separate accounting entity. In other words, we account for the transactions of the entity separately from those of the owners of the business. For example, if Imperial Oil Limited sells gasoline to one of its dealers for $10,000, that sale is recorded in Imperial Oil's books. However, the shareholders of Imperial Oil Limited do not record the sale in their own personal books since Imperial Oil Limited is a separate entity, apart from its shareholders.

In order to ensure consistency among all businesses, accountants set up the records of a business using the "accounting equation," which takes the form:

$$\begin{array}{ccc} \text{Assets} & & \text{Liabilities and Owner's Equity} \\ \text{(left of the equals sign)} & = & \text{(right of the equals sign)} \end{array}$$

Assets are economic resources that a business *owns* that are expected to be of benefit in the future. Examples of assets are cash, inventory, office furniture, land, and buildings. **Liabilities** are amounts *owed* to creditors. Examples of liabilities are bank loans, invoices from suppliers, wages owed to employees, and mortgages. **Owner's equity** represents the *difference* between assets and liabilities. If a proprietorship has $100,000 in assets and $25,000 in liabilities, the owner's equity is $75,000.

Each individual asset, liability, and owner's equity is called an "account." For example, a proprietorship might have a cash account, a bank loan account, and a capital account.

assets
Things that a business owns that are expected to be of value in the future

liabilities
Things that a business owes to creditors

owner's equity
The difference between an organization's assets and its liabilities, representing the investment of the proprietor, shareholders, or partners

FINANCIAL STATEMENTS

The entries in the various accounts that make up the three items from the accounting equation can be used to create three different financial statements: the balance sheet, the income statement, and the statement of changes in financial position. (The statement of changes in financial position is also referred to as a funds flow statement as well as a statement of sources and uses of cash.) Some of the items that make up owner's equity will appear on both the balance sheet and the income statement.

EXHIBIT 18.1 • BALANCE SHEET

The Ski Patrol
123 Main Street
Jasper, Alberta

THE SKI PATROL
Balance Sheet

ASSETS

	As at December 31, 1993		As at December 31, 1994	
Current Assets				
Cash		$10,000		$ 4,000
Marketable Securities		--		15,000
Accounts Receivable	$76,000		$79,000	
Less: Allowance for				
Doubtful Accounts	3,000	73,000	4,000	75,000
Notes Receivable		25,000		22,000
Inventory		65,000		56,000
Prepaid Expenses		8,000		6,000
Total Current Assets		$181,000		$178,000
Fixed Assets				
Store Equipment	$41,000		$71,000	
Less: Accumulated				
Depreciation	10,000	$31,000	15,000	$56,000
Furniture and Fixtures	$ 8,000		$19,000	
Less: Accumulated				
Depreciation	1,000	7,000	4,000	15,000
Total Fixed Assets		$38,000		$71,000
Intangible Assets				
Copyrights		$ 5,000		$ 5,000
Total Intangible Assets		5,000		5,000
Total Assets		$224,000		$254,000

LIABILITY AND OWNERS' EQUITY

	As at December 31, 1993		As at December 31, 1994	
Current Liabilities				
Accounts Payable	$58,000		$41,000	
Current Installments on				
Long-term Debt	15,000		15,000	
Accrued Expenses	3,000		7,000	
Income Taxes Payable	8,000		6,000	
Total Current Liabilities		$84,000		$69,000
Long-term Liabilities				
Long-term Notes Payable	$15,000		$30,000	
Total Long-term Liabilities		$15,000		$30,000
Total Liabilities		$99,000		$99,000
Owners' Equity				
Common Stock		$80,000		$80,000
Retained Earnings		45,000		75,000
Total Owners'Equity		$125,000		$155,000
Total Liabilities and Owners' Equity		$224,000		$254,000

The Balance Sheet

The **balance sheet** is simply a statement of the accounting equation at a particular date, showing assets, liabilities, and owner's equity. Exhibit 18.1 shows the balance sheet for the Jasper Ski Patrol at December 31, 1993, and December 31, 1994.

Assets are separated into two main groups: current and fixed. **Current assets** are the resources used in order to keep the business operating. An asset is defined as "current" if it is capable of being sold, consumed, or converted to cash within the next twelve months. Current assets for the Ski Patrol are made up of six different accounts: cash, marketable securities, accounts receivable, notes receivable, inventory, and prepaid expenses. They are listed in terms of their **liquidity**—how quickly they can be disposed of and turned into cash.

- Cash, funds on hand or in a bank account, is available immediately.
- **Marketable securities** are short-term investments, such as bonds and shares, that can be converted into cash in a very short time.
- Accounts receivable arise when the business makes a sale but does not receive the money right away; in other words, the business is extending credit to its customer. Usually, credit is extended only to those customers who have a history of making their payments to the selling company, and the risk of non-collection is low. However, businesses must make allowances for uncollected accounts, as the Ski Patrol has done.
- Notes receivable are funds the business is owed as described in written documents called "notes." A note specifies the amount to be paid and the time and place of payment.
- Inventory is the product that a business manufactures or stocks to sell to its customer. The sale of inventory is how many companies make money. It is very important that businesses keep track of their inventory to ensure that the level of inventory does not become too high or too low. High levels mean the business has too much money tied up in inventory that is not selling. The inventory may indeed become too old or obsolete. It costs money to carry inventory and, if it does not sell, the business should dispose of it at discounted prices, if necessary. Low inventory levels, on the other hand, mean lost sales since the product is not available to be sold and customers will go elsewhere to make their purchase. A business must implement safeguards to protect its inventory against loss or theft. For example, a jeweller will take special measures to protect its diamond inventory.
- Prepaid expenses are payments that are made now for an asset that will be used up in the future. For example, a business purchases office supplies today that will last for several months. Prepaid expenses are not liquid and consequently are not very useful in assessing the performance of a business. They are usually for small amounts.

Fixed assets are equipment, buildings, and land that the business uses to operate the firm over the long term, that is, more than a year. It is important to remember that most fixed, or long-term, assets do wear out and will eventually have to be repaired or replaced. An allowance, therefore, must be made for depreciation in calculating the value of fixed assets. **Depreciation** is the allocation of the cost of a fixed asset

balance sheet
A statement of an organization's financial position at a particular date, balancing assets against liabilities and owner's equity

current assets
Assets that can be sold, consumed, or converted into cash within twelve months

liquidity
The speed at which an asset can be converted to cash

marketable securities
Short-term investments such as bonds or shares that can be quickly converted to cash

fixed assets
Assets such as equipment and buildings used to operate the firm over the long term

depreciation
An allocation of the cost of a fixed asset over its expected lifespan

intangible assets
Assets such as patents, copyrights, and trademarks with no tangible physical properties

current liabilities
Liabilities such as bank loans and accounts payable that fall due within twelve months

long-term liabilities
Liabilities such as mortgages and bonds that do not fall due within the next year, usually used only to finance fixed assets

income statement
A statement summarizing an organization's income, expenses, and profit or loss over a given period of time

over its expected lifespan. It is usually calculated as a percentage of the original cost of the asset. A third type of asset often listed is **intangible assets**, which include patents, copyrights, and trademarks, which have considerable value but no tangible physical properties. The Ski Patrol, which owns the copyright on its distinctive logo, may license it for use on ski clothing and equipment.

Liabilities are classified as current or long-term. **Current liabilities** include payments due on bank loans, taxes due, and accounts payable. Accounts payable are the opposite of accounts receivable, arising when a company makes a purchase but is not required to pay for it until some time in the future. (An account receivable to the company that makes the sale will be an account payable to the company that makes the purchase.)

Long-term liabilities include mortgages and bonds. Generally, businesses issue long-term liabilities only to finance fixed (long-term) assets.

Owner's equity is the owner's net investment in the business. Owner's equity is referred to by different names, depending on the form of business organization: in a proprietorship, it is called "owner's capital"; in a partnership, it is called "partners' capital"; and in a corporation, it is called "common stock" or "retained earnings."

The Income Statement

The balance sheet presents a snapshot of a business's financial status at a particular time. The **income statement** describes transactions over a certain period of time, usually a year. It is also known as the "statement of revenue and expenses," the "operating statement," and the "profit-and-loss statement." Exhibit 18.2 shows the Jasper Ski Patrol's income statement for the period ending December 31, 1994.

When a business makes a sale, accountants call it "revenue." Matched against revenue are the costs, or expenses, of making that sale. If a company is in the business of selling shoes, the money brought in by the sale of shoes is revenue. However, in order to make that sale, the customer is allowed to leave the store with a pair of shoes that used to belong to the company. What it cost the company to buy the shoes is recorded as the "cost of goods sold." The company has many other expenses in making the sale, such as salaries and advertising.

The income statement is prepared using the accrual concept of accounting. Under this concept, we record sales as they occur (even if they are made on account and the company might not collect the account until a later period). Similarly, we record the purchase of inventory on account as a purchase for the current period even though the company might not have to pay for the inventory until the next period. Thus, the accrual concept gives rise to the need to keep records for accounts receivable and accounts payable.

statement of changes in financial position
A statement outlining differences in various aspects of an organization's finances between one business period and the next

Statement of Changes in Financial Position

The **statement of changes in financial position** tells the user where a business' cash came from and where it was spent. It is also referred to as the "funds flow statement" or the "statement of sources and uses of cash."

EXHIBIT 18.2 • INCOME STATEMENT

The Ski Patrol
123 Main Street
Jasper, Alberta

THE SKI PATROL
Income Statement

For the Year Ended December 31, 1994

Revenues

Gross Sales		$300,000	
Less: Sales Returns and Allowances		8,000	
Net Sales			$292,000

Costs of Goods Sold

Beginning Inventory		$ 65,000	
Purchases during Year	$127,000		
Less: Purchase Discounts	4,000		
Net purchases		123,000	
Cost of Goods Available for Sale		$188,000	
Less: Ending Inventory, Dec. 31		56,000	
Cost of Goods Sold			$132,000

Gross Profit $160,000

Operating Expenses

Selling Expenses

Sales Salaries and Commissions	$51,000		
Advertising	16,000		
Depreciation: Store Equipment	5,000		
Miscellaneous Selling Expenses	3,000		
Total Selling Expenses		$75,000	

General Expenses

Office Salaries	$35,000		
Office Supplies	8,000		
Depreciation: Office Equipment	3,000		
Miscellaneous General Expenses	2,000		
Total General Expenses		48,000	

Total Operating Expenses	$123,000
Net Income Before Taxes	$ 37,000
Less: Income Taxes	7,000
Net Income	$ 30,000

The statement is broken down into three distinct parts:
1. Operating activities: how much cash was generated by selling products or services;
2. Financing activities: how much cash was generated by long-term borrowing; and
3. Investing activities: how much cash was spent to purchase fixed assets.

This statement is considered by many users to be the most informative of the three financial statements since it deals with how much cash the business is capable of generating from operating versus borrowing. This statement is usually required by lenders before granting a bank loan. Exhibit 18.3 shows the Jasper Ski Patrol statement of changes in financial position for the year ending December 31, 1994.

BUSINESS REVIEW 18.1

1. What are GAAP? Why is it important that accountants follow GAAP?

2. What are the three important financial statements and what does each reveal?

DOUBLE-ENTRY BOOKKEEPING

The financial statements we have been examining are based on information painstakingly recorded by bookkeepers throughout the year. How is this information recorded so that accountants can use it in this way?

Each transaction is recorded using the financial equation. This means that whenever there is a change in one side of the equation, an equivalent change must recorded on the other side. In other words, if assets (the left, or "debit," side of the equation) increase, the same increase must be recorded under liabilities and owner's equity (the right, or "credit," side of the equation). Because every transaction has two effects that must be recorded, this type of record keeping is known as **double-entry bookkeeping**.

For example, suppose A started up a proprietorship by putting $1,000 cash into a business on December 1, 1992. The two effects that must be recorded are (1) the receipt of cash (an asset) and (2) the creation of owner's equity. We could record this transaction in what is called a "general journal." The entry would appear as follows:

double-entry bookkeeping
Bookkeeping method that keeps the accounting equation in balance by recording the effect of each transaction on both sides of the equation

	Debits	Credits
December 1, 1992		
Cash	$1,000	
Owner's Equity		$1,000

EXHIBIT 18.3 • STATEMENT OF CHANGES IN FINANCIAL POSITION

The Ski Patrol
123 Main Street
Jasper, Alberta

THE SKI PATROL
Statement of Changes
in Financial Position

For the Year Ended December 31, 1994

Operating Activities:

Net Income	$30,000	
Add: Items not requiring an outlay of cash in current period:		
- Depreciation: Store Equipment	$5,000	
Office Equipment	3,000	
Add/Deduct Changes in Non-cash Capital Items*:		
- Accounts Receivable	(2,000)	
- Notes Receivable	3,000	
- Inventory	9,000	
- Prepaid Expenses	2,000	
- Accounts Payable	(17,000)	
- Accrued Expenses	4,000	
- Income Taxes Payable	(2,000)	
Cash Generated from Operating Activities		35,000
Financing Activities:		
Issue Long-term Notes Payable	15,000	
Cash Generated from Financing Activities		15,000
Investing Activities:		
Purchase Store Equipment	(30,000)	
Purchase Furniture and Fixtures	(11,000)	
Cash Used in Investing Activities		(41,000)
Increase in Cash during the Year	9,000	
Cash, Beginning of the Year	10,000	
Cash, End of the Year		19,000
Cash, End of the Year, is made up of:		
Cash	$ 4,000	
Marketable Securities	15,000	
Cash, End of the Year		19,000

Working capital is defined as current assets minus current liabilities.

Note that assets have increased by $1,000 (the debit column) and owner's equity has also increased by $1,000 (the credit column). If, four days later, the business purchased inventory for $1,000 by borrowing the money from the bank, the two effects are (1) the acquisition of inventory (an asset) and (2) incurring a bank loan (a liability). The entry would be recorded as:

December 5, 1992

Inventory	$1,000	
Bank Loan		$1,000

Note that both sides of the equation have increased. In this case, of course, the increase on the right side is in liabilities, not owner's equity.

Finally, if the business sold this inventory for $2,000 on December 31, the final entry to record the sale would be:

December 31, 1992

Cash	$2,000	
Sales		$2,000
Cost of Goods Sold	($1,000)	
Inventory		($1,000)

Sales affect owner's equity by causing the value of the business to increase. Similarly, expenses (such as the cost of goods sold) cause the value of owner's equity to decrease. However, we do not show both sales and expenses in owner's equity, but rather show only the net effect. The owner's equity represents the proprietor's capital in this business. The sale for $2,000 has increased the owner's capital. At the same time, the business released inventory worth $1,000 in order to make the sale. When inventory is released, we disclose it by debiting an expense account called "cost of goods sold," which reduces (debits) capital. The net effect of both the sale and the expense is an increase in owner's equity of $1,000. Net income is the difference between revenue and expenses.

With this information, we can produce two financial statements: the income statement and the balance sheet.

The sale that was produced and the related cost of goods sold both go into the income statement. The form of the income statement would be:

A Proprietorship
Income Statement
For the Month Ended December 31, 1992

Sales	$2,000
Less: Cost of Goods Sold	(1,000)
Net Income	$1,000

Net income is included as part of capital on the balance sheet. Therefore, capital includes the money that the proprietor put in initially ($1,000) plus net income ($1,000). Therefore, capital totals $2,000.

The balance sheet summarizes all of the assets, liabilities, and owner's equity of the business at a particular time.

A Proprietorship
Balance Sheet
As At December 31, 1992

Assets:		Liabilities:	
Cash	$3,000	Bank Loan:	$1,000
		Owner's Equity	
		Capital:	$2,000
	————	Total Liabilities	————
Total Assets	$3,000	and Owner's Equity	$3,000

Both the income statement and the balance sheet are used extensively by people in business to make decisions regarding their businesses.

RATIO ANALYSIS

What do investors, creditors, and other users do with accounting information once they receive it? How do people who own shares of IBM decide whether to buy more shares or to sell the shares they presently own? How do bankers decide whether or not to lend money to a company? Many users perform a ratio analysis.

A ratio expresses the relationship of one number to another number. For example, as we saw in Exhibit 18.1, the total current liabilities for the Jasper Ski Patrol are $69,000, while the long-term liabilities are $30,000. Therefore, the ratio of current to long-term liabilities is 2.3 to 1, which means that there are $2.30 in current liabilities for every $1.00 in long-term liabilities. This ratio indicates that the Ski Patrol relies more heavily on short-term than on long-term financing. Interest rates on short-term financing tend to vary more than rates on long-term financing. Therefore, the Ski Patrol's reliance on short-term financing could cause problems if interest rates rise.

There are a number of standard ratios that users employ. They are broken down into four main categories:
1. Ability to pay current liabilities
2. Ability to pay long-term liabilities
3. Operating ratios
4. Profitability ratios

Ability to Pay Current Liabilities

The ratio of current assets to current liabilities is referred to as the **current ratio**. This ratio is used by bankers and suppliers to determine whether or not to extend credit to the business. As we saw in Exhibit 18.1, the total current assets of the Ski Patrol are $178,000. The total current liabilities are $69,000. Therefore, the ratio of current assets to current liabilities is:

current ratio
The ratio of current assets to current liabilities, a measure of the ability to pay current debts

$$\text{Current Ratio} = \frac{\text{Current Assets}}{\text{Current Liabilities}} = \frac{\$178,000}{\$69,000} = 2.58:1.$$

In other words, the Ski Patrol has $2.58 in current assets for every $1.00 in current liabilities.

What is an acceptable current ratio? If a business were to run into financial difficulty, bankers and suppliers would like large amounts of current assets on the balance sheet that could be seized to repay the debt. The greater the current ratio, the less the risk of default, as far as bankers and creditors are concerned. However, current assets are not without cost to the business. Cash in the bank earns little or no interest. Similarly, large inventories are expensive to finance. Therefore, businesses do not wish to keep too much in current assets. There is always a tradeoff between having too many and having too few resources tied up in current assets.

A general rule of thumb is a current ratio of 2 to 1. However, not all companies have such a current ratio. The more likely it is that a company can predict its cash flows (utilities and pipelines are examples), the lower its current ratio need be since the business can forecast when it will need to pay current liabilities. On the other hand, businesses in cyclical industries (automobile manufacturers) may require a higher current ratio.

quick ratio
The ratio of cash, marketable securities, and net accounts

A variation of the current ratio is the **quick ratio**, or acid-test ratio. Since inventory may not be converted into cash quickly and prepaid expenses cannot be sold, many users exclude both these items from the calculation, leaving only cash, marketable securities, and net accounts receivable in the numerator. In the case of the Ski Patrol:

$$\text{Quick Ratio} = \frac{\text{Quick Assets}}{\text{Current Liabilities}} = \frac{\$4,000 + \$15,000 + \$75,000}{\$69,000} = 1.77:1.$$

A rule of thumb for the quick ratio is 1 to 1. However, ability to predict cash flows, as discussed earlier with the quick ratio, would change this rule of thumb.

Ability to Pay Long-Term Liabilities

debt-to-asset ratio
The ratio of total assets to total liabilities, a measure of the proportion of assets financed by debt rather than owner's equity

The **debt-to-asset ratio** tells us how much of a business's total assets are financed by liabilities. In the case of the Ski Patrol:

$$\text{Debt-to-Asset Ratio} = \frac{\text{Total Liabilities}}{\text{Total Assets}} = \frac{\$99,000}{\$254,000} = 0.39:1$$

This ratio tell us that 39 percent of the Ski Patrol's total assets are financed by creditors. The other 61 percent must be financed by owners. The lower the debt-to-asset ratio, the less risk the creditors face since the company has a greater amount of assets to support the creditors' claims. Bankers would be more likely to lend to companies with lower than higher debt-to-asset ratios.

Utility and pipeline companies like TransAlta Utilities in Alberta are able to maintain a lower current ratio because its cash flows can be predicted. An important part of TransAlta's cash flows comes in the form of monthly collections from its electric utilities customers.

Operating Ratios

Operating ratios deal with how successful the business is at selling inventory and collecting accounts receivable. The **inventory turnover** tells us the number of times that inventory is bought and sold during the course of a year. The higher the inventory turnover the better, since this means increased profitability and less chance of inventory becoming obsolete. The ratio for the Ski Patrol, based on data in Exhibit 18.2, is:

$$\frac{\text{Inventory}}{\text{Turnover}} = \frac{\text{Cost of Goods Sold}}{\text{Average Inventory}} = \frac{\$132{,}000}{(\$56{,}000 + \$65{,}000)/2} = 2.18 \text{ times.}$$

The ratio should be compared with those of companies in the same industry before a conclusion can be reached. In the food retailing industry, a high inventory turnover would be expected. In office-building construction, inventory turnover would be very low. However, it seems that 2.18 is a fairly low figure. Since there are 365 days in a year, it takes 365/2.18 = 167 days on average from the time inventory is purchased to the time it is sold. The 167 days is called the **average holding period of inventory**.

When a company sells inventory to another company and does not receive payment immediately, the selling company records this transaction as an account receivable. The **accounts receivable turnover** measures a company's ability to collect cash from its credit customers. The higher the ratio, the faster cash is collected.

inventory turnover
The ratio of goods sold in a year to the average inventory, measuring the number of times goods are bought and sold in a year

average holding period of inventory
The average length of time that goods are held before they are sold

accounts receivable turnover
The ratio of credit sales to net accounts receivable, measuring the speed at which cash is received for credit sales

This ratio applies only to credit sales. If 75 percent of the Ski Patrol's net sales were on credit, credit sales would total $292,000 x 75% = $219,000.

$$\text{Accounts Receivable Turnover} = \frac{\text{Credit Sales}}{\text{Net Accounts Receivable}} = \frac{\$219,000}{\$75,000} = 2.92 \text{ times.}$$

This ratio varies widely among industries. Companies in the utility industry tend to have higher accounts receivable turnover since they can cut off service to customers that do not pay. On the other hand, businesses that supply services to the public sector may have lower accounts receivable turnover since many departments in the public sector are slow to pay their bills. It appears the Ski Patrol's accounts receivable turnover is fairly low. Using 365 days in the year, it takes 365/2.92 = 125 days on average to collect its accounts receivable. The 125 days is called the **days sales in accounts receivable**. The average holding period of inventory and days sales in accounts receivable yield some very interesting information when brought together to calculate the **cash conversion cycle**.

After the Ski Patrol purchases inventory, it takes an average of 167 days before the inventory is sold. Once sold, it takes a further 125 days to collect the cash. Therefore, it takes the Ski Patrol a total of 292 days from the time inventory is purchased until the time it collects the cash from the sale of the inventory. However, the Ski Patrol is probably able to purchase inventory on account. The accounts payable deferral period is the time that is allowed for payment. For example, if the Ski Patrol's creditors allowed the company 30 days to pay its bills, the cash conversion cycle would be reduced by that number of days. The cash conversion cycle would be 262 days: the time it takes to convert from cash to inventory to accounts receivable and back to cash again.

days sales in accounts receivable
The average length of time taken to collect accounts receivable

cash conversion cycle
The average length of time between payment being made for inventory and payment being received for goods sold

Inventory Purchased	Accounts Payable Paid	Sale Made	Accounts Receivable Collected and Cash Received
Day 1 ⟶	Day 30 ⟶	Day 167 ⟶	Day 292

The cash conversion cycle is computed as follows:

Average Holding Period of Inventory	=	167 days
Add: Days Sales in Accounts Receivable	=	125 days
Less: Accounts Payable Deferral Period	=	(30 days)
		262 days

Clearly, a company cannot go without cash for long periods of time since cash is needed to make payroll, pay rent, and purchase supplies. Obviously, a company would like to have as low a cash conversion cycle as possible. A high cash conversion cycle means that the company might have to borrow money from its bankers in order to operate. The Ski Patrol is not in this position only because it has so much equity. However, the company's cash conversion cycle does explain why the company has large amounts of accounts receivable and inventory on its balance sheet, but very little cash.

Profitability Ratios

The main objective of any business is to make a profit. Ratios that deal with profitability are informative for a wide variety of users.

One way to view the profitability of a company is through a "pie" chart. The chart in Figure 18.1 tells us how much of the sales of the Ski Patrol went to expenses and how much was left over for profit.

Return on sales tells us how good the company is at retaining a percentage of its sales as profit. The higher the percentage, the better. For the Ski Patrol,

$$\text{Return on Sales} = \frac{\text{Net Income}}{\text{Net Sales}} = \frac{\$30,000}{\$292,000} = 10.27\%$$

return on sales
The ratio of net income to net sales, measuring the ability to make a profit on sales

When a company knows what its return on sales is, it can see what effect the introduction of new products with revised costs and selling prices would have on this ratio. A product that sells with a very high markup could dramatically increase this ratio.

The potential owner of a business can either invest in that business or invest elsewhere. The **return on total equity** looks at how much income the business generated and what resources it took to generate it, which helps the investor make that decision. For the Ski Patrol,

$$\frac{\text{Return on}}{\text{Total Equity}} = \frac{\text{Net Income}}{\text{Total Owner's Equity}} = \frac{\$30,000}{\$155,000} = 19.4\%$$

return on total equity
The ratio of net income to total owner's equity, measuring the profitability of investment in the business

Total owner's equity represents the net amount of resources that the owners have either contributed to the business (common stock) or left in the business (retained earnings). An investor would compare this

FIGURE 18.1 • PERCENTAGE OF NET SALES FOR THE SKI PATROL

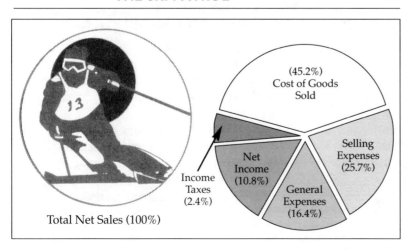

return with what could be earned on other investments, such as bonds or shares in other companies. A 19.4 percent return would be very attractive.

earnings per share (EPS)
Net income divided by the total number of shares outstanding, measuring profit per share

Earnings per share (EPS) is perhaps one of the most widely used ratios. It is the only ratio that is required to be included in the financial statements of publicly traded companies because EPS indicates the amount of income that each share generates. A high EPS is good since it means the company is generating profits that can be used to expand or reduce bank indebtedness. If a company's EPS increases over many years, it usually means that the price of the stock will increase over time. Assume that the Jasper Ski Patrol has 80,000 common shares outstanding (originally sold at $1.00 per share).

$$\text{EPS} = \frac{\text{Net Income}}{\text{No. of Common Shares Outstanding}} = \frac{\$30,000}{80,000} = \$0.375/\text{share}.$$

share price–to–earnings ratio
The ratio of the current price of a share to the earnings per share, measuring the length of time it would take to recover the price of the share

For publicly traded companies, the EPS is usually compared with the price of the stock to produce the **share price–to–earnings ratio**. If the Ski Patrol shares were traded at today's prices on the Toronto Stock Exchange at $3.75 per share, the price-to-earnings ratio would be $3.75/$0.375 = 10 times. The price-to-earnings ratio tells us that if the company were to pay out all of its earnings to shareholders and the company continued to generate the same EPS, it would take ten years for an investor to get back the original price of the stock (i.e., 10 years x $0.375 = $3.75). The share price–to–earnings ratio is the figure that analysts use to compare companies within the same industry. Price–to–earnings ratios are frequently reported in the business section of a newspaper.

All these ratios can be derived from the information provided in financial statements prepared according to GAAP. Issues in Business 18.2 discusses whether this information is adequate for investors.

ISSUES IN BUSINESS 18.2

INFORMATION FOR BUSINESS DECISIONS: HOW ADEQUATE IS INFORMATION SUPPLIED UNDER GAAP?

IN ORDER TO create new jobs and new opportunities, we rely on an industrious private sector. Companies must raise huge sums of money from investors to purchase buildings, machinery, and equipment. These, in turn, are used to create products and services, thereby creating employment.

However, not all companies turn out to be successful. Therefore, investors try to determine which companies are the best investment. Companies are required to follow accounting principles that are standardized (called "generally accepted accounting principles," or GAAP). This is done so that investors can more readily evaluate and compare companies to determine whether those they are interested in have an ability to pay the investor interest or dividends.

(continued)

Investors therefore rely heavily on accountants to ensure that the financial statements are in fact fairly presented and disclose all the information necessary in order to make a well-informed decision.

Questions for Discussion

1. Beyond provision of information in accordance with GAAP, could the organization's accounting function bear some responsibility for success or failure of a company? Explain.

2. Is accounting information enough for an investor who wishes to make a well-informed investment decision? Explain.

ACCOUNTING AND BUDGETING

We think of accounting as dealing with past performance, and our study has examined how financial statements of past performance can be used. We will now consider how accounting information can be used to plan for the future of the business.

The owners of any organization have goals. These goals may be to achieve a 20 percent return on sales, increase market share by 10 percent per year, or launch a new product within six months. Whatever the goals, the owners need the help of employees, especially in larger organizations, in order to achieve those goals. A **budget** is a quantitative expression of the organization's goals against which performance can be assessed. From the budget can be derived how those goals will be achieved and what everyone's role is in achieving them.

Even individuals should budget, as indicated by Lori Petroski's experience in Developing Your Business Skills. In smaller organizations, the budgeting process may be quite informal, with the owner and the employees simply meeting to decide on goals. However, in larger organizations, budgeting is a much more complicated process, requiring several stages of refinement in order to meet the organization's many goals and ensure that it is understood by the many people who must work to it. Such complex budgeting issues are beyond the scope of this text.

budget
A financial plan for meeting the organization's goals, forecasting income, and allotting specific funds to various purposes, against which performance can be assessed

---

DEVELOPING YOUR BUSINESS SKILLS

BUDGETING: A SKILL FOR LIFE

Lori Petroski had finally realized her dream of being accepted into university. She had been preparing for this experience for quite some time and was looking forward to meeting new people and living away from home for the first time in her life. After leaving high school, she had a good summer job and arrived at university with enough money to pay for her tuition, books, and rent, and still had a few hundred dollars left over.

Since she had money, she had not considered a student loan. She felt quite good about her finances until she began to pay other unanticipated costs, such as commuting to campus, lunches, university fees, and entertainment. The additional money from a part-time job just was not

(continued)

enough to make ends meet. Lori confided to a friend, Anne, that she had had no idea that it cost so much to go to school and she was worrying about how she would cope, but she was determined to finish her degree.

Anne suggested that she should try to budget her money by keeping track of when money was coming in to her bank account and when it was going out, so that she would be able to anticipate larger expenditures. Lori did not like the idea of keeping records or budgeting, but she liked worrying about her finances even less, so she decided to try it.

The benefits were immediately apparent to her. Lori had no idea that she was spending so much money on lunches at the cafeteria and that her trips home every other weekend were so expensive. By making sandwiches in her apartment and going home only once a month, she was able to save substantially. Lori believed that she was well on her way to a successful second semester.

Budgeting, unfortunately, is viewed by many people as an onerous and unenjoyable task. However, budgeting simply expresses goals in terms of numbers. If you wish to make it through a year of university, it is crucial that you have enough money to do it. This is not any different from a business that needs to generate money to succeed. By expressing goals on paper in terms of a budget, a business can determine if it is doing the right things in order to achieve those goals. The same applies to a student.

BUSINESS REVIEW 18.2

1. Which financial ratios would you be interested in if you were a bank manager considering a request from a business for a loan to buy new machinery? If you were an investor considering the purchase of shares?

2. Assume the Ski Patrol is about to move to new premises. What expenses would such a move entail? Draw up a budget for the move.

Every business needs to ensure that it has sufficient cash in order to pay its bills as they come due. This is a very important part of the budgeting process. If the organization is expanding, that means it will likely have higher inventory and payroll costs. The organization must ensure that cash is available in order to pay for these items as required. An excellent and simple way to keep track of cash is through the use of a cash budget. Exhibit 18.4 shows the cash budget for the Ski Patrol.

ACCOUNTING IN MANAGEMENT

Is accounting just adding up the numbers? Or can it make a difference to the way a business is run? Issues in Business 18.3 suggests that accountants can be more than bean counters.

EXHIBIT 18.4 · CASH BUDGET

The Ski Patrol
123 Main Street
Jasper, Alberta

THE SKI PATROL
Cash Budget

January to June 1995

	January	February	March	April	May	June
Cash Receipts						
Cash Sales	$35,000	$38,000	$32,000	$20,000	$5,000	$3,000
Collect Accounts Receivable	10,000	7,000	10,000	6,000	2,000	1,000
Total Cash Receipts	45,000	45,000	42,000	26,000	7,000	4,000
Cash Disbursements:						
Purchases	18,000	17,000	15,000	9,000	2,000	1,000
Selling and General Expenses	15,000	15,000	13,000	9,000	8,000	6,000
Total Cash Disbursements	33,000	32,000	28,000	18,000	10,000	7,000
Excess of Cash Receipts Over Cash Disbursements	12,000	13,000	14,000	8,000	(3,000)	(3,000)
Add: Opening Cash Balance	4,000	16,000	29,000	43,000	51,000	48,000
Ending Cash Balance	$16,000	$29,000	$43,000	$51,000	$48,000	$45,000

ISSUES IN BUSINESS 18.3

ACCOUNTING FOR QUALITY

TOTAL QUALITY MANAGEMENT (TQM) and the need for continuous improvement are fast becoming important issues in both the private and government sectors. Organizations that passed up many of the previous management fads are now turning to TQM with much fervour. Business journals are reporting many successes and failures in implementing such programs. Yet little is really understood about the impact these programs are having, because they have not been in operation long enough.

What sets TQM apart from previous fads is the requirement for continuous and accurate measurement of every process that exists within the organization. For example, the time needed to perform a certain task or the volume of waste produced in the manufacturing process would

(continued)

be measured. As a result, one of the main weaknesses in implementing TQM programs is the failure to recognize the need to take these measurements. In the past, accountants simply included waste costs as part of the normal cost of production.

This brings an exciting challenge to the accounting profession—how to help organizations "account for quality." This new approach to accounting must go beyond the traditional reporting of profits, expenses, departmental budgets, and so forth. Organizations are looking to accountants to help them develop ways to measure the actual processes involved in converting to a quality system.

Simply put, TQM is a system for creating competitive advantage by focussing on what is important to the customer. TQM itself can be broken down into:

- "Total": that is, the whole organization is involved and understands that customer satisfaction is everyone's job;
- "Quality": the extent to which products and services satisfy the requirements of internal and external customers;
- "Management": the leadership, infrastructure, and resources that support employees as they meet the needs of those customers.

Accountant Michael Stanleigh recently worked with a pulp-and-paper plant. At the end of his plant tour, the managers told him that they had received many complaints about their product. Their solution had been to establish a quality assurance program. Customers had complained that many rolls of newsprint must have been broken in production because there were a number of visible seams in the paper on the roll. The paper was of variable thickness, which increased the chances of breakage during production. As well, some of the rolls had no visible seams, but the paper thickness varied nonetheless. In addition, some customers had received rolls that were damaged because of poor packaging.

It became obvious that every roll of newsprint needed to be inspected before leaving the plant. Rolls that had more than one seam, were of varying degrees of thickness, or were packaged poorly would not be sent out to the customer.

The results were immediate. Customer complaints waned, and once threatened sales continued. Management felt that the new quality assurance program was a tremendous success. Essentially it meant zero defects for the customer. But the plant had a warehouse full of newsprint rolls rejected on the basis of quality. While recycling them back through the system meant nothing was wasted, how could the managers account for this new step?

The company's solution was to include the cost of running the newsprint through the system again as part of the production cost. However, what management failed to do was to look into the root causes of the problem. Why did the paper break when it was spun onto the roll? Why was the paper thickness inconsistent? Why were rolls improperly packed prior to shipping?

Stanleigh recommended that the company implement a TQM system. This meant developing detailed flow charts of every single process in every department. These charts highlighted the amount of rework required, the amount of waste produced, and any bottlenecks or duplication of work. Essentially, the organization started to look at the sources of some of its problems. Employee teams used a structured problem-solving process to measure the problems, find the root cause or causes, and determine the appropriate solutions. One of the root causes of the inconsistent paper thickness and breaking was found to be the type of wood used in the pulp. Also it was found that employee carelessness and poor equipment were the main factors in the packaging problems.

(continued)

Previously, the quality control figures reported to head office as part of the cost of production were in fact the cost of reworking the pulp. However, a system that accounts for quality needs to report these quality costs separately. The only figures that should ever be included in the cost of production are those that relate directly to the cost of producing a zero-defect end product. All waste, recycling, and the like should be included as a cost of rework. These costs can then be shown separately, and their root causes can be investigated so that sound solutions can be developed and implemented.

The accounting profession is excellent at applying root-cause analysis. It is the job of the accountant to determine the root causes and measure the impact these problems are having before any drastic solutions are taken.

Source: Adapted from Michael Stanleigh, "Accounting for Quality," *C.A. Magazine*, October 1992, p. 40. Reprinted with permission from *CA Magazine*, published by the Canadian Institute of Chartered Accountants, Toronto.

Question for Discussion

1. Stanleigh suggests that breaking out costs into various accounts instead of including virtually everything as "production costs" is important to quality and efficiency. Explain.

Magna International Inc., an auto parts producer, is committed to Total Quality Management (TQM). On site testing equipment and quality verification techniques are implemented to ensure that quality is built into all of Magna's products.

INTERACTIVE SUMMARY AND DISCUSSION QUESTIONS

1. Accounting information is necessary in order for the owner/manager of a business to make sound business decisions. What types of decisions do owners/managers make with accounting information?

2. There are three different accounting organizations in Canada that have input into determining what constitutes generally accepted accounting principles, the principles that accountants follow when preparing financial statements. Why is it necessary for businesses to follow a set of uniform accounting principles?

3. A company's financial statements are normally audited at year end by public accountants. What benefit would there be to a company in having its financial statements audited?

4. Bookkeeping is concerned with recording transactions in accounting journals, while accountants organize this information into financial statements. Accountants also deal with management accounting, which is used by internal managers. Why do you think that both financial statements and management accounting reports are required by companies?

5. Accountants classify all transactions as being assets, liabilities, owner's equity, revenues, and expenses. Briefly explain how each of these items differs from the others and where you would put each in preparing a set of financial statements.

6. Each asset, liability, and owner's equity item is called an "account." Why do you think that it is necessary to keep track of transactions in separate accounts?

7. A balance sheet is prepared at a particular time, while an income statement and a statement of changes in financial position are prepared for a period of time, usually one year. What do you think a user would learn about a business from each of these statements?

8. A ratio is the relationship of one number to another number. Why do you think that comparing certain numbers from the financial statements would be meaningful to a user?

9. A cash budget is used to estimate how much cash will be going into and out of the business for some future period of time. Banks almost always require cash budgets from businesses that wish to borrow money. Why do you think that banks request cash budgets?

10. Frequently, businesses prepare cash budgets only because their bank requires them to. However, budgeting also involves more than just cash budgets. What other types of budgets could a business have? Why is budgeting so important to the survival and growth of a business?

11. Assume that a medium-sized retail chain of women's clothing stores is contemplating buying out a single-unit independent store to add to its chain. What role would an accountant play in the considerations leading up to the decision to purchase? Specifically, how could an accountant help?

CASE 18.1

ACCOUNTING WITH A CONSCIENCE

To WHAT EXTENT should corporations take responsibility for the costs of the environmental factors they require for industrial activities? The following situation considers accounting with a conscience.

Social responsibility accounting (SRA) has been described by Robert Anderson as "a systematic assessment of and reporting on those parts of a company's activities that have a social impact"— a definition easily adapted to environmental accounting, which deals with measurement and reporting issues as well as the notion of corporate responsibility. Unfortunately, the current

(continued)

accounting system does not motivate managers to accept social or environmental responsibility, simply because of the difficulty in measuring and reporting the factors involved.

But external pressures are mounting. Interest in the environment is not going to go away. Today's executives are more aware of and concerned with society's priorities. Their personal beliefs have also shifted. The concept of sustainable development—that "which meets the needs of the present without compromising the ability of the future to meet its own needs"—has gained momentum. In June 1991, the Canadian Institute of Chartered Accountants launched two research projects, "Accounting and Reporting on Environmental Issues within the Existing Financial Reporting Framework" and "Environmental Auditing," that demonstrate its seriousness in implementing an accounting program to meet societal pressures.

But has this serious intent been transcribed into action? For too long, corporations have relied on external economies to support the profit-making system. They have not recorded the financial impact of these economies within their statements. Using a river as a cooling system and not restoring the water to its original temperature serves as an external economy for a corporation because it saves money, but is a social diseconomy because community resources must be used to return water to its original quality. Daniel Rubenstein notes: "The problem here is the failure to recognize the natural capital contributed by society in the form of free goods such as air, water, and other prerequisites for industrial activity which are lent to business for use rather than consumption." R.E. Benedick wrote: "Corporate accounting practices . . . currently discourage environmental protection by failing to reflect the real costs to society of pollution and thoughtless short-term exploitation of such natural resources as forests." The measurement of these real costs is the major stumbling block in the smooth adaptation of an environmentally conscious accounting system.

Why measure the environmental effects of corporate actions? Any decisions regarding resource allocation require careful analysis and must be measured before it can be considered. Some kind of cost/benefit analysis is an important analytical tool. For example, if corporations do not bear the cost of preventing waste gases from being discharged, then the public must. Environmental economies must be allocated. Stopping production to stop pollution may not be a viable option. We may have to accept less than totally pure air and water to provide jobs or economic security. Very slight increases in water and air purity for very large expenditures may not be the appropriate social choice.

Source: Adapted from Michael Stanleigh, "Accounting for Quality," *C.A. Magazine*, October 1992, p. 40. Reprinted with permission from *CA Magazine*, published by the Canadian Institute of Chartered Accountants, Toronto.

Questions for Discussion

1. One reason for some of the economic problems we face today is that our accounting systems have failed to distinguish between desirable and undesirable means to meet economic goals. Discuss.

2. Measuring the costs of environmentally responsible programs is a simple beginning to social responsibility accounting, but does nothing to measure the benefits attained from the expenditures. In what way could benefit/cost accounting practices provide a more realistic measurement of SRA costs?

3. A corporation struggling to survive will not be inclined to spend the energy or resources on environmental responsibility programs. Perhaps the best way to ensure these programs are established is through the enactment of laws and regulations. Comment on the implications of such an approach.

4. Accountants measure a corporation's economic activities and therefore are well suited to developing new methods to assess and report on corporate activities that have an environmental impact. Discuss.

CASE 18.2

MARKET-VALUE OR HISTORICAL COST ACCOUNTING

"MARKET-VALUE ACCOUNTING" is a hot buzzword this season in financial circles and regulatory bodies. Accounting regulators worldwide are trying with unaccustomed boldness to close gaps in company accounts in response to increasing concern in the public and private sectors about the adequacy of financial statement reporting by financial institutions.

Days after Britain's Accounting Standards Board published plans to reform companies' profit-and-loss accounting and the treatment of their financial assets, its American counterpart, the Financial Accounting Standards Board (FASB), launched a controversial new rule forcing all businesses to publish up-to-date values of their financial assets and obligations.

This new rule tackles one of accounting's foggiest areas, the balance sheet. This is supposed to show the value of a firm's assets and liabilities; in practice, it does no such thing. Most items are shown at their original cost, not at what they would cost now. And some do not appear at all.

FASB wants firms to show "fair value" of their financial assets. This is not easy. Historical costs are based on actual prices paid; fair values are a best guess at what the price would be if there were a sale today.

Another problem is posed by the volatile prices of many financial assets, which could result in big swings—up or down—in fair values from one year to the next. Critics of the FASB say this information is misleading, as firms are not, in fact, selling assets at these prices. What they mean is that investors may be scared if the current liquidation value of, say, a bank proves on this measure to be zero.

Under this new rule, a fair value must be shown for all financial instruments. But this number will be shown in a footnote to the accounts, rather than in the headline figures. And a fair value will be required only "where practicable." "Practicable" means that estimating fair value should not involve excessive cost.

The impact of the new rule could be huge: it affects the bulk of banks' balance sheets, as well as up to a quarter of industrial firms' assets and most of their liabilities. It will need fierce policing, though. And there is room for improvement: defining fair value more tightly would help. As common definitions are agreed, the fair values of financial instruments ought to be reflected in the headline numbers—in the profit-and-loss account as well as in the balance sheet. The current values of tangible assets, such as land and buildings, should also be included.

Source: Excerpts from "Think of a Number," *The Economist,* January 4–10, 1992, p. 60 Copyright ©1992 The Economist Newspaper Group, Inc. Reprinted with permission. Futher reproduction prohibited.

Questions for Discussion

1. Assume that you are the manager of a building supply company such as Beaver Lumber. Discuss the considerations and problems involved in switching to a market-value accounting system.

2. Answer the same question for a Dairy Queen operation which owns its own building and parking lot.

PHOTO CREDITS

ACC 18 Photo courtesy of TransAlta Utilities   ACC 24 Photo courtesy of Magna International Inc.

MODULE

◆ FIN ◆

MANAGING THE FIRM'S FINANCES

THE FOCUS OF THIS MODULE

1. To emphasize the importance of sound financial management
2. To describe the key ingredients of a financial plan
3. To outline the major areas of operations that require funding
4. To distinguish between debt financing and equity financing
5. To list the most common sources of short- and long-term funds
6. To examine the advantages and risks of leverage
7. To learn the meaning of the following terms:

KEY TERMS

financial management	prime interest rate
financial plan	line of credit
accounts receivable	revolving credit agreement
debt financing	secured loan
equity financing	factor
trade credit	bond
unsecured loan	venture capital
promissory note	leverage
installment note	treasury bill
demand note	certificate of deposit (CD)

WHEN "SWEET LORRAINE" isn't operating at full capacity, the $500-million coated-paper machine costs its employer a lot of money.

This is not the only investment that caused Repap Enterprises Inc., a Montreal-based pulp-and-paper firm, to struggle to manage its financial affairs. It suffered huge debt problems because of a massive capital spending program. This program included the $2.5-billion purchase of five new coated-paper machines, buying and modernizing the Skeena pulp mill in British Columbia, and taking over Manitoba's old Manfor pulp mill.

Compounding the difficulties, the firm was only able to operate at 10 percent capacity in North America. Profits vanished because of declining prices, poor markets, and the company's heavy interest burden.

Under these pressures, Repap founder/chairman George Petty had to raise $148 million, which he did through a convertible debenture issue. Although analysts said they would have preferred a straight equity issue, the proceeds from the debenture issue kept Repap afloat until product prices rebounded.

With well over $1.3 billion in debt, Repap was not able to fully cover interests costs. In addition to the debenture issue, the company responded to its need for finances by:
- selling two non-strategic investments;
- dropping quarterly dividend payments, thus saving $36 million annually;
- negotiating a delay in principal payments on debt associated with its Midtec, Wisconsin, plant, and a delay in preferred stock dividends;
- negotiating a $60-million Province of New Brunswick loan guarantee;
- arranging equipment sale–and–lease-backs and cutting capital outlays to $51 million;
- exploring joint-venture partnerships on its expensive machinery.

Investors were satisfied with these steps. They felt that they would gain enough time to keep the company going.

Source: Adapted from Robert Gibbens, "Repap Digs In for Paper Turnaround," *The Financial Post*, July 15, 1991, p. 15.

Whether a company is large, as Repap is, or the size of a College Pro Painters franchise, financing it adequately can make a vital difference between its enjoying continued success or failing. Companies require a financial plan, which includes the use of funds, and arrangements to obtain them, in order to pay for operations throughout the life of the firm. This is known as finance.

In other words finance is the management of money. As business becomes more competitive, effective financial management and financial planning are becoming crucial factors in meeting goals and objectives. If the funds are not available at the right times to produce and market goods and services, sales cannot be made, and the company will lose business, become less profitable, and perhaps fail completely. Sound financial management is vital for a large multinational corporation or a small franchise operation, and for individuals planning their future.

FINANCIAL PLANNING

financial management
Raising and spending money to best advantage

Financial management involves planning in two complementary areas: how money is to be raised and how it is to be spent. Raising money requires careful research to determine which sources of funds the firm should draw on. Ensuring that these funds are used to the greatest advantage by the firm demands an awareness of all aspects of the firm's business that involve the use of money. For example, even though the inventory levels and accounts receivable may be the responsibility of other management specialists, the financial manager will stress the importance of not tying up more money than necessary in these areas.

Financial planning is largely based on forecasts of production, purchasing, and sales. The **financial plan** identifies the sums of money that will be needed at specific points to achieve long-term profit objectives, the times that bills will fall due and when funds will be available to meet these obligations, the sources of funds most appropriate to the firm's needs, and the best uses to which money can be put. Thus, the plan co-ordinates the financial activities of the firm and sets in place controls to evaluate performance. It answers three pairs of critical questions:

1. How much money will be needed during the period covered by the plan? How much money will be received?
2. When will money be needed? When will money be available?
3. Where will needed funds come from? How will excess funds be used?

Figure 19.1 shows the components reflected in these questions, with particular focus on the best sources of funds and the most efficient use of those funds.

A company requires funds for daily business activities; to maintain inventory; to cover cash deficiencies created by the normal delay between sales and receipt of payment; to make interest payments on loans; to distribute dividends to shareholders; and to buy land, facilities, and equipment. The firm's financial plan must identify all of these financial obligations and specify when each must be met. Neither expenditures nor revenues tend to flow smoothly or regularly. The financial manager lines up anticipated cash outflows against cash inflows from sales and other sources to pinpoint the need for additional funds at particular times in the business cycle—and also to take

financial plan
A description of upcoming need for funds, the most appropriate sources of them, their most effective use, and the development of controls to ensure that the plan is followed

FIGURE 19.1 • MANAGING FUNDS FLOW THROUGH THE FINANCIAL PLAN

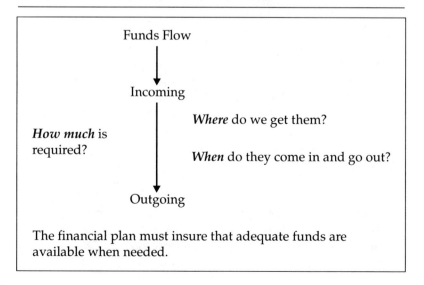

Funds Flow

Incoming

Where do we get them?

How much is required?

When do they come in and go out?

Outgoing

The financial plan must insure that adequate funds are available when needed.

FIGURE 19.2 • FINANCIAL PLANNING REQUIRES DECISIONS

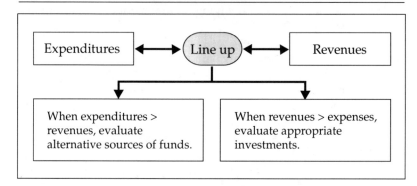

advantage of any surpluses, when cash inflows more than cover the firm's expenses, by making appropriate investments. The process is illustrated in Figure 19.2. Some of the pitfalls of poor financial planning are outlined in Developing Your Business Skills.

DEVELOPING YOUR BUSINESS SKILLS

PLANNING THE SECOND YEAR

Lori Petroski breathed a sigh of relief as she opened her mail and found that she was granted a student loan for the second year of university. She was determined that she was not going to repeat the experience of her first year, when she ran out of money halfway through the second semester. However, she had really needed the money a week earlier, when she was supposed to pay her tuition fees. This meant she was facing late-fee penalties in addition to her normal fees.

Lori had learned about budgeting in her first year of university. After running into some difficulties initially, she developed a budget, and careful adherence to it helped her make it through most of the second semester. Unfortunately, she ran out of cash halfway through March. Lori's immediate reaction was to pay for her remaining expenses with her VISA card. After all, her summer job would start in a month and she would then have enough money to pay the VISA bill. However, she soon realized that the money used to pay VISA meant less money for her second year. When she reviewed her budget, she saw that she would be $1,000 short. Lori realized that if she had planned earlier, she would not have needed to use her VISA card and been forced to pay the high interest rates that credit cards incur. Interest rates on student loans are considerably lower.

This year, Lori planned ahead. She applied for a larger loan than she had originally anticipated for her second year. Since it was a long-term loan, it would not have to be repaid until after she graduated. As her second year started, she was confident that she could make it through the entire year without resorting to credit cards if she continued to manage her finances carefully.

Financial management is not all that different for a student and for the financial manager of an organization. Both face a flow of incoming and outgoing funds and the fact that the former does not always balance the latter. Consequently, the student or manager may have to turn to short-term financing through borrowing. Short-term financing is often expensive, and it may not always be readily available, so a student or manager may then have to turn to longer-term sources of funds.

CASH MANAGEMENT

One of the financial manager's ongoing tasks is the management of the firm's cash balances. The objective, ideally, is to keep just enough cash in the firm's low-interest chequing account to pay bills and meet payrolls, but not more. Other funds should be kept in investments that generate greater revenue, until needed to pay taxes, to pay dividends to shareholders, or to cover interest payments due on loans or mortgages.

Cash management also requires attention to cash flows (receipts and collections) and short-term investment in securities. One common and perfectly acceptable strategy for keeping the amount of cash needed for business operations to a minimum is to pay bills as late as possible without incurring late-payment charges while collecting money owed by customers as quickly as possible. The challenge is to maintain the firm's credit rating, and free up as much money as possible for investment for profit.

The Uses of Credit

Allowing customers to buy now and pay later is an excellent way of attracting sales. It carries with it, of course, not only the risk that the customer will not be able to pay but also the fact that until payment is received the money is not available to carry on the firm's operations. Interest charges on late payments are a way of covering these concerns.

Many factors must be weighed in the decision to allow credit sales: whether the individual sale would take place at all if payment had to be made immediately, whether the availability of credit will attract new customers or retain the loyalty of existing ones, what the reputation of the customer is for honouring financial commitments, what policies are adopted generally in the industry (for example, credit is rarely extended to customers in the retail grocery industry), and what the firm's own credit policies and immediate financial needs are. In establishing a credit policy, the firm's financial plan must consider the balance between raising the level of sales and collecting payment as quickly as possible.

A firm's **accounts receivable** are the amounts due on sales it has made but not yet received payment for. Accounts receivable can represent as much as 15 to 20 percent of a firm's assets, so the decision of how much credit to extend to a customer and on what terms is of prime importance. The key factor is usually the history of the relationship between the company and its customers. If the customer is new, sellers will routinely consult credit-rating agencies such as Dun and Bradstreet and the Credit Bureau of Canada.

accounts receivable
Amounts due from customers on credit sales

MANAGING INVENTORY

The acquisition and storage of inventory represent a considerable investment for most businesses. Inventory must be maintained in order to be able to respond quickly to consumer demand, but the financial manager will want to keep the money invested in raw materials, work in process, and finished goods as low as is practicable.

The rate at which a firm's product sells has a direct effect on the amount of money invested in inventory. For products with a steady stream of sales—for example, most grocery products—a modest inventory can be carried, supplemented by a regular resupply schedule. On the other hand, large quantities of souvenirs must be stocked for a major sporting event such as the Commonwealth Games because the time period during which customers are available and interested in buying is extremely compact, allowing no time to reorder.

FINANCING LAND, PLANT, AND EQUIPMENT

The greatest financial demands faced by most companies, especially new companies, are the acquisition of land, plant facilities, and equipment. These "fixed assets" must be acquired before a company can begin to generate sales and must be maintained to ensure continuing revenue. Financial management involves the choice of the best method to raise the necessary capital and maximize long-term benefits to the firm.

Fixed assets also involve certain tax considerations. Unlike operating costs, which are deducted from revenues before income is calculated for tax purposes, the purchase of fixed assets is not regarded as an expense because the company has merely exchanged money for an asset that still has value: it could be sold for an equivalent amount. Tax law does recognize that some assets depreciate in value over time. Plant facilities, such as buildings, deteriorate, and major equipment, such as conveyor belts, forklift trucks, bakery ovens, and computers, cannot be sold for what they were bought for. Tax regulations,

Long-term benefits of fixed assets like equipment must outweigh the cost of purchase. The Air Jet spinning frames at the E.F. King Plant (Sherbrooke, Quebec) produce yarn 5–10 times faster than, for example, Ring spinning frames. They also clean the yarn, which means the yarn no longer has to go through a separate cleaning process. The Air Jet thus performs two tasks and saves time and money.

therefore, allow the owners of buildings and equipment used in business to deduct a portion of the purchase price from income each year (the percentages vary according to the type of asset) to cover this depreciation. Land, on the other hand, is expected to maintain or even increase its value, so no depreciation allowance applies. Careful management of fixed assets is important in minimizing tax obligations.

BUSINESS REVIEW 19.1

1. What are the critical questions a financial plan should answer?

2. List the main funding requirements a business must plan for.

DEBT AND EQUITY FUNDS

Where do the funds required to operate a business come from? How does a firm find the money to cover the purchase of current assets—supplies and materials that will be consumed or converted to salable product with twelve months? How does it raise the large sums required to purchase fixed assets? The three major methods of raising funds are normal business operations, borrowing on a short-term or long-term basis, and capital provided by owners of the business. These can be further divided into two types of financing: debt financing and equity financing. **Debt financing** is the acquisition of funds through any type of borrowing. Because borrowing is regarded as a normal cost of business, interest charges on most commercial loans are tax deductible. **Equity financing** includes the use of retained earnings (business revenue reinvested in the firm), investments by the present owners of the firm, and the raising of funds through the sale of shares to venture capitalists and members of the general public. Debt and equity funding each have advantages and disadvantages. Table 19.1 summarizes these key sources of funds.

debt financing
The acquisition of funds through borrowing

equity financing
The acquisition of funds by retaining earnings, investment by owners, and the sale of shares

---

TABLE 19.1 • KEY SOURCES OF FUNDS

Regular operations	Short-term funding	Long-term funding
← *Debt financing* →		
Trade credit from suppliers	Promissory notes Lines of credit Secured bank loans	Mortgages Long-term loans Bonds
← *Equity financing* →		
Income before depreciation		Owners' capital investment
Income from investments		Retained earnings
Rental income		New share issues

Operating Revenues

Operating revenues are the main source of cash for everyday purposes. These include sales, rentals, and any other sources of regular capital inflow. After costs are covered, a firm may choose to emphasize future growth, by reinvesting earnings in its operations, or immediate profit, by distributing earnings as dividends to shareholders or as bonuses to employees. The decision may depend on the industry market conditions or company philosophy, or it may be related more to what type of good or service is produced. Mitel traditionally earmarks less than 10 percent of its annual earnings for dividend distribution because of its growth orientation. In contrast, Bell Canada shareholders have come to expect this mature company to distribute as much as 80 percent of its earnings as dividends.

As already mentioned, cash needs and operating revenue fluctuate as the yearly cycle unfolds, often in inverse proportion. For example, a company like Consumers Distributing offers a variety of household, recreational, and other types of goods, and 80 percent of sales are made during the Christmas season. The implications are obvious: Christmas shopping will create enough funds to support operations for many months, but building up inventory just before the following Christmas shopping season will place heavy financial demands on the company. Financing this inventory will require short-term funds in addition to operating revenue. The increasing sales activity during the Christmas season will provide the funds necessary to repay whatever had to be borrowed. This fluctuation of cash surplus and cash needs is represented in Figure 19.3.

For many retail companies, sales are highest during the Christmas season. Advertising campaigns are geared up with special sales offers, bonuses, packagings, Christmas products and other incentives to customers. Lavish Christmas decorations in shopping malls add an extra push to shoppers to visit and shop.

FIGURE 19.3 • SEASONAL CASH INFLOWS AND OUTFLOWS FOR A CATALOGUE RETAILER

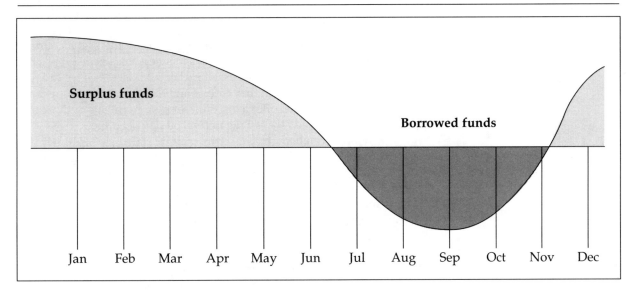

Maximizing cash inflows and planning for cash outflows is a major responsibility. However, extra funds may be needed for reasons other than the normal variations in the business cycle, such as the purchase of equipment or training a work force. For example, the start-up costs of a College Pro Painters franchise include buying a van, ladder, and other equipment.

Even established firms often need funds beyond their revenues, particularly if they want to expand into a new region or invest in new equipment and facilities. The task of evaluating the advantages and disadvantages of borrowing additional funds falls to the financial manager. When none of the borrowing options seems to provide the best solution, the financial manager may opt for raising equity capital, which can be done in a number of ways. These will be discussed in the next section.

SHORT-TERM SOURCES OF FUNDS

When operating revenue falls short of cash needs for the purchase of current assets, the financial manager turns to short-term borrowing. This term is used for any obligations that must be paid within twelve months. The three main sources of short-term funds are trade credit, unsecured bank loans, and secured short-term loans.

Trade Credit

Many firms use trade credit as a normal part of business transactions. Just as an individual consumer may "charge" items and pay for them later, a firm often buys supplies from another firm and usually is not required to pay immediately. In other words, the purchasing firm has an outstanding debt owed to the supplier. Such **trade credit** for the period between delivery and payment represents a major source of short-term financing. Trade credit has become such a standard feature

trade credit
Credit extended by a supplier for a fixed period before payment is due, usually 30 days

of contemporary business that no special paperwork is required. It is clearly understood that payment is due within 30 days from the date of delivery. Typically, the supplier highlights the terms of credit right on the invoice the purchaser receives at the time of shipment.

The supplier extends credit to its regular customers as a courtesy and a service. But the supplier is also a business that needs to consider its own cash flow. As we discussed earlier, all businesses try to minimize the amount of credit they extend and the time a debt is outstanding. So suppliers often offer a discount for cash payments or those that are made well in advance of the normal 30-day deadline.

A typical supplier's credit terms may be stated as "2/10 net 30." The purchaser reads these terms as "a 2 percent discount will be allowed if I pay the invoice within 10 days; otherwise, payment is due in 30 days." But why should the firm pay quickly in order to take advantage of the 2 percent discount? The following time line explains the dollars-and-cents reasons:

March 16: A local Pizza Hut is extended credit terms of 2/10 net 30 on a $1,000 purchase of paper supplies.

March 25: If the manager takes the discount and pays within 10 days, the cost will be $980 ($1,000 less 2%).

April 15: If the discount offer is ignored, the cost will be $1,000 on April 15.

The decision not to take the discount means that the manager is paying $20 to keep the money for an extra 20 days (March 26 to April 15). Because there are slightly more than eighteen 20-day periods in a year, this is the equivalent of an annual interest rate of more than 36 percent. It is wise for the Pizza Hut manager (or any other financial manager) to borrow money from the bank if necessary to take advantage of early-payment discounts of this magnitude.

Unsecured Bank Loans

Unsecured loans from chartered banks are a second principal source of short-term financing. When receiving an **unsecured loan**, the borrower is not required to identify any collateral (such as accounts receivable or inventory) to guarantee repayment. Banks make unsecured loans of this type by evaluating loan requests based on the firm's overall credit rating and the bank's previous dealings with it. This minimizes red tape and delay for both lender and borrower. There are three basic forms of unsecured bank loans: promissory notes, lines of credit, and revolving credit agreements.

A **promissory note** is a written promise to pay, stating the amount borrowed, the interest rate, and when payment is due. There are two common types of promissory notes: installment notes and demand notes.

Installment notes lay down a specific schedule of repayments by the borrower over a fixed time period. This may be a few months or as long as ten years, depending on the circumstances. Installment notes are often used by consumers to finance such items as vacations or new cars.

unsecured loan
A loan made without the borrower designating assets as collateral against repayment on the basis of the borrower's credit rating

promissory note
A written promise to pay, stating the amount, interest rate, and when payment is due

installment note
A promissory note including a schedule for repayment

Demand notes set no specific time limits, though the borrower promises to pay "on demand." They are usually used by businesses that expect to be able to repay the loan in one to three months. For example, a retailer wishing to finance a temporary increase in inventory for the "back to school" sales season might sign a demand note for the necessary funds. Exhibit 19.1 shows a typical demand note.

demand note
A promissory note stating no fixed date for repayment but that payment will be made "on demand"

The note will state the basis on which interest is payable. Sometimes a fixed rate of interest is given. Interest rates are usually stated as so many percentage points "above the bank's prime interest rate." The **prime interest rate** is the lowest rate of interest charged by chartered banks on short-term business loans to large firms with excellent credit ratings. The prime rate is set slightly higher than the Bank of Canada rate, which is announced weekly in reaction to changes in the world money market. The prime rate is a reference point for other lending rates and is known to fluctuate widely with changes in the supply of and demand for short-term unsecured loans.

prime interest rate
The lowest interest rate a bank charges to firms with excellent credit ratings

A **line of credit** is an agreement with a bank that enables a firm to borrow money as it needs it for short terms, provided that the total outstanding never exceeds a stated maximum. The line of credit option speeds up the borrowing process for both parties because the firm's credit-worthiness does not have to be evaluated for each separate loan. Major banks also offer personal lines of credit for individuals. Bank credit cards, such as VISA and MasterCard, are another type of line of credit.

line of credit
An agreement enabling a client to borrow money as needed for short terms provided that the total outstanding never exceeds a stated maximum

Under the usual line of credit agreement, the bank may revoke the agreement at any time and demand immediate payment. A **revolving credit agreement** is a guaranteed line of credit committing the bank to extend credit up to the maximum, regardless of how tight money might be. Because the bank guarantees the availability of funds, it normally charges a small commitment fee on the unused balance of the

revolving credit agreement
A guaranteed line of credit

EXHIBIT 19.1 • A TYPICAL DEMAND NOTE

The First Canadian Bank
Bank of Montreal

1000 Major Ave, Cityville July 6 19 9X $ 8,500.00
Branch

On demand we jointly and severally promise to pay to the order of the Bank of Montreal

the sum of eight thousand, five hundred xx/100 Dollars
and to pay interest monthly at a rate of 1.25 per cent per annum above the Bank of Montreal's prime interest rate per annum in effect from time to time, up to and after maturity, compounded monthly from the due date of such interest until actual payment at the above mentioned branch of the Bank of Montreal. At the date of this note such prime interest rate per annum is 5.5 per cent. Value received.

Alice Partner

Peter Forbes

Prod. 1059207 - Form. 824 (4/81) Litho. CANADA - 204155

Source: Reprinted with permission from the Bank of Montreal.

credit agreement (the money it must have available that the company could borrow but doesn't).

Secured Short-Term Loans

secured loan
A loan made on the basis of designated assets the lender may claim should the borrower be unable to repay

When a firm has already borrowed a lot of money or its credit rating is a little shaky for some other reason, short-term financing may still be available but only through **secured loans**. In other words, it may be necessary to pledge some of its assets as security against repayment for a loan. The exact details are spelled out in the loan agreement, which identifies the pledged assets, or collateral, as well as the amount of the loan, the interest rate, and the due date. Secured loan agreements are filed with the province so that any subsequent lenders can determine what remaining assets a borrower has for use as collateral. Lenders such as chartered banks prefer highly liquid collateral, such as accounts receivable, inventories, and marketable securities. In the event of default, they do not want to have to administer and liquidate collateral. Their objective is to be repaid as scheduled. Because of the higher degree of risk and the additional paperwork, secured short-term loans are normally granted on less favourable terms than unsecured loans.

Factoring: The Sale of Accounts Receivable

factor
A financial institution that purchases accounts receivable from businesses at a discount and accepts all the credit risks

Borrowers may choose to sell their accounts receivable as an option to using them as collateral. In these cases, firms sell such assets to a **factor**, a financial institution that purchases accounts receivable from businesses at a discount. Chartered banks and sales finance companies may also, in some circumstances, offer factoring services to commercial customers. Factors do a fair amount of business with furniture and appliance dealers, whose customers frequently buy on credit. For many firms, this is a very straightforward kind of short-term financing with two immediate benefits: additional funds become available from what amounts to a "cash" sale and the responsibility of collecting payments from customers is transferred to someone else.

Whatever assets are factored are sold at a discount and the factor generally accepts all the credit risks associated with the purchase. In practice, upon conclusion of the sale, the customers with outstanding bills are informed that all future payments must be directed to the factor. While factoring is considered an expensive method of short-term financing, it does relieve firms that routinely use this service of most, if not all, of the expense of maintaining a credit department.

LONG-TERM SOURCES OF FUNDS

Short-term financing can be used for immediate needs, such as the purchase of inventory, when the firm expects to be able to repay the money within the year. Major purchases of land, buildings, or new equipment, however, cannot be covered in a single year of business operations. For these, the financial manager must consider the various sources of long-term financing, such as long-term loans, bonds, and increased equity.

Long-Term Loans

Long-term loans are defined as those made for a period of more than one year. They usually mature in less than five years, though some loans—for example, mortgages—may be extended for twenty years or more. The Federal Business Development Bank (FBDB) offers loans to small businesses, but the most common sources of long-term loans are major financial institutions such as chartered banks, insurance companies, and pension funds. Equipment manufacturers often offer their customers the option of making credit purchases over a period of years.

Long-term loans involve greater risk for the lender because the distant future is more uncertain so they usually carry higher interest rates than short-term loans. A long-term loan agreement specifies the exact term of the loan, the interest rate, the schedule of payments, and the dollar amount of each payment. Interest payments are usually made quarterly.

Bonds

A **bond** represents a method of long-term borrowing by corporations or government agencies. Corporate bonds are issued according to the terms of a legal contract called the bond indenture, which contains the provisions of the loan—amount, interest rate, and maturity date. Exhibit 19.2 shows a corporate debenture, which is a common type of bond. Legally, bond interest and matured bonds must be paid off before shareholders can receive dividends.

Bonds are typically sold in denominations of $1,000. They are purchased by chartered banks, insurance companies, pension funds, and even individuals. Like stocks, they are actively traded and can be bought and sold through any stockbrokerage firm. Their current market prices are quoted daily in the financial sections of newspapers. Issuing bonds to raise money is generally possible only for larger companies with regional or national reputations.

bond
A certificate sold to raise long-term capital, promising to pay a set rate of interest and the principal at a specific maturity date

Equity Financing

Equity funds are provided by the owners of the firm. These funds differ from the debt financing discussed so far in that they do not have to be repaid. Owners provide financing because they expect to recover their investment through increased profits at a later date. A firm can increase equity by retaining earnings from previous business periods, by having owners put more money into the firm, by inviting new partners to invest, or by creating additional shares that investors can buy.

An established firm's *earnings* are the funds that are available after paying all claims, including interest on any loans or bonds and taxes. Instead of having the owners take all earnings as profit or distributing them all as dividends to shareholders, the firm nearly always retains part of the earnings to finance future growth.

The owner of a sole proprietorship can decide to invest more money in the business without consultation. The members of a partnership can agree to do so. Inviting new partners to join a firm is also common, though technically a new partnership is formed whenever a partner enters (or leaves).

EXHIBIT 19.2 • A CORPORATE BOND

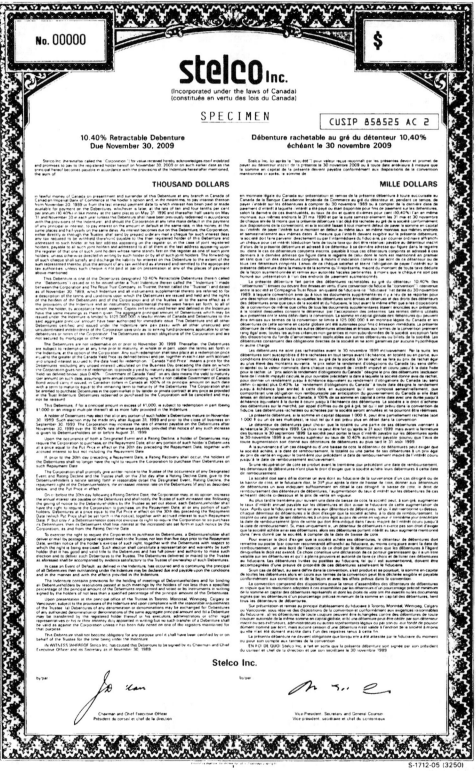

Source: Reprinted with permission from Stelco Inc.

A corporation's shareholders are its owners. Shares of stock are the true equity of the corporation. Like any business owners, shareholders are the ones who take the risk. They are not guaranteed dividends, but receive such payment only after all other claimants, including bond-holders, have been satisfied. Even then, the distribution of dividends is decided on by the firm's board of directors. Subject to certain legal requirements, any corporation can issue new shares to raise additional funds. This, of course, means that existing shares will represent a smaller proportion of the company's total equity. (The trading of exist-ing shares on the stock market does not raise funds for the corpora-tion. The shares are merely changing ownership, and any profit or loss on the transaction falls to the shareholder, not the corporation.)

Raising Venture Capital

Venture capital is provided by investors prepared to risk putting money into small, new, or struggling businesses. Venture capital comes from a very wide variety of sources: corporations, pension funds, large endowment funds, and wealthy individuals. Venture cap-italists lend money at extremely high interest rates or, more often, receive discounted company shares and part ownership in the firm in exchange for their investment. The risk is often great, but venture cap-italists invest because they see the potential for substantial profits as very high. If the firm is successful and issues shares to the general public on the stock market, the venture capitalists often contribute their managerial experience—which may lessen the autonomy of the present owners and managers.

venture capital
Debt or, more usually, equity capital invested in high-risk enterprises in the expectation of substantial profit should the business succeed

Venture capitalists receive a lot of mail. Many firms believe they have good prospects and would grow if they could find outside financing. For the most part, venture capitalists are quite cautious. They look for well-managed firms in growing industries. Recently, high-tech industries such as medical technology, robotics, energy-related firms, and information-processing equipment and software have attracted significant amounts of venture capital.

Financiers weigh three key elements when deciding whether to lend money to a small business:
1. How much of their own money or assets the owners have put on the line. This is an indication of their degree of commitment to the success of the business.
2. The quality and experience of the management.
3. The soundness of the firm's business plan.

Leverage: Borrowing Magnifies the Rate of Return

In high school physics, you learned that, with a lever, we can move an object that we do not have the strength to move unassisted. The lever multiplies our limited resources; analogously, borrowing brings **leverage** to money you want to invest.

leverage
Increasing the rate of return on equity capital through the use of borrowed funds

Say that you need $100,000 to buy a business and have only $10,000 to invest. You could acquire the $100,000 asset by issuing shares worth $100,000 and buying $10,000 worth of them yourself. You would then have to share the return with other shareholders. On the other hand, if you borrowed $90,000, you would have an asset of $100,000, which can produce a much greater return. (You would, of course, have to pay interest on the borrowed funds out of that return.) Borrowing allows you to leverage your $10,000.

Companies expecting high rates of return but in immediate need of cash sometimes apply this concept of leverage to increase the rate of return on investment. Table 19.2 presents strategies by two similar firms. The Leverage Corporation raised 90 percent of its funds by issuing bonds. The Equity Corporation preferred to obtain all the funds it needed by selling shares in the firm. Although each company earned the same profits in Year A, shareholders of the Leverage Corporation received no less than 210 percent on their $10,000 investment—even after paying $9,000 to the bondholders. In contrast, the Equity Corporation earned $30,000, but this represented only a 30 percent return on its shareholders' investment of $100,000.

Leverage has very different consequences if earnings are less than the amount needed to pay interest on borrowed funds. Consider the results should company earnings drop to $5,000, as shown in Table 19.3. The Equity Corporation would earn a modest 5 percent return on its shareholders' investment. However, it would outperform the Leverage Corporation. Because it would have to pay its bondholders $9,000 in interest, the $5,000 gain would in fact end up as a loss of $4,000, or 40 percent, for its shareholders. Thus, leverage works both ways.

Leverage is evidently a risky approach to finance. Issues in Business 19.1 explains how investors can use leverage to take over a company by borrowing funds to buy all its shares, removing them from trade on the stock market.

TABLE 19.2 • SIMPLIFIED INCOME STATEMENTS, YEAR A, FOR THE LEVERAGE CORPORATION AND THE EQUITY CORPORATION

Leverage Corporation			Equity Corporation		
Common stock	$ 10,000		Common stock	$100,000	
Bonds (at 10% interest)	90,000		Bonds	0	
	$100,000			$100,000	
Earnings	$ 30,000		Earnings	$ 30,000	
Less bond interest	9,000		Less bond interest	0	
	$ 21,000			$ 30,000	
Return to shareholders	$\dfrac{\$\,21{,}000}{\$\,10{,}000}$ = 210%		Return to shareholders	$\dfrac{\$\,30{,}000}{\$100{,}000}$ = 30%	

TABLE 19.3 • SIMPLIFIED INCOME STATEMENTS, YEAR B, FOR THE LEVERAGE CORPORATION AND THE EQUITY CORPORATION

Leverage Corporation		Equity Corporation	
Common stock	$ 10,000	Common stock	$100,000
Bonds (at 10% interest)	90,000	Bonds	0
	$100,000		$100,000
Earnings	$ 5,000	Earnings	$ 5,000
Less bond interest	9,000	Less bond interest	0
	–$ 4,000		$ 5,000
Return (loss) to shareholders	$\dfrac{\$\ 4,000}{\$\ 10,000} = (40\%)$	Return to shareholders	$\dfrac{\$\ 5,000}{\$100,000} = 5\%$

ISSUES IN BUSINESS 19.1

WATCH OUT FOR THE LBO

MANY FIRMS HAVE been taken over through a technique known as the LBO (leveraged buy-out). The LBO is a simple concept whose roots date back to the late 1960s. In such a deal, a small group of investors, usually a combination of management and an LBO specialist, borrow big sums of money to take an undervalued company private [to buy its shares when they are trading at a low price on the stock market and then remove the company from public trading].

The debt, often 90 percent or more of the purchase price, is paid off from the company's internal cash flow and by aggressive asset stripping [selling off of assets not central to the business]. Ross Johnson of Nabisco tried to take over the company this way by shedding the company's food divisions and retaining its lucrative cigarette business.

Fortunes can be made if the target companies are worth more than the whole. On the other hand, others are worried about the effect of such a takeover. They argue that the new owners of a company that has been taken through an LBO are more concerned about short-term profits and paying down the debt than building long-term values that make the company competitive. Research and development expenditures, for example, are often the first victims of a newly privatized company.

Source: Eric Reguly, "The Year of the LBO Leaves Many Concerns," *The Financial Post*, December 26, 1988, p. 4.

Questions for Discussion
1. Leveraged capital in an LBO is an interesting cross between equity capital and debt capital. As far as the business is concerned, it is equity capital because it is provided by shareholders. The new shareholders themselves, however, have gone into debt to acquire control of the company. How will their debt affect their approach to financial management? What advice should the financial manager offer to the new shareholders?
2. Are the interests of shareholders and the company the same? Explain.

BUSINESS REVIEW 19.2

1. Differentiate between debt financing and equity financing.
2. Outline the sources of equity funding.
3. List the main sources of short-term funds and discuss the pros and cons of each.
4. If you were a financial manager needing some funds for a two-to-four-year period, would you try to rely on short- or long-term funds? Why?

THE USE OF EXCESS FUNDS

Occasionally, an organization finds itself with more money than it needs to cover its daily expenses. These excess funds may come from high seasonal sales income or a major achievement such as the signing of a licensing agreement with a foreign company. The financial manager, in consultation with other senior managers, is responsible for carefully managing such irregular but substantial cash inflows to generate additional revenue.

Several possible options exist: expand the level of operations, increase productive capacity, modernize facilities, perhaps even acquire other companies. However, the financial manager must consider more immediate needs as well. Will those excess funds be needed six months down the line? Tying up excess funds reduces a firm's current assets and reduces the availability of additional funds if they are needed at short notice. A company may prefer to maintain liquidity rather than automatically plan to make capital expenditures.

Marketable Securities as Substitutes for Cash

If a firm chooses to emphasize liquidity, it has the option of keeping its excess funds in cash. However, liquidity can be maintained in ways that still improve revenue. Most financial managers invest funds not needed for day-to-day operations in marketable securities because they pay higher interest than a savings account at the bank. These have little or no risk of loss for the purchaser. They are easily redeemed for cash, which is why they are identified as "marketable"—in fact, they are often referred to as "near-money." Treasury bills and certificates of deposit are the most common marketable securities.

Every week, the Government of Canada issues **treasury bills** to cover its short-term borrowing needs. They are sold to the highest bidder through banks and investment dealers. The terms are short, usually 91 or 182 days, and rarely exceed one year. The smallest denomination is $1,000, and the largest $1 million. Treasury bills are

treasury bill
Note issued by the federal government to cover short-term funding needs, sold at a discount rather than bearing interest

sold at a discount rather than earning interest: for example, a financial manager might buy a 91-day $10,000 bill for $9,800, thus earning the equivalent of 8 percent interest over the 91-day period. Because treasury bills are issues of the Canadian government, risk is virtually nonexistent. Private investors and financial managers enjoy the ease of buying and selling the bills over the phone. Treasury bills are the most popular marketable securities.

A **certificate of deposit (CD)** is a short-term note issued by a chartered bank. The size and maturity date of a CD are often tailored to the needs of the investor. Normally, the smallest denomination is $10,000, and the minimum maturity is 30 days. CDs are easily resold, and their interest rate is typically slightly higher than the return on treasury bills.

certificate of deposit (CD)
Short-term note issued by a chartered bank

INTERACTIVE SUMMARY AND DISCUSSION QUESTIONS

1. The financial plan involves the following considerations: expenses for various time periods, source of necessary funds, and timing of the funds flow. Develop a hypothetical financial plan for the first two months of operations for a student starting to operate a new College Pro Painters franchise.

2. Organizations must plan in order to meet their short-term requirements. Outline the main funding requirements to be planned for.

3. Most firms have a highly seasonal cash flow. Draw a graph of the likely cash flow for a prairie wheat farmer, a gift shop, and an insurance broker.

4. The two major categories of funding are debt and equity. Compare and contrast the two in terms of: maturity date, claim on assets, claim on income, and right to a voice in management.

5. The use of trade credit can be managed by both buyer and seller. Explain.

6. Bonds are a method of long-term borrowing. However, their use is generally possible only for larger companies or governments. Explain why.

7. Financing education? Assume that Anthony Chen had the following loans in year 2 of his four-year program:

   $475 VISA bill unpaid for two months
   $500 bank overdraft for three months
   $3,000 student loan

   Making whatever assumptions necessary, calculate the total cost for Anthony to have borrowed this money. What lessons can be drawn from your findings?

8. Venture capital is sometimes available for small firms that have good products or ideas. Explain why venture capitalists would be willing to accept the risk of a new venture.

9. Show how the principle of leverage increases the rate of return on investment through the use of borrowed funds.

10. Marketable securities can be viewed as substitutes for cash. Explain.

CASE 19.1

DOMTAR INC.

AS AN OFFENSIVE guard, Pierre Desjardins lined up against some hefty competitors during his career with the Montreal Alouettes. Teammates recognized "Pierre was always the leader. You knew he was going to be a captain in football or industry." This battered lineman is now facing a challenge that makes his gruelling battles look like child's play. In the fall of 1990, Desjardins became the president and CEO of Domtar Inc.

Domtar Inc. is a mini-conglomerate which has interests in pulp and paper, packaging, and construction materials. The company has 10,800 employees scattered around 55 plants. This wide diversification developed over the years as an attempt to achieve growth in Canada's small domestic market.

Unfortunately, in 1990, before Desjardins arrived on the scene, the company had lost $294 million on $2.3 billion in revenue. In 1991, the company lost $148 million, and was showing a slight improvement. Two years previously, common shares traded at $13.50; the recent issue was priced at $6.00 (see Exhibit 1). Domtar, like most forestry companies, had been chopped down by a recession.

It was also being crippled by a billion-dollar debt incurred by the expansion in the 1980s. It was forced to dip into its credit line to cover interest. Operations have gluttonously consumed cash, and the firm faces costly environmental cleanups. But Pierre Desjardins remains confident. "I like sometimes to be on the edge. I don't get all my satisfaction out of things that are easy. When it gets easy, I get bored," he says.

He isn't bored these days, having just finished a gruelling Canada–United States road trip to sell a critical Domtar refinancing. It is a complex $1-billion deal involving a $500-million credit facility, and issues of notes and preferred and common shares.

Desjardins sees the financing as a vote of confidence for his cost cutting since joining the company eighteen months ago. He argues it gives him a few years of breathing space to implement a strategy that will shrink Domtar into a much more focussed firm. However, the financing details are a harsh judgement of the company's perilous condition. Covenants imposed by Domtar's

EXHIBIT 19.3 • DOMTAR: A SUMMARY FINANCIAL PICTURE

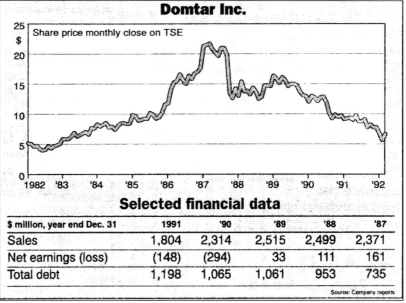

Domtar Inc.

Share price monthly close on TSE

Selected financial data

$ million, year end Dec. 31	1991	'90	'89	'88	'87
Sales	1,804	2,314	2,515	2,499	2,371
Net earnings (loss)	(148)	(294)	33	111	161
Total debt	1,198	1,065	1,061	953	735

Source: Company reports

(continued)

bankers have put it on one of the industry's shortest leashes, and, at a time when the prime rate ranged around 6 percent, it had to issue seven-year notes at a junk-bond rate of 11.75 percent.

Desjardins is adamant the recent financing will suffice for several years. The big capital projects are over, he says, and his financial projections are conservative. Sell-offs will ease the pressure, and cost cutting continues....

Along with the refinancing, Domtar, under Desjardins's leadership, has cut 3,000 jobs. Management layers were trimmed to two from six. The corporate office in Montreal has 120 bodies, down from 800. "Profit improvement and cost reduction are like a religion in this company," the no-nonsense CEO says.

Between the cost cutting and refinancing, Desjardins says he has fashioned a strategic vision. By 1995, the company will be in fewer businesses. Pierre and his management team see salvation in its state-of-the-art fine papers (i.e., sheets used for photocopying, envelopes, computer printouts, writing paper, and various business documents) plant in Windsor, Quebec. This plant will substantially increase its output and margins. Some or all of the rest of the smaller plants will be sold. "The financing plan means we don't have to get into fire sales, so it allows us to enhance the value of all these businesses. And second, it allows a more favourable mergers and acquisitions market to return to dispose of these assets," Desjardins says.

The task is not an easy one for the former football star. But football has taught him self-discipline and a sense of priorities. This rigid control is being transmitted to Domtar, and shareholders hope that it will prove successful.

Source: Adapted from Gordon Pitts, "Desjardins Puts It on the Line at Domtar," *The Financial Post*, March 30, 1992, pp. S18–S19.

Questions for Discussion

1. Why did the company diversify into so many activities and markets?

2. What factors led to the firm's cash-flow problems? Were any of these avoidable?

3. List the financial vehicles used by the company to try to solve the short- and medium-term financial pressures. Why were so many used? Suggest some reasons for the selection of each type.

4. Outline the steps taken by management to reduce expenses and produce profits once again.

5. In addition to the complex financial plan, the company realized that they needed a different strategic plan as well. What are the main elements of that plan?

CASE 19.2

THE LONG ROAD TO RECOVERY

IT'S BEEN A long way back for Frank Stronach, the ebullient founder and chairman of auto-parts producer Magna International Inc. Stronach has led Magna through a strong recovery and has lifted investor confidence. Analyst Steve Garmaise of First Marathon says he expects continued strong growth over the next two years. But the picture has not always been so optimistic for Magna.

After Stronach had made a success of the corporation, he attempted to diversify his product line. He ventured into magazine publishing and an upscale restaurant named after his daughter and Magna director, Belinda. He then left management to run for the Liberals in the 1988 federal

(continued)

election. Critics suggest that these were the seeds of Magna's problems. Stronach denies this and says the company expanded too quickly; too many of its plants were too young to produce the kinds of returns needed to pay down debts, even though the company enjoyed positive cash flow.

Magna began to unravel. Debts stood at $1 billion, causing the company to miss predetermined debt-to-equity ratios set by its lenders. Magna's shares, which are currently trading at $19.00, hit a low of $2.10 apiece during these difficult times. Investors had virtually given up the auto-parts producer for dead.

However, in late 1988, before the winter snow fell on Bay Street, Frank Stronach resumed the company helm and dived into a major restructuring program. This included the selling of three plants, closing the restaurant, stopping publication of two glossy magazines, and cutting back expenses.

First results of Stronach's handiwork came in the final half of 1991, when Magna's profits surged at a time that major auto giants were losing heavily because of declining auto sales. In the first quarter of the 1992 fiscal year, Magna reported net income of $25.5 million, compared with net income of only $16.5 million for all of the previous year, which ended July 31, 1991.

Reassured by that performance, investors quickly snapped up $100 million in new shares in November 1991. The money helped reduce debt to the point where Stronach predicted that Magna would be debt free in about three years. Mr. Stronach set a goal for the company to attain a maximum of 50 cents of debt for every dollar of equity. This goal was to be achieved within the next two years. Profits and cash flow will help Magna retire the $400 million of debt that will be outstanding after $200 million of debentures are converted to shares in this period, Stronach said.

In getting Magna back on its feet, Stronach said he learned some tough personal lessons, including the need to remain focussed, disciplined, and ever-vigilant to ensure that debt does not outstrip equity.

Source: Adapted from Cecil Foster, "A Kinder, Gentler Stronach in Wake of Magna Recovery," *The Financial Post*, January 13, 1992.

Questions for Discussion

1. Discuss the phases Magna has gone through.

2. Analyze the steps taken in Stronach's restructuring plan.

3. One of Magna's goals is to achieve "a maximum of 50 cents of debt for every dollar of equity." What are the implications of this objective?

4. Have Stronach's plans worked? Has he attained his goals? Check this out in the business section of your library.

PHOTO CREDITS

FIN 6   Photo courtesy of Dominion Textile Inc.   FIN 8   The Cadillac Fairview Corporation Limited

MODULE

◆ SEC ◆

INVESTORS AND THE SECURITIES MARKETS

THE FOCUS OF THIS MODULE

1. To describe the nature of securities and the securities market

2. To discuss various types of stock and bonds

3. To describe the securities exchanges and the way that securities are bought and sold

4. To explain how investors can follow the stock market through commonly reported securities transaction information

5. To discuss the reasons why people and institutions invest

6. To describe the nature of mutual funds

7. To define the following terms:

KEY TERMS

securities	callable bond
underwriter	stock exchange
common shares	stockbroker
par value	over-the-counter (OTC) market
book value	futures contract
market value	board lot
pre-emptive right	odd lot
preferred shares	bull
cumulative preferred shares	bear
non-cumulative preferred shares	price–earnings ratio
convertible preferred shares	TSE 300 Composite Index
maturity date	institutional investor
secured bond	individual investor
debenture	speculation
convertible bond	investment
serial bond	yield
sinking fund	mutual fund

ALTHOUGH HER EARLY YEARS on a Saskatchewan farm taught her the value of a dollar, Trudy Poggemiller had no time or money to learn about investing until after she had worked her way though medical school. But, once she began practising family medicine in Don Mills, Ontario, she began reading up on tax shelters. Soon she was tucking $5,500 a year (the maximum allowable) into government investment certificate (GIC)–type registered retirement savings plans (RRSPs). Why GICs? "I wanted something secure, and I wanted to find out what [investment] was all about," Poggemiller says.

She quickly learned to do comparison shopping by calling the big banks. "You ask, is there a front-end [charge]? Is there a back-end [charge]? What is your management fee? What is the percentage [paid in interest]? How much do I have to put in? What terms [to maturity] do you offer?

"It's pretty basic. Anybody can do it."

Anybody can also make a mistake. Hers, she discovered, lay in buying GICs that all mature in the same year. Then she had to roll everything over into new interest-bearing securities just when the rates were far from enticing. From now on, she will stagger the due dates to protect herself from short-term dips in interest rates.

Of course, that one miscue in timing the maturity of her GICs has not affected the return so far. Thanks to yields of 10 to 13 percent, Poggemiller's three GICs have already grown in value, from $16,500 to $20,000. When these savings reach $60,000, she will move on to phase II of a three-phase plan: another $60,000 worth of RRSPs will gradually be invested in various bonds and mutual funds. Phase III, farther in the future, calls for another $60,000 to go into RRSPs invested in common stocks and preferred shares.

Poggemiller has a specific long-term objective. "By the time I am ready to retire, I hope I am over the million [-dollar] mark."

That is no pipedream. Mathematically, if she maintains her annual $5,500 contribution (not including any increased contribution limits that may be allowed) and manages an annual yield of 10 percent, compounded year after year, Trudy Poggemiller will hit her million-dollar target before she is 63 years old.

Source: Excerpt from Hal Tennant, "Head Start on $1 Million," *Your Money*, February 1987, p. 71.

The funds invested by Trudy Poggemiller are typical of the investments made by individuals. If money is invested systematically, the process of compounding interest builds a substantial sum over time. This is why financial counsellors encourage young people to start to save money early and systematically. A young person, aged 22, investing $1,000 per year at 8 percent interest would have built up an asset of more than $122,000 by the time he or she is 52. In another ten years, this amount would more than double, to

$263,000, at the same interest rate, even if no additional investments were made.

Trudy Poggemiller's investment strategy is one side of financing. The other side is the firm trying to raise some funds from potential investors. Don Low's experience shows that other aspect.

DON LOW WAS CONSUMED by a dream: to turn his new venture, Flash Pack Ltd., into a household name by opening a minimum of 150 franchises across Canada within three years. Flash Pack specialized in custom foam packaging, crating, and shipping. In the same way that a travel agent arranges trips, the company finds the best way to send consumers' parcels anywhere. For example, it will ensure that a shipment of fine china to Aunt May in another city can be done safely, easily, and cheaply. It will do the same for business organizations.

Low realized that a great deal of capital would be needed to get the company off the ground and expanding quickly. He had already spent $650,000, and expected to need another $1 million in the next year. He decided to raise this by going public.

Going public means giving up a percentage of the ownership of the business and facing the pressure of shareholders. It is also expensive since a prospectus must be prepared and brokerage commissions must be paid. But the prospect of raising a lot of money outweighed the disadvantages. Many franchisors are content to open one or two stores at a time and grow slowly, but with U.S. competitors already moving into Canada, Low had no time to waste.

His first step was to gain credibility by setting up two franchises. In addition to his own resources, he raised $5 million privately through friends and investors. This paid for the franchises, and his cost of preparation for going public. One significant expense was $85,000 for a prospectus.

His next step was to find one or more stockbrokeraging companies who would underwrite and sell the shares. This was not an easy task. Stockbrokeraging companies had to be convinced that the business idea was a good one, and would be attractive to the market.

By mid-June, 1,050,000 shares were sold at 60 cents. This was down from the $1.00 per share that Low had hoped to raise. Flash Pack was able to raise $550,000 after paying $74,000 in brokerage commissions.

Low was pleased that his company was able to complete the offering. "I'm very proud that we achieved it," he says. On the basis of the funds raised, expansion began with the opening of five Flash Pack stores in Toronto and one in Vancouver. Don Low is now optimistic about the spread of his business throughout the country.

Source: Excerpt from Tim Falconer, "Handle with Care," *Canadian Business*, October 1988, p. 115.

Such investments by individuals are sources of capital for business organizations.

FUNDING A BUSINESS

A firm can use two sources for the funds it needs: equity capital and debt capital. It can generate equity capital by selling shares of stock, giving investors part ownership in the company. It can raise further capital by issuing corporate bonds, promising bondholders a set rate of interest and the return of the principal at a specified date. Companies issue stock and bonds for specific reasons: plant expansion, product development, acquisition of another company, or any of a range of business projects. Thus, investors play an important part in helping business firms grow. Stock (or shares—the terms are used more or less interchangeably) and bonds are **securities**: evidence of ownership or indebtedness. Because these "pieces of paper" are backed by real assets, they are readily bought and sold.

The decision to raise money by selling shares, or bonds, in the market is significant in that the owners are sharing their holdings with others or assuming a considerable debt. A formal process is required, controlled by provincial securities commissions, to ensure a fair and honest offering to the public. First, the company must decide how many dollars are to be raised. Next, it must choose the type of securities (shares or bonds) to be offered. A prospectus describing the offering must be prepared, meeting specific requirements.

The firm also must find one or more brokerage firms to underwrite the offering. An **underwriter** agrees to purchase the shares or bonds (at a set price or on a "best efforts basis") and to bring them to the market, thus guaranteeing their sale. Securities are generally offered to the public the day after the issue is cleared by a provincial securities commission.

COMMON OR PREFERRED SHARES?

Shares of stock are units of ownership in the equity (or stock) of a corporation. Both common and preferred shares represent ownership but bring with them different privileges and offer different rewards. Every corporation issues common shares; it may choose also to issue preferred shares.

Common Shares

Investors buy **common shares** in the hope of future rewards: dividends paid out of the earnings of the corporation and capital gains if the value of their shares increases. They also take the risk that the company may do poorly or fail, in which case there will be no dividends, and the value of their shares will decrease or disappear completely.

Common shareholders have the right to influence the direction and policies of the corporation at shareholders' meetings, by electing the board of directors and voting on other important issues, such as the acquisition or sale of a subsidiary company. Voting is on the basis of one vote per common share; that is, the owner of 1,000 shares has 1,000 votes, and the owner of 10 shares has 10. The privileges of ownership and control carry with them the responsibility to see that the corpora-

securities

Stocks and bonds that, because they are backed by real assets, can be readily bought and sold

underwriter

A stockbroker who agrees to bring a new securities issue to the market, guaranteeing its sale

common shares

Shares whose owners have voting rights and a residual claim to the firm's assets after all creditors and preferred shareholders have been paid

tion's debts and obligations to preferred shareholders are met before common shareholders receive dividends.

How much is a share worth? It depends on one's perspective. The share was initially sold for a certain price. (This is the only time the corporation receives funds in return for the equity represented by the share.) Sometimes that amount is printed on the share certificate, and that is known as the share's **par value**. Because share values change, the par value often soon becomes meaningless, so most firms today issue no-par-value share certificates, with no amount shown. Exhibit 20.1 shows a no-par-value share certificate. More important to investors are the share's book value and its market value. The **book value** is the value of the corporation's assets less all its liabilities and the value of its preferred shares and divided by the number of common shares. The **market value** is the price at which the share is currently being traded and can be ascertained by checking the stock market quotations in the daily newspaper. The market valuation is based on the public's perception of the firm's future prospects as well as its current earnings. Book value and market value are usually close, but seldom identical.

par value
The value printed on some share certificates; that is, the price at which they were first issued

book value (of a share)
The value of the corporation's assets, less its liabilities and the value of its preferred shares, divided by the number of common shares

market value
The price at which a share is currently being traded

EXHIBIT 20.1 • A SHARE CERTIFICATE

Reprinted with permission from Stelco Inc.

Sometimes, a corporation decides to raise additional funds by issuing more common shares. This, of course, dilutes the ownership—and level of control—of existing shareholders. Usually, the corporation gives the existing shareholders a **pre-emptive right** to buy the new shares in proportion to their present ownership before the shares are offered to the general public. In other words, a shareholder who owns 200 shares in a corporation with 10,000 shares that decides to issue another 5,000 shares will have the opportunity to buy 100 of the new shares, maintaining 2 percent ownership.

Preferred Shares

Preferred shares have a more certain rate of return than do common shares. They appeal to more conservative investors who are looking for a reasonably steady source of income. **Preferred shares** receive preferential treatment in the payment of dividends, carrying a fixed dividend (the amount is noted on the share certificate) in each year that a dividend is declared, regardless of the total earnings of the firm. Only after preferred shareholders have received their dividends are payments made on common shares. These may be less—or much greater—than the dividends on preferred shares.

All corporations have common shares but not all choose to issue preferred shares. This type of share offering is made by companies that wish to raise additional equity capital but do not want to dilute the power of the present owners. Preferred shareholders become part owners of the corporation, but because their investment offers less risks, it involves fewer privileges. Preferred shareholders have extremely limited voting rights and therefore little control over the direction and management of the corporation. On the other hand, should the company be dissolved, their claim on the assets of the corporation precedes that of common shareholders, though it is recognized only after all liabilities, including the claims of bondholders, have been met.

Preferred shares may be cumulative or non-cumulative—and the distinction is important. **Cumulative preferred shares** entitle shareholders to receive all dividends in arrears before any dividends are paid to common shareholders. Suppose ABC Corporation has a cumulative preferred share issue carrying a dividend of $3. In the face of poor performance, the board of directors decides not to declare a dividend for two years in succession; this means no shareholders receive dividends in these years. In the third year, performance improves, and the board declares a dividend. Before the common shareholders receive any money, the cumulative preferred shareholders must receive $9 per share—$3 for the current year and $6 to cover the two years in which dividends were not declared. In contrast, suppose DEF Company Ltd. has a **non-cumulative preferred share** issue carrying the same dividend. In a similar situation, the preferred shareholders receive only the $3 for the year in which the dividend was declared.

Frequently, a conversion feature is included as part of a preferred share issue that allows the holder to convert the security into a

---

pre-emptive right
The rights of present shareholders to buy shares in a new issue in proportion to their present ownership before the shares are offered to the general public

preferred shares
Shares whose owners received a fixed dividend in each year that a dividend is declared and have first claim to the firm's assets after all creditors have been paid

cumulative preferred shares
Shares that entitle the shareholder to receive all dividends in arrears before anything is paid to common shareholders

non-cumulative preferred shares
Shares that entitle the shareholder to receive dividends only for the years in which dividends are declared

different type of share. Such an option describes **convertible preferred shares**, and the standard conversion is from preferred shares to common shares at a stated price. A conversion feature adds marketability to a share issue.

convertible preferred shares
Preferred shares with an added feature permitting the holder to convert them to common shares at a stated price

By definition, preferred shares represent equity capital. For the investor, however, their special dividend feature makes them a compromise between bonds and common shares. The stated dividend is usually higher than bonds would bring, but considerably lower than the *possible* earnings on common shares. Unless the firm is in trouble, the shares themselves will maintain a fairly consistent value because the maximum rate of return is fixed. Common shares fluctuate widely in value according to the fortunes of the corporation. The possibility of complete loss, should the corporation fail, is always present.

BONDS

Bonds are a way of raising long-term debt capital. The corporation issuing bonds borrows money from the bondholders, who in return receive specified interest payments (usually semi-annually) and the face value of the bond at the **maturity date**. As creditors rather than owners of a corporation, in the event of bankruptcy, bondholders are entitled to a claim on the firm's assets before any claim can be made by preferred or common shareholders. Corporate bonds are normally issued in denominations from $1,000 to $50,000. Since no ownership is involved, municipal, provincial, and federal governments also use bond issues as sources of funds. Canada Savings Bonds are made available in smaller denominations than most corporate bonds to encourage the average citizen to invest.

maturity date
The date at which the face value of a bond or loan must be repaid

All bonds are fixed income securities in the sense that the issuing corporation agrees to pay a specific rate of interest. However, there are several types of bonds to choose from.

Secured Bonds

Holders of **secured bonds** have first claim to the assets securing those bonds in the event of bankruptcy. These assets could include real property and personal property such as furniture, machinery, and even the stocks and bonds of other companies owned by the borrowing firm. A company such as Canadian Pacific might raise a large proportion of the funds it requires for long-term financing by listing equipment such as locomotives and railcars as collateral for bonds.

secured bond
A bond backed by specific company assets

Like all investors, people who buy bonds balance returns with risks. Because these bonds are secured by a corporation's assets, they involve less risk than do securities not backed by such collateral. Therefore, secured bonds offer purchasers lower interest rates than do unsecured bonds.

Debentures

Many companies do issue unsecured bonds, called **debentures**. These are not secured by specific property but rather by the general reputation of the corporation. Only extremely credit-worthy firms can find buyers for debentures. Bell Canada has used debentures to raise several million dollars.

debenture
An unsecured bond, backed only by the reputation of the issuing organization

Canadian Pacific Limited, one of Canada's largest companies, operates in such diversified areas as transportation, energy, real estate, telecommunications and environmental management. CP offers investors assets which can produce shareholder value. Its top priority in 1994 is to improve the CP Rail System to a competitive level with the American railroad industry, and in so doing, attract investors.

Convertible Bonds

convertible bond
A bond that can be converted into a specified amount of common stock at the option of the bondholder

Some companies offer **convertible bonds** that are covered by a bond indenture, allowing bondholders to convert the bonds into a predefined number of shares of the company's common stock. For example, suppose that, according to the bond indenture, a $1,000 bond is convertible into 50 shares of common stock in GHI Corporation. This means a share price of $20. The bondholder would not convert the bond when shares are $18 each on the day the bond is purchased. However, if the market value increases to $30, the bondholder might choose to convert—or sell the bond for the $1,500 it is now worth.

Retiring Bonds

All bonds have a maturity date, and corporations must have the capital available to repay the face value of the bonds at that time. Before a bond issue is approved by the provincial securities commission, the corporation must demonstrate its plan for retiring the bonds.

serial bond
A bond from an issue of bonds that reach maturity in different years

One approach is to issue **serial bonds**, with parts of the issue reaching maturity in different years. In this way, the corporation will be able to repay only a small proportion of the principal each year. Suppose JKL Corporation floats a $3-million serial bond issue to be retired by 30 years from now. It might arrange to divide the issue into fifteen equal lots, with the first lot maturing fifteen years from now and the others in successive years. It would then repay $200,000 a year, starting in the sixteenth year.

sinking fund
A fund to which a firm makes annual payments to ensure that its bonds can be retired at their maturity

Another approach is to establish a **sinking fund** in which the corporation would make annual payments to provide funds to retire the bonds at maturity. A bond trustee is appointed to ensure that the issuer fulfils its contractual responsibilities.

Some firms issue **callable bonds** that allow them to redeem the bonds, usually for a premium, after a certain period. MNO Corporation might float a twenty-year bond issue at 7 percent interest, callable at any point after ten years. If interest rates fall to 5 percent, the corporation will probably want to call the bonds and pay the premium rather than continue to pay the higher rate. On the other hand, if interest rates rise to 9 percent, the corporation would be more likely to let the bonds reach maturity and meanwhile invest the money more profitably. Table 20.1 lists types of bonds and their characteristics.

callable bond
A bond that the issuing corporation can redeem, usually for a premium, before its maturity date

The Trade in Bonds

Bonds are bought and sold on securities markets, often for more or less than their face value. Assuming that the firm that issued the bond is sound and is expected to be able to redeem the bond on its maturity rate, what affects the price of a bond is the relationship of the current interest rate to that paid by the bond.

Suppose you hold a $1,000 bond that paid 8 percent interest, but current interest rates are only 4 percent. If you decide to sell the bond, you should be able to get more than $1,000 for it, because if the purchaser invested at the current rate, the return would be only half as much. This raises the value of your bond. Conversely, if current interest rates are higher than the rate paid by your bond, you would have to settle for a lower price to compensate the purchaser, who could do better by investing elsewhere. In other words, as interest rates fall, bond prices rise; as interest rates rise, bond prices fall.

TABLE 20.1 • TYPES AND CHARACTERISTICS OF BONDS

Types of Bonds	Characteristics
Secured bonds	Backed by specific pledges of company assets — real or personal property
Unsecured bonds (debentures)	Backed not by specific pledges of assets but by the financial reputation of the issuing corporation
Convertible bonds	Can be converted into common stock at the option of the bondholder
Serial bonds	A large issue, parts of which mature at different dates
Sinking-fund bonds	Backed by yearly deposits by the corporation of funds sufficient to redeem the bonds when they mature
Callable (or redeemable) bonds	Give the issuing corporation the option of redeeming the bonds (usually at a premium) prior to their maturity date

Source: Adapted from New York Stock Exchange, *Fact Book 1981*, p. 28.

BUSINESS REVIEW 20.1

---

1. Describe the nature of securities.
2. What are shares? Outline and define the various types.
3. What are bonds? Outline and define the various types.

THE SECURITIES EXCHANGES

stock exchange
A regulated market for trading stock bonds, and other investment vehicles

Securities exchanges are a regulated marketplace for trading stocks, bonds, and other investment vehicles. They are commonly known as **stock exchanges**. The firms whose securities are traded receive only the proceeds on the initial sale when the stock or bond issue is under-written by stockbrokers. From that point, the firms are not involved in the trading and are not directly affected by stock market gains or losses. It is stockbrokers who handle the initial sale to investors and subsequent trading of securities between investors. The firms are not part of these transactions.

stockbroker
An intermediary, or middleman, who buys and sells securities for clients

Only stockbrokers may trade on the stock exchanges. A **stockbroker** is an intermediary (or middleman) who buys and sells securities for clients.

The Toronto Stock Exchange (TSE)

There are five Canadian stock exchanges, but when investors talk about "the stock market," they are usually referring to the Toronto Stock Exchange (TSE), which is the largest stock exchange in Canada. In order to transact business on the TSE, a brokerage firm must be a member. There are usually about 80 member firms, each having purchased one or more "seats" on the exchange. The price of a seat is around $200,000. Each representative must meet certain basic qualifications of education and be accepted by the exchange management.

The securities of virtually all the major publicly held companies are listed (traded) on the TSE—approximately 1,300 stocks and bond issued by 850 companies. Several million shares are traded daily. Approximately 80 percent of the dollar value, and 45 percent of the total number, of listed shares traded in Canada are traded on the TSE.

Other Canadian Stock Exchanges

The remainder of the trading on Canadian exchanges takes place at four regional and local exchanges. The largest of these is in Montreal; the others are in Vancouver, Calgary, and Winnipeg. Often, companies listed on these exchanges are also listed on the TSE. These exchanges trade mainly in the shares of smaller firms operating within a limited geographic area. As well as the shares of larger companies, many smaller, more speculative stocks are often traded here.

Foreign Stock Exchanges

The world's oldest stock exchange is the Amsterdam Stock Exchange, which started trading in 1611. The London Stock Exchange, listing

The Toronto Stock Exchange is a not-for-profit organization owned and operated by more than 70 member firms, also known as brokerage houses. Membership entitles a brokerage firm to use the Exchange's facilities and 30,000-square-foot trading floor to buy and sell securities for their clients and themselves.

more than 10,000 stocks, goes back to the eighteenth century. The New York Stock Exchange is the world's largest. Many Canadian companies are listed on major foreign exchanges, such as those in Tokyo, Hong Kong, Paris, Zurich, Frankfurt, Johannesburg, Melbourne, and Copenhagen.

THE OVER-THE-COUNTER (OTC) MARKET

Individuals who are interested in investing in certain companies may not find their stocks listed on the Toronto Stock Exchange or on any of the other regional exchanges. There are about 2,100 securities traded in the **over-the-counter (OTC) market**. Actually, the OTC market is not a real place at all. It is simply a method of trading unlisted securities outside the organized securities exchanges. It is a network of securities dealers and brokers throughout Canada who buy and sell unlisted stocks and bonds by telephone. Supply and demand, which determine price, are established through regular contact. Securities dealers in the OTC market often purchase shares in their own name. When a prospective buyer appears, they sell these shares at a profit, if possible. A broker who has none of the wanted shares in inventory will call other brokers to make purchases at the lowest possible price for resale.

over-the-counter (OTC) market
The trading of securities not listed on a stock exchange through a network of dealers and brokers

THE FUTURES MARKET

Actual securities are not the only items traded on the stock exchange. A buyer may also invest in futures contracts. **Futures contracts** guarantee the price at which the number of shares of some stock or amount of some commodity covered by the contract will exchange hands at some specified later date. *Canadian Business* describes futures contracts this way:

futures contract
A commitment to trade a commodity or shares of stock for a set price at a specified later date

Unlike options contracts that give the buyer the right (or the option) to purchase or sell a stock, bond, currency, or amount of gold, futures contracts *commit* the holder to take delivery of commodities or financial instruments for a specified price, at some specified date in the future. Few investors actually do take delivery, of course. The game plan for futures players is to keep an alert eye on the price of, say, soybeans, pork bellies, or treasury bills, and, if the price climbs—thus boosting the value of the contract—to unload the contract at a profit. If the price falls, the investor could easily end up in deep financial trouble.

But this is one of the few remaining corners of the investment supermarket where a tough-skinned, financially liquid speculator can hit the jackpot. Cash requirements for futures trading are low—a margin of 5 to 10 percent of the contract price, depending on the commodity or financial instrument and the broker. If you do pay, say, $3,000 down on a contract for 5,000 bushels of soybeans to be delivered at $6 a bushel next May, however, the margin required to maintain the contract could be raised far and fast if the price of the beans begins to soften. But then, soybeans could soar to $8 a bushel by spring, and your profit on the contract would turn out to be $2 a bushel, or $10,000, minus your $3,000 down payment and commission.

The futures market isn't merely a playpen for speculators, though. Those who *sell* the primary contracts are invariably hedgers. A farmer who borrows cash to plant his corn crop could be asked by his bank to sell two futures contracts (5,000 bushels each) for September delivery at $2.54 a bushel. In other words, the farmer has locked in his price by selling his corn in advance and the bank's loan is guaranteed, even if the price of corn slumps to $2.00. The price of corn could soar by September, of course. But, even so, the farmer is assured of his $2.54 a bushel, so he can repay his loan and turn a nice profit on his remaining crop.

The largest percentage of commodities futures trading in Canada is done on the Winnipeg Commodity Exchange. Trading in financial futures has been the exclusive preserve of the Toronto Stock Exchange and the Montreal Exchange.[1]

BUYING AND SELLING SECURITIES

Investing in securities, as distinct from keeping money in a bank account, requires a stockbroker or investment dealer, who buys and sells securities according to the customer's instructions. Suppose you have $500 you wish to invest. If you do not have a stockbroker, you might ask a friend or colleague to recommend one. Failing that, you can check the stockbrokerage firms listed in the Yellow Pages of your telephone directory. Most cities have offices of major brokerage firms, such as Burns Fry, Midland Walwyn, Nesbitt Thompson, Richardson Greenshields of Canada, and Wood Gundy, as well as smaller firms.

Your broker will want to discuss your objectives. Are you looking for short-term profit? long-term gain? both? The broker will then identify a selection of stocks and bonds that seem to meet your needs. When you have decided what, and how much, you want to buy, the broker places the order.

Suppose, for example, that you have dual goals: income and growth. XYZ Company shares may suit you. Your broker can determine the current trading facts on the stock by referring to a computer that has on-line TSE and other market information.

Stocks are typically traded in multiples known as board lots. A **board lot** is a trading unit made up of a set number of shares; that number depends on the stock price. For securities priced at $1.00 and over, a board lot equals 100 shares; for those priced between $0.10 and $0.99, a board lot equals 500 shares; and for those priced below $0.10, a board lot equals 1,000 shares. You can also buy or sell **odd lots**, a number of shares fewer than a board lot.

At the TSE, stocks priced at less than $5.00 are quoted in dollars and cents. Traditionally, quotations of share prices at and above $5.00 are quoted in eighths of a dollar. For example, a quote of $15⅛ equals $15.125.

Your broker's information shows the most recent sale price for the stock as well as the current quotation (the bid and ask). The *bid* is the highest price anyone is willing to pay for a stock (for example, $16¼). The *ask* is the lowest price at which anyone is willing to sell the stock (e.g., $16⅝). Using this information, you can decide what price you are willing to pay for XYZ shares.

You then authorize your broker to place a market order at the asking price. Or you can place a limit order at some lower price (e.g., $16½), and your order will automatically be traded if sufficient shares become available at that price, or a better one.

The brokerage firm directs your order to the appropriate destination for execution. In the case of the TSE, the days of the hectic floor trading system depicted in the movies has ended. As of 1994, orders sent to the TSE are handled by the Computer-Assisted Trading System (CATS). Orders are entered by traders directly into the market through trading terminals located in the brokerage firm offices. Trades are executed automatically when stock becomes available on the opposite side of the market. Printed trade confirmations are immediately sent to both the buyer's and the seller's brokers.

After your order is filled, your stockbroker will call you to confirm the trade. The brokerage firm will also mail you a written confirmation. You must pay the broker the price of the shares plus the broker's commission within five business days after the day of the trade.

The Costs of Trading

Brokerage firms charge commissions to both buyers and sellers for securities transactions. Charges are usually a percentage of the total value of the trade but can vary among brokers according to volume and services rendered, decreasing as the dollar value of the transaction increases. The fee is a little higher when shares are traded in odd lots to cover the extra paperwork. As with all retailing situations, competition has led to the establishment of discount brokers.

Bulls and Bears

Some investors expect the stock market to rise; others that it will fall. Those investors who believe stock prices will rise are known as **bulls**.

board lot
A trade of 100 shares, the quantity in which the shares are usually traded

odd lot
A trade of fewer than 100 shares, grouped with other odd lots to make one or more board lots

bull
An investor who believes stock prices will increase and who buys to profit from the rise

bear
An investor who believes stock prices
will decrease and who sells to avoid loss

They buy securities in order to profit from the rising prices. A market in which stock prices are rising overall is referred to as a "bull market." In contrast, **bears** are investors who believe stock prices will fall. Bears sell securities to avoid the decline in market prices that they anticipate. A market in which stock prices are decreasing overall is referred to as a "bear market."

Regulating Securities Transactions

Regulation of the sale of securities is under provincial jurisdiction. Provinces have enacted regulatory legislation, and each of the exchanges in Canada is incorporated under provincial law. The exchanges possess self-regulatory powers, and have developed extensive controls over their members through various bylaws and regulations. The basic objective of these controls is to protect investors from securities trading abuses and stock manipulations that have occurred in the past both in Canada and elsewhere by (a) assuring orderly markets, and (b) maintaining the financial responsibilities of member firms.

As discussed earlier, the important requirement for the protection of investors is that full disclosure of relevant financial information must be made by companies desiring to sell new stock or bond issues to the general public. This information is included in a booklet called a prospectus, which must be furnished to purchasers.

Brokers or Promoters?

The broker who negotiates the purchase of shares of XYZ Company for you is unlikely to push one stock to the exclusion of others. You make your own decisions. Under stock market regulations, the broker should merely provide the service of making the purchase, offering advice and perhaps guiding you away from poor investments, but ultimately following your instructions. Stock promoters are interested in gaining investment money for particular firms. The risks of dealing with stock promoters are discussed in Issues in Business 20.1.

ISSUES IN BUSINESS 20.1

STOCK PROMOTERS' HYPE CAN COST YOU YOUR SHIRT

STOCK PROMOTERS ARE a special breed of sales people.... But unless you want to lose your shirt, you had better know how they operate because there are no money-back guarantees.

Promoters fill the void between brokers, who are authorized to offer investment advice under the "full, true and plain disclosure" creed of their industry, and company management, which is charged with developing the business. One exchange that has many promoters is the Vancouver Stock Exchange (VSE).

In theory, a promoter drums up investment for a company and sometimes acts as a market maker, usually in exchange for shares in the company. Sometimes the theory works.

(continued)

When two Ontario prospectors staked the Hemlo gold claim several years ago, they got their drilling money by approaching a Toronto promoter. He brought the deal to Vancouver promoter Murray Pezim, who put the claims into one of his 70 or so VSE-listed companies. Hemlo turned out to be the biggest Canadian gold find in years, making money for a great many people.

But few VSE listings do that well. One study found that only about one in five issues actually increases in value over the long term, while many others fall into inactive oblivion. Many VSE promoters have discovered, for example, that it's often easier to convince the public they have found gold than it is to actually find it.

Not that investors are blameless. Most of them are speculators looking for quick capital gains. They, too, are less interested in the company finding gold than they are in the market thinking it will find gold.

Stock promotion can, and often does, become a paper game where promoters go to great lengths to increase share prices and unload their stocks at or near the top of the market. It's called stock manipulation and many of the techniques are illegal, although hard to prove....

A broker who promises a client that a stock will double in price has broken industry rules and could be disciplined. However, a promoter who does the same thing is just an enthusiastic salesperson.

Promoters are about the only people in the industry who are not licensed in some way, so they can be a real problem. There is no way of disciplining them or controlling what they do.

The VSE is particularly vulnerable to such practices because of the nature of its listings. For the most part, these are junior companies engaged in mining exploration—they either win big or lose completely.

In addition, the number of shares outstanding is relatively low; thus, someone can get a little more control over it. And third, the price is low. Those combinations make ideal targets for somebody who wishes to manipulate stock.

Source: *The Globe and Mail*, July 5, 1985, p. B9. Reprinted with permission of the Canadian Press.

Questions for Discussion

1. What are the advantages of stock promotion?
2. Can the average investor take advantage of the information stock promoters can provide and avoid making mistakes? Explain.

FOLLOWING THE STOCK MARKET

Most daily newspapers include several pages of stock market quotations and news from the world of finance. Keeping up-to-date is important for investors because of the dynamic, rapidly changing nature of the market. The volume of sales and closing prices of all stocks and bonds listed on the major exchanges are given. (It takes a little skill to interpret them, however.) More succinct market news is given on many radio and television newscasts.

Stock Quotations

Exhibit 20.2 is reproduced from *The Financial Times of Canada*. It shows a portion of the weekly stock trend summary on March 12. Suppose we follow the progress of one particular stock, Alberta Natural Gas. The highest price for that stock in the past year was $18.25 per share;

EXHIBIT 20.2 • WEEKLY STOCK SUMMARY

Highest and lowest price for the past 52 weeks. Prices are quoted in fractions; hence, 14¼ is $14.75

Δ **Indicates a weak bullish trend.** The stock's 13-week moving average is above its 40-week moving average, but the short-term price trend is weakening. A long-term trend reversal.

∇ **Indicates a weak bearish trend.** The stock's 13-week moving average is below its 40-week moving average, but the short-term price trend is weakening. A long-term trend reversal.

▼ **Indicates a bearish trend.** The stock's 13-week moving average is below its 40-week moving average, and the short-term price trend is weak.

▲ **Indicates a bearish trend.** The stock's 13-week moving average is above its 40-week moving average, and the short-term price trend is strong.

Abbreviation indicates the name of the company

Price at the close of the week's trading

% change in the price of the stock since last week

Number of shares traded in one week

The relative strength indicator measures a stock's performance relative to the Toronto Stock Exchange Composite 300 Index over the last 13 weeks. Values over 100 indicate the stock is outperforming the TSE 3009. Values under 100 indicate the stock is underperforming the TSE 300. The following + or – signs indicate that relative strength is rising or falling.

Company names are followed by the following footnotes: nv – non-voting, sv – subordinate voting, rv – restricted voting, j – special reporting rules. Stock-trading symbols include: .PR if the stock is a preferred share, .WT if it is a warrant, .UN if it is a unit, .RT if it is a right.

		CLOSE	% CHANGE	VOLUME 100s	REL. STR.	52 WK HI	52 WK LO	YIELD
▼ Aurzon j	ARZ	0.82	1.2	1922	88-	1.09	0.30	
▲ Autrex	AUT.A	1.25	-	31	121-	1.30	0.80	29.6
▼ Autrex	AUT.B	1.00	-	nt ☆	97-	1.25	1.00	37.0
▼ Azco Mining	AZC	3.15	-	924	98-	4.25	1.80	
Aztec Res	AZL	2.40	4.0	149	92-	3.95	2.40	-
▲ BAA	BAA	19.50	-2.5	2 ☆	98-	21.00	13.50	-
▽ Baca j	BZL.A	0.30	-40.0	69 ☆	170-	0.75	0.15	-
▲ Baja Gold	BGJ	1.75	-2.8	2058	161-	2.10	1.01	-
Ballard Powr	BLD	5.75	-4.2	1032 ★	85-	8.00	5.25	-
Ballard P	BLD.WT	1.75	-	3 ☆	65-	2.60	1.12	-
▽ Ballistic Ene	BAL	6.00	4.3	1614	119+	7.00	2.80	-
▲ Banister	BAC	17.38	6.9	1503 ★	105+	17.50	11.00	-
▲ Bank of Mtl	BMO	28.00	-1.3	41075	98-	30.75	22.75	4.3
▼ BMO 4	BMO.PR.D	28.38	-	84 ☆	95-	30.00	27.25	7.9
▲ BMO 1	BMO.PR.E	31.25	-	186	100-	32.25	28.75	7.2
▲ Bank NS	BNS	30.25	-	18076	97-	33.25	23.25	3.8
▲ BNS 1	BNS.PR.A	23.88	-	1962	100-	23.88	20.50	4.0
BNS 3	BNS.PR.B	20.25	-	206 ☆	95-	21.00	20.00	8.7
BNS 4	BNS.PR.C	27.25	-	123 ☆	94-	28.12	26.00	8.3
BNS 5	BNS.PR.D	29.00	0.4	537	95-	29.75	27.25	8.0
Bnk NS	BNS.PR.E	27.50	0.5	298	96-	28.88	25.00	6.5
▼ Barrington j	BPL	5.12	3.5	2711	99+	7.25	3.50	-
▲ Batoa	BNB	7.88	1.6	390	100-	7.88	5.25	-
▼ Battle Creek j	BCV	2.55	4.1	621	104+	4.50	1.90	-
▲ Battl Mount	BMG	15.00	-	nt ☆	115-	15.00	7.25	-
▼ BC Bancorp	BBC	1.27	-	325 ☆	94-	1.81	1.24	39.4
BC Gas	BCG	16.00	0.8	2929	-	17.25	15.12	5.6
BC Gs	BGU.PR.A	25.62	-5.1	1 ☆	86-	29.00	25.38	8.4
BC Rail	BCL.PR.A	26.00	-	86 ☆	95-	27.00	25.38	8.9
△ BC Sugar	BCS.A	10.25	-2.4	1809	98-	11.75	8.88	3.9
▲ BC Sugr	BCS.PR.C	15.00	-	nt ☆	102-	16.00	13.88	6.7
▲ BC Tel	BT.PR.A	65.00	-	nt ☆	99-	65.00	58.50	6.7
▲ BC Tel	BT.PR.B	65.00	-3.0	5z ☆	100-	67.00	57.00	6.9
▲ BC Tel	BT.PR.C	70.00	-	1 ☆	99-	72.00	62.00	6.8
▲ BC Tel	BT.PR.D	72.00	2.8	2	99+	72.00	68.00	6.6
▲ BC Tel	BT.PR.E	20.50	-	25	99-	21.50	16.50	5.9
▲ BC Tel	BT.PR.F	77.00	2.7	1 ☆	99+	77.00	64.00	6.7
▲ BC Tel	BT.PR.G	83.00	-3.5	1 ☆	95-	89.00	73.00	6.9
▲ BC Tel	BT.PR.H	85.50	0.9	11z ☆	94-	86.00	74.00	7.0
▲ BC Tel	BT.PR.J	26.00	4.5	3 ☆	101+	26.25	22.62	6.5
▲ BC Tel	BT.PR.L	25.88	-	nt ☆	98-	26.75	24.00	6.8
▲ BC Telecom	BCT	26.00	-1.0	1791	107-	26.25	18.75	4.6
▲ BCE	B	50.50	3.1	79345 ★	106+	52.12	42.00	5.3
BCE M	B.PR.M	26.50	-2.3	2000 ★	97-	28.25	26.25	7.4
BCE O	B.PR.O	42.75	-0.9	205 ☆	96-	44.00	42.00	6.3
▲ BCE	B.WT	6.00	-20.0	57000 ★	167+	7.12	2.11	-
▲ BCE Mobile	BCX	39.75	-	5072 ★	95-	45.00	36.00	-
▲ BCE Plc	BDF.PR.A	26.00	-1.0	4 ☆	97-	27.00	24.50	7.1
▲ BCE Plc	BDF.PR.B	27.00	-	20	97-	28.50	25.12	7.2
Beamscope	BSP	13.00	-	1824	138-	13.62	6.62	-
▲ Becker nv	BEK.B	10.88	1.2	157 ☆	108-	14.62	5.00	-
▲ Bell Cda	BC.PR.A	28.00	-	15 ☆	97-	29.12	26.25	6.9
Bell Cda	BC.PR.C	27.25	1.4	198 ★	101-	28.00	25.50	6.9
Bell Cd	BC.PR.D	27.50	-	nt ☆	98-	28.25	26.00	6.8
▲ Bema j	BGO	3.05	6.6	4961	94+	3.50	0.75	-

Source: *Financial Times of Canada*, March 12, 1994.

the lowest was $15.00. Last year, the company paid dividends of $0.68. Over the last week, the value of the stock was fairly steady. It closed at $16.88, down 2.2 percent over the week. There were 104,900 shares of Alberta Natural Gas traded on the Toronto Stock Exchange. Earnings per share were $0.85 as at December 1988.

The **price–earnings ratio**, which is the current market price of a share of stock divided by the annual earnings per share, is given as 13 percent. The P/E ratio shows how much investors are willing to pay per dollar of reported profits.

price–earnings ratio
The ratio of the annual earnings of a share to its current market price

Stock Indexes

Daily news reports on radio and television often include current stock indexes. A stock index is an average of the market prices of key stocks and thus indicates overall market activity.

The TSE **300 Composite Index** is the major Canadian index. It is based on the market prices of 300 stocks listed on the Toronto Stock Exchange that form a cross-section of major companies in the country. Individual stocks sometimes do not rise or fall with the index; however, it does provide a general measure of market activity for a given time period. The arbitrary starting level of the TSE 300 index in 1977 was 1,000. Subindexes representing seventeen different industry sectors are also reported.

TSE 300 Composite Index
An average of the market prices of 300 stocks listed on the Toronto Stock Exchange

What happens in one financial market is reflected in markets around the world minutes later. Thus, investors assess the direction and strength of the market by watching other indexes as well as the TSE 300. One of these is the Dow-Jones Industrial Average from the New York Stock Exchange. Others are London's Financial Times 100, Tokyo's Nikkei Index, and Hong Kong's Hang Seng Index. Exhibit 20.3 shows how *The Globe and Mail* reports a range of key market indexes from around the world.

INVESTORS AND THEIR GOALS

Investors in securities can be categorized as institutional or individual. **Institutional investors** include business firms and public-sector organizations such as insurance companies, pension funds, mutual funds, universities, and banks that invest their own financial assets or funds they hold in trust. These investors deal in large blocks of 10,000 shares or more.

institutional investor
A business firm or public-sector institution that invests excess funds or funds held in trust in stocks and bonds

Individual investors, sometimes called "retail investors," also play an important role in the securities market. Although they trade in comparatively small quantities, their vast numbers mean they represent nearly half of all stock market activity. Institutional investors such as mutual funds and insurance companies also have to be aware of the concerns and objectives of the individuals who delegate to them the responsibility of investing their money. At present, only about 10 percent of Canadians invest in the stock market, but more are entering it, so the importance of individual investors is likely to grow.

individual investor
An individual who makes personal investments in stocks and bonds, also called a retail investor

Why do people and institutions buy and sell stocks? Speculation is a frequent motive for many individual investors, and even institutions will occasionally take a calculated risk. Investment is in the interest of those who seek long-term growth, income, safety, or all three.

EXHIBIT 20.3 • KEY MARKET INDEXES

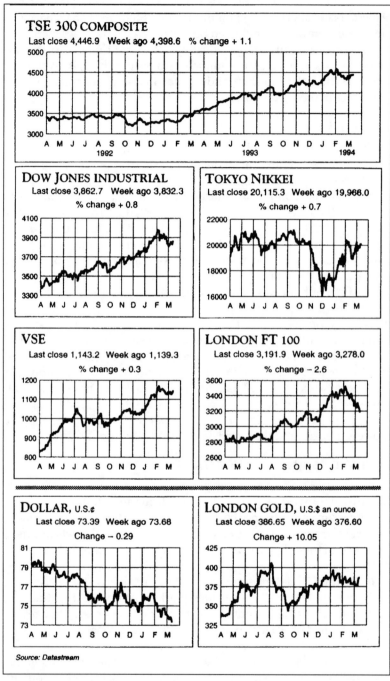

Source: *The Globe and Mail*, March 14, 1994.

Speculation

Some people regard buying and selling shares as an opportunity for **speculation**, hoping to use the stock market to make large gains rapidly. Speculators watch for market fluctuations in the attempt to "buy cheap and sell dear." They tend to buy high-risk stocks, such as "penny stocks" (so called because shares sell for less than a dollar). The hope is that a 10-cent stock will climb quickly to $2, generating a return of twenty times the original cost. The most common penny stocks are those of mining companies and small oil-and-gas companies that have no proven reserves and are trying to raise capital in order to explore their claims. The dream of another Hemlo gold strike fuels much of this speculative activity.

speculation
Buying and selling stocks in the hope of profiting quickly from sudden increases in share prices

Investment

People interested in **investment**, as opposed to speculation, do not anticipate making quick profits. Rather, they are interested in steady growth in the value of their stock, which results from the issuing company's sound financial planning. They also consider the relative safety of their investment, and returns in the form of dividends and interest consistent with the risk they do take.

investment
Trading in the stock market with a focus on long-term growth, regular income, and/or safety for savings

Investors who focus on growth as their motivation for investment choose companies with a track record of increasing earnings. They expect these earnings to continue to grow and also to outpace the earnings of the competition. Investors looking for growth tend to buy shares in the electronics industry, the pharmaceutical industry, and the energy-producing industries. Such companies often pay out small dividends because they reinvest most of their earnings to finance future growth. What investors lose in dividends they expect to gain in the value of their shares.

Many investors are looking for a source of additional income and try to identify and invest in companies that pay substantial dividends. Because dividends come from company earnings, careful investors look at the company's dividend track record, its current profitability, and the likelihood of future success. A company that retains almost none of its earnings, distributing them in dividends instead, may be headed for trouble. Banking, insurance, and public utilities are usually good income stocks.

The **yield** is the return an investor receives on an investment. Yield is expressed as a percent. Suppose you would like to invest $1,500. You are interested in the shares of four companies—Telecommunications Giant, Hardware Supreme, Interprovincial Heat and Light, and Major Department Stores. Table 20.2 presents recent information on their market prices and dividend rates. The yield (annual dividend as a percentage of current market price) for Telecommunications Giant is 7.9 percent, for Hardware Supreme 0.67 percent, for Interprovincial Heat and Light 8.02 percent, and for Major Department Stores 2.4 percent. If your objective is to achieve immediate income, you will likely buy stock in Interprovincial Heat and Light or Telecommunications Giant.

yield
The return an investor receives on an investment, expressed as the percentage of current market price that the annual dividend represents

Once you have made your investment, you should still keep an eye on market prices and dividends. As prices change, the yield will vary.

TABLE 20.2 • MARKET PRICE AND ANNUAL DIVIDEND FOR SELECTED COMPANIES

Company	Recent market price	Recent annual dividend	Yield in %
Telecommunications Giant	$24.63	$1.94	7.90
Hardware Supreme	35.88	.24	0.67
Interprovincial Heat and Light	53.00	4.25	8.02
Major Department Stores	24.88	.60	2.40

For example, a rise in the market price of Telecommunications Giant stock to $50 would generate a yield of 3.9 percent for the investor, not 7.9 percent.

Some people have money to invest but fear unpredictable market swings. In a twelve-month period, Bow Valley Enterprises share prices fluctuated from $16.50 to $11.25, Canadian Tire from $20.50 to $14.25, Ford of Canada from $165.00 to $110.50, Gramma Lee's from $0.40 to $0.10, and Stelco from $26.50 to $4.65. Investors who are unable to absorb a financial setback or cannot handle anxiety will tend to opt for safety as their first objective and choose high-quality bonds and preferred shares that have a high probability of steadily paying a satisfactory return.

Most investors do not put all of their capital in growth or income or safe securities. They have more than one objective in mind. For example, an investor whose main goal is growth may select stocks with at least a modest yield to have the satisfaction of some short-term return. A general guide to the investment objectives met by various types of securities is presented in Table 20.3.

Most experts agree that wise investors work with a range of securities rather than putting all their eggs in one basket. Investment portfolio strategy is discussed in Developing Your Business Skills.

TABLE 20.3 • SECURITIES AND INVESTMENT OBJECTIVES

Security*	Investment Objective		
	Safety	Income	Growth
Bonds	Best	Very steady	Usually none
Preferred shares	Good	Steady	Slight
Common shares	Least	Variable	Best

*It is best to apply the comparisons made here to a given firm's securities.

DEVELOPING YOUR BUSINESS SKILLS

DEVELOPING A PORTFOLIO STRATEGY

Ninety percent of the problems investors will encounter in the next year are already in their portfolios.

That's because most of those so-called portfolios are just grab bags of securities, says Fred Marconi, vice-president and director of Cassels Blaikie & Co. Ltd. of Toronto. They are simply a collection of investments that lack direction.

Most investors cannot afford a professional portfolio manager, and time constraints and lengthy client lists limit how much assistance and review a registered representative can offer. An investor's failing is often not that the wrong security was purchased but that it was not followed closely after it was purchased.

And, Marconi says, following a stock does not mean simply checking the stock listings in the morning to find out how it did the day before. It means watching the industry, changes in company management, new products, profits, and the economy in general. It means spending time and making timely decisions. There's no lack of information; it's a question of knowing what to do with it.

David West, supervisor of education with the Canadian Securities Institute, recommends following the same portfolio management procedure a stockbroker does—know the client; develop and implement the investment strategy; monitor the client, the market, and the economy; and measure and adjust the performance of the portfolio.

The first step is perhaps the most important. Why invest? Some people buy whenever they receive a hot tip. Others try to buy securities that match their needs, but don't bother to make any changes as the companies and their lives change. They forget that a strategy does not hold up forever. Children are born, salaries rise, spouses die, marriages break down, salaries fall, and all along taxes must be paid. Shrewd investors will keep in tune with the economy and with their personal needs.

The investment strategy should reflect lifestyle, income, tax bracket, and temperament, among other factors. Investors under 35 will need cash and savings for emergencies, but they could also (temperament permitting) try higher-risk growth securities. Between the ages of 35 and 50, one might wish to reduce one's savings levels and put more money into higher-risk vehicles. The peak earning years of 50 to 65 would emphasize moderate risk and maximum income to prepare for retirement. Post-65 investments would be risk-adverse and emphasize safety and income.

After defining their goals and determining what types of securities will help achieve them, investors should examine a list of their current assets and evaluate the balance and mix of securities they hold. Is there too much interest income? Are there too many stocks from the same industry? Is there room for growth?

The best advice is to keep the investments that work toward the new goals and get rid of others. From now on, buy only securities that fit into the investment plan and fall within the limits of comfortable risk.

Source: Cathryn Motherwell, "Close Attention Needed to Develop Portfolio Strategy," *The Globe and Mail,* July 22, 1985, p. B9.

BUSINESS REVIEW 20.2

1. What is a securities exchange and how does it function?
2. How are securities bought and sold?
3. What are the main reasons investors have for the purchase of securities?

MUTUAL FUNDS: ANOTHER APPROACH TO INVESTING

It is not unusual for some investors to feel overwhelmed by both the number of investment options and the importance of timing in the purchase of securities. Aware that they have neither the time nor the knowledge to keep up-to-date, they choose to buy shares in one or more mutual funds. A **mutual fund** is a financial intermediary, a company that sells shares to investors and pools the funds to acquire a diversified portfolio of stocks and bonds. This gives investors holdings in a variety of firms, and professional management of these holdings. The mutual fund investor becomes a part owner in each of the companies the fund has invested in, thus spreading the risk.

Mutual funds are managed by highly skilled and experienced professionals who perform the analysis of trends in the overall securities market and of the prospects of specific industries and companies that the individual investor does not have the time, experience, or money to do. As of November 1993, nearly 24 percent of Canadians own shares in one or more of the approximately 650 mutual funds. Mutual funds have become Canada's fastest-growing investment vehicle.

In a discussion of mutual funds, Doug Kelly points out:

Mutual funds can have many different objectives and each is designed to suit the needs of the individual investor at a particular time.

Even though mutual funds simplify the decision for the investor, selecting the right portfolio can still be a major decision. There is a wide variety of mutual funds, designed to fit a range of investment objectives. The following describes the major fund types.

Equity funds. Equity funds buy stocks of several different individual companies. This diversification lessens your dependence on the performance of a single company or sector. Among equity funds, there are growth and blue-chip funds. Blue-chip funds buy higher-quality securities with a potential for slow but steady return.

Fixed-income funds. Fixed-income funds emphasize safety and income by investing in fixed-income securities such as short-term money-market instruments, mortgages and long-term government bonds.

Money-market funds. Money-market funds invest in the money market, where governments, corporations and banks borrow. These are low-risk, short-term securities that pay steady interest, although providing little in the way of capital gains.

Mortgage funds. Mortgage funds invest in residential and commercial mortgages. They offer the chance of a higher rate of return than

mutual fund
A company that sells shares to investors and pools the funds to acquire a diversified portfolio of stocks and bonds

The first trust company to sponsor a mutual fund, Canada Trust is still going strong with mutual funds advertising campaigns like the Everest Funds™. The Everest Funds™ offers 12 different fund options including investments in Asian and European markets.

money-market funds and do not carry the risk of volatile long-term bond funds.

Bond funds. Bond funds buy bonds issued by the federal government, provinces and large corporations. Bond funds tend to be volatile, but offer the possibility of higher returns.

Dividend funds. Dividend funds invest mainly in dividend-paying preferred shares and are therefore suitable for the investor who needs income. They tend to be less volatile than pure equity funds and may offer some tax advantages that go with receiving income from dividends rather than from interest.

Balanced funds. Balanced funds contain both equity and fixed-income securities and give you the strengths and weaknesses of both securities.

Other funds. A number of more specialized forms of mutual funds also exist. *Ethical funds* screen investments according to specific ethical standards. *Real estate funds* buy mainly commercial, income-producing properties and their income is primarily derived from the rent they collect and the capital gains earned when the properties are sold. *Sector funds* allow investors to concentrate in specific industries such as energy and technology. *Global funds* put money in stocks and other securities of foreign companies. *Index funds* reflect the makeup of a particular stock or bond index, such as the TSE 300 Composite Index. [2]

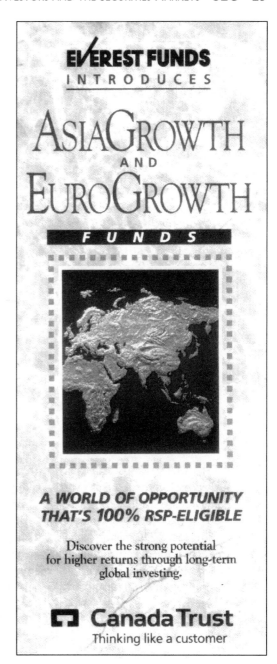

INTERACTIVE SUMMARY AND DISCUSSION QUESTIONS

1. The two sources of funding for long-term capital are equity capital and debt capital. Distinguish between the two.
2. Shares or stocks are units of ownership in a corporation. The two types are common and preferred shares. Explain the difference between the two.
3. When might a company issue common shares, and when would it issue preferred shares?
4. Why might investors purchase common shares, and why might they purchase preferred shares?
5. Long-term debt capital can be raised through the sale of bonds. When might an organization choose to raise capital through the sale of bonds instead of through the sale of common shares?
6. Rank the priority of claim of bondholders, common shareholders, and preferred shareholders

in the event of a firm's dissolution. Explain.
7. What are the main functions of a stock exchange?
8. Trace the process through which a stock is bought and sold.
9. Go to the library and, from an appropriate newspaper, record the daily price movements of a group of five common stocks for a 30-day period. Then prepare a brief report on what you think influenced the price movements in these issues.
10. Individuals who are interested in investing in certain companies may not find their stocks listed on the TSE or regional exchanges. They may have to trade on the over-the-counter market. Explain how this works.

CASE 20.1

THE REVOLUTION ON BAY STREET

THE LATE 1980s and early 1990s were some of the most difficult years since the Great Depression for Canada's 120 brokerages—the very symbol of prosperity through much of the previous decade. The horrendous half-decade peaked in 1990, when members of the Toronto Stock Exchange were bludgeoned by the results of the 1987 stock market crash. That year, TSE firms lost $230 million.

Profitability returned in a big way in 1991, largely because of the booming bond market. For the first nine months of 1991, TSE members' profits were $208.7 million, surpassing the previous all-time high of $160 million in 1986. Cyclical activities in the investment industry are not uncommon.

However, Canada's brokerage scene has recently undergone something much more fundamental than an extended bear market. The industry is being reshaped by a number of factors:
- deregulation of brokerage fees, ownership, and activities
- crisis in public confidence
- retreat of the retail investor from the market
- new technologies
- globalization

Deregulation
Commissions were first deregulated in Ontario and Quebec in 1983. Discount investment houses emerged, grabbing an increasing percentage of the market. In 1987, banks were granted the right to buy securities firms, integrating brokerages into a much broader industry.

In 1988, deregulation opened the doors for foreign firms to buy Canadian brokerages and participate in all areas of the Canadian industry. Under recent revisions to acts governing federally regulated financial institutions, banks, trust and loan, and insurance companies have been granted investment and portfolio management powers. Competition in domestic markets has increased drastically. Large capital-intensive firms, together with new foreign entrants, are competing aggressively for shrinking volumes of business.

Public Confidence

Investor confidence has dropped. This has been brought on by some high-profile shady deals. Insider-trading scandals involving the blue-bloods of the industry have rocked Wall Street. In Japan, some of the country's largest dealers were found to have been compensating favoured clients for investment losses.

In Canada, the spectacular failure of Toronto-based Osler Inc. has taken its toll on public confidence. There are growing doubts about the fairness of the stock markets. Institutional players are dominating, pushing retail investors into a diminishing role.

Retail Investor Retreat

Institutional investors such as pension funds can send stocks soaring or plummeting by buying and selling large blocks. For brokerages, growth of institutional trading has meant only one thing—tighter commissions. "The retail investor is where you make your money," one broker commented.

New Technologies

The industry is being forced to pour millions of dollars into computers and telecommunications just to remain competitive at home and abroad. Clients will soon be able to buy and sell shares on their home computers. Brokers can execute trades directly from their terminals—eliminating the need for an intermediary within the firm.

Globalization

Technology has quickened the pace of internationalization. It has linked stock exchanges and brokers from Tokyo to Vancouver and made round-the-clock trading possible. Canadian firms are no longer just competing against one another. They are now up against major brokerage firms around the world. By maintaining foreign offices and striking global alliances, Canadian brokerages can offer clients portfolios with a more international flavour. The biggest proportion of international trade is made up of debt securities, but experts suggest international equity will soon dominate.

Cyclical trends play a strong role in determining whether a market is a "bear" or a "bull." Consultants from Brendan Wood International Inc. suggest that the investment community must become adaptable to these numerous changes in order to determine "whether to call past successes an indicator of good fortunes...or the end of a good thing."

Source: Adapted from Doug Kelly, "The Revolution on Bay Street," *The Financial Post,* January 6, 1992, pp. 4–5.

Questions for Discussion

1. Deregulation has been a big factor in the changing market. What were the main effects of deregulation?
2. Identify some key trends that led to the deregulation of the investment industry.
3. Discuss the effects on the industry now that banks, insurance companies, and trust companies can buy securities firms.
4. What is the effect on the brokerage industry when foreign firms buy Canadian brokerage companies?

CASE 20.2

FIDELITY INVESTMENTS CANADA LTD.

FIDELITY INVESTMENTS CANADA LTD. is one of the newer independent mutual funds firms. Although the company has grown steadily since its launch in September 1987, it got off to a rocky start. The precipitous stock market drop in October of that year nearly forced the company to close even before it became established. Industry experts say good performance and aggressive marketing have helped put the Canadian operation on the map.

John Simpson, executive vice-president, implemented some key strategies that have contributed to that success. In a bid to boost market share, Fidelity bumped up sales commissions to 4.9 percent from 4 percent on mutual funds that charged redemption fees. The move paid off. Fidelity's increased compensation piqued the interest of brokers and financial planners. Many had traditionally sold the products of some of Canada's major independent mutual funds—Mackenzie Financial Corp., Trimark Investment Management Inc., AGF Management Ltd., and Templeton International. They now began also to sell Fidelity.

In addition, Simpson has criss-crossed the country, visiting brokers and giving public seminars in an effort to increase the public's interest in his firm. The result over the past year was notable. The company more than quadrupled its assets, to $605 million from $127.5 million at the start of the year.

However, to reach the mutual fund major leagues, Simpson says the company must aim to acquire $1 billion in assets. In order to reach this goal, Simpson aims to "hustle, keep our performance in good shape, bring out some new and interesting products, and keep working hard." Simpson believes that the way of the future for Fidelity Canada lies in offering more international funds.

Although there are good growth prospects in Canada, Simpson maintains there are also very compelling prospects in southeast Asia and new markets in Europe and the United States.

One example is the Far East Fund, which was cloned from Fidelity's U.S. company's South East Asia Trust. This fund is sold to Fidelity's British, European, and Asian clients. During the original fund's seven-year existence, it earned an annual compound return of 19 percent.

Similarly, the Growth America Fund replicates their U.S. Stock Selector Fund. With $220 million in assets under administration, the fund earned a 44.3 percent return in 1991—making it the fourth-best performing fund available in Canada last year. Another good example is the International Portfolio Fund. With $100 million in assets under administration, the fund returned 17.7 percent last year.

"We definitely think the growth of the markets is going to be international," Simpson says. "We're trying to get Canadians to diversify a bit more."

Fidelity Canada's thrust may be toward global markets, but veteran Fidelity investment manager George Domolky, manager of the company's Canadian equity-based portfolios, believes successful international fund investing need not extend farther than Canada. Domolky believes this country has been neglected by international fund managers, who in the last few years have ventured to other areas of the world.

His dedication to the Canadian market has earned him the nickname "Captain Canada." He is a champion of Canadian investments. Domolky's Fidelity Canada Fund, which is sold exclusively to U.S. investors, returned 23 percent last year.

(continued)

Fidelity Canada's Capital Builder Fund earned a 13.3 percent return in the same year. Marketed to domestic investors, the Capital Builder Fund has averaged a 9.1 percent return over the past three years, making it one of the top seven Canadian funds over that time.

Fidelity Canada is now drawing more than $2 million in net sales a day. The company had net sales of $397 million last year. As a relative newcomer to the Canadian mutual funds market, Fidelity Canada has clearly made its mark. It looks like the "new kid on the block" is here to stay.

Questions for Discussion

1. What can be learned from this case about the marketing of mutual funds?
2. What advice would you give a potential purchaser about buying mutual funds?
3. Discuss the variations in the rates of returns on the different funds, giving some of the reasons for them.
4. Do you agree with Simpson's strategy of featuring various global funds? What are the potential problems and risks of such a strategy?
5. Does Mr. Domolky's emphasis on Canadian shares make sense in light of the international approach of other Fidelity funds?

Source: Adapted from Sandra Santedicola "Fidelity Taking Aim at Canada," *The Financial Post*, February 17, 1992, p. M4.

NOTES

1. *Canadian Business*, February 1983, p. 37. Reprinted by permission of Canadian Business Magazine ©1994.

2. Doug Kelly, "The Mosaic of Mutual Funds: From Equity to Global," *The Financial Post*, August 12, 1991, p. 15.

PHOTO CREDITS

SEC 8   Canadian Pacific

SEC 11   Photo courtesy of The Toronto Stock Exchange

SEC 23   © Canada Trust™

MODULE
◆ BAN ◆

MONEY AND BANKING

THE FOCUS OF THIS MODULE

1. To describe the characteristics and functions of money

2. To define the money supply and various forms of near-money

3. To describe the purposes and operations of chartered banks and other financial intermediaries

4. To describe the basis on which chartered banks are allowed to operate

5. To describe the role of the Bank of Canada in the Canadian banking system

6. To explain how the Canada Deposit Insurance Corporation (CDIC) protects its depositors

7. To describe the Canadian Payments System

8. To discuss electronic funds transfer

9. To define the following terms:

KEY TERMS

money

medium of exchange

unit of account

store of value

currency

demand deposit

notice deposit

token money

credit card

chartered bank

required cash reserves

trust company

credit union (caisse populaire)

Bank of Canada

secondary reserve requirement

open-market operations

bank rate

Canada Deposit Insurance
  Corporation (CDIC)

cheque

Canadian Payments System

electronic funds transfer
  system (EFTS)

debit card

IT'S 4:00 A.M. and you want to pay your telephone bill. You dial the bank, enter a code, and transfer the correct amount.

Now you can sleep easy. Or so the banks hope. They're introducing a new generation of technology designed to give better service and woo customers in the increasingly competitive banking industry.

Automatic teller machines (ATMs) are enabling people to do more and more—pay bills, make transfers to registered retirement savings plans, and make deposits—as well as dispensing cash. There are still other machines that update a passbook, provide a credit card statement, or balance a chequing account.

At the Canadian Imperial Bank of Commerce, when customers receive their chequing account statement, they no longer see a series of numbers printed on a page but photocopies of the actual cheques. This has been made possible with document-imaging technology, which has the potential to speed and simplify cheque processing within the banks.

And corporate customers are seeing remittances move quicker, with less staff effort, through electronic data interchange arranged by the bank. "The banks want to provide a higher level of more personalized customer service," says Bill Shaw, vice-president of financial-systems marketing for NCR Canada Ltd.

Source: Adapted from Susan Noakes, "Banks Bank on Technology to Serve Customers Better," *The Financial Post*, October 21, 1991, p. 52.

Money makes the wheels of our economy go round. Most of us are happy if we have enough dollars; we rarely stop to try to understand how we use money, how our banks and other financial institutions work, or how the Bank of Canada regulates the financial system. Yet these are the cornerstone of our economic system.

MONEY: WHAT IS IT?

Money is one of the greatest inventions of humanity. Whether as copper, nickel, and silver coins; as paper; or as a digital code in a computer's memory, it is an essential commodity needed by every organization.

money
Anything generally accepted as a medium of exchange for goods or services and as a store of value for future use

Money is anything commonly used and generally accepted as a medium of exchange for goods and services and as a store of value for future use. Today, we usually think of money as coins, folding bills, and the content of chequing and savings accounts. People have also made payment with cattle, stones, wampum, or shark's teeth. What money represents continues to be a source of fascination:

Money bewitches people. They fret for it, and they sweat for it. They devise the most ingenious ways to get it, and most ingenious ways to get rid of it. Money is the only commodity that is good for nothing but to be gotten rid of. It will not feed you, clothe you, shelter you, or amuse you unless you spend it or invest it. It imparts value only in parting. People will do almost anything for money, and money will do almost anything for people. Money is a captivating, circulating, masquerading puzzle. [1]

Money is a versatile means of exchange often taken too much for granted.

SEPARATING BUYING FROM SELLING

The chief purpose of money is to facilitate the act of buying and selling. The acceptance of some medium of exchange of recognized value means that the farmer who wants to buy new cooking pots does not have to search for a potmaker who is willing to trade pots for grain. Instead, the farmer can sell the grain for money to someone who wants it and then go in search of the desired cooking pots—or can keep the money for use on a later occasion if nothing suitable is available.

Most early forms of money were items with intrinsic value in the society in which they were used. For example, pastoral societies have used cattle or goats. Gold and silver have been used as a medium of exchange for at least 4,000 years, often being measured by weight. The idea of stamping standard pieces of metal—"coins"—in official recognition that they represent certain weights of the metals developed less than 3,000 years ago. Paper money, in itself valueless, was at first a promise to pay a specific amount of gold or silver. It came into common use about 200 years ago, although there are reports of this curious practice in China some hundreds of years earlier. An early instance in North America of the use of paper money occurred in New France in 1685. Because of a shortage of coins in the colony, soldiers, civil servants, and suppliers were paid with money printed on playing cards and signed by the governor. This playing-card money was redeemed for coinage or trade goods when the king's ship arrived from France.

PRACTICAL MONEY

The nineteenth-century philosopher John Stuart Mill wrote that money is "a contrivance for sparing time and labour. It is a machinery for doing quickly and commodiously what would be done, though less quickly and commodiously, without it." [2] Few of us would want to carry around the giant stone disks that people on the Pacific island of Yap used as money. What are the features that make money useful, convenient, and reliable?

Divisibility

The cow-owner shopping for a loaf of bread is faced with a very clumsy trading situation. It must be possible to divide money into small units so that items of relatively little value can be paid for. Metallic money could be minted into coins of different sizes and values. Spanish gold doubloons could be broken into pieces of eight; the pound sterling, originally a pound of silver coins, is today divided into 100 pence; one French franc is worth 100 centimes; the German Deutschmark has a value of 100 pfennigs; and our familiar dollar can be traded for pennies, nickels, dimes, and quarters. Today's forms of money facilitate purchase of a newspaper or a condominium because they are so conveniently divisible.

Portability

The people of Yap publicized the extent of their wealth by placing their stone money at the doorway of their houses. However, exchanging it for different items was very cumbersome. Today's lightweight paper currency makes buying and selling comparatively a very uncomplicated process. Canadian paper money comes in denominations of $2, $5, $10, $20, $50, $100, and $1,000.

Durability

Cheese and meat do not make good choices as forms of money. A monetary system works more efficiently if it is based on something that lasts, at least for the foreseeable future. Coins and paper currency satisfy this requirement because deterioration is very slow and replacement is straightforward. The Canadian $2 bill has an average life of approximately ten months and can be folded some 4,000 times without tearing.

Canadian coins are struck at the Royal Canadian Mint in Ottawa. The first coins of the Dominion of Canada were silver nickels, dimes, quarters, and fifty-cent pieces. Bronze pennies were issued a few years later. With the exception of the fifty-cent pieces, which are no longer in circulation, the coins still come in the same denominations along with the recently introduced loonies or dollar coins.

While that may sound impressive, the cost of replacing money is a constant headache for the Canadian mint. The eleven-sided gold-coloured dollar coin affectionately known as "the loonie" was introduced to reduce the demand for smaller coins, especially for use in vending machines. Over the long term, the mint expects the loonie will be cheaper to produce. The comparison of bills and coins in Table 21.1 was made just before the $1 coin was introduced. The mint's costs were not the whole story, however. Banks and retail stores complained that the coins were more expensive to handle, and some suggested that having to carry around several loonies instead of dollar bills would increase the wear and tear on pocket and purse.[3]

Stability

People must trust the value of their money. They need to know that a litre of milk will cost the same tomorrow as it does today. The effects of inflation are quite predictable. People see that a fixed amount of money will buy less and less and that the value of their savings is dwindling. They stop using money as a store of value; instead of keeping money in a bank account, they protect their assets by investing in jewels, land, or fine art. In cases of hyperinflation, when the purchasing power of the currency falls uncontrollably, money also loses its function as a medium of exchange as people resort to barter in order to know they are receiving items of value instead of worthless paper. In the chaos that followed the Second World War, cigarettes were regarded as a more stable form of money than Deutschmarks. In the years following the collapse of the Soviet Union, Moscow factories started to use coupons for food as part of employees' wages because prices were soaring beyond any meagre increase in wages. Many South American countries have also recently experienced bouts of heavy inflation.

Security Against Counterfeiting

Interfering with the money supply is almost as old as the idea of money. Criminals once "clipped" tiny pieces of precious metal off the sides or edges of coins. This process was largely stopped when mints began to "mill" coins by putting serrations around the edges. Protecting paper money presented different challenges. A common procedure is to use a watermark in the paper. If you hold Canadian paper money up to the light, you will notice small green dots (called

TABLE 21.1 • DOLLAR BILLS OR DOLLAR COINS?

	Dollar bills	Dollar coins
Life expectancy	9–12 months	20 years
Annual replacement	270 million	50 million
Cost	$39 per thousand	$170 per thousand

Source: Adapted from Andrew McIntosh, "If Coins Come, the Bills May Go," *The Globe and Mail*, June 11, 1985.

"planchets") that were embedded in the mash when the paper was made. These planchets can be scraped off real bills. Furthermore, the ink used in printing our money never completely dries; it can be smeared. The most common denominations of bills are printed with complicated colour backgrounds. Higher-denomination bills now contain a foil hologram. All these devices make our money difficult to counterfeit.

The production and distribution of counterfeit money is a crime that enables the perpetrators to acquire goods and services without true payment. This kind of criminal interference with a country's legal currency may provide exciting material for novels and movie scripts, but in the real world it can undermine the economy by ruining the currency's value. Security to prevent the theft of currency plates is extremely tight. The Canadian dollar coin shows the loon we know today because the dies for the original design—voyageurs in a canoe—were lost during a flight from Ottawa to the mint in Winnipeg. It was decided that, however unlikely it was that they had fallen into the wrong hands, the risk of keeping to the design on the lost dies was too great to take.

THE FUNCTIONS OF MONEY

medium of exchange
A method of facilitating purchase or sale without the need for a barter system

unit of account
A common factor by which the value of similar or different goods and services can be compared

store of value
A method of accumulating wealth until it is need for purchases

As we have seen, the primary function of money is as a **medium of exchange**, avoiding the problems of a barter system. A closely related function is as a **unit of account**, allowing us to appreciate relative economic value. One type of car might be valued at $20,000; a bicycle at $300; and a monthly transit pass at $65. A meal at an expensive restaurant might cost $120; a week's groceries $75. The same bottle of shampoo might cost $4.29, $3.95, and $2.99 at three different neighbourhood stores. The use of money as a common factor permits important comparisons, not only within one product type but also over the entire range of products and services.

Money also serves as an efficient temporary **store of value**, accumulating until it is needed to make purchases. Other stores of value include stocks, bonds, real estate, works of art, and precious gems. The first three of these examples may generate additional income through dividends, interest payments, or rent. All of them may actually increase in market value. Their drawback is that they cannot always be converted easily or cheaply into cash. Selling stocks and bonds involves the services of a broker, who will charge a commission; redeeming the value of real estate, art, or gems requires the availability of a buyer. And increase in value is not guaranteed: the items may be worth less than when they were bought. Costs of ownership may include maintenance, storage, and insurance.

The advantage of money as a store of value is its liquidity; it can be spent immediately. Simply holding on to money, however, can create a serious problem during a period of inflation. Should prices double, all the bills under the mattress will buy only half the clothes and movie tickets when they're pulled out to be spent. Furthermore, unless it is kept in an interest-bearing chequing/savings account, the money will not earn anything for its owner (and, even then, very little). The key benefit of money, therefore, is that it is immediately available to pay debts or buy goods and services.

THE MONEY SUPPLY

What is money? As strange as it may seem, definitions of money differ. Coins and notes (paper money), or **currency**, form one rather small part—between 4.4 and 49.0 percent, depending on the definition of money used. Chequing accounts are also considered to be money because they are almost instantly available. The Bank of Canada calls these components of the money supply "M1." More specifically, M1 is the sum of Canadian currency in circulation, metal coins and paper money, and Canadian-dollar **demand deposits** (money held in chequing and chequing/savings accounts) in chartered banks, excluding those held by other banks and by the federal government.

This is not the complete picture, however. Another significant group of funds consists of various **notice deposits**. For these, notice must be given to the financial institution ahead of time that they are to be redeemed. Thus, notice deposits cannot be used in ordinary transactions until they are first converted into chequable deposits or currency. Because these items cannot be used immediately, some economists do not consider them to be money, but instead refer to them as "near-money." Examples of near-money include savings accounts, personal and non-personal redeemable fixed-term deposits issued by the chartered banks, share-capital accounts in credit unions (*caisses populaires*), and term deposits and guaranteed investment certificates (GICs) and debentures with less than one year to maturity held by trust and mortgage-loan companies. However, these notice deposits can usually be liquidated prior to maturity (usually at some penalty) and therefore can also be considered part of the money supply. These components, plus M1, the Bank of Canada refers to as "M2."

"M2+" is a logical extension of M2. This money measure includes M2 plus all deposits held by the general public at non-bank depository institutions—trust and mortgage-loan companies and credit unions (*caisses populaires*), personal deposits at Alberta Treasury branches, and deposits at Province of Ontario Savings Offices.

There are several other definitions of money, which are discussed in more advanced textbooks.[4] These definitions are related to different emphases on particular functions or properties of money.

All of the money in use today is **token money**; that is, its value as money exceeds the market value of the materials it is made of. This was not the case when gold coins were in circulation. The present-day monetary system allows a loonie, an official piece of paper such as a $5 bill, or a cheque to work equally well in financial transactions.

Plastic Money: A Substitute for Cash

Plastic money has become a fact of life. Many people think of **credit cards** as substitutes for liquid cash. About 21 million VISA and MasterCards are held by Canadians. Many use three or more cards. Of the total amount banks extended for consumer loans, about 15 percent was attributable to loans under the banks' charge cards, VISA and

currency
Coins and paper money

demand deposit
An account at a bank or other financial institution from which the depositor can withdraw money "on demand"

notice deposit
An account at a bank or other financial institution from which the depositor can withdraw money only after giving notice, usually seven days

token money
Money whose monetary value exceeds the market value of the materials it is made of

credit card
A method of making purchases by borrowing from the card-issuing institution

MasterCard.[5] A major reason for the tremendous increase in credit card business is the widespread acceptance of this method of payment, with co-operation among banks in various countries making many cards acceptable throughout the world. Retail merchants and service-oriented business people everywhere are making credit card transactions more and more convenient. New areas of credit card use are continually developing. Most products can be purchased by simply making a phone call and listing a credit card number and expiry date. Many charitable organizations and political parties send out pledge cards with spaces for credit card numbers.

While the plastic card may function much like money in permitting the holder to make purchases, the monthly statement of card purchases is a tangible reminder that they are *credit* cards—not money. They merely represent a special credit arrangement between the holder and the organization issuing the card. The issuer—usually a bank—permits the cardholder to repay the outstanding balance at the end of the billing period or, in the case of bank credit cards and retail credit cards, to pay at least a stated minimum amount each month and pay interest on the outstanding balance until it is repaid.

Credit card users should be aware that the interest rate on unpaid balances is extremely high—almost any other kind of loan arrangement is considerably cheaper. Developing Your Business Skills discusses credit cards and debt management. However, even if the cardholder does pay the balance in full each month to avoid interest charges, the credit card is not a free service. Merchants who accept credit cards pay a commission on each transaction and must cover their costs in some way.

DEVELOPING YOUR BUSINESS SKILLS

HANDLING A PAYMENT CRISIS

Acquiring the goods we want can be rewarding as long as a positive balance exists in our bank accounts after the purchase. But, although this is the ideal situation, many items are bought on credit. Individuals, as well as businesses, occasionally find that incoming cash flow is not adequate to meet credit payments.

Should you ever find yourself in a negative-balance situation, your credit reputation could be threatened. This could negatively affect your ability to obtain credit in the future. Therefore, here is what you must do:

If you think you are in danger of missing a payment, explain your problem to the creditor instead of waiting for them to take action. This applies to a business owing money, or an individual dealing with a credit card issuer. Such is the recommendation of Duke Stregger, executive director of the non-profit Credit Counselling Service (CCS) of Metropolitan Toronto.

If you have a good credit history, missing one minimum payment (3 to 5 percent of the balance) will not usually trigger an inquiry into your account. But, in the case of credit cards, all accounts more than 90 days in arrears are carefully scrutinized by card issuers. Also, it is important to keep in mind that missing a payment on a credit card increases your interest expenses.

(continued)

Interest charges range from a low of about 16.75 percent for VISA to 28.8 percent for credit cards issued by retailers, such as Eaton's.

Although most people are a little embarrassed to talk about their financial problems, major financial institutions and retailers can be "very considerate." They see there is a lot of goodwill attached to granting small pardons in cases of real hardship, Stregger said. Creditors know that most people in a financial crunch eventually work their way out of it.

©1993 Creators Syndicate Inc.

Consolidation of credit card debt into a single bank loan is a good option. Interest rates for bank debt will normally be lower. However, if you are a "credit junkie," "put your credit cards into a block of ice for a year," Stregger advises.

Source: Adapted from Erik Heinrich, "Easing Credit-Card Blues," *The Financial Post*, May 25, 1992, p. 18.

BUSINESS REVIEW 21.1

1. List the functions of money and give an example of how each function has served you in the past week.

2. Why does the Bank of Canada classify deposits in a chequing account as M1 but those in a savings account as M2?

THE CANADIAN CHARTERED BANKING SYSTEM

The Canadian banking system consists of 68 banks with approximately 7,400 branches. Seven are defined as Schedule I banks; that is, they are domestically owned and widely held, which means that fewer than 25 percent of shares may be held by non-residents of Canada and no one person may own more than 10 percent of the voting stock. Schedule II banks include most trust companies and similar institutions as well as the "foreign" banks that operate in this country, such as HongKong Bank of Canada or Citibank Canada. Schedule II banks may be closely held, which means that one person or organization may own more than 10 percent of the voting shares. For example,

chartered bank
A business based on holding funds deposited with it and using these funds to make loans

Barclays Bank of Canada is a wholly owned subsidiary of Barclays Bank in the United Kingdom, and Gentra (formerly Royal Trustco) is now controlled by the Royal Bank of Canada, even though the bank itself must be widely held by many shareholders. Table 21.2 lists the largest Schedule I banks and Schedule II trust companies.

Chartered banks perform two main functions: (1) they buy and sell loans, bills, and bonds (evidences of debt) and (2) they provide financial services such as safekeeping of funds; serving as paying and receiving stations for currencies; collecting cheques, draft notes, and other obligations for their customers; as well as performing special advisory services for customers. Figure 21.1 describes the operations of chartered banks. Another view of banks follows:

Like Frisbee manufacturers, bankers buy inputs, massage them a bit, burn a little incense, say the magic words, and out pops some output from the oven. If their luck holds, they can sell the finished product for more than it cost to buy the raw materials and process them through the assembly line.

For a banker, the raw material is money. He buys it at a long counter he sets up in the store, then rushes around to the back, polishing it on his sleeve as he goes, sits down behind a huge desk (a little out of breath), and sells it soon as he can to someone else....

About the only way you can tell whether a banker is buying money or selling it is to observe him in his native habitat and see whether he's standing up or sitting down. For some unknown reason, probably an inherited trait, bankers always stand up when they buy money (take your deposit), but invariably sit down when they sell it (make loans or buy securities). [6]

TABLE 21.2 • BANKS AND TRUST COMPANIES

	Revenue $000	Profit $000	Assets $000
Banks			
Royal Bank of Canada	12,199,000	107,000	138,193,000
Cdn. Imp. Bank of Commerce	11,388,000	12,000	132,212,000
Bank of Montreal	8,847,000	640,000	109,035,000
Bank of Nova Scotia	8,420,179	676,224	97,660,809
Toronto-Dominion Bank	6,138,000	408,000	74,133,000
Trust, Savings and Loan			
Imasco Financial	4,371,500	169,800	43,126,400
CT Financial Services	4,094,468	193,227	44,264,510
Canada Trustco Mortgage	3,548,425	155,437	36,984,154
Royal Trustco	2,827,000	–852,000	25,114,000
National Trustco	1,684,608	39,287	16,566,546

Source: *Report on Business 1000*, July 1993, p. 114.

FIGURE 21.1 • THE OPERATIONS OF CHARTERED BANKS

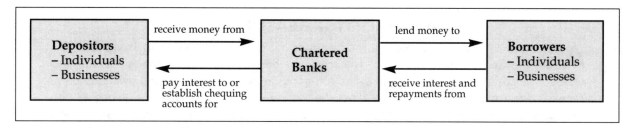

Services Provided by Chartered Banks

Schedule I chartered banks offer literally dozens of services to their customers. As well as the basic deposit and loan facilities, they administer bank credit cards, investment banking, safety deposit boxes, electronic transfers of money to distant locations, low-cost traveller's cheques, the sale of government bonds, and specialized customer services such as financial counselling. Some depositors arrange overdraft chequing accounts that automatically provide small loans at low interest when the balances in their accounts cannot cover the cheques they have written. The automated teller machine (ATM), which reduces both paper and people costs, has changed the way in which most people deal with banks.

Banks use deposits as the basis of the loans they make to individual and business borrowers. Because their income is derived from loans, banks lend most of the currency obtained from their chequing and savings account depositors to borrowers at interest rates higher then the rates paid to depositors. By law, banks must keep **required cash reserves**, a percentage of the money they take in as deposits, in order to cover withdrawals. They must also keep a percentage in treasury bills at the Bank of Canada as working reserves. The percentage of reserves required may vary but is usually in the range of 10 percent for demand deposits and 3 percent for notice deposits.

It has been pointed out that banks are profit-making institutions. Yet when we entrust our hard-earned money to the bank for safe keeping, dutifully pay our service charges, and accept the going interest rates on our savings or borrowings from the bank, it is a little disheartening to hear people say that the banks are profiting enormously from their dealings with us. Issues in Business 21.1 discusses the matter of just how much profit these corporations should make from handling our money.

required cash reserves
Percentage of deposits required to be kept in cash by banks to cover withdrawals

Farcus by David Waisglass Gordon Coulthart

Hey, only three more months and my student loan will be paid off.'

ISSUES IN BUSINESS 21.1

BANK PROFITS—REASONABLE?

A RECENT NEWS RELEASE revealed the health of the banking business. "Big Banks Get 'Gift from the Gods'," the headline ran. The article continued to describe some unrelenting successes. "Canada's six major chartered banks got a shot in the arm in their fiscal third quarter… Year-over-year net income for the Big Six in the quarter ended July 31 was up a strong 13 percent, to $938.2 million. Net income for the nine months edged down 2 percent, to $2.7 billion. Fee income was an important factor helping to prop up third-quarter earnings. 'Given the economic environment, fee income is surprisingly strong,' Alain Tuchmaier of McLean McCarthy Ltd. said. 'That's a real positive because… it is a recurring part of the banks' business.'"

Apart from higher service charges generated from retail banking, the article continued, a key part of the growth in fee income came from the banks' brokerage arms, which have seen an upturn in business. In addition, although provisions for loan losses in the third quarter were up substantially from a year ago, analysts say stabilization in non-performing loans over the preceding quarter indicates problem loans have bottomed out. This is expected to give added momentum to current-year earnings.

In the third quarter, Royal Bank had the biggest return on assets—a key measure of bank performance—with 80 cents per $100 of assets, followed by Scotiabank and TD, at 75 cents and 69 cents, respectively. Scotiabank posted the best quarterly return on equity (16.3 percent), followed by the Royal Bank (16.1 percent) and the Bank of Montreal (15 percent).

The banking system is profiting quite nicely from the services it provides to consumers, i.e., loans, brokerage fees, and other service fees.

Source: Excerpts from Erik Heinrich, "Big Banks Get 'Gift from Gods," *The Financial Post*, September 9, 1991.

Questions for Discussion

1. What may be some of the reasons why the banks continue to be profitable?
2. Consider the various return calculations given above. Do you think they are high? Why or why not?
3. Should bank returns be an issue of concern to the public?

THE BANKS' COMPETITORS

More and more Canadians are banking at trust companies and credit unions (*caisses populaires*). These financial institutions perform most of the functions that the Schedule I banks do. In particular, they act as go-betweens for savers with funds to lend and investors with the need to borrow.

trust company
A business that acts as a financial trustee and administers funds for individuals and businesses, offering a range of banking services

Trust companies were originally set up to act as executors of wills, as administrators of estates for living people, as guardians of children, as trustees for bond issues, and so forth. In carrying out their duties to invest the funds in their care, they extended their activities into granting mortgages and other loans. In recent years, their acceptance of funds "in trust" has developed into a deposit account system very like that of the chartered banks. Trust companies have gradually expanded the scope of their activities. They are major competitors of banks in deposit markets, commercial and mortgage lending, and personal loans.

Canada's 3,600 **credit unions (*caisses populaires*)** are financial co-operatives owned by their members. They trace their origin to the mutual savings banks in Europe of the eighteenth century and the People's Bank movement of the nineteenth century. They have traditionally stressed the virtues of mutuality and thrift, as well as the provision of deposit and credit facilities for the "common people." Credit unions perform many of the regular banking functions and serve as sources for consumer loans at competitive rates for their members. They tend to be affiliated with companies, unions, professional associations, or religious groups. Their goal is to provide more personalized and accessible banking services to owner members. The close relationship sometimes makes the availability of loans easier because the basis of the loan goes beyond purely objective criteria such as collateral available.

credit union (caisse populaire)
A financial co-operative, offering deposit and credit facilities to its members

The Need for a Central Banking Authority

What would happen if all a bank's depositors decided to withdraw their funds at once? The bank would be unable to return the depositors' money—unless it could borrow the needed funds from another bank. But if the demand for currency instead of chequing and savings accounts spread to other banks, the result would be a bank panic. Banks would have to close their doors until they could obtain payments from their borrowers. Until the 1920s, such panics often resulted in bank failures. In 1933, a royal commission on banking and currency recommended the establishment of a central banking authority, partly to ensure the safety of the banking system.

THE BANK OF CANADA

In 1934, Parliament passed the Bank of Canada Act, thereby creating a central bank for Canada. The act provided a new legal framework for the chartered banks and gave the **Bank of Canada** a mandate "to regulate credit and currency in the best interest of the economic life of the nation, to control and protect the external value of the national monetary unit and to mitigate by its influence fluctuations in the general level of production, trade, prices, and employment, so far as possible within the scope of monetary action." [7]

In practice, the Bank of Canada is a banker's bank. The chartered banks are required to submit regular reports on their operations to the minister of finance and the Bank of Canada. Most important, they are required to keep reserve deposits with the Bank of Canada.

The Bank of Canada is expected to formulate and execute monetary policy for Canada. The work of the Bank is carried out through several departments, including Securities (to handle open-market operations), Research, and International Transactions. Through its nationwide network of offices and its role as the ultimate clearing agency, the Bank regulates monetary operations in the country.

Although a government agency, the Bank of Canada is designed to be fairly free from political interference. The governors of the Bank of

Bank of Canada
Canada's central bank with responsibility for issuing paper money, administering government bonds and treasury bills, controlling the money supply, and setting the bank rate

Canada have tried to maintain a tradition of independence. Of course, the government, as the sole shareholder and as the body that is responsible for overall economic policy, has ultimate control over the Bank. There is regular, close consultation between the minister of finance and the governor of the Bank, and in case of serious disagreement, it is clearly the minister who has the upper hand. [8]

The most important function of the Bank of Canada is monetary management or control of the money supply in order to promote economic growth and a stable dollar. Control of the money supply includes the control of credit conditions. Three tools of monetary management are the Bank's secondary reserve requirements, its open-market operations, and the bank rate.

Reserve Requirements

The strongest weapon in the Bank of Canada's arsenal for controlling the money supply is the **secondary reserve requirement**, which dictates the proportion of a bank's chequing and savings accounts that

secondary reserve requirement
The requirement that banks hold a percentage of the deposits made to chequing and savings accounts in treasury bills

Established in 1935, the Bank of Canada is owned by the Government of Canada. It is the monetary manager responsible for issuing paper currency, acting as fiscal agent and banker for the government, setting the bank rate and helping to formulate and implement monetary policies.

must be held in treasury bills. (Treasury bills are promissory notes of the Government of Canada. They are the shortest-term marketable debt instrument of the government and are one of the ways that the government borrows the money for its enormous needs.)

By changing the percentage of reserves required from the chartered banks, the Bank of Canada can directly affect the amount of money available for making loans. For example, if it should choose to stimulate the economy by increasing the amount of funds available for borrowing, it may lower the reserve requirement, allowing the banks to buy fewer treasury bills.

Changing reserve requirements was a little-used tool until the past two decades, which have been characterized by dramatic inflation. A variation of as little as 1 percent in the reserve requirement significantly changes the amount of money banks are able to lend. Therefore, the Bank of Canada prefers to use its other two instruments of monetary management—open-market operations and changes in the bank rate.

Open-Market Operations

The most important and most frequently used instrument of monetary management is **open-market operations** in the buying and selling of government bonds. Suppose the Bank of Canada decides it wants to increase the money supply. It could do this by lowering the reserve requirement, but it can also simply buy government bonds in the open market. The exchange of money for bonds releases more money into the economy, which in turn increases the amount available to member banks. Conversely, when the Bank of Canada sells government bonds, the overall money supply is reduced.

open-market operations (of the Bank of Canada)
Buying and selling government bonds on the open market

The Bank of Canada uses open-market operations when small adjustments in the money supply are desired. The process is more flexible and has less effect on public attitudes. In contrast, when the Bank of Canada announces a change in reserve requirements, the reaction of banks, business people, and the stock market is immediate and predictable: they interpret the decision as introducing a period of "tighter" or "easier" money.

The Bank Rate

As the "banker's bank," the Bank of Canada lends money on a short-term basis to chartered banks when they need it to make loans. The interest rate charged by the Bank of Canada is called the **bank rate**.

bank rate
The interest rate charged by the Bank of Canada to the chartered banks

The bank rate is usually higher than the rate on other sources of funds (for example, savings accounts or term deposits of individuals or businesses). The banks naturally borrow money from the cheapest source available, so they will use Bank of Canada funds only if the bank rate is low enough for them to make a profit on the loans they offer to individuals and businesses. When the bank rate is high, the cost of such loans goes up, fewer loans are likely to be made, and money is "tight." Conversely, if the bank rate goes down, more loans are made and the money supply is increased. Changes in the bank rate also produce considerable psychological effect. Banks and other lenders tend to change their rates in accordance with movements in the bank rate.

The bank rate, therefore, affects the money supply and, indirectly, the rate of inflation. Like the reserve requirement, it is a blunt instrument that can have a dramatic effect on buying and selling activities, particularly in industries that are highly sensitive to interest rate changes such as the automobile and housing industries. Changes in the bank rate send messages quickly and effectively to all parts of society about the Bank of Canada's attitude to the money supply.

Table 21.3 shows how each of these tools of the Bank of Canada can stimulate or slow the economy.

Setting the Bank Rate

The bank rate is set weekly through the auctioning of 91-day treasury bills each Tuesday. The "life" of a treasury bill begins when Finance Canada and the Bank of Canada decide on the number and amount of bills to be issued. Although the amount depends primarily on the government's need for cash and on debt management policy, the total issue outstanding is watched closely. The Bank of Canada calls for bids (or tenders) one week in advance. The chartered banks, the larger investment dealers (a dozen or so), and the Bank of Canada itself bid regularly at each weekly auction. Others may also submit tenders. Bids are usually submitted electronically. The highest bidder obtains all the bills it bid for at that price; the second- and third-highest bidders are themselves similarly accommodated, and so on until the entire issue has been sold.

The process is quick. When the auction is over, calculations of allotments and of the average price and yield are made by computer. Bids may be submitted until noon, and by 2:00 P.M. successful bidders are informed by telephone, and the press release is circulated.

The bill rate is the key short-term rate from which the bank rate and the entire spectrum of interest rates are derived. The bank rate is set 0.25 percent higher than the bill rate. Through increasing or decreasing its own holdings of treasury bills, the Bank of Canada can effect changes in its monetary policy through changes in short-term interest rates. [9]

INSURANCE FOR DEPOSITORS: THE CDIC

What if your bank fails? Most Canadians had paid little or no attention to the question until the failure of the Canadian Commercial and Northland banks in 1985. The last bank failure had been in 1923,

---

TABLE 21.3 • THE TOOLS OF THE BANK OF CANADA AND HOW THEY AFFECT THE ECONOMY

Tools	Stimulate the economy	Slow the economy
Reserve requirement	Lower	Raise
Open-market operations	Buy	Sell
Bank rate	Lower	Raise

although trust companies have also failed. Bank failures can have catastrophic results for depositors. Individuals and businesses deposit money in financial institutions for one major reason: to safeguard their funds, including protection against inflation through interest payments. Few depositors anticipate the collapse of the financial institution itself. However, the remote fear that it might happen and evidence of collapse in other countries have encouraged depositors to lobby for protection against the possible loss of their deposits.

The **Canada Deposit Insurance Corporation (CDIC)** is a federal government agency that insures deposits up to a maximum of $60,000 for all deposit accounts in one institution and sets requirements for sound banking practices. As well, joint deposit accounts are insured separately from deposits in one name. Insurable deposits include savings and chequing accounts, guaranteed investment certificates, debentures other than bank debentures, money orders, deposit receipts, and certified drafts or cheques. To be insurable, a deposit must be payable in Canada, in Canadian currency, and must be repayable on demand on or before the expiration of five years. Shareholders, as owners of the bank rather than depositors, are not covered.

In Quebec, deposits in all financial institutions other than the chartered banks are guaranteed by the Quebec Deposit Insurance Board. All chartered banks, and trust and loan companies outside Quebec, must subscribe to the CDIC. Members must display the CDIC's official membership sign.

As well as insuring deposits in failed institutions, the CDIC protects the safety of deposits in institutions insured by examining and supervising the financial affairs and management of these institutions; it may prevent an institution from failing by providing financial and management assistance.

The CDIC was established in 1967. Despite the failures of 1985, deposit insurance is not of such vital importance to the survival of Canadian Schedule I chartered banks. Any bank within the Canadian banking system is part of a huge national operation, and it is unlikely that it would encounter the type of liquidity problems that would face a single-unit bank, which is common in the United States. Deposit insurance is far more important to depositors in the smaller financial intermediaries—the trust companies and credit unions—and places these institutions in a more secure position in competing with banks for the depositor's dollar.

THE CANADIAN PAYMENTS SYSTEM

When you write a cheque, how do you know that the money will be received by the person or business you want to pay it to? Do you even know what a cheque is?

A **cheque** is an unconditional promise to pay, directing a bank to pay out a certain sum of money under specified conditions. The concept of cheques has been around for almost 3,000 years, permitting us to do business without forcing us to handle currency. Almost all cheques are written on special chequebook paper, but they need not be. Cheques have been written on many curious surfaces: on hand-

Canada Deposit Insurance Corporation (CDIC)
An agency that provides insurance for depositors in the case of bank, credit union, or trust company failure

cheque
An authorization to a bank to pay from a specific account a certain sum of money to a specified recipient

Farcus   by David Waisglass
Gordon Coulthart

**Good news, Smitsberg! The boss agrees
you should have a bigger paycheque.**

Canadian Payments System
The means by which a cheque travels
from the recipient's bank to the cheque
drawer's bank and the designated funds
are transferred

**electronic funds transfer system
(EFTS)**
A method of using computer technology
to transfer funds

kerchiefs, cigarette paper, calling cards, fragile
valentines, and newspapers. One written on the
shell of a hard-boiled egg was cashed without
trouble by the Canadian Imperial Bank of
Commerce. A Western lumberman made out so
many cheques on his own brand of shingle that
his bank had to construct a special type of filing
cabinet for them.

Most business transactions and many personal ones use cheques. These are cleared
through the banking system by the remarkably
efficient **Canadian Payments System**, run by
the Canadian Payments Association (an
agency of the banks and other similar financial
institutions).

Suppose that Jean Martin has purchased a
new battery from Canadian Tire. Her cheque, in
the amount of $107.04, has authorized the Royal
Bank in Moncton to reduce her chequing account
by paying this amount to Canadian Tire. If both
parties had chequing accounts in the same bank,
cheque processing would be a simple matter of increasing the
chequing account of Canadian Tire by $107.04 and reducing Martin's
account by that amount.

But Canadian Tire has its chequing account in Toronto. In this situation, the Canadian Payments System enters the picture to act as col-
lector for intercity transactions. The system handles approximately 39
million cheques every week. In the majority of cases, a cheque will
clear a bank account on the same day that it is presented for payment
in a Canadian bank branch. Figure 21.2 shows the journey of Martin's
cheque through the system. If you receive cheques from your bank
each month, you can trace the route each of them has taken by examining the endorsement stamps on the back of it.

ELECTRONICS AND BANKING

The banking industry has adopted the efficiencies computers provide
with open arms. Each year, Canadian businesses handle more than a
billion cheques. Accounting for them is a task computers are ideally
designed to handle.

More and more, banks recognize that many payment processes
could be faster if "paper" were not involved. They look forward to the
"cashless society." This will be some time in coming, but many elements of it exist today. All banks use some form of **electronic funds
transfer system (EFTS)** that significantly reduces the paper trail, the
most familiar being automated teller machines and automated cash
dispensers found in supermarkets, airports, and service stations.

Integrated networks such as INTERAC allow a Royal Bank customer
to use the automatic bank teller of the Bank of Montreal if it is handier.
INTERAC now extends around the world. This author visits Hong
Kong regularly but carries along only a small amount of Hong Kong

FIGURE 21.2 • A CHEQUE'S JOURNEY THROUGH THE CANADIAN CLEARING AND SETTLEMENT SYSTEM

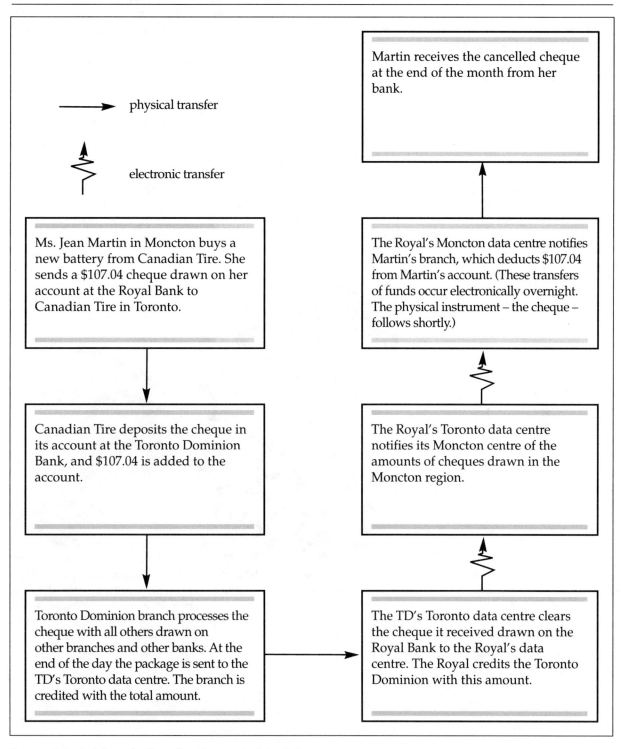

→ physical transfer

⚡ electronic transfer

Ms. Jean Martin in Moncton buys a new battery from Canadian Tire. She sends a $107.04 cheque drawn on her account at the Royal Bank to Canadian Tire in Toronto.

Canadian Tire deposits the cheque in its account at the Toronto Dominion Bank, and $107.04 is added to the account.

Toronto Dominion branch processes the cheque with all others drawn on other branches and other banks. At the end of the day the package is sent to the TD's Toronto data centre. The branch is credited with the total amount.

Martin receives the cancelled cheque at the end of the month from her bank.

The Royal's Moncton data centre notifies Martin's branch, which deducts $107.04 from Martin's account. (These transfers of funds occur electronically overnight. The physical instrument – the cheque – follows shortly.)

The Royal's Toronto data centre notifies its Moncton centre of the amounts of cheques drawn in the Moncton region.

The TD's Toronto data centre clears the cheque it received drawn on the Royal Bank to the Royal's data centre. The Royal credits the Toronto Dominion with this amount.

Source: Adapted from the Canadian Payments Association.

debit card

A method of making purchases by authorizing immediate electronic withdrawal of funds from an account at a financial institution

funds because he can access his Canadian account there as easily as at home.

The EFTS is finding its way into supermarkets and other retail settings. In some places, a customer merely swipes a bank card (or a **debit card**) through the sensing machine, then authorizes the amount, and payment is made electronically to the store. The EFTS reduces paperwork, is convenient for customers, and increases efficiency for both buyer and seller. The important distinction for the consumer between a credit card and a debit card is that, when the latter is used, the money is withdrawn from the user's account immediately, not when a cheque is written to pay a monthly balance. This may mean the loss of interest on dollars in a savings account—and is thus a source of additional revenue for the bank.

Canadian banks are world leaders in technology. They are often testing new methods to make it easier for the consumer to use their services. Debit cards represent an example of such an innovation. Issues in Business 21.2 considers whether the debit card is of more benefit to the consumer or to the financial institution.

Royal Bank's Personal Touch Payment allows its clients a convenient and safe way of shopping without having to carry cash. Upon purchase, the store clerk passes the client card through a special terminal, directly withdrawing the amount from the account. This becomes even more convenient than a credit card.

ISSUES IN BUSINESS 21.1

ARE DEBIT CARDS OF MORE BENEFIT TO THE CONSUMER OR THE BANK?

DEBIT CARDS ALLOW consumers to electronically transfer money directly from their bank account to a retailer's account by using a magnetic-stripped card such as their bank card. Debit card machines have gradually become available across the country. By using the debit cards, consumers no longer need worry about having cheques accepted at certain stores.

These cards have the potential to benefit financial institutions as well as their customers. "From the banks' perspective, the cards reduce costs because there's less cheque and cash handling, and therefore fewer staff needed to process paperwork," says Colin Davies, associate partner, banking industry group at Toronto-based Andersen Consulting. "Debit cards would also drastically reduce security and servicing costs for automated instant tellers and guards."

The banks play down such benefits, saying it will be a long time before they realize any return on their large investments in software and other systems for debit cards.

However, the debit cards will help the banks to attract business. "The banks can get a segment of retailers they haven't traditionally had access to," says Davies. For instance, liquor stores and grocery stores that don't take credit cards and rarely take cheques will accept debit cards. The banks, which charge about 25 cents a transaction for the debit service, will benefit from this charge each time people don't use cash.

Banks are realizing they have to offer debit cards as part of a bundle of services. If they already have a VISA relationship and cash-management service for a merchant, debit cards are a logical extension to that service. Offering debit cards as part of a package protects the banks against loss of business that might result from not offering them. Credit card business is profitable for banks, and they risk erosion of that business if competitors take advantage of the debit platform and they don't.

There is still some question as to whether debit cards will be accepted. In both Britain and the United States, they have been abandoned—in Britain, because of failure to get support from merchants, and in the United States because of the highly fractionalized banking system. However, experts feel that because Canadian banks are world leaders in technology and the banking system is strong, debit cards will work in Canada.

Source: Excerpts from Kirsteen MacLeod, "Cashing In on Debit Cards," *The Financial Post*, September 16, 1991, p. 38.

Questions for Discussion
1. Are there any significant benefits to the consumer who uses a debit card?
2. Do the advantages to the banks outweigh those to the customer?
3. What are the risks to banks of introducing the debit card system?

BUSINESS REVIEW 21.2

1. Differentiate between Schedule I and Schedule II banks and give examples of financial institutions in each category.

2. Reserve requirements, open-market operations, and the bank rate are used by the Bank of Canada to control the money supply. Explain how each is used to this end.

3. Discuss the use of electronics in banking and predict what the situation will be like ten years from now.

INTERACTIVE SUMMARY AND DISCUSSION QUESTIONS

1. Money is something that everyone knows about—or is it? Ideal characteristics that money should possess include *divisibility, portability, durability, stability*, and *difficulty* to counterfeit. Explain each of these characteristics as it relates to money.

2. The functions of money are to serve as a medium of exchange, a unit of account, and a temporary store of value. Explain.

3. The Canadian money supply comprises many components, among them: coins, paper money, demand deposits, and chequing/savings accounts. Differentiate between demand deposits and savings accounts.

4. Chartered banks are profit-making businesses that perform two basic functions: they hold deposits, and they use these deposits to make loans. How do they earn profits?

5. The Bank of Canada was created to provide monetary leadership for the country. What are some of the main ways that it does so?

6. "The strongest weapon in the Bank of Canada's arsenal for controlling the money supply is the *secondary reserve requirement*." Describe how this works.

7. The Bank of Canada sets the *bank rate* every Tuesday. How does this process work?

8. If your trust company, credit union, or bank should fail, you would likely be protected through the Canada Deposit Insurance Corporation. How would this work and what are the limitations?

9. Cheques are cleared from the Canadian Payments System. Describe how the system works.

CASE 21.1

EUROPEAN BANK FOR RECONSTRUCTION AND DEVELOPMENT

IN HIS SPACIOUS office on Leadenhall Street, not far from the Bank of England, Jacques Attali pauses for a moment before describing the main achievements of this year-old European Bank. "The bank exists," he says simply, as if that in itself is quite an achievement. And it is.

The London-based European Bank for Reconstruction and Development, to give the world's newest international financial institution its full name (the name is similar to that of the International Bank for Reconstruction and Development, more commonly referred to as the World Bank, which was started after the Second World War), "exists as a forum, as a place of

(continued)

expertise, political and economic," says the institution's controversial French president. With a subscribed capital base of ECU 10 billion ($7 billion) and a Triple A credit rating, the bank's heft in the marketplace is now certainly hard to miss.

It is also very much Attali's own creation. Attali, although not a banker by training, came up with the idea of a bank to help in the reconstruction of newly liberalized Eastern and Central Europe. In 1989, his concept was taken before the European Parliament by French president François Mitterrand. The next year, an agreement to establish the bank was signed in Paris, and it was inaugurated in April 1991, with 40 countries, including Canada, as members.

Membership includes the three Baltic states and eleven of the former Soviet republics. However, the European Bank is much more than just an international bank. It is a political body. "It is not just an institution for finance," Attali says unabashedly, "but also for influence." As well as financing the transformation of Eastern Europe and the former Soviet Union, the bank has a wide mandate to foster multiparty democracy, help draft new constitutions, protect minority rights, restore and improve the environment, and promote freer markets and entrepreneurial initiatives.

Freer trade is the real key to assisting the emerging nations of Eastern and Central Europe, Attali believes. He points to the North American Free Trade Agreement between Canada, the United States, and Mexico as a good model. It is "bold and positive," he says, holding it up as an example of what could be done to create trade links in Europe among economies at very different stages of economic development. Attali also believes it is imperative that the West give massive investment assistance to the newly liberalized nations, specifically to channel funds into restructuring projects, including conversion of military plants to civilian use, and wide-scale retraining.

The European Bank has been very successful so far. Attali reported lending and investments by the bank so far of ECU 625 million and had mobilized another ECU 2.1 billion in co-financings from private institutions. These have involved twenty projects in half a dozen countries. Among them are district heating and cold-storage enterprises in Poland, packaging and telecommunications in Hungary, power-generating equipment in Romania, a drilling company in Siberia, and food processing in Czechoslovakia. More than half the transactions have involved the private sector or institutions being privatized.

Some critics remain suspicious of what they fear will be an interventionist philosophy on the part of the bank, rather than a truly deep commitment to the free market. But Attali is adamant that it is not the bank's intention to compete with private-sector banks and investment firms, as some have also feared—just the reverse. "We are here to open doors to them," he says. He wants the European Bank to be a front runner for the commercial banks. "We [can] put an international stamp on projects for them." There has also been speculation that the bank would try to push aside other international financial institutions involved in the area in which it operates. However, Attali says the bank works in close co-ordination with the International Monetary Fund and the World Bank as well as private-sector institutions. "We want to be a catalyst for other efforts," he says.

The European Bank is also helping to train managers in the financial sectors of the countries in which it operates. So far, it has organized ten training programs, and wants to do more. "It is just a beginning and will take time," Attali says.

Source: Adapted from Neville Nankivel, "Jacques Attali Banks on Socialism's Ruins," *The Financial Post*, May 4, 1992, p. S28.

Questions for Discussion

1. Discuss how the availability of funds for projects in the former Eastern Bloc can make a difference beyond the individual organization that is receiving the funds.

(continued)

2. Many banks have operations around the world. Does it make sense to have a special bank such as the European Bank for Reconstruction and Development? Why wouldn't private commercial banks fill this need?

3. What are the potential disadvantages of operating a bank such as this, which has motivations beyond purely economic ones?

CASE 21.2

THE BANK OF MONTREAL

AFTER A DECADE of being savaged by investment analysts for lacklustre performance, the Bank of Montreal, under the leadership of Matthew Barrett, is beginning to deliver an acceptable return to shareholders. However, in the wake of record 1991 profits at four of the six major banks—including the Bank of Montreal—banking chief executives are facing accusations of excessive profits at a time when many clients are engaged in life-and-death financial struggles.

"This is not manna from heaven—we have worked hard to earn it," Barrett declared. Under Barrett's direction, the Bank of Montreal has developed into a viable, competitive business. The Bank of Montreal has spent heavily on research, technology, infrastructure, and training, and that is finally paying off. It has also reduced its non-interest expenses.

In two years as chairman and CEO, Barrett has presided over a public relations turnaround for Canada's oldest and third-largest bank with nearly $100 billion in assets. He has also earned the status of a caring, socially aware manager for the 1990s.

Once dismissed as a cold, remote institution, the B of M enjoys an image of scrappy competitiveness in an industry of undifferentiated me-tooism. The bank has won applause for its feisty interest rate policy. An accurate call on declining rates allowed it to pursue highly profitable lending and money market activities. Its tactic of cutting prime rates consistently ahead of the opposition has become a powerful and inexpensive marketing tool.

The bank has exploited this headline-grabbing "prime policy" to attract off-the-street business and reclaim shares of neglected markets in consumer and small to medium–sized business lending. Asset growth, which lagged in the troubled 1980s, is coming back strongly. Before Mr. Barrett's time, the Bank of Montreal had alienated many customers by taking commercial loans officers out of local branches. Barrett has moved decision making closer to markets, and resurrected the community bank, which tries to be more things for a larger segment of customers.

Mr. Barrett is known by his colleagues as an effortless communicator; one who has taken his vision of continuous improvement, customer service, and teamwork directly to the bank's 32,000 employees. "We have a culture of continuous improvement in the bank. We're not at all complacent," he says. Meanwhile, the B of M works hard to cultivate its image as a bank alert to the concerns of its communities. It is committed to promoting women in management and to upgrading staff training.

The logic of economies of scale has driven financial institutions to get much bigger. Deregulation of financial services allows banks to diversify into trust and insurance services. However, Barrett has distanced himself from deregulation. He prefers to concentrate on rebuilding the B of M's core banking business, which lost ground during the decade before Barrett became CEO. Its distribution system of 1,200 branches suggests "a natural market share" of 17 to

(continued)

18 percent. But, in crucial areas such as consumer and small-business loans, its share has languished at around 11 percent. Barrett just wants to get back to the starting line.

He also aims at building a large North American bank, working from a strong base in Canada and in the Chicago area, where the B of M owns the well-regarded Harris Bank, purchased in 1984 for $718 million.

In business terms, there is little denying the success of the strategies Barrett is employing. "Strategically, they're doing all the right things," says investment analyst Hugh Brown of Burns Fry Ltd. Proof of success lies in the numbers in banking as in any other business. In fiscal 1990, the bank returned to solid profitability after losing money in 1987 and 1989. It reported record earnings of $595 million for the year ended 1991, up almost 14 percent from a year earlier.

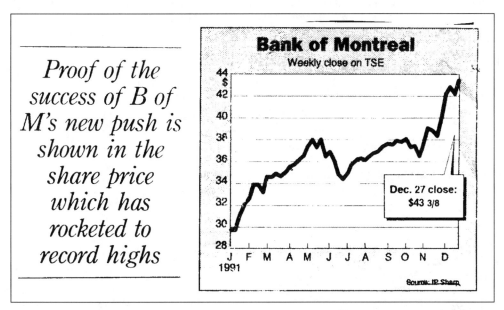

Proof of the success of B of M's new push is shown in the share price which has rocketed to record highs

Source: Adapted from Gordon Pitts, "Champion of Rate Cuts Lifts B of M," *The Financial Post*, January 6, 1992, pp. S8–9.

Questions for Discussion

1. How was the Bank of Montreal positioned in the market before Matthew Barrett became CEO? And after?

2. What main tactic gave the B of M the competitive edge when restructuring? Would this alone bring about the changes experienced by the bank? Explain.

3. Discuss the distribution system employed by this business. In what ways can the bank's mission statement of "continuous improvement" be applied to banking?

NOTES

1. "Creeping Inflation," *Federal Reserve Bank of Philadelphia Business Review*, August 1957, p. 3. Quoted in Campbell R. McConnell, *Economics* (New York: McGraw-Hill, 1975), p. 289.

2. Excerpt from *Principles of Money, Banking and Financial Markets*, 7th Ed., by Lawrence S. Ritter and William L. Silber. Copyright ©1974 by Basic Books, Inc., copyright ©1977, 1980, 1983, 1986, 1989, 1991 by Lawrence S. Ritter and William L. Silber. Reprinted by permission of HarperCollins Publishers, Inc.

3. Andrew McIntosh, "If Coins Come, the Bills May Go," *The Globe and Mail*, June 11, 1985.

4. See, for example, Gordon F. Boreham and Ronald G. Bodkin, *Money, Banking and Finance: The Canadian Context* (Toronto: Dryden, 1993).

5. Boreham and Bodkin, *Money, Banking and Finance*, p. 115.

6. Lawrence S. Ritter and William L. Silber, *Principles of Money, Banking and Financial Markets* (New York: Basic Books, 1974), pp. 385–86.

7. Alan Toulin, "Bank of Canada Role on the Line," *The Financial Post*, November 18, 1991, p. 5.

8. Edwin G. Dolan and Roy Vogt, *Basic Economics* (Toronto: Holt, Rinehart and Winston of Canada, 1981), pp. 192–93.

9. "Treasury Bills—What They Are and How the Weekly Auction Works," *Canadian Bankers' Association Bulletin*, April 1980.

PHOTO CREDITS

MODULE

◆ FUT ◆

THE FUTURE OF CANADIAN BUSINESS

THE FOCUS OF THIS MODULE

1. To comment upon recent major changes in the way Canadians live and work and why it is difficult to predict future changes

2. To evaluate the current economic, social, global, and technological trends affecting business

3. To discuss the concept of sustainable development

4. To identify the challenges facing Canadian business and the executive of the future

5. To define the following terms:

KEY TERMS

jobless growth

technology

high-technology firm

artificial intelligence (AI)

virtual reality

biotechnology

sustainable development

automation

Business must be able to predict the future extent and direction of economic, societal, global, and technological change if it is to successfully meet the industrial challenges of the 1990s and the twenty-first century. But change is difficult to predict.

Business cannot assume that what happened yesterday or today will be true tomorrow. The pace of change has clearly quickened. In 1970, Alvin Toffler's *Future Shock* pointed out that humankind's last 50,000 years of existence can be divided into 800 "lifetimes" of about 62 years each. The first 650 of these lifetimes were spent in caves. Writing has existed for only the past 70 lifetimes. Most of the products used today have been developed within the present lifetime.

CHANGES IN THE WAY WE LIVE AND WORK

In *The Third Wave*, published in 1980, Toffler argued that the economies of developed nations were entering a new era. According to Toffler, the first wave in history occurred when permanent settlements replaced nomadic lifestyles. The second wave was marked by the Industrial Revolution, when work shifted out of the home and into factories and offices, changing family structures in the process. This second-wave, or nuclear family, as Toffler labels it, was characterized by a breadwinning husband, a housekeeping wife, and two children.

Toffler points out that the nuclear family is no longer the norm, accounting for only 7 percent of the U.S. population. He cites the tremendous increase in single-person households, the high incidence of childless couples, and the growth of a service-oriented economy as some of the causes of a third wave in human history. Toffler also concludes that work, often computer-based, would begin to shift back into the home, similar to the pattern that existed in the first wave. Most children would grow up in a home that doubled as a workplace, and this changed work/living environment would affect male–female relationships. Non-family members would join households as part of the new work organizations, forming a new version of the extended family.

Many of Toffler's predictions have already come true. The work force, once dominated by men who held one job throughout their working lives, now reflects the changing status of women, the acceptance of career shifts for both men and women, and the oversupply of workers skilled in yesterday's jobs. This oversupply has forced business, governments, and labour to take a hard look at the current Western economic situation and at what they perceive as the future of the industrial base.

It is not easy to predict trends. In 1988, the famous futurist himself admitted that he had miscalculated. The numbers of people working at home in "electronic cottages" were already far greater than he had imagined. [1]

As Vancouver small-business consultant Douglas Gray explains in *Home Inc.*, a guide to home-based business, "some people are rejecting the corporate rate race and choosing to 'cocoon'—creating a home-centred business that doesn't require commuting and eliminates the stresses of working in a corporate office. Others have opted for a home-based business as a method of balancing a career with raising children." [2] But, though some home workers are self-employed or operating independent businesses, many also work at home for others. "Telecommuters" save time and money by avoiding the daily commute; they also save their companies office space and related expenses. Indications are that workers in a familiar, low-stress environment are more productive than those working in a busy office with its constant distractions and interruptions. Working at home also allows people with disabilities to be gainfully employed. [3] Toffler prophesies that the development of the electronic cottage will allow the home partially to regain its place as "the centre of society."

Despite the difficulties of prediction, it is easy to see that trends in the economy, in society, in technology, and in the environment do affect business. Effective managers must recognize these trends and how they are influencing their operations if they are to develop appropriate strategies to deal with the problems and opportunities these trends present.

ECONOMIC TRENDS

If managers of twenty or even ten years ago were suddenly to find themselves in the economy of the mid-1990s, they would discover that their companies' relationship to the global marketplace, the employment situation, and even the foundations on which the Canadian economy rests, was profoundly different. Inflation, unemployment, recession, currency fluctuations, and changing trade agreements have had enormous impacts.

People are becoming more conscious than they were a decade ago of how economic factors affect everyday life. Some are alarmed by the high unemployment and double-digit inflation of recent years. Others fear economic domination by U.S. or Japanese firms or the competition of cheap labour in Mexico or Southeast Asia. But Canada is still a wealthy nation and an effective competitor in the world marketplace.

Still, the economic changes noted above indicate the importance of business people's thorough understanding of the competitive system. No firm is far removed from the basic economic changes that occur in society, and effective managers must be aware of current economic events affecting their businesses.

The failures of the political and economic systems in Eastern Europe and in Russia have been grim lessons for Canada and our business people who planned and depended upon joint ventures. These devastating examples have given us a sober view of what can happen. On the other hand, these threats to our economic well-being must also be seen as important opportunities to be seized. It is clear that politics and economics are contiguous players on the world stage.

Success in economic relations will naturally hinge on the international political climate. But business's advance guard has the satisfaction of knowing that commercial ties bring East and West closer together. [4]

From classroom to board room, the basic unit of economic study in the future will be the globe. Global trends promise to make business a tougher and more exciting calling—and a major contributor to planet-wide unification.

THE GLOBAL MARKETPLACE

Globalization is a necessary response to a world market made smaller by telecommunications and larger by a more balanced division of wealth. In 1960, the United States accounted for 40 percent of global GNP; as of 1991, the U.S. share is 20 percent, Europe has 22 percent, and East Asia 22 percent. These figures remain similar today.

As a result, we'll see more transborder joint ventures and mergers as corporations seek global hook-ups. In the airways, Canadian Pacific has ties with American Airlines and Air Canada with Continental. We'll see global niche consolidation. Canada's CAE Industries Ltd. in 1989 bought the four military simulation divisions of the Link Co. in the United States and became the world's largest simulator maker. There will be a predatory wave as trading blocs produce giant corporations that attempt overseas acquisitions, forcing potential target firms to expand on the eat-or-be-eaten principle. Mergers in the Canadian economy are just an early tremor in a global shake-up.[5]

Issues in Business 22.1 considers the impact of global trends on the Canadian economy and provides some conclusions and recommendations for managing change.

ISSUES IN BUSINESS 22.1

MANAGING CHANGE

As CANADA PREPARES for the twenty-first century, business and government will need to do some new thinking. The impact of globalization on the Canadian economy signals a profound change in the way that business is to be conducted. Everyone in Canada will be affected by international forces.

In the manufacturing sector, Canadian business is already involved in global action. Some business leaders have already started to develop a new vision of Canada that is outward-looking and responsive to worldwide changes affecting production, marketing, and human resource management.

Canada's major problem is that many people in government, and in the service industries, do not yet share this global vision. Yet, 70 percent of Canadians work in the service sector. A major theme of this study is the need to develop an awareness of the international facts of life for all sectors, including services, and for government policies in all sectors to be more responsive to global forces.

Until the manufacturing and service sectors share the same vision for Canada with government, the future will be clouded. Responsible government policies and successful corporate strategies are possible in Canada once the nature of global competition is fully realized. The Canada–U.S. Free Trade Agreement was a step in the right direction. Much more needs to be done to build upon this foundation and bring a broader constituency to the table of international activity.

Canada already has a high degree of international trade and investment. Much of Canada's manufacturing sector builds value-added into resource-based industries and is successful in global competition. While both large and small manufacturers are affected by international forces,

(continued)

Labatt's, a successful Canadian beer company, has carved a name for itself among pub goers and beer drinkers in Britain where it accounts for 96% of all Canadian lager sold. In fact, it ranks among the top ten beers sold in the U.K. and is number three in Italy.

most of Canada's service sector is dominated by small business in local or regional markets (with the exception of those large banks and other financial services operating internationally).

Conclusion

Canadian business is now faced with domestic markets that are turning into global markets. Both Canada's manufacturing and service sectors need to improve their ability to operate at international standards. The nature of international competitiveness demands knowledge-intensive skills. An appropriate role of government is to work with business and labour in generating a more innovative and effective educational system. Workers and managers need to have an international outlook plus the knowledge, managerial expertise, and entrepreneurial skills to help all sectors of Canada's business become globally competitive.

Recommendations

Reduce Fiscal Deficits

Curbing the seemingly insatiable appetites of Canadian governments for increasing fiscal deficits remains the first priority in economic policy. Establishment of the proper economic environment for development of international competitiveness cannot proceed far without responsible government policy.

Business leaders have an important role to play. They must continue to keep up the pressure on governments to find ways to bring order to their fiscal regimes. They must ensure that their voices continue to be heard on this issue, particularly since business is one of the few stakeholder groups able to speak effectively on behalf of economic rationality.

Change the Protectionist Mindset

For decades, Canadian business and government have assumed that government policy could effectively isolate the domestic economy from the forces of international competition. The protectionist mindset is still central to the Canadian vision of economic development. This must be changed.

It is a dangerous illusion to believe that the forces of globalization and international competition can be restrained by Canadian government policy. The protectionist mindset must be replaced by a truly international perspective that seeks Canada's future prosperity in the competitive abilities of its businesses rather than in measures to attenuate the impact of global competition. Canadian businesses have to learn to look within themselves for the means to address the problems they face rather than turn to governments for help.

Balance Manufacturing and Service Activities

Services represent a large and growing component of manufacturing costs; they are a key determinant of the international competitiveness of Canadian industry. Government policies and corporate strategies need to understand the balanced nature of manufacturing and service activities.

Canada will prosper in the new international environment if its businesses develop the management systems and competencies for operating knowledge-intensive businesses. As they advance toward these structures and systems, Canadian businesses will find that the distinctions between manufacturing and services businesses will become less sharp and that the two types of operations will converge in essential managerial characteristics. Manufacturing businesses will have a larger service content while service business will have to adopt the productivity approaches of knowledge-intensive manufacturing. This corporate imperative will need an appropriate response from governments, which need to understand that manufacturing and service activities are equally important if Canadian business is to be globally competitive.

(continued)

A New Role for Government

After putting its fiscal house in order, government too needs to learn a new role in the development of globally competitive Canadian business. Instead of concentrating on policies of subsidization and protectionism, governments must become more effective in encouraging Canadian businesses to open up to the rest of the world. This will require greater efforts to complete the unfinished business of the Canada–U.S. Free Trade Agreement and to push for broader market access in the GATT and other international forums. Instead of advocating unrealistic R&D policies aimed

With the service sector dominating the job market, "service" has become an important word in advertisements. Manufacturers have either shifted their focus from product to service or broadened it to include service. Industries like travel agencies, banks and hotels must consistently emphasize friendly staff and efficent services.

at making Canada a major creator of new scientific knowledge and commercial technology, governments needs to devote their energies to helping Canadian businesses become more adept consumers of the science and know-how of the rest of the world. Instead of putting government resources into physical resources such as bricks and mortar, governments need to pay more attention to the development of the human resources of Canada.

Better Education and Training

The conversion of the Canadian economy into a truly modern knowledge-intensive one will not proceed without major efforts to change our educational system. At all levels (school, technical college, university, and in-house), business education and training must be revamped to provide the knowledge and skills needed to build competitive businesses. Canada must develop a national competitive advantage in its people. Canadians can be as intelligent and hard-working as workers and managers in other countries. What is needed is vision and a guiding hand through better corporate and government training programs.

In particular, Canadian businesses have to learn to address their education and training agendas with the same level of competence and attention they now devote to the financial and capital budgeting processes. They have to make international business considerations central to their human resource programs. Canadian firms can build upon and further develop business skills in well-educated and motivated people. Together, Canadian workers and Canadian firms can improve Canada's international competitiveness. The challenge for the future for all sectors in Canadian society is to develop and share a global vision.

Source: Excerpt from Alan M. Rugman and R. D'Cruz, "New Visions for Canadian Business," *Kodak Canada*, 1991, pp. 9–10.

(continued)

Question for Discussion

1. Examine each of Rugman and D'Cruz's recommendations and explain why you agree or disagree. Give examples of successful or unsuccessful Canadian enterprises to illustrate your points.

The Job Market

The transformation of Canada's economy imposed by more rapid technological change and tougher competition from overseas has generated human costs that are impossible to calculate. In addition to those who have actually been out of work, there are countless thousands who have been forced to accept shorter hours, a lateral transfer, or a cut in pay to keep their jobs. The unemployment rate of around 11 percent for the mid-1990s, coupled with the underemployment rate, is a problem in need of a solution. And, at the same time, those who are still employed are forced to work longer and harder.

Some of the forces at work are:

- The emergence of low-cost resource suppliers in developing countries make many mines and mills uneconomical to operate.
- The arrival of low-cost imports of high-quality goods forces fabricating and finishing plants to undertake major changes in products, processes, or the obtaining of materials. Often some aspects of the operation are relocated to low-cost areas overseas.
- New technologies such as banking machines and other automated devices allow companies to rethink completely their way of serving clients and using their employees.
- The slowdown in population growth and tax revenues forces governments not only to curtail the growth in public-sector employment but also to seek ways to deliver public services at lower costs.

Not only has growth been slower in the 1990s, but pressures from technology and import competition have forced employers in those industries to find ways to produce more with fewer people. Some people call this process **jobless growth**.

At the same time, dramatic changes have also taken place in the nature of jobs within the workplace. The introduction of computers and advanced electronic equipment is blurring the distinction between clerical and technical staff, and between technical staff and production workers. Changes in distribution systems have reduced the need for workers in shipping, storing, and receiving. Middle and even senior management jobs are being eroded as new management information systems evolve and companies adopt leaner organization structures. The daunting fact is that the transformation process is only beginning. Canadian firms are in the early stages of the modernization and adaptation programs needed to compete in the markets of the 1990s.

What hope does all this offer the unemployed and those who will be entering the labour force? For the young, there are few promising signs in the immediate future, as indicated in Issues in Business 22.2. Their experience is in many ways similar to that of people over the age of 55 who are being forced off the payroll now by various forms of early retirement and who are probably the ones who find it most difficult to train or adapt.

jobless growth
Growth in the economy unaccompanied by any increase in employment

ISSUES IN BUSINESS 22.2

A LOST GENERATION?

THE RECESSION HAS had such a disastrous effect on the job prospects of young Canadians that it may actually have created a lost generation.

On March 2, 1994, Statistics Canada published its first examination of what the recession did to employment trends among citizens aged 15 to 24. The article, by Deborah Sunter in the quarterly *Perspectives,* catalogues a tale of woe:

- Unprecedented numbers of young Canadians have been wrestled out of the work force;
- Proportionately, more of them lost their jobs than did adults;
- It will take years longer for them to gain back jobs than it will for adults.

"I don't know if you're a baby boomer, but I have guilt," Ms. Sunter said in an interview.

It's a dramatic change for a generation once touted as having the world by the tail. Because this group is smaller in number than the baby boomers, its members were expected to be much in demand as they reached working age.

At the end of the 1980s, for example, the media carried articles on how various companies in the service sector—the traditional employer of the young—were forced to hire senior citizens because the young were in such short supply.

By the early 1990s, it was a completely different picture. For example, in 1989, before the recession hit, 62.3 percent of Canadians aged 15 to 24 were employed. By November 1992, the numbers had fallen to 50 percent. Adult employment, meanwhile, had overtaken the levels it had reached before the recession. . . .

And while more young Canadians are turning to school to fill their days (Statistics Canada says 56 percent of young people were in school full-time in November 1993, compared with 49 percent in November 1989), this avenue, too, is being barricaded with steep increases in tuition fees and much tougher entrance guidelines.

Not only that, this additional education does not guarantee a good job if the jobs are nowhere to be found, says Lars Osberg, an economist at Dalhousie University. "Going back to school only delays the problem. It doesn't actually solve it."

Others said it is possible that by the time the economy does produce good jobs, a fresh generation of better-trained, better-educated young people will be vying for them.

The prospect that all of these factors could produce a lost generation appears currently to be in the offing. He said that trying to achieve a lower interest rate and exchange rate would go a long way toward creating new jobs.

Gordon Betcherman, director of a labour research group at Queen's University in Kingston, said that this generation of Canadians may not find its niche in the job market until the end of the century, when the oldest batch of baby boomers begins to retire. The boomers "are sort of jamming up the system," he said.

He said he believes that the government should step forcefully into the issue by devising policies to help young, skilled Canadians into what he called the "good jobs" sector.

Source: Alanna Mitchell, "Future Is Bleak for Youth, Study Says," *The Globe and Mail,* March 3, 1994, pp. A1, A2.

Question for Discussion

1. What steps can a young person take to improve the chances of getting a job?

Many older people worked all their lives in primary industries and manufacturing, which have declined in relative importance since 1980 and will continue to do so, while the service sector will mushroom to control more than 70 percent of employment. Virtually all jobs created since 1985 are in the service sector.

For the next decade, the labour market in Canada will be characterized by more competition between generations. That competition will mean stress (if not economic hardship) for some senior managers, who will find themselves being asked to leave just at the point where they had expected to sit back and enjoy the respect and privileges that go with a senior executive position.

There will also be more competition between the sexes, as both men and women get crowded out of certain stereotyped occupations (there are now fewer opportunities in both the female-dominated retail trade, service, and clerical positions, and male-dominated production-line, transportation, and construction jobs). This may be a setback for women, whose employment has been enhanced by the rapid growth of service-sector jobs.

There will be a growing need for retraining of employees to help them adapt, which will offer a rapidly expanding market for post-secondary education services, a market that many colleges and universities still are ill-equipped to serve.

The best odds for survival in the coming job market will be with those who have power, seniority, adaptability, or a good level of technical/computer literacy. Inevitably, many individuals will find their lives disrupted by corporate reorganization. That is the human side of a process with major consequences for our economic future.

The Economic Base

Canada's growth prospects for the 1990s will depend heavily on how well we manage economic transformation from an economy based on resources and a narrow line of manufactured goods. Decisions made now will determine not only whether we can produce efficiently but also whether we produce the range of products that people want to buy. The challenge is to emerge trim and fit, equipped with the right skills and products.

High technology is not just another buzzword, like "industrial strategy" or "concentration." It has become the key to survival for many, if not most, Canadian industries.

Underlying economic pressures are forcing Canada to transform the impetus for economic growth from the exploitation of physical resources—land and labour—to the mobilization of intellectual knowledge. In the past, Canada's growth has been generated primarily by extracting more raw materials from the land, employing more workers, and increasing the amount of capital invested in plant and equipment. A small but significant proportion of growth was generated by doing things in smarter ways—exploiting advances in knowledge, improving the skills of the work force and the quality of capital equipment, and achieving economies of scale.

The fundamental economic challenge is to shift the balance more in the direction of smarter solutions. One reason we must do this is that it is becoming increasingly difficult to achieve growth in resource industries. Big chunks of our resource sector are on the decline, for these reasons:

- A number of developing countries have a low-cost resource base that can be developed using low-cost labour: coal in Colombia, copper in Chile, and pulpwood in Brazil, for example. During the 1970s, those countries made major commitments to develop their resources. Many of the companies involved are government-owned or -controlled, while the invested capital has come mainly from foreign lenders and development agencies.

- New projects, both at home and abroad, added to global production capacity of such commodities as copper, nickel, and iron ore at a time when those minerals began to encounter increasing competition for novel industrial materials—a side effect of new technologies. Copper is being replaced in electrical circuitry by fibre-optic products that offer greater capacity, speed, and flexibility in many key uses. Iron ore and nickel are falling in demand as steel is replaced by plastics and light metals such as aluminium in many applications.

- Commodity exports are the sole source of foreign exchange earnings for many developing countries—their only means of raising the money needed to pay interest on foreign debts and buy essential imports. Accordingly, producers in those countries are not driven by the profit motive, but continue to export regardless of market conditions to keep gross revenues steady. If prices are depressed because of weak demand, such producers may even increase output to try to maintain a given level of export earnings.

Many Canadian resource companies, therefore, face exceptionally tough competitive conditions. Global excess capacity, at a time when materials substitution is causing significant and unpredictable erosion of demand, has depressed market prices. The weakness in prices has been exacerbated by competition from new resource producers that are often insensitive to short-term fluctuations in price. In this global context, many existing Canadian production facilities look unprofitable. Some are being closed permanently because they have no hope of competing with other countries where reserves are of high quality and can be exploited at lower cost. Some are being scaled back and investments are being made to reduce unit production costs in the hope that the facility will become competitive again when markets improve. Some have been closed temporarily until world demand has a chance to catch up with global supply.

The unavoidable conclusion is that resource development will not be the engine of economic growth in Canada that it has been in the past. It will be some time before new capacity is needed. And, when that time comes, there will be low-cost reserves in other countries competing for the development opportunities.

Canada's comparative advantage at one time was that the resources existed here and they could be reliably developed and produced (with significant help from foreign investors). Now, other countries are attracting that development activity more easily.

This does not mean we should write off the whole resource sector. There will be segments of strong growth, especially in the energy field, and sales from existing facilities will increase as economic growth gradually brings demand and supply back into balance. In short, most existing mines and mills will continue to operate and may eventually be expanded or replaced. The missing element will be the drive to develop new reserves and add substantial amounts of new capacity. That development activity has been an important engine of growth in Canada throughout the country's history, but has been slowing relative to other sectors for several decades. Exports of food (mainly wheat) and crude and fabricated materials accounted for more than 80 percent of Canada's exports in the 1960s, but for only half by the early 1990s. In the same period, machinery and consumer goods, especially automobiles and parts, increased from 15 to 45 percent.

The erosion of our comparative advantage in resource exports forces Canadian industry to shift the focus of production into goods and services with a higher value-added: that is, where more technical, managerial, and marketing skills are required to produce the end product.

In the 1960s, Canadians were highly dependent on their ability to hew wood and draw water—extracting and fabricating materials from the land. The major shift since then has been into mass production of relatively homogeneous end products such as autos, parts, machinery, consumer goods, and so on. That type of activity, however, is also experiencing vigorous competition from newly industrialized countries such as South Korea and Singapore.

As with resources, Canadian firms can, by using the most modern technology to reduce unit costs, preserve a share of the market for mass-produced goods. The real challenge, though, is to carve out a niche in areas where Canadians have a unique touch, offering one of these things:
- a special quality (as in high-fashion clothing)
- a unique combination of skills (such as engineering services)
- the application of leading-edge ideas (such as the Canadarm used on space-shuttle missions)

In effect, economic success in the developing countries is forcing Canadian industry out of its traditional market niche and into activities where it must make creative use of new technologies to carve out a market position for the 1990s.

SOCIAL TRENDS

Change in population density both in the world and within Canada, the ethnic makeup of the country, age distribution, and gender equality at home and at work will affect how companies operate and what businesses are profitable.

Population Changes

The so-called population explosion is a well-documented fact. In 1750, the world's population stood at about 800 million. It doubled by 1900 and doubled again by 1964. By 1993, it was estimated at close to 6 billion. Probably it will stabilize at about 11 billion late in the twenty-first century.

Economically disadvantaged nations traditionally have higher birthrates. The population of less-developed countries is rising at a rate faster than that of economically advanced regions such as Canada, the United States, Europe, and Japan. But people in developed nations typically have longer life expectancies. For example, a male in Canada is expected to live to 73.8 years and a female to 80.4. By contrast, in India neither men nor women are expected to live much beyond 40.

Population growth in Canada and elsewhere has always meant expanding markets for business. The 1991 census set Canada's population at 27 million. It is expected to hit 30 million by 2001. But the composition of the Canadian population will change even more significantly.

A lowered birthrate means that Canada will have an aging population. By 2001, 40 percent of Canadians will be 50 years or more. In 2031, nearly a quarter will be over 65, compared with 11 percent in 1986. The increasing numbers of elderly people will represent a larger proportion of the Canadian voting population. They will command more public attention as well as exerting more influence on economic, political, and social policies. For business, an older population will produce several effects: increased financial pressure on private and government pension plans, possible labour shortages, and marketing's gradual move away from youth-oriented advertising. Until recently, few advertisers focussed on consumers aged 50-plus. That is changing. As baby boomers turn grey, old is becoming gold.

Ad gurus are already formulating catchy labels: the successors to yuppies may be "woopies"—well-off older people. "Many in the 50-to-65 age bracket, their nest-building finished, have more time and money for leisure, clothing, and cars," notes Prudential-Bache Securities Canada Ltd. "The boomers are used to prosperity and will carry their free-spending habits into old age."

Ads in the 1990s are increasingly targeting the older consumer's interests. Food ads emphasize low cholesterol. Car ads will tout the ease of getting in and out. Ad dollars will shift more toward print. "With increasing age and education levels, there is greater propensity to read," explains Stephen Rosenblum, vice-president with Young & Rubican Ltd. "Still, the boomers are a TV generation, and alongside lifestyle programming in the *Golden Girls* mould, TV will surfeit on elderly wisdoms about reliable brands."[6]

Attitudes and Lifestyle

Many social trends affecting business involve either social responsibility or the quality of life. People want socially responsible decisions from executives and protest actions that are not in line with this thinking. Canadian citizens have filed lawsuits against producers of poor products, picketed supermarkets, boycotted companies that indulge in questionable resource extraction or marketing techniques, and demanded stronger legislation to control certain business practices. Shareholders expect responsibility from the companies they invest in, as indicated in Issues in Business 22.3.

They are also increasingly concerned about the quality of life. While most people seek material possessions, there is now a greater interest in living fuller, more personally rewarding lives. Individuals must decide on the lifestyle that is right for them, which includes work and personal styles.

Recent years have seen a growing trend in the media to dispel the myth of the frail, bedridden elderly. Advertisements for such industries as tourism and travel agencies are now targeting older Canadians with more time and money. They are portrayed as healthy, happy and active.

ISSUES IN BUSINESS 22.3

SHAREHOLDER ACTIVISM

THERE IS GREATER activism on the part of the individual investor. At BCE Inc., for example, we are experiencing a steadily growing stream of correspondence and phone calls from a wide variety of individuals. These communications cover matters as diverse as our financial performance, product or service complaints, federal-provincial economic and constitutional issues, and employment equity. In 1990, we received several hundred written questions and comments from shareholders in all parts of Canada, with many more phone calls. Roy Thomson Hall was filled for our 1990 shareholders' meeting, which lasted almost three hours.

In the old days, the activist shareholder was considered a gadfly, and every CEO had a means of dealing with gadflies. It involved terrifying stares and withering sarcasm delivered from great heights on a podium. We can all recall the great Canadian CEOs of the past who could nail an annual-meeting gadfly at 40 paces. Today, however, corporations are hearing from investors about the Valdez principles (a set of pro-environmental guidelines named after the *Exxon Valdez* disaster) as well as the MacBride principles (based on investment in Northern Ireland). Investors are equally interested in so-called sin investments, investments or business dealings with South Africa, in poison pills, and in golden parachutes.

Knowing what concerns investors is vital; an unpleasant surprise can be costly. One good example can be drawn from the famous RJR-Nabisco leveraged-buyout fight. Initially, there was considerable investor and public sympathy for management until *The New York Times* revealed a draft document detailing some $2 billion in executive gains from the proposed management buy-out. Unaware of investor and public sensitivities, RJR-Nabisco management did not, at first, take the revelation seriously. Consequently, investor and public sentiment swung to the opposition (Kohlberg, Kravis and Roberts) and ultimately so did ownership of RJR-Nabisco.

Another good example of where ignoring investor concerns can be detrimental to the company is Stelco, a well-established Canadian steel maker with a fine reputation. Not long ago, the company was experiencing financial setbacks as the result of a prolonged strike combined with poor market conditions. Stelco wanted to raise additional capital from its shareholders but initial attempts were singularly unsuccessful. Shareholders had little understanding of the circumstances in which the company found itself. They insisted on hearing firsthand from senior management about the company's plans so they could make an informed judgement before investing further. Senior management then had to spend considerable time and effort informing shareholders, ultimately winning their support.

Shareholder activism can be viewed as something to be warded off, or as something to be incorporated explicitly in management's decision-making process. I believe that the most successful corporate managers of the 1990s will also have the best-informed and most supportive owners.

Source: Excerpts from L.R. (Red) Wilson, "The '90s Need Not Be Nasty," *Business Quarterly,* Spring 1992, pp. 113–115. Reprinted with permission of *Business Quarterly,* published by the Western Business School, The University of Western Ontario, London, Ontario, Canada.

Question for Discussion

1. Why is it important for managers to be aware of shareholders' concerns?

Balancing Work and Family

Through most of the twentieth century, a "normal" family life implied a father who went to work to support the family; a mother who stayed at home to take care of the children, keep house, and prepare meals; and children who were in the care of their mother until they reached school age and then expected to come home to Mother after school hours. It is worth noting that this pattern is probably less than 200 years old. In earlier times, the home was the workplace, and both parents—and children too—contributed to earning the family income.

In the past few decades, women have increasingly sought work outside the home. In some part, this has been the result of women's growing desire for freedom and independence, but for many women it has been a matter of economic necessity: the single income that supported a family in the 1950s and 1960s was no longer adequate. In many ways, business and government have yet to face the new concerns that women's participation in the work force bring. These concerns are outlined in Issues in Business 22.4.

ISSUES IN BUSINESS 22.4

WOMEN'S NEEDS IN THE NEW ECONOMY

TO ECONOMISTS, restructuring means learning to survive in a world of intense competition, new technology, and rapid change. To millions of Canadian women, restructuring means the balancing act between work and family responsibilities is getting more difficult than ever.

Clerical jobs, with 9-to-5 hours and a secure paycheque, are disappearing. Factory jobs, with regular shifts and decent wages, are already gone. Jobs in the service sector—where 85 percent of women now work—tend to be part-time and low-paying.

Employers want workers who are cheap, flexible, and eager to retrain. Women want some predictability in their lives so they can look after their children, care for elderly parents, and run their homes.

Until recently, no one linked these two realities. Now, that is about to change.

Women and Economic Restructuring has one basic message: if the new economy that Canada is struggling to build ignores the needs and priorities of women, it will fail.... The task force writing the report comprised six prominent women—three business leaders and three top union officials. In spite of their varied backgrounds, the authors noticed that certain problems plague working women in almost every segment of the economy.

The most common is that politicians and employers still regard day-care as a luxury Canada cannot afford. Although 69 percent of women with pre-schoolers are in the work force, Canadian decision makers refuse to acknowledge that child care has become an economic necessity.

The task force would like to see the government, employers, and parents share the cost of a national child-care program. But, recognizing this is not likely to happen soon, it urges business to provide on-site day-care and unions to negotiate child-care funding as part of their collective agreements.

(continued)

An increasingly prevalent problem is that women are struggling to look after aging parents, while working full-time.

The task force does not offer any specific recommendations, but warns that elder care is too big an issue to leave to families alone. It urges government, business, and labour to get involved.

A third problem is that training programs tend to be geared toward men. The early ones were designed to help displaced workers in male-dominated industries such as steel making or heavy equipment.

But the adjustment process is quite different in industries such as garment making and fish processing, which employ large numbers of women. Jobs are converted from full-time to part-time. Factory work is converted to piecework done at home, for lower pay and no benefits.

The task force urges policy makers to develop specific training programs to help women in dying industries.

Finally, women trying to start their own businesses have trouble convincing the banks that they are a good credit risk.

Statistics show that enterprises launched by women enjoy a success rate double that of male-owned businesses. Nevertheless, women face a double handicap when they try to borrow money; banks don't like lending to small businesses and they are nervous about female entrepreneurs.

Without their own companies, women cannot change corporate culture. They cannot develop new work patterns that accommodate family life.

The task force acknowledges that moving from a comfortable, resource-based economy to a competitive knowledge-based one is going to cause pain and dislocation for everyone.

Women aren't the only victims of economic restructuring. They just happen to be the ones who usually get overlooked.

Source: Carol Goar, "Task Force Outlines Women's Needs in New Economy," *The Toronto Star*, March 3, 1994, p. A23. Reprinted with permission — The Toronto Star Syndicate.

Question for Discussion

1. Suggest some specific measures government, business, financial institutions, labour groups, and working families can undertake to assist working women.

BUSINESS REVIEW 22.1

1. What are some of the changes that the "third wave" of development is bringing to the way Canadians live and work?

2. Describe the stresses and opportunities that the global marketplace is bringing to the Canadian economy.

3. What social changes are affecting the way business operates?

TECHNOLOGICAL TRENDS

Technology is the methods, practical science, and engineering used to supply a society with the things it needs or wants. In our society, new technology is being introduced faster than ever before.

Technological changes lead to other changes in business and industry. Production methods must be updated, employees retrained, and management thinking restructured. Much knowledge acquired in school is outdated within ten years of graduation or less, and certain jobs become obsolete. Society has thus begun to emphasize lifelong education and training so people can remain productive for more than a few years.

High-technology firms are defined as companies whose research and development expenditures and proportion of technical employees are twice as great as the average for all manufacturing firms. These firms are expected to experience major growth in the future Canadian economy.

High-tech entrepreneurship is a risky business, but Canada needs these industries or it will lose high-tech jobs to foreign countries. Attracting high-tech industries is a current issue, with many provinces and communities now offering incentives to such firms to locate in their regions. It is important to note that affordable labour is the most attractive factor. However, shifting the unemployed and unskilled from smokestack industries to high technology requires training facilities and new attitudes.

Recent technological breakthroughs in the areas of electronic control devices, **artificial intelligence (AI)**, **virtual reality**, and **biotechnology** that Canadians might explore are discussed in Issues in Business 22.5.

technology
The methods, practical science, and engineering a society uses to supply its needs

high-technology firm
A company whose research and development expenditures and proportion of technical employees are twice the average for manufacturing firms

artificial intelligence (AI)
"Expert systems": computers programmed to analyze data by drawing on the thinking patterns and behaviour of experts in the field

virtual reality
A computer simulation that allows viewers to feel they are actually within a simulated environment

biotechnology
The application of technology to the study of biology and to the actual changing of biological processes

---

ISSUES IN BUSINESS 22.5

USES OF TECHNOLOGY

The Smart House

TEN YEARS FROM now, you'll consider your home a dumb place to live. Oh, you'll smarten it up with timing and control devices, but ultimately you'll concede that the Jones' darling new Smart House has a higher IQ.

In the Joneses' house, a single cable distributes power, telecommunications and audio/video signals, eliminating separate wiring for cable television, phones, stereo speakers, alarms, and appliances. Smart appliances for Smart Houses communicate with one another: the microwave triggers a message on the television, for example, to inform Mr. Jones his dinner is ready.

It will be possible to phone any electrical device in the Smart House. "Suppose your washer is on the blink. Rather than send a repairman, the manufacturer will use the phone to get into the appliance and find the problem."

The Smart House has been under development in the United States, sponsored by the National Association of Home Builders and several high-tech and appliance companies. Two trailer trucks roam the United States, exhibiting smart rooms to the public, and construction of

(continued)

the prototype got under way in October 1988. Although the Smart House consortium is in a leading position to shape tomorrow's home, "the Japanese and Europeans are pursuing the same idea, and even in the United States different firms are developing their own systems," notes Norm Aspin, president of the Electrical and Electronic Manufacturers Association of Canada, which has joined with Ontario Hydro, Hydro-Québec, Bell Canada, and the National Research Council to champion the automated house concept in this country.

Artificial Intelligence (AI)

The greatest computer-related triumph in the 1990s will be the spread of artificial intelligence (AI) software. AI programs, known as expert systems, make human-like inferences by drawing from databases containing facts, paradigms, and precepts relating to particular fields of expertise. Linked to sensors and robots, expert systems will lead an industrial transformation.

Among early AI applications is an expert system developed by Canadian Pacific Ltd. that analyzes lubricant samples from diesel locomotives, then indicates which engine parts need maintenance. Ultimately, AI computers, feasting on data streaming from sensors, will make thousands of such decisions to run automated plants. Mining giant Noranda Minerals Inc., for example, is developing an expert system to control milling processes. As expert systems come to the fore, says Gordon MacNabb, president and CEO of Precarn Associates Inc. of Nepean, Ontario, an AI and robotics research consortium, "we will depend on this technology to compete with the rest of the world."

AI will enable robots with vision systems to locate specific items in complex environments. The U.S. military is experimenting with an AI robot vehicle ultimately intended to recognize obstacles and geographical features. Consumer spin-offs will include robot vacuum cleaners and lawn mowers. "AI's potential is almost unlimited," says George Sekely, CP vice-president for computers and communications. "Whatever can be quantified can be done."

Cyberspace

The architect is walking his client through the new office building he's designed.

They're in the main lobby, and it's quite a sight: marble floors, high ceilings, specially commissioned art on the walls. But the client isn't quite satisfied. The reception desk—a massive oak-and-marble thing sporting the company logo in bronze—is in the wrong place.

No problem. The architect picks the desk up with one hand and plunks it down closer to the elevators. The client smiles.

The architect hasn't even worked up a sweat, because that two-tonne desk doesn't really exist. Neither does the building—there's just a big hole in the lot where it's supposed to go.

It's all cyberspace—an incredibly detailed, life-like computer simulation that puts people in the middle of whatever world they and their computers can dream up. . . .

In a sense, cyberspace—the term was coined by Vancouver science fiction writer William Gibson—is a logical extension of the trend that sees computers becoming simpler to use as their power expands exponentially. Twenty-five years ago, you used a stack of coded computer cards. Fifteen years ago, you memorized an arcane set of computer commands. Next, you used a "mouse"—a little wheeled box that rolls around on a tabletop—to manipulate familiar-looking objects on a computer screen.

So, why not just reach out and grab something that looks like it's right in front of you?

(continued)

Artists at Aareas by Design Inc. (TM), a Canadian computer graphics company, use Computer Assisted Design (CAD) to render architectural plans into 3-dimensional images for commercial and residential builders. The final images are then transferred onto photo-like prints and/or animated into video tape. Now clients can tour every corner of a house or building, open its doors and windows before it is even built, via a TV screen. Changes and upgrades can be made without the expenses of actual models. Such an innovation is predicted to change the future of real estate marketing.

In the late 1980s, NASA researchers Mike McGreavy and Scott Fisher cobbled together a cyberspace rig with a helmet visor to see and a glove to control simple computer-generated environments. They used their gadget to fly to Mars. Put it on, make a fist, and point in any direction. You "fly" in that direction. There goes the moon, over your shoulder.

As remarkable as the rig McGreavy and Fisher built was the fact that it was built using off-the-shelf technology. News of cyberspace technology excited everyone "from senators to the heads of small companies, to various other carnivorous blades of grass," said futurist Stewart Brand in 1989.

Work on cyberspace was progressing so fast, Brand said, that "instead of it being decades before it's commercially viable, it'll probably be months before cyberspace virtual reality . . . is upon us."

Nintendo, the people who made Super Mario Brothers your kid's best friends, introduced the Power Glove. Kids—or Mom and Dad—put the glove on and control the video game just by waving their hands around.

It's just a video game, you say. But so was Pong, the numbingly simple TV tennis set that started the whole video-game revolution in the mid-1970s.

And the distance between Pong and Super Mario Brothers is, at today's rate of change, roughly the distance between Nintendo's Power Glove and our friend the architect.

(continued)

Biotechnology

Though we tend to think of technological change in terms of computer technology and the information superhighway, the biggest changes may come in the area of biotechnology. As far as business is concerned, major interest started in the mid-1980s when the U.S. Supreme Court allowed companies to patent genetically engineered products. This opportunity for future gain sent research and development in biotechnology surging ahead. Two fields are particularly likely to be affected: medicine and agriculture.

Genetic engineers and medical specialists all over the world, including Canada, are working on the Human Genome Project, a massive attempt at mapping the entire human genetic structure. Already, this project has identified genes that cause a number of genetically inherited diseases, such as cystic fibrosis, Huntington's disease, and some forms of Alzheimer's disease. Identifying the cause is a major step toward prevention, though that may be a long way in the future. Meanwhile, research continues in the battle against viral diseases, from AIDS to the common cold.

Biotechnology's greatest impact in the near future will be in agriculture, worth $22 billion in annual cash receipts in Canada alone. Agricultural biotech is creating new plants and animals by gene manipulations or transfers. Work is under way to make wheat frost-resistant by importing into its DNA a fish's antifreeze gene. The earth's entire genetic heritage, human included, may be mixed to produce commercially useful creatures such as meatier livestock or faster-growing crops. In fact, crops could be preset to a desired shape and size to reduce waste at the processing stage.

We are far from transferring a few genes and then, presto, you have corn that grows in the desert. But in the 1990s, we should see engineered plants that resist disease and have greater nutritive value.

Several hundred new plants, animals, and microbes have already been created—Monsanto Co. of St. Louis, Missouri, has produced pest-resistant tomatoes, for instance—but there is still much to learn. When U.S. researchers implanted a human growth hormone gene into pigs, for example, the animals developed side effects, including lameness and internal bleeding.

And there are hazards: the unwitting release of a destructive organism into the environment would be the biotech equivalent of the Chernobyl disaster. In the United States, groups of Rifkinites, named for ecological activist Jeremy Rifkin, have opposed the commercialization of altered microbes and, moreover, have contested Harvard University's 1988 patent on a drug-test mouse—the world's first patented animal—genetically designed to contract cancer.

Some people oppose patenting lifeforms because it might one day be extended to humans. But farmers own plants and animals, whereas if you own humans, that's slavery. Can't we distinguish along those lines? The short-term answer is yes: watch for Canada, following the U.S. example, to stimulate R&D by allowing lifeform patents. Federal funding plus industrial spending here add up to only $400 million annually on biotech, including manufacturing, compared with U.S. $5 billion on R&D alone south of the border.

Sources: Ian Allaby, "The Future Now! Priming Your Business for the 1990s," *Canadian Business,* March 1989, pp. 56, 57; and Paul Wells, "Here Come the '90s," *The Montreal Gazette,* December 31, 1989, p. B4, B5.

Question for Discussion

1. These descriptions of technological innovations were written in 1989. Which of them are in use today? What further uses of technology do you expect in the next ten years?

International Competition and Co-operation

Technology is a driving force of our civilization, as nations compete to develop the tools and techniques that will fashion tomorrow's economies. Canada, however, is barely in the race, with R&D spending stagnant at just above a paltry 1.3 percent of GDP since 1983. The massive cost of crossing technological frontiers makes international co-operation mandatory. Canada has an aggressive export-oriented high-tech community, but with government support weak, companies may increasingly latch on to international ventures, imitating the success of our aerospace industry, a participant in both the U.S. and European space programs.

Construction of a manned, U.S. led international space station will begin in the late 1990s. Canada's contribution, a $1.2-billion mobile robotic arm system, will help assemble the station. Much space investment will come from private companies or consortia.

Should space activity continue, benefits will go beyond the development of new alloys, semiconductor crystals, and medicines in zero-gravity labs:

Space and moon bases will constitute a colonial market dependent upon Earth for goods from plumbing to paint. Space folks will need minigyms to keep them in form, cookbooks to tempt their palates, entertainments to enliven long hours of duty. Zero-gravity clothes washers, toilets, and showers have been a constant problem, although NASA may replace showers with mist sprays and suction systems. We don't think much about soap foam on Earth, but in space that foam quickly fills waste tanks. "Space products must be compatible with on-board water and atmosphere recycling," says Bill Seitz, former head of systems development in NASA's man-systems division, which looks to "task out" elements of its space habitation project.[7]

Technology and You

Some people worry that technology is out of control. A few even believe that humans will some day be the slaves of computers or of "super machines." Issues in Business 22.6 discusses the particular concerns roused by some of the uses to which technology can be put in the workplace. Most business executives, however, believe that technology has been and will continue to be a way of improving the efficiency of business, the standard of living, and the quality of life.

ISSUES IN BUSINESS 22.6

TECHNOLOGY AND PRIVACY

TECHNOLOGY HAS MADE the most remarkable impact on our continued erosion of privacy. "You have to wonder," says Tom Wright, Ontario's privacy commissioner, "whether anyone has thought anything about other than the gee-whiz of technology, or what it means to how we define privacy."

Brian Bawden, a specialist in computer law with the Toronto firm Osler, Hoskin & Harcourt, believes that society is sadly lacking in coming to terms with the relationship between technology and privacy.

In his research, Bawden has discovered that 20 million workers, about 10 percent of the work force in the United States, are subject to on-the-job electronic surveillance.

In the Canadian context, he assumes that about 2 million Canadians are being monitored electronically. He lists how it is done:

- While bugging isn't new, many more cases of employer eavesdropping are being documented. Bawden says it was recently alleged, for example, that Northern Telecom has bugged its employees for years, and has used the information to fight union-organizing campaigns.
- Some U.S. employers have the ability to track the movements of employees in the workplace by requiring them to wear a special badge containing a microchip.
- The Computer Workers of America estimate that 400 million employee telephone calls are monitored each year in the United States.
- A telephone device has been developed to assess an employee's speech patterns to determine stress levels and gauge honesty.
- Voice-mail systems, which record incoming telephone calls, are saved in a central system, which makes voice-mail vulnerable to interception.
- In some U.S. companies, chair sensors record how long an employee remains seated and measures restlessness while the employee is seated.
- New software allows supervisors to call up the screens of employees without the employees knowing it.
- Brain-wave testing is still in a development stage, but it's predicted it can be used to determine a prospective employee's concentration ability and suitability for certain tasks.
- The technology is available to test genetic makeup of employees to weed out those with undesirable traits.

Bawden likens technology to letting a genie out of a bottle. "On all fronts, we are scrambling to catch up and wrap our minds around ways to keep ourselves as the master of technology rather than becoming its slave."

As for Wright, he believes that privacy is not a barrier to technology. "People like to portray it as technology versus privacy, and that's absolutely the wrong way to put it because it sets up a confrontation.

"A better way to look at it is that, when new technology is being developed and designed, there's an obligation on the part of the developer to consider the impact, that there is a right to privacy."

(continued)

Source: Excerpt from Warren Gerard, "The Coming End of Privacy," *The Toronto Star*, March 5, 1994, pp. B1, B4. Reprinted with permission — The Toronto Star Syndicate.

Question for Discussion

1. Which of the uses of electronic surveillance listed in the article do you consider legitimate concerns of management and which do you consider invasions of employee privacy? Would your answers have been the same ten years ago? Will they be the same ten years in the future?

THE CHANGING BIOSPHERE

Like all other human activity, business is affected by pollution, global warming, the thinning of the ozone layer, and the disappearance of fishing stocks. It must be acknowledged that past and current business practices have helped create these problems. As we recognize these and other ecological challenges, they will change the way business operates, bringing new limitations, but also creating opportunities for new products and new approaches. Issues in Business 22.7 examines the concept of **sustainable development** as good business practice.

sustainable development
Development that can be sustained in the future because it does not impair the environment

ISSUES IN BUSINESS 22.7

BUSINESS AND THE ENVIRONMENT

SURE, THE EARTH is afflicted with acid rain and toxic chemicals, chlorofluorocarbons (CFCs) attack the ozone layer, a miasma of CO_2 slowly stews us. But let's suppose, for once, that we will control our environmental problems. The question is: what will make that possible? Answer: a change in the social psyche that will affect industry, consumers, retailers, and governments.

Surveys reveal a surprising amount of support among voters for environmentalism. "Polls say that 80 percent of the population is worried. The environment will be a mainstream concern in the next decade," predicts Colin Isaacs, executive director of Toronto's Pollution Probe, whose role until recently was to bemoan public apathy.

Governments will toughen pollution laws and increasingly tax products—such as throwaway items—that sully the environment. Seals of approval have been issued for environment-friendly products, including those made from recycled materials or enclosed in biodegradable packaging.

Industry will take matters into its own hands. Already, most Canadian producers have ceased to use CFCs as propellants in aerosol cans, aside from medical sprays. U.S. chemical giant E.I. du Pont de Nemours & Co. has announced a complete withdrawal from CFC production by 2000, and the company has found replacements for most of the CFCs used in solvents and refrigeration systems.

There's a greening of corporate board rooms. Industry won't push the environment to the edge any more. Aside from the moral concern, there are the financial liabilities.

Industry was often blamed for environmental problems. Now we see economic growth as the engine for improving conditions. We have to bring jobs and knowledge to the Third World.

(continued)

Third World poverty has led to the destruction, for economic gain, of the CO_2-absorbing forests that are our best resistance to the greenhouse effect.

The new economic watchword, however, will be "sustainable development" signifying that current growth should not undermine future growth by impairing the environment.

Waste recycling is here to stay, not because it's lucrative—although one day it might be—but because the number of cheap, safe, and politically acceptable dump sites has dwindled. Many North American communities now require residents to recycle. Many Canadian municipalities have recycling programs that encourage residents to place newspapers, bottles, and cans in curbside boxes for collection. Consumer concern is shown by the fact that the participation rate is extremely high.

Although such programs often depend on governments and private-sector subsidies, recycling will become financially attractive as Earth's rising population makes greater demands on energy and materials.

The potential of recycling will be maximized with monetary incentives. Alberta's recycling depots reimburse people for glass, metal, or plastic containers. Depot operators earn fees from the companies whose containers they collect. Non-refillable glass bottles are crushed and shipped to a glass plant. Metal is sold as scrap. Plastics go to a recycler who makes them into household items such as flower pots. The depots are licensed and guaranteed an exclusive territory to ensure their financial viability. The depots make money, judging by how actively licences are sought.

A conserver society need not be a poorer society. It will simply be smarter. "Japan has spectacular growth yet cut its energy and materials input about 60 percent in eleven years," notes the Canadian Environmental Advisory Council. Besides, a conserver society will mean new entrepreneurial and job opportunities. There's lots of cleaning up to do.

Source: Adapted from Ian Allaby, "The Future Now! Priming Your Business for the 1990s," *Canadian Business*, March 1989, p. 62.

Question for Discussion

1. Should business take voluntary action that might cause loss of income to the business in order to protect the environment or should it do only what is required by law?

BUSINESS STRATEGY CHANGES

Changes in business strategy over the years have had a direct effect on how firms operate today. Some of these changes include:

1. Computer-based management information systems (MIS). An efficient MIS is one that gets the appropriate data (and only the appropriate data) to the responsible decision maker in time for a considered decision.

2. **Automation**—the replacement of people with machines that can perform tasks faster or cheaper than humans. Some experts point out that workers are required to make the new machines, so the labour force is only partially reduced. The problem is that the displaced workers may not be qualified to handle the new jobs. Issues in Business 22.8 examines the changing distribution of workers in manufacturing industries.

automation
The use of machinery and electronic devices to do work previously done by human beings

3. More extensive cost-control programs, within which accountants and other managers find new ways to hold down the rising costs of doing business. These programs are very important, especially during periods of inflation or sales decline.
4. New ways of acquiring the energy and materials necessary to operate business. The importance of this change is obvious, because the costs of energy and raw materials are rising.
5. Management awareness and understanding of the attitudes and problems of workers. The labour force is composed of a multitude of different groups requiring different managerial approaches. Management must be sure that leadership styles match the work situation.

ISSUES IN BUSINESS 22.8

DELAYERING THE PLANT

MOST CANADIANS PROBABLY know that the recession hit factories faster and harder than any other sector. In 1989, a full year before other parts of the economy began to contract, manufacturers were tightening their belts and laying people off. By 1993, factory employment had dropped by over 15 percent.

But most Canadians may not know just how selective manufacturing executives were about which employees would get the chop. Quite simply, they cut from the bottom first: blue-collar and clerical workers bore the brunt of the job losses.

Managers and other white-collar professionals, as a rule, were the last to be cut and the first to be hired. By 1993, there were almost 5 percent more managers and administrators than there were in 1989, but almost 18 percent fewer workers at every other level. Almost 20 percent of blue-collar jobs and 15 percent of the clerical jobs disappeared.

Blue-collar workers accounted for fully 275,000 of the 326,000 factory jobs that evaporated between 1989 and 1993. The clerical, sales, and service group wasn't far behind: 51,000 jobs disappeared there, with the clerical workers accounting for pretty well all of the drop. Factory owners added a handful of people to their sales staffs and trimmed about the same number from the group that services their products.

The top echelon of managers and other professionals—including engineers, systems analysts, and accountants—suffered only a slight dip in employment of about 6 percent before returning in 1993 to where they had been in 1989.

Indeed, for all the talk about streamlining cumbersome management structures—"delayering" in business jargon—Canadian factories are more managed now than ever. In 1993, there were 12.8 managers and administrators for every 100 people employed, up from 10.3 in 1989.

Manufacturers may be more competitive now than they were in the late 1980s, but they've achieved all their productivity gains on the shop floor and on the clerical side, not by creating leaner management structures. The extra managers and professionals, it appears, are the people charged with figuring out which new computer and robot systems will help the company cut jobs and raise productivity. . . .

(continued)

On the surface, the 1993 increase of 12,000 factory jobs suggests that manufacturers were beginning to hire gain. That was true for blue-collar jobs (up 4,000), but the job losses continued for clerical, sales, and service workers (down 16,000). Management jobs, however, increased by almost 20,000.

With fewer people on the shop floor, fewer clerks keeping the paper flowing, and more white-collar managers and experts in the front office, the factory is a very different place now than it was only a few years ago. And given the extraordinary pace at which factories have been buying machinery and equipment that can replace people, the odds are that this trend will persist.

Source: Adapted from Bruce Little, "In the Recession, Some Managed to Find Work," *The Globe and Mail,* March 7, 1994, p. A11.

Questions for Discussion

1. Why has the ratio of managers to blue-collar workers increased?

2. Can you account for the fact that clerical workers declined in numbers, while sales people were largely unaffected?

One critical question remains: what will be your role in facing tomorrow's challenges? Virtually every sector of society and every career field is influenced by contemporary business—directly or indirectly. And business offers exciting opportunities for a rewarding future. Developing Your Business Skills examines the manager of tomorrow.

DEVELOPING YOUR BUSINESS SKILLS

EXECUTIVES OF THE YEAR 2000

The executive of the future will have to be knowledgeable and sophisticated not only about international business conditions, but also about international politics. As recent events have so decisively shown in Eastern Europe, politics, economics, and business are inseparable.

Nor will a business succeed abroad without some sense of the distinctiveness of the consumer; the work force; and the structures of distribution, agriculture, and credit. Call it the history and culture of the place.

But the most difficult challenge for the executive will be to understand the nature of political and economic change itself. Why did Eastern European regimes fall so fast? What will be the future of the governing gerontocracy of China? What does the humiliation of Marxism mean for the countries of Latin America and Africa?

The changes which are occurring in Eastern Europe, the Western European single market, the rapid growth of Asia, the consequences of the North American Free Trade Agreement with the United States and Mexico, and the evolution of Latin America and Africa will challenge

(continued)

Canadians in general and Canadian business people in particular in ways we can scarcely imagine. Foreign competition crashing into our markets is only the most obvious sign of globalization. Immigration, world environmental trends, the international finance system, and political instability abroad will all have direct consequences for Canadians and Canadian companies.

What skills will be required for executives to deal with all this? Foreign languages, an appreciation and experience of other people's cultures, and an aptitude for political and economic analysis would be a good starting point.

Science and technology are also going to dominate the lives of many of our executives. Whether we are talking about the primary sector, manufacturing, or the service industries, there is no getting away from the challenge and promise of rapid technological change. The executives of the future must be comfortable with technologies to understand their role in our economy.

In manufacturing, for example, not only the next ten years but probably the next half-century will be dominated by five key areas of technology: (1) advanced materials (polymers, ceramics, high-temperature and "smart" materials); (2) sensors—devices linking machines and data-processing systems to their environment—which react to light, position, temperature, chemicals; (3) computing; (4) advanced manufacturing (associated with CAD/CAM); and (5) biotechnology.

But technological change requires new sets of organizational and analytical skills. We can envisage the proliferation of new corporate positions, like Chief Technology Officer whose job it will be to analyze and acquire new technologies on a far more systematic and thorough basis than before, and to be part of the team of the Office of the Chief Executive, so that his or her views will be reflected in all major decisions.

Similarly, the relatively new organizational science of integrated logistics, which deals with the movement of materials in a manufacturing operation from their raw state, through production, through product distribution, to the delivery of the finished product, will require a new breed of executive, a top-level manager who cuts across traditional frontiers like customer service, order processing, design, marketing, transportation, and warehousing.

There is a special challenge for English-Canadian executives in the year 2000: they have not reflected on what it means to be a Canadian business person in the way in which Quebec business people have. They have not sorted out how to deal constructively with the Canadian state. They have been so enthusiastic about free trade and privatization that some have forgotten the national interest.

Quebec has found the knack. So have the French, the Germans, the Japanese, and even the Americans—all of them form teams with their national governments, but not English Canadians. Instead, all we do here is prattle about the beauties of the market while the other national teams eat our lunch.

Well, that was the easy part: defining the problem. So, what do we do about it? Can our educational system produce these paragons of virtue, our mythical Canadian executives of the year 2000? What should the high school graduate do if he or she wants to be a future business leader?

Our super executive will not take a commerce degree at the undergraduate level. Instead, a more likely route will be to major in the liberal arts at the undergraduate level.

If we think that our executives must be worldly in the best sense of the term, they must have the skills that will enable them to understand the world. They must know languages, and there is a good case for studying the history and culture of other countries as well.

We need a new kind of science course that is also integrated but takes as its starting point the great technological concerns of the day. Whether it is the dramatic failures of technology—

(continued)

Chernobyl, the Challenger crash, Bhopal, the Exxon Valdez—or the challenges of the environment, from polychlorinated biphenyls to global warming, or the tragic mystery of AIDS, our world provides us with plenty of raw material to capture the interest of any curious young person. The trick is to locate a scientific or technological problem in its broader context: political, economic, cultural, moral, for this is the kind of thinking that will be required not only for future Canadian executives but also for future Canadian leaders.

But the education of undergraduates must be seen as a total experience. Whether it is forming student societies or taking part in student politics, whether it is debating or doing theatre or playing sports, the complete undergraduate life will help form our future executives. And their summers will play an important part as well. Wherever possible, they should travel, starting with Canada, then going as widely afield as possible. They should work abroad and study languages. They should try different work experiences, from factories to offices, so they will have some sense of what the working world is like.

The graduate level is the place to acquire more disciplined, analytical, technical skills, whether it is law, an MBA, engineering, or an advanced degree in science. But the mind must be kept open to new experiences, new ideas, new sensations. Summers, once again, should be spent travelling and working abroad. Of course, there is a lot to be said for doing one's graduate degree outside of Canada as well.

After graduation, perhaps a further spell of working abroad would be appropriate, in Africa perhaps, or in the Hong Kong money markets.

What does it all add up to? The demands of the year 2000 and the specific needs of the Canadian executive mean that we will have to rethink radically both what our model of the ideal executive is and how we educate such a person. We need a fundamentally different kind of person from what we have needed in the past. That person will in some ways be like the Levantines of old, those bold, cosmopolitan wheeler-dealers who still haunt the eastern Mediterranean, the sort of people who can open a McDonald's in Moscow and still let the Americans think they did it!

But that person will also understand technology and its impact on people. That person will not simply be a technician but a humanist. That person will be open to new ideas while being intellectually rigorous and analytical, and will have the interpersonal skills necessary to be a team player, a sensitive colleague, and a socially aware employer and citizen.

Equally important, that person will understand what it means to be a Canadian business executive, with all of the attendant political, social, and public obligations that entails.

And, most important, that person will have a central core of belief, a reflective quality, and a set of values that will provide guidance not only for business and public life but for all of life.

Source: John Godfrey, "Canadian Executives of the Year 200." *The Financial Post*, July 10, 1990, p. 10.

BUSINESS REVIEW 22.2

1. How will changes in technology affect the workplace of the future?
2. What effect will pollution, global warming, and the destruction of the ozone layer have on business and enterprise?
3. What skills will the executive of the future need?

BALANCING THE POSITIVE AND NEGATIVE ASPECTS OF CHANGE

Assessments of the future of business often assign more importance to negative influences than to positive ones. Indeed, many factors and circumstances may well have an adverse impact on forecasts: inflation, unemployment, and bureaucratic red tape are but a few. Still, there are favourable situations balancing the negative inputs to assessments of our future, including:

1. Recognition of the importance of continued capital investment is strong. Some recent tax proposals illustrate this vital concern.
2. Former Communist nations such as Russia and Eastern Europe are viewed as opportunities for future business investments and marketing efforts.
3. Canada, with a leading position in communications and other high-technology industries, has an opportunity to play a major role in building the information superhighway.
4. The decline in the value of the Canadian dollar in the early 1990s has reduced the price of Canadian goods on the world market, and lower interest rates have made it easier for firms to borrow funds.
5. Tariff and non-tariff barriers on manufacturing and agricultural products in other countries have been reduced under the Uruguay Round of the General Agreement on Tariffs and Trade. The net effect of these changes is to reduce tariff rates in most of the major industrialized countries to the lowest levels in the present century. The North American Free Trade Agreement provides even greater opportunities within Canada, the United States, and Mexico.

TOMORROW'S CHALLENGES

Many of today's challenges will be present tomorrow. But management must also watch for the new challenges that will appear. Some of today's vexing situations may seem minor when compared with the complexities to be faced in the future.

Tomorrow's challenges require today's preparation. Business executives must learn to adapt to events that may be unheard of now. Management must be flexible, prepared to meet new situations with strategies designed for the future—an approach requiring a sound education. Qualified executives must have a solid understanding of the business system and must be able to adapt to change.

The only thing constant about Canadian business, in fact, is change. It is a vital part of everyday business life. Change was yesterday's challenge. It is today's challenge. And it will be tomorrow's challenge.

INTERACTIVE SUMMARY AND DISCUSSION QUESTIONS

1. You are involved in a debate surrounding Alvin Toffler's position that a third wave has taken place in our history. You are to take the position that it has. Support your position.
2. Why has home work in the electronic cottage become so appealing?
3. As Canada prepares for the twenty-first century, what initiatives might business and government work on and plan together as a result of the impact of globalization on the Canadian economy?
4. What contributions will high technology make at the close of this century in fields such as information, medicine, and agriculture?
5. What are some positive factors that are likely to affect the future of Canadian business and the private-enterprise economic system?
6. What are the major challenges facing Canadian executives for the next decade? the next century? Discuss politics, education, and technology in framing your response.

CASE 22.1

TOWARD A SANER, SIMPLER WORKSTYLE

AS NEVER BEFORE, employers and employees are experimenting with sabbaticals, flexible hours, four-day work weeks, permanent part-time work, job sharing, and early retirement.

That's not to say it's sweeping the nation. It is a small movement, as yet. But it has arrived not a moment too soon. Canadian wage earners seem more stressed out than ever before. And if it seems a tad churlish to whine about long hours when Canada boasts 1.6 million unemployed, in fact the high rate of joblessness is a big part of the problem. To put it bluntly, all these clever new workstyles, from the companies' point of view, represent a palatable, even *nouveau chic*, way of chopping the work force but not the work. In other words, heaping extra tasks on the survivors. And the huge supply of ready, willing, but unemployed individuals acts as a pretty effective threat in keeping the noses of the employed pressed tightly to the grindstone.

The statistics prove that more employees than ever are working longer hours. The proportion who put in 50 hours or more a week was 14.4 percent in 1993, says Statistics Canada, up from 13.7 percent in 1992. Not only that, up to 1 million people work overtime each week, says a recent Statscan study.

Europeans would regard this noxious North American practice of extra-long hours as a farce. In Europe, unions are in the throes of demanding, along with high pay, a four-day work week (four *normal* days, not five days compressed into four). And just as the work week is becoming shorter, Europe's vacations and school days are growing longer. Not only that, Europeans have excellent day-care systems.

It adds up to an eye-opening model for how to make work life more livable.

In Canada, by contrast, union members have intimated they would appreciate the chance to do a little less overtime, if you please. Annual hours of school—already far shorter than those in Europe—are getting even shorter in some provinces, making working parents scramble that much harder.

Economists say a similarly sane workstyle is possible in Canada too. Already, perhaps one in ten Canadian companies is making serious efforts toward flexible work practices, says Gordon Betcherman, director of a labour research group at Queen's University in Kingston, Ontario.

(continued)

These firms tend to be large, have a preponderance of female employees, and operate in non-traditional areas of the economy, such as in business services.

But not everyone agrees. Workplace specialists who scoff say nothing short of a cataclysm will produce the sort of reform Dr. Betcherman envisions. And if it does occur, they say, it will happen at the employer's behest, not because an employee wants a pleasanter life.

What no one disputes, though, is that the pressure for a break from work is intense. It's part of what economists characterize as one half of a mismatch: on the one hand, you have part-time workers who clamour to work full-time (not to mention the unemployed who want a job, any job) and, on the other, you have full-time workers who yearn to work part-time, so long as the jobs are stable and show some possibility of promotion.

Why? For employees, it's to reclaim some fun in life. Even sanity.

For employers, it's a chance to nurture a strung-out work force back to vigour and potentially save the costs of training newcomers to replace the fallen. It's also a canny way to trim wage costs without cutting staff.

The need for such a rethinking of work could hardly be more apparent. We've all heard the cautionary tales about overwork; the co-worker who works so hard he drops dead a month after he retires; the doctor at the peak of her career who has a nervous breakdown; the entrepreneur who needs a bottle of scotch to get through the day.

The pressure does not diminish when workers return home at the end of the day. The work force today contains more mothers of small children than ever; 71 percent of married women with children under age 18 hold jobs outside the home. This is ripe territory for a lot of guilt, the kind of guilt that shows up in frantic attempts by both parents to catch up with children's lives during the brief time they have.

There are also fewer hours to devote to housework. Hence, both men and women devote weekends to laundry, buying groceries, and mopping floors, not to savouring a glass of Chardonnay over dinner.

In short, for many, time has become the ultimate luxury, and absolutely unattainable. And that translates into stress.

Source: Adapted from Alanna Mitchell, "Toward a Saner, Simpler Workstyle," *The Globe and Mail*, March 5, 1994, p. B1.

Questions for Discussion

1. Why, in a time of high unemployment, are so many people working overtime and under stress at work?

2. Do you think a "European" approach to working hours, vacations, and child care could be achieved in North America?

CASE 22.2

BELL'S CEO LOOKS TO THE FUTURE

That we are living in a period of unprecedented change is an obvious understatement. Furthermore, even a brief review of developments that have taken place over the past 50 years, the past 10 years—not to mention last year alone—indicates that the pace of change is, in fact, accelerating.

(continued)

For example, almost 30 years ago, Marcel Vincent, the president and CEO of Bell Canada at that time, gave a speech entitled "The Year 2064 as It Appears from 1964." In it, he forecast a whole host of new-age techno-wonders—like miniature computers the size of wrist watches, worldwide voice-activated computer networks, and computers that would create exotic musical sounds.

We are only on the threshold of the twenty-first century, but most of what Mr. Vincent predicted already exists today. Much of this new technology, however, arrives so fast that it is only dimly understood when it is applied. And often it is obsolete before we have figured out how to benefit from it.

In a period of both rapid change and moving goalposts, how can managers keep abreast of these changes? And how will we be able to distinguish trends from fundamental sea changes?

Success, in this larger, more general sense, will depend heavily, as it always has, on effective leadership. But it must be leadership that is able to prioritize, to judge what is important, and ultimately to act decisively. This, in my view, is what will make the difference.

None of us likes to make mistakes, but every manager, every corporation, has made mistakes in the past and will do so again in the future. Caution certainly has its place, but prudence should not always be linked to caution. Frankly, I do not think that when Boris Yeltsin leaped up on the Soviet tank he worried whether his speech notes were complete and tidy.

On the other hand, the incidence of mistakes can be reduced if the right questions are asked and information is properly gathered and processed beforehand. An example: during the 1960s, Bell Canada participated with AT&T in the development of the videophone. The technology was perfected twenty years ago and soon every Bell Canada executive had a videophone sitting on his or her desk.

At first it was exciting—a brave new world. Then people grew to resent it, and ultimately to hate it. The great thing about the ordinary telephone is visual privacy; other people cannot see you reading your mail or doodling as you talk with them. You can even come out of the shower and take a call dripping wet. The videophone, as we were to discover, was technology in search of a market.

We have since recycled that experience into video conferencing, however, now coming into its own as travel has become so time-consuming and expensive. Recently, for example, I attended a Northern Telecom International Operations Committee meeting with participants from Hong Kong and London via video—at a cost of only several hundred dollars.

Getting the right information at the right time is a prerequisite of avoiding costly errors. Unfortunately, in a typical corporate hierarchical structure, negatives can be filtered out or information held back when it contradicts strongly held opinions.

Today, as many companies have discovered to their dismay and to that of their investors, hierarchical structures tend to breed bureaucratic cultures. That was the downfall of the command economies of Eastern Europe, and it has been the debilitating weakness of many businesses in Canada and elsewhere.

Modern communications technology permits greater delegation of authority to line managers who have the necessary information to respond quickly. Foremen on the factory floor are best positioned to place orders for just-in-time supply. Sales representatives know best what the customer wants. And feedback and reporting to senior management can be timely and more comprehensive.

Bell Canada, for example, used to have a hierarchy that was viewed as a quasi-military organization. This has changed markedly in recent years as authority continues to be delegated down the ranks.

Another good example is Montreal Trust, where information management is a two-way street. There, employees met with senior management in focus groups to discuss an agenda set by the employees. Out of this came a formal report that was subsequently distributed to all participants. This project involved some 700 people, a sizable group for a firm with 2,000 employees.

(continued)

Even with these good examples of organizational changes and their implications for improvement in information flow, our ability to look ahead and successfully manage change is limited. Some years ago, Bell Canada introduced videotex technology to Canada. Technically, the product was good—it seemed like a great idea—but the concept was new and we could only estimate the potential market.

Alex, as it is known, still has not caught on. Clearly, we did not judge adequately the extent of customer resistance or reluctance to pay phone-line charges to interact with computer-stored information bases.

On the other hand, the opposite also happens. Two examples: when Bell Canada launched mobile cellular service, estimates of the market were relatively modest. This product was thought to be of interest largely to doctors, lawyers, travelling sales people, real estate agents, and busy executives. Not so, apparently. Since Bell Cellular began operation in 1986, the customer base has increased ten times and we have one of the largest continuous cellular coverage areas in the world, some 207,000 square kilometres. Clearly, the market growth for mobile communications caught most of us by surprise.

To prosper in the coming years, business will need managers who understand not just the customer's needs and concerns as well as those of the shareholders, but also the political and social context in which the company operates. They must also be able to gather and assimilate information from many different sources and communicate effectively and efficiently among all levels within the corporation. These are abilities not necessarily developed by mastering a particular skill such as engineering, law, or accounting. They require the capacity to think in larger terms; to see beyond immediate problems toward clear, long-term goals; and to know how to achieve these goals by practical means. In other words, we need leaders who are both visionary and pragmatic.

In an increasingly complex world, corporate managers will most certainly need the assistance of external professional advisers to serve as catalysts, agents for change, and problem solvers. We need to be informed and educated, to be encouraged to adapt to change and to be provided with disinterested viewpoints on complex and often emotional issues.

The future, it is said, is a "different country," but the tasks we will be performing there will be perfectly recognizable from where we stand today. But we must be prepared to do them better and faster and with a greater sense of personal commitment and accountability. It is a future, I believe, that, with enlightened management, and perhaps most important a full measure of good luck, can and will be better for all of us.

Source: Excerpts from L.R. (Red) Wilson, "The '90s Need Not Be Nasty," *Business Quarterly*, Spring 1992, pp. 113, 115–117. Reprinted by permission of *Business Quarterly*, published by the Western Business School, The University of Western Ontario, London, Ontario, Canada.

Questions for Discussion

1. In developing products, in what instances has Bell Canada accurately perceived future trends? In what instances has the company failed to do so?

2. What does Red Wilson see as the role of technology and information in management?

NOTES

1. "Here Come the '90s," *Royal Bank Reporter*, Fall 1984, p. 14.
2. Quoted in Laura Ramsay, "Home Office Revolution: More People Choose to Work in Slippers," *The Financial Post*, April 16, 1990, p. 37.
3. Tom Forester, *High Tech Society: The Story of the Information Technology Revolution*, quoted in "Here Come the '90s," *Royal Bank Reporter*, Fall 1989, p. 14.
4. Ian Allaby, "The Future Now! Priming Your Business for the 1990s," *Canadian Business*, March 1989, pp. 54, 55.
5. Allaby, "The Future Now!," p. 54.
6. Allaby, "The Future Now!," p. 59.
7. Allaby, "The Future Now!," pp. 56, 58.

PHOTO CREDITS

INDEX

Those terms and page references appearing in boldface type indicate the location of the margin glossary definitions.

Absenteeism, PEO26–27
Absolute advantage, GLO22–23
Accountability, ORG7
Accounting
 vs. bookkeeping, ACC5–6
 and budgeting, ACC21–22, 23
 and computers, INF4
 defined, ACC5
 and double-entry bookkeeping,
  ACC12–15
 and financial statements, ACC7–12
 and GAAP, ACC4–5, 20–21
 inadequate, ACC6–7
 information, ACC3–4, 20–21
 market-value, ACC28
 profession of, ACC4–5
 ratio analysis in, ACC15–20
 social responsibility in, ACC26–27
 and top quality management,
  ACC23–25
Accounting equation, ACC7
Accounts payable, ACC10
Accounts receivable, ACC9, FIN5
Accounts receivable turnover,
 ACC17–18
Achievement needs, PEO8
Acid rain, SOC19
A.C. Nielsen Company, INF10, 13,
 14
Acquired needs theory, PEO7–8
Adams, J. Stacey, PEO11
Administered VMS, DIS6
Administrative agencies, LEG20, 21
Advertising
 defined, COM3
 as function of marketing, MKT6
 media, COM11–12
 and product life cycle, COM8–9
 trends in, COM10–11
 types of, COM6
Advisory Council for the Status of
 Women, HRM9
Affiliation needs, PEO8
Affirmative action, SOC8–13, *see also*
 Employment equity
AFL-CIO, LR5, 7
Agency, LEG16
Agent, LEG16
Aging, FUT13
Agriculture, Department of, SOC24

Agriculture, and perfect competi-
 tion, BUS23
Aikenheads, DIS12
Air Canada, FUT3, PEO27–28, PRI3
Alderfer, C.P., PEO7
Alternate work schedules, PEO20–21
American Express, SOC12
American Federation of Labor
 (AFL), LR5
Amsterdam Stock Exchange, SEC10
Anticipatory inventory, OP16
Anti-Dumping Tribunal, GLO14,
 LEG21
Apple Computer Inc., LEG12
Apprenticeship, HRM20
Aptitude and attitudinal testing,
 HRM10
Arbitration, LR14–15, 20–21
Artificial intelligence, FUT17–20
Asian countries, trade with,
 GLO10–11, 18–19
Assembly line, OP8–9
Assessment centre, HRM22
Assets, ACC7, 9
Atomic Energy Control Board,
 LEG21
AT&T, PEO19
Australian Tourist Commission,
 COM8
Authority, ORG7
Autocratic leader, MGT17–18
Automated teller machines (ATMs),
 BAN2, 11
Automation, FUT24
Automobile Protection Association,
 SOC16–17
Average holding period of
 inventory, ACC17
Avon Canada Inc., OP17–18

Badley, Bernard, ORG27–28
Bagel Works, ENT29–30
Balance of payments, GLO19–20
Balance sheet, ACC9–10
Balance of trade, GLO19, 20
Bank of Canada, OWN19, SOC25
 and bank rate, BAN15–16
 defined, BAN13
 and open-market operations,
  BAN15

 and reserve requirements,
  BAN14–15
Bank of Montreal, BAN24–25,
 OWN17, SOC12
Bank rate, BAN15–16
Bankruptcy, LEG17–18
Bankruptcy Act, LEG17
Banks, *see* Chartered banks
Bargaining unit, LR9
Bargaining zone, LR11–12
Bata Canada, DIS18–19
Batch processing, OP7–8
Bay, The, DIS6, ORG5
BCE, Inc., BUS13–15, OWN12
Bears, SEC14
Beaver Lumber, DIS14
Bell Canada, FIN8, FUT31–33,
 HRM22, OWN17
Bell Helicopter, ORG16
Bell Laboratories, OP27
Benetton, COM7
Benihana, OP7–8
Bennett, R.B., BUS12
Better Business Bureau, SOC27
Bill of materials (BOM), OP13
Biotechnology, FUT17, 20
Black & Decker, DIS6
Blue-collar workers, and job loss,
 FUT25–26
Board of directors, OWN13–16
Board lot, SEC13
Body Shop, The, SOC22
Bombardier Inc., ACC2–3
Bonds
 defined, FIN13
 retirement of, SEC8–9
 trade in, SEC9
 types of, SEC7–9
Bonus, HRM26
Bookkeeping
 defined, ACC5
 double-entry, ACC12–15
Book value, SEC5
Bowditch, James, PEO10
Bramalea Ltd., HRM26, OWN17
Brand, PRI9–11
Breakeven analysis, PRI15–16
Breakeven point, PRI15
British North America (BNA) Act,
 LEG3–4

Broker, DIS4
Budget, ACC21, 23
Budget Car and Truck Rentals, ENT18
Budgeting, ACC21–22
Buffer inventory, OP16
Bulls, SEC13–14
Buono, Anthony, PEO10
Bureau of Competition Policy, LEG19
Business
in Canada, BUS10–15
defined, BUS4
and the environment, FUT23–24, SOC18–24
family-owned, ENT24
and the future, FUT29, 31–33
globalization of, FUT3–7, GLO4–5
government regulation of, LEG18–20
and inflation, SOC24–25
international, *see* International business
and the judiciary, LEG20–24
process of, BUS25–26
regulating behaviour of, SOC5–7
social responsibility of, *see* Social responsibility
and sports, BUS2–3
and strategy changes, FUT24–25
and unemployment, SOC25–27
women in, ENT24–26
Business associates, business' responsibility to, SOC13
Business Depot, DIS12
Business law, LEG5, *see also* Law
Business plan, ENT14, 15
Buying, MKT6

CAE Inc., FUT3–4, GLO3
Caisse de dépôt et placement du Québec, OWN20
Caisses populaires (credit unions), BAN13, OWN22
Callable bond, SEC9
Campbell Soup Co. Ltd., OP4
Canada
aging population in, FUT13
balance of trade in, GLO19, 20
banking system in, BAN9–12
crown corporations in, OWN17–21
currency of, BAN4–5
economy of, BUS10–15, FUT9–11
employment equity legislation in, HRM15

and global competition, FUT4–11, GLO28
human rights legislation in, HRM13
and international trade, GLO23–27
job market in, FUT7–9
labour legislation in, LR7–9, 17
labour unions in, LR4–7
largest advertisers in, COM5
largest corporations in, OWN10–11
largest retailers in, DIS7
legal system in, LEG3–4
mixed economy in, BUS10
productivity in, BUS20–21, OP3
resource industries in, FUT9–11
small business in, ENT5
stock exchanges in, SEC10
union membership in, LR6
Canada Deposit Insurance Corporation (CDIC), BAN16–17
Canada Employment Centre, HRM9
Canada Labour Code, HRM29, LR7
Canada Post, OWN17, 20
Canada Safety Code, HRM28, **29**
Canada Savings Bonds, SEC7
Canada Trust, SEC23
Canada–U.S. Free Trade Agreement (FTA), BUS13, FUT4, 6, GLO4, OP4, SOC26
Canadian Association of Family Enterprise, ENT24
Canadian Auto Workers, LR7, 12–14
Canadian Booksellers Co-operative, OWN22
Canadian Broadcasting Corporation (CBC), ORG13, OWN19
Canadian Business, SEC11
Canadian Charter of Rights and Freedoms, HRM12, LEG3–4
Canadian Classification and Dictionary of Occupations, HRM9
Canadian Congress of Labour (CCL), LR5
Canadian Consumers' Association, SOC14–15
Canadian Federation of Independent Business (CFIB), ENT15–16, 17
Canadian Federation of Labour, LR7
Canadian General Electric, HRM22, ORG13, 16
Canadian Human Rights Act, HRM12
Canadian Human Rights

Commission, HRM12, 17
Canadian Imperial Bank of Commerce, BAN2, HRM31–32
Canadian Institute of Chartered Accountants (CICA), ACC5, SOC14
Canadian Labour Congress (CLC), LR5, 6, 7
Canadian Marconi, ORG16, 17
Canadian National Institute for the Blind, SOC8
Canadian National Railways (CNR), LEG11, ORG5, OWN19
Canadian Pacific Limited, BUS11, FUT3, ORG5, SEC7, 8
Canadian Payments System, BAN17–18
Canadian Radio-television and Telecommunications Commission (CRTC), LEG19, 20, 21
Canadian Tire Corporation, DIS3, 4, 6
Canadian Transport Commission, LEG21
Canadian Waste Materials Exchange, SOC20
CANSIM, INF10
Capacity, OP14
Capital, BUS19
Capitalism, BUS6
Career change, PEO2–3
Cash conversion cycle, ACC18–19
Cash management, FIN5
Catalogue showroom, DIS11–12
CCL Industries Inc., GLO2
Census, INF14
Centralization, ORG8
Central Mortgage and Housing Corporation, OWN19
Certificate of deposit (CD), FIN19
Certified General Accountants Association of Canada, ACC5
CFCs (chlorofluorocarbons), SOC5–7
Chain store, DIS11
Channel of distribution, DIS3
Chartered banks
defined, BAN10
profits of, BAN12
services provided by, BAN11
Chatelaine magazine, COM11
Checkpoint Systems, ACC4
Cheques, BAN17–18, 19
Chief executive officer (CEO), MGT7–8, 23–25, **OWN16**, *see also*

Child labour, LR4

China, communism in, BUS7

Christmas season, FIN6, 8

Chrysler Corporation, LR4, OP32–33, PEO18–19

Civil Code (*Code civil*), LEG4, 16

Civil law, LEG15

Class action, LEG25–26

Classroom training, HRM20–21

Clearly Canadian Beverage Corporation, MKT1–3

Closed shop, LR8

Coca-Cola Ltd., PRI10

Codes of conduct, SOC3–5

Cod stocks, SOC18

COIN database, ENT14

Coins, BAN4

Coles the Book People, OWN22

Collective agreements, LR9–16

Collective bargaining, LR9–16

Color Your World, DIS5–6

Combines Investigation Act (1985), BUS24, 25, ENT3, LEG19, SOC15–16

Command economy, BUS9

Commission, HRM26

Committee structure, ORG18

Common carrier, DIS14–15

Common law, LEG4

Common market, GLO17

Common shares, OWN12, SEC4–6

Communication, MKT13

Communism, BUS7, 9

Communist Manifesto, The, BUS7

Community, business' responsibility to, SOC17

Comparative advantage, GLO22–23

Compensation, HRM25–29

Competition, BUS16–17

and government regulation, LEG19–20

invisible hand of, BUS6

monopolistic, BUS24

perfect, BUS23

and private enterprise system, BUS9, 18

Competitiveness

defined, BUS21

and physical distribution, DIS16

and productivity, OP4

and quality, BUS29–30

requirements for, BUS22

Competitive priorities, OP4

Compressed workweek, PEO22

Compulsory arbitration, LR15

Computer-Assisted Trading System

(CATS), SEC13

Computers

business applications of, INF4–7

and crime detection, INF18–19

development of, INF2–4

and production planning, OP14–15

Computer simulation training, HRM20

Computer software, and copyright infringement, LEG11, 12

Conceptual skills, MGT7

Conciliation, LR14

Confederation of National Trade Unions, LR6, 7

Conference Board of Canada, INF10

Congress of Democratic Trade Unions, LR6

Congress of Industrial Organizations (CIO), LR5

Constitution Act (1982), LEG4

Consumer behaviour, MKT10–11

Consumer and Corporate Affairs Canada, COM15, LEG19, SOC15

Consumerism, SOC14

Consumer movement, SOC14–17

Consumer Packaging and Labelling Act, SOC15

Consumer products, PRI3–5

Consumer Protection Office (Quebec), SOC16–17

Consumers Distributing, DIS12, FIN8, OP12

Consumers' Gas Co. Ltd., HRM33

Consumers' Protection Agency, SOC27

Content theories of motivation, PEO4–8

Continuous flow, OP8–9

Contract carrier, DIS14

Contracts, LEG13–15

Contractual VMS, DIS6

Controlling, MGT19–20

Convenience products, PRI4

Convenience store, DIS11

Conventional arbitration, LR15

Convertible bonds, SEC8

Convertible preferred shares, SEC7

Cooke, Jack Kent, BUS27–28

Co-operative advertising, COM3

Co-operatives

defined, OWN21

largest, OWN23

Copyright, LEG10–12

Copyright Act, LEG10

Corporate irresponsibility,

SOC28–29

Corporate VMS, DIS5–6

Corporations, *see also* Incorporation

board of directors of, OWN13–16

crown, OWN17–21

defined, OWN7

50 largest Canadian, OWN10–11

growth of, OWN17

private or closely held, OWN12

public or publicly held, OWN12

shareholders of, OWN12–13

structure of, OWN12–16

top management of, OWN16

Costco, DIS12

Cost-push inflation, SOC25

Counselling, employee, HRM23

Counselling Assistance to Small Enterprise (CASE), ENT13

Counterfeiting, BAN5–6

Countertrade, GLO21–22

Coupon, COM14

Court system, *see* Judiciary

Craft union, LR3

Crawford, Purdy, MGT23–25

Creative selling, COM16

Credit, FIN5, 9–10, 11

Credit Bureau of Canada, FIN5

Credit cards, BAN7–9, FIN11

Credit unions (caisses populaires), BAN13, OWN22

Creelman, George, ORG25–27

Criminal law, LEG15

Cross-border shopping, DIS9, 10

Crown corporations

defined, OWN17

largest, OWN21

CTV, OWN19

Cumulative preferred shares, SEC6

Currency, BAN7, *see also* Money

Current assets, ACC9

Current liabilities, ACC10

Current ratio, ACC15–16

Customer departmentalization, ORG5

Customers, business' responsibility to, SOC14–17

Customs union, GLO17

Cyberspace, FUT18–19

Cycle inventory, OP16

Daniel et Daniel, ENT11

Data

external, INF9

government sources of, INF9–10

internal, INF9

primary, INF11, 16
private sources of, INF10–11
qualitative, INF8
quantitative, INF8
secondary, INF9–11, 16
Data analysis, INF4–5
Davis, Les, LEG9–10
Days sales in accounts receivable,
ACC18
Debenture, SEC7
Debit cards, BAN20, 21, INF6
Debt-to-asset ratio, ACC16
Debt financing, FIN7
Decentralization, ORG8
Decision making, MGT21–22
Deed, LEG7
Delayering, FUT25–26
Delegation, ORG7
Demand curve, PRI13
Demand deposit, BAN7
Demand forecasting, OP12
Demand note, FIN11
Demand-pull inflation, SOC25
Deming, Edwards, OP27, 29
Democratic leader, MGT18
Departmentalization, ORG5–6
Department store, DIS10
Depreciation, ACC9–10
Depression, Great, BUS12
Devaluation, GLO20
Direct international trade, GLO6
Direct investment, GLO7
Direct marketing, COM12, DIS12
Disabilities, and employment
equity, SOC8–13
Discount store, DIS11
Discrimination
defined, HRM12
in job specifications, HRM8–9
prohibited grounds for, HRM13
Dismissal, HRM24, 31–32
Distribution, *see also* Retailing
channels of, DIS3–6
defined, **MKT13**
density of, DIS13–14
exclusive, DIS13
intensive, DIS13
physical, MKT6, DIS14–16
selective, DIS14
Distribution strategy, OP25–26
Dividends, OWN12
Domtar Inc., FIN20–21
Dormant (secret) partners, OWN4
Double-entry bookkeeping,
ACC12–15

Doughnut-shaped chart, ORG22
Dow-Jones Industrial Average,
SEC17
Drucker, Peter, BUS15, MGT12, PEO16
Dumping, GLO14
Dun & Bradstreet, FIN5, INF11
Du Pont Canada, GLO4
Dutailier Inc., PRI24–25

Earnings per share (EPS), ACC20
Earth Summit, SOC24
Eastern Europe, BUS7, FUT3, 29
Eaton, Kenneth, ENT13
Eaton, Timothy, DIS10
Eaton's, BUS16, DIS4, 17–18, ORG13,
OWN12
Ecology, SOC18
Economic systems, BUS4–10
capitalism, BUS6
communism, BUS7
mixed economies, BUS9–10
and private enterprise, BUS9
socialism, BUS6
Economy
business' responsibility to,
SOC24–27
Canadian, BUS10–15
sunrise, BUS13–15
trends in FUT3–11
Edmonton Telephone Corporation,
SOC4–5
Electronic banking, BAN18, 20, 21
Electronic cottage, FUT2
Electronic data interchange (EDI),
INF17–18
Electronic funds transfer system
(EFTS), BAN18–20
Embargo, GLO14
Employee(s)
business' responsibility to,
SOC7–13
compensation, HRM25–29
counselling, HRM23
selection process for, HRM10
skills, HRM19–23
turnover, HRM23–25
Employee benefits, HRM28
Employee stock ownership plan
(ESOP), HRM26
Employment equity, HRM12–17,
SOC8–13
Employment and Immigration
Canada, HRM9
Endorsement, LEG17
Energy, wise use of, SOC23

Energy, Mines and Resources,
Department of, SOC24
Energy Supplies Allocation Board,
LEG21
Engel, Blackwell, and Miniard
Consumer Decision Process
Model, MKT10–11
Engels, Friedrich, BUS7
ENIAC, INF2
Entrepreneurs, BUS17, ENT4–5
defined, **BUS17, ENT4**
women as, ENT24–26
Entrepreneurship, BUS19–20, *see also*
Small business
university courses in, ENT27–28
Environment, Department of, SOC24
Environmental issues, FUT23–24,
SOC18–24, 31–32
Environmental labelling and
advertising, COM15
Equilibrium price, PRI13
Equipment assets, *see* Fixed assets
Equity financing, FIN7, 13–15
Equity theory, PEO11–12
ERG theory, PEO7, 8
Esteem needs, PEO5
Etherington, Bill, ORG8
Ethnicity, and employment equity,
SOC8–10
European Bank for Reconstruction
and Development, BAN22–24
European Community (EC), GLO17
European Free Trade Area (EFTA),
GLO17
Excess funds, use of, FIN18–19
Exchange control, GLO14
Exchange rate, GLO20–21
Exclusive distribution, DIS13
Existence needs, PEO7
Expectancy, PEO10
Expectancy theory, PEO10–11
Experimental design, INF13
Export strategy, GLO8–9
Express warranty, LEG9
External Affairs, Department of,
SOC24
External data, INF9
Exxon Corp., SOC2

Factor, FIN12
Factors of production, BUS18–20
Family-owned business, ENT24
Featherbedding, LR22
Federal Business Development
Bank, ENT13, **14,** FIN13

Federal courts, LEG22
Feudal system, BUS4–5
Fidelity Investments Canada Ltd., SEC26–27
Fiedler, Fred, MGT18
Final-offer arbitration, LR15
Financial management, FIN2
Financial plan, FIN3
Financial planning, FIN2–4
Financial Post, The, HRM9, INF10
Financial statements, ACC7–12
Financial Times of Canada, The, SEC15
Financial Times 100, SEC17
Financing, FIN7–18, MKT7
Finished goods inventory, OP16
First Choice Haircutters, OP6
Fisher, Douglas, LR4
Fisheries, Department of, SOC24
Fixed assets
  defined, ACC9
  financing, FIN6–7
Fixed cost, OP15, PRI15
Fixed exchange rate, GLO21
Flexible manufacturing, OP10–11
Flextime, PEO20–21
Floating exchange rate, GLO21
Food distributors, largest Canadian, DIS7
Food and Drug Act, SOC15
Ford, Henry, OP8, 9
Ford Motor Company, BUS16, COM6, LR8, OP17, 20–22
Franchise agreements, ENT19–20
Franchisee, ENT17
Franchises
  advantages/disadvantages of, ENT18
  defined, ENT17
Franchising, ENT17–24
Franchisor, ENT17
Freedom of choice, BUS18
Freedom to compete, BUS18
Free-rein leader, MGT18
Free trade, BUS13, GLO4, *see also* Canada–U.S. Free Trade Agreement; North American Free Trade Agreement
Free trade area, GLO17
Freight forwarder, DIS15
Friedman, Milton, SOC7
Friendship, commerce, and navigation treaties, GLO15
Frisco Bay Industries, OWN6
Frustration–regression principle, PEO7

Fullerton, Ronald A., MKT8
Functional departmentalization, ORG6
Functional organization, ORG14, 15
Fur trade, BUS10–11
Futures contract, SEC12–13
Future Shock, FUT1

Gap, The, DIS11
Gemini Fashions, GLO5
General Agreement on Tariffs and Trade (GATT), FUT29, GLO15–17
General Electric, *see* Canadian General Electric
General Foods Corporation, PEO19
Generally accepted accounting principles (GAAP), ACC4–5, 20–21
General Motors, BUS16, HRM21, INF3, LEG5–7, OP20, 24–25, ORG16
General partner, OWN4
General store, DIS10
Generic product, PRI11
Geographic departmentalization, ORG5
George Weston, OWN17
Gillette Canada Inc., GLO4
Glegg Water Conditioning, BUS28–29
Globalization, FUT3–11, GLO4–5
Global warming, SOC23
Globe and Mail, The, SEC18
Globe and Mail Report on Business, The, HRM9
Goals
  defined, MGT11
  and management by objectives, PEO17
  and profits, MGT12–13
Goal-setting theory, PEO11, 17
Gold standard, GLO20
Goods, vs. services, PRI2–3
Government
  and crown corporations, OWN17–21
  and the environment, SOC23–24
  powers affecting business, LEG4, 5
  regulation of business, LEG18–20, SOC6–7
  regulation of securities transactions, SEC14
  and small business, ENT3, 13, 14, 15–16
  as source of data, INF9–10
Grapevine, ORG24

Gray, Douglas, FUT2
Great-West Life Assurance, COM17
Grievance, LR18
Grievance arbitration, LR20
Grievance procedures, LR18–20
Groseillers, Médard Chouart des, BUS10–11
Gross National Product (GNP), BUS20
Guinness Book of World Records, PEO5–6

Handbook of Canadian Consumer Markets, INF10
Hang Seng Index, SEC17
Harassment, HRM17–19
Harlequin Enterprises, OWN17
Hawthorne effect, PEO4
Hawthorne studies, PEO3–4, 23
Hazardous Product Act, SOC15
Health and Welfare Canada, SOC24
Herzberg, Frederick, PEO7
Hewlett-Packard Ltd., LEG12
Hibernia, OWN19
Hierarchy of needs, PEO5–7, 8
Hierarchy of organizational objectives, ORG5, 6
High-technology firms, ENT7, FUT17
Hillier, Robert, OP4
Hiring from within, HRM6, 9
HMV, DIS11
Holiday Inn, ENT18
Home Inc., FUT2
Horizontal organization, ORG18–21
Hudson's Bay Company, BUS11, OWN8, *see also* Bay, The
Human relations approach to management, PEO4
Human relations skills, MGT6
Human resource department, responsibilities of, HRM4
Human resource forecast, HRM5
Human resource management, HRM4
Human resource planning, HRM5
Human rights, and employment, HRM12–19
Hygiene factors, PEO7
Hyperinflation, BAN5, SOC25
Hypermarché Laval, DIS12
Hypermarket, DIS12

IBM, HRM22, INF2, MKT9, OP14, ORG8, SOC12

IKEA, PRI19
Image goals, PRI18
Imperial Oil Ltd., HRM6, SOC12
Implied warranty, LEG9
Import quota, GLO14
Inco Ltd., LR4, SOC19
Income statement, ACC10, 11
Income Tax Act, LEG5
Incorporation, OWN7–11, *see also*
　　Corporations
　advantages of, OWN8, 9
　disadvantages of, OWN8, 9–10
　and misuse of corporate funds,
　　OWN26–27
Indexes, stock, SEC17, 18
Indirect international trade, GLO6
Individual investor, SEC17
Industrial distributor, DIS4
Industrial products, PRI3, 5
Industrial Revolution, BUS6, FUT2,
　　LR3
Industrial union, LR3
Industry, Trade and Commerce
　　Canada, ENT3
Inflation
　cost-push, SOC25
　currency and, BAN5
　defined, PRI19, SOC24
　demand-pull, SOC25
　and GNP, BUS20
　hyper-, SOC25
　and prices, PRI19–20
Informal organization, ORG24
Information
　and privacy, INF15
　transfer of, INF6–7
　types of, INF7–8
Inputs, defined, OP2
Installment note, FIN10
Institutional advertising, COM6
Institutional investor, SEC17
Instrumentality, PEO10
Intangible assets, ACC10
Intangible personal property, LEG7
Intangible private property, BUS17
Intellectual and industrial property
　　law, LEG9–12
Intellectual property, BUS17, LEG7
Intensive distribution, DIS13
Intentional tort, LEG15
Interac, BAN18
Interactive voice technology (IVT),
　　INF7
Interest arbitration, LR14–15
Intermediary (middleman), DIS4

Internal data, INF9
International Aviation
　　Transportation Association
　　(IATA), ORG16
International business
　arguments for, GLO22–23
　barriers to, GLO12–15
　and export strategy, GLO8–9
　levels of involvement in, GLO6–7
　and national/international law,
　　GLO15–19
　requirements for, GLO7–8
　social/cultural factors of,
　　GLO10–12
　terminology of, GLO19–22
International joint venture, GLO7
International law, GLO15–19
International Monetary Fund
　　(IMF), GLO15
Interviews, INF12–13
Inventory
　anticipatory, OP16
　in balance sheet, ACC9
　buffer, OP16
　cycle, OP16
　finished goods, OP16
　just-in-time (JIT), OP16–18
　materials, OP16
　pipeline, OP16
　work-in-progress, OP16
Inventory control, DIS16
Inventory costs, OP15
Inventory management, FIN5–6,
　　OP15–18
Inventory turnover, ACC17
Investment, SEC19–20
Investment Canada, LEG21
Investors
　business' responsibility to, SOC14
　in securities, SEC17–20
Invisible hand of competition, BUS6
Irving, K.C., BUS27–28
Ivory Soap, PRI6

Japan
　conducting business in, GLO11–12
　job satisfaction in, PEO23–25
　management styles in, PEO22–23
Job analysis, HRM7
Job description, HRM7, 8
Job enlargement, PEO19
Job enrichment, PEO18–22
Job evaluation, and compensation,
　　HRM25
Job interview, HRM10–11

Jobless growth, FUT7
Job market, and globalization,
　　FUT7–9
Job orientation, HRM11
Job rotation, HRM21
Job satisfaction, PEO23–25
Job sharing, PEO22
Job shop, OP4–7, 9
Job specifications
　avoiding discrimination in,
　　HRM8–9
　defined, HRM7
Joint venture, OWN4
Journal, ACC5
Judiciary, LEG20–24
Just-in-time inventory control
　　(JIT), OP16–18

Kapital, Das, BUS7
Kentucky Fried Chicken, ENT18
Kibbutzim, BUS7
Kierkegaard, Søren, PEO5
Klein, Chips, ENT25
Kmart, DIS8

Labatt Breweries of Canada, FUT4,
　　ORG25–27
Labour, BUS19
Labour, Department of, SOC24
Labour legislation, LR7–9, 17
Labour unions
　and collective agreements, LR9–16
　concerns facing, LR21–23
　and contracts, LR18–20
　and co-operation with manage-
　　ment, LR22–23, 26–27
　defined, LR3
　and dues, LR8
　future of, LR24
　history of, LR3–7
　largest Canadian, LR6
　and legislation, LR7–9
　membership, LR6
　setting up, LR9
　and technological change, LR22
　and white-collar workers, LR23
Lamarre, Bernard, SOC28–29
Land assets, *see* Fixed assets
Lao-tzu, PEO5
Lateral transfer, HRM23
Law
　of agency, LEG16
　and bankruptcy, LEG17–18
　business, LEG5
　civil, LEG15

common, LEG4
and contracts, LEG13–15
criminal, LEG15
defined, LEG3
and government regulation,
    LEG18–20
intellectual and industrial
    property, LEG9
and international trade, GLO15–19
and the judiciary, LEG20–24
and negotiable instruments,
    LEG16–17
origins of, LEG4
property, LEG7–12
real estate, LEG7–8
of sale, LEG8–9
statutory, LEG4
of torts, LEG15–16
Law of supply and demand,
    BUS22–23, PRI13
Lawyers, in-house, LEG5–7
Layoff, HRM24
Leaders
    traits of, MGT17
    types of, MGT17–18
Leading, MGT17–19
Lease, LEG7
Leverage, FIN15–17
Leveraged buyout (LBO), FIN17
Lever Brothers, SOC6
Liabilities, ACC7, 10
Licensing, GLO6
Lien, LEG8
Limited partner, OWN4
Linamar Machine Ltd., OP5
Line of credit, FIN11
Line flow, OP8
Line-and-staff structure, ORG15–16
Line structure, ORG13
Liquidity, ACC9
Listerine, COM4
List price, PRI15
Loans, FIN10–12, 13
Loblaws, BUS17, DIS12, HRM21,
    OWN17, PRI2, SOC15
Local area networks (LANs), INF6
Locke, E.A., PEO11
Lockout, LR16
London Stock Exchange, SEC10–11
Long-term liabilities, ACC10
Lunney, Bob, MGT9–10

McClelland, David, PEO7–8
McDonald's, COM12, HRM21, MKT9,
    15, PRI9, SOC5

McGregor, Douglas, PEO12–13
Maclean Hunter, ORG5
Magazines, and advertising, COM11
Magna International Inc., ACC25,
    FIN21–22
Mail interview, INF13
Make-up Art Cosmetics (M.A.C.),
    COM2, 3
Management
    and accounting, ACC22, 23–25
    and computers, INF2–4
    and decision making, MGT21–22
    defined, MGT3
    and delayering, FUT25–26
    functions of, MGT13–21
    future of, FUT26–28
    and goals, MGT11–12
    human relations approach to,
        PEO4
    Japanese vs. North American
        styles of, PEO22–23
    levels of, MGT4–5
    and mission, MGT11
    and objectives, MGT12
    ownership, ORG8–10
    scientific, PEO4
    skills, MGT6–7, 9–10
Management development pro-
    grams, HRM21
Management hierarchy, MGT4
    and management functions,
        MGT21
    and management skills, MGT6
Management information system
    (MIS), INF8
Management by objectives
    (MBO), PEO16–18
Management process
    controlling, MGT19–20
    leading, MGT17–19
    organizing, MGT14
    planning, MGT13–14
Managers
    leadership traits of, MGT17
    middle, MGT5
    roles of, MGT10–11
    supervisory, MGT4–5
    top, MGT5, 7–8, 9–10
Manual of Sex-free Occupational
    Titles, HRM9
Manufacturing resource planning
    (MRP II), OP14
Marantz, Gordon, LEG18
Marketable securities, ACC9,
    FIN18–19

Market economy, BUS9
Marketing, *see also* Retailing
    approaches to, MKT8–9
    concept of, MKT3–5
    and consumers, MKT9–12
    defined, MKT7
    strategy, MKT12
    tools of, MKT5–7
    trends in, MKT14
Marketing boards, BUS23
Marketing channel, DIS3–6, MKT13
Marketing communications
    and advertising, COM5–12
    defined, COM3
    elements of, COM3
    objectives of, COM4–5
    and packaging, COM14–15
    and personal selling, COM15–18
    and sales promotion, COM13–14
Marketing mix, MKT12–13
Marketing niche, ENT11, MKT11–12,
    PRI5
Marketing plan, MKT12–13
Marketing research
    defined, INF9, MKT5
    and experimental design, INF13
    and observation method, INF13
    primary data in, INF11
    sampling in, INF14–15
    secondary data in, INF9–11
    and surveys, INF12–13
Market orientation, MKT9
Markets, types of, BUS23–25
Market segment, MKT9
Market share, PRI18
Market value, SEC5
Market-value accounting, ACC28
Mark I, INF2
Marks & Spencer, DIS11
Markup, PRI14–15
Marx, Karl, BUS7
Maslow, Abraham, PEO5–7
Materials inventory, OP16
Materials requirement planning
    (MRP), OP14
Matrix structure, ORG16–18
Maturity date, SEC7
Mayo, Elton, PEO3–4
Meadowlands Investments,
    COM21–22
Meany, George, LR5
Mediation, LR14
Medical examinations, HRM11
Medium of exchange, BAN6
Mennonites, BUS7

Mentor, HRM21
Mercury poisoning, SOC19
Merger, OWN17, 18
Merrell Dow Canada, SOC1–3
Merrill Lynch, HRM22
Mesta, OWN21–22
Metric system, LEG18–19
Mexico, BUS13
Michelin Tires, DIS6
Microsoft Corporation, INF3, LEG12
Middleman (intermediary), DIS4
Middle managers, MGT5
Mill, John Stuart, BAN3
Mintzberg, Henry, MGT10–11
Mission, MGT11
Missionary selling, COM16
Mission statement, MGT11
Mitel Corporation, FIN8
Mixed economies, BUS9–10
Molson Breweries, LEG16
M1 (money supply), BAN7
Money
    characteristics of, BAN3–6
    defined, BAN2
    functions of, BAN6–7
    origins of, BAN3
    supply, BAN7–8
    token, BAN7
Monopolistic competition, BUS24
Monopoly, BUS24–25
Montreal Symphony Orchestra,
    BUS5
Montreal Trust, OWN17
Moody's, INF11
Morale, PEO13–14
Mother Parker's Foods, SOC20
Motivation
    acquired needs theory of, PEO7–8
    content theories of, PEO4–8
    equity theory of, PEO11–12
    ERG theory of, PEO7, 8
    expectancy theory of, PEO10–11
    goal-setting theory of, PEO11, 17
    and hierarchy of needs, PEO5–7, 8
    and job enrichment, PEO18–22
    and management by objectives,
        PEO16–18
    and morale, PEO13–14
    process theories of, PEO10–12
    Theory X, PEO12–13
    Theory Y, PEO12–13
    Theory Z, PEO22–23
    two-factor theory of, PEO7, 8
    and worker input, PEO15–16
Motivators, PEO7

Motive, PEO4
Mountain Equipment Co-op,
    OWN22
M2 (money supply), BAN7
M2+ (money supply), BAN7
**Multinational corporation (MNC),
    GLO7**
Mutual funds, SEC22–23, 27–28

Narrowcasting, COM12
National Energy Board, LEG21
National Harbours Board, LEG21
National Policy, BUS11
Natural resources, BUS19
Needs
    defined, PEO4
    hierarchy of, PEO5–7
Negotiable instruments, LEG16–17
Neilson Cadbury Canada,
    GLO30–32
Networking, INF6–7
Newspapers, and advertising,
    COM11
New York Stock Exchange, SEC11,
    17
Niche marketing, *see* Marketing
    niche
Nichol, Dave, BUS17, PRI2
Nikkei Index, SEC17
Nissan, COM6
**Non-cumulative preferred shares,
    SEC6**
**Non-profit (not-for-profit) organi-
    zations, BUS4**
Non-renewable resources, SOC23
Non-tariff barriers, GLO14–15
North American Free Trade
    Agreement (NAFTA), BUS13,
    FUT29, GLO4, 17, SOC26
Northern Telecom, OWN17
North West Company, BUS11
Notes receivable, ACC9
Notice deposit, BAN7
Not-for-profit organizations, *see*
    Non-profit organizations

Objectives, MGT12, PEO17
Observation method, INF13
Occupational safety, HRM28–29
Odd lot, SEC13
Odd pricing, PRI19
Oligopoly, BUS24
Olivetti Canada, COM19–21
Olympia and York, OWN17
On-the-job training, HRM20

Onkyo, COM4
**Open-market operations (Bank of
    Canada), BAN15**
Operating ratios, ACC17–19
Operating revenues, FIN8–9
Operations function, OP3
Operations management, *see also*
    Production process
    and change, OP29–30
    defined, OP2
    and productivity, OP3–4
Orchestra, as line structure, ORG14
Order processing, COM16, DIS16
Organization(s)
    defined, ORG3
    horizontal, ORG18–21
    informal, ORG24
    non-profit (not-for-profit), BUS4
    structure of, ORG4–28
Organizational chart
    defined, 21
    doughnut-shaped, ORG22
Organizational structure(s)
    and centralization, ORG8
    committee, ORG18
    comparison of, ORG19
    and delegation, ORG7
    and departmentalization, ORG5–7
    forms of, ORG12–24
    functional, ORG14, 15
    and growth, ORG11–12
    and hierarchy of organizational
        objectives, ORG5
    horizontal, ORG18–21
    influences on, ORG4–12
    line, ORG13
    line-and-staff, ORG15–16
    matrix, ORG16–18
    and span of control, ORG7–8
Organizing, MGT14
Ostensible partners, OWN4
Ostry, Sylvia, GLO17
Ouchi, William, PEO22
Outdoor advertising, COM12
Outputs, defined, OP2
Outside director, OWN14
**Over-the-counter (OTC) market,
    SEC11**
Owen, Robert, BUS6, 7
Owner's equity, ACC7, 10

Packaging, COM14–15, PRI12, 20
Parent company, OWN17
Parkinson, C. Northcote, ORG11–12
Parkinson's Law, ORG11–12

advantages/disadvantages of, OWN4–5, 6
defined, **OWN3**
types of, OWN4
Par value, SEC5
Patents, LEG9–10, 12
Pay equity, HRM12, 33
Pay for performance, HRM27
Peel Regional Police, MGT9–10
Penetration price strategy, PRI22
People Jewellers, OWN17
Pepsi-Cola, HRM6
Perfect competition, BUS23
Performance appraisal, HRM22–23
Perrier Group, SOC2
Personal interview, INF12
Personal selling
defined, **COM3**
types of, COM16
Peters, Tom, INF3
Petro-Canada Ltd., ORG2–3, 6, OWN19, SOC31–32
Physical distribution, DIS14–16, MKT6
Physiological needs, PEO5
Picketing, LR15, 16
Piecework, HRM26
Pipeline inventory, OP16
Pizza Hut, MKT13
Pizza Pizza, ENT21–24
Planning, MGT13–14
Plant assets, *see* Fixed assets
Point-of-purchase, COM13
Pollution, SOC19–20
Population change, FUT12
Portfolio strategy, SEC22
Positioning, COM4
Power needs, PEO8
Pre-emptive right, SEC6
Preference products, PRI4
Preferred shares, OWN13, SEC6–7
Premium, COM14
Prepaid expenses, ACC9
President's Choice, BUS17, PRI2–3, 10, SOC15
Price Club, DIS12
Price–earnings ratio, SEC17
Price lining, PRI16–17
Prices
and consumers, PRI19
and inflation, PRI19–20
and law of supply and demand, BUS22–23, PRI13–14
and quality, PRI19
setting, PRI13–17

Pricing
and breakeven analysis, PRI15–16
defined, **MKT13**
and downsizing, PRI20
and image goals, PRI18
new products, PRI21–22
odd, PRI19
and product promotion objectives, PRI19
and profitability objectives, PRI17–18
psychological, PRI19
and social policy objectives, PRI18
and status quo objectives, PRI18
and volume objectives, PRI18
Primary data, INF11, 16
Prime interest rate, FIN11
Principal, LEG16
Privacy, FUT22–23, INF15
Private brand, PRI10
Private carrier, DIS14
Private or closely held corporation, OWN12
Private enterprise system
defined, **BUS9**
and entrepreneurs, BUS17
ground rules of, BUS17–18
and public affairs, OWN20–21
Private property, BUS17
Privatization, BUS10, OWN20
Probability sample, INF14
Process departmentalization, ORG6
Process theories of motivation, PEO10–12
Procter and Gamble, ORG16, PRI6
Product(s)
and brand identification, PRI9–11
classification of, PRI3–5
consumer, PRI3–5
defined, **MKT12**–13, **PRI3**
industrial, PRI3, 5
life cycle of, PRI5–8
management, PRI11–12
and market niches, PRI5
packaging, PRI12
Product advertising, COM6
Product departmentalization, ORG5
Production process
assembly line, OP8–9
batch processing, OP7–8
continuous flow, OP8–9
and equipment maintenance, OP19–20
flexibility in, OP5, 10–11

and inventory management, OP15–18
job shop, OP4–7, 9
and labour management, OP20–22
planning, OP12–15
and purchasing, OP22–25
and priorities, OP11
and quality control, OP27–29
and warehousing/distribution strategy, OP25–26
Productivity
and competitiveness, OP4
defined, **BUS20**–21
growth, OP3
operations management and, OP3–4
Product liability, LEG15–16
Product life cycle
and advertising, COM8–9
decline stage of, PRI8
defined, **PRI6**
growth stage of, PRI7
introductory stage of, PRI7
maturity stage of, PRI8
Product management, PRI11–12
Product orientation, MKT8
Product/process matrix, OP11
Product promotion objectives, PRI18–19
Profit
and business ethics, SOC30–31
defined, **BUS4**
and goals, MGT12–13
and pricing, PRI17–18
and private enterprise, BUS18
and product life cycle, PRI7
Profitability objectives, PRI17–18
Profitability ratios, ACC19–20
Profit maximization, PRI17
Profit sharing, HRM26
Promissory note, FIN10
Promotion, HRM23
Promotion contests, COM14
Property, LEG7
Property law, LEG7–12
Protective tariff, GLO12
Provigo, DIS12
Provincial courts, LEG21–22
Proxy, OWN13
Psychological pricing, PRI19
Public ownership, *see* Crown corporations
Public or publicly held corporation, OWN12
Pulling strategy, COM3

Purchasing management, OP22–25
Pushing strategy, COM3

Quaker Oats Co., COM8–9
Qualitative data, INF8
Quality
  and competitiveness, BUS29–30
  defined, OP27
  and price, PRI19
  in production process, OP28–29
  and productivity, OP29
Quality of life, BUS20
Quality of work life (QWL), PEO15
Quantitative data, INF8
Quebec Deposit Insurance Board,
  BAN17
Questionnaires, INF13
Quick ratio, ACC16

Radio, and advertising, COM12
Radio Shack, ENT18
Radisson, Pierre, BUS10, 11
Rand, Ivan, LR8
Rand formula, LR8–9
Ratio analysis, ACC15–20
Raymond Industrial Equipment
  Ltd., OP30–32
Real estate law, LEG7–8
Real property, LEG7
Recessions
  and bankruptcy, LEG18
  and Canadian economy, BUS12–13
  and jobs, FUT8
  and inflation, SOC25
  and small business, ENT12
Regulated industries, LEG19
Regulatory agencies, *see*
  Administrative agencies
Reimer Express, DIS15
Relatedness (social interaction)
  needs, PEO7
Renewable resources, SOC23
Repap Enterprises Inc., FIN1–2
Repository for Integrated
  Computer Imaging (RICI),
  INF18–19
Repossession, LEG8
Required cash reserves, BAN11
Resource industries, FUT9–11
Resources, SOC23
Responsibility, ORG7
Restaurants, BUS16–17
Restrictive Trade Practices Act,
  ENT3
Restrictive Trade Practices

  Commission, LEG19
Retailer(s)
  defined, DIS4
  largest Canadian, DIS7
  types of, DIS10–12
Retailing
  and computers, INF5–6
  evolution of, DIS6–7
  as marketing function, MKT6
  marketing planning for, DIS9
  and repositioning, DIS13
  and small business, ENT6
  wheel of, DIS8, 9
Retirement, HRM23–24
Return on sales, ACC19
Return on total equity, ACC19
Revaluation, GLO21
Revenue Canada, MGT2, 4
Revenue tariff, GLO12
Revlon, PRI3
Revolving credit agreement, FIN11
Ricardo, David, GLO23
Ricardo theory, GLO23
Robert Campeau Corporation,
  OWN17
Rogers Cablesystems Ltd., SOC12
Roman Catholic Church, ORG13
Roosevelt, Franklin, BUS12
Rose, Billy, GLO23
Routing sheet, OP13, 14
Royal Bank, BAN20, PEO20, SOC12
Royal Canadian Mint, BAN4–5
Royal Trustco, HRM26, ORG9–10,
  OWN14–15
Royalty payment, LEG10
Rumball, Donald, ENT12
Russia, BUS7, 8–9, FUT3, 29

Safety needs, PEO5
Safeway, DIS12
Saint-Simon, Henri de, BUS6, 7
Salary, HRM25
Sale, law of, LEG8–9
Sales management, COM17–18
Sales and Marketing Management,
  INF10
Sales maximization, PRI18
Sales orientation, MKT8–9
Sales promotion, COM3, 13–14
Sample (market research), **INF14–15**
Sample (sales promotion), **COM14**
Save-on Foods, DIS12
School Workplace Apprenticeship
  Program, HRM20
Scientific American, INF2

Scientific management, PEO4
Scope mouthwash, COM4
Scrambled merchandising, DIS8
Sears Canada, BUS16, HRM22
Secondary data, INF9–11, 16
Secondary reserve requirement,
  BAN14–15
Second Cup Coffee Company,
  ENT18
Secret (dormant) partners, OWN4
Secured bond, SEC7
Secured loan, FIN12
Securities
  buying/selling, SEC12–13
  defined, SEC4
  regulating sale of, SEC14
Securities exchanges, SEC10–11
Seldane, SOC1–3
Selective distribution, DIS14
Self-actualization needs, PEO5–6
Self-sufficiency, GLO22
Selling, MKT7, *see also* Personal
  selling
Seniority, HRM23
Separation, HRM23
Serial bond, SEC8
Service firms, ENT6
Service planning, OP18
Services, vs. goods, PRI2–3
Set-up costs, OP15–16
7-Eleven, COM4
Sexual harassment, HRM17–19
Shareholder activism, FUT14
Shareholders, OWN12–13, SEC4–5
Share price–to–earnings ratio,
  ACC20
Shares
  buying and selling, SEC12–13
  common, OWN12, SEC4–6
  and incorporation, OWN8
  non-voting, OWN13
  preferred, OWN13, SEC6–7
Shewart, Walter, OP27
Shopping products, PRI4
Short list, HRM9
Shostack, Lynn, PRI3
Sinking fund, SEC8
Skills, employee, HRM19–23
Skimming price strategy, PRI21
Small business
  and business plan, ENT14–15
  characteristics of, ENT10–17
  defined, ENT4
  and entrepreneurs, ENT4–5
  family-owned, ENT24

and franchising, ENT17–24
and government, ENT3, 13, 14, 15–16
importance of, ENT3–4
vs. large business, ENT10
and recessions, ENT12
statistical profile of, ENT5
types of, ENT6–7
and women as entrepreneurs, ENT24–26
Small Business Loan Act, ENT14
Small Business Secretariat, ENT3
Smart House, FUT17–18
Smith, Adam, BUS6, OP20, SOC7
Smith, Donald, BUS11
Smithbooks, DIS11, OWN22
Socialism, BUS6, 9
Social issues
affecting people, SOC7–18
economic, SOC24–27
environmental, SOC18–24
Social needs, PEO5
Social policy pricing objectives, PRI18
Social responsibility
to business associates, SOC13
to the community, SOC17
and corporate irresponsibility, SOC28–29
to customers, SOC14–17
defined, SOC3
to employees, SOC7–13
and the environment, SOC18–24
and inflation, SOC24–25
to investors, SOC14
and profit, SOC30–31
scorecard on, SOC27–28
and unemployment, SOC25–27
Social responsibility accounting (SRA), ACC26–27
Social trends, FUT11–16
Society of Management Accountants of Canada, ACC5
Softimage Inc., ENT7–9
Sole proprietorship
advantages/disadvantages of, OWN2–3, 4
defined, OWN2
Soviet Union, *see* Russia
Span of control, ORG7–8
Specialization, GLO22–23
Specialty advertising, COM13
Specialty products, PRI4–5
Specialty store, DIS11
Speculation, SEC19

Sports, and business, BUS2–3
Spreadsheet analysis, INF4–5
Stakeholder, SOC7
Standard of living, BUS20
Standard & Poor's, INF11
Stanford, Jim, ORG2–3
Statement of changes in financial position, ACC10–12, 13
Statistics Canada, GLO18, INF9–11
Statistics Canada Catalogue, INF10
Status quo pricing objectives, PRI18
Statutory law, LEG4
Stevenson, Robert Louis, PEO5
Stock, OWN8, SEC4–8, *see also* Shares
Stockbrokers
challenges facing, SEC24–25
defined, SEC10
Stock exchange, SEC10
Stockholders, *see* Shareholders
Stock indexes, SEC17, 18
Stock promotion, SEC14–15
Stock quotations, SEC15–17
Stock turnover, PRI14–15
Store of value, BAN6
Strategic business units, ORG8
Strategic planning, MGT14
Strict product liability, LEG16
Strikebreakers, LR16, 17
Strikes, LR1–3, **15**, 18
Stronach, Frank, FIN21–22
Strong Equipment Corp., OWN24–25
Subjobber, DIS4
Subsidiary, OWN17
Succession planning, HRM6
Sunkist Growers, OWN22, PRI9
Sunrise economy, BUS13–15
Supermarket, DIS12
Supervisory managers, MGT4
Supply curve, PRI13
Supreme Court of Canada, LEG22
Survey of Buying Power, INF10
Survey of Markets, INF10
Surveys, INF12–13
Sustainable development, FUT23, SOC18
Sweden, socialism in, BUS6
Swift, Catherine, ENT16–17
Systems contract, OP22–23

Tactical planning, MGT14
Tangible personal property, LEG7
Tangible private property, BUS17
Target market, MKT9, 10
Target return goal, PRI18

Tariffs, FUT29, **GLO12**–13
Task forces, MGT15–17
Taylor, Claude, PEO27–28
Taylor, Frederick, ORG14
Teams, MGT15–17
Technical skills, MGT6
Technology
defined, FUT17
and privacy, FUT22–23
trends in, FUT17–23
Telecommuting, FUT2
Telephone interview, INF12–13
Television, and advertising, COM11–12
Theory X, PEO12–13
Theory Y, PEO12–13
Theory Z, PEO22–23
Third Wave, The, FUT2, INF3
Thomas Cook Group (Canada) Ltd., HRM2–3
Throughput time, OP9
Time wage, HRM26
Tip Top Tailors, DIS6
Title, LEG8
Toffler, Alvin, FUT1, 2, INF3
Token money, BAN7
Top managers/management, MGT5, 7–8, OWN16
Toronto-Dominion Bank, SOC12
Toronto Star, The, OWN17
Toronto Stock Exchange (TSE), SEC10, 11, 13, 17
Torstar Corporation, OWN17
Torts, LEG15–16
Total productive maintenance (TPM), OP19–20
Total quality management (TQM), ACC23–25
Townsend, Robert, ORG22
Trade credit, FIN9–10
Trademark, LEG10–12, PRI9
Trademark Act, LEG10
Trade shows, COM13
Trades and Labor Congress (TLC), LR5
Trading blocs, compared, GLO17
Trading stamps, COM14
Training, HRM20–21
Transaction processing system (TPS), INF8
TransAlta Utilities, ACC17
Transfers, HRM23
Transportation, DIS14–15, MKT6
Treasury bill, FIN18
Troll dolls, PRI8–9

TSE 300 Composite Index, SEC17
Two-factor theory, PEO7, 8

Ukraine, trade with, GLO29–30
Underwriter, SEC4
Unemployment, FUT7–8, SOC25–27
Union Gas, HRM21
Unions, *see* Labour unions
Union shop, LR8
Unit of account, BAN6
United Auto Workers, LR4, 7
United Co-operatives of Ontario,
   OWN22
United States
   capitalism in, BUS6
   labour unions in, LR4–5, 7
United Steelworkers of America,
   LR4
Universal product code, INF5–6
Unsecured loan, FIN10
Up the Organization, ORG22
Uruguay Round, FUT29, GLO16

Valence, PEO10
Vancouver Stock Exchange (VSE),
   SEC14–15
Variable cost, OP15, PRI15
Vending machine, DIS12
Venture capital, FIN15
Venture capitalists, ENT14

Vertical marketing system (VMS),
   DIS5–6
Via Rail, BUS24
Victoria General Hospital (Halifax),
   ORG27–28
Virtual reality, FUT17, 18–19
Volume objectives, PRI18
Voluntary abritration, LR15
Volvo, PEO19
Vroom, Victor, PEO10

Wages
   defined, HRM25
   and piecework, HRM26
   and productivity, BUS20–21
   time, HRM26
Wal-Mart, DIS6
Warehouse club, DIS12
Warehousing, DIS16, OP25–26
Warner-Lambert Canada, SOC9–10
Warranties, LEG9
Waste management, SOC20–21
Wealth of Nations, The, BUS6, OP20
Weights and Measures Act, SOC15
Weight Watchers, ENT18
Westar Mining Ltd., LR24–25
West Edmonton Mall, DIS6, 7
Wholesaler, DIS4
Wholesaling, MKT6
Wildcat strike, LR18

Wings of Eastern Ontario, ENT11
Winnipeg General Strike, LR5, 16
Women
   and employment equity,
      HRM16–17, SOC8–10, 30
   as entrepreneurs, ENT24–26
   and harassment, HRM17–19
   and job specification laws,
      HRM8–9
   in legal profession, LEG2–3, 27
   and the new economy, FUT15–16
   and pay equity, HRM12, 33
Wood, Carol, ENT11
Woolco, DIS4
WordPerfect Corporation, LEG11
Word processing, INF5
Workaholism, PEO9–10
Worker input, PEO15–16
Workers' compensation act, HRM29
Work-in-progress inventory, OP16
Work to rule, LR18
Workstyles, FUT30–31
World Commission on
   Environment and Development,
      SOC18
World War II, BUS12

Yield, SEC19–20

Zellers, DIS11

READER REPLY CARD

We are interested in your reaction to *Canadian Business: A Contempory Perspective* by Steven H. Appelbaum and M. Dale Beckman. With your comments, we can improve this book in future editions. Please help us by completing this questionnaire.

1. What was your reason for using this book?
   _____ university course
   _____ college course
   _____ continuing education course
   _____ professional development
   _____ personal interest
   _____ other (please specify)

2. If you are a student, please identify your school and course. If you used this text for a program, what was the name of the program.
   _____

3. Which modules did you use. _____

4. Approximately how much of each module did you use.
   _____ all _____ 3/4 _____ 1/2 _____ 1/4

5. Which sections of the modules were omitted from your course?
   _____

6. What did you like best about this modular format?
   _____

7. What advantages did this format bring for you?
   _____

8. In terms of the content, what is the best aspect of this text?
   _____

9. Is there anything that should be added? _____
   _____

10. Was the information in this text presented in a manner helpful to teaching and learning? _____
    _____

11. Would you support the modular format for future major texts? Why?_____

12. Please add any comments or suggestions. _____
    _____

(fold here and tape shut)

MAIL **POSTE**

Canada Post Corporation / Société canadienne des postes

Postage paid   **Port payé**
If mailed in Canada   si posté au Canada

Business   **Réponse**
Reply   **d'affaires**

0116870399   01

0116870399-M8Z4X6-BR01

Scott Duncan
Publisher, College Division
HARCOURT BRACE & COMPANY, CANADA
55 HORNER AVENUE
TORONTO, ONTARIO
M8Z 9Z9